MENTAL CAPACITY ACT MANUAL

MENTAL CAPACITY ACT MANUAL

THIRD EDITION

by

RICHARD M.JONES M.A. (Kent and Brunel)
Solicitor, C.Q.S.W.
Consultant, Morgan Cole, Solicitors

 THOMSON REUTERS

SWEET & MAXWELL

First edition 2005
Second edition 2007
Third edition 2008

Reprinted 2009

Published in 2008 by Thomson Reuters (Legal) Limited
(Registered in England & Wales, Company No 1679046. Registered Office
and address for service: 100 Avenue Road, London, NW3 3PF)
trading as Sweet & Maxwell

Typeset byHobbs, Totton, Hampshire
Printed and bound by MPG Books Ltd, Bodmin, Cornwall

For further information on our products and services, visit
www.sweetandmaxwell.co.uk

ISBN: 978 1 84703 561 5

No natural forests were destroyed to make this product, only farmed
timber was used and replanted.

CIP catalogue record for this book is available from the British Library.

PREFACE

The Mental Capacity Act has been substantially amended by the Mental Health Act 2007 to provide for a procedure that can be used to authorise the deprivation of liberty of a mentally incapacitated person. The new procedure represents the Government's response to the finding of the European Court of Human Rights in *HL v United Kingdom* (the "Bournewood" case). The Government could have achieved its objective by making minor amendments to the Mental Health Act 1983. Instead, a procedure has been created that is hugely complex, voluminous, overly bureaucratic and difficult to understand, and yet provides mentally incapacitated people with minimum safeguards.

The Joint Committee on Human Rights in its "Legislative Scrutiny: Mental Health Bill" (HL Paper 40; HC 288) said at para.90:

"The proposals to amend the Mental Capacity Act are detailed and complex, and we question whether they will be readily understood by proprietors of residential care homes, even with the benefit of professional advice".

The Mental Capacity Act vitally affects the lives of a significant and growing proportion of the population. When it was passed in 2005, the Act was comprehensible to a reasonably informed lay person who was required to make decisions on behalf of a mentally incapacitated individual. The fact that key elements of the Act have been rendered largely incomprehensible to both lay people and to many professionals represents a significant failure on the part of both Government and Parliament.

Transitional arrangements for England

The Department of Health issued the following note on September 9, 2008:

"The Mental Capacity Act 2005 deprivation of liberty safeguards will be implemented from April 1, 2009. These safeguards will impact significantly on local authorities, Primary Care Trusts (PCTs), care homes and hospitals. The purpose of this note is to explain the transitional arrangements that will apply in England for the month of April 2009 only.

It is proposed to introduce transitional arrangements to ease the handling of the higher number of assessments requested by managing authorities (care homes and hospitals) of supervisory bodies (local authorities and PCTs) that might be expected following the implementation of the safeguards on April 1, 2009.

The proposed transitional arrangements will be placed before Parliament within a Commencement Order and details of the proposed arrangements are being shared now in advance of the laying of a Commencement Order in order to assist and inform local planning. The arrangements will not become law until they have successfully completed the Parliamentary process.

The proposed transitional arrangements will provide an extension of the urgent and standard deprivation of liberty authorisation assessment timescales. Managing authorities will still be required to apply for deprivation of liberty authorisations from April 1, 2009 but transitional arrangements will be in place for one month.

It is proposed that urgent authorisations given during April 2009 will be

effective for a period of 21 days rather than the usual 7 days (as provided for in paragraph 78(2) of Schedule A1 to the Mental Capacity Act 2005).
For urgent authorisations given on May 1, 2009 and thereafter, the usual period of 7 days will apply.

In respect of requests for standard authorisations received by supervisory bodies during April 2009, it is proposed that the timeframe for assessment will be 42 days, rather than the usual 21 days (as provided for in regulation 13 of The Mental Capacity (Deprivation of Liberty: Standard Authorisations, Assessments and Ordinary Residence) Regulations 2008 (SI No. 2008/1858)). In respect of requests for standard authorisations received by supervisory bodies on May 1, 2009 and thereafter, the usual period of 21 days to complete the standard authorisation process will apply.

The effect of these proposed transitional arrangements is to allow for the possibility that supervisory bodies may take longer to process requests for assessments in the first month of the new arrangements. The objective is to alleviate the pressures that supervisory bodies and managing authorities may face in the initial stages of the deprivation of liberty safeguards implementation process. It is important that both supervisory bodies and managing authorities plan ahead, ideally jointly, to ensure that they are well prepared for the beginning of the new arrangements".

In preparing this edition I have taken into account of judicial decisions and other material that was available to me on October 1, 2008.

Richard Jones
e-mail: richard.jones2@morgan-cole.com

PREFACE TO THE FIRST EDITION

The Mental Capacity Act 2005 is a measure which is likely to touch the lives of everyone because, at some point, all adults will probably be affected by a lack of capacity to make decisions relating to their everyday lives, either personally, or through contact with people who are unable to make decisions for themselves. As the Government has noted, a

> "wide range of conditions can result in incapacity to take decisions. In some cases, the capacity to take decisions is never attained (for example in the case of some people with a learning disability). In other cases, capacity is attained but is subsequently lost. This may occur for a number of reasons, including medical disorders or traumatic injury. The loss of capacity may be temporary for example during a toxic confusional state, which might result from an illness, or use of drugs. In some cases, capacity may fluctuate during periods when they are well, but may lose it during periods of illness. Finally, the loss of capacity may be permanent, as for example in some cases of dementia or the persistent vegetative state" (*Who Decides? Making Decisions on Behalf of Mentally Incapacitated Adults*, Cm. 3803, para.2.1).

The following factors can be said to have driven the process that cumulated in the passing of the Act: the legal context, demographic tends and improvements in healthcare, the community care policy, and the protection of human rights.

The legal context

As is pointed out in the "Introduction and General Note" to the Act, the legal context that confronted the Law Commission when it commenced its investigation into the adequacy of legal procedures for decision-making on behalf of mentally incapacitated adults was most unsatisfactory. It was described as "one of incoherence, inconsistency and historical accident" (Law Comm. No.231, para.2.45). The High Court had attempted to respond to this situation by using the doctrine of necessity and the declaratory jurisdiction to determine the legality of action proposed to be taken in respect of a mentally incapacitated person, but this approach, which is aimed at responding to individual problems, was ill-suited to developing a coherent legal framework It was clear that the law did not offer sufficient protection either for the mentally incapacitated, or for those who look after them.

Demographic trends and improvements in healthcare

The number of elderly people is rising steadily in the population. The mental faculties of the elderly often decline with age and the number of persons suffering from dementia, which leads to a progressive loss of mental capacity, is increasing markedly. More than 700,000 people in the United Kingdom are estimated to suffer from dementia and this is projected to rise to around 840,00 by 2010 (The Alzheimer's Society (January 2004)). Recommendation 1035 (1986) of the Parliamentary Assembly of the Council of Europe on ageing of populations in Europe noted that during the period from 1990 to 2020:

"increases of 20% and more are expected in the 45–60 age group and of 15–20% in the 65 and over and there will be a disproportionate growth in the number of very old people, aged 80 and over, which would be one-third of the size of this group".

In the United Kingdom context, the House of Lords Select Committee on Economic Affairs estimated that the proportion of the population aged 65 or over as a percentage of those aged 16–64 would be 24.4% in 2000, 32.8% in 2025, and 39.2% in 2050 (Session 2002–03, 4th Report, *Aspects of the Economics of an Ageing Population*, Vol.1, p.10).

Medical advances, in particular the development of antibiotics, have saved the lives of many people who would in earlier times have died from disease or trauma. Some of those who survive will do so with impaired mental capacity or even, exceptionally, lapse into a persistent vegetative state. In the case of Tony Bland, a young man who as a result of being crushed at the Hillsborough disaster was in a persistent vegetative state, Lord Browne-Wilkinson expressed his concern about the "scale of the problem that is presented by modern technological developments" and said that it seemed to him "imperative that the moral, social and legal issues raised by this case should be considered by Parliament" (*Airedale NHS Trust v Bland* [1993] 1 All E.R. 821 at 878, 879, HL). Also, as the Law Commission noted, the

"achievements of medical science have also created difficult dilemmas about the appropriate measure of medical care which should be given at the end of life, particularly where unconscious or incapacitated people have, in advance, indicated an unwillingness to be kept alive once their health has deteriorated" (Law Comm. No.231, para.2.38).

A further concern in the medical context was the recognition that certain procedures involving the mentally incapacitated were almost certainly unlawful. The most prevalent example was the practice of carrying out research on a person who was mentally incapable of consenting to participating in it, and where that person would receive no benefit from the results of the research.

The community care policy

The community care policy comprises two distinct threads. The first relates to the policy of discharging mentally disordered people from large, isolated long-stay hospitals into community based provision. This has lead to significant changes to the ways in which such people are cared for. The second thread concerns the manner in which social care needs of the population should be assessed and provided for. The White Paper *Caring for People: Community Care in the Next Decade and Beyond* (1989) Cm. 849, states at para.1.1:

"Community care means providing the services and support which people who are affected by problems of ageing, mental illness, mental handicap or physical or sensory disability need to be able to live as independently as possible in their own homes, or in 'homely' settings in the community. The Government is firmly committed to a policy of community care which enables such people to achieve their full potential."

One of the consequences of this approach, which has been delivered through the legislative framework of the National Health Service and Community Care Act 1990, has been the emphasis on avoiding institutional care for elderly and disabled people unless their particular needs positively require such an outcome.

The combination of these two policy initiatives has lead to a decrease in reliance on institutional care for the mentally disabled. Institutional care tends to encourage a paternalistic approach to meeting patient/resident needs, while community based care increases the opportunities for mentally disabled individuals to make many of the decisions that occur in everyday life either by themselves or with support. Some of the decisions that may be required to be taken will raise the question of whether the person concerned possesses the required level of mental capacity to make the decision in question. If the answer is in the negative, disputes, in particular about the most appropriate living situation for the person, can sometimes arise between relatives, or between relatives and a public authority.

The protection of human rights

The Act is indicative of a growing shift in attitude toward those who, for whatever reason, lack the mental capacity to make key decisions for themselves. In particular, there has been a growing international recognition of the unacceptability of discrimination against the mentally disabled. In 1971, the United Nations proclaimed the Declaration of the Rights of Mentally Retarded Persons. Its seven paragraphs read:

"1. The mentally retarded person has, to the maximum degree of flexibility, the same rights as other human beings.

2. The mentally retarded person has a right to proper medical care and physical therapy and to such education, training, rehabilitation and guidance as will enable him to develop his ability and maximum potential.

3. The mentally retarded person has a right to economic security and to a decent standard of living. He has a right to perform productive work or to engage in any other meaningful occupation to the fullest possible extent of his capabilities.

4. Whenever possible, the mentally retarded persons should live with his own family or with foster parents and participate in different forms of community life. The family with which he lives should receive assistance.

5. The mentally retarded person has a right to a qualified guardian when this is required to protect his personal well-being and interests.

6. The mentally retarded person has a right to protection from exploitation, abuse and degrading treatment. If prosecuted for any offence, he shall have a right to due process of law with full recognition being given to his degree of mental responsibility.

7. Whenever mentally retarded persons are unable, because of the severity of their handicap, to exercise all their rights in a meaningful way or it should become necessary to restrict or deny some or all of these rights, the procedure used for that restriction or denial of rights must contain proper legal

safeguards against every form of abuse. This procedure must be based on an evaluation of the social capability of the mentally retarded person by qualified experts and must be subject to periodic review and to the right of appeal to higher authorities."

Although a Declaration of the United Nations is not legally binding, the Declaration on the Rights of Mentally Retarded Persons was supported by the UK Government when it was adopted by the General Assembly. The Declaration can therefore be categorised as identifying non-binding "soft law" principles which provide guidance to the UK Government when it legislates in this field. Despite is dated terminology, the Declaration represents an important milestone in that it established some important rights, in particular the person with a learning disability has "the same rights as other human beings" which cannot be restricted without due process that "must contain proper legal safeguards against every form of abuse". The Law Commission paid "careful regard" to aspects of the Declaration when it made its final report (Law Comm. No.231, para.2.27). The philosophy that lies behind the Declaration is one of minimum intervention in the lives of the learning disabled, consistent with providing proper care and protection and maximum help to enable them to realise their full potential and make best use of their abilities. Many countries have enacted legislation embodying its principles: see *Report on Incapable Adults,* Scottish Law Commission, Cm. 2962, para.1.5.

Subsequent to the 1971 Declaration, the General Assembly proclaimed the Declaration on the Rights of Disabled Persons in 1975, and adopted twenty-five "Principles for the protection of persons with mental illness and the improvement of mental health care" (Resolution 46/119 of December 17, 1991). Principle 23.1 requires States to "implement [the] Principles through appropriate legislative, judicial, administrative, educational and other measures, which they shall review periodically." In the European context, Recommendation No.(99)4 of the Committee of Ministers of the Council of Europe on Principles Concerning the Legal Protection of Incapable Adults, and the Convention on Human Rights and Biomedicine, together with its Additional Protocol, are reproduced as Annexes A to C[1].

The only international instrument against which UK law can be judicially tested is the European Convention on Human Rights. Although the Convention is not part of substantive domestic law, the Human Rights Act 1998 makes Convention rights enforceable in domestic courts. The Joint Committee on Human Rights said that the provisions of the Draft Mental Incapacity Bill:

"engage a wide range of [Convention] rights, including the right to respect for family life, the right to property, and the right to be free of degrading treatment. In our view, however, the safeguards built into the Draft Bill are sufficient to ensure that there is no significant risk of the implementation of the Draft Bill leading to an incompatibility with any of them" (Session 2002–03, 15th Report, *Scrutiny of Bills and Draft Bills: Further Progress Report* (HL 149/HC 1005), para.4.7).

Further reports of the Joint Committee were more questioning of whether particular provisions of the Bill risked violating either Arts 2, 3, 5, or 8 of the

---

[1] Not reproduced in this edition.

Convention. Generally speaking, the Committee was satisfied with the responses that it received from the Government either in terms of amendments to the Bill, or from assurances the it received regarding the contents of the *Code of Practice* (Session 2004–05, 4th Report (HL 26/HC 224), Ch.4).

Another aspect of the rights based approach to the provision of services has been an increasing demand for the mentally incapacitated to enjoy the benefits of a lay advocate. In particular, it is considered that the support of an advocate would be beneficial in respect of an incapacitated person who did not enjoy the benefits of an involvement with caring relatives.

Running in tandem with the development of a rights agenda for the mentally incapacitated has been a gradual abandonment of the paternalistic approach to medical provision for the mentally capacitated, and a growing recognition of the principle of patient autonomy. The House of Lords Select Committee on Medical Ethics (1993–94) commented that the principle of patient autonomy "has become important in relation to medical treatment as the relationship between doctor and patient has changed to one of partnership" (HL 21–1, para.40). One manifestation of this trend has been the recognition at common law of the right of a capacitated patient to make a "living will". At the European level, the importance of patients being empowered to make informed choices in healthcare is reflected in the European Charter of Patients' Rights which proposes fourteen rights that all patients in Europe should be granted. The Charter, which was developed by the Italian patients' rights organisation Cittadinazattiva—Active Citizens Network, was launched in Rome in 2002.

Ten years elapsed between the publication of the Law Commission's Mental Incapacity Bill on February 28, 1995 and the Mental Capacity Act receiving its Royal Assent on April 7, 2005. This delay can be partly explained by the sensitivity of successive Governments to concerns that had been expressed by a number of bodies about the prospect of the provisions on advance decisions enabling euthanasia to be introduced "by the backdoor". This concern, which was a recurring issue throughout the parliamentary debates on the Bill, led to the enactment of s.62. The fact that the legislation had been the subject of detailed scrutiny over a number of years did not prevent the Bill being amended frequently during its passage through Parliament. Although the amendments improved the Bill, they did not ameliorate the following concerns:

- The fact that the Act provides for advance decisions to be made orally will inevitably result in many purported oral advance decisions being invalid because they will not be applicable to the treatment in question for one or more of the reasons set out in s.25(4).

- There is much to be said in favour of the opinion of House of Lord's Select Committee on Medical Ethics that advance decisions should be advisory only. A number of witnesses to the Joint Committee pointed out that healthy patients tend not to make the same choices as sick ones.

- Although the potential for the donee of a lasting power of attorney to act in a manner which is contrary to the best interests of the donor was recognised by the Government, the Act does not provide sufficient safeguards to protect the donor from such acts.

Apart from these concerns, there can be no doubt that the Mental Capacity Act represents a major advance in that it provides a comprehensive statutory framework for assisting those lacking capacity to make decisions for themselves wherever possible and for proper decisions to be made by others when that is not possible. However, the framework could prove to be an empty vessel if it is not "accompanied by changes in attitude which recognise the rights of those lacking capacity and the need to instil respect and good practice in dealing with them" (Joint Committee, para.30).

CONTENTS

Table of Cases

PART 1

MENTAL CAPACITY ACT 2005

(2005 c.9)

ARRANGEMENT OF SECTIONS

1

Part 2

The court of protection and the public guardian

The Court of Protection

Supplementary powers

Practice and procedure

Fees and costs

The Public Guardian

Court of Protection Visitors

Part 3

Miscellaneous and general

Declaratory provision

Private international law

General

66. Existing receivers and enduring powers of attorney etc.
67. Minor and consequential amendments and repeals
68. Commencement and extent
69. Short title

[SCHEDULE A1

HOSPITAL AND CARE HOME RESIDENTS: DEPRIVATION OF LIBERTY]

SCHEDULE 1

LASTING POWERS OF ATTORNEY: FORMALITIES

[SCHEDULE 1A

PERSONS INELIGIBLE TO BE DEPRIVED OF LIBERTY BY THIS ACT]

SCHEDULE 2

PROPERTY AND AFFAIRS: SUPPLEMENTARY PROVISIONS

SCHEDULE 3

INTERNATIONAL PROTECTION OF ADULTS

SCHEDULE 4

PROVISIONS APPLYING TO EXISTING ENDURING POWERS OF ATTORNEY

SCHEDULE 5

TRANSITIONAL PROVISIONS AND SAVINGS

SCHEDULE 6

MINOR AND CONSEQUENTIAL AMENDMENTS

SCHEDULE 7

REPEALS

An Act to make new provision relating to persons who lack capacity; to establish a superior court of record called the Court of Protection in place of the office of the Supreme Court called by that name; to make provision in connection with the Convention on the International Protection of Adults signed at the Hague on 13th January 2000; and for connected purposes. [7th April 2005]

PROGRESS OF THE BILL
1–002 *Hansard*, HL Vol.667, col.1333 (1 R).

Hansard, HC Vol.422, col 928 (1 R); Vol.425 col.22 (2R), (Prog), (MR), (Carry-over Motion); Vol.428, cols 101 (1R), 1531 (Prog), (RS); Vol.432, cols 1362 (Prog), (Lords' Amendments), 1641 (Royal Assent); Vol.668 cols 11 and 42 (2R); Vol.669 cols 102,191, 734 (Comm),1101 (MfA); Vol. 670, cols 845 (MfA), 1275, 1441 and 1483 (Rep.); Vol.671, cols 412 (3R), 950 (Royal Assent).

INTRODUCTION AND GENERAL NOTE

The Law Commission's Fourth Programme of Law Reform (1989, Law Com. No. 185) **1–003** proposed an investigation into the adequacy of legal and other procedures for decision-making on behalf of mentally incapacitated adults. There followed an extensive consultation exercise in the course of which the Commission published the following consultation papers.

- Mentally Incapacitated Adults and Decision-Making: An Overview (CP No.119)
- Mentally Incapacitated Adults and Decision-making: A New Jurisdiction (CP No.128)
- Mentally Incapacitated Adults and Decision-Making: Medical Treatment and Research (CP No.129)
- Mentally Incapacitated and Other Vulnerable Adults: Public law Protection (CP No.130)

The current state of the law was described by the Commission at para.1.1 of its Final Report "Mental Incapacity" (Law Com. No.231) which was published in March 1995:

"It is widely recognised that, in this area, the law as it now stands is unsympathetic and full of glaring gaps. It does not rest on clear or modern foundations of principle. It has also failed to keep up with developments in our understanding of the rights and needs of those with mental disability."

The Report sought to provide:

"A new set of coherent answers to a single question. The question, put simply, is 'who decides?' Although it may be asked in a variety of situations and for a variety of reasons, it arises whenever a person lacks the mental capacity to make a legally effective decision for himself or herself. There are various supplementary questions which must then be put. 'On what basis?' and 'with what formalities?' are examples of these. The types of decision which may be called for can be divided into three broad categories: 'personal welfare' decisions, 'health care' decisions and 'financial' decisions" (para.2.1).

A draft "Mental Incapacity Bill" was appended to the Report. This was intended to "provide a unified and comprehensive scheme within which people can make decisions for themselves" (para.3.1).

Lord Mackay, the Lord Chancellor, announced in January 1996 that the "Government has decided not to legislate on the basis of the Law Commission's proposals in their current form and has also concluded that it would be inappropriate to make any proposals to Parliament in the absence of full public consultation" (Lord Chancellor's Department, Press Notice, January 16,1996).

The incoming Labour Government issued a consultation paper "*Who Decides? Making Decisions on Behalf of Mentally Incapacitated Adults*", Cm.3803 (1997) which was based on the Commission's proposals. It also took into account the report of the House of Lords Select Committee on Medical Ethics (HL Paper 21-1) which had considered the issue of advance statements about healthcare. The consultative paper sought views on a possible framework for providing protection for mentally incapacitated adults and those who look after them, and for providing an organised framework of law to manage the welfare and affairs of mentally incapacitated adults. The consultation resulted in over 4,000 responses being received. The Government's response to the consultation was published in October 1999 as "*Making Decisions: The Government's proposals for making decisions on behalf of mentally incapacitated adults*", Cm.4465. The proposals were largely based on the Law Commission's recommendations. The Lord Chancellor, Lord Irvine, announced in November 1999 that the Government had decided to bring forward legislation "to empower mentally incapacitated adults, so far as can safely be allowed, to make provision for the care they want before they lose capacity, and to ensure that when decisions come to be made about their care and welfare, they contain adequate safeguards and protection, they are made consistently and in line with each individual's particular best interests" (speech to the Law Society's Conference on Mental Incapacity, November 10,1999).

Judicial support for legislation was expressed in a number of cases. In *F (Adult: Court's Jurisdiction), Re* [2000] 2 F.L.R.512, CA, Butler-Sloss P. said at 524:

"The assumption of jurisdiction by the High Court on a case-by-case basis does not, however, detract from the obvious need expressed by the Law Commission and by the Government for a well-structured and clearly defined framework of protection of vulnerable, mentally incapacitated adults, particularly since the whole essence of declarations under the inherent jurisdiction is to meet a recognised individual problem and not to provide general guidance for mentally incapacitated adults. Until Parliament puts in place that defined framework, the High Court will still be required to help out where there is no other practicable alternative."

A "Draft Mental Incapacity Bill" (Cm.5859-1) was presented to Parliament in June 2003. In July 2003 the House of Commons and House of Lords appointed a Joint Committee to scrutinise the Draft Bill. The Joint Committee's Report, which contained 99 recommendations and was mainly supportive of the principles underlying the draft Bill, was published in two volumes in November 2003 (HL Paper 189-1, 2; HC 1083-1, 2). The Government's response to the report was published in February 2004 (Cm.6121). The great majority of the Joint Committee's recommendations were accepted by the Government.

Several witnesses to the Joint Committee suggested that the title "Mental Incapacity Bill" was inappropriate and had negative connotations and preferred "Mental Capacity Bill" which they saw as a more accurate description of the Bill, as well as being more positive and reassuring. The Joint Committee considered that the Bill "should avoid the pejorative implications of incapacity and instill confidence in those it is intended to serve" and recommended "that consideration should be given to changing the Bill's title to 'Mental Capacity Bill'" (paras 362–364). The Government accepted this recommendation.

The objectives of the legislation, which has the general aim of seeking to strike a balance between respect for individual autonomy and the need to protect the vulnerable, were explained by the Secretary of State for Constitutional Affairs and Lord Chancellor, Lord Falconer, when he moved the second reading of the Bill:

"The Bill seeks to do six main things. First, it allows adults to take as many decisions as they can for themselves and, in any event, to put them at the centre of the decision-making process about themselves.

Secondly, when adults fear that they may not be able to take decisions about their medical treatment in the future, it allows them, if they wish, and subject to effective safeguards, to make decisions in advance of incapacity about whether treatment should be carried out or continued.

Thirdly, where adults cannot make decisions and have not made any decision in advance about their own personal welfare or other property or affairs, the Bill ensures that the decisions which are made for them are made in their best interests.

Fourthly, where an adult lacks capacity to make a decision for himself about serious medical treatment, accommodation in a hospital or care home, or other residential accommodation, and they have no friends or family to be consulted, the Bill will require the relevant NHS body or local authority to appoint an independent [mental capacity advocate] to support the person in these most difficult decisions.

Fifthly, the Bill will provide protection against subsequent legal liability for those carers who have honestly and reasonably sought to act in the best interests of the person for whom they have cared.

Finally, the Bill will provide clarity and safeguards around the carrying out of research in relation to people who lack capacity" (*Hansard*, HL Vol.668, col.12).

The view of the Joint Committee on Human Rights is that the legislation "should be broadly welcomed from a human rights perspective, because it enhances the ability of people who lack capacity to make their own decisions where they can and makes it more likely that sound decisions will be made on their behalf where they cannot make those decisions for themselves" (Fourth Report, HL 26/HC 224, para.4.5). In *B v Secretary of State for Work and Pensions* [2005] EWCA Civ 929, para.25, Sedley L.J. said: "Mental capacity, although not listed in Art.14 [of the European Convention on Human Rights], is arguably at least as sensitive a personal characteristic, in relation to discrimination, as race or sex".

Research into the operation of the Adults with Incapacity (Scotland) Act 2000 (asp 4) found that lack of publicity about the Act and how it might benefit adults and carers was perceived as one of the main barriers to access (The Adults with Incapacity (Scotland) Act 2000: Learning from Experience (2004), Scottish Executive). The Department of Health has been proactive in publicising the Mental Capacity Act by producing a leaflet and a number of information booklets on the Act which are tailored to meet the needs of different audiences. They can be downloaded from the Department of Health's website (see Annex A).

Territorial Extent
This Act only extends to England and Wales, apart from the two exceptions set out in s.68(5). **1–004**

Territorial Application: Wales
The Welsh Ministers may make regulations under ss.30 and 34 and issue guidance under s.32(3). They may also make regulations under ss.35, 36, 37 and 41. Section 68(2) provides that ss.30–41 will come into force by order made by the Welsh Ministers. Section 43(1) provides that the Welsh Ministers must be consulted by the Lord Chancellor before a *Code of Practice* is prepared or revised. **1–005**

Matters not covered by this Act
The most significant omission from the Act relates to the recommendations that the Law Commission made in Pt IX of its Final Report for the protection of vulnerable people at risk. In particular, the Commission recommended that, where local authorities have reason to believe that a vulnerable person in their area is suffering or is likely to suffer significant harm or serious exploitation, they should be under a statutory duty to investigate and to provide or arrange community care services or to take other action to protect that person (Law Comm. No.231, para.9.16). **1–006**

Appointees
If an incapacitated person has little capital and receives income only from state benefits, the necessary financial arrangements can be made under reg.33 of the Social Security (Claims and Payment) Regulations 1987 (SI 1987/1968) which provides that the Secretary of State may appoint someone aged 18 or over (the "appointee") to act on behalf of the claimant. The appointee has no power to deal with the claimant's capital but can: **1–007**

  (i) exercise any rights and duties that the claimant has under the social security legislation;

  (ii) receive any benefits payable to the claimant; and

  (iii) deal with the money received on the claimant's behalf in the interests of the claimant or his or her dependants.

Concern has been expressed about the nature of the enquiries conducted before appointments are made, and about the absence of regular supervision or monitoring of the performance of appointees: see R. Lavery and L. Lundy "The Social Security Appointee System" (1994) *Journal of Social Welfare and Family Law* 313.

The Government resisted amendments to the Bill which would have brought the appointee system under the jurisdiction of the Court of Protection. However, Baroness Andrews, speaking during the committee stage in the House of Lords, said:

"The Bill has enabled us to take stock of the arrangements for appointees and to improve them in the light of the Bill's principles. Officials and Ministers from the Department for Constitutional Affairs and Department for Work and Pensions have been discussing how they can use the Bill to improve the appointeeship system ...

During the process a DWP official—a benefits official—will visit the person lacking capacity and the prospective appointee. The official needs to be sure that the person does in fact lack the capacity to look after their own benefits, and that the appointee will act in their best interests. That process will be enhanced by the Bill and the code of practice. For example, it will be useful for the officials carrying out those visits to have the benefit of the extra advice on assessing capacity. DWP and DCA officials will work together to ensure that DWP guidance reflects the principles of the Bill and places best interests at its heart.

In addition DWP acknowledges that the question of monitoring needs to be addressed, and it will look at options for introducing a monitoring system. With half a million appointees, that is not going to be easy; but it is clearly important, and there will be visits, paper reviews, targeted monitoring—all those sorts of things can be looked at in the light of the Bill. DWP will act quickly to revoke appointments where allegations of misman-agement are made" (*Hansard*, HL Vol.668, col.1463).

The DWP has produced an "Agents, Appointees and Receivers Guide" which can be accessed on its website (see Annex A).

Guidance on how an appointee can open a bank account and manage money on behalf of the claimant is contained in "Banking for mentally incapacitated customers" which can be downloaded from the website of the British Bankers Association (see Annex A).

The appointee should carry out his or her functions in accordance with the provisions of this Act, in particular ss.1 to 4.

COMMENCEMENT

1–008   See s.68.

ABBREVIATIONS

1–009   "ANH": artificial nutrition and hydration
"Code of Practice": the *Code of Practice* laid before Parliament in draft in February 2007, pursuant to ss.42 and 43 of the Act, and approved in April 2007
"CPR": the Court of Protection Rules 2007 (SI 2007/1744)
"EPA": Enduring Powers of Attorney
"Explanatory Notes": Explanatory notes on the Mental Capacity Bill prepared by the Department for Constitutional Affairs and the Department of Health
"IMCA": independent mental capacity advocate
"Joint Committee": House of Lords, House of Commons, Joint Committee on the Draft Mental Incapacity Bill, Session 2002–3
"LPA": lasting power of attorney
"Oral and written evidence": House of Lords, House of Commons, Joint Committee on the Draft Mental Incapacity Bill, Session 2002–3, Volume II: Oral and written evidence, HL Paper 189-II, HC 1083-II
"the Bill": the Mental Capacity Bill
"the court": the Court of Protection
"the 1983 Act": the Mental Health Act 1983 (c.20)
"the 1985 Act": Enduring Powers of Attorney Act 1985 (c.29)

Throughout the Act, the capital letter "P" is used to refer to a person who lacks capacity or is believed to lack capacity to make a decision about a particular matter, and the capital letter "D" is used to refer to a person exercising powers in relation to P.

PART 1

PERSONS WHO LACK CAPACITY

The principles

The principles

1.—(1) The following principles apply for the purposes of this Act. **1–010**

(2) A person must be assumed to have capacity unless it is established that he lacks capacity.

(3) A person is not to be treated as unable to make a decision unless all practicable steps to help him to do so have been taken without success.

(4) A person is not to be treated as unable to make a decision merely because he makes an unwise decision.

(5) An act done, or decision made, under this Act for or on behalf of a person who lacks capacity must be done, or made, in his best interests.

(6) Before the act is done, or the decision is made, regard must be had to whether the purpose for which it is needed can be as effectively achieved in a way that is less restrictive of the person's rights and freedom of action.

GENERAL NOTE

The Joint Committee recommended that a statement of principles should appear on the **1–011** face of the Act. The Committee believed "that such a statement inserted as an initial point of reference could give valuable guidance to the courts, as well as helping non-lawyers to weigh up difficult decisions. Evidence given to us indicates that this be welcome to a wide range of those who have to deal with the problems of substitute decision-making in practice. We also believe that such a statement would be valuable in helping to frame the Codes of Practice based upon the [Act]" (para.43). The principles apply to all actions and decisions taken under this Act by both lay and professional people and the judiciary. The statement set out in s.2(3) can be added to the principles contained in this section.

The status of this section is that decisions and actions carried out under the Act should be tested against the principles which act as benchmarks for decision makers. Although there is no duty placed on persons or bodies to apply the principles, a failure to do so could be cited in legal proceedings as evidence of unlawful conduct.

Subsection (1)

Although the principles apply "for the purposes of this Act", they are integral to the defi- **1–012** nition of capacity in s.2 which is imported as the test of capacity in the Civil Procedure Rules 1998 Part 21(as inserted by SI 2007/2204). Importing the definition therefore imports the principles into Part 21 (*Saulle v Nouvet* [2007] EWHC 2902 (QB), para.46).

Subsection (2)

This establishes the fundamental principle that persons over the age of 16 (s.2(5)) are **1–013** assumed to be mentally capable of making their own decisions. This assumption of personal autonomy can only be overridden if the person concerned is assessed as lacking the mental capacity to make a particular decision for him or herself at the relevant time. Thus, in the absence of a capacity assessment, any doubts have to be resolved in favour of capacity. The consent of a mentally capable person to care or treatment provides the carer or clinician with legal authority to provide the care or treatment. Such a person's refusal of care or treatment must be respected even though the refusal might have drastic consequences, including death, for that person.

The approach to be taken when making the assessment is set out in ss.2 and 3. In legal proceedings, the burden of proof will fall on the person who asserts that capacity is lacking.

Subsection (3)

1–014   This provision, which is aimed at maximising the decision making capacity of individuals, is expanded upon in s.3(2).

The Explanatory Notes suggest that "all practicable steps" could include "making sure the person is in an environment in which he is comfortable or involving an expert in helping him express his views" (para.20). The nature of the help provided will depend upon the condition of the person, the available resources and the nature and urgency of the decision to be taken. Family and legal and medical advisers could be involved where appropriate to "ensure that [the person] has proper explanations of information required for the decision, and that he takes decisions when he is in the right frame of mind to do so" (*Saulle v Nouvet*, above, para.48). The Joint Committee said that such steps "might include using specific communication strategies, providing information in [a] more accessible form, or treating an underlying mental disorder to enable a person to regain capacity" (para.70). Providing information over time may allow a person to assimilate information more completely, thereby maximising their actual understanding. Consideration could be given to postponing the decision if it is felt that the person might regain capacity over time. Chapter 3 of the *Code of Practice* considers the steps that can be taken to help people make their own decisions.

It is important not to equate "practicable" with "possible" (*Owen v Crown House Engineering* [1973] 3 All E.R. 618, 622 NIRC). In *Dedman v British Building and Engineering Appliances Ltd* [1974] 1 W.L.R. 171, 179, CA, Scarman L.J. said:

> "The word 'practicable' is an ordinary English word of great flexibility: it takes its meaning from its context. But, whenever used, it is a call for the exercise of common sense, a warning that sound judgment will be impossible without compromise. Sometimes the context contemplates a situation rarely to be achieved though much to be desired: the word then indicates one must be satisfied with less than perfection ... [S]ometimes ... what the context requires may have been possible, but may not for some reason have been 'practicable'. Whatever its context, the quality of the word is that there are circumstances in which we must be content with less than 100 per cent: and it calls for judgment to determine how much less."

During the second reading debate in the House of Lords, Lord Brennan cited a dramatic example of the impact that appropriate help can have on the ability of a disabled person to communicate:

> "[A] client whom I represented had for 12 years, while being able to walk and grunt but not talk, been treated as a zombie, because his family did not believe that he was capable of any cognitive function. After obtaining a judgment on liability and getting an interim payment, at the second meeting with a speech therapist who knew about communication my client was able to converse with her. When challenged by me in conference, he readily spelt the word 'encyclopaedia'. Yet his family—his carers—were convinced for 12 years that his life was pretty well worthless" (*Hansard*, HL Vol.668, col.84).

In *AK (Adult Patient) (Medical Treatment: Consent), Re* [2001] 1 F.L.R. 129, a patient who had lost the use of virtually all his muscles, apart from those in one of his eyelids, through motor neurone disease was assisted to communicate by means of a device known as an "E transport" which involved the painstaking spelling out of words letter by letter by a process linked to the line of sight.

Although all practicable steps must be taken to help a person make a decision, those assisting the person must beware of subjecting the person to undue influence. In the context of consent to medical treatment, Lord Donaldson M.R. said in *T (Adult: Refusal of*

Treatment), Re [1992] 4 All E.R. 649, 662 that while it is acceptable for the patient to receive advice or for the patient to have been subject to the strong persuasion of others in reaching a decision, such persuasion must not "overbear the independence of the patient's decision". His Lordship identified the real question in each case as being: "does the patient really mean what he says or is he merely saying it for a quiet life, to satisfy someone else or because the advice and persuasion to which he has been subjected is such that he can no longer think and decide for himself? In other words, is it a decision expressed in form only, not in reality?" His Lordship identified two aspects of the effect of outside influence that could be of "crucial importance": the strength of will of the patient and the relationship of the "persuader" to the patient. With regard to the former, a patient who is "very tired, in pain or depressed will be much less able to resist having his will overborne than one who is rested, free from pain and cheerful". With regard to the relationship between the persuader and the patient, his Lordship spoke of the potential strength of the parental and marital relationship, especially with regard to arguments based on religious belief. Other outside influences that could vitiate a person's consent include fraud, misrepresentation and duress. For the effect of a person's vulnerability to exploitation on the assessment of their mental capacity, see *Lindsay v Wood* [2006] EWHC 2895 (QB) which is noted in the General Note to s.3. Undue influence in the context of financial transactions was considered by the House of Lords in *Royal Bank of Scotland v Etridge* [2001] UKHL 44; [2001] 4 All E.R. 449.

Research into the decision-making capabilities of persons with learning disabilities has shown that the presentation of information in a user-friendly manner makes it possible to move some people from being assessed as incapable to being assessed as capable (M.J. Gunn, J.G. Wong, I.C.H. Clare and A.J. Holland, "Decision-making capacity" (1999) 7(3) Med. L. Rev. 269). Confirmation that capacity is not static, even among patients who have engaged in self-harm, is contained in a study which found that the number of patients judged to have capacity increased significantly following the presentation of an information sheet about the specific treatment being proposed, together with a verbal explanation (R. Jacob, I.C.H. Clare, A.J. Holland, P.C. Watson, C. Maimaris and M.J. Gunn "Self-Harm, Capacity, and Refusal of Treatment: Implications for Emergency Medical Practice" (2005) 22 *Emergency Medical Journal* 799.

For a publication which offers practical help in assisting with communication, see N. Grove and B. McIntosh, "Communication for Person Centred Planning" (2006) *Foundation for People with Learning Disabilities*. Models available from psychology that might be helpful in identifying means to improve capacity are identified in "Assessment of Capacity in Adults: Interim Guidance for Psychologists" (2006) *British Psychological Society*, p.25.

Guidance on creating the right environment for assessing capacity is given in *Assessment of Mental Capacity: Guidance for Doctors and Lawyers*, (2004) BMA/Law Society, para.2.3.

Subsection (4)

This provision underpins the right to personal autonomy by preserving the right of a per- **1–015** son to make an irrational, unusual or eccentric decision which, viewed objectively, is not in that person's best interests without the person being treated as being mentally incapable by virtue of that decision alone. It does not prevent a capacity assessment being undertaken in respect of a person who makes an unwise decision, a series of unwise decisions, a decision that puts that person at risk, or who makes a decision which does not reflect that person's values, beliefs or approach to risk-taking. The making of such decisions might suggest that the person is susceptible to undue influence, or it could be an indication of inadequate understanding or a lack of information being provided to the person about the decision in question. The Joint Committee "considered carefully the dilemma created when a person with apparent capacity was making repeatedly unwise decisions that put him/her at risk or resulted in preventable suffering or disadvantage". While the Committee recognised that "the possibility of over-riding such decisions would be seen as unacceptable to many user groups", they suggested that "such a situation might trigger the need for a formal assessment of capacity" (Vol.1, para.78).

That the nature of the decision taken might be indicative of a lack of capacity on the part of the decision maker was emphasised by Kennedy L.J. in *Masterman-Lister v Brutton & Co* [2002] EWCA Civ 1889; [2003] 3 All E.R. 162, para.54, where his Lordship said that although the role of the court was the investigation of capacity not outcomes, outcomes "can often cast a flood of light on capacity".

In the context of consent to medical treatment, Lord Donaldson M.R. said:

"Prima facie every adult has the right and capacity to decide whether or not he will accept medical treatment, even if a refusal may risk permanent injury to his health or even lead to premature death. Furthermore, it matters not whether the reasons for the refusal were rational or irrational, unknown or even non-existent. This is so notwithstanding the very strong public interest in preserving the life and health of all citizens" (*T (Adult: Refusal of Treatment), Re* [1992] 4 All E.R. 649, CA, at 664).

Butler-Sloss P., in confirming that a mentally competent person is entitled to refuse treatment even if she does not give good reasons for doing so, said that "there is a point at which refusal and irrationality, as others might see it, tips the usually competent person over into a situation where the person, for however long or short a period, is actually unable to see through the consequences of the act, because that capacity to see through those consequences is inhibited by the panic situation in which the patient finds [her]self" (*Bolton Hospitals NHS Trust v O* [2003] 1 F.L.R. 824, para.15).

The approach taken in this provision is consistent with the finding of the European Court of Human Rights in *Winterwerp v Netherlands* (1979–80) 2 E.H.R.R. 387, para.37, that Art.5 of the European Convention on Human Rights does not permit the detention of a person "simply because his views or behaviour deviate from the norms prevailing in a particular society."

Subsection (5)

1–016   The best interest principle, which must guide all actions done for or decisions made on behalf a person who lacks capacity, is expanded upon in s.4.

A clinician who follows a valid and applicable advance decision (see ss.24–26) is not acting "for or on behalf of a person who lacks capacity", he or she is acting on the instructions of a capacitated individual. It follows that the best interests principle does not apply to such decisions and healthcare professionals must comply with a valid and applicable advance decision, even though they do not consider that it would be in the patient's best interests to do so.

Subsection (6)

1–017   Someone making a decision or acting on behalf of a mentally incapacitated person must consider whether it is possible to decide or act in a way that would interfere less with the person's rights and freedom of action, or whether there is a need to act at all. Put another way, the intervention should be proportional to the particular circumstances of the case. As only "regard" must be had to this principle, an option which is not the least restrictive option can still be in the person's best interests.

The Parliamentary Under-Secretary of State for Constitutional Affairs gave the following example of an approach that would satisfy this principle: "A care assistant might be worried about residents with dementia wandering into the kitchen of the establishment unsupervised in case they come into contact with cleaning fluids. However, to steer them away from the kitchen would be unnecessary if staff ensured that all dangerous liquids were locked in a cupboard. That would not interfere with the freedom of action of the person suffering from dementia" (St.Comm.A, col.25).

Preliminary

People who lack capacity

2.—(1) For the purposes of this Act, a person lacks capacity in relation to a **1–018** matter if at the material time he is unable to make a decision for himself in relation to the matter because of an impairment of, or a disturbance in the functioning of, the mind or brain.

(2) It does not matter whether the impairment or disturbance is permanent or temporary.

(3) A lack of capacity cannot be established merely by reference to—

(a) a person's age or appearance, or

(b) a condition of his, or an aspect of his behaviour, which might lead others to make unjustified assumptions about his capacity.

(4) In proceedings under this Act or any other enactment, any question whether a person lacks capacity within the meaning of this Act must be decided on the balance of probabilities.

(5) No power which a person ("D") may exercise under this Act—

(a) in relation to a person who lacks capacity, or

(b) where D reasonably thinks that a person lacks capacity, is exercisable in relation to a person under 16.

(6) Subsection (5) is subject to section 18(3).

DEFINITIONS
"enactment": s.64(1). **1–019**

GENERAL NOTE

This section sets out the Act's definition of a person (i.e. a person over the age of 16 **1–020** (subs.(5)) who lacks capacity, bearing in mind the assumption is that a person has capacity (s.1(2)). The definition applies for "the purposes of this Act" only (Subs.(1)). Schedule 6 makes consequential amendments to statutes to ensure that the definition contained in this Act is used in relation to other relevant proceedings. Common law definitions of capacity, such as the capacity to make a will (*Banks v Goodfellow* (1869-70) L.R. 5 Q.B. 549) and to marry (*Sheffield City Council v E* [2004] EWHC 2808 (Fam); [2005] Fam 326), are not affected.

An assessment should take place whenever there is a concern that an individual might lack the mental capacity to make the proposed decision; see further, the General Note to s.3. If a person satisfies the "diagnostic test" set out in this section, that person's capacity to make the particular decision in question is assessed using the formula set out in s.3. Therefore, the fact that a person may be suffering, for example, from a mental illness does not of itself render that person mentally incapable of making a particular decision. A finding of incapacity can only be made if it is established under s.3 that the impact of the mental illness on the person is sufficient to render him or her incapable of making that decision. If the person fails to satisfy the diagnostic test, there can be no finding of incapacity for the purposes of this Act.

The Law Commission proposed a "diagnostic threshold" to ensure that the test of capacity "is stringent enough not to catch large numbers of people who make unusual or unwise decisions" (Law Com. No.231, para.3.8).

J. Beckett and R. Chaplin report that the capacity of patients with schizophrenia has been extensively studied and has shown a broad range from the significantly impaired to full capacity in both the acute and chronic stages of the illness, and that patients with depression have shown relatively unimpaired capacity. Their own study found that many patients hospitalised with mania have capacity to make an informed choice regarding treatment even when compulsorily detained ("Capacity to consent to treatment in patients with acute mania" (2006) 30 *Psychiatric Bulletin* 419).

Subsection (1)

1–021 *Impairment of, or a disturbance in the functioning of, the brain or mind.* A wide range of conditions can result in incapacity to make decisions. In some cases, the capacity to take decisions is never attained (for example a person born with a severe leaning disability). In other cases, capacity is attained but is subsequently lost, either on a temporary or permanent basis. The Explanatory Notes state that the diagnostic test contained in this provision could "cover a range of problems, such as psychiatric illness, learning disability, dementia, brain damage or even a toxic confusional state, as long as it has the necessary effect on the functioning of the mind or brain, causing the person to be unable to make the decision" (para.22). It will "clearly also apply to patients with grave physical illnesses, which, by reason of vital organ failure and consequent biochemical disturbances, will cause either confusion or impairment of consciousness" (Dr Fiona Randall, Oral and written evidence, Ev 301). It could also cover people who are suffering from the effects of pain, shock or exhaustion or who are drunk or under the influence of drugs. A person who is rendered unconscious will clearly satisfy the test.

Although medical evidence supporting a conclusion that the test has been satisfied is not required, it would be advisable for the assessor to seek such evidence in difficult or controversial cases; see further, the General Note to s.3.

Subsection (2)

1–022 The temporary nature of P's incapacity matters for the purposes of decision making because a decision should be delayed if the person's mental capacity might return and the delay would be consistent with the person's best interests (see s.4(3)). Temporary loss of capacity could be caused by the effect of excessive alcohol consumption, the misuse of drugs, the nature of a person's mental disorder, the effect of prescribed medication or an emotional crisis. Also see the note on s.24(1).

Subsection (3)

1–023 This provision is aimed at preventing unjustified assumptions being made about a person's mental capacity. It "gives further emphasis to the Bill's principle that everyone should be assumed to have capacity until it is shown that they do not. For example, it is not acceptable to say, on the assumption that someone has a learning disability, that he cannot or will not want to make decisions about where to live", *per* Baroness Andrews (*Hansard*, HL Vol.670, col.1319). Also see the notes to s.4(1).

Subsection (4)

1–024 "The balance of probability standard means that a court is satisfied an event occurred if the court considers that, on the evidence, the occurrence of the event was more likely than not", *per* Lord Nicholls in *H (Minors) (Sexual Abuse: Standard of Proof)*, Re [1996] A.C. 563 at 586.

Subsections (5) and (6)

1–025 Although the powers under this Act only generally arise where the person lacking capacity is 16 or over, powers in relation to property might be exercised in relation to a younger person who has disabilities which will cause the incapacity to last into adulthood (see s.18(3)). Any overlap with the jurisdiction under the Children Act 1989 (c.41) can be dealt with by an order made under s.21. Further exceptions to the general rule that this Act applies to those who are 16 and over are:

1. A lasting power of attorney can only be made be a person who has reached 18 (s.9(2)(c)).
2. An advance decision can only be made by a person who reached 18 (s.24(1)).

3. The standard and urgent authorisation procedure in Sch.A1 only applies to a person who has reached 18 (Sch.A1, para.13).
4. The offence of ill-treatment or neglect of a mentally incapacitated person established by s.44 has no age limit.

This Act does not effect the legal right of a person with parental responsibility over a child to consent to the medical treatment of that child on the child's behalf.

Inability to make decisions

3.—(1) For the purposes of section 2, a person is unable to make a decision for **1–026** himself if he is unable—
(a) to understand the information relevant to the decision,
(b) to retain that information,
(c) to use or weigh that information as part of the process of making the decision, or
(d) to communicate his decision (whether by talking, using sign language or any other means).

(2) A person is not to be regarded as unable to understand the information relevant to a decision if he is able to understand an explanation of it given to him in a way that is appropriate to his circumstances (using simple language, visual aids or any other means).

(3) The fact that a person is able to retain the information relevant to a decision for a short period only does not prevent him from being regarded as able to make the decision.

(4) The information relevant to a decision includes information about the reasonably foreseeable consequences of—
(a) deciding one way or another, or
(b) failing to make the decision.

DEFINITIONS
"emergency worker": s.2(3)   **1–027**

GENERAL NOTE
This section sets out the test for determining whether a person who has satisfied the diag- **1–028** nostic test set out in s.2 is "unable to make a [particular] decision" and therefore lacks capacity for the purposes of this Act. The approach taken is a "functional" approach to capacity as the definition relates to the ability of the person to make a particular decision at a particular moment in time, not on the person's ability to make decisions generally. The assessment of a person's capacity must therefore relate to the decision to be made. The functional approach can be contrasted with the "outcome" approach which uses the consequence of the decision-making process as the criterion for determining capacity, and the "status" or "diagnostic" approach under which a person's capacity is determined by his or her membership of a specific population, such as those who have a particular psychiatric diagnosis. With regard to the status approach T. Grisso and P. Appelbaum have pointed out that a "patient may be psychotic, seriously depressed, or in a moderately advanced stage of dementia, yet still found competent to make some or all decisions" (*Assessing Competence to Consent to Treatment* (1998), p.18). The rejection of the outcome approach, which is confirmed in s.1(4), was emphasised in *Masterman-Lister v Jewell* [2002] EWHC 417 (QB); [2002] W.T.L.R. 563, at para.19 where Wright J. said that "in principle, legal capacity depends on understanding rather than wisdom; the quality of the decision is irrelevant as long as the person understands what he is deciding". The appropriateness of adopting the functional approach has been confirmed by research that has shown that people with mild intellectual disabilities may have the capacity to make some financial

decisions but not others (W.M.I. Suto, I.C.H. Clare, A.J. Holland and P.C. Watson "Capacity to make financial decisions among people with mild intellectual disabilities", Journal of Intellectual Disability Research (2005) 49, 199–209).

The functional approach, which allows individuals to have the maximum decision-making powers possible, reflects the position that obtained under common law. In *Masterman-Lister v Brutton & Co* [2002] EWCA Civ 1889; [2003] 3 All E.R. 163, Chadwick L.J. said at paras 57–58:

> "English law requires that a person must have the necessary mental capacity if he is to do a legally effective act or to make a legally effective decision for himself. The authorities are unanimous in support of two broad propositions. First, that the mental capacity required by the law is capacity in relation to the transaction which is to be effected. Second, that what is required is the capacity to understand the nature of that transaction when it is explained."

In *Sheffield City Council v E* [2004] EWHC 2808 (Fam); [2005] Fam 326, para.19, Munby J. said:

> "The general rule of English law, whatever the context, is that the test of capacity is the ability (whether or not one chooses to exercise it) to understand the nature and quality of the transaction."

The functional approach allows for a temporary loss of capacity, for example, unconsciousness following a road traffic accident, and for persons to lack capacity in relation to one matter but not in relation to another (perhaps more complex) matter. A striking example of a situation where a person was found to be capable of making a decision in relation to one matter, but not in relation to another is the deceased who on the same day was found by Karminski J. to have had capacity to marry (*Park, In the Estate of* [1954] P. 89), and by Pearce J. and a jury not to have had capacity to make a will (*Park, Culross v Park* (1950) *The Times*, December 2, 1950) (cited by Munby J. in *Sheffield City Council v E*, above, para.25).

1–029   As s.1(2) of this Act establishes a presumption of capacity in respect of persons over the age of 16, a capacity assessment by a potential decision maker should only be undertaken if there is evidence to suggest that the presumption might be rebutted. Although, strictly speaking, this section requires a fresh capacity assessment to be undertaken in respect of every decision that the person might be required to make, with a person who is profoundly mentally incapacitated this could result in a large number of separate capacity assessments having to be made during the course of a single day. For routine decisions such as what clothes the person should wear, what food he or she should eat, or whether he or she should go for an accompanied walk, it is likely that the capacity assessment, if it happens at all, will be undertaken in a perfunctory manner. It would be appropriate for the approach that formal carers should adopt in relation to such matters to be incorporated into the person's care plan. If there is a challenge as to whether the person had capacity, the decision-maker would need to show that he or she had reasonable grounds for believing that the person lacked the capacity to make the decision in question at that particular time: see s.5. It is suggested that formal capacity assessments should be undertaken in respect of significant, complex or controversial decisions, decisions which would involve placing the incapacitated person at risk, or where the mental capacity of the person is disputed.

If there is any doubt as to whether a person lacks capacity, this should be decided on a balance of probabilities (s.2(4)). Prior to reaching a conclusion that a person lacks the capacity to make a particular decision, all practicable steps must be taken to help him or her to make the decision (s.1(3)). A person who wishes to challenge a finding of capacity can, if the matter cannot be resolved by discussion, mediation or the provision of a second opinion, make an application to the Court of Protection for a declaration (s.15(1)(a)).

The person who is required to assess an individual's capacity will be the person who has the power to make the decision in respect of, or to act on behalf of the person in question. This Act does not establish any formal procedure for the assessment of capacity and no statutory form confirming incapacity needs to be completed. Neither is there a requirement for a particular professional, such as a psychologist or a psychiatrist, to be involved in the assessment. In the context of decision making by multi-disciplinary care teams, it is not sufficient for a decision to be categorised as a "team decision": the person who has professional accountability for a decision relating to an individual who may lack capacity must be identified, and it is that person who must undertake the capacity assessment. The assessment of a person's capacity to make most day-to-day decisions will be made by the appropriate carer and will not require the involvement of a professional. Where consent to medical treatment is required, the doctor proposing the treatment is responsible for the capacity assessment. If a professional, such as a psychiatrist or a psychologist, is brought in to assist the potential decision-maker with an assessment of the person's capacity to make a complex or serious decision, the ultimate decision about capacity is that of the potential decision-maker and not the psychiatrist or psychologist whose role is that of an advisor. The *Code of Practice*, at para.4.53, suggests that:

"Professional involvement might be needed if:

- the decision that needs to be made is complicated or has serious consequences
- an assessor concludes a person lacks capacity, and the person challenges the finding
- family members, carers and/or professionals disagree about a person's capacity
- there is a conflict of interest between the assessor and the person being assessed
- the person being assessed is expressing different views to different people—they may be trying to please everyone or telling people what they think they want to hear
- somebody might challenge the person's capacity to make the decision—either at the time of the decision or later (for example, a family member might challenge a will after a person has died on the basis that the person lacked capacity when they made the will)
- somebody has been accused of abusing a vulnerable adult who may lack capacity to make decisions that protect them
- a person repeatedly makes decisions that put them at risk or could result in suffering or damage."

It is a striking fact that during the Parliamentary debates on the Bill no-one questioned **1–030** the ability of professionals, let alone lay people, to assess mental capacity. The available evidence suggests that professional competence in this area is poor (see the studies cited below). In the context of medical practice, T. Grisso and P. Appelbaum suggest that doctors approach the issue of capacity assessments intuitively:

"Whether they recognise it or not, most clinicians assess their patients' decision-making abilities as part of every encounter. Ordinarily, this occurs unconsciously, as clinicians take notice of patients' dress, demeanour, communicative skills, intelligence, ability to attend to a conversation, apparent understanding, and ability to reach a decision. Since we all assume, appropriately, that people with whom we deal are competent to make decisions about their own lives—indeed the law makes a similar assumption—only when our unconscious monitoring detects something unexpected do we attend to it directly" (above, p.61).

The authors suggest that the following factors alert clinicians to the need for a capacity assessment: abrupt changes in patients' mental states, patients' refusal of recommended treatment, patients' consent to specially invasive or risky treatment, and the presence of one or more risk factors to impaired decision making, such as diagnosis or age (above, pp.62–76).

A systematic review of studies of capacity to consent to treatment for psychiatric patients found, inter alia, that "although there is no gold standard criterion of capacity, it may be that formal assessments, although reliable, lack specificity and tend to 'overdiagnose' incapacity compared with the clinicians' assessments" (D.Okai, G.Owen, H.McGuire, S.Singh,

R.Churchill and M.Hotopf, "Mental capacity in psychiatric patients", British Journal of Psychiatry (2007), 191, 291–297, 295).

1–031   For a person to be assessed as being mentally incapable or making a decision he or she must: (1) be suffering from an impairment of, or disturbance in the functioning of, the mind or brain (s.2(1)); and (2) fail to satisfy any one of the requirements set out in paras (a)–(d) of subs.(1). Paragraphs (a), (b) and (c), which will cover the vast majority of cases, are taken from the decision of the Court of Appeal in *MB (Medical Treatment), Re* [1997] 2 F.L.R. 426 at 437, where Butler-Sloss L.J. identified the test of capacity in medical cases in the following terms:

> "A person lacks capacity if some impairment or disturbance of mental functioning renders the person unable to make a decision whether to consent to or refuse treatment. That inability to make a decision will occur when:
>
> (a) the patient is unable to comprehend and retain the information which is material to the decision, especially as to the likely consequences of having or not having the treatment in question;
> (b) the patient is unable to use the information and weigh it in the balance as part of the process of arriving at the decision."

As the approach adopted by this section is based on the common law test of capacity ("there is no relevant distinction" between them: *Local Authority X v MM and KM* [2007] EWHC 2003 (Fam); [2007] M.H.L.R. 173, para.74, per Munby J.), the Court of Protection will use the existing caselaw on capacity as a guide to interpretation.

The finding of Lord Donaldson in *T (Adult: Refusal of Treatment), Re* [1992] 4 All E.R. 649 at 661 that the required capacity is the capacity which is "commensurate with the gravity of the decision" which the person is purporting to make is likely to be followed under this Act. Thus the more serious the decision, the greater the level of capacity required. This issue is considered by A.Buchanan in "Mental capacity, legal competence and consent to treatment", Journal of the Royal Society of Medicine 2004; 97: 415–420.

To be valid, a consent must be truly that of the mentally capable person, given freely and uncontaminated by the undue influence of others. The nature of undue influence is considered in the note on s.1(3). Paragraph 3.1 of the *Reference Guide to Consent for Examination or Treatment* (Department of Health, 2001) considers the validity of consent given in a prison or psychiatric hospital environment:

> "When patients are seen and treated in environments where involuntary detention may be an issue, such as prisons and mental hospitals, there is a potential for treatment offers to be perceived coercively, whether or not this is the case. Coercion invalidates consent and care must be taken to ensure that the patient makes a decision freely. Coercion should be distinguished from providing the patient with appropriate reassurance concerning their treatment, or pointing out the potential benefits of treatment for the patient's health. However, threats such as the withdrawal of any privileges or loss of remission of sentence for refusing consent, or using such measures to induce consent are not acceptable."

In *B (Consent to Treatment: Capacity), Re* [2002] EWHC 429 (Fam); [2002] 1 F.L.R. 1090, at para.100, Butler-Sloss P. stressed the importance of distinguishing between capacity and best interests in the context of consent to medical treatment:

> "If there are difficulties in deciding whether the patient has sufficient mental capacity, particularly if the refusal may have grave consequences for the patient, it is most important that those considering the issue should not confuse the question of mental capacity with the nature of the decision made by the patient, however grave the consequences. The view of the patient may reflect a difference in values rather than an absence of competence and the assessment of capacity should be approached with this firmly in mind. The doctors must not allow their emotional reaction to or strong disagreement with the

decision of the patient to cloud their judgment in answering the primary question whether the patient has the mental capacity to make the decision."

A person's ambivalence about whether to receive medical treatment is only relevant to the issue of capacity "if, and only if, the ambivalence genuinely strikes at the root of the mental capacity of the patient", *per* Butler-Sloss P. in *B (Consent to Treatment: Capacity), Re* above, at para.35. In this case the President said at para.94: "Unless the gravity of the illness has affected the patient's capacity, a seriously disabled patient has the same rights as the fit person to respect for personal autonomy".

If there is concern or doubt about the mental capacity of a person to consent to medical treatment, that doubt should be resolved as soon as possible, by doctors within the hospital or NHS trust or by other normal medical procedures. In the meantime, while the question of capacity is being resolved, the person must be cared for in accordance with the judgment of the doctors as to the person's best interests. In the rare case where disagreement still exists about competence, it is of the utmost importance that the person is fully informed of the steps being taken, such as enlisting independent outside expertise, and made part of the process. Those in charge must not allow a situation of deadlock or drift to occur. If all appropriate steps to seek independent assistance from medical experts outside the hospital have failed, the hospital should not hesitate to make an application to the Court of Protection or seek the advice of the Official Solicitor (*NHS Trust v T (Adult Patient: Refusal of Medical Treatment)* [2004] EWHC 1279 (Fam) ; [2005] 1 All E.R. 387, para.42).

A judge is not required to accept the evidence of psychiatrists as to a person's mental **1–032** capacity (*W (Adult: Refusal of Medical Treatment), Re* [2002] EWHC Fam 901). In *Masterman-Lister v Jewell*, above, Wright J. said at para.16:

"Although the opinions of skilled and experienced medical practitioners are a very important element in the evidence to be considered by the court, that element has to be considered in conjunction with any other evidence that there may be about the manner in which the subject of the enquiry actually has conducted his everyday life and affairs."

The evidence of the patient's wife was preferred to the medical evidence in *Lindsay v Wood* [2006] EWHC 2895 (QB), largely because of the "difference between 'real life', as it is described, and the artificial conditions of medical assessment" (para.49). Stanley Burnton J. said at para.18:

"When considering the question of capacity, psychiatrists and psychologists will normally wish to take into account all aspects of the personality and behaviour of the person in question, including vulnerability to exploitation. However, vulnerability to exploitation does not of itself lead to the conclusion that there is a lack of capacity. Many people who have full capacity are vulnerable to exploitation, or more so than most other people. Many people make rash and irresponsible decisions, but are of full capacity. The issue is ... whether the person concerned has the mental capacity to make a rational decision."

Although the test set out in this section is easily understandable and, perhaps, gives the impression that the assessment of a person's mental capacity is a relatively straightforward task, the reality is that the assessment can sometimes be extremely difficult. Baroness Finlay of Llandaff gave evidence to the Joint Committee on this point:

"If I can give you two specific and very common instances, one where patients have been anxious, which is understandable because they are facing dying, and where the benzodiazepine group of drugs such as Midazolam are used to remove the churning drive of anxiety without sedating the patients so they can still function but they are relived in part of this desperate feeling of anxiety, butterflies and churning inside. With some of these patients you can have a conversation and they appear to understand everything that is said and have recall. The following day they have no recall whatsoever of that conversation. It may have been a few hours later in some patients. Another situation which arises is where patients' calcium goes up and that occurs in about ten per cent of all cancer patients. They become confused. That is a gradual onset and the outset is difficult to diagnose. They may appear to be arguing rationally but when their calcium level has been brought down and is treated they then are behaving differently and they have no recall of that previous conversation or the direction that they were trying to give in expressing what they wanted. Also they may completely change their mind which is a terribly important situation for a clinician. The difficulty is in judging whether they have capacity or not because at any one point in time the conversation appears to be logical and consequential. There are lots of other situations which arise, particularly with patients on steroids where the steroids may have created a very mild steroid psychosis which can be difficult to diagnose and just presents as emotional immobility. Again, their thinking and perception is distorted" (Oral and Written Evidence, Ev 126).

This Act requires judgments to be made about a person's mental capacity by people without a clinical background who will probably have had no training or experience in making such assessments. There must be a very considerable doubt as to their ability to do this. Similar doubts can be expressed about the competence of some medical practitioners to undertake this task. In its evidence to the Joint Committee, the Alzeheimer's Society emphasised the need for a skilled capacity assessment. One of its members wrote of her experiences:

"As a former nurse, my mother was extremely good at covering up her problems and was extremely plausible. Her doctor reacted with shocked amazement at our suggestion that my mother had dementia.—'There's nothing wrong with your mother. I saw her only the other day and had a conversation with her. She's fine.' This was at a time when my mother was putting the electric kettle on the gas ring, entertaining phantom meetings of teachers in her front room, turning up at the hairdressers at 2a.m. and living on a diet of biscuits having forgotten how to cook" (Oral and Written Evidence, Ev 384).

1–033   It has been noted that competency is rarely questioned when the patient consents to treatment (B. Hoffman and J. Srinivasan "A study of competence to consent to treatment in a psychiatric hospital" (1992) 37 *Canadian Journal of Psychiatry* 179). Also see R. Cairns, C. Maddock, A. Buchanan, A.S. David, P. Hayward, G. Richardson, G. Szmukler and M. Hotopf., "Reliability of mental capacity assessments in psychiatric in-patients" (2005) 187 *British Journal Psychiatry* 372, where the researchers found a probable bias towards judging a patient as having capacity if they made the apparently "correct" decision of agreeing to treatment.

Research into the application of the functional approach to capacity has been undertaken: see M.J. Gunn, J.G. Wong, I.C.H. Clare and A.J. Holland, "Decision-making capacity" (1999) 7(3) Med. L. Rev. 269. The authors concluded that the approach "can work, albeit the interface between legal definition and clinical practice is not a simple one to bridge" (at 306). Suto and her colleagues found that the quality of capacity assessment made by medical practitioners under Part VII of the 1983 Act, including those undertaken by psychiatrists, was poor and that most assessors relied on the status approach. The authors found little evidence of the use of the functional approach (W.M.I. Suto, I.C.H. Clare and A.J. Holland, "Substitute financial decision-making in England and Wales: a study of the Court of Protection" (2002) 24(1) *Journal of Social Welfare and Family Law* 37). There is also evidence that psychiatrists can be inconsistent in their approach to the assessment of patients' capacity to consent to treatment (A. Shah and S. Mukherjee, "Ascertaining Capacity to Consent: A survey of approaches used by psychiatrists" (2003) 43 *Medicine, Science and the Law* 231). A study of the recognition of the mental incapacity of acutely ill medical hospital in-patients found that clinical teams rarely identified patients who did not have the required mental capacity (V. Raymont, W. Bingley, A Buchanan, S. David, P. Hayward, S. Wessely, and M. Hotopf, "Prevalence of mental incapacity in medical inpatients and associated risk factors: cross sectional study" (2004) 364 *Lancet* 1421). The Royal College of Psychiatrists summarised the available research evidence by stating that "at present few doctors understand and are knowledgeable about capacity assessments, and many would fail to recognise that a person lacked capacity" ("Assisted Dying for the Terminally Ill Bill—Statement form the Royal College of Psychiatrists on Physician Assisted Suicide", April, 2006).

For an extensive analysis of the assessment of capacity from a psychological perspective, see "Assessment of Capacity in Adults: Interim Guidance for Psychologists" (2006) *British Psychological Society.* Also see, *Assessment of Mental Capacity: Guidance for Doctors and Lawyers* (2004) BMA/Law Society and M. Church and S. Watts, "Assessment of mental capacity: a flow chart guide" Psychiatric Bulletin (2007), 31: 304–307.

Subsection (1) para.(a)
The nature of understanding is considered by T. Grisso and P. Appelbaum, above, at p.38: **1–034**

"As basic as the concept of understanding may seem, the psychological process related to it are not easily defined. A person's accurate assimilation of information involves a complex series of events. First the information must be received as presented, a process that is influenced not only by sensory integrity, but also by perceptual functions such as attention and selective awareness. Whatever is received then undergoes cognitive processing and is encoded in a manner consistent with the person's existing fund of information and concepts, which in turn influences how, and how well, the message is recorded and stored in the memory."

The authors point out that many medical conditions, as well as chronic mental disorders and disabilities, can "have a substantial negative influence on these functions" (p.39).

In the context of an individual's capacity to execute an instrument, it has been held that the degree or extent of the understanding required is relative to the particular transaction which it is to effect (*Re Beaney (deceased)* [1978] 2 All E.R. 585).

The information provided must include the information specified in subs.(4). As the information must be "relevant to the decision", the person should not be burdened with peripheral information. The information, which should be devoid of unnecessary technical jargon, should be given in an appropriate manner in the person's first language (subs.(2)). It is suggested that the person must have the ability to understand that the information provided applies to him or herself. All practicable steps should be taken to assist the person to understand the information (s.1(3)), with account being taken of any cultural or religious factors relating to the person which might inhibit communication.

In the context of consent to medical treatment, an explanation in "broad terms" of the nature of the procedure which is intended and its likely effects would be sufficient for the person's consent to be "real" (*Chatterton v Gerson* [1981] 1 QB 432 at 442). In *R v Mental Health Act Commission Ex p. X* (1998) 9 B.M.L.R. 77 at 87, DC, Stuart-Smith L.J. said that he could not "accept that a patient must understand the precise physiological process involved before he can be said to be capable of understanding the nature and likely effects of the treatment or can consent to it". The finding in *Chatterton v Gerson* was followed by the House of Lords in *Sidaway v Board of Governors of the Bethlem Royal Hospital* [1985] 1 All E.R. 643, where it was held that the decision on what risks should be disclosed to a patient was primarily a matter of clinical judgment and in making that judgment a doctor was required to act in accordance with a practice accepted at the time as proper by a responsible body of medical opinion. It would not matter that there may be another body of responsible medical opinion which takes a different view, However, Lords Keith and Bridge, speaking with the majority, considered that the court might in certain circumstances come to the conclusion that disclosure of a particular risk was so obviously necessary to an informed choice on the part of the patient that no reasonably prudent doctor would fail to make it. This approach was confirmed by the House of Lords in *Bolitho (Deceased) v City and Hackney HA* [1997] 4 All E.R. 771, where it was held that in a rare case, if it could be demonstrated that the medical opinion was not capable of withstanding logical analysis, the judge would be entitled to hold that the body of opinion was not reasonable or responsible.

Sidaway and *Bolitho* were considered by the Court of Appeal in *Pearce v United Bristol Healthcare NHS Trust* (1999) 48 B.M.L.R.118, para.23, where Lord Woolf held that:

"[I]f there is a significant risk which would affect the judgment of a reasonable patient then in the normal course it is the responsibility of a doctor to inform the patient of that significant risk, if the information is needed so that the patient can determine for him or herself as to what course that he or she should adopt."

Whether a risk is "significant" cannot be determined simply in terms of percentages. The doctor will have to:

"take into account all the relevant considerations, which include the ability of the patient to comprehend what he has to say to him or her and the state of the patient at the particular time, both from the physical point of view and the emotional point of view" (para.24).

If a patient asks about a risk, it is the doctor's legal duty to give an honest answer (*per* Lord Woolf at para.5).

In *R (A Minor) (Wardship: Medical Treatment), Re* [1991] 4 All E.R.177, a case concerning the capacity of a child to consent to treatment, Lord Donaldson M.R. said at 187:

"[W]hat is involved is not merely an ability to understand the nature of the proposed treatment—in this case compulsory medication—but a full understanding and appreciation of the consequences both of the treatment in terms of intended and possible side effects and, equally important, the anticipated consequences of a failure to treat."

The treating doctor should therefore provide the patient with information about what would happen to the patient if the treatment is provided, the likely consequences to the patient if the treatment is not provided, and the risks and side effects of the treatment. In the studies examined by Diana Rose and her colleagues, approximately half of those who received electroconvulsive therapy felt that they had been given insufficient information about the procedure ("Information, consent and perceived coercion: patient's perspectives on electroconvulsive therapy" (2005) 186 *British Journal of Psychiatry* 54).

The following passage from the General Medical Council's guidelines "Consent: patients and doctors making decisions together" (2008) suggests that doctors have a therapeutic privilege that allows for certain information to be withheld from patients:

"You should not withhold information necessary for making decisions . . . unless you believe that giving it would cause the patient serious harm. In this context 'serious harm' means more than the patient might become upset or decide to refuse treatment" (Pt.2, para.16).

Given that the notion of professional paternalism has been effectively buried by the recommendations made by *Learning from Bristol: the report of the public inquiry into children's heart surgery at the Bristol Royal Infirmary* 1984–1995 (Cm.5207), it is suggested that Andrew Hockton is correct when he states that doctors invoke therapeutic privilege "at their peril" (*The Law of Consent to Medical Treatment*, 2002, para.1–002).

Subsection (1) para.(b)

1–035 RETAIN. See subs.(3).

Subsection (1) para.(c)

1–036 Understanding the information is not sufficient: the person must also be able to use the information as part of the process of arriving at a decision. In using the information, the person can be assisted by relevant professional advice (*Masterman-Lister v Brutton & Co* [2003] 3 All E.R.162, CA), and by support from the person's care network. The *Code of Practice*, at para.4.22, offers the following examples of persons who able to understand, but not "use or weigh" the information:

"For example, a person with the eating disorder anorexia nervosa may understand information about the consequences of not eating. But their compulsion not to eat might be too strong for them to ignore. Some people who have serious brain damage might make impulsive decisions regardless of information they may have been given or their understanding of it."

In order to "use or weigh" information, the person must not be prevented by mental disorder from believing the information because "the specific requirement of belief is subsumed in the more general requirements of understanding and of ability to use and weigh information" (*Local Authority X v MM and KM* [2007] EWHC 2003 (Fam); [2007] M.H.L.R. 173, para.81, per Munby J.). In *B v Croydon HA* (1994) 22 B.M.L.R. 13, 20, Thorpe J. said that in the context of consent to medical treatment there is a difference between outright disbelief (due to mental disorder) which meant being "impervious to reason, divorced from reality, or incapable of adjustment after reflection", and "the tendency which most people have when undergoing medical treatment to self assess and then puzzle over the divergence between medical and self assessment". In *R (on the application of B) v Dr. SS, Dr. AC and the Secretary of State for Health* [2005] EWHC 86 (Admin), paras 188, 190, Charles J. found that the patient was refusing treatment because he did not accept or believe that he is, or may be, mentally ill. It therefore followed that the patient lacked capacity because he "does not believe or accept a cornerstone of the factors to be taken into account in considering the information he has been given about his proposed treatment and therefore is not able to use and weigh in the balance the relevant information as to his proposed treatment in reaching a decision to agree to it or to refuse it".

In *Re MB*, above, the court said that if a compulsive disorder or phobia from which the patient suffers dominates her thinking, the decision may not be a true one. In this case the patient's phobia to needles induced such panic in her that "at that moment the needle or mask dominated her thinking and made her quite unable to consider anything else" (at 431). *Re MB* was applied in *Re H (Adult Patient)* [2006] EWHC 1230 (Fam) where Potter P. said, at para.22, that "a compulsive disorder or phobia may prevent the patient's decision from being a true one, particularly if conditioned by some obsessional belief or feeling which so distorts the judgment as to render the decision invalid". Similar considerations apply if the patient's thinking is dominated by factors such as confusion, shock, fatigue, pain or drugs (*Re T (Adult: Refusal of Treatment* [1992] 4 All E.R. 649).

A person who is subject to the undue influence of another would be unable to give a valid consent: see the notes on s.1(3).

Subsection (1) para.(d)

The rationale for this provision is explained in the Explanatory Memorandum at para.27: **1–037**

"This is intended to be a residual category and will only affect a small group of persons, in particular some of those with the very rare condition of 'locked-in syndrome'. It seems likely that people suffering from this condition can in fact still understand, retain and use information and so would not be regarded as lacking capacity under subs.(1)(a)-(c). Some people who suffer from this condition can communicate by blinking an eye, but it seems that others cannot communicate at all. [This provision] treats those who are completely unable to communicate their decisions as unable to make a decision. Any residual ability to communicate (such as blinking an eye to indicate 'yes' or 'no' in answer to a question) would exclude a person from this category."

Although the blinking of an eye or the squeezing of a hand can be used to communicate a decision without undue difficulty, it would be less easy to use such methods to identify whether the person has understood and applied the information provided. In *AK (Adult Patient) (Medical Treatment: Consent), Re* [2001] 1 F.L.R. 129, a patient who could only communicate by blinking one eyelid was held to be mentally capable of making a decision to refuse life-sustaining treatment.

This provision is concerned with people who are "unable" to communicate their decision; it does not encompass people who are unwilling to communicate their decision. If a person falls into the latter category, he or she must be assumed to be mentally capable unless the decision-maker assesses that person as lacking the capacity to make the decision in question (s.1(2)). If the failure of the person to communicate is assessed as being the consequence of "an impairment of, or a disturbance in the functioning of, [that person's] mind or brain" (s.2(1)), the decision-maker must consider whether the identified impairment or disturbance results in a failure of the person to satisfy the requirements of paras (a),(b) or (c). If there is such a failure, the person will lack the capacity to make the decision.

Subsection (2)

1–038   This provision, which expands upon the principle set out in s.1(3), was added at the third reading of the Bill so that there "is no longer any doubt: no one should be labelled incapable merely because insufficient efforts have been made to help him understand and communicate", *per* the Parliamentary Under-Secretary of State (*Hansard*, HC Vol.428, col.1632).

AN EXPLANATION. The explanation must be sufficiently specific to enable the person to use or weigh the information as required by subs.(1)(c).

Subsection (3)

1–039   This provision allows for situations where the person's mental capacity fluctuates.

SHORT PERIOD. The person must be able to retain the information for the time that it takes to make the decision. Most decisions will therefore require the information to be retained for a brief period only. Significant or difficult decisions might require the person to retain the information over a number of days before a decision is made. The assessment process can be repeated if the information has been forgotten.

In "Summing up—a Judge's Perspective", [2006] Crim. L.R. 817, H.H. Judge Nic Madge makes reference to Professor Robert H. Margolis's review of the literature that shows that patient's retain about 50 per cent of the information provided to them by health care professionals. Of the information recalled, about half is remembered incorrectly, i.e. patients remember correctly only about a quarter of what they are told. An equally disturbing finding is that patient's often forget their own medical diagnoses. Information presented in a simple, easy to understand format is remembered better than information presented in a more complex manner. The more information presented, the lower the proportion that is recalled by the patient. When verbal presentation is supplemented by written explanations, recall can be significantly enhanced: see "Boosting Memory with Informational Counselling" *The ASHA Leader* (August 3, 2004) pp.10–11, 28, available at *www.asha.org/about/publications/leader-online/archives/2004/040803*.

Best interests

1–040   **4.**—(1) In determining for the purposes of this Act what is in a person's best interests, the person making the determination must not make it merely on the basis of—

(a) the person's age or appearance, or

(b) a condition of his, or an aspect of his behaviour, which might lead others to make unjustified assumptions about what might be in his best interests.

(2) The person making the determination must consider all the relevant circumstances and, in particular, take the following steps.

(3) He must consider—

(a) whether it is likely that the person will at some time have capacity in relation to the matter in question, and

(b) if it appears likely that he will, when that is likely to be.

(4) He must, so far as reasonably practicable, permit and encourage the person to participate, or to improve his ability to participate, as fully as possible in any act done for him and any decision affecting him.

(5) Where the determination relates to life-sustaining treatment he must not, in considering whether the treatment is in the best interests of the person concerned, be motivated by a desire to bring about his death.

(6) He must consider, so far as is reasonably ascertainable—

(a) the person's past and present wishes and feelings (and, in particular, any relevant written statement made by him when he had capacity),

(b) the beliefs and values that would be likely to influence his decision if he had capacity, and

(c) the other factors that he would be likely to consider if he were able to do so.

(7) He must take into account, if it is practicable and appropriate to consult them, the views of—

(a) anyone named by the person as someone to be consulted on the matter in question or on matters of that kind,

(b) anyone engaged in caring for the person or interested in his welfare,

(c) any donee of a lasting power of attorney granted by the person, and

(d) any deputy appointed for the person by the court, as to what would be in the person's best interests and, in particular, as to the matters mentioned in subsection (6).

(8) The duties imposed by subsections (1) to (7) also apply in relation to the exercise of any powers which—

(a) are exercisable under a lasting power of attorney, or

(b) are exercisable by a person under this Act where he reasonably believes that another person lacks capacity.

(9) In the case of an act done, or a decision made, by a person other than the court, there is sufficient compliance with this section if (having complied with the requirements of subsections (1) to (7)) he reasonably believes that what he does or decides is in the best interests of the person concerned.

(10) "Life-sustaining treatment" means treatment which in the view of a person providing health care for the person concerned is necessary to sustain life.

(11) "Relevant circumstances" are those—

(a) of which the person making the determination is aware, and

(b) which it would be reasonable to regard as relevant.

DEFINITIONS
    "treatment": s.64(1)   **1–041**
    "lasting power of attorney": s.64(1)
    "deputy": s.64(1)
    "the court": s.64(1)

GENERAL NOTE

    Section 1(5) establishes the principle that "an act done, or decision made, under this Act **1–042** for or on behalf of a person who lacks capacity must be done, or made, in his best interests". This section sets out a checklist of factors which must be considered before the decision is made, or the act is carried out. In effect, the checklist establishes the course of action that should be followed in order to reach a determination whether a decison is in the person's best interests, a term which is not defined in this Act: it deals with the process of acquiring evidence, rather than specifying the criteria of best interests. A considerable latitude is therefore granted to the decision-maker when reaching a reasonable belief as to where P's best interests lie. In its report on *Mental Incapacity*, the Law Commission acknowledged that "no statutory guidance could offer an exhastive account of what is in the persons best interests, the intention being that the individual person and his or her individual circumstances should always determine the result" (Law Com. No. 231, para.3.26). As well as being in the person's best interests, the decision should also aim to satisfy the least restrictive option principle set out in s.1(6).

Any person or body that intervenes on behalf of P must believe that their act or decision is in that person's best interests and that belief will have to be reasonable (subs.(9)). The test of best interests is therefore an objective one. It is the best interests of P that is at issue, not the best interests of another. In *Local Authority X v MM and KM* [2007] EWHC 2003 (Fam); [2007] M.H.L.R. 173, para.108, Munby J. said: "Parental rights and responsibilities, and the rights and responsibilities of partners and other carers, have in the final analysis to give way to the best interests of a vulnerable adult." The test applies to all decisions made or actions taken under this Act, ranging from a decision of the Court of Protection to a minor decision made by an informal carer. It is unrealistic to imagine that the process established by this section will be followed in respect of every minor decision that will need to be taken on behalf of P.

It is noteworthy that while the law requires a "significant harm" test to be satisfied before a child can be removed from the family home against parental wishes (Children Act 1989, s.31(2)), the court can order the removal of a mentally incapable adult from the family home under this Act merely on the basis that removal would be in the adult's best interests. This issue is considered in the note on *Best interests and living arrangements*, below.

Only one course of action can be in the best interests of P. The practical effect of subs.(6) is to attempt to ascertain what P's subjective preference would have been had he or she been mentally capable. However, the effect of this is not to require the decision maker to make a form of substituted judgment on behalf of P as the matters itemised in subs.(6) must merely be considered by the decision-maker who may come to a decision which P would not have wanted. For example, "if someone had a lifelong aversion to needles, a decision could still be taken to give them the necessary injection when they were unconscious after a car crash", *per* the Parliamentary Under-Secretary of State, St.Comm. A, col.73. The concept of substituted judgment has been developed by the American courts and rejected by the English courts; see, for example, the observations of Lord Goff and Lord Mustill in Airedale *NHS Trust v Bland* [1993] 1 All E.R.821 at 872–3, and 891–2 respectively.

The provisions of subss.(3)–(7) do not provide an exhaustive list of factors that need to be taken into account as the decision maker must consider "all the relevant circumstances" (subs.(2)). The assessment of a P's best interests is clearly going to be influenced by either the personal or professional relationship that the decision-maker has with P. If P's incapacity is likely to be temporary, it might be possible for the decision to be postponed until capacity is regained: see subs.(3).

If someone disagrees with the best interests determination that has been made, the Department of Constitutional Affairs Consultation Paper CP 10/06, at pp.10–11, identifies the following options that may be explored:

- involving an advocate, who is independent of all the parties, to work with the person who lacks capacity and help them understand the situation or act as an advocate of their best interests;
- getting a second opinion in cases where the decision relates to medical treatment;
- holding a formal or informal case conference if the decision relates to medical treatment or social care;
- using the informal or formal complaints processes if the decision in question is to be taken by the health, social or other welfare services; or
- participating in mediation or other forms of dispute resolution. This may be most appropriate to decisions on the day-to-day care or welfare of a person.

If all attempts to resolve a dispute fail, it may be appropriate to apply to the Court of Protection for a ruling on what particular decision or course of action is in P's best interests. The *Code of Practice* states at para.5.15:

"Any staff involved in the care of a person who lacks capacity should make sure a record is kept of the process of working out the best interests of that person for each relevant decision, setting out:

- how the decision about the person's best interests was reached
- what the reasons for reaching the decision were
- who was consulted to help work out best interests, and
- what particular factors were taken into account.

This record should remain on the person's file."

Best interests and medical treatment

As the approach taken in this section is founded on the common law, an account of com- **1–043** mon law rules relating to best interests in the context of the provision of medical treatment is set out below.

A patient's best interests are not limited to best medical interests (*Re M.B. (Medical Treatment)* [1997] 2 F.L.R. 426, CA); they encompass "medical, emotional and all other welfare issues" (*per* Butler-Sloss P. in *A (Mental Patient: Sterilisation)*, Re [2000] 1 F.L.R. 549 at 555). *Re MB* was applied in *Trust A v H (An Adult Patient)* [2006] EWHC 1320 (Fam); (2006) 9 C.C.L.R 474, where Potter P. said at paras 25–26:

"In English law 'best interests' are not confined to best medical interests and the court is not tied to the clinical assessment of what is in the patient's best interests, being itself obliged to take into account a broad spectrum of medical, social, emotional and welfare issues before reaching its own conclusion on the basis of a careful consideration of the evidence.

When considering those best interests the court assesses the advantages and disadvantages of various treatment and management options, the viability of each such option, and its likely effect on the patient and the enjoyment of his or her life. Any likely benefit of the treatment has to be balanced and considered in the in the light of any additional suffering such treatment might entail."

In *Y (Mental Patient: Bone Marrow Donation)*, *Re* [1996] 2 F.L.R. 787, Connell J. held that it was in the best interests of an incompetent patient to donate bone marrow to her gravely ill sister. Having heard evidence that the death of the sister would have a particularly adverse effect upon the mother, with whom the patient enjoyed a very close relationship, and, in particular, would significantly handicap her ability to visit the patient, his Lordship held that the procedure would be to the patients "emotional, psychological and social benefit".

The sanctity of life is a fundamental principle and there is a very strong presumption in favour of a course of action which will prolong life (*B (A Minor) (Wardship: Medical Treatment)*, *Re* [1981] 1 W.L.R. 1421). Lord Goff said in Airedale *NHS Trust v Bland* [1993] 1 All E.R. 821, at 865–866:

". . . the fundamental principle is the principle of the sanctity of human life - a principle long recognised not only in our own society but also in most, if not all, civilised societies throughout the modern world, as is indeed evidenced by its recognition both in Art.2 of the European Convention on Human Rights and in Art. 6 of the International Covenant on Civil and Political Rights

But this principle, fundamental though it is, is not absolute We are concerned with circumstances in which it may be lawful to withhold from a patient medical treatment or care by means of which his life may be prolonged. But here too there is no absolute rule that the patient's life must be prolonged by such treatment or care, if available, regardless of the circumstances."

This approach is illustrated by the case of *D (Medical Treatment: Mentally Disabled* **1–044** *Patient)*, *Re* [1998] 2 F.L.R. 22 where Sir Stephen Brown P. granted a declaration that "notwithstanding the [patient's] inability to consent to or refuse medical treatment, it is lawful as being in the best interests of the patient that the [NHS Trust] do not impose hae-modialysis upon him in circumstances in which, in the opinion of the medical practitioners responsible for such treatment, it is not reasonable practicable so to do". This was a case where it had proved to be impossible to treat a gravely ill, physically protesting, incompetent patient. The doctors had sought a declaration to protect themselves from any liability arising from a failure to carry out the treatment.

In *W Healthcare NHS Trust v H* [2004] EWCA Civ 1324, reference was made to the following passage from para.1.2 of the BMA's "Withholding and Withdrawing Life Prolonging Medical Treatment: Guidance for decision making" (2000):

"Where, however, the disability is so profound that individuals have no or minimal levels of awareness of their own existence and no hope of recovering awareness the question arises as to whether continuing to provide treatment aimed at prolonging that life would provide a benefit to them."

Brooke L.J. said at para.30:

"English law, as it stands at present, places a very heavy burden on those who are advocating a course which would lead inevitably to the cessation of a human life."

In *R (on the application of Burke) v The General Medical Council* [2005] EWCA Civ 1003; [2005] H.R.L.R. 35, Lord Phillips M.R. said at para.33:

"The courts have accepted that where life involves an extreme degree of pain, discomfort or indignity to a patient, who is sentient but not competent and who has manifested no wish to be kept alive, these circumstances may absolve the doctors of the positive duty to keep the patient alive. Equally the courts have recognised that there may be no duty to keep alive a patient who is in a persistent vegetative state. In each of these examples the facts of the individual case may make it difficult to decide whether the duty to keep the patient alive persists."

In *Re J (A Minor) (Wardship: Medical Treatment)* [1991] Fam 33, Lord Donaldson M.R. said in a case where two NHS trusts sought declarations that it would be lawful not to provide further aggressive treatment to a gravely ill child:

"We know that the instinct and desire for survival is very strong. We all believe in and assert the sanctity of human life . . . even very severely handicapped people find a quality of life rewarding which to the unhandicapped may seem manifestly intolerable. People have an amazing adaptability. But in the end there will be cases in which the answer must be that it is not in the interests of the child to subject it to treatment which will cause increased suffering and produce no commensurate benefit, giving the fullest possible weight to the child's, and mankind's desire to survive."

The Lord Chancellor said at the second reading of the Bill in the House of Lords that "in some cases it will be in the best interests of the person to withhold treatment or to give palliative care that might incidentally shorten life" (*Hansard*, HL Vol.668, col.15). In support of this approach, he quoted from the Roman Catholic Archbishop of Cardiff who had said:

". . . it is not the church's position that life must be sustained at all costs. On the contrary, one can quite reasonably, and consistently with one's responsibilities for oneself and others, decide to refuse treatment—even life sustaining treatment—which one judges burdensome or futile, knowing that forgoing the treatment will shorten one's life."

In *Re A*, above, Thorpe L.J. said at 560:

"[T]he first instance judge with the responsibility to make an evaluation of the best interests of a claimant lacking capacity should draw up a balance sheet. The first entry should be of any factor or factors of actual benefit Then on the other sheet the judge should write any counterbalancing dis-benefits to the applicant Then the judge should enter on each sheet the potential gains and losses in each instance making some estimate of the extent of the possibility that the gain or loss might accrue. At the end of that exercise the judge should be better placed to strike a balance between the sum of the certain and possible gains against the sum of the certain and possible losses. Obviously, only if the account is in relatively significant credit will the judge conclude that the applicant is likely to advance the best interests of the claimant."

Adopting this "balance sheet" approach is recommended for practitioners who are faced **1–045** with particularly difficult or contentious decisions.

In *Re A*, the question whether third party interests, such as the interests of potential sexual partners of the patient, should ever be considered in a case concerned with the best interests of a patient was left open. During the Bill's passage through Parliament, the BMA sought assurances that it would be possible to conduct a diagnostic test on an incapacitated person primarily for the benefit of a family member in the case of genetic diseases, or to a nurse or doctor if a needlestick accident had occurred during the person's treatment. The Minister of State responded to these concerns as follows:

"[T]he Bill will allow for acts whose primary purpose is to benefit a third party, provided that those acts are in P's best interests. I reassure the House that the interpretation of best interests could be broader than P's medical best interests. I can confirm that the Bill will not prevent a genetic test for a familial cancer, for example, that might not be essential to P's medical care but would provide considerable benefit to some other family member. Similarly, HIV testing would be lawful if there were a needlestick injury to a nurse involved in P's care and if a timely diagnosis of HIV status would be in P's best interests, so that treatment could be started. There is the ability for a medical professional in those circumstances—if they reasonably think that a person might have HIV /AIDS or hepatitis C and they might have been affected by it—to request a test so that treatment of P could start" (*Hansard*, HC Vol.428, col.1601).

Although it is likely that a court would confirm the lawfulness of the assurances given by the Minister, the best interests principle would not be satisfied in a situation where the procedure in question resulted in no tangible or intangible benefit to P. It could be argued in a situation where the primary purpose of the intervention is to benefit a third party that an intangible benefit would be the desire of P, had he or she been capable, to be seen to be "a normal decent person, acting in accordance with contemporary standards of morality" (*C (Spinster and Mental Patient), Re* [1991] 3 All E.R. 866, *per* Hoffmann J. at 870).

Where there is no alternative treatment available for a mentally incapacitated patient and the disease is progressive and fatal, it is reasonable to consider experimental treatment with unknown benefits and risks, but without significant risks of increased suffering to the patient, in cases where there is some chance of benefit to the patient (*Simms v Simms* [2002] EWHC Fam 2734; [2003] 1 All E.R. 669). Butler-Sloss P. said at para.57: "A patient who is not able to consent to pioneering treatment ought not to be deprived of the chance in circumstances where he would be likely to consent if he had been competent". Her Ladyship stressed, at para.64, that in such cases the views of the family of the patient about the proposed treatment would carry great weight in the wider considerations of the best interests test.

Although, in the absence of an appropriate lasting power of attorney, the next of kin of a mentally incapable patient has no legal right either to consent or to refuse treatment on behalf of the patient, it is not necessarily undesirable for such consent to be sought if the interests of the patient will not be adversely affected by any consequential delay. This is because "contact with the next of kin may reveal that the patient has made an anticipatory choice which, if clearly established and applicable in the circumstances—two major 'ifs'— would bind the practitioner" (*NHS Trust v T (Adult Patient: Refusal of Medical Treatment)*, above, *per* Lord Donaldson M.R. at 649).

Where a clinician concludes that a treatment that has been requested by a relative of the patient is inimical to the patient's best interests and his professional conscience, intuition or hunch confirms that view, he may refuse to act and cannot be compelled to do so, though he should not prevent another from so acting, should that clinician feel able to do so (*Re Wyatt* [2005] EWHC 2293 (Fam); [2005] 4 All E.R. 1325, para.36).

In the absence of a valid and applicable advance decision, the supposed view of the patient, as identified by relatives, will be no more than a factor to be taken into account in determining where his or her best interests lie.

Best interests and living arrangements

1–046   In *Re S (Adult Patient) (Inherent Jurisdiction: Family Life)* [2002] EWHC 2278 (Fam); [2003] 1 F.L.R. 292, para.48, Munby J. said:

> "I am not saying that there is in law any presumption that mentally incapacitated adults are better off with their families: often they will be; sometimes they will not be. But respect for our human condition, regard for the realities of our society and . . . common sense . . ., surely indicate that the starting point should be the normal assumption that mentally incapacitated adults will be better off if they live with a family rather than in an institution—however benign and enlightened the institution may be, and however well integrated into the community—and the mentally incapacitated adults who have been looked after within their family will be better off if they continue to be looked after within the family rather than by the State."

His Lordship returned to this issue in *Local Authority X v MM and KM* [2007] EWHC 2003 (Fam); [2007] M.H.L.R. 173, where he said:

1. There is a need "to be conscious of the limited ability of public authorities to improve on nature. We need to be careful not to embark upon 'social engineering'" (para.116).
2. If the State is to justify removing "vulnerable adults from their relatives, partners, friends or carers it can only be on the basis that the State is going to provide a *better* quality of care than that which they have hitherto been receiving" (para.117).
3. The court is entitled to intervene to protect a vulnerable adult from the risk of future harm "so long as there is a real possibility, rather than a merely fanciful risk of such harm. But the court must adopt a pragmatic, common sense approach to the identification, evaluation and management of perceived risk" (para.119). The "emphasis must be on a sensible risk appraisal, not striving to avoid all risk, whatever the price, but instead seeking a proper balance and being willing to tolerate manageable or acceptable risks as the price appropriately to be paid in order to achieve some other good—in particular to achieve the vital good of the elderly or vulnerable person's *happiness*. What good is it making someone safer if it merely makes them miserable?" (para.120).

Subsection (1)

1–047   Although the Government resisted an amendment to insert an anti-discrimination principle in s.1 for technical reasons and because it "would be inconceivable that giving someone less favourable treatment because of his disability, sex, age, race or sexual orientation could ever be considered to be in his best interests" (*per* the Parliamentary Under-Secretary of State (*Hansard*, HL Vol.668, col.1194)), the question of including some form of anti-discrimination or equal consideration provision in the Bill was a recurrent theme in the Parliamentary debates. The Government's response to this concern was to amend this provision at report stage in the House of Lords to "make sure that no one began a best interests determination with unjustified assumptions or prejudices. [The provision now] makes it clear that decision-making must start from a blank slate. People cannot say, 'She is very old so it is not necessary to give her this treatment' or, 'He has very severe physical disabilities, so it is obviously not in his best interests to have an operation'. Instead there must be a full and objective best interests assessment in every situation", *per* Baroness Andrews (*Hansard*, HL Vol.670, col.1320).

A PERSON'S BEST INTERESTS. The best interests criterion does not apply to advance decisions: see the note on s.1(5).

APPEARANCE. This covers "visible medical problems, disabilities, the colour of someone's skin, religious dress, and so on", *per* Baroness Andrews, above.

CONDITION. The condition, which might relate to either a mental or physical disorder, could be temporary.

Subsection (2)

ALL THE RELEVANT CIRCUMSTANCES. In the Bill as originally drafted, this phrase read "all the **1–048** circumstances appearing to him to be relevant". The amendment, together with the addition of subs.(11), were made in order to emphasise the objective nature of the best interests test (*Hansard*, HC Vol.428, col.1631).

IN PARTICULAR. None of the considerations set out in the indicative "checklist" contained in subss.(3)–(7) take precedence over any other consideration. The Government's view is the "any prioritising of factors within the best interests checklist would have the effect of unnecessarily fettering the application of all factors in the checklist. We believe that the checklist as it is in the draft Bill is sufficiently flexible to allow the factors to be applied to any particular individual in their particular circumstances" (*The Government Response to the Scrutiny Committee's Report on the draft Mental Incapacity Bill*, (Cm.6121)).

Subsection (3)

If the person is likely to regain his or her capacity at some point in the future, the decision **1–049** should be postponed until then if such a delay is consistent with the person's best interests. Paragraph 5.28 of the *Code of Practice* identifies "some factors which may indicate that a person may regain or develop capacity in the future". They "are:

- the cause of the lack of capacity can be treated, either by medication or some other form of treatment or therapy
- the lack of capacity is likely to decrease in time (for example, where it is caused by the effects of medication or alcohol, or following a sudden shock)
- a person with learning disabilities may learn new skills or be subject to new experiences which increase their understanding and ability to make certain decisions
- the person may have a condition which causes capacity to come and go at various times (such as some forms of mental illness) so it may be possible to arrange for the decision to be made during a time when they do have capacity
- a person previously unable to communicate may learn a new form of communication."

Subsection (4)

This provision complements the principle contained in s.1(3). The decision-maker might **1–050** wish to seek the help of others when complying with this obligation to involve the person to the fullest practicable extent in both the decision-making process and the consequences of the decision.

REASONABLY PRACTICABLE. This is an objective requirement. "[T]here will always be cases where, for urgent or non-emergency reasons, it would be inappropriate and not in a person's best interests to delay acting, which is why the words 'reasonably practicable' are in clause 4(4). It is also unrealistic to expect all people affected by the Bill to be able to participate in decisions. The Bill applies to people in a coma, as well as to those who are seriously distressed or who need urgent care. While in some cases it would be possible to wait until the person is capable of making the decision themselves, in other cases it clearly would not", *per* the Parliamentary Under-Secretary of State, St. Comm. A, col.92.

IMPROVE HIS ABILITY TO PARTICIPATE. Using communication support where this is appropriate.

Subsection (5)

1–051   This provision was inserted at the Committee stage in the House of Lords in an attempt to respond to the concern of those who considered that decisions concerning life-sustaining treatment could lead to euthanasia by omission. Its purpose is to "make it absolutely clear that no person, whether doctor, attorney, deputy or court, can, when making a best interests determination, have the motive of causing death, regardless of what would be in his best interests" (Joint Committee on Human Rights, Fourth Report, Session 204–2005, Appendix 4, para.41). The Joint Committee expressed its concern that proving the motive of a person making a best interests determination will in practice "be extremely difficult" (para.4.42). This concern was shared by some members of the House of Lords who drew a distinction between intent, which can be objectively identified by examining the act, and motive, which is a state of mind which cannot be objectively verified: see, for example, Lord St John of Fawsley at *Hansard*, HL Vol.668, cols 1167–1170.

The Parliamentary Under-Secretary of State said that this provision "does not change the law as it stands at the moment. But it does put it beyond doubt. All that matters is that the decision maker considers the range of treatment options available and the patient's objective best interests in respect of those treatments. [Subsection (5)] cannot be interpreted to mean that doctors are under an obligation to provide, or to continue to provide, life-sustaining treatment where that treatment is not in the best interests of the patients. That is the case even when the patient's death is foreseen" (*Hansard*, H.C. Vol.670, cols.1293–1294). Medical treatment that is judged to be in the best interests of P because, for example, it would provide effective pain control can therefore be given even if one of the adverse consequences of the treatment would be to shorten P's life. This provision would also allow for the cessation of treatment where the motive is to end futile or burdensome treatment.

If there is any ambiguity in either an advance decision or a lasting power of attorney about a purported refusal of life-sustaining treatment, the treatment should be provided.: see s.11(8) and *HE v A Hospital NHS Trust* [2003] EWHC 1017 (Fam); [2003] 2 F.L.R. 408, noted under s.24. The scope of this provision in the context of the sanctity of life doctrine is considered by J. Coggon in "Ignoring the moral and intellectual shape of the law after *Bland*: the unintended side effect of a sorry compromise", Legal Studies 27 (2007) 110–125.

LIFE-SUSTAINING TREATMENT. Is defined in subs.(10).

Subsection (6)

1–052   The factors set out in this provision cannot determine the decision: they must be considered by the decision-maker and weighed against other factors. In the absence of a written record, it may be difficult to establish whether the decision-maker has taken these factors into account when reaching a decision.

In *Ashan v University Hospitals Leicester NHS Trust* [2006] EWHC 2624 (QB), Judge Hegarty QC held that a patient who has been left in a persistent vegetative state following elective surgery should be cared for at home by her family rather than at a specialist private nursing and rehabilitation centre funded by the Trust. The patient's "immediate family are devout Muslims. They firmly believe that she should be cared for at home in a Muslim environment where they could pray together in her presence and ensure the proper observance of Muslim traditions and practices" (para.43). The judge concluded that "the wishes and beliefs of [the patient's] family and, so far they can properly be attributed to her, those which she herself would have held had she continued to have the capacity to do so, are factors which can and should be taken into account in determining whether it is reasonable for her to be cared for at home, even though no tangible benefits, whether physical or emotional, are likely to flow from a recognition of those wishes and beliefs in view of her profound mental incapacity and lack of awareness" (para.56). The judge said, at para.54, that this approach "appears to be entirely consistent" with this provision and subs.(7)(b).

Paragraph (a)

"Wishes and feelings" about a particular issue can be expressed orally, in writing, or **1–053** through behaviour. The past or present wishes and feelings of the person would normally carry substantial weight in the determination of that person's best interests, especially if they are well thought out, written down and signed. The person's present wishes and feelings about a particular issue might be expressed in the form of a "crisis card" that the person might carry on his or her person.

Although the person may lack mental capacity, he or she may be able to indicate present wishes and feelings or preferences through expressions of pleasure or distress. These indications, which might be accessed through the use of psychological techniques, should be given serious consideration by the decision maker. As the incapacity might have the effect of altering the person's perception about what he or she might find acceptable, where past wishes and feelings conflict with present wishes and feelings, greater weight should be given to the latter.

The person's ascertainable wishes and feelings must be considered by the decision-maker who could be faced with the task of balancing a person's wishes and feelings against a contrary course of action which is objectively believed to be in that person's best interests. For example, the person could have been subject to significant psychological strain when the wishes and feelings were expressed. The *Code of Practice* states at para.5.38: "[The person's] wishes and feelings, beliefs and values will not necessarily be the deciding factor in working out their best interests. Any such assessment must consider past and current wishes and feelings, beliefs and values alongside all other factors, but the final decision must be based entirely on what is in the person's best interests."

In *R. (on the application of Wilkinson) v Broadmoor Special Hospital Authority* [2001] EWCA Civ 1545; [2002] 1 W.L.R. 419, para.64, Hale L.J. said:

"The wishes and feelings of the incapacitated person will be an important element in determining what is, or is not, in his best interests. Where he is actively opposed to course of action, the benefits which it holds for him will have to be carefully weighed against the disadvantages of going against his wishes, especially if force is required to do this."

If a person falls just below the borderline of capacity, "the more weight must in principle be attached to her wishes and feelings, because the greater the distress, the humiliation and indeed it may be the anger she is likely to feel the better she is able to appreciate that others are taking on her behalf decisions about matters which vitally affect her—matters, it may be, as here, of an intensely private and personal nature" (*Local Authority X v MM and KM* [2007] EWHC 2003 (Fam); [2007] M.H.L.R. 173, para.124, per Munby J.).

There will clearly be occasions when, having undertaken the consultations set out in subs.(7), it would be difficult for the decision-maker to establish whether the person's past expression of wishes and feelings as reported by others represent that person's actual wishes and feelings expressed at that time. This situation could occur when the reporter has a vested interest in the decision. It is also important for the decision-maker to be alert to the possibility of the person's expression of his or her past or present wishes and feelings having been subject to the undue influence of another (see the note on s.1(3)).

The context within which the wishes and feelings were expressed should be carefully examined, e.g. a person might have expressed a desire not to live at a time when he or she was clinically depressed or was ignorant about the true prognosis of an illness or of the treatment that could be offered. The person might also have been misinformed about a crucial component of an issue that was being considered. It is also the case that a person's wishes and feelings can undergo dramatic shifts due to a change of personal perspective. One disabled witness to the Joint Committee wrote that she had had a settled wish that she wanted to die "that lasted about ten years, and during the first five of those years I made serious suicide attempts several times. I was saved only because my friends refused to accept my view that my life had no value, and made sure I received emergency treatment in hospital, which was given against my will. Then I was extremely angry with them; now I am eternally grateful. What has changed is not my medical condition, but my outlook on life. If advance decisions had been legally binding then, I have no doubt that I would have written one" (Alison Davis, Oral and written evidence, Ev 359).

RELEVANT WRITTEN STATEMENT. The purpose of the words in parenthesis "is to clarify that if someone with capacity has written down their wishes and feelings in respect of a matter, including positive preferences, those must be explicitly taken into account in a best-interests determination", *per* the Parliamentary Under-Secretary of State (*Hansard*, HC Vol.670, col.1442). In the context of medical treatment, where someone has sought to make a written advance decision that does not qualify under ss.24 and 25, but there is a reasonable belief that the written statement is an expression of the person's wishes, it must be taken into account under this provision. A decision maker who does not follow a written statement should record the reasons for his decision (*Code of Practice*, para.5.43). Also see the note on "advance statements" in the General Note to s.24.

Paragraph (b)

1–054   Beliefs and values may be evidenced by factors such as the person's cultural background, religious and/or political affiliation, memberships of societies, subscriptions to charitable causes and known past behaviour and expressions of conviction. If P has never had capacity, it will be extremely difficult to ascertain his or her beliefs and values. In this situation, it is suggested that an assumption should be made that P would be "a normal decent person, acting in accordance with contemporary standards of morality" (*C (Spinster and Mental Patient), Re* [1991] 3 All E.R. 866, *per* Hoffmann J. at 870).

Paragraph (c)

1–055   OTHER FACTORS. Such as emotional bonds, family obligations or concern for others.

Subsection (7)

1–056   The purpose of the consultation is to seek information which would assist the decision-maker in making the best interests determination; it is not to ask the consultees what decision they would make. As the procedure set out in this section has to be followed in respect of every decision that is taken on behalf of an incapacitated person, it is likely that the decision-maker would conclude that it would not be "appropriate" to consult where trivial decisions have to be made.

The decision-maker must bear in mind P's right to confidentiality when undertaking the consultation(s). Disclosure in confidence can be made to someone who has a proper interest in having the information in question (*R (on the application of S) v Plymouth City Council* [2002] EWCA Civ 388; [2002] M.H.L.R. 118, para.49) if such disclosure is the best interests of P. It is likely that appropriate consultees would have such an interest.

If there is no-one apart from a paid carer in the categories set out in this provision with whom it would be appropriate to consult about P's best interests, an independent mental capacity advocate must be consulted in the situations set out in ss.37–39.

The decision-maker must *consider* consulting the persons listed. Such persons may be able to assist with providing information relevant to the issues set out in subs.(6).The consultations might also disclose the existence of an advance decision made by P. Whether it is "practicable and appropriate" to undertake the consultation will depend upon a number of factors including the urgency and nature of the decision. The views of the consultees about P's best interests may differ from P's own views as identified under subs.(6)(a).

A decision-maker must be able to justify a decision that it was not "practicable and appropriate" to consult someone identified in this provision. It is important not to equate "practicable" with "possible" (*Owen v Crown House Engineering* [1973] 3 All E.R. 618, 622 NIRC). In *Dedman v British Building and Engineering Appliances Ltd* [1974] 1 W.L.R. 171, 179, CA, Scarman L.J. said:

> "The word 'practicable' is an ordinary English word of great flexibility: it takes its meaning from its context. But, whenever used, it is a call for the exercise of common sense, a warning that sound judgment will be impossible without compromise. Sometimes the context contemplates a situation rarely to be achieved though much to be desired: the word then indicates one must be satisfied with less than perfection . . . [S]ometimes . . . what the context requires may have been possible, but may not for some reason have been 'practicable'. Whatever its context, the quality of the word is that there are circumstances in which we must be content with less than 100 per cent: and it calls for judgment to determine how much less."

Given this interpretation, although reasonable steps should be taken in an attempt to make contact with the persons named in this provision, the decision-maker would not be required either to act as a private detective in order to discover a person's whereabouts or to use a disproportionate amount of time in the attempt.

The weight to be given to the views expressed by the consultees will depend on a number of factors including the extent of their knowledge of P, the amount of contact that they have with P, whether they have a vested interest in the decision to be taken and their relationship with P. It is unlikely that it would be "appropriate" to consult with a person who has a history of ill-treating or neglecting P.

It should be noted that studies have shown that relatives' perception of the patient's likely views often differ substantially from the patient's own wishes; see, for example, A.B. Seckler *et al*, "Substituted judgment: how accurate are proxy predictions?" (1991) 115(9) Ann. Intern. Med. 92–8. Studies on social comparison processes suggest that "we are not particularly good at assessing other people's opinions, abilities, or future behaviour" and that the "dominant view is that we tend to be egocentric", i.e. people judge others in the same way that they judge themselves. (N. Harvey, M. Twyman and C. Harries "Making Decisions for other People: The Problem of Judging Acceptable Levels of Risk" (Jan, 2006) 7(1) *Forum: Qualitative Social Research* (On-line Journal) Art.26, para.21, available at: *www.qualitative-research.net/fqs-texte/1-06/06-1-26-e.htm*.

Paragraph (b)
Carers UK in its evidence to the Joint Committee expressed concern that this provision **1–057** gives "equal decision-making weight to both professionals and to carers" (Oral and written evidence, Ev 338). It should be noted in this context that there have been occasions when the sustained opposition of family carers to the firmly held views of professionals about the care needs of an incapacitated person has been proved to have been correct; see, for example, the "Report on an Investigation into Complaint No.02/C/17068 against Bolton Metropolitan Borough Council" (November 2004).

INTERESTED IN HIS WELFARE. The decision-maker should consider the nature of the interest and its motivation before consulting persons in this category. The Parliamentary Under-Secretary of State for Constitutional Affairs said that an advocate could fall into this category (St. Comm. A, col.100).

ANYONE ENGAGED IN CARING FOR THE PERSON. The carer identified in this provision need not be a relative of P. "Care" is not defined. It is suggested that the approach that should be adopted when determining whether a person qualifies as a carer under this provision should mirror the approach that the Court of Appeal took in *Re D (Mental patient: habeas corpus)* [2000] 2 F.L.R. 848 when explaining the meaning of the term "cared for" in s.26(4) of the Mental Health Act 1983. Having described the phrase as containing clear and everyday words, the court held that in order to justify a finding that a relative is caring for the patient, the services provided must be more than minimal and they need not have been provided in the long term. The court was asked to consider the situation of a relative who assisted the patient in managing his financial affairs, checked whether he was eating appropriately and took away his soiled clothing and bed clothes. In finding that the relative was caring for the patient, the court said that there "was more than sufficient evidence to pass the 'cared for' test, wherever one sets the threshold of services amounting to 'cared for'. In other words, the services were not merely minimal. They were services which were substantial and sustained." It is clear from this case that a person may be engaged in caring for P even if they do not share the same residence.

Subsection (8)

1–058   This applies the duties contained in this section to the following situations: (1) any decision made by a donee acting under a lasting power of attorney; and (2) where the person concerned does not in fact lack capacity but where the decision-maker reasonably believes the person lacks capacity.

Subsection (9)

1–059   If the decision-maker, having satisfied the requirements of subss.(1)–(7) reasonably believes that what has been done or decided is in the best interests of the P, he or she will have complied with this section. Reasonable belief is an objective test and the decision-maker will therefore need to identify objective reasons to support the contention that he or she believed that the decision was in the P's best interests.

Subsection (10)

1–060   This definition, which applies throughout this Act (s.64(1)), was subject to a Government amendment to delete the word "his" before "life" because "in the case of a pregnant woman we want to ensure that the life of the baby, not only the life of the mother, must be considered", *per* the Parliamentary Under-Secretary of State (*Hansard*, HL Vol.668, col.1184).

The nature of life sustaining treatment is considered in the *Code of Practice* at para.5.30:

> "Whether a treatment is 'life-sustaining' depends not only on the type of treatment, but also on the particular circumstances in which it may be prescribed. For example, in some situations giving antibiotics may be life-sustaining, whereas in other circumstances antibiotics are used to treat a non-life-threatening condition. It is up to the doctor or healthcare professional providing treatment to assess whether the treatment is life-sustaining in each particular situation."

Subsection (11)

1–061   This provision recognises that the decision-maker might not be aware of all of the circumstances of P, or of the decision in question.

[Restriction on deprivation of liberty

1–062   **4A.**—(1) This Act does not authorise any person ("D") to deprive any other person ("P") of his liberty.

(2) But that is subject to—

(a) the following provisions of this section, and

(b) section 4B.

(3) D may deprive P of his liberty if, by doing so, D is giving effect to a relevant decision of the court.

(4) A relevant decision of the court is a decision made by an order under section 16(2)(a) in relation to a matter concerning P's personal welfare.

(5) D may deprive P of his liberty if the deprivation is authorised by Schedule A1 (hospital and care home residents: deprivation of liberty).]

AMENDMENT
This section was inserted by the Mental Health Act 2007, s.50(2).   **1–063**

DEFINITIONS
"deprivation of liberty": s.64(5), (6).   **1–064**
"the court": s.64(1).

GENERAL NOTE
This section prohibits the deprivation of the liberty of a person under this Act other than   **1–065**
in the following situations: first, where the court under has made an order under s.16(2)(a);
second, where it is authorised for life-sustaining or other emergency treatment (s.4B); and,
third where the procedure set out in Sch.A1 is used. It follows that a deprivation of liberty
cannot take place on the authority of s.5, or through the actions of the donee of an LPA or a
court appointed deputy. The detaining authority can be either a public or a private body
(s.65(6)).
   As an authorisation under Sch.A1 can only apply to the detention of a person in a hospital
or a care home, an application must be made to the Court of Protection if detention takes
place elsewhere.
   Detention under this Act does not entitle the institution to do anything other that detain
the patient or resident for the purposes of the order or authorisation.

[Deprivation of liberty necessary for life-sustaining treatment etc

4B.—(1) If the following conditions are met, D is authorised to deprive P of his   **1–066**
liberty while a decision as respects any relevant issue is sought from the court.
   (2) The first condition is that there is a question about whether D is authorised to
deprive P of his liberty under section 4A.
   (3) The second condition is that the deprivation of liberty—
   (a) is wholly or partly for the purpose of—
      (i) giving P life-sustaining treatment, or
      (ii) doing any vital act, or
   (b) consists wholly or partly of—
      (i) giving P life-sustaining treatment, or
      (ii) doing any vital act.
   (4) The third condition is that the deprivation of liberty is necessary in order
to—
   (a) give the life-sustaining treatment, or
   (b) do the vital act.
   (5) A vital act is any act which the person doing it reasonably believes to be
necessary to prevent a serious deterioration in P's condition.]

AMENDMENT
This section was inserted by the Mental Health Act 2007, s.50(2).   **1–067**

DEFINITIONS
"deprivation of liberty": s.64(5), (6).   **1–068**
"the court": s.64(1).
"life-sustaining treatment": s.64(1).

1–069   This section enables a person to be derived of his liberty for the purpose of providing him with emergency medical treatment for either a physical or mental disorder while a decision as respects "any relevant issue" is sought from the court. In order for the deprivation to be lawful, the conditions set out in subss.(2) to (4) must be satisfied.

This section cannot be invoked if P is ineligible within the meaning of Sch.1A, i.e. he comes within a category where the Mental Health Act 1983 must be used. This is because the court cannot make an order under s.16(2)(a) if P is ineligible (s.16A).

Acts in connection with care or treatment
1–070   **5.**—(1) If a person ("D") does an act in connection with the care or treatment of another person ("P"), the act is one to which this section applies if—

    (a) before doing the act, D takes reasonable steps to establish whether P lacks capacity in relation to the matter in question, and

    (b) when doing the act, D reasonably believes—

        (i) that P lacks capacity in relation to the matter, and

        (ii) that it will be in P's best interests for the act to be done.

(2) D does not incur any liability in relation to the act that he would not have incurred if P—

    (a) had had capacity to consent in relation to the matter, and

    (b) had consented to D's doing the act.

(3) Nothing in this section excludes a person's civil liability for loss or damage, or his criminal liability, resulting from his negligence in doing the act.

(4) Nothing in this section affects the operation of sections 24 to 26 (advance decisions to refuse treatment).

1–071   The aim of this section is to clarify aspects of the common law principle of necessity which enable decisions to be taken for people who lack capacity. It does not create any new powers of intervention or duties to act, but offers protection against civil and criminal liability for certain acts done in connection with the care or treatment of P and which would normally require that persons consent, e.g. helping P to dress, wash or to eat, entering P's house, moving P from his own home to a care home, taking P to the dentist, and providing P with medical treatment. Such acts, which could be performed by a range of professional and lay people, are not limited to "day to day" or emergency situations, as they could include, for example, performing a serious planned operation on P. Without the protection of this section, such acts could amount to civil wrongs, such as trespass, or crimes, such as assault. Liability for negligent acts is unaffected (subs.(3)). Subject to the limitations set out in s.6, this section enables steps to be taken on behalf of P by family members, carers, and health and care professionals without the need for any formal authority or involvement of the Court of Protection as long as the steps are in the P's best interests. Some decisions cannot be made without the involvement of an independent mental capacity advocate (see s.25 *et seq.*). Section 27 lists those decisions that can never be made on behalf of a person who lacks capacity.

There is no requirement for decisions taken to be documented or for any person or body to be informed of the decisions taken. The protection will apply in any setting where P is being cared for or where services are being provided to him or her, e.g. at P's home, a care home, a day centre or a hospital. As one person does not have power to act to the exclusion of others, it is likely that a number of persons will be acting under the powers contained in this section during the course of a day. It is surely unrealistic to expect lay carers, the majority of whom are unlikely to have received any training on this Act, to undertake a capacity assessment and a best interests determination in respect of the decisions that they need to make in respect of P.

The established common law position that no-one has the power to make decisions on behalf of a mentally incapacitated person is unchanged (*F v West Berkshire HA* [1989] 2 All E.R. 545, HL) as this section does not confer power on anyone to make substitute decisions on behalf of the person or to give substitute consent. As a large number of people are unlikely to have made provision for their incapacity through creating lasting powers of attorney, the "operational reality of [this section] is likely to be crucial" (Joint Committee, para.103).

If P is subject to guardianship under the Mental Health Act 1983, D should not take decisions or act in a manner which conflicts with the exercise of the statutory powers of the guardian (see s.8 of the 1983 Act) as such decisions or acts could constitute the offence of obstruction under s.129 of that Act.

A decision made by either a donee under a lasting power of attorney or a deputy appointed by the court will take priority over any action that might be taken under this section (s.6(6)).

The point at which it would be unwise to rely on the protection provided by this section, and when an application should be made to the Court of Protection for an order or to have a deputy appointed is unclear.

Paragraph 6.18 of the *Code of Practice* states that the Court of Protection must be asked to make decisions relating to:

"• the proposed withholding or withdrawal of artificial nutrition and hydration (ANH) from a patient in a permanent vegetative state (PVS)
• cases where it is proposed that a person who lacks capacity to consent should donate an organ or bone marrow to another person
• the proposed non-therapeutic sterilisation of a person who lacks capacity to consent (for example, for contraceptive purposes)
• cases where there is a dispute about whether a particular treatment will be in a person's best interests."

Consideration should also be given to making an application to the court for a declaration if the legality of the proposed action is in doubt.

This provision does not provide any procedural safeguards aimed at preventing the inappropriate use of "section 5 acts". If there is concern about the manner in which P is being cared for, consideration could be given to invoking the multi-agency adult protection procedure. In extreme cases, the offence of ill-treatment or wilful neglect might be committed under s.44.

Subsection (1)

Paragraph (a) emphasises the Act's "ethos of empowerment and personal autonomy, and **1–072** the key obligation of all carers to support and maximise the decision-making capacity of the person who lacks capacity", *per* the Parliamentary Under-Secretary of State for Constitutional Affairs, St. Comm. A, col.107.

The *Code of Practice*, at para.6.5, states that actions that might be covered by this section include:

"Personal care

• helping with washing, dressing or personal hygiene
• helping with eating and drinking
• helping with communication
• helping with mobility (moving around)
• helping someone take part in education, social or leisure activities
• going into a person's home to drop off shopping or to see if they are alright
• doing the shopping or buying necessary goods with the person's money
• arranging household services (for example, arranging repairs or maintenance for gas and electricity supplies)
• providing services that help around the home (such as homecare or meals on wheels)

- undertaking actions related to community care services (for example, day care, residential accommodation or nursing care). . .
- helping someone to move home (including moving property and clearing the former home).

Healthcare and treatment

- carrying out diagnostic examinations and tests (to identify illness, condition or other problem)
- providing professional medical, dental and similar treatment
- giving medication
- taking someone to hospital for assessment or treatment
- providing nursing care (whether in hospital or in the community)
- carrying out any other necessary medical procedures (for example, taking a blood sample) or therapies (for example, physiotherapy or chiropody)
- providing care in an emergency."

A healthcare professional is not authorised under this section to provide medical treatment to P if he or she is aware that the treatment in question is specified in a valid and applicable advance decision that has been made by P: see s.26.

A PERSON. Including a person who instructs another to act. This Act does not specify who has the authority to take a particular decision or to undertake a particular act.

DOES AN ACT. Acting on a reasonable belief that P lacks capacity, and having concluded that there are reasonable grounds for believing that the decision or act is in P's best interests. The steps taken to establish the reasonableness of the belief and the reasonableness of the grounds will reflect the status of the decision-maker and the significance of the decision being taken: a healthcare professional would be expected to adopt a more rigorous approach than a lay carer, and a routine care intervention would require less investigation than a serious medical decision. It will also be the case that the urgency of the action required, for example, the provision of emergency medical treatment, will dictate the extent of the steps that can be taken.

CARE. This term is not defined. Payment for something that is arranged for P's care or treatment is provided for by s.8.

TREATMENT. Includes a diagnostic or other procedure (s.64(1)).

REASONABLY BELIEVES. Formal assessments of capacity will rarely be required with most day to day decisions, but D must be able to identify objective reasons to explain why he or she believes P lacks capacity. A formal capacity assessment should be undertaken where a decision is either contentious, significant or is likely to be challenged. Professional assistance should be sought by a lay carer in these circumstances. The starting point is a presumption of capacity (s.1(2)). The other relevant principles set out in s.1 should also be applied.

LACKS CAPACITY. In relation to the particular decision that needs to be made. Many of those who will be making a judgment about P's capacity, using the test set out in s.3, will be lay people.

BEST INTERESTS. The checklist contained in s.4 must be followed, and the least restrictive principle contained in s.1(6) should be applied. The amount of time devoted to ascertaining the best interests of P will, in non-urgent cases, depend upon the significance of the decision under consideration.

Subsection (3)
Consent is not a defence to a claim in the tort of negligence and there are some criminal **1–073**
offences, such as manslaughter, which depend on a finding of negligence as defined in civil
law. This provision therefore makes it clear that liability for negligence is unaffected by this
section.

Subsection (4)
A valid and applicable advance decision relating to the person's healthcare is unaffected **1–074**
by this section which gives no protection from liability if the decision is not followed.

Section 5 acts: limitations
6.—(1) If D does an act that is intended to restrain P, it is not an act to which **1–075**
section 5 applies unless two further conditions are satisfied.
(2) The first condition is that D reasonably believes that it is necessary to do the
act in order to prevent harm to P.
(3) The second is that the act is a proportionate response to—
(a) the likelihood of P's suffering harm, and
(b) the seriousness of that harm.
(4) For the purposes of this section D restrains P if he—
(a) uses, or threatens to use, force to secure the doing of an act which P resists,
or
(b) restricts P's liberty of movement, whether or not P resists.
(5) [*Repealed by the Mental Health Act 2007, s.50(4)(a)*]
(6) Section 5 does not authorise a person to do an act which conflicts with a
decision made, within the scope of his authority and in accordance with this
Part, by—
(a) a donee of a lasting power of attorney granted by P, or
(b) a deputy appointed for P by the court.
(7) But nothing in subsection (6) stops a person—
(a) providing life-sustaining treatment, or
(b) doing any act which he reasonably believes to be necessary to prevent a
serious deterioration in P's condition,
while a decision as respects any relevant issue is sought from the court.

DEFINITIONS
"the Human Rights Convention": s.64(1)   **1–076**
"public authority": s.64(1)
"lasting power of attorney": s.64(1)
"deputy": s.64(1)
"the court": s.64(1)
"life-sustaining treatment": s.64(1)

GENERAL NOTE
This section sets two important limitations to the protection from liability given to "sec- **1–077**
tion 5 acts".
The first (subss.(1) to (5)) relates to restraint, which is defined in subs.(4). Restraint can
only be used when: (1) the person using it reasonably believes that it is necessary to prevent
harm to P and; (2) its use is proportionate both to the likelihood and seriousness of the harm.
The restraint must also be in P's best interests (s.1(5)). Restraint that does not meet these
conditions is unlawful. The practical result of this is that only the minimum amount of
restraint for the shortest duration should be used to prevent the harm occurring. This
reflects the "least restrictive option" principle in s.1(6).

This section, together with s.5, provides authority for taking P to hospital and providing P with treatment at the hospital, even if taking P to the hospital and the subsequent treatment involves restricting P's liberty (subs.(4)(b)). The use of restraint which results in P being deprived of his or her liberty would constitute a violation of P's rights under Art. 5 of the European Convention of Human Rights. A deprivation of P's liberty can only be authorised under this Act in the situations set out in s.4A. The nature of a "deprivation of liberty" is considered in Part 2. Depriving a person of their liberty for a short period in order to respond to an emergency does not constitute a violation of Art.5 (*X v United Kingdom* (1982) 4 E.H.R.R. 188, para.41).

Although this provision does not provide for the restraint of P in order to prevent harm to others, such action is authorised under common law powers to prevent a breach of the peace. In *Albert v Lavin* [1981] 3 All E.R. 878, the House of Lords confirmed that under common law "every citizen in whose presence a breach of the peace is being, or reasonably appears to be about to be, committed has the right to take reasonable steps to make the person who is breaking or threatening to break the peace refrain from doing so; and those reasonable steps in appropriate cases will include detaining him against his will" (*per* Lord Diplock at 880). A breach, which can take place in public or on private property, occurs when "harm is actually done or is likely to be done to a person or in his presence to his property or a person is in fear of being so harmed through an assault, an affray, a riot, an unlawful assembly or other disturbance" (*R. v Howell* [1981] 3 All E.R. 383, *per* Watkins L.J. at 389). Restraining P from causing harm to others could be justified under this provision if it was considered that P's actions would provoke a reaction that would cause harm to P. If there is concern about the manner in which a donee of a lasting power of attorney or a court appointed deputy is restraining P, a complaint may be made to the Public Guardian (s.58(1)(h)).

The second limitation (subss.(6) and (7)) is that a valid decision by a donee or a deputy takes priority over any action which might be taken under s.5. There is an important proviso to this limitation. If there is a dispute as to whether a decision of a donee or deputy either prevents life-sustaining treatment being given to P or might cause a serious deterioration of Ps condition, action can be taken to sustain life or prevent serious deterioration while the dispute is referred to the Court of Protection.

Subsection (1)

1-078 RESTRAIN. Acts of restraint could include steadying P's shaking arm to enable an injection to be given safely, holding P down whilst administering a sedative, using reasonable force to take P to hospital to receive necessary treatment, using barriers to prevent P from falling out of bed, preventing P from running into the road, putting a car seatbelt on P, telling P that he will be restrained if he persists in a particular activity, securing the external doors of a care home to prevent P from leaving, assisting P to undress, and preventing P from harming himself.

The Government did not adopt the recommendation of the Joint Committee on Human Rights that the use or threat of force or other restrictions of liberty of movement be expressly confined to emergency situations for the following reason:

> "Sometimes it is not always in a person's best interests for matters to be left until it is an urgent situation. For example, restraint may be necessary in order to undertake a diagnostic procedure. If such a procedure is left until there is an urgent need or an emergency, then the resulting harm to the person may be worse. If a person needs treatment for a bad tooth, it will generally be in that person's best interests to be restrained, and to have the tooth treated, rather than to wait until it is so bad as to count as an emergency requiring intervention" (Letter from the Parliamentary-Under Secretary of State to the Chair of the Committee, December 16, 2004, Annex, para.4).

The use of restraint to ensure that mentally incapacitated patients are provided with artificial nutrition and hydration is considered by G.M. Sayers and S.M. Gabe in "Restraint in order to feed: justifying a lawful policy for the UK", European Journal of Health Law 14 (2007) 3–20.

Subsection (2)

REASONABLY BELIEVES. D must be able to identify objective reasons to justify the necessity **1–079** of acting to prevent P from suffering harm.

HARM. This term, which is not defined, is not confined to physical harm. It could include preventing P from causing financial harm to him or her self by, for example, restraining P from ripping up bank notes or from spending money recklessly. It could also include the prevention of psychological harm by, for example, restraining P from acting in a manner which could result in him or her suffering verbal abuse from members of the public.

The *Code of Practice*, at para.6.45, provides the following examples of harmful situations:

"• a person with leaning disabilities might run into a busy road without warning, if they do not understand the dangers of cars
 • a person with dementia may wander away from home and get lost, if they cannot remember where they live
 • a person with manic depression might engage in excessive spending during a manic phase, causing them to get into debt
 • a person may also be at risk of harm if they behave in a way that encourages others to assault or exploit them (for example, by behaving in a dangerously provocative way)."

Subsection (3)

PROPORTIONATE RESPONSE. In terms of both the degree and duration of the restraint. It fol- **1–080** lows that (a) the minimum amount of restraint should be used in order to prevent harm occurring, and (b) the level of restraint used should diminish as the risk of harm diminishes. The *Code of Practice* provides the following example at para.6.47:

"[A] carer may need to hold a person's arm while they cross the road, if the person does not understand the dangers of roads. But it would not be a proportionate response to stop the person going outdoors at all. It may be appropriate to have a secure lock on a door that faces a busy road, but it would not be a proportionate response to lock someone in a bedroom all the time to prevent them from attempting to cross the road."

In the context of restraint used in the provision of medical treatment, the following decisions were made prior this Act coming into force:

(i) The extent of force or compulsion that may become necessary in ensuring that medical treatment is provided to a mentally incapacitated patient can only be judged in each individual case and by health professionals. It may become for them a balance between continuing treatment that is forcibly opposed and deciding not to continue with it (*Re M.B. (Medical Treatment)* [1997] 2 F.L.R. 426, CA, at 439).

(ii) It is lawful "to overcome non-co-operation of a resisting patient by sedation and a moderate and reasonable use of restraint" in order to provide treatment if such treatment "is in the patient's best interests. The lawfulness of such restraint has to be carefully considered when assessing the balance of benefit and disadvantage in the giving of the proposed medical treatment and where the best interest of the patient truly lies. A patient . . . has . . . the right not to be subjected to degrading treatment under Article 3 of the European Convention on Human Rights" (*Trust A v H (an Adult patient)* [2006] EWHC 1230; (2006) 9 C.C.L.R. 474, *per* Sir Mark Potter P. at para.27).

(iii) In *R. (on the application of Wilkinson) v The Responsible Medical Officer Broadmoor Hospital* [2001] EWCA 1545; [2002] 1 W.L.R. 419, para.64, Hale

L.J. said that where a mentally incapacitated patient is "actively opposed to a course of action, the benefits which it holds for him will have to be carefully weighed against the disadvantages of going against his wishes, especially if force is required to do this."

The Department of Health and Department of Education and Skills has issued "Guidance on restrictive physical interventions for people with learning disabilities and autistic spectrum disorder, in health, education or social care settings" (July 2002). This guidance was issued under s.7 of the Local Authority Social Services Act 1970 (c.42). Similar guidance was issued by the Wales Assembly Government entitled "Framework for restrictive physical intervention policy and practice."

Subsection (4)

1–081   The definition contained in this provision includes verbal restraint, such as threatening P with the use of force, and locking P in a room even if P does not indicate any objection to the confinement.

RESTRICTS P'S LIBERTY. Restrictions on P's liberty are not confined to emergency situations as P could be subjected to restrictions of his or her liberty for an indefinite period without such restrictions constituting a deprivation of his or her liberty.

Subsection (6)

1–082   If a carer or doctor wishes to challenge a decision made by a donee or deputy on the ground that the decision of the donee or deputy is not in P's best interests, an application could be made to the Court of Protection to determine the issue. In the absence of such action, the decision of the donee or deputy must be respected as a failure to do so would be unlawful.

DOES AN ACT. It is submitted that this phrase includes an instruction to another to do an act.

Subsection (7)

1–083   This provision does not apply where a complaint has been made to the Public Guardian under s.58(1)(h) about the decision of the donee or deputy.

LIFE-SUSTAINING TREATMENT. Is defined in s.4(10).

Payment for necessary goods and services

1–084   **7.**—(1) If necessary goods or services are supplied to a person who lacks capacity to contract for the supply, he must pay a reasonable price for them.

(2) "Necessary" means suitable to a person's condition in life and to his actual requirements at the time when the goods or services are supplied.

GENERAL NOTE

1–085   In general, a contract entered into by a person who lacks capacity (P) is voidable and can be set aside if the other person knew or must be taken to have known of the lack of capacity. Under s.3(2) of the Sale of Goods Act 1979 (c.54), this rule does not apply if "necessaries" are supplied and P must pay a "reasonable price" for the goods. There is also a matching common law rule about "necessary" services. This section combines these rules to set out a single statutory rule to cover "necessary" goods and services. Subsection (2) repeats the established legal definition of what is "necessary". Thus, for example, a cleaner who carries on cleaning the house of P, who has a progressive dementia, can expect to be paid. As P lacks the capacity both to order or to pay for necessaries, ss.5 and 8 allows for a carer to do both.

At the committee stage in the House of Lords, the Government resisted an amendment to extend the existing powers to set aside a contract made by a person who lacks capacity to a situation where: (1) the other party was not aware of the incapacity; and (2) the contract can be set aside without loss to the other party, or where the person lacking capacity has been persuaded to enter into a plainly disadvantageous contract. However, the Government committed itself "to carrying out scoping research work to assess whether there is a problem arising from the current law and, if so, the extent of that problem. This will take into account people who lack capacity and the broader group of vulnerable consumers more generally. The Department of Constitutional Affairs (now the Ministry of Justice) will also commit to working with the Department of Trade and Industry as part of the implementation strategy of the Bill to ensure that policy on consumer strategy, credit and indebtedness is sensitive to the needs of consumers who lack capacity", *per* the Parliamentary Under-Secretary of State (*Hansard*, HL Vol.670, cols 1471–1472).

Subsection (2)

CONDITION IN LIFE. This means the living circumstances of P, in particular the standard of **1–086** life that P enjoys. The *Code of Practice* states, at para.6.58, that the aim of this provision "is to make sure that people can enjoy a similar standard of living and way of life to those they had before lacking capacity. For example, if a person who now lacks capacity previously chose to buy expensive designer clothes, these are still necessary goods—as long as they can still afford them. But they would not be necessary for a person who always wore cheap clothes, no matter how wealthy they were". Deciding whether goods and services are "necessary" can therefore depend upon a identifying a number of subtle factors that shape a person's lifestyle.

Expenditure

8.—(1) If an act to which section 5 applies involves expenditure, it is lawful for **1–087** D—

(a) to pledge P's credit for the purpose of the expenditure, and

(b) to apply money in P's possession for meeting the expenditure.

(2) If the expenditure is borne for P by D, it is lawful for D—

(a) to reimburse himself out of money in P's possession, or

(b) to be otherwise indemnified by P.

(3) Subsections (1) and (2) do not affect any power under which (apart from those subsections) a person—

(a) has lawful control of P's money or other property, and

(b) has power to spend money for P's benefit.

DEFINITIONS

"property": s.64(1)   **1–088**

GENERAL NOTE

If D, acting under s.5, arranges something for P's care or treatment that costs money then **1–089** D can either promise that P will pay (i.e. D may pledge the credit of P), use money which P has in his possession, pay himself back from P's money in his possession or consider himself owed by P. Nothing in this section allows D to gain access to P's funds where they are held by a third party such as a bank or building society. Such funds cannot be accessed until formal steps are taken, such as registering a relevant power of attorney, or making an application to the Court of Protection for a deputy to be appointed or for a single order to be made. This section does not authorise D to sell any of P's property or to gain access to any of P's assets other than cash that is in P's possession.

D cannot make a decision that conflicts with a decision made by either a donee of a lasting power of attorney ("LPA") or a deputy (s.6(6)).

D could be appointed under reg.33 of the Social Security (Claims and Payments) Regulations 1987 (SI 1987/1968) to be the "appointee" to act on behalf of P. Appointeeship is considered in the Introduction and General Note to this Act.

Although there is no requirement placed on D to keep records of the financial transactions undertaken on behalf of P, given the potential for allegations of financial abuse to be made it would clearly be sensible for D to do so.

Subsection (2)

1–090   INDEMNIFIED. If D cannot be compensated by cash that is in the possession of P, an application should be made to the court if it is not possible to claim reimbursement from a donee of a LPA or a deputy who has been granted appropriate powers by the court.

Subsection (3)

1–091   This recognises that people may have control over P's money or property by other routes, for example by virtue of being appointed as P's appointee. A donee or a deputy appointed by the court could also have lawful control over P's money.

Lasting powers of attorney

Lasting powers of attorney

1–092   **9.**—(1) A lasting power of attorney is a power of attorney under which the donor ("P") confers on the donee (or donees) authority to make decisions about all or any of the following—

   (a) P's personal welfare or specified matters concerning P's personal welfare, and

   (b) P's property and affairs or specified matters concerning P's property and affairs, and which includes authority to make such decisions in circumstances where P no longer has capacity.

   (2) A lasting power of attorney is not created unless—

   (a) section 10 is complied with,

   (b) an instrument conferring authority of the kind mentioned in subsection (1) is made and registered in accordance with Schedule 1, and

   (c) at the time when P executes the instrument, P has reached 18 and has capacity to execute it.

   (3) An instrument which—

   (a) purports to create a lasting power of attorney, but

   (b) does not comply with this section, section 10 or Schedule 1,

confers no authority.

   (4) The authority conferred by a lasting power of attorney is subject to—

   (a) the provisions of this Act and, in particular, sections 1(the principles) and 4 (best interests), and

   (b) any conditions or restrictions specified in the instrument.

DEFINITIONS

1–093   "property": s.64(1)

GENERAL NOTE

1–094   A power of attorney is a legal document under which one person (the "donor") empowers another person (the "attorney" or "donee") or persons to act in his or her stead, either generally or for specific purposes. An act done by a donee can be treated as an act done by the donor, so as to affect the donor's relations with third parties. Prior to the Enduring Powers of Attorney Act 1985 (c.29), a power of attorney would be automatically revoked if the donor lost mental capacity. That Act introduced Enduring Powers of Attorney ("EPA") which enabled donors to continue to act on behalf of the donor's property and affairs after the donor ceased to have capacity if certain formalities were satisfied. This section, together with ss.10–14, creates a new form of power of attorney, a "lasting power of attorney" ("LPA"). These replace the EPA and the 1985 Act is repealed by Sch.7. A key distinction between an EPA and a LPA is that the former were confined to the donor's property and affairs, while the latter can also extend to personal welfare matters, which can include health care decisions (s.11(7)(c)). The legal effect of existing EPAs is preserved and integrated into the scheme of this Act by s.66(3) and Sch.4. A person with mental capacity who has made an EPA before this Act comes into force can either destroy it and then make a LPA, or can do nothing. An EPA cannot be made after this Act has come into force (s.66(3)). The power to make an ordinary power of attorney under the Powers of Attorney Act 1971(c.27) is unaffected by this Act.

A LPA can only be executed by a mentally capable adult (subs.(2)(c)), and it will only be valid if it complies with s.10, and the instrument conferring the authority is made in the form prescribed by the Lasting Powers of Attorney, Enduring Powers of Attorney and Public Guardian Regulations 2007 (SI 2007/1253) and registered with the Public Guardian in accordance with Sch.1 (subss.(2)(a)(b), (3)) and Part 2 of SI 2007/1253. There is nothing to prevent a person who is detained under the Mental Health Act 1983 from executing a LPA as long as he or she has the capacity to do so. Publicly funded legal advice through the Legal Help scheme cannot be provided to assist an individual to create a LPA (Access to Justice Act 1999, Sch.2, para.1(ea)). The Public Guardian is required to establish and maintain a register of LPAs (s.58(1)(a)), and will receive reports from donees (s.58(1)(f)).

Decisions made by the donee must be in P's best interests and he or she must act in accordance with the principles set out in s.1 (subs.(4)(a)). The donee must also comply with any conditions or restrictions that P has put in the LPA (subs.(4)(b)). If the donee is granted the power to refuse consent to life sustaining treatment, his or her decision must not be motivated by a desire to bring about the donor's death (ss.4(5),11(8)). The donee, who acts as the agent of P (see the General Notes to s.10), is subject to the restrictions on restraint set out in s.6 (s.11(1)–(6)), and to any advance decision made by P (s.11(7)(b); but see s.25(2)(b)). The Public Guardian can investigate a complaint about the way in which a donee is exercising his or her powers (s.58(1)(h)). This function can be discharged in co-operation with other persons who are involved in the care of treatment of P(s.58(2)). The Public Guardian can direct a Court of Protection Visitor to investigate the complaint and report to him (s.58(1)(d)). The Public Guardian could then report to the court which could decide to revoke the LPA (s.22(4)(b)). The court can also interpret the terms of an LPA or give directions as to its exercise (s.23), but it does not have power to extend or amend the terms of the LPA as granted by the donor.

By making an LPA, the donor (P), confers on the donee or donees authority to make decisions about P's personal welfare and/or property and affairs or specified matters concerning those areas. The authority to make decisions includes, where appropriate, the authority to act on decisions made (s.64(2)). The LPA must include authority for the donee/s to make decisions when P no longer has capacity to make those decisions (subs.(1)).

If P wishes, a LPA relating to P's property and affairs can operate as an "ordinary" power of attorney while P has mental capacity as long as it will continue to have effect after P loses capacity. Section 11(7)(a) prevents a personal welfare LPA having similar effect: it can only be used once the donor has lost capacity.

Separate LPAs can be created for welfare and financial matters. It is not possible for a single LPA to cover both matters. In her evidence to the Joint Committee, the Health Minister acknowledged the need, in some cases, to appoint different donees in relation to different types of decision:

"From the health care side it may be that people might want different attorneys for different decisions. Somebody that you trust with your finances may not be the same as somebody that you wanted to make decisions about your health and welfare" (Q754).

The Joint Committee expressed its concern about evidence that it has received "indicating that financial abuse occurs in approximately 10–15% of cases involving EPAs. Further evidence estimated that that abuse was as high as 20%" (para.138). These figures relate to unethical conduct. It is estimated that 2%–3% of cases involve criminal conduct (Oral and written evidence, Ev 188). This Act attempts to reduce the risk of financial abuse by requiring an LPA to be executed and registered before it can be used (see subs.(2)), thereby reducing the difficulties associated with the monitoring of EPAs. A report prepared for the Public Guardianship Office, "The role of the Public Guardianship Office in safeguarding vulnerable adults against financial abuse" (undated) by Hilary Brown *et al*, suggests that further action will be required to tackle the financial abuse of incapacitated persons who are subject to LPAs. There are also potential conflicts of interest between P and the donee in relation to welfare matters. For example, a decision by the donee to authorise the placement of P in a care home might have the effect of diminishing the potential inheritance of the donee. The powers of the Court of Protection in relation to LPAs are set out in ss.22 and 23. They include the power to revoke a LPA if the donee is not acting in P's best interests (s.22(3)(4)). The Public Guardian can receive reports from donees (s.58(1)(f)).

Baroness Andrews outlined the manner in which the Act can be utilised to prevent financial abuse by donees:

"[D]onors of financial LPAs will be advised that they can, if they so choose, stipulate in their financial LPA that they wish the [donee] to provide annual accounts to the Public Guardian or to any other third party for checking. That is a front-line defence. Therefore, the Public Guardian can check accounts not only if he is asked to do so but also if someone raises a concern. Concerns can be raised by different sorts of objectors at all stages. If an objector raises concerns about a prospective [donee] at the registration stage, the Court may add a requirement for the [donee] to lodge accounts if that would alleviate the concerns of the objector. That is a second line of defence.

Anyone can raise a concern with the Office of the Public Guardian if they fear that [a donee] of a registered LPA is not acting properly. The Court will then be able to direct that the [donee] should lodge accounts. We believe that is robust. They could be 'one-off' accounts or annual accounts. They could be lodged with the Court, a solicitor, an accountant or, indeed, a third party.

In the broader context the *Code of Practice* makes it clear to financial [donees] that they should keep accounts. We intend to issue guidance to reinforce that message" (*Hansard*, HL Vol.669, cols 771–772).

The British Bankers' Association has published a booklet on "Banking for people who lack capacity to make decisions" (October 2007).

The House of Lords Select Committee on Medical Ethics in its comments on proxy decision-making on healthcare matters, observed that, "whilst the idea of the patient appointed proxy is in many ways attractive, it is vulnerable to the same problems as advance directives, and indeed to a greater degree" (HL Paper 21–1, para.268). The Committee observed that personal relationships are not immutable, and that the choice of proxy might soon become out of date. The Committee also noted the practical difficulties of ascertaining what choice the patient would have made, that previous statements of preference form an unreliable basis for future decisions, and the difficulty in ensuring the objectivity of the proxy (even when acting in good faith).

The Law Society has issued a Practice Note on lasting powers of attorney (2007). Paragraph 5.2 states that there "may be circumstances where an LPA may not be appropriate, and a later application to the Court of Protection for deputyship, with oversight of the Office of the Public Guardian, may be preferable. This may be advisable, for example:

- where there are indications of persistent family conflicts suggesting that an LPA may be contested, or
- where the assets are more substantial or complex than family members are accustomed to handle, or
- in cases where litigation may lead to a substantial award of damages for personal injury."

Subsection (1)

DONOR. See subs.(2)(c). Only individuals can make LPAs. There is no provision for joint **1–095** LPAs to be made by, for example, a husband and wife. The donor is not required to live in England or Wales.

AUTHORITY TO MAKE DECISIONS. A donee will be provided with protection by ss.5 and 6 for acts done outside the scope of the LPA.

Subsection (1)(a)

PERSONAL WELFARE. The donee has no power to act under the authority of a welfare LPA if **1–096** the donor has the mental capacity to make the decision in question (s.11(7)(a)). The *Code of Practice*, at para.7.21, states that personal welfare LPAs might include decisions about:

"• where the donor should live and who they should live with
- the donor's day-to-day care, including diet and dress
- who the donor may have contact with
- consenting to or refusing medical examination and treatment on the donor's behalf
- arrangements needed for the donor to be given medical, dental or optical treatment
- assessments for and provision of community care services
- whether the donor should take part in social activities, leisure activities, education or training
- the donor's personal correspondence and papers
- rights of access to personal information about the donor, or
- complaints about the donor's care or treatment."

A welfare LPA which gives general powers to the donee would include all of the above powers. A welfare LPA which is not drafted in general terms can either specify the powers that the donee is granted, or can specify the types of decisions that the donee is not empowered to make.

There is a potential overlap between financial and welfare LPAs. For example, a decision that it would be in the best interests of P to live in a care home, which is a welfare decision, would require a financial decision to be made in that the care home fees would need to be paid. If the LPA provides for separate donees for financial and welfare matters, this could lead to the decision of the welfare donee being thwarted by the refusal of the financial donee to pay the fees. In such a situation, both donees must act in the best interests of P. If the dispute cannot be resolved, a complaint should be made to the Public Guardian who can require a Court of Protection Visitor to report to him on the matter (s.58(1)(d)).

The implications of providing healthcare decision making powers to a donee are considered in the General Note to s.11.

Subsection (1)(b)

PROPERTY AND AFFAIRS. Subject to any restrictions contained within it, the donee of a finan- **1–097** cial LPA can act under it as soon as it has been registered with the Public Guardian. The term "property and affairs" means "business matters, legal transactions and other dealing of a similar kind" (*F v West Berkshire HA* [1989] 2 All E.R. 545, HL, *per* Lord Brandon at 554). The *Code of Practice*, at para.7.36, states that financial LPAs might include decisions about:

"• buying or selling property
• opening, closing or operating any bank, building society or other account
• giving access to the donor's financial information
• claiming, receiving and using (on the donor's behalf) all benefits, pensions, allowances and rebates (unless the Department for Work and Pensions has already appointed someone and everyone is happy for this to continue)
• receiving any income, inheritance or other entitlement on behalf of the donor
• dealing with the donor's tax affairs
• paying the donor's mortgage, rent and household expenses
• insuring, maintaining and repairing the donor's property
• investing the donor's savings
• making limited gifts on the donor's behalf . . .
• paying for private medical care and residential care or nursing home fees
• applying for any entitlement to funding for NHS care, social care or adaptations
• using the donor's money to buy a vehicle or any equipment or other help they need
• repaying interest and capital on any loan taken out by the donor."

A financial LPA may grant the donee general powers, in which case the donee will be authorised to undertake any of the acts set out above. As an alternative, the donor might wish to grant the donee specific powers, or could specify the types of decisions the donee is not empowered to make.

Subsection (2)(b)

1–098   REGISTERED. The donor could either register the instrument straight away, or could leave it with the proposed donee with a request that it be registered when he or she believes that the donor has lost the capacity to make the decision to register. In both cases, the LPA cannot be used until the Public Guardian has registered it.

Subsection (2) (c)

1–099   REACHED 18. This ensures that there is no overlap with the Children Act 1989 or the wardship jurisdiction of the High Court.

Subsection (2)(c)

1–100   CAPACITY. The donor must have the capacity to execute the instrument at the time when it is executed. The fact that a capacious donor is detained under the Mental Health Act 1983 does not disqualify him or her from executing an LPA. In *Re K, Re F* [1998] 1 All E.R. 358, a case on the 1985 Act, Hoffman J. held that the donor should be able to understand:

1. If such be the terms of the power, that the donee will be able to assume complete authority over the donor's affairs.
2. If such be the terms of the power, that the donee will in general be able to do anything with the donor's property which he himself could have done.
3. That the authority will continue if the donor should be or become mentally incapable.
4. That if he should be or become mentally incapable, the power will be irrevocable without confirmation by the court.

This test, which was described by Sir Christopher Staughton in the Court of Appeal in *Re W* [2001] 4 All E.R. 88, 92, as a "sound indication of what the donor must understand if the power is to be valid", is a broader test than that set out in Sch.1, para.2(1)(e).

Subsection (3)

CONFERS NO AUTHORITY. Note, however, that the court can declare an instrument that is not **1–101** in the prescribed form to be treated as if it were, if it is satisfied that the person executing the instrument intended it to create a LPA (Sch.1, para.3(2)).

Subsection (4)

BEST INTERESTS. The donee must therefore apply the s.4 check list before any decision is **1–102** made on behalf of P.

ANY CONDITIONS OR RESTRICTIONS. Even if the condition or restriction, viewed objectively, does not serve the best interests of P. The scope of a donee's power is also limited by the fact that he or she acts as the agent of P: see the General Note to s.10.

Appointment of donees

10.—(1) A donee of a lasting power of attorney must be— **1–103**
(a) an individual who has reached 18, or
(b) if the power relates only to P's property and affairs, either such an individual or a trust corporation.

(2) An individual who is bankrupt may not be appointed as donee of a lasting power of attorney in relation to P's property and affairs.

(3) Subsections (4) to (7) apply in relation to an instrument under which two or more persons are to act as donees of a lasting power of attorney.

(4) The instrument may appoint them to act—
(a) jointly,
(b) jointly and severally, or
(c) jointly in respect of some matters and jointly and severally in respect of others.

(5) To the extent to which it does not specify whether they are to act jointly or jointly and severally, the instrument is to be assumed to appoint them to act jointly.

(6) If they are to act jointly, a failure, as respects one of them, to comply with the requirements of subsection (1) or (2) or Part 1 or 2 of Schedule 1 prevents a lasting power of attorney from being created.

(7) If they are to act jointly and severally, a failure, as respects one of them, to comply with the requirements of subsection (1) or (2) or Part 1 or 2 of Schedule 1—
(a) prevents the appointment taking effect in his case, but
(b) does not prevent a lasting power of attorney from being created in the case of the other or others.

(8) An instrument used to create a lasting power of attorney—
(a) cannot give the donee (or, if more than one, any of them) power to appoint a substitute or successor, but
(b) may itself appoint a person to replace the donee (or, if more than one, any of them) on the occurrence of an event mentioned in section 13(6)(a) to (d) which has the effect of terminating the donee's appointment.

DEFINITIONS
"lasting power of attorney": s.64(1) **1–104**
"property": s.64(1)
"trust corporation": s.64(1)
"bankrupt": s.64(3)

GENERAL NOTE

1–105   This section sets out requirements relating to the appointment of donees and how they should act. The maximum number of donees that a donor of an LPA may specify is five (Lasting Powers of Attorney, Enduring Powers of Attorney and Public Guardian Regulations 2007 (SI 2007/1253, reg.6). An individual donee must be an adult and, if the LPA relates to property and affairs, not be a bankrupt (subss.(1)(a),(2)). A trust corporation, as well as an individual, can be appointed as donee to a LPA that relates only to property and affairs (subs.(1)(b)). Apart from where a trust corporation is appointed, the appointment of a donee is personal. This contrasts with the appointment of a deputy who can be the holder of an office or position (s.19(2)). If an individual is appointed, it is important for the donor to be confident that the chosen donee would be likely to act in his or her best interests when performing functions under this Act. The Act does not place an obligation on a donee to accept appointment.

A donee acts as the agent of the donor. Under the law of agency, an act of an agent done within the scope of his authority binds his principal, in this case P. As an agent the donee is bound by a number of common law duties toward P, including the duty to act with due care and skill, to act in good faith, not to delegate his or her functions to another, to keep the donor's affairs confidential apart from where the disclosure of information is allowed by the LPA or is otherwise required, to keep accounts of monies received and paid on P's behalf, to keep money belonging to P separate from his or her own funds and not to permit his or her own interests to conflict with the duties owed to P. The relationship of the donee to the patient is that of a fiduciary and like all fiduciaries the donee should not benefit from the relationship (*Bunting v W* [2005] EWHC 1274 (Ch), para.31). The donee also has a duty to act within the scope of the LPA (s.9(4)(b)) although he or she has implied authority to do what is necessary for or incidental to the effective execution of the powers granted. The donee also has a duty to act in the donor's best interests, to be guided by the best principals set out in s.1, to have regard to the *Code of Practice* (s.42(4)(a)), and to comply with any directions that the Court of Protection might make. The duties of an agent are described in the *Code of Practice* at paras 7.58–7.68. For a comprehensive account of the law of agency, see Francis M.B. Reynolds, *Bowstead and Reynolds on Agency*, (18th ed., Sweet & Maxwell, London, 2006).

In this Act references to making decisions, in relation to a donee, include, where appropriate, acting on decisions made (s.64(2)).

Any concerns about the way in which the donee in undertaking his or her functions, including a concern that the donee might lack mental capacity, should be reported to the Public Guardian or, if criminal behaviour is suspected, the police. The donee of a financial LPA who is dishonestly abusing his position could be guilty of an offence under s.4 of the Fraud Act 2006. The Public Guardian may decide to direct a Court of Protection Visitor to visit P and/or the donee (s.58(1)(d)). In serious cases, the Public Guardian will refer the matter to the court. Also see the note on adult protection procedures in s.44.

The *Code of Practice*, at para.7.70, states that signs that a donee may be exploiting the donor (or failing to act in the donor's best interests) include:

"• stopping relatives or friends contacting the donor – for example, the attorney may prevent contact or the donor may suddenly refuse visits or telephone calls from family and friends for no reason
  • sudden unexplained changes in living arrangements (for example, someone moves in to care for a donor they've had little contact with)
  • not allowing healthcare or social care staff to see the donor
  • taking the donor out of hospital against medical advice, while the donor is having necessary medical treatment
  • unpaid bills (for example, residential care or nursing home fees)
  • an attorney opening a credit card account for the donor
  • spending money on things that are not obviously related to the donor's needs
  • the attorney spending money in an unusual or extravagant way

- transferring financial assets to another country."

A number of witnesses to the Joint Committee expressed their concern about the situation that could arise when a donee who is a close relative of P appears not to be acting in the best interests of the P because of a conflict of interest. This difficulty was said to be "not common but neither is it rare" (Oral and written evidence, Ev 472). An example of how such a conflict can arise has been given by Baroness Finlay:

> "A lady aged 59 was very ill. Her family appeared to be very concerned about her pain and constantly asked for her diamorphine to be increased. However, we remained unconvinced that her pain was really that severe. In fact, the patient declined increasing doses of diamorphine. Her 60th birthday arrived and was passed with minimal celebration, after which the family visited very little. She became depressed and spoke to one of the night nurses, explaining that the problem was that on her 60th birthday, her fixed-term life insurance policy expired. The family would not now inherit what they thought they would if she had died, and if her drugs had been duly increased" (*Hansard*, HL Vol.642, col.766).

Donees who are close relatives might not accurately reflect P's wishes as studies have shown that relatives' perception of the patient's likely views often differ substantially from the patient's own wishes; see, for example, A.B. Seckler *et al*, "Substituted judgment: how accurate are proxy predictions?" (1991) 115(9) Ann. Intern. Med. 92–98; also see the studies cited in R. Schiff *et al*, "Living wills and the Mental Capacity Act: a postal questionnaire survey of UK geriatricians" (2006) 35 *Age and Ageing* 116 and the notes to s.4(7).

In its *"Response to the Scrutiny Committee's Report on the draft Mental Incapacity Bill"* (Cm.6121), the Government recognised "that there may be potential for conflict of interest in an LPA" and agreed "that donors should be given information about this and more generally about the seriousness of making an LPA".

Subsection (1)

INDIVIDUAL. A professional donee, such as an accountant or a solicitor, must be referred to **1–106** by name. For example, it is not possible to refer to "a partner in Sue, Grabit and Run".

TRUST CORPORATION. Is defined in the Trustee Act 1925 (c.19), s.68(1) as "the Public Trustee or a corporation either appointed by the court in any particular case to be a trustee, or entitled by rules made under s.4(3) of the Public Trustee Act 1906 (c.55), to act as custodian trustee." A trust corporation is "often parts of banks or other financial institutions" (*Code of Practice*, para.7.9).

Subsection (2)

The Parliamentary Under-Secretary of State announced that the Government had **1–107** "decided that the Office of the Public Guardian will check to see if prospective financial attorneys are bankrupt when an LPA is registered" (*Hansard*, HL Vol.668, col.1417). If the donee is bankrupt, then the LPA will be invalid. There is nothing to prevent a bankrupt from being appointed to act as a donee of a welfare LPA.

Subsection (4)

This provides that where two or more people are appointed as donees, they may be **1–108** appointed either to act jointly (so that they must all join together in any decision), or to act jointly and severally (which means that they can act either independently or all together) or to act jointly in respect of some matters and jointly and severally in respect of others. The donor therefore "has all possible options when wanting to appoint more than one donee", *per* the Parliamentary Under-Secretary of State (*Hansard*, HL Vol.670, col.1473). If the donor does not specify, it will be assumed that the donees were appointed jointly (subs.(5)).

Subsection (6)

1–109   For joint donees, any breach by one of them of the requirements concerning how LPAs are made will prevent a LPA from being created.

Subsection (7)

1–110   Where donees are appointed jointly and severally, a breach by one of them of the requirements concerning how LPAs are made will only prevent the appointment taking affect in his or her case; a valid LPA is created in respect of the other donee(s).

Subsection (8)

1–111   This enables a donor to provide in the LPA for the replacement of the donee(s) on the occurrence of an event mentioned in s.13(6)(a)–(d) which would normally terminate a donee's powers. One of these events is the death of the donee. It would therefore be possible, for example, for a donor to appoint his spouse as donee, but nominate his child as a replacement donee. Under para.(a), a donee cannot be given power by the LPA to choose a successor.

Lasting powers of attorney: restrictions

1–112   **11.**—(1) A lasting power of attorney does not authorise the donee (or, if more than one, any of them) to do an act that is intended to restrain P, unless three conditions are satisfied.

(2) The first condition is that P lacks, or the donee reasonably believes that P lacks, capacity in relation to the matter in question.

(3) The second is that the donee reasonably believes that it is necessary to do the act in order to prevent harm to P.

(4) The third is that the act is a proportionate response to—

(a) the likelihood of P's suffering harm, and

(b) the seriousness of that harm.

(5) For the purposes of this section, the donee restrains P if he—

(a) uses, or threatens to use, force to secure the doing of an act which P resists, or

(b) restricts P's liberty of movement, whether or not P resists,

or if he authorises another person to do any of those things.

(6) [*Repealed by the Mental Health Act 2007, s.50(4)(b)*]

(7) Where a lasting power of attorney authorises the donee (or, if more than one, any of them) to make decisions about P's personal welfare, the authority—

(a) does not extend to making such decisions in circumstances other than those where P lacks, or the donee reasonably believes that P lacks, capacity,

(b) is subject to sections 24 to 26 (advance decisions to refuse treatment), and

(c) extends to giving or refusing consent to the carrying out or continuation of a treatment by a person providing health care for P.

(8) But subsection (7)(c)—

(a) does not authorise the giving or refusing of consent to the carrying out or continuation of life-sustaining treatment, unless the instrument contains express provision to that effect, and

(b) is subject to any conditions or restrictions in the instrument.

DEFINITIONS

1–113   "lasting power of attorney": s.64(1)

"the Human Rights Convention": s.64(1)

"treatment": s.64(1)

"life-sustaining treatment": s.64(1)

GENERAL NOTE

Subsections (1)–(5) place restrictions on the use of restraint by donees similar to those **1–114** that apply to "section 5 acts" (see s.6) and deputies (see s.20). Reference should be made to the notes on s.6.

A donee has no power to bring or defend legal proceedings on behalf of the donor. The authority of the court could be sought for the donee to act as the donor's litigation friend.

Under subs.(7), a personal welfare LPA:

(i) can only take effect after P loses capacity. Decision making will therefore fluctuate between the donor and donee in cases where the donor has fluctuating capacity. It is also the case that P could be capable of making some simple personal welfare decisions, but not other, more complex, decisions. This could give rise to considerable practical difficulties. A healthcare professional who is proposing to provide medical treatment for P must also assess P's capacity. Any dispute between donee and the professional about the assessment of P's capacity that remains unresolved should be referred to the Court of Protection for a declaration under s.15(1)(a);

(ii) is generally subject to any advance decision that P has made: see the note on subs.(7)(b), below; and

(iii) can authorise the donee to give or refuse consent to the carrying out or continuation of health care for P. This power is subject to any conditions or restrictions in the LPA and to subs.(8) which prohibits the donee from refusing life-sustaining treatment for P unless the LPA expressly allows for this. A LPA does not provide the donee with a power to demand that a specific form of medical treatment be provided to P.

In order to make a healthcare decision on behalf of P, the donee should have received the same information about the nature of the treatment being proposed and its consequences as P would have received had he or she had been mentally capable. The power to make a LPA which enables the donee to make healthcare decisions has been criticised on the ground that patients' views about the medical treatment that they would wish to receive are not fixed; they adapt to circumstances (see further the note on s.25(4)(c)). An application to the Court of Protection should be made if the donee is asked to consent to a non-therapeutic treatment, such as an organ donation, if such treatment is not specified in the LPA.

The fact that the donee has the power to refuse medical treatment on behalf of P represents a significant change in the doctor patient relationship in that a non-medical donee can override the doctor's clinical judgment as to what treatment his or her patient should receive. If a doctor wishes to challenge a decision made by a donee not to consent to treatment for P, the doctor could consider making an application to the Court of Protection for on order overriding the donee's decision on the ground that the donee was not acting in P's best interests. But as the briefing note on the Mental Capacity Bill by the Catholic Bishops' Conference of England and Wales (July 2004, at para.24) notes, how many doctors "will have the time, energy and motivation to ask a court to override a[donee] whose determination of best interests appears to them to be defective or questionable?" If the decision of the donee to refuse treatment either stops the doctor from providing life-sustaining treatment or would be likely to lead to a serious deterioration in P's condition, the treatment can continue until the decision of the court is made (s.6(6), (7)).

A donee cannot refuse the provision of basic care for P, such as the provision of hydration and nutrition by non-artificial means and keeping P clean, because the cessation of such care would never be in P's best interests.

A healthcare professional who treats P despite the existence of a LPA which provides for a donee to make the decision in question will be protected from legal liability by virtue of s.5 unless, at the time, he is satisfied that such a LPA exists. If an urgent healthcare decision needs to be taken in respect of P and there is no time to contact the donee, the healthcare professional should proceed to treat P in his or her best interests and then report to the donee.

Subsection (7)

1–115　Make decisions. See s.64(2).

Subsection (7) para.(a)

1–116　Reasonably believes. The donee must be able to satisfy this objective test by identifying the grounds that he or she had for believing that P lacked capacity.

Subsection (7) para.(b)

1–117　Generally, a LPA is subject to the terms of an advance decision. However, if the LPA is made after the advance decision it overrides the advance decision if it confers on the donee the power to refuse treatments specified in the advance decision (s.25(2)(b)).

Subsection (7) para.(c)

1–118　The LPA does not provide a donee with the power to require that a particular medical treatment be given to P if such treatment is not considered by healthcare professionals to be in the best interests of P.

Subsection (8)

1–119　The power of a donee to prevent life-sustaining treatment to be given to P, which is subject to the restriction contained in s.4(5), was the subject of considerable criticism during the Bill's passage through Parliament. For example, Earl Howe said:

> "In very many cases—perhaps the majority—the doctor and the [donee] will be in agreement about what is in the patient's best interests, and no problem will therefore arise. The problems arise when doctor and [donee] are in disagreement.

> Both of them are required under the Bill to work in the patient's best interests. But the interpretation of 'best interests' is open to difference. What the Bill is saying is that, in the worst case, [a donee] with no medical knowledge whatever can take it on himself to gainsay a doctor whose professional advice is that the patient whose life is at stake should receive certain treatment. It might be perfectly possible for the [donee] to maintain, with some justification, that his decision to refuse consent was taken in the best interests of P. But the doctor, who had close knowledge and experience of the treatment, might not think that a fair and reasonable view of best interests.

> What happens then? The Bill allows the doctor to seek a ruling from the Court [of Protection] where there is such disagreement. But let us take the example of a doctor who has no previous knowledge of the patient and who is confronted by a [donee] with no medical expertise and articulates his views plausibly and forcefully. Are we going to imagine that every doctor in that position will have the strength of purpose and the degree of self-belief to refer the matter to the Court? I find that unlikely. Doctors are professional people, but they are also human. I very much fear that some will be browbeaten into agreeing to a course of action that runs contrary to their better judgment" (*Hansard*, HLVol.670, col.1484).

This provision is compatible with Art.2 of the European Convention on Human Rights which provides for a "right to life" because the donee is chosen by a competent adult and can only act under this Act in the best interests of that person.

Scope of lasting powers of attorney: gifts

1–120　**12.**—(1) Where a lasting power of attorney confers authority to make decisions about P's property and affairs, it does not authorise a donee (or, if more than one, any of them) to dispose of the donor's property by making gifts except to the extent permitted by subsection (2).

　(2) The donee may make gifts—

(a) on customary occasions to persons (including himself) who are related to or connected with the donor, or

(b) to any charity to whom the donor made or might have been expected to make gifts,

if the value of each such gift is not unreasonable having regard to all the circumstances and, in particular, the size of the donor's estate.

(3) "Customary occasion" means—

(a) the occasion or anniversary of a birth, a marriage or the formation of a civil partnership, or

(b) any other occasion on which presents are customarily given within families or among friends or associates.

(4) Subsection (2) is subject to any conditions or restrictions in the instrument.

DEFINITIONS

"lasting power of attorney": s.64(1)   **1–121**
"property": s.64(1)

GENERAL NOTE

This section limits the power of a donee of a financial LPA to dispose of P's property by **1–122** making gifts. Only gifts coming within the categories set out in subs.(2) are allowed.The donee must also act in accordance with any conditions or restrictions on his or her power to make gifts which are specified in the LPA, and satisfy the best interests criterion (s.9(4)(a)). If the donee wishes to make a gift which exceeds his or her authority under the LPA, an application should be made to the court under s.18(1)(b). The court has power to authorise gifts that are more substantial than those permitted by subs.(2) if satisfied that these would be in P's best interests (s.23(4)).

Subsection (2)

NOT UNREASONABLE. This is for the donee to determine. The donee is not required to obtain **1–123** consent from anyone before making the gift. The authorisation of the Court of Protection should be obtained if it is proposed to make a substantial gift in order to reduce P's tax liability.

Subsection (3)

ANY OTHER OCCASION. Taking into account P's past and present wishes and feelings **1–124** (s.4(6)(a)).

Revocation of lasting powers of attorney etc

13.—(1) This section applies if—   **1–125**

(a) P has executed an instrument with a view to creating a lasting power of attorney, or

(b) a lasting power of attorney is registered as having been conferred by P,

and in this section references to revoking the power include revoking the instrument.

(2) P may, at any time when he has capacity to do so, revoke the power.

(3) P's bankruptcy revokes the power so far as it relates to P's property and affairs.

(4) But where P is bankrupt merely because an interim bankruptcy restrictions order has effect in respect of him, the power is suspended, so far as it relates to P's property and affairs, for so long as the order has effect.

(5) The occurrence in relation to a donee of an event mentioned in subsection (6)—

(a) terminates his appointment, and

(b) except in the cases given in subsection (7), revokes the power.

(6) The events are—

(a) the disclaimer of the appointment by the donee in accordance with such requirements as may be prescribed for the purposes of this section in regulations made by the Lord Chancellor,

(b) subject to subsections (8) and (9), the death or bankruptcy of the donee or, if the donee is a trust corporation, its winding-up or dissolution,

(c) subject to subsection (11), the dissolution or annulment of a marriage or civil partnership between the donor and the donee,

(d) the lack of capacity of the donee.

(7) The cases are—

(a) the donee is replaced under the terms of the instrument,

(b) he is one of two or more persons appointed to act as donees jointly and severally in respect of any matter and, after the event, there is at least one remaining donee.

(8) The bankruptcy of a donee does not terminate his appointment, or revoke the power, in so far as his authority relates to P's personal welfare.

(9) Where the donee is bankrupt merely because an interim bankruptcy restrictions order has effect in respect of him, his appointment and the power are suspended, so far as they relate to P's property and affairs, for so long as the order has effect.

(10) Where the donee is one of two or more appointed to act jointly and severally under the power in respect of any matter, the reference in subsection (9) to the suspension of the power is to its suspension in so far as it relates to that donee.

(11) The dissolution or annulment of a marriage or civil partnership does not terminate the appointment of a donee, or revoke the power, if the instrument provided that it was not to do so.

DEFINITIONS

1–126   "lasting power of attorney": s.64(1)

"property": s.64(1)

"bankrupt": s.64(3)

"trust corporation": s.64(1)

GENERAL NOTE

1–127   This section identifies the way in with an LPA can be revoked, whether before or after registration. A donor who has revoked the LPA must follow the procedure set out in the Lasting Powers of Attorney, Enduring Powers of Attorney and Public Guardian Regulations 2007 (SI 2007/1253), reg.21. The death of the donor revokes the LPA; see reg.22.

P can revoke an LPA at any time while he or she has capacity to do so (subs.(2)). P's bankruptcy will revoke a LPA that relates to P's property and affairs, but not a personal welfare LPA or that part of a LPA giving authority to make personal welfare decisions (subs.(3)). An interim bankruptcy restrictions order merely suspends a financial LPA (subs.(4)).

The events relating to the donee which are set out in subs.(6) terminate his or her appointment and also revoke the LPA, apart from when the terms of the LPA replace the donee or where the donee is acting jointly and severally with others and, after the event, there is at least one remaining donee (subs.(7)).

The Public Guardian should be informed if a LPA is revoked as this would enable him to cancel the registration (Sch.1, para.17).

P might have the capacity to revoke the power by, for example, saying "I don't want X **1–128** deciding things for me any more", but not have the capacity to make the decision in question. This power can be exercised during a period of temporary capacity. In *Re S*, unreported, March 13, 1997, Master Lush held that in order to revoke an EPA, a donor should have the capacity to understand who the attorneys are; what authority they have; why it is necessary of expedient to revoke the power; and the foreseeable consequences of revoking the power.

Subsection (3)
BANKRUPTCY. See s.64(3) and (4). **1–129**

Subsection (4)
BANKRUPTCY RESTRICTIONS ORDERS. These are provided for in Sch.4A of the InsolvencyAct **1–130** 1986 (c.45).

Subsection (6)
DISCLAIMER OF THE APPOINTMENT. The procedure set out in reg.20 SI 2007/1253 must be **1–131** followed.

BANKRUPTCY OF THE DONEE. But see subss.(8)–(10).

DISSOLUTION OR ANNULMENT OF A MARRIAGE, OR CIVIL PARTNERSHIP. But see subs.(11). A civil partnership is a registered relationship between two people of the same sex which ends only on death, dissolution or annulment, as provided for in the Civil Partnership Act 2004.

LACK OF CAPACITY OF THE DONEE. Although the matter is not free from doubt, it is submitted that a temporary incapacity of the donee would not revoke the LPA.

Protection of donee and others if no power created or power revoked

14.—(1) Subsections (2) and (3) apply if— **1–132**
(a) an instrument has been registered under Schedule 1 as a lasting power of attorney, but
(b) a lasting power of attorney was not created,
whether or not the registration has been cancelled at the time of the act or transaction in question.

(2) A donee who acts in purported exercise of the power does not incur any liability (to P or any other person) because of the non-existence of the power unless at the time of acting he—
(a) knows that a lasting power of attorney was not created, or
(b) is aware of circumstances which, if a lasting power of attorney had been created, would have terminated his authority to act as a donee.

(3) Any transaction between the donee and another person is, in favour of that person, as valid as if the power had been in existence, unless at the time of the transaction that person has knowledge of a matter referred to in subsection (2).

(4) If the interest of a purchaser depends on whether a transaction between the donee and the other person was valid by virtue of subsection (3), it is conclusively presumed in favour of the purchaser that the transaction was valid if—
(a) the transaction was completed within 12 months of the date on which the instrument was registered, or
(b) the other person makes a statutory declaration, before or within 3 months after the completion of the purchase, that he had no reason at the time of

the transaction to doubt that the donee had authority to dispose of the property which was the subject of the transaction.

(5) In its application to a lasting power of attorney which relates to matters in addition to P's property and affairs, section 5 of the Powers of Attorney Act 1971 (c. 27) (protection where power is revoked) has effect as if references to revocation included the cessation of the power in relation to P's property and affairs.

(6) Where two or more donees are appointed under a lasting power of attorney, this section applies as if references to the donee were to all or any of them.

DEFINITIONS
1–133   "lasting power of attorney": s.64(1)
"purchaser": s.64(1)
"property": s.64(1)

GENERAL NOTE
1–134   This section provides legal protection to donees and others who act on invalid LPAs.

Subsection (1) outlines the situations to which subss.(2) and (3) apply. It gives protection to donees and others who rely on registered LPAs which later turn out to be invalid. The protection applies whether or not the registration has been cancelled. Broadly, both donees and third parties will be protected from legal liability if they were unaware that the LPA was invalid.

Subsections (4) and (5) deal with property. If either para.(a) or (b) of sub.(4) is satisfied, a purchaser of property from a donee of an invalid LPA will be protected unless the purchaser was aware of the invalidity.

General powers of the court and appointment of deputies

Power to make declarations
1–135   **15.**—(1) The court may make declarations as to—
  (a) whether a person has or lacks capacity to make a decision specified in the declaration;
  (b) whether a person has or lacks capacity to make decisions on such matters as are described in the declaration;
  (c) the lawfulness or otherwise of any act done, or yet to be done, in relation to that person.
  (2) "Act" includes an omission and a course of conduct.

DEFINITIONS
1–136   "the court": s.64(1)

GENERAL NOTE
1–137   This section provides the Court of Protection with the power to make declarations about whether an individual has mental capacity, and whether an act or proposed act was or would be lawful. A declaration may be refused on the ground that no such declaration is needed. For example, in *H (Mental Patient: Diagnosis), Re* (1993)1 F.L.R. 28, the judge held that a C.T. scan for a schizophrenic patient with a suspected brain tumour was not one of those cases where it was either necessary or desirable to grant a declaration. He did not wish to "send a signal" that this and similar procedures should be delayed pending a costly application to the court.

The power to make declarations regarding a person's capacity is likely to be exercised where: (a) healthcare professionals cannot resolve a dispute about a person's capacity to make a serious decision regarding the provision of medical treatment; or (b) there is a dispute as to whether a person was mentally capable when either an advance decision or a lasting power of attorney was made. Declarations regarding the lawfulness of an act are likely to be made most frequently in cases involving controversial or particularly serious decisions regarding the provision of care or medical treatment for the incapacitated person. Subsection (2) confirms that the court can be asked to make declarations on an omission to act (for example, the withholding or withdrawing of medical treatment), as well as on a course of conduct. As a superior court of record, the Court of Protection has the same powers as the High Court (see s.45(1)).

The inherent jurisdiction of the High Court to make declarations relating to adults (see below) is not ousted by this Act. In *Re SA (Vulnerable Adult with Capacity: Marriage)* [2005] EWHC 2942 (Fam); [2006] 1 F.L.R. 867, Munby J. held, following *G (an Adult) (Mental Capacity: Court's Jurisdiction), Re*, below, that in certain circumstances the inherent jurisdiction can be exercised for the protection of vulnerable adults who do not lack capacity to make the decision in question. His Lordship said at para.79:

"The inherent jurisdiction can be invoked wherever a vulnerable adult is, or is reasonably believed to be, for some reason deprived of the capacity to make the relevant decision, or disabled from making a free choice, or incapacitated or disabled from giving or expressing a real and genuine consent. The cause may be, but is not for this purpose limited to, mental disorder or mental illness. A vulnerable adult who does not suffer from any kind of mental incapacity may nonetheless be entitled to the protection of the inherent jurisdiction if he is, or is reasonably believed to be, incapacitated from making the relevant decision by reason of such things as constraint, coercion, undue influence or other vitiating factors."

His Lordship elaborated by stating that (1) "constraint" involved "some significant curtailment of the freedom to do those things which in this country free men and women are entitled to do"; (2) undue influence occurs "where a vulnerable adult's capacity or will to decide has been sapped or overborne by the improper influence of another"; and (3) other disabling circumstances include "circumstances that may so reduce a vulnerable adult's understanding and reasoning powers as to prevent him from forming or expressing a real and genuine consent, for example, the effects of deception, misinformation, physical disability, illness, weakness (physical, mental or moral), tiredness, shock, fatigue, depression, pain or drugs" (para.78). A vulnerable adult is "someone who, whether or not mentally incapacitated, and whether or not suffering from any mental illness or mental disorder, is or may be unable to take care of him or herself, or unable to protect him or herself against significant harm or exploitation, or who is deaf, blind or dumb, or who is substantially handicapped by illness, injury or congenital deformity. This, I emphasise, is not and is not intended to be a definition. It is descriptive, not definitive; indicative rather than prescriptive" (para.82).

Confirmation that the inherent jurisdiction is not ousted by this Act was given by the Court of Appeal in *KC and NNC v City of Westminster Social and Community Services Department and IC (a protected party, by his litigation friend the Official Solicitor)*, [2008] EWCA Civ 198 where the court approved the following finding made by Roderic Wood J. at first instance:

"[S]ave where to do so would be demonstrably inconsistent with the will of Parliament, the inherent jurisdiction remains alive, in appropriate cases, to meet circumstances unmet by the scope of the legislation."

The Declaratory Jurisdiction of the High Court

As the Court of Protection's jurisdiction to make declarations is founded on the inherent **1–138** jurisdiction of the High Court to make declarations and as the inherent jurisdiction is not ousted by this Act (see above), an account of the development of this jurisdiction in so far as it relates to personal welfare matters is given below.

The question of the lawfulness of treating patients who are incapable of giving consent because they are unconscious in circumstances where the operation or other treatment cannot safely be delayed until consciousness is recovered or because they are deemed to be mentally incapable of making a decision whether to receive treatment was considered in the House of Lords in *F v West Berkshire HA* [1989] 2 All E.R. 545. Their Lordships held that:

1. Under the common law doctrine of necessity a doctor can lawfully operate on, or give other treatment to, adult patients who are incapable, for one reason or another, of consenting to his doing so, provided that the operation or other treatment concerned is the best interests of such patients. The operation or other treatment will be in the best interests of patients if, but only if, it is carried out in order either to save their lives or ensure improvement or prevent deterioration in their physical or mental health. Lord Brandon said at 551: "in many cases it will not only be lawful for doctors, on the grounds of necessity, to operate on or give other medical treatment to adult patients disabled from giving their consent: it will be their common law duty to do so."

2. A doctor will be deemed to have acted in the best interests of a mentally incapable patient and will be immune from liability in trespass to the person if he establishes that he acted in accordance with a practice accepted at the time as proper by a responsible body of medical opinion skilled in the particular form of treatment in question (*Bolam v Friern Hospital Management Committee* [1957] 2 All E.R.118 applied).

3. Special considerations apply in the case of an operation for the sterilisation of an adult woman who is physically perfectly healthy because such treatments cannot be considered to be either curative or prophylactic. No court now has jurisdiction either by statute or derived from the Crown as parens patriae to give or withhold consent to such operations in the case of a mentally incapable adult. However, the High Court does have jurisdiction to make a declaration that the proposed operation is lawful on the ground that in the circumstances it is in the best interests of the patient. Although a declaration is not necessary to establish the lawfulness of the operation, in practice the court's jurisdiction should be invoked prior to the operation taking place, since a declaration would establish by judicial process whether the proposed operation was in the best interests of the patient and therefore lawful.

The purpose of the declaratory jurisdiction was explained by Sir Thomas Bingham MR in *S (Hospital Patient: Court's Jurisdiction) (No.1), Re* [1996] Fam. 1 at 18:

"[I]n cases of controversy and cases involving momentous and irrevocable decisions, the courts have treated as justicable any genuine question as to what the best interests of a patient require or justify. In making these decisions the courts have recognised the desirability of informing those involved whether a proposed course of conduct will render them criminally or civilly liable; they have acknowledged their duty to act as a safeguard against malpractice, abuse and unjustified action; and they have recognised the desirability, in the last resort, of decisions being made by an impartial independent tribunal."

In *Re SA (Vulnerable Adult with Capacity: Marriage)*, above, paras.44, Munby J. observed that since the *F* case, above, the inherent jurisdiction is now exercisable in relation to a wide range of other questions, including questions where the doctrine of necessity is not engaged at all and that the court can now "regulate everything that conduces to the incompetent adult's welfare and happiness".

In *R (on the application of Burke) v The General Medical Council* [2005] EWCA Civ 1003; [2005] H.R.L.R 35, para.80, the Court of Appeal, having considered the decision of the European Court of Human Rights in *Glass v United Kingdom* [2004] 1 F.L.R 1019, held that:

1. A declaration does not "authorise" treatment that would otherwise be unlawful. The court makes a declaration whether or not proposed treatment or the withdrawal of treatment will be lawful.

2. Good practice may require medical practitioners to seek such a declaration where the legality of proposed treatment is in doubt. This is not, however, something that they are required to do as a matter of law.

The nature of the High Court's declaratory jurisdiction over mentally incompetent adults was reviewed by Munby J. in *A (A Patient) v A Health Authority* [2002] EWHC 18 (Fam Div/Admin); [2002] Fam 213. His Lordship held that:

(i) the jurisdiction could be invoked by anyone whose past or present relationship with the incompetent adult, whether formal or informal, gave him or her a genuine and legitimate interest in obtaining a decision, rather than being a stranger or officious busybody. Thus proceedings can be brought by a relative, a carer, a local authority or a NHS Trust;

(ii) the jurisdiction may regulate all that conduces to the incompetent adult's welfare and happiness, including companionship and his or her domestic and social environment;

(iii) the jurisdiction, which extended no further than the parens patriae jurisdiction in relation to children, extended not merely to declaratory relief but also to the grant of injunctive relief—at least interlocutory injunctive relief to preserve or regulate the status quo;

(iv) cases which involved only issues of public law should be litigated by way of an application in the Administrative Court for judicial review. Private law cases about the best interests of the adult were to be litigated in the Family Division notwithstanding the fact that issues of public law might be involved; and

(v) if the task facing the judge was to come to a decision for and on behalf of an incompetent adult then the welfare of that person had to be the paramount consideration. If the task of the judge was to review the decision of the public authority taken in the exercise of some statutory power then the governing principles were those of public law.

In *St Helens Borough Council v PE (by her litigation friend the Official Solicitor)* [2006] EWHC 3460 (Fam); [2007] M.H.L.R. 169, Munby J. said that in best interests proceedings where the court is exercising its protective jurisdiction and the doctrine of necessity was not engaged it was sufficient for declaratory relief to state that a particular course of action was in the incapacitated person's best interests, *i.e.* it was not necessary to declare that the action was "lawful".

Subsequent to the decision in *F*, the courts have held that declarations relating to the medical treatment of mentally incapable patients should also be applied for in the following circumstances: where it is proposed to withdraw artificial feeding from a patient in a persistent vegetative state (*Airedale NHS Trust v Bland* [1993] 1 All E.R. 821, HL), where there is doubt about the mental capacity of the patient (*St George's Healthcare NHS Trust v S* [1998] 3 All E.R. 673), where it was anticipated that force might have to be used to administer an anaesthetic to a patient who required a CT scan (*Doncaster and Bassetlaw Hospitals NHS Trust v C* [2004] EWHC 1657 (Fam Div)), and where it is proposed to harvest bone marrow from the patient (*Y (Mental Patient: Bone Marrow Donation), Re* [1996] 2 F.L.R. 787). Declarations have been applied for in a number of cases where it was proposed to sterilise a mentally incompetent patient. The test for making an application for a declaration in such cases was established by Sir Stephen Brown P. in *GF (Medical Treatment), Re* [1992] 1 F.L.R. 293 when he said at 294:

"I take the view that no application for leave to carry out [a sterilisation] operation need be made in cases where two medical practitioners are satisfied that the operation is (1) necessary for therapeutic purposes, (2) in the best interests of the patient, and (3) there is no practicable, less intrusive means of treating the condition."

In *LC (Medical Treatment: Sterilisation), Re* [1997] 2 F.L.R. 258, Thorpe J. held that leave to perform the sterilisation operation could not be justified upon the basis of some vague and unsubstantiated fear that the patient would be exposed to the risks of pregnancy from which she is presently protected. A similar approach was taken in *S (Medical Treatment: Adult Sterilisation, Re* [1998] 1 F.L.R. 994, where Johnson J. refused to grant a declaration on an application by the patient's mother in "the absence of any risk [of pregnancy] that can be called identifiable rather than speculative". A sterilisation can be in the best interests of the patient even if the risk of pregnancy is small (*W (An Adult: Mental Patient) (Sterilisation), Re* [1993] 1 F.L.R. 381).

In *An NHS Trust v D* [2003] EWHC 2793 (Fam Div), Coleridge J. considered the following question: when should an NHS Trust make an application to the High Court for a declaration that the proposed termination of the pregnancy of a mentally incapacitated patient is lawful? His Lordship held that where there is any doubt as to either the mental capacity of the patient or whether the termination would be in her best interests, an application to the court should be made. In particular, the following circumstances would ordinarily warrant the making of an application:

1. Where there is a dispute as to capacity, or where there is a realistic prospect that the patient will regain capacity, following a response to treatment, within the period of her pregnancy or shortly thereafter;
2. Where there is a lack of unanimity amongst the medical professionals as to the best interests of the patient;
3. Where the procedures under s.1 of the Abortion Act 1967 (c.87) have not been followed (i.e. where two medical practitioners have not provided a certificate);
4. Where the patient, members of her immediate family, or the foetus's father have opposed, or expressed views inconsistent with, a termination of the pregnancy; or
5. Where there are other exceptional circumstances (including where the termination may be the patient's last chance to bear a child).

1–139   If any case is considered to fall anywhere near the boundary line in relation to any of the above criteria, it should for the avoidance of doubt be referred to the court (*S (Adult Patient: Sterilisation: Patient's Best Interests), Re* [2001] Fam.15, *per* Thorpe L.J. at 32).

It is essential for protocols to be put in place to deal with the possible termination of the pregnancy of patients in psychiatric hospitals. Such protocols should be designed to address the issue in good time and should ensure that the patient is referred at an early stage to independent legal advice whether from the Official Solicitor or from the solicitor who represented her at the Mental Health Review Tribunal (*SS (Medical Treatment: Late Termination), Re* [2002] 1 F.L.R. 445).

Declarations can be applied for in respect of treatment in the future (*NHS Trust v T (Adult Patient: Refusal of Medical Treatment)* [2004] EWHC 1279 (Fam Div); [2005] 1 All E.R. 387). In this case Charles J. confirmed that an interim declaration could be made pursuant to CPR Part 25.1(1)(b). His Lordship said, at para.45, that when the court is faced with an emergency situation where treatment cannot be delayed because of an imminent high risk to life the court should make every effort to ensure that the person who it is proposed should be treated in reliance of any declaration has an opportunity to make representations (either directly or indirectly) to the court (and thus in cases of emergency out of hours to the Duty Judge). It would then be for the Judge to decide on capacity and then if appropriate on best interests by applying the normal civil standard on the best evidence then available. It is submitted that in extreme emergencies where there is no time to seek the assistance of the court, any doubt that may exist about the patient's capacity must be resolved in favour of society's interest in upholding the concept that all human life is sacred and that it should be preserved if at all possible.

In *Re Wyatt* [2005] EWHC 2293 (Fam); [2005] 4 All E.R. 1325, Hedley J. held that, in exceptional circumstances, a declaration can be used to resolve a future dispute which can be clearly identified and reasonably anticipated. This finding was upheld on appeal, although the Court of Appeal expressed reservations about judges making open-ended declarations which they may have to re-visit if circumstances change (*Wyatt v Portsmouth Hospital NHS Trust* [2005] EWCA Civ 1181, para.118).

In *G (An Adult) (Mental Capacity: Court's Jurisdiction), Re* [2004] EWHC 2222 (Fam Div), an incapacitated young woman had been made the subject of interim declarations to protect her from the actions of her father. The evidence was that after a period of being subject to the interim declarations the daughter would regain her mental capacity and her mental health would improve, but that once the protection of the court was withdrawn the daughter's mental health would deteriorate and she would lose her mental capacity. Bennett J. held that in these circumstances he had jurisdiction to make declarations to ensure that the continuing protection of the court was not withdrawn simply because the daughter had regained her mental capacity, given the likely consequences if the court withdrew its protection. The judge said, at para.104, that if the declarations sought were in the daughter's best interests, the court, by intervening, far from depriving her of her right to make decisions, will be ensuring that her now stable and improving mental health is sustained, that she has the best possible chance of continuing to be mentally capable, and of ensuring a quality of life that prior to the court's intervention she was unable to enjoy.

A declaration will not be used to require a doctor to act against his or her clinical judgment. In *National Health Service Trust v D* [2000] 2 F.L.R. 677, Cazalet J. said at 686:

> "[I]t is well-established that there can be no question of the court directing a doctor to provide treatment which he or she is unwilling to give and which is contrary to that doctor's clinical judgment."

In recent years declarations have been made to regulate the care of mentally incapable adults in cases where there is a dispute about the care that the adult either is receiving or will receive in the future. It is now possible for the High Court to make declarations as to the lawfulness of proposed actions in relation to the adult in circumstances where the issue in question cannot be resolved by recourse to the Mental Health Act 1983. By using this jurisdiction the High Court is able to effectively resolve disputes such as who should have responsibility for the future care of the adult, who the adult should have contact with and under what circumstances, and the powers that staff can use when providing the adult with care, including the use of restraint and detention. In *F (Adult: Court's Jurisdiction), Re* [2000] 2 F.L.R. 512, CA, the local authority was concerned that T, an 18 year old with an intellectual age of 5–8 years, who was being accommodated in one of the authority's specialist establishments contrary to her mother's wishes, would be at risk of neglect and exposure to sexual exploitation if she were to return to her home. As T was not mentally impaired within the meaning of the Mental Health Act 1983, the local authority was unable to protect T by making her the subject of a guardianship application under that Act. The authority therefore sought declarations from the High Court, the effect of which were to keep T in the accommodation and to restrict and supervise her contact with her family. In determining the question of the jurisdiction of the High Court to make such declarations, the Court held that:

(i) the application of the common law doctrine of necessity (see *F v West Berkshire HA*, above), is not limited to medical and similar matters; it embraces the problems that arose in this case;

(ii) the doctrine, which can be invoked by both an authority and an individual, may properly be invoked side by side with the 1983 Act (*R. v Bournewood Community and Mental Health NHS Trust Ex p. L* [1998] 3 All E.R. 289, HL);

(iii) the jurisdiction of the High Court under its inherent jurisdiction to grant relief by way of declarations was therefore not excluded by the 1983 Act;

(iv) the jurisdiction will only be invoked if there is a serious justicable issue; and

(v) in making a declaration the judge will be guided by the patient's best interests on an application of a welfare test analogous to that applied in wardship cases.

Sedley L.J. said at 529: "[N]either the mother nor the (imaginary) sister nor the local authority possesses by virtue of their status any power to detain T. Nor, however, does T have the capacity to choose one of them as an appropriate carer. If the role of carer is contested, it is the court alone which has the power—and in my judgment the duty—to make that choice in T's best interests. From the choice will follow the exercise of care; and from the exercise of care, if absolutely necessary, some restraint may follow."

1–140   In *A Local Authority v BS* [2003] EWHC 1909 (Fam Div); [2003] 2 F.L.R.1235, a case where it was alleged that a mentally incapacitated adult had been struck by her father, interim declarations were made on a without notice basis rendering it lawful for the local authority to (1) place the adult in a residential placement; (2) to prohibit her father from removing her from that placement; and (3) to limit the contact between the adult and her father to supervised contact. Wall J. said, at para.21, that although in a field as complex as care for the mentally disabled, a high degree of pragmatism is inevitable, in each case there are four essential building blocks. First, is mental incapacity established? Secondly, is there a serious justicable issue relating to welfare? Thirdly, what is it? Fourthly, with the welfare of the incapable adult as the court's paramount consideration, what are the balance sheet factors which must be drawn up to decide which course of action is in his or her best interests? His Lordship said at, para.18, that in certain circumstances, the court will have to make findings of fact about disputed historical matters but that this would only be necessary if they are required to determine the identification of the incapable person's best interests. There will plainly be cases which are very fact specific. There will be others in which the principle concern is the future, and the relative suitability of the plans which each party can put forward for both the short term and the long term care of the mentally incapable adult.

The inherent jurisdiction was invoked in *A London Borough Council v T and T B*, November 1, 2001, where detailed declarations and injunctions were made by the court on the application of the local authority in a situation where there had been a breakdown of trust between a mentally incapacitated adult's mother and the authority which had led to the parties becoming polarised in their positions. The judge found that "there have been occasions where the mother has behaved either in an illogical fashion or in a fashion which can perhaps be most aptly described as not constructive". The relief was designed to provide for the care of the adult by the authority for the foreseeable future and for regulating contact between the mother and her daughter. Constant and relentless complaints by the mother resulted in the judge approving the appointment of an independent non-legal advocate for the client who would provide a channel "for the time to be investigated and dealt with". A penal notice was added to some of the orders because of the past breaches of the undertakings that the mother had given to the court.

In *S (Adult Patient) (Inherent Jurisdiction; Family Life), Re* [2002] EWHC 2278; [2003] 1 F.L.R. 292, above, the jurisdiction was used to determine a dispute between the local authority and the father of a mentally incapacitated adult about the future place of residence of the adult. Munby J. described at, para.6, the court's role in this case, a case which fell entirely within the confines of private law, as acting as "a surrogate decision maker on behalf of [the adult]". His Lordship said at para.20:

"[T]he doctrine of necessity enables [the parents of a mentally incapacitated adult] not merely to assume the responsibility for the day-to-day care of their child, with all the routine decision-making which that entails, but also to decide, no doubt, where appropriate, in conjunction with suitable professional advisors, more important matters such as where their child should live, who he should see, what services offered by public authorities he should make use of, what medication he should take and what nursing, dental and medical treatment he should receive. [Cases should only come before the court] if disputes erupt between those seeking to care for the patient."

His Lordship reminded himself of the following point made by Lord Goff in *F v West Berkshire HA*, above, at 566:

"officious intervention cannot be justified by the principle of necessity. So intervention cannot be justified when another more appropriate person is available and willing to act."

The jurisdiction was invoked in *Re S.* because there is no presumption of the right of contact between a parent and an adult child, even one under a disability (*D-R (Adult: Contact), Re* [1999] 1 F.L.R.1161, *per* Butler-Sloss L.J. at 1165), and neither the local authority nor the father had the legal authority to decide where the adult should live. The judge had to weigh the father's rights under Art.8 of the European Convention on Human Rights against the son's Art.8 rights. Munby J. held, at para.39, that where there is a conflict between these rights, the State, in the form of the local authority, may have a positive obligation to intervene, even at the risk of detriment to the father's family life, if such intervention is necessary to ensure respect for the son's Art.8 rights. His Lordship further held that in proceedings under the inherent jurisdiction concerning mentally incapable adults:

(i) there is nothing analogous to the threshold requirements contained in ss.31 and 100 of the Children Act 1989 requiring the State to establish, before intervention takes place, either the risk of significant harm and/or parenting which falls short of the reasonable;

(ii) although there is no presumption that mentally incapacitated adults are better off with their families, other things being equal, the parent, if he or she is willing and able, is the most appropriate person to look after such an adult; not some public authority, however well meaning and seemingly well equipped to do so; and

(iii) the Court has jurisdiction to identify a third party (a "surrogate decision maker") as the most appropriate person to be responsible not merely for the adult's care but also for taking important decisions about his life.

A noteworthy feature arising from the cases noted above is that the threshold for remov- **1–141** ing a mentally incapable adult from the parental home is substantially lower than that required to remove a child in that there is no requirement to establish that the adult is either suffering, or is likely to suffer significant harm. All that is required is that the balance sheet exercise identified by Thorpe L.J. in *Re A*, above, indicates that removal is in the adult's best interests. Where allegations are made, the burden of proving each allegation is upon the maker, and the requisite standard of proof is the balance of probability (*London Borough of Ealing v KS and others* [2008] EWHC 636 (Fam), para.49).

In *City of Sunderland v PS and CA* [2007] EWHC 623 (Fam), para.22, Munby J. said that "proper compliance with s.6 of the Human Rights Act 1998 requires the judges to mould and adapt the inherent jurisdiction so that it is compatible with the requirement of Art.5 [of the European Convention on Human Rights], as well as Art.8". Applying this principle to cases where it was in the best interests of mentally incapable adults to be detained in care homes, his Lordship said, at para.23, that the following minimum requirements must be satisfied in order to comply with Art.5:

1. The detention must be authorised by the court on application made by the local authority and *before* the detention commences.

2. Subject to the exigencies of urgency or emergency the evidence must establish unsoundness of mind of a kind or degree warranting compulsory confinement. In other words, there must be evidence establishing at least a prima facie case that the individual lacks capacity and that confinement of the nature proposed is appropriate.

3. Any order authorising detention must contain provision for an adequate review at reasonable intervals, in particular with a view to ascertaining whether there still persists unsoundness of mind of a kind or degree warranting compulsory confinement.

His Lordship also held that the power under s.37 of the Supreme Court Act 1981 for the court to appoint a receiver could be invoked by the court in the exercise of the inherent jurisdiction even though there was an available statutory remedy under Pt VII of the Mental Health Act 1983 (now see this Act). His Lordship said at para.34:

"It is necessary for PS's interests for her income and savings to be put under proper control, but it would be an unnecessary burden and, in my judgment, wholly disproportionate to the very modest amounts involved, to condemn the parties to the trouble and expense of separate proceedings in the Court of Protection. In the circumstances it seemed to me that the appropriate course was for me to appoint an appropriate officer of the local authority to be PS's receiver."

In *A Local Authority v Z* [2004] EWHC 2817 (Fam Div); [2005] H.R.L.R. 2, Hedley J. considered the extent of the duty owed by a local authority when the welfare of a vulnerable adult (who may or may not be mentally incapacitated) in their area is threatened by the criminal (or other wrongful) act of another. In this case a husband was intending to assist his severely disabled wife in her desire to commit suicide. Assisting the suicide of another is a crime (Suicide Act 1961 (c.60) , s.2(1)). His Lordship held that in such a case the local authority incurred the following duties:

1. To investigate the position of a vulnerable adult to consider what was her true position and intention.
2. To consider whether she was legally competent to make and carry out her decision and intention.
3. To consider whether any other (and if so, what) influence may be operating on her position and intention and to ensure that she has all the relevant information and knows all the available options.
4. To consider whether to invoke the inherent jurisdiction of the High Court so that the question of competence could be judicially investigated and determined.
5. In the event of the adult not being competent, to provide all such assistance as may be reasonably required both to determine and give effect to her best interests.
6. In the event of the adult being competent, to allow her in any lawful way to give effect to her decision although that should not preclude the giving of advice or assistance in accordance with what are perceived to be in her best interests.
7. Where there are reasonable grounds to suspect that the commission of a criminal offence may be involved, to draw that to the intention of the police.
8. In very exceptional circumstances, to invoke the jurisdiction of the court under s.222 of the Local Government Act 1972 (c.70) in order to seek an injunction to restrain a criminal act.

1–142   Although a local authority can invoke the inherent jurisdiction in order to determine whether a mentally vulnerable adult has the capacity to marry, the High Court has no jurisdiction to determine whether it is in the best interests of that adult to marry a particular person (*Sheffield City Council v E* [2004] EWHC 2808 (Fam Div); [2005] Fam 326). A person is capable of entering into a marriage if he or she is capable of understanding the nature of the contract of marriage, i.e. an understanding of the duties and responsibilities that normally attach to marriage, namely the agreement to live together, love each other as husband and wife, and establish a relationship of mutual and reciprocal obligations, typically involving the sharing of a common home and a common domestic life and the right to enjoy each other's society, comfort and assistance. The contract is, in essence, a simple one which does not require a high degree of intelligence to comprehend (*Sheffield City Council v E and S* [2004] EWHC 2808 (Fam); [2007] M.H.L.R. 131). The person concerned must be also able to understand the nature of sexual intercourse and its foreseeable consequences, which is not an onerous test (*Local Authority X v MM and KM* [2007] EWHC 2003 (Fam); [2007] M.H.L.R. 173). In *MM* Munby J. had to make declarations in a complex case where P had the capacity to consent to sexual relations, but lacked the capacity to make decisions with respect to contact and residence, which included contact with the person with whom she had a sexual relationship. In *X City Council v MB, NB and MAB* [2006] EWHC 168 (Fam); [2007] M.H.L.R. 155, Munby J. held that the court may intervene to protect a vulnerable adult if there is a real possibility of harm resulting from an arranged marriage.

Butler-Sloss P. invoked the inherent jurisdiction to grant an injunction to prevent the publication of a report that had been prepared by a local authority subsequent to its decision to remove a number of foster children and vulnerable adults from the home of their foster mother (*Local Authority v Health Authority (Disclosure: Restriction on Publication)*), above). Her Ladyship found that the publication of the report would be "deeply damaging and detrimental" to the welfare of the mentally incapacitated adults.

In *NHS Trust v Bland*, above, Lord Goff at 864–865 reiterated his opinion that declaratory relief was justified, while recognising:

> "that strong warnings have been given against the civil courts usurping the function of the criminal courts, and it has been authoritatively been stated that a declaration as to the lawfulness or otherwise of future conduct is 'no bar to criminal prosecutions, no matter the authority of the court which grants it': see *Imperial Tobacco Ltd v Attorney General* [1980] 1 All E.R. 866."

The court has jurisdiction to grant whatever relief in declaratory form is necessary to safeguard and promote the incapacitated adult's welfare and interests (*S (Adult Patient) (Inherent Jurisdiction: Family Life), Re*, above, para.50). This can include injunctive relief, including interlocutory injunctive relief, the making of tipstaff orders (location orders, collection orders and passport orders) and orders enabling third parties to take protective steps in relation to an incapacitated adult: see *Re SA*, above, paras 84–95. Guidance on the making of without notice applications to the court was provided by Charles J. in *B Borough Council v Mrs S and Mr S (by the Official Solicitor)* [2006] EWHC 2584 (Fam), at paras 38–43, 158.

The wardship jurisdiction of the High Court should be invoked if the individual that needs protecting is a child and intervention under the Children Act 1989 is either not possible or inappropriate (*F (Mental Health Act: Guardianship), Re* [2000] 1 F.L.R. 192).

Subsection (1) para.(a)

WHETHER A PERSON HAS OR LACKS CAPACITY. The court will apply the tests set out in ss.2 and **1–143** 3. In *Masterman-Lister v Brutton & Co* [2002] EWCA Civ 1889; [2003] 3 All E.R.162, para.29, Kennedy L.J. said that the "conclusion that in law capacity depends on time and context means that inevitably a decision as to capacity in one context does not bind a court which has to consider the same issue in a different context". This case is also authority for the proposition that although the final decision as to capacity rests with the court, in almost every case "the court will need medical evidence to guide it".

Subsection (1) para.(c)

A declaration cannot be used to authorise what would otherwise be unlawful, nor can it **1–144** render unlawful that which would otherwise be lawful (*R (on the application of Burke) v General Medical Council*, above, para.71).

In *Re P (Adult Patient) (Consent to medical treatment)* [2008] EWHC 1403 (Fam), paras.31, 32, Sir Mark Potter P. agreed with the finding made by Charles J. in *Surrey Council v MB* [2007] EWHC 3085 (Fam). The President said:

> "Charles J held (at para.46 of the judgment) that the statutory provision granting the Court discretion under Section 15(1)(c) to make declarations as to the lawfulness or otherwise of any act done or yet to be done in relation to P, is a free standing provision which co-exists with the provisions of the Mental Health Act, and he went on to hold that he considered the language wide enough to include the making of a declaration permitting compulsory removal and detention for the purposes of medical treatment, if found to be in the best interests of P, and that such an order would not be in breach of Article 5 of the ECHR, provided that the conditions enumerated by Munby J in *City of Sunderland v PS* [2007] EWHC 623 (Fam); [2007] M.H.L.R. 196 were met. Those conditions are that P is incapable of making a decision whether or not to go to the place of treatment ('the unit') and/or to stay within it; that a requirement to go to and remain in the unit would be in his best interests; that the Court has declared in advance that it is in the best interests of P to be taken there and to be compelled to remain there by using reasonable and

proportionate measures; and that there is a mechanism for timely and ongoing review of P's capacity and best interests with regard to his remaining in the relevant unit."

On the basis of case law under the inherent jurisdiction, the *Code of Practice* states, at para.8.18, that cases involving any of the following decisions should be brought before the court:

"• decisions about the proposed withholding or withdrawal of artificial nutrition and hydration (ANH) from patients in a permanent vegetative state (PVS)
• cases involving organ or bone marrow donation by a person who lacks capacity to consent
• cases involving the proposed non-therapeutic sterilisation of a person who lacks capacity to consent to this (e.g. for contraceptive purposes) and
• all other cases where there is a doubt or dispute about whether a particular treatment will be in a person's best interests."

Powers to make decisions and appoint deputies: general

1–145   **16.**—(1) This section applies if a person (P) lacks capacity in relation to a matter or matters concerning—

(a) P's personal welfare, or
(b) P's property and affairs.

(2) The court may—

(a) by making an order, make the decision or decisions on P's behalf in relation to the matter or matters, or
(b) appoint a person (a deputy) to make decisions on P's behalf in relation to the matter or matters.

(3) The powers of the court under this section are subject to the provisions of this Act and, in particular, to sections 1(the principles) and 4(best interests).

(4) When deciding whether it is in P's best interests to appoint a deputy, the court must have regard (in addition to the matters mentioned in section 4) to the principles that—

(a) a decision by the court is to be preferred to the appointment of a deputy to make a decision, and
(b) the powers conferred on a deputy should be as limited in scope and duration as is reasonably practicable in the circumstances.

(5) The court may make such further orders or give such directions, and confer on a deputy such powers or impose on him such duties, as it thinks necessary or expedient for giving effect to, or otherwise in connection with, an order or appointment made by it under subsection (2).

(6) Without prejudice to section 4, the court may make the order, give the directions or make the appointment on such terms as it considers are in P's best interests, even though no application is before the court for an order, directions or an appointment on those terms.

(7) An order of the court may be varied or discharged by a subsequent order.

(8) The court may, in particular, revoke the appointment of a deputy or vary the powers conferred on him if it is satisfied that the deputy—

(a) has behaved, or is behaving, in a way that contravenes the authority conferred on him by the court or is not in P's best interests, or
(b) proposes to behave in a way that would contravene that authority or would not be in P's best interests.

DEFINITIONS
    "property": s.64(1)   **1–146**
    "the court": s.64(1)

GENERAL NOTE

This section sets out the core jurisdiction of the Court of Protection, which is to make **1–147** substitute decisions for persons lacking the required mental capacity to make decisions for themselves about either their personal welfare or their property and affairs, or to appoint a deputy to do so if this is in their best interests. The court does not have jurisdiction to supply consent to any matter on behalf of P. Sections 17 and 18 indicate to extent of the court's powers with regard to the personal welfare and the property and affairs of P. A decision of the court is to be preferred to the appointment of a deputy who, if appointed, should be granted powers as limited in scope and duration as is reasonable practicable (subs.(4)). This requirement is consistent with the least restrictive intervention principle set out in s.1(6). The deputy's appointment can be revoked or his or her powers varied if the court considers that the deputy's past, present or future actions will not serve P's best interests (subs.(8)). The court has power to act on its "own motion" to make whatever order is in P's best interests (subs.(6)), and can vary or discharge existing orders (subs.(7)). When exercising this jurisdiction, the court must adhere to the principles set out in s.1 and must make decisions which are in the best interests of the P (subs.(3)). The court can make any order or appointment which is in the best interests of P, regardless of the nature of the application made to it.

The Public Guardian is required to establish and maintain a register of orders appointing deputies, and to supervise deputies (s.58(1)(b) and (c)), and will receive reports from deputies (s.58(1)(f)). The Public Guardian can investigate a complaint about the way in which a deputy is exercising his or her powers (s.58(1)(h)). Ultimately the matter could be referred to the court which has power to either discharge the order appointing the deputy or to vary the deputy's powers (subs.(7)). The supervision and investigatory functions of the Public Guardian can be discharged in co-operation with other persons who are involved in the care of treatment of P (s.58(2)).

Subsection (2)(a)

MAKING AN ORDER. The *Code of Practice* states at paras 8.27–8.28:   **1–148**

"In some cases, the court must make a decision, because someone needs specific authority to act and there is no other route for getting it. These include cases where:

- there is no EPA or property and affairs LPA in place and someone needs to make a financial decision for a person who lacks capacity to make that decision (for example, the decision to terminate a tenancy agreement), or
- it is necessary to make a will, or to amend an existing will, on behalf of a person who lacks capacity to do so.

Examples of other types of cases where a court decision might be appropriate include cases where:

The court can make an order the effect of which is to deprive P of his or her liberty (s.4A(3),(4)), apart from situations where P is ineligible within the meaning of Sch.1A (s.16A).

- there is genuine doubt or disagreement about the existence, validity or applicability of an advance decision to refuse treatment . . .
- there is a major disagreement regarding a serious decision (for example, about where a person who lacks capacity to decide for themselves should live)
- a family carer or a solicitor asks for personal information about someone who lacks capacity to consent to that information being revealed (for example, where there have been allegations of abuse of a person living in a care home)

- someone suspects that a person who lacks capacity to make decisions to protect themselves is at risk of harm or abuse from a named individual (the court could stop that individual contacting the person who lacks capacity)."

Article 8 of the European Convention on Human Rights may impose on a local authority not merely the power but in appropriate circumstances the duty to apply to the court for an order if that is necessary to protect a vulnerable adult from possible harm at the hands of his family. In *S (Adult Patient) (Inherent Jurisdiction; Family Life), Re* [2002] EWHC 2278; [2003] 1 F.L.R. 292, para.39, Munby J. said:

". . . as *Botta v Italy* [(1998) 26 E.H.R.R. 241] shows, the State, even in this sphere of relations between purely private individuals, may have positive obligations to adopt measures which will ensure effective respect for the son's private life. Thus the State, in the form of the local authority, may have a positive obligation to intervene, even at the risk of detriment to the father's family life, if such intervention is necessary to ensure respect for the son's Article 8 rights. And the State, in the form of the High Court, has a positive obligation to act in such a way as to ensure respect for those rights."

Where, in accordance with an order made under this provision, a person has been authorised to carry out a transaction for a person who lacks capacity, the Public Guardian has the functions set out in reg.45 of the Lasting Powers of Attorney, Enduring Powers of Attorney and Public Guardian Regulations 2007 (SI 2007/1253).

Subsection (2)(b)
APPOINT A PERSON (A DEPUTY). The appointment of deputies is governed by s.19. Where a deputy has been appointed under this provision, the fee prescribed in the Schedule to the Public Guardian (Fees, etc) Regulations 2007 (SI 2007/2051) shall be payable by P within 30 days of the date of the invoice for the fee (regs 3 and 7). After the appointment, the Public Guardian must determine the level of supervision required by s.58(1)(c) and the level of fee as set out in the Schedule is payable accordingly. The three levels of supervision are type I (highest), type II (lower) and type III (minimal), (reg.8(3)); see further the General Note to s.19.

A deputy's power to make decisions on behalf of P is limited to the matters specified by the court. Where possible, the court will seek to make a single order (subs.(4)(a)). Given the terms of s.5, it is likely that the appointment of a deputy to make personal welfare decisions in relation to P will be made rarely. The Government said its response to recommendation 54 of the Joint Committee's Report (Cm.6121):

"We would only expect deputies to be given healthcare powers in rare cases, for example, where there is a dispute between family members as to who has the patient's best interests at heart and where the patient has chronic and/or degenerative health problems calling for repeated assessments and decisions by doctors and carers."

In these circumstances, the "court is unlikely to appoint as a deputy someone who is unknown to the person. Appointing someone who has no particular insight into the person's wishes, feelings, values or healthcare needs would not be in the person's best interests. The court must appoint a deputy only if that appointment would be in the best interests of the person lacking capacity under [s.16(3)]", *per* the Parliamentary Under-Secretary of State, St. Comm. A, para.195.

The *Code of Practice* states at paras 8.38–8.39:

"Deputies for personal welfare decisions will only be required in the most difficult cases where:

- important and necessary actions cannot be carried out without the court's authority, or
- there is no other way of settling the matter in the best interests of the person who lacks capacity to make particular welfare decisions.

Examples include when:

- someone needs to make a series of linked welfare decisions over time and it would not be beneficial or appropriate to require all of those decisions to be made by the court. For example, someone (such as a family carer) who is close to a person with profound and multiple learning disabilities might apply to be appointed as a deputy with authority to make such decisions
- the most appropriate way to act in the person's best interests is to have a deputy, who will consult relevant people but have the final authority to make decisions
- there is a history of serious family disputes that could have a detrimental effect on the person's future care unless a deputy is appointed to make necessary decisions
- the person who lacks capacity is felt to be at risk of serious harm if left in the care of family members. In these rare cases, welfare decisions may need to be made by someone independent of the family, such as a local authority officer. There may even be a need for an additional court order prohibiting those family members from having contact with the person."

The need for a deputy to be appointed to manage the person's property and affairs is **1–149** likely to arise in the same circumstances that governed the appointment of receivers under Pt VII of the Mental Health Act 1983, in particular when property needs to be sold or if the person has financial resources that the court considers requires management by a deputy. The Public Accounts Committee stated that for "a receivership to be successful [under the 1983] Act, it is crucial that the receiver appointed is trustworthy and reliable. It is also important that the receiver is competent to manage the patient's affairs and should take an active interest in the patient's welfare" (House of Commons, Session 1993–1994, Thirty-ninth Report, para.5). The following cases decided under the 1983 Act on the position of receivers are relevant to the position of deputies under this Act:

1. As well as establishing that the receiver acts as the patient's agent (see the note on s.19), the case of *EG, Re* [1914] 1 Ch. 927 established that a solicitor instructed by the receiver in connection with the patient's affairs is the solicitor of the patient and not that of the receiver.
2. The effect of an appointment of a receiver is not to create a liability to a third party that would not otherwise exist. A receiver's duty to satisfy a patient's legal liabilities is entirely dependent on there being such liabilities in existence (*Bell v Todd* [2002] Lloyd's L.R.12, para.22).
3. A person who has been rendered a patient as the result of the actions of a tortfeasor is entitled to require the tortfeasor to bear the costs of the receiver as part of the damages (*Cassel v Riverside HA* [1992] P.I.Q.R. Q168).

A financial deputy who is dishonestly abusing his position could be guilty of an offence under s.4 of the Fraud Act 2006.

Subsection (4) para. (a)
See the General Note, above. **1–150**

Subsection (4) para. (b)
LIMITED IN SCOPE AND DURATION. This provision reflects the fact that many disabled people **1–151** have capacity to take many day-to-day decisions and would only require the assistance of a deputy in relation to a limited range of matters.

Subsection (5)
If a deputy considers that the powers conferred by the court are insufficient to carry out **1–152** the necessary duties toward the person lacking capacity, he or she should apply to the court either to vary the powers in the order of appointment, or for the court to make a particular decision itself. The court "will be able to grant powers to the deputy on condition that it first

obtains the Public Guardian's consent for certain actions. It is important that deputies are, of course, properly supervised, but it would be disproportionately burdensome and costly to require them to apply to the court all the time for authority to act. That supervisory role should properly be undertaken by the Public Guardian", *per* the Parliamentary Under-Secretary of State (*Hansard*, HL Vol.670, col.1474).

Subsection (7)

1–153   See s.18(5).

Subsection (8)

1–154   This provides the court with similar powers to those it has with respect to donees: see s.22(3), (4).

[Section 16 powers: Mental Health Act patients etc

1–155   **16A.**—(1) If a person is ineligible to be deprived of liberty by this Act, the court may not include in a welfare order provision which authorises the person to be deprived of his liberty.

(2) If—

(a) a welfare order includes provision which authorises a person to be deprived of his liberty, and

(b) that person becomes ineligible to be deprived of liberty by this Act,

the provision ceases to have effect for as long as the person remains ineligible.

(3) Nothing in subsection (2) affects the power of the court under section 16(7) to vary or discharge the welfare order.

(4) For the purposes of this section—

(a) Schedule 1A applies for determining whether or not P is ineligible to be deprived of liberty by this Act;

(b) "welfare order" means an order under section 16(2)(a).]

AMENDMENT

1–156   This section was inserted by the Mental Health Act 2007, s.50(3).

DEFINITIONS

1–157   "deprivation of liberty": s.64(5),(6).
"the court": s.64(1).

GENERAL NOTE

1–158   This section prevents the court from making an order under s.16(2)(a) authorising the deprivation of P's liberty if P is ineligible to be deprived of his liberty within the meaning of Sch.1A, i.e. he comes within a category where the Mental Health Act 1983 must be used. It also, in subs.(2), provides that an existing order under s.16(2)(a) authorising P to be deprived of his liberty ceases to have effect on P becoming ineligible.

Section 16 powers: personal welfare

1–159   **17.**—(1) The powers under section 16 as respects P's personal welfare extend in particular to—

(a) deciding where P is to live;

(b) deciding what contact, if any, P is to have with any specified persons;

(c) making an order prohibiting a named person from having contact with P;

(d) giving or refusing consent to the carrying out or continuation of a treatment by a person providing health care for P;

(e) giving a direction that a person responsible for P's health care allow a different person to take over that responsibility.

(2) Subsection (1) is subject to section 20 (restrictions on deputies).

DEFINITIONS
"treatment": s.64(1)   **1–160**
"deputy": s.64(1)

GENERAL NOTE
This section sets out in subs.(1) the types of personal welfare matters that, under s.16, the **1–161**
Court of Protection may either determine itself or appoint a deputy to make decisions about
on P's behalf. The power of deputies to make decisions is subject to the restrictions set out
in s.20 (subs.(2)) and is limited to the matters specified by the court (s.16(2)(b)).

The list in subs.(1) which is indicative, not exhaustive, is based on matters that have been
dealt with by the High Court in the exercise of its inherent jurisdiction to make declarations:
see the General Note to s.15. It is not a list of decisions that must always go the court for
determination; rather it provides examples of decisions that could go to the court for determination if it would be appropriate to do so.

Subsection (1) (a)
This power enables a judge to prevent P from being taken to another country if this would **1–162**
be contrary to his or her health and welfare (*KC and NNC v City of Westminster Social and
Community Services Department and IC (a protected party, by his litigation friend the
Official Solicitor),* [2008] EWCA Civ 198, para.13).

As the court only has power to make any decision that P could have made, this power
cannot be used to override the provisions of either s.47 of the National Health Service
and Community Care Act 1990 (c.19), which provides for the assessment by a local authority of a person's need for community care services (which includes the provision of
accommodation), or the National Assistance Act (Choice of Accommodation) Directions
1992.

Subsection (1) (c)
A restraining order could be made where the named person presents a risk of abuse, or **1–163**
where continued contact with that person will harm or distress P. The power restrain a
named person cannot extend to any interference with other rights of that person, such as
the right to occupy property.

Subsection (1) (d)
By virtue of s.26(1), the court cannot make an order which is inconsistent with the terms **1–164**
of a valid and applicable advance decision.

In the consultation paper *"Who Decides"* (Cm.3803 at 7.26), the Government expressed
its concern that a deputy "might have less prior knowledge of a patient's wishes regarding
treatment than the patient's doctor". The fact that a deputy has the power to refuse treatment on behalf of P represents a significant change in the doctor patient relationship in
that a non-medical deputy can override the doctor's clinical judgment as to what medical
treatment his or her patient should receive; see further the General Note to s.11. This power
is subject to the limitation set out in s.20(5).

The deputy does not have the power to direct that a different person should take over
responsibility for P's health care (s.20(2)(b)). Neither does the deputy have the power to
require a doctor to provide treatment which is not considered to be in P's best interests.
This is because if P were capable, he or she would not have such a power.

1–165   This allows for the court to order that the responsibility for P's healthcare be transferred to another doctor where P's doctor has a conscientious or clinical objection to a treating P.

Section 16 powers: property and affairs

1–166   **18.**—(1) The powers under section 16 as respects P's property and affairs extend in particular to—

(a) the control and management of P's property;

(b) the sale, exchange, charging, gift or other disposition of P's property;

(c) the acquisition of property in P's name or on P's behalf;

(d) the carrying on, on P's behalf, of any profession, trade or business;

(e) the taking of a decision which will have the effect of dissolving a partnership of which P is a member;

(f) the carrying out of any contract entered into by P;

(g) the discharge of P's debts and of any of P's obligations, whether legally enforceable or not;

(h) the settlement of any of P's property, whether for P's benefit or for the benefit of others;

(i) the execution for P of a will;

(j) the exercise of any power (including a power to consent) vested in P whether beneficially or as trustee or otherwise;

(k) the conduct of legal proceedings in P's name or on P's behalf.

(2) No will may be made under subsection (1)(i) at a time when P has not reached 18.

(3) The powers under section 16 as respects any other matter relating to P's property and affairs may be exercised even though P has not reached 16, if the court considers it likely that P will still lack capacity to make decisions in respect of that matter when he reaches 18.

(4) Schedule 2 supplements the provisions of this section.

(5) Section 16(7) (variation and discharge of court orders) is subject to paragraph 6 of Schedule 2.

(6) Subsection (1) is subject to section 20 (restrictions on deputies).

DEFINITIONS
1–167   "property": s.64(1)

GENERAL NOTE
1–168   This section, which is supplemented by Sch.2, provides a non-exhaustive, indicative list of the matters relating to P's property and affairs that come within the jurisdiction of the Court of Protection under s.16. The Court may either determine the matter itself or appoint a deputy to make decisions on P's behalf. The power of deputies to make decisions is subject to the restrictions set out in s.20 (subs.(6)) and is limited to the matters specified by the court (s.16(2)(b)).

Like s.17, subs.(1) does not contain a list of matters which must always be referred to the court; it provides an indication of the types of order the court might make if an application is made.

It is submitted that the court may make an order if the provisions of a financial LPA do not enable P's best interests to be satisfied: see *Re C*, Rattee J., unreported, January 23, 1996.

If P's sole source of income is social security benefits, the Department of Work and Pensions can appoint an "appointee" to receive and deal with the benefits on P's behalf: see the Introduction and General Note to this Act under the heading "Appointees".

This largely reproduces the list which applied to the Court of Protection under s.96 of the **1–169** Mental Health Act 1983.

Paragraph (a)

PROPERTY. This includes papers held by the Official Solicitor in an action in which he acts **1–170** as the patient's litigation friend (*E (Mental Health Patient), Re* [1985] 1 All E.R. 609, CA). In *E* the court held that the parents of a patient had no absolute right to see such papers, although they were the patient's property, but must obtain the authority of the Court of Protection to order disclosure of them as necessary or expedient for the benefit of the patient.

Paragraph (b)

GIFT. The court will adopt the stance that it takes to the making of wills: see *C, Re* and *S,* **1–171** *Re*, noted under para.(i), below. Although it is proper to propose a gift where one of the objectives is to reduce liability for tax, this should not be the sole objective (*CWM, Re* [1951] 2 K.B. 714).

Any view expressed by the P about a gift can be taken into account by the court but cannot be regarded as determinative. The court will be concerned to establish whether P has been subjected to the undue influence of the proposed recipient of the gift. The criteria for capacity to make a gift were set out in *Beaney (Deceased), Re* [1978] 2 All E.R. 595 at 601:

> "The degree or extent of understanding required in respect of any instrument is relative to the particular transaction which it is to effect Thus, at one extreme, if the subject-matter and value of a gift are trivial in relation to the donor's other assets, a low degree of understanding will suffice. But, at the other, if its effect is to dispose of the donor's only asset of value and thus, for practical purposes, to pre-empt the devolution of his estate under [the donor's] will or intestacy, then the degree of understanding required is as high as that required for a will, and the donor must understand the claims of all potential donees and the extent of the property to be disposed of."

DISPOSITION OF P'S PROPERTY. Provisions relating to the preservation of interests in property disposed of on behalf of P are contained in paras 8 and 9 of Sch.2.

Paragraph (h)

Paragraphs 5 and 6 of Sch.2 are concerned with the making of settlements on behalf of P. **1–172** Settlements are likely to be created, with or without the appointment of a deputy, where P has been awarded substantial damages for personal injury.

In *L(WJG), Re* [1966] Ch. 135, at 144 and 145, Cross J. considered the approach to be adopted by a judge in determining whether and how he should exercise his discretion in regard to the making of a settlement where one of the objects of the exercise was to save death duties. His Lordship said: "As the state had maintained [P] free of charge for many years, it would be a little shabby to deprive it of the chance of recouping some of that expenditure by way of death duties."

Paragraph (i)

Paragraphs 2 to 4 of Sch.2 apply to the making of a will on behalf of P. Paragraph 4(3) **1–173** provides that a will made under this Act has the same effect as a will made by a competent testator. The will must be executed in accordance with para.3(2).

An application for a statutory will can be made without the permission of the court by any of the persons specified in s.50 and rr.51(1) and 52(4) of the CPR 2007. The procedure for making an application, including an urgent application, is considered in Ch.20 of *Heywood and Massey: Court of Protection Practice*, Sweet and Maxwell. The areas that should be covered in evidence to the court are set out in Practice Direction 9F. P must be an adult before a will can be made (subs.(2)). In *D(J), Re* [1982] 2 All E.R. 37 at 42 and 43, Megarry V-C. identified five considerations which the court should have in mind when deciding on what provisions should be inserted in a will made under a similar provision in the Mental Health Act 1959. They are:

1. It is to be assumed that the patient is having a brief lucid interval at the time when the will was made.
2. During the lucid interval the patient has full knowledge of the past and a full realisation that as soon as the will is executed he will relapse into the actual mental state that previously existed, with the prognosis as it actually is.
3. It is the actual patient who has to be considered and not a hypothetical patient.
4. During the hypothetical lucid interval, the patient is to be envisaged as being advised by competent solicitors.
5. In all normal cases, the patient is to be envisaged as taking a broad brush to the claims on his bounty, rather than an accountant's pen.

In *C (Spinster and Mental Patient), Re* [1991] 3 All E.R. 866, Hoffmann J., in applying *Re D(J)*, held that in the case of a person who has never enjoyed a rational mind the court when called upon to interpret the phrase "the patient might be expected to provide" in s.95(1)(c) of the 1983 Act should assume that the patient would have been a normal decent person who would have acted in accordance with contemporary standards of morality. In appropriate cases this could result in the patient making charitable gifts and bequests. *Re C* was considered in *S (Gifts by Mental Patient), Re* [1997] 1 F.L.R. 96, 99 where Ferris J. said on the question of dispositions to charity: "It seems to me that I ought not authorise the making of dispositions to charity except to the extent that I have a reasonable degree of confidence that not only is it objectively reasonable but that it is something which the patient herself would have wished to be done if she were of full capacity and aware of the circumstances."

The court will not make a new will under this provision unless it is satisfied that there are grounds for making a change. In *Re S*, above, Ferris J. said at 99:

"[M]y approach gives weight to the undesirability of the court exercising its jurisdiction in such a way as to change the existing position in circumstances where it is not fully satisfied that the change is something which the patient herself would have desired."

The court has no jurisdiction to determine the validity of an existing will and, in particular, whether P had the required mental capacity when he made it. The test for testamentary capacity (the capacity required to make a will) was set out by the Court of Appeal in *Banks v Goodfellow* (1870) L.R. 5 Q.B. 549:

"It is essential that a testator shall understand the nature of the act and its effects; shall understand the extent of the property of which he is disposing; shall be able to comprehend and appreciate the claims to which he ought to give effect; and, with a view to the latter object, that no disorder of mind shall poison his affections, pervert his sense of right, or prevent the exercise of his natural faculties—that no insane delusion shall influence his will in disposing of his property and bring about a disposal of it which, if the mind had been sound, would not have been made."

In *Scammell v Farmer* [2008] EWHC 1100 (Ch), para.24, Stephen Smith QC, sitting as a deputy High Court judge, said that there "was a large measure of agreement between counsel that the test of mental capacity under s.3 of the 2005 Act is a modern restatement of the test propounded in *Banks v Goodfellow* . . . There is, however, an obvious difference between the position at common law and the position under the 2005 Act, in that the onus of proof of incapacity under the 2005 Act (s.1(2)) is from the outset, and remains, on the complainant. At common law, the position is different."

Paragraph (k)

The conduct of legal proceedings need not be confined to proceedings relating either to **1–174**
P's personal welfare or his property and affairs *(W (EEM), Re* [1971] Ch.123).

Subsection (3)

This provision enables the court to take a long term view where a brain damaged child **1–175**
has been awarded a large sum of damages and there is no prospect of the child ever gaining
the capacity to manage that money.

Appointment of deputies

19.—(1) A deputy appointed by the court must be— **1–176**
(a) an individual who has reached 18, or
(b) as respects powers in relation to property and affairs, an individual who has
    reached 18 or a trust corporation.

(2) The court may appoint an individual by appointing the holder for the time
being of a specified office or position.

(3) A person may not be appointed as a deputy without his consent.

(4) The court may appoint two or more deputies to act—
(a) jointly,
(b) jointly and severally, or
(c) jointly in respect of some matters and jointly and severally in respect of
    others.

(5) When appointing a deputy or deputies, the court may at the same time
appoint one or more other persons to succeed the existing deputy or those
deputies—
(a) in such circumstances, or on the happening of such events, as may be speci-
    fied by the court;
(b) for such period as may be so specified.

(6) A deputy is to be treated as P's agent in relation to anything done or decided
by him within the scope of his appointment and in accordance with this Part.

(7) The deputy is entitled—
(a) to be reimbursed out of P's property for his reasonable expenses in discharg-
    ing his functions, and
(b) if the court so directs when appointing him, to remuneration out of P's prop-
    erty for discharging them.

(8) The court may confer on a deputy powers to—
(a) take possession or control of all or any specified part of P's property;
(b) exercise all or any specified powers in respect of it, including such powers
    of investment as the court may determine.

(9) The court may require a deputy—
(a) to give to the Public Guardian such security as the court thinks fit for the due
    discharge of his functions, and
(b) to submit to the Public Guardian such reports at such times or at such inter-
    vals as the court may direct.

DEFINITIONS
"deputy": s.64(1) **1–177**
"the court": s.64(1)
"property": s.64(1)
"trust corporation": s.64(1)
"Public Guardian": s.64(1)

GENERAL NOTE

1-178   A deputy appointed by the Court of Protection must be an adult who consents to the appointment, with the exception that a trust corporation can be appointed in respect of P's property and affairs (subss.(1) and (3)). Most deputies are likely to be a member of P's family. More that one deputy can be appointed for P (subs.(4)). When appointing a deputy, the court will exercise its discretion so as to satisfy the best interests of P(s.1(5)). A deputy will not be appointed if the court can satisfactorily deal with the matter itself by making an order (s.16(4)). The spouse of P has no right to be appointed (*Davy (Laura), Re* [1892] 3 Ch. 38). The court will decide the extent of the powers to be conferred on the deputy (s.16(5)). A deputy has no power to act if he or she believes that P has the capacity to make the proposed decision (s.20(1)). The powers of the deputy will also be subject to the other restrictions contained in s.20. The deputy's powers can be varied by the court, which can also revoke the appointment (s.16(8)). A deputy will be provided with protection by ss.5 and 6 for acts done outside the scope of the appointment. There is no time limit attached to the appointment.

Those applying to become deputies would need to demonstrate why an appointment is necessary. There is no requirement for the court to be satisfied as to the suitability of an individual for appointment by, for example, investigating any actual or potential conflict of interest, although the Public Guardian is required to supervise deputies (s.58(1)(c)). Unlike a donee under a lasting power of attorney, the deputy can be the holder of a specified office, such as a Director of Adult Services (subs.(2)). Where there is more than one deputy, they can be appointed to act either jointly or jointly and severally, i.e. they must either act together with the agreement of all donees (jointly), or each donee can act independently of the other (severally). As an alternative, the donees can be appointed to act jointly in respect of some matters and jointly and severally in respect of others (subs.(4)). When making the appointment, the court has the power to appoint a successor or successors to the original appointee(s) and to specify the circumstances under which this could occur (subs.(5)). The *Code of Practice* states at para.8.44:

> "Appointment of a successor deputy might be useful if the person appointed as deputy is already elderly and wants to be sure that somebody will take over their duties in the future, if necessary."

A deputy can claim reasonable expenses and, if the court directs, the deputy can be paid for his or her services. Both expenses and the payments will be made out of P's property (subs.(7)). The expenses of an officer of a local authority who applies to the court for appointment as a deputy may be defrayed by the authority (National Assistance Act 1948, s.49). The deputy can be provided with the power to deal with all matters concerning the control and management of P's property, including being able to invest (subs.(8)). The court will be able to require a deputy to give the Public Guardian security against misbehaviour and to direct the deputy to file reports with the Public Guardian at specified intervals (subs.(9)). Although case law has established that receivers appointed Court of Protection under Pt VII of the Mental Health Act 1983 are statutory agents of the person who lacks capacity (*EG, Re* [1914] 1 Ch. 927), it was considered "helpful to make statutory provision to that effect in relation to deputies" (Explanatory Notes, para.73). This is done in subs.(6). An act of an agent, done within the scope of his authority binds his principal, in this case P. As as agent the deputy is bound by a number of common law duties toward P, including the duty to act with due care and skill, to act within the scope of the authority granted by the court, to act in good faith, not to delegate his or her functions to another without authority, to keep the affairs of P confidential, to keep accounts of monies recieved and paid on P's behalf, and not to permit his own interests to conflict with his duties to P. The duties of an agent are set out in the *Code of Practice* at paras 8.55–8.67. In addition to these duties, the deputy is required to act in P's best interests (s.20(6)), to apply the principles set out in s.1 and to have regard to the *Code of Practice* (s.42(4)(b)). *EG, Re* is authority for the propositions that the property of P does not vest in the deputy (at 933), and that the deputy is not personally liable for the costs of those he or she employs in the course of acting for P (at

935). The deputy should notify any third party with whom he is dealing of the fact that he is acting as deputy for P, as it is a general principle of the law of agency that an agent is personally liable on any contract made in his own name on behalf of a principal where the name or existence of the principal (P) is undisclosed at the time of contracting. Also see the comment on the law of agency in the General Note to s.10.

Any concerns about the manner in which a deputy is performing his or her functions **1–179** should be reported to the Public Guardian who is responsible for supervising the activities of deputies (s.58(1)(c)). The Public Guardian may decide to direct a Court of Protection Visitor to visit P and/or the deputy. Allegations of serious criminal conduct, such as physical or sexual abuse, should be reported directly to the police, and the Public Guardian informed. Also see the note on adult protection procedures in s.44.

The Public Guardian has published a "Guide to the supervision of Deputies" (OPG507). Pages 8–10 deal with the level of supervision that Deputies will receive:

"When a Deputy is appointed, the OPG carries out an assessment to decide the appropriate level of supervision and support. You will be allocated either a Type I, II or III level of supervision.

Type I cases are supervised more closely than Type II cases. In Type III cases the OPG would have minimal contact with you following assessment of the supervision level.

The OPG decides on the level of supervision appropriate for you by looking at the factors that are relevant to your case. Criteria include:

- the complexity and value of the estate of the person who lacks capacity;
- the relationship and amount of contact between you and the person who lacks capacity;
- the type of decisions you are being asked to make;
- your experience or past record as a Receiver/Deputy; and
- support provided to the person who lacks capacity by family, friends and/or professionals.

Examples of when the OPG might decide that a Type I supervision level is appropriate include:

- where you have been appointed as a property and affairs Deputy or a personal welfare Deputy in a case involving a substantial damages award and there are financial or care arrangements to set up;
- where you have been appointed as a property and affairs Deputy and have a poor credit history; or
- where concerns have been reported to the Court or the OPG about your management of the person's affairs.

The OPG is likely to decide that a Type II supervision level is appropriate when, for example, the person whose affairs you manage has limited assets, there was no objection to your appointment, and you are closely related to the person, or you are a professional Deputy.

The OPG is likely to decide that a Type III supervision level is appropriate where you have been appointed as property and affairs Deputy, the assets you manage are less than £16,000 and there are no other factors that mean the OPG will need to maintain regular contact with you.

You will be notified in writing of the assessment decision and given a summary of the reasons. This will be done as soon as possible after you receive the Court order appointing you as Deputy."

Further information about the supervision regimes can be found on the website of the Office of the Public Guardian.

In this Act references to making decisions, in relation to a deputy, include, where appropriate, acting on decisions made (s.64(2)).

Subsection (1)

1–180 APPOINTED BY THE COURT. An application for the appointment of a deputy is made by using the procedure set out in Part 9 of the CPR 2007. For a detailed analysis, see Ch.8 of *Heywood and Massey: Court of Protection Practice*, Sweet and Maxwell.

Subsection (6)

1–181 "A key principle governing deputies is that they cannot do more than the person could do if he or she had capacity", *per* the Parliamentary Under-Secretary of State, St. Comm. A, para.191.

AGENT. The duties of an agent are set out above.

Subsection (9)(a)

1–182 SECURITY. See CPR 2007, r.200 and the Lasting Powers of Attorney, Enduring Powers of Attorney and Public Guardian Regulations 2007 (SI 2007/1253), regs 33 to 37.

Subsection (9)(b)

1–183 SUBMIT TO THE PUBLIC GUARDIAN . . . REPORTS. See regs 38 to 40 of SI 2007/1253.

Restrictions on deputies

1–184 **20.**—(1) A deputy does not have power to make a decision on behalf of P in relation to a matter if he knows or has reasonable grounds for believing that P has capacity in relation to the matter.

(2) Nothing in section 16(5) or 17 permits a deputy to be given power—

(a) to prohibit a named person from having contact with P;

(b) to direct a person responsible for P's health care to allow a different person to take over that responsibility.

(3) A deputy may not be given powers with respect to—

(a) the settlement of any of P's property, whether for P's benefit or for the benefit of others,

(b) the execution for P of a will, or

(c) the exercise of any power (including a power to consent) vested in P whether beneficially or as trustee or otherwise.

(4) A deputy may not be given power to make a decision on behalf of P which is inconsistent with a decision made, within the scope of his authority and in accordance with this Act, by the donee of a lasting power of attorney granted by P (or, if there is more than one donee, by any of them).

(5) A deputy may not refuse consent to the carrying out or continuation of life-sustaining treatment in relation to P.

(6) The authority conferred on a deputy is subject to the provisions of this Act and, in particular, sections 1 (the principles) and 4 (best interests).

(7) A deputy may not do an act that is intended to restrain P unless four conditions are satisfied.

(8) The first condition is that, in doing the act, the deputy is acting within the scope of an authority expressly conferred on him by the court.

(9) The second is that P lacks, or the deputy reasonably believes that P lacks, capacity in relation to the matter in question.

(10) The third is that the deputy reasonably believes that it is necessary to do the act in order to prevent harm to P.

(11) The fourth is that the act is a proportionate response to—

(a) the likelihood of P's suffering harm, [and]

(b) the seriousness of that harm.

(12) For the purposes of this section, a deputy restrains P if he—

(a) uses, or threatens to use, force to secure the doing of an act which P resists, or

(b) restricts P's liberty of movement, whether or not P resists,

or if he authorises another person to do any of those things.

(13) [*Repealed by the Mental Health Act 2007, s.50(4)(c)*]

AMENDMENT
The word in square brackets in subs.(11) was substituted by the Mental Health Act 2007, **1–185** s.51.

DEFINITIONS **1–186**
"deputy": s.64(1)
"property": s.64(1)
"lasting power of attorney": s.64(1)
"life-sustaining treatment": s.64(1)
"the Human Rights Convention": s.64(1)
"public authority": s.6(1)

GENERAL NOTE
This section sets out a number of limitations on the powers of deputies, who must always **1–187** act in P's best interests (subs.(6)).

Subsection (1) specifies that a deputy cannot act where P is able to act for himself. The Explanatory Notes state at para.75:

"In some cases the person may have fluctuating capacity, for example as a result of mental health problems, and it is not acceptable for a deputy to carry on making substitute decisions when the person concerned has in fact recovered."

As it is can be difficult to determine whether a person with fluctuating mental capacity is enjoying a lucid interval, the deputy should consider seeking professional assistance if he suspects that P is able to act for himself.

Subsections (2) and (3) list matters which must always be dealt with by the court, not a deputy.

Subsection (4) provides that a deputy cannot be given power to override a valid decision made by a donee under P's LPA. If there is concern or a dispute about the way the donee is carrying on his or her responsibilities under the LPA, the court must use its powers under ss.22 and 23 rather that seeking to appoint a deputy.

Subsection (5) prevents deputies from refusing consent to the carrying out or continuation of life-sustaining treatment.

Subsections (7)–(12) impose limitations on a deputy's power to restrain P. They match those imposed in relation to "section 5 acts" by s.6 and on donees by s.11, and reference should be made to the notes on s.6. The deputy will have to be acting within the scope of an authority expressly conferred on him by the court (subs.(8)).

Subsection (2) (a)
If a deputy is concerned about someone's conduct toward P, he or she can apply to the **1–188** court for a relevant order to be made, or apply for a non-molestation order under Pt IV of the Family Law Act 1996 (c.27) as P's litigation friend.

Subsection (6)
All deputies, both professional and lay, will need to be familiar with the principles set out **1–189** in s.1 and with the "checklist" approach used in best interest determinations made under s.4.

Transfer of proceedings relating to people under 18

1–190   **21.**—[(1)] The [Lord Chief Justice, with the concurrence of the Lord Chancellor] may by order make provision as to the transfer of proceedings relating to a person under 18, in such circumstances as are specified in the order—

(a) from the Court of Protection to a court having jurisdiction under the Children Act 1989 (c. 41), or

(b) from a court having jurisdiction under that Act to the Court of Protection.

[(2) The Lord Chief Justice may nominate any of the following to exercise his functions under this section—

(a) the President of the Court of Protection;

(b) a judicial office holder (as defined in section 109(4) of the Constitutional Reform Act 2005).]

AMENDMENTS

1–191   The amendments to this section were made by SI 2006/1016, art.2, Sch.1, para.31.

GENERAL NOTE

1–192   Generally speaking, this Act is concerned with people aged 16 and over who lack capacity (s.2(5); but see s.18(3)), while the Children Act 1989 is mainly concerned with people under the age of 18. This section deals with any overlap between the two jurisdictions by providing the Lord Chancellor with a power to make transfer of proceedings orders. The Parliamentary Under-Secretary of State gave the following example of the need for a transfer:

"[I]f the parents of a 17 year-old who has profound learning difficulties are in dispute with each other about residence or contact, it might be more appropriate for the Court of Protection to deal with that, since a s.8 order made under the Children Act 1989 would expire on the child's eighteenth birthday at the latest" (*Hansard*, HL Vol.668, col.1485).

Subsection (1)

1–193   MAY BY ORDER. See the Mental Capacity Act 2005 (Transfer of Proceedings) Order 2007 (SI 2007/1899) which is reproduced in Pt 3.

[Powers of the court in relation to Schedule A1

Powers of court in relation to Schedule A1

1–194   **21A.**—(1) This section applies if either of the following has been given under Schedule A1—

(a) a standard authorisation;

(b) an urgent authorisation.

(2) Where a standard authorisation has been given, the court may determine any question relating to any of the following matters—

(a) whether the relevant person meets one or more of the qualifying requirements;

(b) the period during which the standard authorisation is to be in force;

(c) the purpose for which the standard authorisation is given;

(d) the conditions subject to which the standard authorisation is given.

(3) If the court determines any question under subsection (2), the court may make an order—

(a) varying or terminating the standard authorisation, or

(b) directing the supervisory body to vary or terminate the standard authorisation.

(4) Where an urgent authorisation has been given, the court may determine any question relating to any of the following matters—

(a) whether the urgent authorisation should have been given;

(b) the period during which the urgent authorisation is to be in force;

(c) the purpose for which the urgent authorisation is given.

(5) Where the court determines any question under subsection (4), the court may make an order—

(a) varying or terminating the urgent authorisation, or

(b) directing the managing authority of the relevant hospital or care home to vary or terminate the urgent authorisation.

(6) Where the court makes an order under subsection (3) or (5), the court may make an order about a person's liability for any act done in connection with the standard or urgent authorisation before its variation or termination.

(7) An order under subsection (6) may, in particular, exclude a person from liability.]

AMENDMENT

This section was inserted by the Mental Health Act 2007, s.50(7), Sch.9, Pt.1, para.2.

DEFINITION

"the court": s.64(1).

GENERAL NOTE

This section gives the court jurisdiction for the purposes of Art.5(4) of the ECHR to review the authorisation of a person's detention and to terminate the authorisation if it is not lawful. The court is also given power to determine key issues relating to the authorisation, to vary the authorisation, and to order either the supervisory body (for standard authorisations) or the managing authority (for urgent authorisations) to either vary or terminate the authorisation.

If the court makes an order, it may also make an order about a person's liability for any act done before the variation or termination of the authorisation, and this includes an order excluding a person from liability (subss.(6),(7)).

For applications under this section, see s.50(1),(1A).

Powers of the court in relation to lasting powers of attorney

Powers of court in relation to validity of lasting powers of attorney

22.—(1) This section and section 23 apply if—   1–195

(a) a person (P) has executed or purported to execute an instrument with a view to creating a lasting power of attorney, or

(b) an instrument has been registered as a lasting power of attorney conferred by P.

(2) The court may determine any question relating to—

(a) whether one or more of the requirements for the creation of a lasting power of attorney have been met;

(b) whether the power has been revoked or has otherwise come to an end.

(3) Subsection (4) applies if the court is satisfied—

(a) that fraud or undue pressure was used to induce P—

   (i) to execute an instrument for the purpose of creating a lasting power of attorney, or

   (ii) to create a lasting power of attorney, or

  (b) that the donee (or, if more than one, any of them) of a lasting power of attorney—

   (i) has behaved, or is behaving, in a way that contravenes his authority or is not in P's best interests, or

   (ii) proposes to behave in a way that would contravene his authority or would not be in P's best interests.

 (4) The court may—

  (a) direct that an instrument purporting to create the lasting power of attorney is not to be registered, or

  (b) if P lacks capacity to do so, revoke the instrument or the lasting power of attorney.

 (5) If there is more than one donee, the court may under subsection (4)(b) revoke the instrument or the lasting power of attorney so far as it relates to any of them.

 (6) "Donee" includes an intended donee.

DEFINITIONS

1–196 "lasting power of attorney": s.64(1)
  "the court": s.64(1)

GENERAL NOTE

1–197 This section and s.23 set out the powers of the Court of Protection where a person has drawn up a document (an "instrument") which is either intended to be registered as a lasting power of attorney (LPA) at some time in the future, or has already been registered as a LPA. The court is provided with a power to determine questions about the validity and revocation of LPAs (subs.(2)), and can direct that the instrument should not be registered, or where it has been registered and P lacks capacity, that it should be revoked if any of the grounds in subs.(3) are satisfied (subs.(4)). Although this section does not provide the court with the power to override a valid decision of a donee, the court can revoke the power if it determines that the donee is not acting in P's best interests (subs.(3)(b)). This section also provides that where there is more than one donee, the court may revoke the instrument or the LPA so far as it relates to any of them provided that P lacks capacity (subss.(5), (6)).

 An application for an order under this section should be made using the procedure set out in Pt 9 of the CPR 2007.

Subsection (3)

1–198 Is SATISFIED. The burden of proof is placed on the person who is challenging the validity of the LPA.

 UNDUE PRESSURE. Although the concepts are different, it is likely that the court will have regard to the caselaw on "undue influence" when considering this term. In *Re T (Adult: Refusal of Medical Treatment)* [1992] 4 All E.R. 649, 662, CA, Lord Donaldson said that, while it is acceptable for a patient to receive advice or for the patient to have been subject to the strong persuasion of others in reaching a decision, such persuasion must not "overbear the independence of the patient's decision". His Lordship identified the real question in each case as being:

  "does the patient really mean what he says or is he merely saying it for a quiet life, to satisfy someone else or because the advice and persuasion to which he has been subjected is such that he can no longer think and decide for himself? In other words, it is a decision expressed in form only, not in reality?"

His Lordship identified two aspects of the effect of outside influence that could be of "crucial importance": the strength of will of the patient and the relationship of the "persuader" to the patient. With regard to the former, a patient who is "very tired, in pain or depressed will be much less able to resist having his will overborne than one who is rested, free from pain and cheerful". With regard to the relationship between the persuader and the patient, his Lordship spoke of the potential strength of the parental and marital relationship, especially with regard to arguments based on religious belief. These factors should make the doctor alert to the possibility that the patient may not mean what he or she says. Other outside influences that could vitiate a patient's consent include fraud, misrepresentation and duress. Also see the note on undue influence in s.1(3).

Powers of court in relation to operation of lasting powers of attorney

23.—(1) The court may determine any question as to the meaning or effect of a **1–199**
lasting power of attorney or an instrument purporting to create one.

(2) The court may—

(a) give directions with respect to decisions—

   (i) which the donee of a lasting power of attorney has authority to make, and

   (ii) which P lacks capacity to make;

(b) give any consent or authorisation to act which the donee would have to obtain from P if P had capacity to give it.

(3) The court may, if P lacks capacity to do so—

(a) give directions to the donee with respect to the rendering by him of reports or accounts and the production of records kept by him for that purpose;

(b) require the donee to supply information or produce documents or things in his possession as donee;

(c) give directions with respect to the remuneration or expenses of the donee;

(d) relieve the donee wholly or partly from any liability which he has or may have incurred on account of a breach of his duties as donee.

(4) The court may authorise the making of gifts which are not within section 12(2) (permitted gifts).

(5) Where two or more donees are appointed under a lasting power of attorney, this section applies as if references to the donee were to all or any of them.

DEFINITIONS
   "the court": s.64(1) **1–200**
   "lasting power of attorney": s.64(1)

GENERAL NOTE
This section provides the Court of Protection with powers to decide any questions about **1–201**
the "meaning or effect" of a LPA or an instrument purporting to create one (subs.(1)), to give directions to donees where P lacks capacity (subs.(2)(a)), and to give any consent or authorisation which P might have given had he or she not lacked capacity (subs.(2)(b)). If P is incapacitated, the court also has power to give the donee directions in relation to producing reports, accounts, records and information, determining a donee's remuneration and expenses, and relieving a donee from some or all of the liabilities arising from a breach of his or her duties as donee (subs.(3)). The Court may also authorise the making of gifts beyond the scope of what is permitted by s.12(2) (subs.(4)).

An application for an order under this section should be made using the procedure set out in Pt 9 of the CPR 2007.

Subsection (1)

1–202   MEANING OR EFFECT. This gives the court power to determine any point of construction arising on the LPA, and whether a donee has power to carry out a particular act.

Subsection (2)

1–203   The purpose of para.(b) was explained by the Parliamentary Under-Secretary of State:

"[Donees] are in law regarded as agents and are therefore affected by the law of agency as well as the provisions of the Bill. [Under the law of agency] it is sometimes necessary for the [donee] to give the consent or authorisation of the donor before they can act. The obvious example is where the donee would like to purchase the donor's property. The donor would make it a condition of the power of attorney that the [donee] must get their consent. In other words, if I wanted to buy the house of someone for whom I acted as [donee], I would need to get their consent to do so. However, if they lack capacity, I cannot get their consent. Yet, it would be wrong for me to purchase their house without consent. In those circumstances, the court would step in and give the consent. So, it is a protection, but a protection in circumstances where the law of agency applies" (*Hansard*, HL Vol.668, col.1426).

Subsection (3) para.(a)

1–204   As, generally speaking, the court will not exercise any supervision over the conduct of a donee, the giving of directions relating to the production of reports etc is likely to be triggered by concerns being raised by persons who are in close contact with P.

Subsection (3) para.(c)

1–205   REMUNERATION. The directions could override a provision for remuneration contained in the LPA.

Subsection (3) para.(d)

1–206   ANY LIABILITY. Note the breath of this power. Unlike the power to relieve trustees from breaches of trust under s.61 of the Trustee Act 1925, there is no requirement for the donee to have acted "honestly and reasonably".

Subsection (4)

1–207   This provision could be used to authorise gifts for tax planning purposes. Also see s.18(1)(b).

Advance decisions to refuse treatment

Advance decisions to refuse treatment: general

1–208   **24.**—(1) "Advance decision" means a decision made by a person (P), after he has reached 18 and when he has capacity to do so, that if—

(a) at a later time and in such circumstances as he may specify, a specified treatment is proposed to be carried out or continued by a person providing health care for him, and

(b) at that time he lacks capacity to consent to the carrying out or continuation of the treatment,

the specified treatment is not to be carried out or continued.

(2) For the purposes of subsection (1)(a), a decision may be regarded as specifying a treatment or circumstances even though expressed in layman's terms.

(3) P may withdraw or alter an advance decision at any time when he has capacity to do so.

(4) A withdrawal (including a partial withdrawal) need not be in writing.

(5) An alteration of an advance decision need not be in writing (unless section 25(5) applies in relation to the decision resulting from the alteration).

DEFINITIONS
    "treatment": s.64(1) **1–209**

GENERAL NOTE

Sections 24–26 deal with advance decisions to refuse medical treatment. As they broadly **1–210** "seek to codify and clarify the current common law rules" relating to advance directives (Explanatory Notes, para.84), a brief account of these rules is set out below. An advance directive made before the commencement of this Act will take effect as an advance decision if it complies with the relevant provisions of this Act. The Government's cautious approach to legislating in this area is illustrated by the following extract from "*Who Decides? Making Decisions on Behalf of Mentally Incapacitated Adults*" (Cm.3803):

> "The Government recognises the strength of feeling on this subject. This was the area of the Law Commission's work which aroused the greatest public concern, and it is clear that this is a matter on which many have deep rooted personal, moral, religious and ethical views. The Government does not believe that it would be appropriate to reach any conclusions in this area in the absence of fresh consultation—not just on the detailed plans put forward by the Law Commission, but also on the need for and the merits of legislation in this area generally" (para.4.2).

This caution was, to a certain extent, explained by the conclusion of the House of Lords Select Committee on Medical Ethics which had commended the development of advance directives, but decided that "it could well be impossible to give advance directives in general greater legal force without depriving patients of the benefit of the doctor's professional expertise and of new treatments and procedures which may have become available since the directive was signed" ((1993–94) HL Paper 21–1, para.185).

Advance Directives

The case of *C (Adult: Refusal of Medical Treatment)*, Re [1994] 1 All E.R. 819, was the **1–211** first occasion when an English Court had been invited to rule directly on the legal validity of an advance directive. Thorpe J. held that a refusal of treatment could take the form of a declaration of intention never to consent in the future or never to consent in some future circumstances. The effect of this ruling was that an advance refusal of treatment for either a physical or mental disorder made when the patient is mentally capable survives any supervening incapacity, even if the refusal leads to the patient's death. His Lordship accepted that a patient might have capacity to make a present refusal but lack the capacity to make an anticipatory refusal.

The criteria required for an advance directive to be valid were identified by Hughes J. in *AK (Adult Patient) (Medical Treatment: Consent), Re* [2001] 1 F.L.R.129 (points 1 and 2), and by Munby J. in *HE v A Hospital NHS Trust* [2003] EWHC 1017 (Fam Div); [2003] 2 F.L.R. 408 (points 3–9). They are:

1. The treating doctor must be satisfied that the patient was mentally capable at the time when the patient made it known that he or she would not consent to the treatment in question.
2. All the circumstances in which the expression of wishes was given will have to be investigated. In particular, care must be taken to (a) ensure that the anticipatory declaration of wishes still represent the wishes of the patient; (b) investigate how long ago the expression of wishes was made; and (c) investigate with what knowledge the expression of wishes was made.
3. There are no formal requirements for avalid advance directive. An advance directive may be oral or in writing.

4. There are no formal requirements for the revocation of an advance directive. An advance directive, whether oral or in writing, may be revoked either orally or in writing. A written advance directive or an advance directive executed under seal can be revoked orally.

5. An advance directive is inherently revocable. Any condition in an advance directive purporting to make it irrevocable, any even self-imposed fetter on a patient's ability to revoke an advance directive, and any provision in an advance directive purporting to impose formal or other conditions upon its revocation, is contrary to public policy and void. So, a stipulation in an advance directive, even if in writing, that it shall be binding unless and until it is revoked in writing is void as being contrary to public policy.

6. The existence and continuing validity and applicability of an advance directive is a question of fact. Whether an advance directive has been revoked or has for some other reason ceased to be operative is a question of fact.

7. The burden of proof is on those who seek to establish the existence and continuing validity and applicability of an advance directive.

8. Where life is at stake the evidence must be scrutinised with especial care. Clear and convincing proof is required. The continuing validity and applicability of the advance directive must be clearly established by convincing and inherently reliable evidence.

9. If there is doubt that doubt falls to be resolved in favour of the preservation of life.

In *R. (on the application of Burke) v The General Medical Council* [2005] EWCA Civ 1003; [2005] H.R.L.R. 35, the Court of Appeal confirmed that an advance directive provides a competent patient with a right to refuse treatment after he ceased to be competent; it cannot be used to require that a patient be provided with any form of treatment that he might consider to be in his own best interests.

If a patient makes a valid advance directive to the effect that he or she is not to be resuscitated if he or she is found in an unconscious state after attempting suicide, the directive must be respected *(W (Adult: Refusal of Medical Treatment), Re* [2002] EWHC 901 (Fam Div)). A failure to respect a valid advance directive can result in a claim for battery being made against the clinician *(Airedale NHS Trust v Bland* [1993] 1 All E.R. 821, HL).

For advance directives and psychiatric treatment, see A. Halpern and G. Szmukler, "Psychiatric advance directives: reconciling autonomy and non-consensual treatment" (1997) 21 *Psychiatric Bulletin* 323. Dr A. Treloar identifies major potential problems with the use of advance directives in "Advance directives: limitations upon their application in elderly care" (1999) 14 *International Journal of Geriatric Psychiatry* 1039. A study by T. Thompson, R. Barbour and L. Schwartz found that advance directives are open to widely varying interpretations in that some of the clinicians interviewed justified treatment contrary to an advance directive on the basis of the patient's best interests ("Adherence to advance directives in critical care decision making: vignette study" (2003) 327 *British Medical Journal* 1011). An anonymous postal questionnaire survey of members of the British Geriatrics Society found that the majority of geriatricians who responded were strongly in favour of the use of living wills by older people despite recognising their potential for problems. Over half had cared for patients who has living wills, and most felt positively about the experience (R. Schiff *et al.* "Living wills and the Mental Capacity Act: a postal questionnaire survey of UK geriatricians" (2006) 35 *Age and Ageing* 116). For an analysis of advance directives/advance decisions under common law and under this Act, see Sabine Michalowski, "Advance Refusals of Life-Sustaining Medical Treatment: The Relativity of an Absolute Right" (2005) 68(6) M.L.R. 948.

Advance Decisions

1–212   This section defines an advance decision, sometimes referred to as a "living will". The person making the advance decision need not refer to it as such. An advance decision can only be made by a mentally capable person aged 18 or over and the decision must specify the treatment that is being refused.The decision could have been made a considerable time before the coming into force of this Act. The effect of an advance decision is to enable the person to refuse the specified treatment when that person loses the capacity to give or refuse consent to that treatment. In other words, an advance decision which is valid and applicable (s.25) is as effective as a contemporaneous decision made by a mentally capable person in that healthcare professionals are bound by it (s.26), even if they or the patient's relatives or carers consider the decision to be unwise (s.1(4)).

Although this section is concerned with refusals of medical treatments and cannot be used to require a doctor to provide a particular form of medical treatment (*R. (on the application of Burke) v The General Medical Council*, above), the person making the advance decision could attempt to achieve this objective by refusing all but the preferred method of treatment for a particular disorder.

The advance decision can specify particular circumstances in which the refusal may apply. Both the treatment and the circumstances may be specified in lay (i.e. non-medical) terms. Section 25(5) and (6) comes into play if the person wishes the advance decision to apply to a refusal of life sustaining treatment. An advance decision cannot be used to give effect to an unlawful act such as euthanasia, which is a deliberate intervention with the express aim of ending life (s.62).

The best interests criterion does not apply to the application of an advance decision as the person concerned has identified his or her best interests when making the advance decision: see the General Note to s.26.

An advance decision can be overridden by the provisions of ss.57, 58 and 63 of the Mental Health Act 1983 (see s.28), so that a decision that refuses a specific treatment for a mental disorder will be rendered ineffective if a person is detained under a section of the 1983 Act which comes within the scope of Pt IV of that Act. An exception to this general rule is s.58A of the 1983 Act.

Apart from an advance decision that relates to life-sustaining treatment (see s.25(5),(6)), this Act does not establish any procedures or formalities that must be followed for an advance decision to be made. The advance decision can be oral or written and there is no procedure that must be followed to establish that the person was mentally capable at the time when the advance decision is made. The advanced decision need not be witnessed and can be made without the benefit of professional advice. Publicly funded legal advice through the Legal Help scheme cannot be provided to assist an individual to make an advance decision (Access to Justice Act 1999, Sch.2, para.1(eb)). To avoid possible legal challenge, it would be sensible for advanced decisions to be written, witnessed and to contain a statement that, in the opinion of the witness, the person was mentally capable of making the decision at the time when it was made, together with a confirmation that the medical consequences of the decision have been explained to the person by a named doctor. A written advance decision could be supplemented by a video recording of the person's verbal confirmation of their decision. There is no provision requiring the advance decision to be reviewed over time, although this is clearly desirable. A written advance directive can be withdrawn or altered orally.

It might be very difficult for a treating doctor to be confident that a patient who is said to have made an oral advance decision during the course of a conversation with a relative had the mental capacity to make the decision at that time (the presumption of capacity set out in s.1(2) will apply) and was provided with sufficient information to enable an informed decision to be made (it is difficult to see how appropriate information could be provided without the involvement of a healthcare professional). It might also be difficult to establish whether the person was subject to the undue influence of the relative at the relevant time (see the note on s.1(3)), or had subsequently revoked the advance decision. Indeed, it may be difficult to establish whether the reported conversation took place at all. Disputes about the existence, validity or applicability of an advance decision can be referred to the Court of Protection (s.26(4)). In *HE v A Hospital NHS Trust*, above, Munby J. said at para.34:

"The absence of anything in writing goes only to the practicability of proof. For it may be difficult to establish the existence of a binding oral advance directive given, first, the need for clear and convincing proof founded on convincing and inherently reliable evidence and, secondly, the need to demonstrate that the patient's expressed views represented a firm and settled commitment and not merely an offhand remark or informally expressed reaction to other people's problems."

The Minister assured members of the Standing Committee which considered the Bill that "including oral decisions does not mean that any casual statement would count as an advance decision. There would be a world of difference between someone remarking casually to a friend that they would never like to be kept alive artificially and someone with Alzheimer's discussing with a doctor charged with their care how they might expect the condition to progress and making an oral decision to refuse certain interventions as their condition worsens. I remind the Committee that the Bill requires tough tests to be passed if an advance decision is to apply. The decision must be specific and made with capacity to be valid and applicable to the treatment in question. Where there is any doubt, a clinician can safely treat someone and receive protection from liability for a claim for damages, tort, criminal liability or assault [see s.26(2)]", *per* the Parliamentary Under-Secretary of State, St. Comm. A, para.225.

The *Code of Practice* states, at para.9.19, that it would be helpful for the following information to be included in a written advance decision:

"• full details of the person making the advance decision, including date of birth, home address and any distinguishing features (in case healthcare professionals need to identify an unconscious person, for example)
• the name and address of the person's GP and whether they have a copy of the document
• a statement that the document should be used if the person ever lacks capacity to make treatment decisions
• a clear statement of the decision, the treatment to be refused and the circumstances in which the decision will apply
• the date the document was written (or reviewed)
• the person's signature (or the signature of someone the person has asked to sign on their behalf and in their presence)
• the signature of the person witnessing the signature, if there is one (or a statement directing somebody to sign on the person's behalf)."

With regard to oral advance decisions made to a member of the patient's healthcare team, the Code suggests, at para.9.23, that the following information be included in the patient's medical notes:

"• a note that the decision should apply if the person lacks capacity to make treatment decisions in the future
• a clear note of the decision, the treatment to be refused and the circumstances in which the decision will apply
• details of someone who was present when the oral advance decision was recorded and the role in which they were present (for example, healthcare professional or family member), and
• whether they heard the decision, took part in it or are just aware that it exists."

1–213 If healthcare professionals are alerted to the possibility that a patient might have made an advance decision, reasonable efforts, such as contacting relatives of the patient and the patient's GP, should be made to establish whether this is the case. Treatment should not be delayed while attempts are made to establish whether an advance decision has been made if the delay would prejudice the patient's health.

Healthcare professionals who have a conscientious objection to respecting a patient's valid and applicable advance directive should ensure that the care of the patient is transferred to the care of another healthcare professional. The following extract from correspondence between the Parliamentary Under-Secretary of State for Health and the Opposition spokesperson on health was read into the record during the report stage of the Bill in the House of Lords at *Hansard*, H.L.Vol.670, col.1306:

"I promised to check GMC and BMA guidance on provisions for when a doctor does not want to carry out treatment. Doctors are entitled to have their personal beliefs respected and will not be pressured to act contrary to those beliefs. As I stated during the Committee, where a doctor has a conscientious objection they may withdraw from the care of the patient. In doing so however they must ensure, without delay, that arrangements have been made for another suitably qualified colleague to take over their role, so that the patient's care does not suffer. The individual doctor does not necessarily have to arrange personally for a transfer of care, provided there are alternative means of doing so. However, the doctor must not abandon the patient or otherwise cause their care to suffer."

Also of relevance in this context is the following guidance given by Butler-Sloss P. in *B (Consent to Treatment: Capacity), Re* [2002] EWHC 429 (Fam Div); [2002] 2 All E.R. 449 at para.100(viii):

"If there is no disagreement about competence but the doctors are for any reason unable to carry out the wishes of the patient, their duty is to find other doctors who will do so."

Where a transfer to other healthcare professionals cannot be agreed, the court can issue a direction under s.17(1)(e).

Guidance on conscientious objection is given in the *Code of Practice* at paras 9.61–9.63. Freedom of thought, conscience and religion is provided for in Art.9 of the European Convention on Human Rights.

As an alternative to making an advance decision, the person could either leave decision making in the hands of healthcare professionals, make an advance statement (see below), or appoint someone to act as their donee under a lasting power of attorney (see s.9). A personal welfare LPA does not take effect until the donor loses capacity (s.11(7)(a)).

The provisions of the Bill relating to advance decisions caused considerable controversy, particularly because of evidence that suggested that well people tend not to make the same decisions as sick people; see further, the notes to s.25(4)(c). The Joint Committee set out some of the concerns that had been raised in paras 195–200 of its Report:

"A very considerable number of written submissions were received expressing grave concern about this aspect of the draft Bill. Many argued from a standpoint of moral conviction that it was wrong to introduce a statute that could enable decisions that would effectively shorten life. Others argued that it was wrong to require a doctor not to give treatment that the doctor believed was in the patient's best clinical interests.

A considerable body of written evidence claimed that the inclusion of advance decisions meant that the Bill was introducing 'euthanasia by the back door'. We took evidence on this matter and considered the issues at length. For several faith organisations and the Guild of Catholic Doctors the omission of treatment that might prolong life even if for a short period of time was considered unacceptable unless such treatment was likely itself to result in undue suffering. We noted that there was nothing in the Bill that allowed for an act that had the clear intent to end a person's life. This was confirmed in oral evidence by the Parliamentary Under-Secretary of the Department for Constitutional Affairs, Lord Filkin.

Allied to these concerns numerous witnesses objected to the fact that the draft Bill allows life sustaining treatment (e.g. artificial ventilation) to be refused. They drew attention to the Court ruling in the case of Bland that the provision of hydration and nutrition by artificial means amounted to 'treatment'. They argued that withdrawal of nutrition and hydration would result in undue suffering and an unpleasant and undignified death.The BMA in their evidence suggested that, while the use of artificial means of nutrition and hydration amounted to treatment and could therefore be refused, the Bill should stipulate that basic care could not be refused.

Witnesses from the medical profession also put to us that: (a) people when capable could not foresee how they might wish to act if they were to become incapable and therefore could not commit themselves to a course of action from which they could not withdraw having become incapable; (b) unforeseen circumstances, such as the development of a new treatment the use of which would be in their best interests, could arise after the advance decision had been made; and (c) the course of action specified in the advance decision might prolong suffering rather than relieving it. We heard evidence from Professor the Baroness Finlay of the difficulties she and her medical and nursing colleagues faced working in palliative care services. She told us that her personal choice would be that advance decisions should be advisory 'but case law seems to have taken us beyond that point already'.

Those who believed that advance decisions should be included argued that this was a logical and appropriate continuation of respect for a patient's individual autonomy in matters of medical treatment. The law already recognises that a capable person can refuse treatment even if that refusal might end their life. But for a doctor to proceed with treatment under such circumstances would be unlawful. Thus it was argued that the draft Bill only proposed to regularise the existing status quo and that it was a logical extension of the established principle of autonomy. For these reasons the making Decisions Alliance, for example, strongly supported the inclusion of advance decisions to refuse treatment in the Bill. Several witnesses regretted that the draft Bill did not require advance decisions to be made in writing, witnessed or made with the benefit of professional advice. Other feared that people might make advance decisions while in a state of despair or depression that they would not have made under more normal circumstances. The risk of advance decisions being made under coercion was also raised."

Advance statements

1–214   Unlike an advance decision, an advance statement is a non-legally binding document which may identify a person's views and preferences on a large range of medical and other issues. Under s.4(6)(a), such a statement would need to be taken into account when decisions are made subsequent to the patient's mental incapacity. The Making Decisions Alliance briefing document on the second reading debate on the Bill states, at p.19, that "advance statements would enable an individual to express their views and preferences on a large range of issues, including:

- domestic arrangements
- treatment preferences
- financial arrangements
- childcare arrangements
- clarification of who to disclose information to, and the limits of what can be discussed
- dietary requirements."

The literature is replete with examples of a failure to appreciate the distinction between advance directives and advance statements: see the studies cited by T. Exworthy in "Psychiatric advance decisions—an opportunity missed" (September 2004) *Journal of Mental Health Law* 129 at p.132.

Subsection (1)

1–215   DECISION. A decision can only be made after full consideration of all relevant matters, including the consequences for the patient if the treatment is not given (*W Healthcare NHS Trust v H* [2004] EWCA Civ 1324; [2005] 1 W.L.R. 834, para.17). This information can be given in to the patient in broad terms: see the note on s.3(1)(a).

AGED 18. The 16 years of age cut off specified in s.2(4) is not used here as the refusal of a 16 or 17 year old to receive medical treatment may be overridden by a person with parental responsibility for the child, or by the court.

CAPACITY. The doctor should assume that the patient was capable in the absence of evidence to the contrary (s.1(2)).

Subsection (1) para.(a)

SUCH CIRCUMSTANCES AS HE MAY SPECIFY. For example, the treatment is not to be given if **1–216** there is no realistic prospect of P ever regaining mental capacity.

SPECIFIED TREATMENT. Care should be taken to ensure that there can be no doubt about the identity of the particular treatment that is being refused. In *W Healthcare NHS Trust v H*, above, para.21, the Court of Appeal found that a statement made by the patient that she would not wish "to be kept alive by machines" was not "an advance directive which was sufficiently clear to amount to a direction that she preferred to be deprived of food and drink for a period of time which would lead to her death in all circumstances". General statements indicating a desire not to be treated, such as "I should not be given any treatment that is likely to prolong my life", would also be invalid. "Treatment" is widely defined in s.64(1). It can include the provision of nutrition and hydration to the patient by artificial means (*Airedale NHS Trust v Bland* [1993] 1 All E.R. 821, HL). The Joint Committee on Human Rights expressed its concern that the "classification of artificial nutrition and hydration as 'treatment' may not be well known to lay people" (23rd Report, para.2.46).

This Act distinguishes between "treatment" and "care": see, for example, s.5(1). The provision of "basic care" such as feeding and hydration which is not medically assisted, and care to maintain bodily cleanliness cannot be categorised as treatment and can therefore not be subject to an advance decision.

AT THAT TIME HE LACKS CAPACITY. Section 2(2) states that "it does not matter" if the patient's incapacity is temporary or permanent. This provision will cause difficulty in cases where P has made an advance decision refusing treatment, P becomes incapacitated and P's capacity could be restored if P was treated. It is likely that s.25(4)(c) would apply in such a situation.

Situations can arise when it will only become apparent that a seemingly incapable person is, in fact, perfectly capable of making the decision in question if considerable time and trouble is taken in an attempt to communicate with that person. In a powerful and moving speech on the second reading of the Bill (*Hansard*, HC Vol.425, cols.64–67), Mrs Claire Curtis-Thomas MP recounted how her mother, who had been hospitalised after having suffered a massive stoke which had left her paralysed, was considered to be mentally incapable and was not being fed. Mrs Curtis-Thomas's mother had made an advance directive refusing treatment subsequent to her recovery from a previous stoke. Mrs Curtis-Thomas's attempts to communicate with her mother, which lasted a number of weeks, eventually succeeded and her mother was able to blink out "I want to live". This had the effect of revoking the advance directive. Mrs Curtis-Thomas said: "If my mother had not had me, all I believe would have happened is that she would have starved to death. I do not think that anybody would have taken the time or known her well enough to realise that she was actually present and capable of making decisions." The principle contained in s.1(3) is applicable to the situation described by Mrs Curtis-Thomas.

THE SPECIFIED TREATMENT IS NOT TO BE CARRIED OUT. An advance decision cannot be used to require that a patient be provided with any form of treatment that he might consider to be in his own best interests. However, s.4 requires an invalid advance decision of this nature to be taken into account when considering what is in the best interests of a patient if it is clear that the patient was attempting to refuse a particular treatment: see s.5(6)(a) and *R (on the application of Burke) v The General Medical Council* above, para.57.

Subsection (2)

1–217   Lay terms can be used as long as the use of such terms does not lead to any ambiguity about the identity of the treatment that is being refused. In *W Healthcare NHS Trust v H*, above, the Court of Appeal held that a purported advance directive was not valid partly on the ground that the patient, who has stated that she did not want to be kept alive by machines, had not specifically considered and refused artificial hydration and nutrition.

Subsection (3)

1–218   There is no procedure for withdrawing or altering an advance decision. A simple statement by a mentally capable person such as, "I no longer wish my advance decision to stand", would be sufficient to withdraw a decision. An alteration has to be in writing, and the formalities set out in s.25(6) complied with, if the decision relates to a life-sustaining treatment (subs.(5)).

Subsection (4)

1–219   It is therefore possible for a capable patient to withdraw a written advance decision immediately before an anaesthetic is administered, even if the treatment refused is life-sustaining treatment.

Validity and applicability of advance decisions

1–220   **25.**—(1) An advance decision does not affect the liability which a person may incur for carrying out or continuing a treatment in relation to P unless the decision is at the material time—

(a) valid, and

(b) applicable to the treatment.

(2) An advance decision is not valid if P—

(a) has withdrawn the decision at a time when he had capacity to do so,

(b) has, under a lasting power of attorney created after the advance decision was made, conferred authority on the donee (or, if more than one, any of them) to give or refuse consent to the treatment to which the advance decision relates, or

(c) has done anything else clearly inconsistent with the advance decision remaining his fixed decision.

(3) An advance decision is not applicable to the treatment in question if at the material time P has capacity to give or refuse consent to it.

(4) An advance decision is not applicable to the treatment in question if—

(a) that treatment is not the treatment specified in the advance decision,

(b) any circumstances specified in the advance decision are absent, or

(c) there are reasonable grounds for believing that circumstances exist which P did not anticipate at the time of the advance decision and which would have affected his decision had he anticipated them.

(5) An advance decision is not applicable to life-sustaining treatment unless—

(a) the decision is verified by a statement by P to the effect that it is to apply to that treatment even if life is at risk, and

(b) the decision and statement comply with subsection (6).

(6) A decision or statement complies with this subsection only if—

(a) it is in writing,

(b) it is signed by P or by another person in P's presence and by P's direction,

(c) the signature is made or acknowledged by P in the presence of a witness, and

(d) the witness signs it, or acknowledges his signature, in P's presence.

(7) The existence of any lasting power of attorney other than one of a description mentioned in subsection (2)(b) does not prevent the advance decision from being regarded as valid and applicable.

DEFINITIONS

"advance decision": s.64(1)   **1–221**
"treatment": s.64(1)
"lasting power of attorney": s.64(1)
"life-sustaining treatment": s.64(1)

GENERAL NOTE

This section states that a person shall not be legally liable for providing treatment to a **1–222**
patient who has made an advance decision unless the decision is both valid and applicable.
It then proceeds to define both "valid' and "applicable'. In *HE v A Hospital NHS Trust*
[2003] EWHC 1017 (Fam Div); [2003] 2 F.L.R. 408, Munby J. said at para.24:

"Where life is at stake the evidence must be scrutinised with special care. Clear and convincing proof is required. The continuing validity and applicability of the advance directive must be clearly established by convincing and inherently reliable evidence."

Establishing whether an advance decision is both valid and applicable could lead to a significant increase in the workload of medical practitioners. As the Law Commission pointed out, the existence of a formal document is no guarantee of either validity or applicability, nor is the absence of such a document any guarantee that a valid and applicable advance decision has not been made (Law Com No.231, para.5.29).

An advance decision is not valid if P has withdrawn the decision while he or she had the mental capacity to do so, has made a subsequent lasting power of attorney (which has the effect of overriding the decision by enabling the donee to refuse consent to the treatment specified in the decision), or has acted in a manner which is clearly inconsistent with the terms of the decision (subs.(2)). In addition, an advance decision will not be valid if it was made either by a child or by an adult who lacked capacity (s.24(1)). Although an adult should be assumed to have been mentally capable at the time when the decision was made (s1(2)), the medical practitioner should investigate any factors that suggest that this assumption could be rebutted.

An advance decision will not be applicable if P is capable of making the treatment decision at the time the treatment is proposed (subs.(3)). It will also not be applicable to treatments not specified in the decision, if the circumstances specified in the decision are absent, or if there are reasonable grounds for believing that that the current circumstances were not anticipated by P and, if they had been anticipated they would have affected P's decision (subs.(4)). Finally, an advance decision is not applicable to life-sustaining treatment unless P has specified in writing that it should be, and the decision is signed and witnessed (subss.(5) and (6)).

A valid and applicable advance decision to refuse treatment will be as legally effective as a contemporaneous refusal of consent. It cannot be overridden by the Court of Protection, a deputy appointed by the court, the donee of a LPA made before the advance decision was made, or a person acting under s.5 (s.5(4)). Although the court may make declarations as to the existence, validity and applicability of an advance decision (s.15(1)(c)), it has no power to override a valid and applicable advance decision on the ground that it would not serve P's best interests. Life sustaining treatment or action to prevent a serious deterioration of the patient's condition may be provided while a decision is being sought from the court (s.26(5)).

In a survey of UK geriatricians, advice concerning the validity of "living wills" was sought by 44 per cent, most frequently from hospital lawyers (R. Schiff *et al.* "Living wills and the Mental Capacity Act: a postal questionnaire survey of UK geriatricians" (2006) 35 *Age and Ageing* 116).

Advance Decisions refusing life-sustaining treatment made before October 1, 2007

Article 5 of the Mental Capacity Act 2005 (Transitional and Consequential Provisions) Order 2007 (SI 2007/1898) gives effect, in certain circumstances, to advance decisions refusing life-sustaining treatment, notwithstanding that they do not comply with all of the requirements of this section. Article 5 states:

"Advance decisions to refuse life-sustaining treatment

1–223   **5.**—(1) An advance decision refusing life-sustaining treatment shall be treated as valid and applicable to a treatment and does not have to satisfy the requirements mentioned in paragraph (3) if the conditions in paragraph (2) are met.

(2) The conditions that must be met are that—

    (a) a person providing health care for a person ("P") reasonably believes that—

        (i) P has made the advance decision refusing life-sustaining treatment before 1 October 2007, and

        (ii) P has lacked the capacity to comply with the provisions mentioned in paragraph (3) since 1 October 2007;

    (b) the advance decision is in writing;

    (c) P has not—

        (i) withdrawn the decision at a time when he had capacity to do so, or

        (ii) done anything else clearly inconsistent with the advance decision remaining his fixed decision;

    (d) P does not have the capacity to give or refuse consent to the treatment in question at the material time;

    (e) the treatment in question is the treatment specified in the advance decision;

    (f) any circumstances specified in the advance decision are present; and

    (g) there are no reasonable grounds for believing that circumstances exist which P did not anticipate at the time of the advance decision and which would have affected his decision had he anticipated them.

(3) The requirements that do not have to be satisfied are as follows—

    (a) the requirement for the decision to be verified by a statement by P to the effect that the advance decision is to apply to that treatment even if life is at risk (section 25(5)(a) of the Act); and

    (b) the requirement for a signed and witnessed advance decision (section 25(6)(b) to (d) of the Act).

(4) In this article, "advance decision" has the meaning given in section 24(1) of the Act."

A person who has made an advance directive refusing life-sustaining treatment and who has capacity on or after October 1, 2007, should make an advance decision that complies with subss.(5) and (6).

Subsection (1)

1–224   The healthcare professional must be aware of the existence of the advance decision if he or she is to incur legal liability for providing the treatment (s.26(2)). If the healthcare professional has knowledge of the advance directive, the treatment can proceed if the professional considers that it is either invalid and/ or not applicable to the treatment.

Subsection (2) para.(a)

1–225   A written advance decision can be withdrawn orally. In the absence of evidence to the contrary, the healthcare professional should assume that the patient was capable of withdrawing the decision (s.1(2)).

Patients can change their minds about having treatment at a very late stage. The difficulties of relying on an advance decision that has not been revoked can be seen from the following clinical example given by Baroness Finlay to the Joint Committee concerning a patient who had taken a massive overdose of paracetamol:

> "He did not want to come to hospital but was persuaded to. He flatly refused any intervention or any treatment. Two psychiatrists spent a lot of time negotiating with him for several days and explained absolutely everything that might happen to him in graphic detail and he was adamant he wanted no treatment. They warned him of every scenario, including coughing up blood as he started to haemorrhage to death. When he started vomiting blood, he changed his mind and requested treatment. He ended up being transferred to King's [College Hospital] for a liver transplant" (Oral and Written Evidence, Ev 131).

If this patient had lost capacity at the point where he started to vomit blood, the doctors would have been bound by his advance decision (which, subsequent to the implementation of this Act, would have to comply with subss.(5),(6)) and the patient would have died. However, there must be a doubt as to whether a patient in this situation would have had the required capacity to make a valid advance decision. A high level of capacity would be required to make such a decision (*T (Adult: Refusal of Treatment), Re* [1992] 4 All E.R. 649, CA).

Subsection (2) para.(b)
It would be sensible for the advance decision to be withdrawn if a LPA of this nature is **1–226** created as there could be a danger of the healthcare professional being unaware of the LPA. Also see the note on s.11(7)(b).

Subsection (2) para. (c)
The inconsistent behaviour would indicate that P has had a change of mind. An example **1–227** of such behaviour is to be found in *HE v A Hospital NHS Trust*, noted under s.24 above, where the patient, when a Jehovah's Witness, had made an advance directive refusing blood. Subsequent to this she had become betrothed to a Muslim man upon condition that she would revert to being a Muslim, and had ceased attending Jehovah's Witness meetings. The judge held that the advance directive was founded entirely on the patient's faith and could not survive the abandonment of that faith.

Although the matter is not free from doubt, it is likely that the inconsistent behaviour of a mentally incapable patient would not qualify under this provision. This interpretation is consistent with s.24(3) which does not allow a mentally incapacitated patient to withdraw an advance decision.

Subsection (4) para.(a)
As an advance decision is a refusal of a specific treatment, a suicide note written by a **1–228** capable person which does not specify a treatment that should not be given in the event of a suicide attempt that leads to mental incapacity is not an advance decision. Neither is a general statement such as: "If I become mentally incapacitated I do not wish my life to be sustained."

Subsection (4) para.(b)
The advance decision should be specific about the circumstances where it is to apply as a **1–229** generally written decision could give rise to a situation where the decision applies in unintended circumstances.

Subsection (4) para.(c)
It is anticipated that this paragraph will be frequently invoked as it is unlikely that **1–230** patients will have been able to precisely predict the circumstances that they will be in subsequent to the onset of their mental incapacity. In order to determine whether the unanticipated circumstances "would", rather than "may" have affected P's decision, the health care professional will need to step into P's shoes by effectively making a substituted

judgment on behalf of P. An obvious and relevant change of circumstances could be the development of new treatments that radically change the prognosis for a particular condition. A significant change in P's family and/or personal circumstances could also be a relevant consideration.

Patients' views about the medical treatment that they would wish to receive are not fixed; they adapt to circumstances. In particular, healthy patients tend not make the same choices as sick ones as they may not fully comprehend what the future might hold for them should they become mentally incapacitated. It has been argued that patients need to experience a situation to know how they would feel about it and hence how they wish to be treated (Dr David Kingsley, Oral and written evidence, Ev 322). In *MB (Caesarean Section), Re* [1997] 2 F.L.R. 426, CA at 436 in a case concerning the mental capacity of a patient who was refusing to be anaesthetised in order to have a caesarean section, Butler-Sloss L.J. said that a "feature of some of the cases to which we have referred has been the favourable reaction of the patient who refused treatment to the subsequent medical intervention and successful outcome." A number of witnesses to the Joint Committee gave examples of patients who had made advance directives refusing life-prolonging treatment and had subsequently agreed to such treatment (see, for example, Dr Fiona Randall, Oral and written evidence, Ev 303). In her evidence to the Joint Committee, Baroness Finlay said:

> "It is a feature of people who are suddenly facing the reality that they are dying that they could not preconceive how they would feel at the time. That is also a situation that one sees in people who are very seriously ill" (Oral and written Evidence, Ev 127).

These issues should be considered by those who make advance decisions and by those who advise them. In particular, those who have made advance decisions should review them at regular intervals to ensure that they reflect their current view as evidence suggests that people may change their minds following experience of either an illness or its treatment: see J.R. Bach "Threats to 'informed' advance directives for the severely physically challenged?" (2003) 84 *Archives of Physical Medicine and Rehabilitation* 23 and L.L. Emanuel "Advance directives and advancing age" (2004) 52 *Journal of the American Geriatrics Society* 641.

Subsection (5)

1–231   This provision and subs.(6) were moved by the Government at the committee stage in the House of Lords to meet concerns that had been raised by Parliamentarians, outside bodies, and the Joint Committee on Human Rights. They are aimed at tipping "the balance of advance decisions even further in favour of preserving life", *per* the Parliamentary Under-Secretary of State (*Hansard*, HL Vol.668, col.1486).

If there is a dispute about the validity and/or applicability of an advance decision that relates to life sustaining treatment, P can be treated until the issue is determined by the court (s.26(5)). Any doubt as to the validity and/or applicability of an advance decision to refuse life-sustaining treatment should be resolved by the court in favour of preserving life (*HE v A Hospital NHS Trust,* above).

LIFE-SUSTAINING TREATMENT. The reference to "life" includes the life of an unborn child: see the note on s.4(10). A woman of child-bearing age should therefore consider whether she would want the advance decision to apply to her unborn child. If she did not wish it to apply to her unborn child, the terms of the decision should reflect this.

It might be difficult to identify whether a treatment is a "life-sustaining treatment" in those cases where, for example, drugs do not have single, targeted effects. Treatments may be life-sustaining in some circumstances, and in others not. This concern has been addressed by the requirement that P must verify that the decision is to apply to the specified treatment "even if life is at risk". In other words, life-sustaining treatment is treatment that is needed to keep P alive.

With regard to artificial nutrition and hydration (ANH), "there can be no doubt that ANH constitutes life-sustaining treatment. Thus, if a person has not specified that the refusal is still to apply where ANH is necessary to sustain life then ANH (if in the person's best interests) will have to be given" (Letter from the Parliamentary-Under Secretary of State to the Chair of the Joint Committee on Human Rights, December 16, 2004, Annex, para.28).

Subsection (6)

For the validity of advance directives made before the implementation of this Act on   **1–232**
October 1, 2007, see art. 5 of the Mental Capacity Act 2005 (Transitional and Consequential Provisions) Order 2007 (SI 2007/1898) which is reproduced above.

Given the difficulties that can arise when determining the validity and/or applicability of oral advance decisions, it is suggested that the approach set out in this provision be adopted for all advance decisions.

IN WRITING. There is no statutory form. "I want to make it clear what 'in writing' can mean. It means that an advance decision can be written by a family member or recorded in medical notes by a doctor or healthcare professional, and it can include electronic records', *per* the Parliamentary Under-Secretary of State (*Hansard*, HL Vol.668, col.1487).

IS SIGNED. The decision can be signed in P's presence and by his or her direction. This is to ensure that there is "no discrimination against people who, for whatever reason, are unable to write but have the capacity to make decisions", *ibid.*

Effect of advance decisions

26.—(1) If P has made an advance decision which is—   **1–233**
(a) valid, and
(b) applicable to a treatment,
the decision has effect as if he had made it, and had had capacity to make it, at the time when the question arises whether the treatment should be carried out or continued.

(2) A person does not incur liability for carrying out or continuing the treatment unless, at the time, he is satisfied that an advance decision exists which is valid and applicable to the treatment.

(3) A person does not incur liability for the consequences of withholding or withdrawing a treatment from P if, at the time, he reasonably believes that an advance decision exists which is valid and applicable to the treatment.

(4) The court may make a declaration as to whether an advance decision—
(a) exists;
(b) is valid;
(c) is applicable to a treatment.

(5) Nothing in an apparent advance decision stops a person—
(a) providing life-sustaining treatment, or
(b) doing any act he reasonably believes to be necessary to prevent a serious deterioration in P's condition,
while a decision as respects any relevant issue is sought from the court.

DEFINITIONS
   "advance decision": s.64(1)   **1–234**
   "treatment": s.64(1)
   "the court": s.64(1)
   "life-sustaining treatment": s.64(1)

GENERAL NOTE

1–235   If an advance decision is both valid and applicable as defined in s.25, it has the same effect as a contemporaneous refusal of treatment by a person with capacity (subs.(1)). Subject to subs.(5), this means that the treatment specified in the decision cannot lawfully be given. If the treatment is given, the patient would be able to claim damages for the tort of battery and the person who provided the treatment could face criminal liability for assault. However, a treatment provider will be protected from legal liability unless satisfied that there is a valid and applicable advance decision (subs.(2)); and a treatment provider may safely withhold or withdraw treatment as long as he or she has reasonable grounds for believing that there is a valid and applicable advance decision (subs.(3)). The responsibility for determining whether an advance directive is both valid and applicable is that of the healthcare professional who would be responsible for providing the treatment specified in the decision.

A clinician who follows a valid and applicable advance decision is not acting "for or on behalf of a person who lacks capacity" for the purposes of s.1(5); he or she is acting on the instructions of a capacitated individual. Such a decision must therefore be complied with even if it conflicts with an objective evaluation of the patient's best interests. This is the case even if complying with the decision would lead to the patient's death. The principle of the sanctity of human life must yield to the principle of patient self-determination as long as the terms of s.25(5) and (6) are satisfied.

Any dispute about the existence, validity or applicability of an advance decision can be determined by the court (subs.(4)). However, action may be taken to prevent the death of the person concerned, or a serious deterioration to his or her condition, whilst a ruling is sought (subs.(5)).

The *Code of Practice* states at para.9.60:

"Some situations might be enough in themselves to raise concern about the existence, validity or applicability of an advance decision to refuse treatment. These could include situations when:

- a disagreement between relatives and healthcare professionals about whether verbal comments were really an advance decision
- evidence about the person's state of mind raises questions about their capacity at the time they made the decision
- evidence of important changes in the person's behaviour before they lost capacity that might suggest a change of mind.

In cases where serious doubt remains and cannot be resolved in any other way, it will be possible to seek a declaration from the court."

Subsection (2)

1–236   SATISFIED. In order to be satisfied that an advance decision is both valid and applicable, the clinician would need to make enquiries about (1) any doubts that might exist about the patient's mental capacity at the time when the purported advance decision was made; (2) the information that the patient received about the consequences of his or her decision; (3) the circumstances surrounding the making of the purported advance decision; (4) the possible effect of undue influence on the patient's decision; and (5) whether the purported advance decision is applicable to the proposed treatment and was intended to apply in the circumstances that have arisen. It is likely that few oral statements made by patients to lay people that are said to constitute advance decisions would survive such scrutiny, especially if the statements were made a considerable time ago. It is submitted that this provision would provide a clinician with a defence in an action for battery if the clinician made a mistaken assumption that the patient lacked capacity when making the purported advance decision, as long as the mistake was made on reasonable grounds. If the clinician is satisfied that no valid and applicable advance decision has been made, the treatment can be given. However, it would be advisable to ask the court to determine the issue in cases where the argument in favour of the existence of a valid and applicable advance decision is finely balanced or where there is a dispute between the clinician and the patient's family about whether such an advance decision has been made.

If the purported advance decision is invalid but it is clear that P was attempting to refuse a particular treatment, the decision should be treated as if it were an expression of the patient's wishes for the purpose of s.4(6)(a).

Subsection (3)

REASONABLY BELIEVES. This is an objective standard. The healthcare professional's belief must be supported by evidence. **1–237**

Subsection (4)

The court has no power to determine that a valid and applicable advance decision is not in P's best interests. **1–238**

Subsection (5)

As this provision is only available in respect of an "apparent" advance decision, it arguable that it cannot be invoked if the doctor is satisfied that the advance decision is both valid and applicable (subs.(2)). However if the validity or applicability of the advance decision is being challenged and the challenge is neither frivolous nor vexatious, the doctor should invoke this provision and seek the guidance of the Court of Protection. **1–239**

Excluded decisions

Family relationships etc

27.—(1) Nothing in this Act permits a decision on any of the following matters to be made on behalf of a person— **1–240**
- (a) consenting to marriage or a civil partnership,
- (b) consenting to have sexual relations,
- (c) consenting to a decree of divorce being granted on the basis of two years' separation,
- (d) consenting to a dissolution order being made in relation to a civil partnership on the basis of two years' separation,
- (e) consenting to a child's being placed for adoption by an adoption agency,
- (f) consenting to the making of an adoption order,
- (g) discharging parental responsibilities in matters not relating to a child's property,
- (h) giving a consent under the Human Fertilisation and Embryology Act 1990 (c. 37).
- (2) "Adoption order" means—
- (a) an adoption order within the meaning of the Adoption and Children Act 2002 (c. 38) (including a future adoption order), and
- (b) an order under section 84 of that Act (parental responsibility prior to adoption abroad).

GENERAL NOTE

This section lists decisions that can never be made by the Court of Protection, a deputy appointed by the court, the donee of a LPA, or a person acting under s.5 on behalf of a person who lacks capacity. Also see s.29. **1–241**

Mental Health Act matters

28.—(1) Nothing in this Act authorises anyone— **1–242**

(a) to give a patient medical treatment for mental disorder, or

(b) to consent to a patient's being given medical treatment for mental disorder,

if, at the time when it is proposed to treat the patient, his treatment is regulated by Part 4 of the Mental Health Act.

[(1A) Subsection (1) does not apply in relation to any form of treatment to which section 58A of that Act (electro-convulsive therapy, etc.) applies if the patient comes within subsection (7) of that section (informal patient under 18 who cannot give consent).]

[(1B) Section 5 does not apply to an act to which section 64B of the Mental Health Act applies (treatment of community patients not recalled to hospital).]

(2) "Medical treatment", "mental disorder" and "patient" have the same meaning as in that Act.

AMENDMENTS

1–243 Subs.(1A) was inserted by the Mental Capacity Act 2005, s.28(1), and subs.(1B) was inserted by s.35(5) of that Act.

DEFINITIONS

1–244 "Mental Health Act": s.64(1)

GENERAL NOTE

1–245 If a mentally disordered patient who is also mentally incapacitated has been detained under the long term provisions of the Mental Health Act 1983, the patient is subject to the regulatory regime for the treatment of his or her mental disorder which is set out in Pt IV of that Act. With the exception of the situation covered by subs.(1A), this section ensures that the provisions of this Act do not apply to any treatment given to a patient which is provided under the authority of Pt IV of the 1983 Act. In other words, the consent to treatment provisions contained in Pt IV will "trump" the provisions of this Act. This means that: (1) treatment for the patient's mental disorder cannot be given under the authority of this Act; (2) neither a donee of a LPA nor a deputy appointed by the court can either consent to or refuse treatment for mental disorder on the patient's behalf; and (3) with the exception of treatments regulated by s.58A of the 1983 Act, an advance decision made by the patient that refuses treatment for mental disorder is not binding on the treating psychiatrist. Treatment decisions relating to mentally incapacitated patients which fall outside the scope of Pt IV, such as decisions about whether the patient should receive treatment for a physical disorder and treatments given to patients detained under the emergency provisions of the 1983 Act, are governed by this Act. This section does not prevent a treatment which is regulated by s.58 or s.58A of the 1983 Act being provided to a mentally incapacitated patient who has not been detained under that Act.

Subsection (1A)

1–246 This provides that the exclusion set out in subs.(1) does not apply in relation to treatments provided under s.58A of the 1983 Act (currently ECT) if the patient comes within s.58A(7). Section 58A(7) states:

"This section shall not by itself confer sufficient authority for [an informal patient under the age of 18 years to be given a treatment regulated by s.58A] if he is not capable of understanding the nature, purpose and likely effects of the treatment (and cannot therefore consent to it)."

This means that if the child is informal and incapable of consenting to the ECT, the treatment is provided under the authority of s.5 of this Act for children over the age of 16 and by virtue of parental consent for younger children.

Where treatment for mental disorder is being provided to an adult community patient **1–247** under s.64B of the 1983 Act (treatment of incapacitated adult patient on supervised community treatment), this provision prohibits the treatment from being provided under s.5 of this Act. It does not preclude treatment decisions authorised by a donee or a court deputy.

Subsection (2)
Under s.145(1) of the 1983 Act, "medical treatment" is defined as including "nursing, **1–248** psychological intervention and specialist mental health habilitation, rehabilitation and care", and "patient" is defined as "a person suffering or appearing to be suffering from mental disorder". "Mental disorder" is defined in s.1 of that Act as meaning "any disorder or disability of mind".

Voting rights
29.—(1) Nothing in this Act permits a decision on voting at an election for any **1–249** public office, or at a referendum, to be made on behalf of a person.

(2) "Referendum" has the same meaning as in section 101 of the Political Parties, Elections and Referendums Act 2000 (c. 41).

GENERAL NOTE
This section excludes decisions on voting at an election for public office, or at a refer- **1–250** endum, from the remit of this Act.

Research

Research
30.—(1) Intrusive research carried out on, or in relation to, a person who lacks **1–251** capacity to consent to it is unlawful unless it is carried out—

(a) as part of a research project which is for the time being approved by the appropriate body for the purposes of this Act in accordance with section 31, and

(b) in accordance with sections 32 and 33.

(2) Research is intrusive if it is of a kind that would be unlawful if it was carried out—

(a) on or in relation to a person who had capacity to consent to it, but

(b) without his consent.

(3) A clinical trial which is subject to the provisions of clinical trials regulations is not to be treated as research for the purposes of this section.

(4) "Appropriate body", in relation to a research project, means the person, committee or other body specified in regulations made by the appropriate authority as the appropriate body in relation to a project of the kind in question.

(5) "Clinical trials regulations" means—

(a) the Medicines for Human Use (Clinical Trials) Regulations 2004 (S.I. 2004/ 1031) and any other regulations replacing those regulations or amending them, and

(b) any other regulations relating to clinical trials and designated by the Secretary of State as clinical trials regulations for the purposes of this section.

(6) In this section, section 32 and section 34, "appropriate authority" means—

(a) in relation to the carrying out of research in England, the Secretary of State, and

(b) in relation to the carrying out of research in Wales, the National Assembly for Wales.

GENERAL NOTE

1–252   The Draft Mental Incapacity Bill made no provision to enable incapacitated adults to take part in medical research. While recognising that "this is an ethically difficult area", the Joint Committee concluded that a clause should be included in the Bill "to enable strictly-controlled medical research to explore the causes and consequences of mental incapacity and to develop effective treatment for such conditions. This clause must include rigorous protocols to protect incapacitated adults from being exploited or harmed" (para.288). In its response to the Joint Committee's report (Cm.6121), the Government accepted that the Bill "should include provision for strictly-controlled research to fill the gap that exists in the current law and the uncertainty and inequality this creates." The provisions attempt to "balance the importance of properly conducted research into the treatment and care of people who lack capacity with the need to protect their interests and respect their current and previously expressed wishes and feelings", *per* Lord Hunt of Kings Heath, *Hansard*, HL Vol.689, col.GC107).

The Joint Committee also recommended, at para.289, that the Bill "should set out the key principles governing research, such as those enshrined by the World Medical Association [in the Helsinki Declaration]. Those key principles should include the following:

- research involving people who may be incapacitated must be reviewed by a properly established and independent ethics committee and can only proceed if ethical permission is granted.
- where a person has the capacity to consent then his decision whether or not to partake in research must be respected.
- considerable care should be taken to ensure that under these circumstances consent to participate was freely given and not a consequence of coercion.
- the inclusion of people in research, who lacked the capacity to consent, must only occur when such research has the potential for direct benefit to those with that particular problem and could not have been done through the involvement of those with capacity.
- those undertaking research involving people lacking the capacity to consent must respect any indications that a person did not wish to participate (i.e. was dissenting). any discomfort or risk involved in the research must be, at the most, minimal."

The Government agreed that "key principles are important" and stated that it would "explore the extent to which these need be in statute, or whether they are already covered by existing Good Practice Guidance". Those carrying out research under this Act are required to act in accordance with the principles set out in s.1 and to have regard to the guidance contained in the *Code of Practice* (s.42(4)(c)). The Government has published a *Research Governance Framework for Health and Social Care* (Department of Health, 2nd ed., 2005) which outlines principles of good governance that applies to all research within the remit of the Secretary of State for Health.

This section, together with ss.31 to 34, make provision for "intrusive" research to be lawfully carried out on, or in relation to a person who lacks the capacity to consent to it, where the research is part of a research project which has been approved by the "appropriate body", as defined in subs.(4), and is carried out in accordance with the conditions set out in ss.32 and 33 (subs.(1)). Intrusive research is research that would require consent if it involved a person with capacity (subs.(2)). Observational research that would breach the subject's right to respect for private life under Art.8 of the ECHR would fall into this category. Intrusive research undertaken on people who lack capacity which does not satisfy the requirements of this Act is unlawful. In addition to the obligations placed on them by this Act, researchers must also comply with their wider legal obligations such as their duties under the data protection and health and safety legislation.

If a person with capacity has consented to his involvement in research, the fact that he subsequently loses capacity does not mean that he has to be withdrawn from the research, in so far as it relates to the matter that he has consented to, because the fact that he given his consent means that the research is not intrusive (see subs.(2)). Baroness Andrews said: "The Bill does not apply to research during temporary incapacity, such as general anaesthesia during surgery, providing that consent was obtained in advance. Consent endures the temporary loss of capacity" (*Hansard*, HL Vol.670, col.1521). However, if the research is a continuing project rather than a one-off event, any further research would be research undertaken without consent and would therefore be intrusive research that would trigger the procedures set out in ss.31–33. For example, if the person consents to a sample of blood being taken as part of a research project, the sample can be taken even if the person loses capacity before that point. The taking of any further samples would constitute intrusive research because of the absence of the person's consent. Transitional provisions are contained in s.34.

Clinical trials that are regulated by the clinical trials regulations, which are concerned with the conduct of clinical trials of medicines for human use, are excluded (subss.(3) and (5)) because the regulations already make provision for trials involving participants who lack capacity. The 2004 Regulations (as amended by SI 2005/2754, SI 2005/2759 and SI 2006/1928) were amended by the Medicines for Human Use (Clinical Trials) Amendment (No.2) Regulations 2006 (SI 2006/2984) which are aimed at making the regulations consistent with this Act in so far as they relate to emergency research conducted on mentally incapacitated patients.

Paragraph 11.7 of the *Code of Practice* states:

"There are circumstances where no consent is needed to lawfully involve a person in research. These apply to all persons, whether they have capacity or not:

- Sometimes research only involves data that has been anonymised (it cannot be traced back to individuals). Confidentiality and data protection laws do not apply in this case.
- Under the Human Tissue Act 2004, research that deals only with human tissue that has been anonymised does not require consent . . . This applies to both those who have capacity and those who do not. But the research must have ethical approval, and the tissue must come from a living person.
- If researchers collected human tissue samples before 31 August 2006, they do not need a person's consent to work on them. But they will normally have to get ethical approval.
- Regulations made under section 251 of the NHS Act 2006 (formerly known as section 60 of the Health and Social Care Act 2001) allow people to use confidential patient information without breaking the law on confidentiality by applying to the Patient Information Advisory Group for approval on behalf of the Secretary of State."

The ethical and legal issues arising from medical research on mentally incompetent adults are considered by M.J. Gunn, J.G Wong, I.C.H. Clare and A.J. Holland in "Medical Research and Incompetent Adults" (2000) *Journal of Mental Health Law* 60. For the application of these Regulations to emergency medicine, see T.J. Coats, "Consent for emergency care research: the Mental Capacity Act 2005" (2006) 23 *Emergency Medical Journal* 893.

Research that began before October 1, 2007

Sections 30 to 34 come into force in England on October 1, 2008 in respect of any **1–253** research which (a) began before October 1, 2007; and (b) was approved before October 1, 2007 by a committee established to advise on, or on matters which include, the ethics of research in relation to people who lack capacity to consent to it (Mental Capacity Act 2005 (Commencement No.1) Order 2006 (SI 2006/2814), reg.4 (as amended by SI 2006/3473, art.2)).

The Human Tissue Act 2004

1–254   The Human Tissue Act 2004 sets up a framework to regulate the storage and use of human organs and tissues from the living and the removal, storage and use of tissues and organs from the deceased, for specified health related purposes and public display. The Act establishes a regulatory authority, the Human Tissue Authority, to regulate these activities and transplantation. Although consent is a fundamental principle underpinning the operation of the Act, the Human Tissue Act 2004 (Persons who lack Capacity to Consent and Transplants) Regulations 2006 (SI 2006/1659) make provision as to the circumstances in which activities may be carried out in relation to material from the body of a person who lacks capacity to consent for the purposes of certain provisions of the Act, including DNA analysis. The regulations were drafted "to ensure that, given the Human Tissue Act 2004 will be brought into force before the Mental Capacity Act 2005, legitimate activities will not fall foul of one Act pending implementation of the other" (Explanatory Memorandum on SI 2006/1659, para.7.2).

Subsection (4)

1–255   By virtue of reg.2 of the Mental Capacity Act 2005 (Appropriate Body) (England) Regulations 2006 (SI 2006/2810), the appropriate body in England for the purpose this section, s.31 and s.33 is a research ethics committee, i.e. "a committee—

(a) established to advise on, or on matters which include, the ethics of intrusive research in relation to people who lack capacity to consent to it; and
(b) recognised by that purpose by the Secretary of State".

SI 2006/2810 came into force on July 1, 2007 for the purposes of enabling applications for ethical approval of research to be made and determined under this Act, and on October 1, 2007 for all other purposes (*ibid.,* art.1, as amended by SI 2006/3474, art.2). A similar definition of appropriate body is made for Wales, with the same commencement dates, by the Mental Capacity Act 2005 (Appropriate Body) (Wales) Regulations 2007 (SI 2007/833 (W.71)) with the exception that the committee has to be recognised by the National Assembly for Wales (now the Welsh Ministers, see below).

The background to research ethics committees is set out in para.7.5 of the Explanatory Memorandum to the Mental Capacity Act 2005 (Appropriate Body) (England) Regulations 2006:

"NHS research ethics committees were established in England in 1991 following the publication of Department of Health guidance HSG (91)5. The appointing authorities for NHS research ethics committees are the Strategic Health Authorities in England. NHS research ethics committees are independent of the researcher and the organisation funding and hosting research. Training and accreditation for NHS committees is provided by the Central Office of Research Ethics Committees (COREC) to ensure national consistency. Before it can proceed, all research involving NHS patients requires approval from an NHS research ethics committee. Research governance is a core standard for health care and health care organisations have to take this standard into account in discharging their duty of quality under section 45 of the Health and Social Care (Community Health and Standards) Act 2003."

Guidance on applying for the ethical review of research involving mentally incapacitated adults has been published by the National Research Ethics Service: see "Research involving adults unable to care for themselves" (Version 1 June 2007).

Subsection (5)

The 2004 Regulations, which came into force on May 1, 2004, implement European **1–256** Clinical Trials Directive 2001/20/EC on "the approximation of the laws, regulations and administrative provisions of the Member States relating to the implementation of good clinical practice in the conduct of clinical trials on medicinal products for human use". The Regulations define "clinical trials" as meaning:

"any investigation in human subjects, other than a non-interventional trial, intended—

(a) to discover or verify the clinical, pharmacological or other pharmacodynamic effects of one or more medicinal products,

(b) to identify any adverse reactions to one or more such products, or

(c) to study absorption, distribution, metabolism and excretion of one or more such products

with the object of ascertaining the safety or efficacy of those products" (reg.2(1)).

Part 5 of Sch.1 to the regulations contains conditions and principles which apply to incapacitated adults.

Subsection (6) para.(b)

The functions of the National Assembly for Wales are performed by the Welsh Ministers **1–257** (Government of Wales Act 2006, s.162, Sch.11, para.30).

Requirements for approval

31.—(1) The appropriate body may not approve a research project for the pur- **1–258** poses of this Act unless satisfied that the following requirements will be met in relation to research carried out as part of the project on, or in relation to, a person who lacks capacity to consent to taking part in the project (P).

(2) The research must be connected with—

(a) an impairing condition affecting P, or

(b) its treatment.

(3) "Impairing condition" means a condition which is (or may be) attributable to, or which causes or contributes to (or may cause or contribute to), the impairment of, or disturbance in the functioning of, the mind or brain.

(4) There must be reasonable grounds for believing that research of comparable effectiveness cannot be carried out if the project has to be confined to, or relate only to, persons who have capacity to consent to taking part in it.

(5) The research must—

(a) have the potential to benefit P without imposing on P a burden that is disproportionate to the potential benefit to P, or

(b) be intended to provide knowledge of the causes or treatment of, or of the care of persons affected by, the same or a similar condition.

(6) If the research falls within paragraph (b) of subsection (5) but not within paragraph (a), there must be reasonable grounds for believing—

(a) that the risk to P from taking part in the project is likely to be negligible, and

(b) that anything done to, or in relation to, P will not—

(i) interfere with P's freedom of action or privacy in a significant way, or

(ii) be unduly invasive or restrictive.

(7) There must be reasonable arrangements in place for ensuring that the requirements of sections 32 and 33 will be met.

DEFINITIONS

"appropriate body": s.30(4)   **1–259**

GENERAL NOTE

1–260   This section sets out the requirements that must be satisfied before the Secretary of State and the Welsh Ministers can approve a research project involving people who lack capacity. It does not preclude either observational or epidemiological research being undertaken. The research does not have to be undertaken in healthcare settings. Paragraph 11.2 of the *Code of Practice* states:

> "The Act does not have a specific definition for 'research'. The Department of Health and National Assembly for Wales publications *Research governance framework for health and social care* both state:
>
> > 'research can be defined as the attempt to derive generalisable new knowledge by addressing clearly defined questions with systematic and rigorous methods'.
>
> Research may:
>
> - provide information that can be applied generally to an illness, disorder or condition
> - demonstrate how effective and safe a new treatment is
> - add to evidence that one form of treatment works better than another
> - add to evidence that one form of treatment is safer than another, or
> - examine wider issues (for example, the factors that affect someone's capacity to make a decision)."

Research that can be undertaken under this provision includes "research on a person—involving direct contact with that person" and "research in relation to a person—indirect research on tissues, materials, data or information otherwise collected from the person" (Explanatory Memorandum to the Mental Capacity Act 2005 (Appropriate Body) (England) Regulations 2006, para.2).

There is a clear tension between the nature of some research contemplated by this section and the best interests principle established in s.1(5). This tension is illustrated by subss.(5) and (6) which contemplate research being undertaken which would be inconsistent with s.1(5). The Parliamentary Under-Secretary of State said that "the research procedures provide an alternative to a best interests determination" (*Hansard*, HL Vol.669, col.135). The Minister of State described the application of the best interests principle to research as being "difficult" (St. Comm. A, col.278), and that the principle is "interpreted slightly differently" when applied to research (*Hansard*, HC Vol.428, col.1604). At the third reading of the Bill, she said:

> "[I]t is always difficult to prove that [research] can be in someone's best interests. We can only say that it is of potential benefit to that person, or might benefit him or her in the longer term, or might benefit him or her indirectly once more research has been done, or might benefit others with the same condition now or in the future" (*Hansard*, HC Vol.428, col.1603).

The Parliamentary Under-Secretary of State said:

> "The purpose of [sections] 30 to 33 is to make provision for acts in connection with research that cannot necessarily be shown precisely to coincide with the person's best interests. It may be that the research procedure involves different or additional approaches to a person's care, which might not meet a narrow assessment of best interest" (*Hansard*, HL Vol.669, col.135).

Although the provisions of this Act relating to research are partly based on the Council of Europe Convention on Human Rights and Biomedicine (ETS No.164) (the Oviedo Convention), the UK Government has not ratified the Convention. The Convention was supplemented by an Additional Protocol concerning Biomedical Research, which was opened for signature by the signatories to the Convention on January 25, 2005. The Oviedo Convention and the Additional Protocol are reproduced in the first edition of this Manual.

The Joint Committee on Human Rights concluded that the "nature of the benefit from the research required in [subs.(5)] has the effect of lowering the threshold of when research will be permissible compared with the standards contained in the Convention" (23rd Report, para.2.60). The Government responded to this comment as follows:

"We have taken careful note of the Oviedo Convention, but are conscious that it does not appear to extend across the breadth of research activities that we wish to cover. For example, Arts.15–17 of the Oviedo Convention are concerned with research 'on a person', which is further clarified in the Explanatory memorandum as 'research on human beings' and in the Additional Protocol which refers to 'research activities in the health field involving interventions on human beings'. We wished to cover wider aspects of research that would not normally require consent from a person with incapacity, including research into medical records, or observation of P in a social care setting. We hope that this helps to explain why, in some cases, we have departed from the language used in the Oviedo Convention" ("Memorandum submitted to the Joint Committee on Human Rights in response to their letter of 18 November 2004 as published in their 23rd Report", paras 59 and 60).

Subsection (1)
APPROPRIATE BODY. See s.30(4).   **1–261**

Subsections (2) and (3)
These provisions identify the scope of the research that can be undertaken. Baroness **1–262** Andrews explained:

"The emphasis is now more clearly on the requirement that the research must be connected to an impairing condition that the person has. It concedes that the relationship between the impairing condition and the impairment of, or disturbance in, the functioning of the mind or brain is sometimes not perfectly understood. It makes it clearer that it may be valid to conduct properly designed research to see whether the condition and the impairment or the disturbance are linked.

The amendment makes it clear that research, for example, to prevent kidney failure in a person in a coma following a car accident or heart attack would be permissible if the other safeguards are met. The impairing condition would be the trauma or shock following the sudden crash or heart attack. The research ethics committee would have to be satisfied that there was a good case for believing that the research into kidney failure was connected to the impairing condition, or its treatment" (*Hansard*, HL Vol.670, col.1500).

IMPAIRMENT OF, OR DISTURBANCE IN THE FUNCTIONING OF THE MIND OR BRAIN. See the note to s.2(1).

Subsection (4)
This provision was subject to a Government amendment to bring it closer to the wording **1–263** of Art.17.1 iii of the Oviedo Convention which states that "research of comparable effectiveness cannot be carried out on individuals capable of giving consent".

Subsection (5) para. (a)
POTENTIAL TO BENEFIT P. If something is done which is intended to be of direct benefit to P, **1–264** it would constitute treatment rather than research.

BURDEN THAT IS DISPROPORTIONATE. "By 'burden' we mean the risk or inconvenience of a trial. For example, researchers might submit a proposal to use an MRI scanner to understand the brain structures of people with dementia or schizophrenia. It might be of potential benefit to their treatment. But if the use of an MRI scanner required long confinement—we know that people with mental capacity or those suffering from cancer or claustrophobia can be very vulnerable to extreme worry in these situations—or perhaps regular and frequent scans, an ethics committee might decide that the research would simply not bring enough benefit to justify the extra scans or trauma that might be involved", *per* Baroness Andrews, (*Hansard*, HL Vol.669, col.154).

Subsection (5) para. (b)

1–265   The Explanatory Notes state, at para.98, that this category or research "might include indirect research on medical notes, or on tissue already taken for other purposes. It may also include interviews or questionnaires with carers about health or social-care services received by the person or limited observation of the person. And it could include taking samples from the person, e.g. blood samples, specifiacally for the research project". It would also include research into how the incapacity, and the medical and other complications that are associated with it, might impact upon the care regime for the mentally incapacitated. Note that s.33(3) states that the "interests of the person must be assumed to outweigh those of science and society".

TREATMENT. This provision allows for research into diagnostic procedures (s.64(1)).

Subsection (6)

1–266   Paragraphs 11.18 and 11.19 of the *Code of Practice* state:

"Any risk to people involved in this category of research must be 'negligible' (minimal). This means that a person should suffer no harm or distress by taking part. Researchers must consider risks to psychological wellbeing as well as physical wellbeing. This is particularly relevant for research related to observations or interviews.

Research in this category also must not affect a person's freedom of action or privacy in a significant way, and it should not be unduly invasive or restrictive. What will be considered as unduly invasive will be different for different people and different types of research. For example, in psychological research some people may think a specific question is intrusive, but others would not. Actions will not usually be classed as unduly invasive if they do not go beyond the experience of daily life, a routine medical examination or a psychological examination".

Consulting carers etc

1–267   **32.**—(1) This section applies if a person (R)—

    (a) is conducting an approved research project, and

    (b) wishes to carry out research, as part of the project, on or in relation to a person (P) who lacks capacity to consent to taking part in the project.

    (2) R must take reasonable steps to identify a person who—

    (a) otherwise than in a professional capacity or for remuneration, is engaged in caring for P or is interested in P's welfare, and

    (b) is prepared to be consulted by R under this section.

    (3) If R is unable to identify such a person he must, in accordance with guidance issued by the appropriate authority, nominate a person who—

    (a) is prepared to be consulted by R under this section, but

    (b) has no connection with the project.

    (4) R must provide the person identified under subsection (2), or nominated under subsection (3), with information about the proj ect and ask him—

    (a) for advice as to whether P should take part in the project, and

    (b) what, in his opinion, P's wishes and feelings about taking part in the project would be likely to be if P had capacity in relation to the matter.

(5) If, at any time, the person consulted advises R that in his opinion P's wishes and feelings would be likely to lead him to decline to take part in the project (or to wish to withdraw from it) if he had capacity in relation to the matter, R must ensure—

(a) if P is not already taking part in the project, that he does not take part in it;

(b) if P is taking part in the project, that he is withdrawn from it.

(6) But subsection (5)(b) does not require treatment that P has been receiving as part of the project to be discontinued if R has reasonable grounds for believing that there would be a significant risk to P's health if it were discontinued.

(7) The fact that a person is the donee of a lasting power of attorney given by P, or is P's deputy, does not prevent him from being the person consulted under this section.

(8) Subsection (9) applies if treatment is being, or is about to be, provided for P as a matter of urgency and R considers that, having regard to the nature of the research and of the particular circumstances of the case—

(a) it is also necessary to take action for the purposes of the research as a matter of urgency, but

(b) it is not reasonably practicable to consult under the previous provisions of this section.

(9) R may take the action if—

(a) he has the agreement of a registered medical practitioner who is not involved in the organisation or conduct of the research project, or

(b) where it is not reasonably practicable in the time available to obtain that agreement, he acts in accordance with a procedure approved by the appropriate body at the time when the research project was approved under section 31.

(10) But R may not continue to act in reliance on subsection (9) if he has reasonable grounds for believing that it is no longer necessary to take the action as a matter of urgency.

DEFINITIONS
    "appropriate authority": s.30(6)   **1–268**
    "lasting power of attorney": s.64(1)
    "deputy": s.64(1)
    "appropriate body": s.30(4)

GENERAL NOTE
    This section provides that before any decision is taken to involve P in approved research, **1–269** the researcher (R) must take reasonable steps to identify either an unpaid carer or a person who is interested in P's welfare in a non-professional capacity who is prepared to be consulted about P's involvement in the research (subss.(1), (2)). This person could be a deputy or a donee of a lasting power of attorney as long as that person is not acting in a paid or professional capacity (subs.(7)). If there is no such person, R must nominate (in accordance with guidance issued by the appropriate authority) a person who is willing to be consulted, but has no connection with the project (subs.(3)). This person could have a professional relationship with P, for example, his GP. The role of the consultee is to provide information to R; he or she does not provide consent for the research to proceed.

    Subsection (4) identifies the purpose of the consultation. If the consultee advises R that, in his or her opinion, P would have been likely to decline to take part if he or she had capacity, P cannot be involved in the research, or if it is already underway P must be withdrawn from it (subs.(5)). However, if P has been receiving treatment as part of the research it should not be withdrawn if to do so would place P's health at significant risk (subs.(6)).

Subsections (8) and (9) allow for cases where P is being, or is about to be, provided with urgent treatment, research into that treatment must also be undertaken as a matter of urgency, and it is not reasonable practicable for R to consult. R may proceed to involve P in the research if he has the agreement of a doctor who is not concerned in the organisation or conduct of the research project, or, if there is no time to do this, he follows an approved procedure. R cannot continue to use these provisions if there is no longer an urgent need to act (subs.(10)). The Explanatory Notes, at para.104, state that examples of this type of research "may involve action by a paramedic or doctor to make measurements in the first few minutes following a serious head injury or stroke".

Subsection (2)

1–270 A PERSON. Such as a family member, advocate or friend.

GUIDANCE. See "Guidance on nominating a consultee for research involving adults who lack capacity to consent", issued by the Secretary of State and the Welsh Ministers in February 2008, which sets out the principles to which researchers must adhere in nominating a consultee and provides advice on ways of meeting this requirement in different research settings, including emergency research.

ENGAGED IN CARING FOR. See the note on "anyone engaged in caring for the person" in s.4(7)(b).

Subsection (3)

1–271 APPROPRIATE AUTHORITY. See s.30(6).

CONNECTION WITH THE PROJECT. This phrase "would certainly include someone involved with, or connected to, either the study itself or a member of the research team. It would also cover wider connections, such as someone with a direct link to funding decisions for the study, for example, or who was involved with the research ethics committee" *per* Baroness Andrews (*Hansard*, HL Vol.670, col.1515).

Subsection (4)

1–272 Paragraph (b) requires R to ask the consultee to exercise a substituted judgment on behalf of P. This will be an almost impossible task to perform if the consultee has had no previous contact with P. Professor Coats argues that in this situation the consultee "will simply reason that most people wish to improve medical treatment and for most trials, most of the patients approached agree to participate in research projects. Therefore, the incapacitated patient would probably agree to be included in the trial. Without any prior knowledge of the patient the 'consultee' will therefore always agree to patient entry. . ." (T.J. Coats, "Consent for emergency care research: the Mental Capacity Act 2005" (2006) 23 *Emergency Medical Journal* 893).

Subsection (5)

1–273 If P is withdrawn part way through the project, this provision does not provide that information collected with respect to P up to that point must be disregarded for the purposes of the project.

Subsection (7)

1–274 DEPUTY. "[W]e will amend the *Code of Practice* to make it clear that if a deputy has no relationship to, or knowledge of, P before their appointment, they should not be consulted on the question of P's participation in research", *per* the Minister of State (*Hansard*, HC Vol.428, col.1605).

Subsection (9)

1–275 MAY TAKE THE ACTION. i.e. involve P in the research.

REGISTERED MEDICAL PRACTITIONER. The doctor to be consulted may be involved in the treatment of P. Baroness Andrews said:

"We want provide that a doctor who can be consulted may well be a consultant surgeon or even a GP whose patient suffers a sudden cardiac arrest or goes into septic shock, for example.

If the emergency happens in the community—outside the hospital—it is perfectly possible that a person's GP can be involved and give approval for research to be initiated by, for example, a paramedic attending the person at home. It is important to think that research in such a case may simply be the taking of a blood sample. As I hope is clear, those doctors are usually best placed to advise the researcher, as they are familiar with the patient's medical history" (*Hansard*, HL Vol.670, col.1501).

APPROPRIATE BODY. See s.30(4).

Additional safeguards

33.—(1) This section applies in relation to a person who is taking part in an **1–276** approved research project even though he lacks capacity to consent to taking part.

(2) Nothing may be done to, or in relation to, him in the course of the research—

(a) to which he appears to object (whether by showing signs of resistance or otherwise) except where what is being done is intended to protect him from harm or to reduce or prevent pain or discomfort, or

(b) which would be contrary to—

(i) an advance decision of his which has effect, or

(ii) any other form of statement made by him and not subsequently withdrawn,

of which R is aware.

(3) The interests of the person must be assumed to outweigh those of science and society.

(4) If he indicates (in any way) that he wishes to be withdrawn from the project he must be withdrawn without delay.

(5) P must be withdrawn from the project, without delay, if at any time the person conducting the research has reasonable grounds for believing that one or more of the requirements set out in section 31(2) to (7) is no longer met in relation to research being carried out on, or in relation to, P.

(6) But neither subsection (4) nor subsection (5) requires treatment that P has been receiving as part of the project to be discontinued if R has reasonable grounds for believing that there would be a significant risk to P's health if it were discontinued.

DEFINITIONS
"advance decision': s.64(1)   **1–277**

GENERAL NOTE
This section provides that P's involvement in research must cease without delay if it **1–279** appears that he objects to what is being done (this requirement is subject to the exceptions contained in subs.(2)(a)), if what is being done is contrary to either an advance decision made by P or to some other statement made by P, or if P indicates that he wishes to be withdrawn from the research (subss.(2),(4)). These provisions are subject to the principle that the interests of P must be assumed to outweigh those of science and society (subs.(3)). P must also be withdrawn from the research if the person conducting the research believes that one or more of requirements for approval is no longer met (subs.(5)). Subsection (6)

makes it clear that any withdrawal from research does not require beneficial treatment to be halted.

Researchers have a duty to have regard to the guidance contained in the *Code of Practice* (s.42(4)(c)).

Subsection (3)

1–280   This principle is taken from section A.5 of the World Medical Association's Declaration of Helsinki on Ethical Principles for Medical Research Involving Human Subjects.

Loss of capacity during research project

1–281   **34.**—(1) This section applies where a person (P)—

(a) has consented to take part in a research project begun before the commencement of section 30, but

(b) before the conclusion of the project, loses capacity to consent to continue to take part in it.

(2) The appropriate authority may by regulations provide that, despite P's loss of capacity, research of a prescribed kind may be carried out on, or in relation to, P if—

(a) the project satisfies prescribed requirements,

(b) any information or material relating to P which is used in the research is of a prescribed description and was obtained before P's loss of capacity, and

(c) the person conducting the project takes in relation to P such steps as may be prescribed for the purpose of protecting him.

(3) The regulations may, in particular,—

(a) make provision about when, for the purposes of the regulations, a project is to be treated as having begun;

(b) include provision similar to any made by section 31, 32 or 33.

DEFINITIONS

1–282   "appropriate authority": s.30(6)
"prescribed": s.64(1)

GENERAL NOTE

1–283   The purpose of this section was explained by the Baroness Andrews:

"[This section establishes] a transitional regulation-making power to cover ongoing research and provides for the necessary flexibility in the provisions for approval of research by a research ethics committee, with consultation of carers and additional safeguards. Why do we need transitional regulations? Primarily because it is necessary to smooth the transition for researchers from the current common law position to the new statutory safeguards for research involving those who lose capacity. We need them to avoid stopping ongoing and essential research

We already have the flexibility to cater for the majority of those in the ordinary powers for making transitional provisions in [s.65], but we need to provide for more comprehensive regulation-making powers to cover projects that enrol people with capacity who go on to lose capacity during the research projects

Our aim is to ensure that a research project can continue in relation to samples or data obtained from people before they lost capacity, subject to certain specified safeguards" (*Hansard*, HL Vol.670, cols 1520–1522).

The Mental Capacity Act 2005 (Loss of Capacity during Research Project) (England) Regulations 2007 (SI 2007/679), which are reproduced in Part 3, have been made under this section (for Wales, see SI 2007/837 (W.72)). They only apply where a person has consented to take part in a research project which started before October 1, 2007, but before the end of the project loses capacity. The person's consent to take part in the project must be given before March 31, 2008. The regulations allow the researcher to continue to use information or material obtained with consent *before* the loss of capacity. They do not apply to situations where the researchers wish to go back to a person who lacks capacity in order to obtain more information or material. Such projects will need to have approval under s.30. The regulations will have a long-term effect. The Minister gave the following example: "[A] person could join an existing study in October 2007 or January 2008 and lose capacity in the 2020s, and, if the study is continuing, the regulations would apply" (*Hansard*, HL Vol.689, col.GC108).

Subsection (2)
APPROPRIATE AUTHORITY. See s.30(6). **1–284**

REGULATIONS. Regulations made under this power are subject to the affirmative resolution procedure (s.65(4)).

Independent mental capacity advocate service

Appointment of independent mental capacity advocates

35.—(1) The appropriate authority must make such arrangements as it con- **1–285** siders reasonable to enable persons (independent mental capacity advocates) to be available to represent and support persons to whom acts or decisions proposed under sections 37, 38 and 39 relate [or persons who fall within section 39A, 39C or 39D].

(2) The appropriate authority may make regulations as to the appointment of independent mental capacity advocates.

(3) The regulations may, in particular, provide—

(a) that a person may act as an independent mental capacity advocate only in such circumstances, or only subject to such conditions, as may be prescribed;

(b) for the appointment of a person as an independent mental capacity advocate to be subject to approval in accordance with the regulations.

(4) In making arrangements under subsection (1), the appropriate authority must have regard to the principle that a person to whom a proposed act or decision relates should, so far as practicable, be represented and supported by a person who is independent of any person who will be responsible for the act or decision.

(5) The arrangements may include provision for payments to be made to, or in relation to, persons carrying out functions in accordance with the arrangements.

(6) For the purpose of enabling him to carry out his functions, an independent mental capacity advocate—

(a) may interview in private the person whom he has been instructed to represent, and

(b) may, at all reasonable times, examine and take copies of—

  (i) any health record,

  (ii) any record of, or held by, a local authority and compiled in connection with a social services function, and

  (iii) any record held by a person registered under Part 2 of the Care Standards Act 2000 (c.14),

which the person holding the record considers may be relevant to the independent mental capacity advocate's investigation.

(7) In this section, section 36 and section 37, "the appropriate authority" means—

(a) in relation to the provision of the services of independent mental capacity advocates in England, the Secretary of State, and

(b) in relation to the provision of the services of independent mental capacity advocates in Wales, the National Assembly for Wales.

AMENDMENT

1–286   In subs.(1) the words in square brackets were substituted by the Mental Health Act 2007, s.50(7), Sch.9, Pt.1, para.3.

GENERAL NOTE

1–287   Sections 35–41 create a scheme designed to provide the input of an independent mental capacity advocate ("IMCA") who will act as a representative and supporter of particularly vulnerable persons who lacks capacity where certain decisions need to be taken. Such people "may include older people with dementia who have lost contact with all friends and family, or people with severe learning disabilities or long term mental health problems who have been in residential institutions for long periods and lack outside contacts" (Explanatory Notes, para.109). The IMCA will become involved where there is no person, other than a professional or paid carer, to be consulted with about P's best interests. An IMCA will not become involved if one of the persons set out in s.40 can be consulted about P's best interests. The Minister of State said:

> "We estimate that about 20 per cent of people in England and Wales who lack capacity when major decisions are being taken about their living arrangements, care or treatment, have no friends or family to consult. The [IMCA] safeguard will provide the person with someone who is on their side so that there is never a closed relationship between the decision maker and the person lacking capacity.
>
> . . . The [IMCA] will clearly have the right to talk to the person lacking capacity and a right of access to relevant records. They will find out as much as they possibly can about the likely wishes of the person and explore a range of possible outcomes that may be open to that individual. We want to give the person those powers so that they can take a broad view of what will eventually be in the best interests of the individual, which they can then recommend to the decision maker" (St. Comm. A, cols 314 and 315).

This section places a duty on the Secretary of State for Health and the Welsh Ministers to make arrangements for the provision of an IMCA service (subss.(1)–(4) and (7)) and provides the IMCA with the power to interview P in private and to examine relevant records (subs.(6)). The requirements set out in regulations made under subs.(2) must be satisfied before a person can be appointed to act as an IMCA. The IMCA, who could be remunerated for his or her services (subs.(5)), will act in P's best interests (ss.1(5)). However, as the role of the IMCA is to support and represent the person lacking capacity, he or she will not make the best interests judgment. The particular functions of IMCAs are set out in regulations (s.36). If the decision maker decides not to accept the advice proffered, the IMCA will need to consider whether take the matter further by, for example, using the NHS or local authority complaints procedure or, if the matter is particularly serious, seeking permission to refer the matter to the Court of Protection.

By virtue of reg.2 of the Mental Capacity Act 2005 (Independent Mental Capacity Advocates) (Expansion of Role) Regulations 2006 (SI 2006/2883), arrangements made by the Secretary of State under this section may include such provision as she considers reasonable for the purposes of enabling IMCAs to be available to represent and support persons in the circumstances specified in reg.3 or 4 of those regulations. SI 2006/2883 is reproduced in Part 3.

Information from the Department of Health on aspects of implementing the IMCA service, together with *The First Annual Report of the Independent Mental Capacity Advocacy Service, April 2007–March 2008,* can be found at *www.dh.gov.uk/imca.*

Subsection (1)
APPROPRIATE AUTHORITY. See subs.(7). **1–288**

Subsection (2)
See reg.5 of the Mental Capacity Act 2005 (Independent Mental Capacity Advocates **1–289** (General) Regulations 2006 (SI 2006/1832) which is reproduced in Part 3. Provision for the appointment of IMCAs in Wales is made by the Mental Capacity Act 2005 (Independent Mental Capacity Advocates) (Wales) Regulations 2007 (SI 2007/852 (W.77)), reg.5.

Under reg.5(3) of SI 2006/1832 and reg.5(8) of SI 2007/852 (W.77), criminal record certificates are required in determining whether a person meets the appointment requirements as to good character. The Police Act 1997 (Criminal Records) (Amendment No.2) Regulations 2006 (SI 2006/2181) amend the Police Act 1997 (Criminal Records) Regulations 2002 (SI 2002/233) to enable an enhanced criminal record certificate to be obtained in respect a person who is applying to act as an IMCA. An enhanced disclosure is not confined to checking the Police National Computer; it also includes a check of local police force records for information considered relevant to the position applied for. SI 2006/2181 also provides for applicants to be checked against the Protection of Vulnerable Adults (PoVA) list as part of the CRB disclosure application. The PoVA list system will be superseded in 2008 by the vetting and barring scheme established by the Safeguarding of Vulnerable Groups Act 2006. IMCAs have been named as a group that will be subject to mandatory checking under this scheme.

Subsection (6) para.(a)
The responsibility for determining the mental capacity of the person who is the subject of **1–290** the decision is that of the decision-maker, not the IMCA.

Subsection (6) para.(b)
It is the responsibility of the record holder to determine whether a record is "relevant" to **1–291** the IMCA's investigation. The record holder should therefore examine the record and ensure that the IMCA only has access to relevant material. The disclosure of irrelevant material to the IMCA would constitute a breach of P's right to confidentiality and respect for private life under Art.8 of the European Convention on Human Rights. If the IMCA is denied access to records that he or she considers are relevant to the investigation, a complaint should be made to the body that holds the record. Ultimately the IMCA could apply to the court for the record to be disclosed. The IMCA is subject to a duty of confidentiality in respect of information that is disclosed under this provision.

Subsection (7) para.(a)
SECRETARY OF STATE. In practice, the Secretary of State for Health. **1–292**

Subsection (7) para.(b)
The functions of the National Assembly for Wales are performed by the Welsh Ministers **1–293** (Government of Wales Act 2006, s.162, Sch.11, para.30).

Functions of independent mental capacity advocates

36.—(1) The appropriate authority may make regulations as to the functions of **1–294** independent mental capacity advocates.

(2) The regulations may, in particular, make provision requiring an advocate to take such steps as may be prescribed for the purpose of—

(a) providing support to the person whom he has been instructed to represent (P) so that P may participate as fully as possible in any relevant decision;

(b) obtaining and evaluating relevant information;

(c) ascertaining what P's wishes and feelings would be likely to be, and the beliefs and values that would be likely to influence P, if he had capacity;

(d) ascertaining what alternative courses of action are available in relation to P;

(e) obtaining a further medical opinion where treatment is proposed and the advocate thinks that one should be obtained.

(3) The regulations may also make provision as to circumstances in which the advocate may challenge, or provide assistance for the purpose of challenging, any relevant decision.

DEFINITIONS

1–295   "appropriate authority": s.35(7)

"independent mental capacity advocate": s.64(1)

"prescribed': s.64(1)

GENERAL NOTE

1–296   This section enables the Secretary of State and the Welsh Ministers to make regulations as to the functions of IMCAs. The primary function of the IMCA is to advocate on behalf of P in respect of decisions that require an IMCA involvement. The Mental Capacity Act 2005 (Independent Mental Capacity Advocates) (General) Regulations 2006 (SI 2006/1832) have been made under this section. They apply not only where the IMCA is instructed under ss.37 to 39 but also where he or she is instructed under regulations made under s.41. Regulation 6 set out the steps an IMCA must take once he or she has been instructed to act in a particular case. Note that the IMCA is only required to carry out the functions identified in reg.6(4)(b) and (c) "to the extent that it is practicable and appropriate to do so". The meaning of "practicable" is considered in the note to s.4(7). For Wales, see the Mental Capacity Act 2005 (Independent Mental Capacity Advocates) (Wales) Regulations 2007 (SI 2007/852 (W.77)), reg.6, which contains the same terminology.

Subsection (2) para.(c)

1–298   WOULD BE LIKELY TO BE. As this provision would require the IMCA to make a substituted judgment on behalf of P, the IMCA should beware of the danger of expressing an opinion which merely reflects his or her views about the matter in question.

Subsection (3)

1–299   Under reg.7 of SI 2006/1832, above, once a decision has been made about P in a matter where an IMCA has been instructed, the IMCA "has the same rights to challenge the decision as he would have if he were a person (other than an IMCA) engaged in caring for P or interested in his welfare" (for Wales, see SI 2007/852 (W.77), reg.7). Paragraph 7.8 of the Explanatory Memorandum states that "it is intended that IMCAs will use existing complaints mechanisms to resolve disputes locally as far as possible, before making use of statutory procedures. In certain cases the IMCA may want to apply to the Court of Protection and he will be able to do this." Challenges can include a challenge to the decision that the person lacks capacity.

Provision of serious medical treatment by NHS body

1–300   **37.**—(1) This section applies if an NHS body—

(a) is proposing to provide, or secure the provision of, serious medical treatment for a person (P) who lacks capacity to consent to the treatment, and

(b) is satisfied that there is no person, other than one engaged in providing care or treatment for P in a professional capacity or for remuneration, whom it would be appropriate to consult in determining what would be in P's best interests.

(2) But this section does not apply if P's treatment is regulated by Part 4 of the Mental Health Act.

(3) Before the treatment is provided, the NHS body must instruct an independent mental capacity advocate to represent P.

(4) If the treatment needs to be provided as a matter of urgency, it may be provided even though the NHS body has not been able to comply with subsection (3).

(5) The NHS body must, in providing or securing the provision of treatment for P, take into account any information given, or submissions made, by the independent mental capacity advocate.

(6) "Serious medical treatment" means treatment which involves providing, withholding or withdrawing treatment of a kind prescribed by regulations made by the appropriate authority.

(7) "NHS body" has such meaning as may be prescribed by regulations made for the purposes of this section by—

(a) the Secretary of State, in relation to bodies in England, or

(b) the National Assembly for Wales, in relation to bodies in Wales.

DEFINITIONS
   "treatment": s.64(1)   **1–301**
   "Mental Health Act": s.64(1)
   "independent mental capacity advocate": s.64(1)

GENERAL NOTE

This section applies where "serious medical treatment" (apart from treatment regulated **1–302** under Pt 4 of the Mental Health Act 1983 (subs.(2)) is to be provided by the NHS for a person who lacks capacity and there is no-one apart from a professional or paid carer for the treatment-provider to consult in determining what would be in P's best interests (subs.(1)). In this situation the treatment-provider must instruct an IMCA to represent P and any information given, or submissions made, by the IMCA must be taken into account when decisions are made about treating P (subs.(3),(5)). Such consultation is not required if the need for the treatment is urgent (subs.(4)). The particular types of treatment that will trigger the involvement of an IMCA have been prescribed by SI 2006/1832 and SI 2007/ 852 (W.77): see subs.(6). A conclusion that "serious medical treatment" might have to be provided to P should alert clinicians to the possible need to seek a declaration from the Court of Protection that the proposed treatment is lawful as it in P's best interests.

Proper records should be taken by the treatment-provider of how the IMCA's representations has been taken into account and, where relevant, the reasons for disagreeing with or ignoring those representations. Where a disagreement arises, every effort must be made to resolve the disagreement at the earliest possible stage, where necessary using the authority's dispute resolution or complaint's procedure. If an unresolved disagreement relates to doubts over P's mental capacity or whether the proposed treatment is in P's best interests, consideration should be given to referring the matter to the court. The IMCA would be advised to contact the Official Solicitor for advice before an application to the court is made. Under reg.7 of SI 2006/1832 once a decision has been made about P in a matter where an IMCA has been instructed, the IMCA "has the same rights to challenge the decision as he would have if he were a person (other than an IMCA) engaged in caring for P or interested in his welfare".

An IMCA can obtain a further medical opinion regarding P's condition (SI 2006/1832, regs.6(4)(d),(5)(d)), and a request for such an opinion can also be made by a deputy or donee if the making of such a request comes within the scope of their authority.

1–303   NHS BODY. See subs.(7). Paragraph 10.9 of the *Code of Practice* states:

"For decisions about serious medical treatment, the responsible body will be the NHS organisation providing the person's healthcare or treatment. But if the person is in an independent or voluntary sector hospital, the responsible body will be the NHS organisation arranging and funding the person's care, which should have arrangements in place with the independent or voluntary sector hospital to ensure that an IMCA is appointed promptly."

Subsection (1) para.(a)
1–304   SECURE THE PROVISION OF. The duty under this section will arise if the NHS is funding P's treatment in the private sector.

PERSON. The obligation to appoint an IMCA applies if P is in prison.

Subsection (1) para.(b)
1–305   APPROPRIATE. It is for the responsible body to decide whether there is anyone, apart from those listed in s.40, who comes within this category. It would not be appropriate to consult with a person who:

(a) has a history of abusing or ill-treating P;
(b) is likely to be the cause of distress to P if P was aware of the consultation;
(c) is not available to be consulted with because his or her whereabouts are unknown;
(d) could only be consulted with if a disproportionate amount of time was used in an attempt to contact that person;
(e) only has very limited knowledge of P;
(f) is unwilling to be a consultee; or
(g) is suffering from a mental disorder which disables him or her from acting as a consultee.

Subsection (2)
1–306   Treatments regulated by Part 4 of the Mental Health Act are excluded because Part 4 provides its own safeguards for patients.

Subsection (3)
1–307   This provision does not apply if a person listed in s.40 is available to be consulted.

Subsection (6)
1–308   By virtue of reg.4 of the Mental Capacity Act 2005 (Independent Mental Capacity Advocates) (General) Regulations 2006 (SI 2006/1832), serious medical treatment "is treatment which involves providing, withdrawing or withholding treatment in circumstances where—

(a) in a case where a single treatment is being proposed, there is a fine balance between its benefits to the patient and the burdens and risks it is likely to entail for him,
(b) in a case where there is a choice of treatments, a decision as to which one to use is finely balanced, or
(c) what is proposed would be likely to involve serious consequences for the patient."

These criteria, which define serious medical treatment by reference to the characteristics of the treatment, allow for a significant amount of discretion to be exercised by the treating clinician. The wording of the criteria is such that electro-convulsive therapy, a treatment that would be regarded as being "serious" by most patients, might not be regarded by the clinician as coming within the terms of reg.4 if the treatment is being provided as a final treatment option in order to preserve life. It is also the case that relatively minor treatments could come within the scope of paras (a) and (b).

The term "likely" in para.(c) suggests a high degree of probability of serious consequences; a mere possibility would not be sufficient. Paragraph 10.44 of the *Code of Practice* states:

"'Serious consequences' are those which could have a serious impact on the patient, either from the effects of the treatment itself or its wider implications. This may include treatments which:

- cause serious and prolonged pain, distress or side effects
- have potentially major consequences for the patient (for example, stopping life-sustaining treatment or having major surgery), or
- have a serious impact on the patient's future life choices (for example, interventions for ovarian cancer)."

A similar definition of serious medical treatment has been established in relation to Wales by the Mental Capacity Act 2005 (Independent Mental Capacity Advocates) (Wales) Regulations 2007 (SI 2007/852 (W.77)), reg.4. The only difference between the two definitions is that the Welsh regulations refer to "a person (P)" rather than to "the patient".

Subsection (7)

For the purposes of this section and s.38, "NHS body" means a body in England which **1–309** is—

(a) a Strategic Health Authority;
(b) an NHS foundation trust;
(c) a Primary Care Trust;
(d) an NHS Trust; or
(e) a Care Trust (SI 2006/1832, reg.3).

In Wales, "NHS body" means—

(a) a Local Health Board;
(b) an NHS trust all or most of whose hospitals, establishments and facilities are situated in Wales;
(c) a Special Health Authority performing functions only or mainly in respect of Wales (SI 2007/852 (W.77), reg.3).

Provision of accommodation by NHS body

38.—(1) This section applies if an NHS body proposes to make **1–310** arrangements—

(a) for the provision of accommodation in a hospital or care home for a person (P) who lacks capacity to agree to the arrangements, or
(b) for a change in P's accommodation to another hospital or care home,

and is satisfied that there is no person, other than one engaged in providing care or treatment for P in a professional capacity or for remuneration, whom it would be appropriate for it to consult in determining what would be in P's best interests.

(2) But this section does not apply if P is accommodated as a result of an obligation imposed on him under the Mental Health Act.

[(2A) And this section does not apply if—

(a) an independent mental capacity advocate must be appointed under section 39A or 39C (whether or not by the NHS body) to represent P, and
(b) the hospital or care home in which P is to be accommodated under the arrangements referred to in this section is the relevant hospital or care home under the authorisation referred to in that section.]

(3) Before making the arrangements, the NHS body must instruct an independent mental capacity advocate to represent P unless it is satisfied that—

(a) the accommodation is likely to be provided for a continuous period which is less than the applicable period, or

(b) the arrangements need to be made as a matter of urgency.

(4) If the NHS body—

(a) did not instruct an independent mental capacity advocate to represent P before making the arrangements because it was satisfied that subsection (3)(a) or (b) applied, but

(b) subsequently has reason to believe that the accommodation is likely to be provided for a continuous period—

(i) beginning with the day on which accommodation was first provided in accordance with the arrangements, and

(ii) ending on or after the expiry of the applicable period,

it must instruct an independent mental capacity advocate to represent P.

(5) The NHS body must, in deciding what arrangements to make for P, take into account any information given, or submissions made, by the independent mental capacity advocate.

(6) "Care home" has the meaning given in section 3 of the Care Standards Act 2000 (c.14).

(7) "Hospital" means—

(a) a health service hospital as defined by [section 275 of the National Health Service Act 2006 or section 206 of the National Health Service (Wales) Act 2006], or

(b) an independent hospital as defined by section 2 of the Care Standards Act 2000.

(8) "NHS body" has such meaning as may be prescribed by regulations made for the purposes of this section by—

(a) the Secretary of State, in relation to bodies in England, or

(b) the National Assembly for Wales, in relation to bodies in Wales.

(9) "Applicable period" means—

(a) in relation to accommodation in a hospital, 28 days, and

(b) in relation to accommodation in a care home, 8 weeks.

[(10) For the purposes of subsection (1), a person appointed under Part 10 of Schedule A1 to be P's representative is not, by virtue of that appointment, engaged in providing care or treatment for P in a professional capacity or for remuneration.]

AMENDMENT

1–311   Subss.(2A) and (10) were inserted by the Mental Health Act 2007, s.50(7), Sch.9, Pt.1, para.4.

In subs.(7)(a), the words in square brackets were substituted by the National Health Service (Consequential Provisions) Act 2006, s.2, Sch.1, para.278.

DEFINITIONS

1–312   "Mental Health Act": s.64(1)

"independent mental capacity act advocate": s.64(1)

GENERAL NOTE

1–313   This section applies if a NHS body intends to arrange for P to be accommodated in a hospital (either NHS or private) or a care home for a period likely to exceed 28 days (for a hospital) or eight weeks (for a care home), or for P to be moved between such accommodation, and there is no-one apart from a professional or paid carer for the NHS body to consult in determining what would be in P's best interests (subss.(1) and (9)). In this situation the NHS body must instruct an IMCA to represent P and must take into account any information given, or submissions made, by the IMCA when a decision is made about what arrangements to make for P (subss.(3) and (5)). Such consultation need not take place if the P is likely to stay in the accommodation for less than the applicable period or if the need for the move is urgent, for example, where P requires an emergency hospital admission, or where a care home place will be lost if P is not moved immediately (subs.(3)). However, the consultation must take place after the arrangements have been made if the NHS body subsequently believes that P will be accommodated at the hospital or care home for the applicable period (subs.(4)). This section does not apply if an IMCA has to be appointed under s.39A or 39C (subs.2A). It will also not apply if P is accommodated in the hospital or the care home as a result of an obligation imposed on him or her under the Mental Health Act 1983 (subs.(2)), as that Act contains its own safeguards. It will apply to decisions about providing accommodation for P if P is about to be discharged from detention under the 1983 Act.

Where an NHS body has made arrangements as to P's accommodation under this section and it is then proposed to review those arrangements, an IMCA may (not must) be instructed to represent P at the review: see the Mental Capacity Act 2005 (Independent Mental Capacity Advocates) (Expansion of Role) Regulations 2006 (SI 2006/2883), reg.3. The equivalent provision for Wales is the Mental Capacity Act 2005 (Independent Mental Capacity Advocates) (Wales) Regulations 2007 (SI 2007/852 (W.77)), reg.8.

Proper records should be taken by the responsible authority of how the IMCA's representations have been taken into account and, where relevant, the reasons for disagreeing with or ignoring the representations. Where a disagreement arises, every effort must be made to resolve the disagreement at the earliest possible stage, where necessary using the authority's dispute resolution or complaint's procedure. If the IMCA continues to believe that either the proposed or present placement is not in the best interests of P, he or she could seek advice from a solicitor to ascertain whether the decision could be subject to a legal challenge. Under reg.7 of the Mental Capacity Act 2005 (Independent Mental Capacity Advocates) (General) Regulations 2005 (SI 2006/1832), once a decision has been made about P in a matter where an IMCA has been instructed, the IMCA "has the same rights to challenge the decision as he would have if he were a person (other than an IMCA) engaged in caring for P or interested in his welfare". Challenges can include the decision that the person lacks capacity. For Wales, see SI 2007/852 (W.77), reg.7.

Subsection (1)

NHS BODY. See subs.(8). Paragraphs 10.10 to 10.12 of the *Code of Practice* state: **1–314**

"For decisions about admission to accommodation in hospital for 28 days or more, the responsible body will be the NHS body that manages the hospital. For admission to an independent or voluntary sector hospital for 28 days or more, the responsible body will be the NHS organisation arranging and funding the person's care. The independent or voluntary hospital must have arrangements in place with the NHS organisation to ensure that an IMCA can be appointed without delay.

For decisions about moves into long term accommodation (for eight weeks or longer), or about a change of accommodation, the responsible body will be either:

- the NHS body that proposes the move or change of accommodation (e.g. a nursing home), or
- the local authority that has carried out an assessment of the person under the NHS and Community Care Act 1990 and decided the move may be necessary.

Sometimes NHS organisations and local authorities will make decisions together about moving a person into long-term care. In these cases, the organisation that must instruct the IMCA is the one that is ultimately responsible for the decision to move the person. The IMCA to be instructed is the one who works wherever the person is at the time that the person needs support and representation."

HOSPITAL. See subs.(7).

CARE HOME. See subs.(6).

PROFESSIONAL CAPACITY OR FOR REMUNERATION. See subs.(10).

APPROPRIATE. See the note to s.37(1)(b).

Subsection (2)

1–315   OBLIGATION IMPOSED ON HIM UNDER THE MENTAL HEALTH ACT. Such as a condition imposed by a Mental Health Review Tribunal under s.73 of the Act requiring the patient to reside at a particular place, a similar requirement imposed by the patient's guardian under s.8 of the Act, or a condition attached to the patient's leave of absence granted under s.17 of the Act requiring him to reside at a particular address. Such placements are excluded because the Mental Health Act provides its own safeguards for patients.

Subsections (3), (4)

1–316   These provisions do not apply if a person listed in s.40 is available to be consulted.

APPLICABLE PERIOD. See subs.(9).

Subsection (4)

1–317   BEGINNING WITH. Including the day on which the accommodation was first provided (*Zoan v Rouamba* [2000] 2 All E.R. 620, CA).

Subsection (8)

1–318   See the note on s.37(7).

Provision of accommodation by local authority

1–319   **39.**—(1) This section applies if a local authority propose to make arrangements—

(a) for the provision of residential accommodation for a person (P) who lacks capacity to agree to the arrangements, or

(b) for a change in P's residential accommodation,

and are satisfied that there is no person, other than one engaged in providing care or treatment for P in a professional capacity or for remuneration, whom it would be appropriate for them to consult in determining what would be in P's best interests.

(2) But this section applies only if the accommodation is to be provided in accordance with—

(a) section 21 or 29 of the National Assistance Act 1948 (c. 29), or

(b) section 117 of the Mental Health Act,

as the result of a decision taken by the local authority under section 47 of the National Health Service and Community Care Act 1990 (c.19).

(3) This section does not apply if P is accommodated as a result of an obligation imposed on him under the Mental Health Act.

[(3A) And this section does not apply if—

(a) an independent mental capacity advocate must be appointed under section 39A or 39C (whether or not by the local authority) to represent P, and

(b) the place in which P is to be accommodated under the arrangements referred to in this section is the relevant hospital or care home under the authorisation referred to in that section.]

(4) Before making the arrangements, the local authority must instruct an independent mental capacity advocate to represent P unless they are satisfied that—

(a) the accommodation is likely to be provided for a continuous period of less than 8 weeks, or

(b) the arrangements need to be made as a matter of urgency.

(5) If the local authority—

(a) did not instruct an independent mental capacity advocate to represent P before making the arrangements because they were satisfied that subsection (4)(a) or (b) applied, but

(b) subsequently have reason to believe that the accommodation is likely to be provided for a continuous period that will end 8 weeks or more after the day on which accommodation was first provided in accordance with the arrangements,

they must instruct an independent mental capacity advocate to represent P.

(6) The local authority must, in deciding what arrangements to make for P, take into account any information given, or submissions made, by the independent mental capacity advocate.

[(7) For the purposes of subsection (1), a person appointed under Part 10 of Schedule A1 to be P's representative is not, by virtue of that appointment, engaged in providing care or treatment for P in a professional capacity or for remuneration.]

AMENDMENTS

Subss.(3A) and (7) were inserted by the Mental Health Act 2007, s.50(7), Sch.9, Pt.1, **1–320** para.5.

DEFINITIONS

"local authority": s.64(1)   **1–321**
"treatment": s.64(1)
"Mental Health Act": s.64(1)
"independent mental capacity act advocate": s.64(1)

GENERAL NOTE

This section applies if a local authority intends to arrange for P to be provided with long- **1–322** stay residential accommodation provided under s.21 of the National Assistance Act 1948 (c.29) or s.117 of the Mental Health Act 1983 (c.20), or for the accommodation to be changed, and there is no-one apart from a professional or paid carer for the authority to consult in determining what would be in P's best interests (subss.(1) and (2)). In this situation the authority must instruct an IMCA to represent P and any information given, or submissions made, by the IMCA must be taken into account when a decision is made about what arrangements to make for P (subss.(4) and (6)). Such consultation need not take place if the P is likely to stay in the accommodation for less than eight weeks or if the need for the accommodation is urgent (subs.(4)). However, the consultation must take place after the placement has been effected if the authority subsequently believes that the accommodation will be provided for P for at least eight weeks (subs.(5)). This section does not apply if an

IMCA has to be appointed under s.39A or 39C or if the accommodation is provided as a result of an obligation imposed on P under the 1983 Act (subs.(3)).

Where a local authority has made arrangements as to P's accommodation under this section and it is then proposed to review those arrangements, an IMCA may (not must) be instructed to represent P at the review: see the Mental Capacity Act 2005 (Independent Mental Capacity Advocates) (Expansion of Role) Regulations 2006 (SI 2006/2883), reg.3. The equivalent provision for Wales is the Mental Capacity Act 2005 (Independent Mental Capacity Advocates) (Wales) Regulations 2007 (SI 2007/852 (W.77)), reg.8.

Proper records should be taken by the responsible authority of how the IMCA's submissions have been taken into account and, where relevant, the reasons for disagreeing with or ignoring the submissions. Where a disagreement arises, every effort must be made to resolve the disagreement at the earliest possible stage, where necessary using the authority's dispute resolution or complaint's procedure. If the IMCA continue to believe that the proposed placement is not in the best interests of P, he or she could seek advice from a solicitor to ascertain whether the decision could be subject to a legal challenge. Under reg.7 of the Mental Capacity Act 2005 (Independent Mental Capacity Advocates) (General) Regulations 2005 (SI 2006/1832), once a decision has been made about P in a matter where an IMCA has been instructed, the IMCA "has the same rights to challenge the decision as he would have if he were a person (other than an IMCA) engaged in caring for P or interested in his welfare". Challenges can include the decision that the person lacks capacity. For Wales, see SI 2007/852 (W.77), reg.7.

Subsection (1)

1–323   Local authority. See the note on "NHS body" in s.37(1).

Professional capacity or for remuneration. See subs.(7).

Appropriate. See the note to s.37(1)(b).

Subsection (2)

1–324   A local authority may itself provide accommodation under s.21 or it can make arrangements under s.29 of the 1948 Act for the accommodation to be provided by a third party. In *R. (on the application of Batantu) v Islington LBC* (2001) 4 C.C.L. Rep. 445, Henriques J. said that the meaning of accommodation under the 1948 Act is wide and flexible and embraces care homes, ordinary and sheltered housing, housing association and other registered social housing, and private sector housing which may have been purchased by the local authority. It would also include hostel accommodation. When making a placement decision under s.21, a local authority in England must comply with the National Assistance Act (Choice of Accommodation) Directions 1992 (reproduced at para.D4–001 of the *Encyclopedia of Social Services and Child Care Law*) which require the authority to provide the prospective resident with their preferred accommodation if certain conditions are satisfied. If prospective residents lack the mental capacity to express a preference for themselves, it "would be reasonable to expect councils to act on the preferences expressed by their advocate, carer or legal guardian in the same way that they would on the resident's own wishes, unless that would in the council's opinion be against the best interests of the resident" (Department of Health Circular LAC (2004) 20 *Guidance* para.5.1). An IMCA should be treated as an "advocate" for the purposes of this guidance.

Section 117 of the 1983 Act places a duty on the relevant NHS Trust and local authority to provide after-care services to patients who have been discharged from non-emergency detention under that Act. The after-care services can include accommodation that is required to meet the mental health needs of P. Accommodation provided under s.117 must be provided free of charge (*R. v Manchester City Council Ex p. Stennett* [2002] UKHL 34; [2002] 4 All E.R. 124).

Section 47 of the 1990 Act places a duty on local social services authorities to assess the care needs of any person who appears to be in need of community care services and decide in the light of the assessment whether services should be provided to that person.

Subsection (3)
See the note on s.38(2). 1–325

Subsections (4), (5)
These provisions do not apply if a person listed in s.40 is available to be consulted. 1–326

[Person becomes subject to Schedule A1
39A.—(1) This section applies if— 1–327
(a) a person ("P") becomes subject to Schedule A1, and
(b) the managing authority of the relevant hospital or care home are satisfied that there is no person, other than one engaged in providing care or treatment for P in a professional capacity
or for remuneration, whom it would be appropriate to consult in determining what would be in P's best interests.
(2) The managing authority must notify the supervisory body that this section applies.
(3) The supervisory body must instruct an independent mental capacity advocate to represent P.
(4) Schedule A1 makes provision about the role of an independent mental capacity advocate appointed under this section.
(5) This section is subject to paragraph 161 of Schedule A1.
(6) For the purposes of subsection (1), a person appointed under Part 10 of Schedule A1 to be P's representative is not, by virtue of that appointment, engaged in providing care or treatment for P in a professional capacity or for remuneration.]

AMENDMENT
This section was inserted by the Mental Health Act 2007, s.50(7), Sch.9, Pt.1, para.6. 1–328

DEFINITIONS
"independent mental capacity advocate": s.64(1). 1–329
"treatment": s.64(1).

GENERAL NOTE
This section requires a supervisory body to appoint an IMCA for P if the managing auth- 1–330
ority has notified it that: (1) P is "subject to Sch.A1"; and (2) there is no appropriate person (other than one engaged in providing care or treatment for P in a professional capacity or for remuneration) to consult in determining P's best interests. The circumstances in which P becomes subject to Sch.A1 are set out in s.39B.
The general functions of an IMCA are set out in s.36 and SI 2006/1832. An IMCA who has been appointed under this section is given additional functions in paras 57, 58, 69(7)–(8), 82, 86, 90, 132, 135, 136, 161 of Sch.A1.
The duty to appoint an IMCA under this section does apply in the circumstances set out in s.40.

[Section 39A: supplementary provision
39B.—(1) This section applies for the purposes of section 39A. 1–331
(2) P becomes subject to Schedule A1 in any of the following cases.

(3) The first case is where an urgent authorisation is given in relation to P under paragraph 76(2) of Schedule A1 (urgent authorisation given before request made for standard authorisation).

(4) The second case is where the following conditions are met.

(5) The first condition is that a request is made under Schedule A1 for a standard authorisation to be given in relation to P ("the requested authorisation").

(6) The second condition is that no urgent authorisation was given under paragraph 76(2) of Schedule A1 before that request was made.

(7) The third condition is that the requested authorisation will not be in force on or before, or immediately after, the expiry of an existing standard authorisation.

(8) The expiry of a standard authorisation is the date when the authorisation is expected to cease to be in force.

(9) The third case is where, under paragraph 69 of Schedule A1, the supervisory body select a person to carry out an assessment of whether or not the relevant person is a detained resident.]

AMENDMENT

1–332 This section was inserted by the Mental Health Act 2007, s.50(7), Sch.9, Pt.1, para.6.

GENERAL NOTE

1–333 This section identifies the three circumstances that determine when P becomes "subject to Schedule A1" for the purposes of s.39A. An account of the Sch.A1 procedure can be found in Pt 2.

[Person unrepresented whilst subject to Schedule A1

1–334   **39C.**—(1) This section applies if—

  (a) an authorisation under Schedule A1 is in force in relation to a person ("P"),

  (b) the appointment of a person as P's representative ends in accordance with regulations made under Part 10 of Schedule A1, and

  (c) the managing authority of the relevant hospital or care home are satisfied that there is no person, other than one engaged in providing care or treatment for P in a professional capacity

or for remuneration, whom it would be appropriate to consult in determining what would be in P's best interests.

(2) The managing authority must notify the supervisory body that this section applies.

(3) The supervisory body must instruct an independent mental capacity advocate to represent P.

(4) Paragraph 159 of Schedule A1 makes provision about the role of an independent mental capacity advocate appointed under this section.

(5) The appointment of an independent mental capacity advocate under this section ends when a new appointment of a person as P's representative is made in accordance with Part 10 of Schedule A1.

(6) For the purposes of subsection (1), a person appointed under Part 10 of Schedule A1 to be P's representative is not, by virtue of that appointment, engaged in providing care or treatment for P in a professional capacity or for remuneration.]

AMENDMENT

1–335 This section was inserted by the Mental Health Act 2007, s.50(7), Sch.9, Pt.1, para.6.

"independent mental capacity advocate": s.64(1). **1–336**

This section requires a supervisory body to appoint an IMCA for P if a managing auth- **1–337** ority has notified it that: (1) P is subject to Sch.A1; (2) the appointment of P's Part 10 representative ends; and (3) there is no appropriate person (other than one engaged in providing care or treatment for P in a professional capacity or for remuneration) to consult in determining P's best interests.

The circumstances in which P becomes subject to Sch.A1 are set out in s.39B. However, an IMCA will only be appointed under this section when a standard authorisation is in place because a Part 10 representative is only appointed following such an authorisation (Sch.1, para.139). The appointment will come to an end once a new Part 10 representative has been appointed.

The general functions of an IMCA are set out in s.36 and SI 2006/1832. An IMCA who has been appointed under this section will also perform the functions of the Part 10 representative under a new one is appointed (Sch.A1, para.159(2)).

The duty to appoint an IMCA under this section does apply in the circumstances set out in s.40.

[Person subject to Schedule A1 without paid representative

39D.—(1) This section applies if— **1–338**
  (a) an authorisation under Schedule A1 is in force in relation to a person ("P"),
  (b) P has a representative ("R") appointed under Part 10 of Schedule A1, and
  (c) R is not being paid under regulations under Part 10 of Schedule A1 for acting as P's representative.

  (2) The supervisory body must instruct an independent mental capacity advocate to represent P in any of the following cases.

  (3) The first case is where P makes a request to the supervisory body to instruct an advocate.

  (4) The second case is where R makes a request to the supervisory body to instruct an advocate.

  (5) The third case is where the supervisory body have reason to believe one or more of the following—
  (a) that, without the help of an advocate, P and R would be unable to exercise one or both of the relevant rights;
  (b) that P and R have each failed to exercise a relevant right when it would have been reasonable to exercise it;
  (c) that P and R are each unlikely to exercise a relevant right when it would be reasonable to exercise it.

  (6) The duty in subsection (2) is subject to section 39E.

  (7) If an advocate is appointed under this section, the advocate is, in particular, to take such steps as are practicable to help P and R to understand the following matters—
  (a) the effect of the authorisation;
  (b) the purpose of the authorisation;
  (c) the duration of the authorisation;
  (d) any conditions to which the authorisation is subject;
  (e) the reasons why each assessor who carried out an assessment in connection with the request for the authorisation, or in connection with a review of the authorisation, decided that P met the qualifying requirement in question;

(f) the relevant rights;

(g) how to exercise the relevant rights.

(8) The advocate is, in particular, to take such steps as are practicable to help P or R—

(a) to exercise the right to apply to court, if it appears to the advocate that P or R wishes to exercise that right, or

(b) to exercise the right of review, if it appears to the advocate that P or R wishes to exercise that right.

(9) If the advocate helps P or R to exercise the right of review—

(a) the advocate may make submissions to the supervisory body on the question of whether a qualifying requirement is reviewable;

(b) the advocate may give information, or make submissions, to any assessor carrying out a review assessment.

(10) In this section—

"relevant rights" means—

(a) the right to apply to court, and

(b) the right of review;

"right to apply to court" means the right to make an application to the court to exercise its jurisdiction under section 21A;

"right of review" means the right under Part 8 of Schedule A1 to request a review.]

AMENDMENT

1–339   This section was inserted by the Mental Health Act 2007, s.50(7), Sch.9, Pt.1, para.6.

DEFINITION

1–340   "independent mental capacity advocate": s.64(1).

GENERAL NOTE

1–341   Where an authorisation under Sch.A1 is in force in relation to P and P has a Part 10 representative (R) who is not being paid for acting as such, the supervisory body must instruct an IMCA to act for P if:

(i) either P or R make a request to the supervisory body to instruct an IMCA; or

(ii) the supervisory body have reason to believe that without the help of an advocate, P and R would be unable to exercise one or both of the relevant rights as defined in subs.(10), or have failed to exercise a relevant right (see subs.(10)) when it would have been reasonable to exercise it, or would be unlikely to exercise a relevant right when it would be reasonable to exercise it.

If a supervisory body has already appointed an IMCA under this provision at the request of R or because they had reason to believe one or more of the things in s.39D(5), they must appoint a further advocate if P requests it (s.39E).

Apart from the general functions of the IMCA set out in s.36 and SI 2006/1832, an IMCA appointed under this section has the additional functions set out in subss.(7) to (9) and in Sch.A1, paras 49, 95.

The duty to appoint an IMCA under this section does apply in the circumstances set out in s.40.

[Limitation on duty to instruct advocate under section 39D

1–342   **39E.**—(1) This section applies if an advocate is already representing P in accordance with an instruction under section 39D.

(2) Section 39D(2) does not require another advocate to be instructed, unless the following conditions are met.

(3) The first condition is that the existing advocate was instructed—

(a) because of a request by R, or

(b) because the supervisory body had reason to believe one or more of the things in section 39D(5).

(4) The second condition is that the other advocate would be instructed because of a request by P.]

AMENDMENT

This section was inserted by the Mental Health Act 2007, s.50(7), Sch.9, Pt.1, para.6. **1–343**

GENERAL NOTE

See the General Note to s.39D. **1–344**

[Exceptions

40.—[(1)] The duty imposed by section 37(3), 38(3) or (4) [, 39(4) or (5), **1–345**
39A(3), 39C(3) or 39D(2)] does not apply where there is—

(a) a person nominated by P (in whatever manner) as a person to be consulted on matters to which that duty relates,

(b) a donee of a lasting power of attorney created by P who is authorised to make decisions in relation to those matters, or

(c) a deputy appointed by the court for P with power to make decisions in relation to those matters.]

[(2) A person appointed under Part 10 of Schedule A1 to be P's representative is not, by virtue of that appointment, a person nominated by P as a person to be consulted in matters to which a duty mentioned in subsection (1) relates.]

AMENDMENT

This section was substituted by the Mental Health Act 2007, s.49. The amendments to it were made by s.50(7), Sch.9, Pt.1, para.7 of that Act.

DEFINITIONS

"lasting power of attorney": s.64(1) **1–346**
"deputy": s.64(1)

GENERAL NOTE

This section confirms that the independent mental advocacy scheme does not apply **1–347**
where there is a suitable person who can be consulted about P's best interests. An IMCA would have to be appointed if the person had not been either nominated or authorised to be consulted about, or to make decisions in relation to, the relevant matter.

Paragraph (a)

The nomination may be written or oral. The decision-maker must be satisfied that the **1–348**
nomination was made when P was mentally capable and that the nominee is willing to be consulted.

Power to adjust role of independent mental capacity advocate

41.—(1) The appropriate authority may make regulations— **1–349**

(a) expanding the role of independent mental capacity advocates in relation to persons who lack capacity, and

(b) adjusting the obligation to make arrangements imposed by section 35.

(2) The regulations may, in particular—

(a) prescribe circumstances (different to those set out in sections 37, 38 and 39) in which an independent mental capacity advocate must, or circumstances in which one may, be instructed by a person of a prescribed description to represent a person who lacks capacity, and

(b) include provision similar to any made by section 37, 38, 39 or 40.

(3) "Appropriate authority" has the same meaning as in section 35.

DEFINITIONS

1–350 "independent mental capacity advocate": s.64(1)

GENERAL NOTE

1–351 This section provides that scope of the independent mental advocacy scheme can be extended by regulations made by the Secretary of State or the Welsh Ministers. The Mental Capacity Act 2005 (Independent Mental Capacity Advocates) (Expansion of Role) Regulations 2006 (SI 2006/2883), which are reproduced in Part 3, have been made under this section. The equivalent provision for Wales is the Mental Capacity Act 2005 (Independent Mental Capacity Advocates) (Wales) Regulations 2007 (SI 2007/852 (W.77)), regs 8 and 9. These regulations do not prevent an NHS body or local authority from instructing an IMCA in other circumstances. However, the regulations only provide authority for the Secretary of State to make arrangements (i.e. provide funding) for IMCAs to be available in the circumstances set out in the regulations.

The Mental Capacity Act 2005 (Independent Mental Capacity Advocates (General) Regulations 2006 (SI 2006/1832), which are considered in the notes to s.37, apply where an IMCA has been instructed under regulations made by virtue of this section (*ibid.*, reg.2(2)).

Subsection (1)

1–352 REGULATIONS. Regulations made under this power are subject to the affirmative resolution procedure (s.65(4)).

Subsection (2) para. (a)

1–353 MUST, OR . . . MAY. This phrase was substituted for "must" at the report stage in the House of Lords "for two reasons. First, concerns have been expressed about extending the [scheme] compulsorily to situations where there are family members. We agree that that it is not necessarily desirable or helpful. It is fair to say that family carers are at the heart of decision-making in many circumstances. We would not wish to get in the middle of that relationship, particularly when we know what a critical and crucial role family members play in supporting their loved ones. We will ensure that the *Code of Practice* refers to the central role at the heart that unpaid carers play, and makes it clear that they will often be the best people to speak up for the person lacking capacity. In addition, we believe that where people have successful, loving and supportive relationships, the obligatory use of an independent mental advocacy scheme would neither be helpful, nor an effective use of resources, frankly. Also, we want to ensure the maximum flexibility to enable us to accommodate all possible outcomes of the consultation on extending the service. Following the consultation, consensus may or may not favour the use of a discretionary power. By tabling the amendment, we are simply allowing for that possibility", *per* the Parliamentary Under-Secretary of State (*Hansard*, HL Vol.670, col.1528).

Miscellaneous and supplementary

Codes of practice
42.—(1) The Lord Chancellor must prepare and issue one or more codes of **1–354**
practice—
- (a) for the guidance of persons assessing whether a person has capacity in relation to any matter,
- (b) for the guidance of persons acting in connection with the care or treatment of another person (see section 5),
- (c) for the guidance of donees of lasting powers of attorney,
- (d) for the guidance of deputies appointed by the court,
- (e) for the guidance of persons carrying out research in reliance on any pro-vision made by or under this Act (and otherwise with respect to sections 30 to 34),
- (f) for the guidance of independent mental capacity advocates,
- [(fa) for the guidance of persons exercising functions under Schedule A1,
- (fb) for the guidance of representatives appointed under Part 10 of Schedule A1,]
- (g) with respect to the provisions of sections 24 to 26 (advance decisions and apparent advance decisions), and
- (h) with respect to such other matters concerned with this Act as he thinks fit.
  (2) The Lord Chancellor may from time to time revise a code.
  (3) The Lord Chancellor may delegate the preparation or revision of the whole or any part of a code so far as he considers expedient.
  (4) It is the duty of a person to have regard to any relevant code if he is acting in relation to a person who lacks capacity and is doing so in one or more of the fol-lowing ways—
- (a) as the donee of a lasting power of attorney,
- (b) as a deputy appointed by the court,
- (c) as a person carrying out research in reliance on any provision made by or under this Act (see sections 30 to 34),
- (d) as an independent mental capacity advocate,
- [(da) in the exercise of functions under Schedule A1,
- (db) as a representative appointed under Part 10 of Schedule A1,]
- (e) in a professional capacity,
- (f) for remuneration.
  (5) If it appears to a court or tribunal conducting any criminal or civil proceed-ings that—
- (a) a provision of a code, or
- (b) a failure to comply with a code,
is relevant to a question arising in the proceedings, the provision or failure must be taken into account in deciding the question.
  (6) A code under subsection (1)(d) may contain separate guidance for deputies appointed by virtue of paragraph 1(2) of Schedule 5(functions of deputy conferred on receiver appointed under the Mental Health Act).
  (7) In this section and in section 43, "code" means a code prepared or revised under this section.

AMENDMENTS
1–355   The words in square brackets in subss.(1) and (4) were inserted by the Mental Health Act 2007, s.50(7), Sch.9, Pt.1, para.8.

DEFINITIONS
1–356   "treatment": s.64(1)
"lasting power of attorney": s.64(1)
"deputy": s.64(1)
"the court": s.64(1)
"independent mental capacity advocate": s.64(1)
"advance decision": s.64(1)
"Mental Health Act": s.64(1)

GENERAL NOTE
1–357   This section requires the Lord Chancellor to publish a *Code of Practice* (or *Codes of Practice*) to address the issues set out in subs.(1). The Code can be revised (subs.(2)). These responsibilities may be delegated (subs.(3)). The Code sets out how the legal rules contained in this Act and the associated regulations will work in practice. Donees, deputies, professionals, researchers, independent mental capacity advocates and paid workers acting on behalf of a person who lacks capacity must have regard to the Code (subs.(4)) The Code can be used as evidence in court or tribunal proceedings and, if relevant, will be taken into account in the determination (subs.(5)). However, no legal liability arises from a breach of the Code itself.

A *Code of Practice* was laid before Parliament in draft in February 2007, pursuant to this section and s.43 and was approved in April 2007. The Introduction to the Code states at p.1:

"The Act does not impose a legal duty on anyone to 'comply' with the Code – it should be viewed as guidance rather than instruction. But if they have not followed relevant guidance contained in the Code then they will be expected to give good reasons why they have departed from it."

The *Code of Practice* can be accessed at the Department of Health's website (see Annex A). A supplement to the Code, dealing with the deprivation of liberty safeguards, was published in July 2008 and is reproduced in Part 5.

Subsection (1)
1–358   GUIDANCE. In *R. v Secretary of State for the Environment Ex p. Lancashire* CC [1994] 4 All E.R. 165, 173, Jowitt J. said:

"The concept of guidance goes beyond simply providing a checklist of factors which should be taken into account. To guide someone is to lead, steer or point someone in a particular direction."

Subsection (1) para. (b)
1–359   Note the scope of this category, which includes informal and family carers. Such carers are not placed under an obligation to "have regard" to the Code (subs.(4)). The position of informal and family carers was examined by the Joint Committee:

"The position is different with regard to guidance issued to assist non-professional or informal decision makers, such as family members and unpaid carers acting under [s.5]. It is essential that family members and carers carrying out such responsibilities are provided with appropriate guidance and assistance, both to promote good practice and also to impress upon them the seriousness of their actions and the need to be accountable for them. We accept that it would be inappropriate to impose on them a strict requirement to act in accordance with the Code of Practice" (Vol.1, para.232).

While such an approach is understandable, this Act places unrealistic expectations on lay carers in that it does not recognise any distinction between lay and professional carers when it comes to adherence to the principles set out in s.1, the requirement to assess capacity under ss.2 and 3, and the determination of best interests under s.4. The Introduction to the Code states that lay carers "should follow the guidance in the Code as far as they are aware of it" (p.2).

Subsection (1) para.(c)

Although an attorney acting under an Enduring Power of Attorney is not placed under an obligation to have regard to the Code, he or she should use it as guidance. **1–360**

Subsection (2)

The Code will "be revised fairly frequently", *per* the Parliamentary Under-Secretary of State (*Hansard*, HL Vol.669, col.758). **1–361**

Subsection (4)

HAVE REGARD TO. The Introduction to the Code states at p.2: **1–362**

"Certain categories of people are legally required to 'have regard to' relevant guidance in the Code of Practice. That means they must be aware of the Code of Practice when acting or making decisions on behalf of someone who lacks capacity to make a decision for themselves, and they should be able to explain how they had regard to the Code when acting or making decisions."

In *R. (on the application of Munjaz) v Mersey Care National Health Service Trust* [2005] UKHL 58; [2006] 4 All E.R. 736, the House of Lords considered the legal status of the *Code of Practice* issued pursuant to s.118 of the Mental Health Act 1983. Although there are differences in the wording of s.118 and this section, the decision in *Munjaz* can be regarded as a clear indication of the approach that a court might adopt when interpreting the status of the Code issued under this Act. In *Munjaz* it was contended that the policy of Ashworth Hospital relating to the seclusion of patients was unlawful because it provided for less frequent medical reviews, particularly after the first week of seclusion, than that laid down in the Mental Health Act *Code of Practice*. Ashworth had also adopted a definition of seclusion that differed from that set out in the Code. It was held that:

1. The Code does not have the binding effect which a statutory provision or a statutory instrument would have. It is what it purports to be, guidance and not instruction.
2. The guidance in the Code should be given great weight. Although it is not instruction, the Code is much more than mere advice which an addressee is free to follow or not as it chooses.
3. The Code contains guidance which should be considered with great care, and should be followed unless there are cogent reasons for not doing so. The requirement that cogent reasons must be shown for any departure sets a high standard which is not easily satisfied. The reasons must be spelled out clearly, logically and convincingly.
4. In reviewing any departures from the Code, the court should scrutinise the reasons given for departure with the intensity which the importance and sensitivity of the subject matters requires.
5. For the purpose of determining whether Ashworth's policy was compatible with the European Convention on Human Rights, the Code is irrelevant: if the policy is incompatible, consistency with the Code will not save it; if it is compatible, it requires no support from the Code.

The following circumstances could provide cogent reasons for not following the guidance contained in the Code issued under this section:

1. The best interests of P (or a group of persons who share particular well-defined characteristics) would not be satisfied if the guidance was followed.

    2. There has been a determination of the High Court that a particular aspect of the guidance is not legally accurate.

    3. Legal advice has been received which casts a significant doubt on the legal correctness of an aspect of the guidance.

    4. Following the guidance would involve breaching P's Convention rights.

    5. A judgment is taken that a particular aspect of the guidance should not be followed for safety or other legitimate reason.

If a person fails to comply with the guidance contained in the Code, he or she must be prepared to give reasons to explain the non-compliance. It would be sensible for a contemporaneous record of such reasons to be made.

Subsection (4) para.(f)

1–363   For remuneration. For example, a care assistant who works in a care home where the residents lack capacity.

Codes of practice: procedure

1–364   **43.**—(1) Before preparing or revising a code, the Lord Chancellor must consult—

    (a) the National Assembly for Wales, and

    (b) such other persons as he considers appropriate.

    (2) The Lord Chancellor may not issue a code unless—

    (a) a draft of the code has been laid by him before both Houses of Parliament, and

    (b) the 40 day period has elapsed without either House resolving not to approve the draft.

    (3) The Lord Chancellor must arrange for any code that he has issued to be published in such a way as he considers appropriate for bringing it to the attention of persons likely to be concerned with its provisions.

    (4) "40 day period", in relation to the draft of a proposed code, means—

    (a) if the draft is laid before one House on a day later than the day on which it is laid before the other House, the period of 40 days beginning with the later of the two days;

    (b) in any other case, the period of 40 days beginning with the day on which it is laid before each House.

    (5) In calculating the period of 40 days, no account is to be taken of any period during which Parliament is dissolved or prorogued or during which both Houses are adjourned for more than 4 days.

GENERAL NOTE

1–365   This section sets out the procedure for issuing and revising the *Code of Practice* and requires the Lord Chancellor to publish the Code in an appropriate format.

Subsection (1)(a)

1–366   The functions of the National Assembly for Wales are performed by the Welsh Ministers (Government of Wales Act 2006, s.162, Sch.11, para.30).

Subsection (2)

1–367   This procedure is known as the "negative resolution" procedure.

Ill-treatment or neglect

1–368   **44.**—(1) Subsection (2) applies if a person (D)—

(a) has the care of a person (P) who lacks, or whom D reasonably believes to lack, capacity,

(b) is the donee of a lasting power of attorney, or an enduring power of attorney (within the meaning of Schedule 4), created by P, or

(c) is a deputy appointed by the court for P.

(2) D is guilty of an offence if he ill-treats or wilfully neglects P.

(3) A person guilty of an offence under this section is liable—

(a) on summary conviction, to imprisonment for a term not exceeding 12 months or a fine not exceeding the statutory maximum or both;

(b) on conviction on indictment, to imprisonment for a term not exceeding 5 years or a fine or both.

DEFINITIONS

"lasting power of attorney": s.64(1) **1–369**

"deputy": s.64(1)

"the court": s.64(1)

GENERAL NOTE

This section creates the offence of ill-treatment or wilful neglect of a person who lacks **1–370** capacity or is believed to lack capacity. It is "aimed at capturing those individuals who are in a position of trust, care or power over people who are then ill-treated or neglected. That could be a donee of a lasting power of attorney, a deputy appointed by the court or a person who has the care of someone who lacks capacity, such as a member of staff in a hospital or care home or a family member", *per* the Parliamentary Under-Secretary of State, St. Comm. A, col.383. It could also include an attorney of an EPA.

In *R. v Newington (Susan)* (1990) 91 Cr. App. R. 247, a case under s.127 of the Mental Health Act 1983, the Court of Appeal said that "ill-treatment" could not be equated with "wilfully to neglect". The court therefore advised the Crown Prosecution Service that, when proceedings were brought, charges of "ill-treatment" and of "wilfully to neglect" should be put in separate counts in the indictment. This ruling applies to proceedings brought under this section.

The Government rejected recommendation 80 of the Joint Committee that this section be "extended to include the misappropriation of the person's property and financial assets" on the ground that a person who uses the funds of someone who lacks capacity for his own benefit may be prosecuted for the offence of theft and that a new offence of "misappropriation" would be very similar to that offence (*The Government Response to the Scrutiny Committee's Report on the Draft Mental Incapacity Bill*, Cm 6121).

The English "No Secrets" and the Welsh "In Safe Hands" guidance set out the multi-agency procedures to be followed when a vulnerable adult is believed to be suffering abuse. Abuse is defined as "a violation of an individual's human and civil rights by any other person or persons" (*No Secrets*, para.2.5). The Government rejected the Joint Committee's recommendation, at para.266, that the statutory authorities should be given additional powers of investigation and intervention in cases of alleged physical, sexual or financial abuse of people lacking the capacity to protect themselves from the risk of abuse:

"The Committee recommended that the draft Bill should go further in the protection it offers against abuse and exploitation of those lacking capacity. However, the Government is already taking action to protect vulnerable adults against abuse. In particular, the 'No Secrets' guidance requires Councils to liaise with other public authorities and other agencies in their area and to produce written and agreed local procedures for handling incidents of abuse concerning vulnerable adults. The new Public Guardian under the Bill would have a role working with Councils and other agencies. The new criminal offence of ill-treatment or wilful neglect would also be another valuable tool in tackling potential abuse" (Cm.6121).

This section is drafted in broader terms than s.127 of the Mental Health Act 1983. Section 127 creates two separate offences that could apply to incapacitated people who are also suffering from a mental disorder within the meaning of s.1 of that Act at the time when the offence was committed. Firstly, under subs.(1) it is an offence for an employee or manager of a hospital, independent hospital or care home to ill-treat or wilfully to neglect an in-patient or out-patient of that hospital or home. Secondly, under subs.(2) it is an offence for a guardian appointed under the 1983 Act or some other person who has the custody or care of a mentally disordered person who is living in the community to ill-treat or wilfully to neglect that person.

A donee of a lasting power of attorney, a deputy appointed by the court or a carer who abuses his or her position could be guilty of the offence of "fraud by abuse of position" under s.4 of the Fraud Act 2006. Section 4 reads:

"(1) A person is in breach of this section if he:
    (a) occupies a position in which he is expected to safeguard, or not act against, the financial interests of another person,
    (b) intends, by means of the abuse of that position—
        (i) to make a gain for himself or another, or
        (ii) to cause loss to another or to expose another to a risk of loss.

(2) A person may be regarded as having abused his position even though his conduct consisted of an omission rather than an act."

Sections 30 to 41 of the Sexual Offences Act 2003 create a number of offences "against persons with a mental disorder impeding choice."

Subsection (1) para.(a)

1–371   An offence under this section could be committed if either D is unaware of P's incapacity, or if D's belief that P lacks capacity is incorrect.

CARE. This is not defined. In *Minister of Health v Royal Midlands Counties Home for Incurables at Lemington Spa* [1954] Ch 530, Denning L.J. defined care as "the homely art of making people comfortable and providing for their well being so far as their condition allows".

PERSON. Of any age. Incapacity arising solely from the fact that P is not old enough to be considered capable would not qualify as incapacity for the purpose of this section.

CAPACITY. It is unclear what capacity means in this context as the functional test of capacity set out in s.3 is not obviously applicable to an offence. It is suggested that a person lacks capacity for the purposes of this provision if (i) he or she is vulnerable due to a mentally disability arising from "an impairment of, or a disturbance in the functioning of, the mind or brain" (see s.2(1)), and (ii) the vulnerability eliminates or significantly reduces that persons ability to resist the ill-treatment or neglect by D.

Subsection (2)

1–372   ILL-TREATS. There is Crown Court authority to support the proposition that it is not necessary to establish a course of conduct as a single act, such as slapping a person's face on one occasion, could constitute ill-treatment (*R. v Holmes* [1979] Crim. L.R. 52, Crown Court (Bodmin)). As it is likely that there is no need for the prosecution to show that the treatment in question caused actual injury to the victim, "ill treatment" encompasses a wide range of conduct.

It is submitted that for the offence of ill-treatment to be proved, the prosecution would have to prove: (1) deliberate conduct by the accused which could properly be described as ill-treatment irrespective of whether it damaged or threatened to damage the victims health; (2) a guilty mind involving either an appreciation by the accused that he was inexcusably ill-treating a person or that he was reckless as to whether he was inexcusably acting in that way; and (3) that the victim was a person without capacity (*R. v Newington* (Susan), above). In *Newington* the court disapproved of a direction given by the trial judge "that violence would inevitably amount to ill-treatment" on the ground that violence necessarily used for the reasonable control of a patient would not amount to ill-treatment.

WILFULY NEGLECTS. The meaning to be attributed to the expression "wilful neglect" may vary according to the context but generally the expression should be taken to mean that there has been an intentional or purposive omission to do something that the person in question knows he or she has a duty to do (*De Maroussem v Commissioner of Income Tax* [2004] UKPC 43, para.41). In the context of a verdict of neglect made at a Coroner's inquest, Sir Thomas Bingham MR said the neglect "means a gross failure to provide adequate nourishment or liquid, or provide or procure basic medical attention or shelter or warmth for someone in a dependent position (because of youth, age, illness or incarceration) who cannot provide it for himself. Failure to provide medical attention for a dependent person whose physical condition is such as to show that he obviously needs it may amount to neglect. So it may be if it is the dependent person's mental condition which obviously calls for medical attention (as it would, for example, if a mental nurse observed that a patient had a propensity to swallow razor blades and failed to report this propensity to a doctor, in a case where the patient had no intention to cause himself injury but did thereafter swallow razor blades with fatal results). In both cases the crucial consideration will be what the dependent person's condition, whether physical or mental, appeared to be" (*R. v Humberside and Scunthorpe Coroner, ex p. Jamieson* [1994] 3 All E.R. 972, at 990, 991).

The leading case on the term "wilfully" is *R. v Sheppard (James Martin)* [1981] A.C. 394, HL, a case brought under s.1(1) of the Children and Young Persons Act 1933 (c.12). Lord Keith said at 418:

> "It is used here to describe the mental element, which, in addition to the fact of neglect, must be proved The primary meaning of 'wilful' is 'deliberate'. So a parent who knows that his child needs medical care and deliberately, that is by conscious decision, refrains from calling a doctor, is guilty under the sub-section. As a matter of general principle, recklessness is to be equiparated with deliberation. A parent who fails to provide medical care which his child needs because he does not care whether it is needed or not is reckless of his child's welfare. He too is guilty of an offence. But a parent who has genuinely failed to appreciate that his child needs medical care, through personal inadequacy or stupidity or both, is not guilty."

A direction of the kind suggested by Lord Keith's reasoning, suitably tailored to the facts of the case, should be given by the trial judge hearing a case under this section (*R. v Morrell (Karen Victoria)* [2002] EWCA Crim 2547). In *Morrell,* the court said that the fact that the neglect is committed by a professional cannot make it automatically "wilful", since "there is or can be a room for genuine mistake, even with an experienced practitioner".

PART 2

THE COURT OF PROTECTION AND THE PUBLIC GUARDIAN

The Court of Protection

The Court of Protection

1–373   **45.**—(1) There is to be a superior court of record known as the Court of Protection.

(2) The court is to have an official seal.

(3) The court may sit at any place in England and Wales, on any day and at any time.

(4) The court is to have a central office and registry at a place appointed by the Lord Chancellor [, after consulting the Lord Chief Justice].

(5) The Lord Chancellor may [, after consulting the Lord Chief Justice] designate as additional registries of the court any district registry of the High Court and any county court office.

[(5A) The Lord Chief Justice may nominate any of the following to exercise his functions under this section—

(a) the President of the Court of Protection;

(b) a judicial office holder (as defined in section 109(4) of the Constitutional Reform Act 2005).]

(6) The office of the Supreme Court called the Court of Protection ceases to exist.

AMENDMENTS

1–374   The amendments to this section were made by SI 2006/1016, art.2, Sch.1, para.32.

GENERAL NOTE

1–375   This section establishes a superior court of record called the Court of Protection which has a comprehensive jurisdiction over the health, welfare and financial affairs of people who lack capacity. The court combines the inherent jurisdiction of the High Court that Judges in the Family Division developed in recent years relating to personal welfare decisions made in respect of mentally incapacitated adults, with the property and financial jurisdiction of the previous Court of Protection, which is abolished by subs.(6). The court has the same powers, rights, privileges and authority as the High Court (s.47(1)). The new court will be able to sit anywhere in England and Wales (subs.(3)), with the general rule being that a hearing is to be held in private (CPR 2007, Pt.13). The Explanatory Notes state, at para.130, that it "is intended that the Court of Protection will have a regional presence but will have a central office and registry as designated by the Lord Chancellor. Additional registries (being High Court district registries or county courts) may also be designated". The Court will initially sit in the following locations:

- Birmingham
- Bristol
- Cardiff
- Manchester
- Newcastle
- Preston.

Any document required to be filed with the court must be filed at the court's central registry. Its address is:

Court of Protection,
Archway Tower,
2 Junction Road,
London N19 5SZ.
DX 141150 Archway 2.

In addition to the powers contained in s.16 to make an order and to appoint a deputy and the powers contained in ss.22 and 23 relating to lasting powers of attorney, the court also has the power under s.15 to make declarations on whether a person has capacity to make a particular decision, and whether an act done, or proposed to be done, in relation to a person who lacks capacity is lawful. The court does not have jurisdiction to authorise the use of powers under the Mental Health Act 1983. When reaching a decision about a mentally incapacitated person the court must apply the principles set out in s.1. Provision for applications to be made to the court is made in s.50.

It is prima facie a contempt of court to publish information relating to proceedings which are brought under this Act and which are heard in private (Administration of Justice Act 1960, s.12).

However, the court has power to make an order authorising the publication of information specified in r.91(2) of the 2007 Rules.

The Human Rights Act 1998
In *Winterwerp v Netherlands* (1979) 2 E.H.R.R. 38, para.75, the European Court of **1–376** Human Rights, in holding that the capacity to deal personally with one's property involves the exercise of private rights and hence affects "civil rights and obligations" for the purposes of Art.6(1) of the ECHR, said:

"Whatever the justification for depriving a person of unsound mind of the capacity to administer his property, the guarantees laid down by Art.6(1) must nevertheless be respected."

Article 6 is also applicable where the purpose of the proceedings is to determine whether or not legal capacity can be restored to the applicant to enable him to carry out certain legal acts (*Matter v Slovakia* (2001) 31 E.H.R.R. 32, para.51).

Transitional Provisions
Transitional provisions for proceedings about P's personal welfare begun in the High **1–377** Court before October 1, 2007 are contained in Art.3 of the Mental Capacity Act 2005 (Transitional and Consequential Provisions) Order 2007 (SI 2007/1898):

"Proceedings begun in the High Court before 1 October 2007
3.—(1) This article applies to any proceedings about P's personal welfare begun in the **1–378** High Court before 1 October 2007 in respect of which the Court of Protection would, but for this article, have jurisdiction on and after that date under section 16 of the Act.

(2) The proceedings may continue to be dealt with, until they are finally decided, in accordance with the arrangements existing immediately before 1 October 2007.

(3) For the purposes of paragraph (2), an application is finally decided when it is determined and there is no possibility of the determination being reversed or varied on an appeal.

(4) In dealing with proceedings under this article, the High Court retains all the powers and jurisdiction in relation to any matter that is the subject of the proceedings that it had immediately before the commencement of the Act.

(5) In this article—
    (a) "P" means any person (other than a protected party) who lacks, or so far as consistent with the context is alleged to lack, capacity to make a decision or

decisions in relation to any matter that is the subject of an application to the court and references to a person who lacks capacity are to be construed in accordance with the Act;

    (b) "personal welfare" is to be construed in accordance with section 17 of the Act; and

    (c) "protected party" means a party, or an intended party (other than P or a child), who lacks capacity to conduct the proceedings."

Subsection (3)

1–379   The Law Commission anticipated a need for there to be at least one venue for each of the six court circuits in England and Wales (Law Com No.231, para.10.16).

The judges of the Court of Protection

1–380   **46.**—(1) Subject to Court of Protection Rules under section 51(2)(d), the jurisdiction of the court is exercisable by a judge nominated for that purpose by—

    (a) the [Lord Chief Justice], or

  [(b) where nominated by the Lord Chief Justice to act on his behalf under this subsection –

    (a) the President of the Court of Protection;

    (b) a judicial office holder (as defined in section 109(4) of the Constitutional Reform Act 2005).]

  (2) To be nominated, a judge must be—

    (a) the President of the Family Division,

    (b) the Vice-Chancellor,

    (c) a puisne judge of the High Court,

    (d) a circuit judge, or

    (e) a district judge.

  (3) The [Lord Chief Justice, after consulting the Lord Chancellor,] must—

    (a) appoint one of the judges nominated by virtue of subsection (2)(a) to (c) to be President of the Court of Protection, and

    (b) appoint another of those judges to be Vice-President of the Court of Protection.

  (4) The [Lord Chief Justice, after consulting the Lord Chancellor,] must appoint one of the judges nominated by virtue of subsection (2)(d) or (e) to be Senior Judge of the Court of Protection, having such administrative functions in relation to the court as the Lord Chancellor[, after consulting the Lord Chief Justice,] may direct.

AMENDMENTS

1–381   The amendments to this section were made by SI 2006/1016, art.2, Sch.1, para.33.

DEFINITIONS

1–382   "the court": s.64(1)

GENERAL NOTE

1–383   The jurisdiction of the Court of Protection will be exercised by judges nominated by the Lord Chancellor, or a person acting on his behalf, from the list set out in subs.(2). One of the nominated judges must be appointed as President of the Court of Protection and another to be Vice-President (subs.(3)). A judge must also be appointed to be Senior Judge of the Court of Protection (subs.(4)). He or she will have various administrative responsibilities.

Subsection (3)
Sir Mark Potter, the President of the Family Division, has been appointed President and **1–384** Sir Andrew Morritt, the Vice-Chancellor, has been appointed Vice-President.

Subsection (4)
Article 4 of the Mental Capacity Act 2005 (Transitional and Consequential Provisions) **1–385** Order 2007 (SI 2007/1898) states:

"The person who, immediately before the commencement of Part 2 of the Act, holds the office of Master of the Court of Protection [i.e. Master Denzil Lush], shall be treated as—
  (a) being a circuit judge nominated under section 46(1) of the Act to exercise the jurisdiction of the Court of Protection; and
  (b) having been appointed the Senior Judge of the Court of Protection under section 46(4) of the Act."

Supplementary powers

General powers and effect of orders etc
47.—(1) The court has in connection with its jurisdiction the same powers, **1–386** rights, privileges and authority as the High Court.

(2) Section 204 of the Law of Property Act 1925 (c. 20) (orders of High Court conclusive in favour of purchasers) applies in relation to orders and directions of the court as it applies to orders of the High Court.

(3) Office copies of orders made, directions given or other instruments issued by the court and sealed with its official seal are admissible in all legal proceedings as evidence of the originals without any further proof.

DEFINITIONS
  "the court": s.64(1)   **1–387**
  "purchaser": s.64(1)

GENERAL NOTE

Subsection (1)
This gives the Court of Protection the same powers as the High Court, for example in **1–388** relation to witnesses, injunctions, contempt, and enforcement.

Subsection (2)
Section 204 of the 1925 Act reads: **1–389**

"(1) An order of the court under any statutory or other jurisdiction shall not, as against a purchaser, be invalidated on the ground of want of jurisdiction, or of want of any concurrence, consent, notice, or service, whether the purchaser has notice of any such want or not.
 (2) This section has effect with respect to any lease, sale, or other act under the authority of the court, and purporting to be in pursuance of any statutory power notwithstanding any exception in such statute.
 (3) This section applies to all orders made before or after the commencement of this Act."

Interim orders and directions
48.—The court may, pending the determination of an application to it in **1–390** relation to a person (P), make an order or give directions in respect of any matter if—

(a) there is reason to believe that P lacks capacity in relation to the matter,

(b) the matter is one to which its powers under this Act extend, and

(c) it is in P's best interests to make the order, or give the directions, without delay.

DEFINITIONS

1–391   "the court": s.64(1)

GENERAL NOTE

1–392   This section enables the court to make interim orders even if evidence of lack of capacity is not yet available, where there is reason for the court to believe that the person lacks capacity in respect of a particular matter within the jurisdiction of the court and it is in the best interests of the person for the court to act without delay.

In *B Borough Council v Mrs S and Mr S (by the Official Solicitor)* [2006] EWHC 2584 (Fam), Charles J. said at para.44:

> "When the Mental Capacity Act comes into force it will provide statutory jurisdiction for [granting interim declaratory and injunctive relief]. In my view the procedure relating to, and the evidence required for a without notice application will not alter materially when the applications are based on that statutory jurisdiction."

Guidance on the making of without notice applications to the court under the inherent jurisdiction was provided by his Lordship at paras 38–43 and 158.

Power to call for reports

1–393   **49.**—(1) This section applies where, in proceedings brought in respect of a person (P) under Part 1, the court is considering a question relating to P.

(2) The court may require a report to be made to it by the Public Guardian or by a Court of Protection Visitor.

(3) The court may require a local authority, or an NHS body, to arrange for a report to be made—

(a) by one of its officers or employees, or

(b) by such other person (other than the Public Guardian or a Court of Protection Visitor) as the authority, or the NHS body, considers appropriate.

(4) The report must deal with such matters relating to P as the court may direct.

(5) Court of Protection Rules may specify matters which, unless the court directs otherwise, must also be dealt with in the report.

(6) The report may be made in writing or orally, as the court may direct.

(7) In complying with a requirement, the Public Guardian or a Court of Protection Visitor may, at all reasonable times, examine and take copies of—

(a) any health record,

(b) any record of, or held by, a local authority and compiled in connection with a social services function, and

(c) any record held by a person registered under Part 2 of the Care Standards Act 2000 (c.14),

so far as the record relates to P.

(8) If the Public Guardian or a Court of Protection Visitor is making a visit in the course of complying with a requirement, he may interview P in private.

(9) If a Court of Protection Visitor who is a Special Visitor is making a visit in the course of complying with a requirement, he may if the court so directs carry out in private a medical, psychiatric or psychological examination of P's capacity and condition.

(10) "NHS body" has the meaning given in section 148 of the Health and Social Care (Community Health and Standards) Act 2003 (c. 43).

(11) "Requirement" means a requirement imposed under subsection (2) or (3).

DEFINITIONS
  "the court": s.64(1)   **1–394**
  "Court of Protection Visitor": s.64(1)
  "local authority": s.64(1)
  "Court of Protection Rules": s.64(1)
  "social services function": s.64(1)

GENERAL NOTE
  This section makes provision for reports to be made to assist the Court of Protection in **1–395** determining a case relating to P. The court can require either written or oral reports to be made by the Public Guardian, a Court of Protection Visitor, a local authority or a NHS body (subss.(2), (3) and (6)). The report, which could assist the court in determining whether an oral hearing of a case is needed, must deal with such matters as the court and/or the Court of Protection Rules direct (subss.(4) and (5)). It is the duty of the person making the report to assist the court on the matters within his or her expertise (CPR 2007, r.117(2)). Unless the court otherwise directs, the matters to be covered in the report are set out in r.117(3). Written questions may be put to the report writer (r.118(1)). The Public Guardian and a Court of Protection Visitor are given power to examine and take copies of relevant records and to interview P in private (subss.(7) and (8)). Where a Court of Protection Visitor is a Special Visitor (see s.61(2)), he or she may, on the directions of the court, carry out in private medical, psychiatric or psychological examinations of P's capacity and condition (subs.(9)).

Subsection (2)
  A case heard under the Mental Health Act 1959 (c.2) suggests that in initial applications **1–396** for the appointment of a deputy and in applications to determine proceedings, where the ultimate issue is whether an individual should either become or remain subject to the court's jurisdiction, the court should lean towards disclosing the Visitor's report, and the individual should be permitted to test the report by putting questions to the Visitor. The court should only withhold disclosure where this is deemed to be in the person's best interests. In all other cases, the judge should only direct disclosure if he sees a positive advantage in doing so, either in the interests of the person generally, or because he feels it would assist the judge in the exercise of his functions (*WLW, Re* [1972] Ch 456 at 457, *per* Goff J.).

  It is a contempt of court to interfere with the discharge of a Visitor's duties (*Anon, Re* (1875–90) 18 Ch.D 26, *per* James L.J. at 27).

  REPORT. Guidance on the preparation, form and structure of the report is set out in Practice Direction 14E.

Subsection (3)
  Paragraph (b) covers the situation where the local authority or NHS body has subcont- **1–397** racted its work to someone else.

  NHS BODY. See subs.(10).

Subsection (5)
  See r.117 of the CPR 2007.   **1–398**

Subsection (6)
1–399   ORALLY. The power to receive oral reports will be particularly helpful in cases of urgency.

Subsections (7), (8) and (9)
1–400   REQUIREMENT. See subs.(11)

Subsection (10)
1–401   Under s.148 of the 2003 Act, an English NHS body means a Primary Care Trust, a Strategic Health Authority, an English NHS trust and a NHS foundation trust. A Welsh NHS body means a Local Health Board, a Welsh NHS trust and a Special Health Authority performing functions only or mainly in respect of Wales. A "NHS body" also includes a cross-border Special Health Authority which means a SHA not performing functions only or mainly in respect of England or only or mainly in respect of Wales.

Practice and procedure

Applications to the Court of Protection
1–402   **50.**—(1) No permission is required for an application to the court for the exercise of any of its powers under this Act—
    (a) by a person who lacks, or is alleged to lack, capacity,
    (b) if such a person has not reached 18, by anyone with parental responsibility for him,
    (c) by the donor or a donee of a lasting power of attorney to which the application relates,
    (d) by a deputy appointed by the court for a person to whom the application relates, or
    (e) by a person named in an existing order of the court, if the application relates to the order.
    [(1A) Nor is permission required for an application to the court under section 21A by the relevant person's representative.]
    (2) But, subject to Court of Protection Rules and to paragraph 20(2) of Schedule 3 (declarations relating to private international law), permission is required for any other application to the court.
    (3) In deciding whether to grant permission the court must, in particular, have regard to—
    (a) the applicant's connection with the person to whom the application relates,
    (b) the reasons for the application,
    (c) the benefit to the person to whom the application relates of a proposed order or directions, and
    (d) whether the benefit can be achieved in any other way.
    (4) "Parental responsibility" has the same meaning as in the Children Act 1989 (c. 41).

AMENDMENT
1–403   Subs.(1A) was inserted by the Mental Health Act 2007, s.50(7), Sch.9, Pt.1, para.9.

DEFINITIONS
1–404   "the court": s.64(1)
    "lasting power of attorney": s.64(1)
    "deputy": s.64(1)
    "Court of Protection Rules": s.64(1)

GENERAL NOTE

This section provides that persons listed in subs.(1) can make as application to the Court **1–405** of Protection as of right. The representative of a person detained under the authority of Sch.A1 also has such a right when making an application under s.21A (subs.(1A)). Other potential applicants have to obtain the permission of the court (CPR 2007, r.50), apart from those listed in, r.51. The factors that the court must have regard to when considering whether to grant permission are set out in subs.(3). They "are designed to ensure that any proposed application will promote the interests of the person concerned, rather than causing unnecessary distress or difficulty for him" (Explanatory Notes, para.136). It is anticipated that the majority of applications to the court will be decided on the basis of the judge's consideration of the papers without any of the parties attending.

The *Code of Practice* deals with the identity of the applicant at paras 8.7–8.10:

"The person making the application will vary, depending on the circumstances. For example, a person wishing to challenge a finding that they lack capacity may apply to the court, supported by others where necessary. Where there is a disagreement among family members, for example, a family member may wish to apply to the court to settle the disagreement—bearing in mind the need, in most cases, to get permission beforehand.

For cases about serious or major decisions concerning medical treatment . . . the NHS Trust or other organisation responsible for the patient's care will usually make the application. If social care staff are concerned about a decision that affects the welfare of a person who lacks capacity, the relevant local authority should make the application.

For decisions about the property and affairs of someone who lacks capacity to manage their own affairs, the applicant will usually be the person (for example, family carer) who needs specific authority from the court to deal with the individual's money or property.

If the applicant is the person who is alleged to lack capacity, they will always be a party to the court proceedings. In all other cases, the court will decide whether the person who lacks, or is alleged to lack, capacity should be involved as a party to the case. Where the person is a party to the case, the court may appoint the Official Solicitor to act for them."

As the European Court of Human Rights has identified that the State may have positive obligations designed to secure respect for private and family life under Art.8 of the European Convention on Human Rights (see, for example, *Glasser v United Kingdom* (2001) 33 E.H.R.R. 1), it is arguable that a local authority has an obligation to make an application to the court if a mentally incapacitated adult is assessed as being likely to suffer harm if he remained with his family. Also see *S (Adult Patient) (Inherent Jurisdiction; Family Life), Re* [2002] EWHC 2278; [2003] 1 F.L.R. 292, noted under s.16(2).

In *Shtukaturov v Russia*, March 27, 2008, para.73, the ECtHR held that the decision of the judge to decide to deprive the applicant of his legal capacity on the basis of documentary evidence, without seeing or hearing the applicant, was unreasonable and in breach of the principle of adversarial proceedings enshrined in Art.6.1 of the Convention.

Subsection (1) (a)

Rule 143 of the CPR 2007 enables the court to appoint a litigation friend to act for this **1–406** person.

Court of Protection Rules

51.—[(1) Rules of court with respect to the practice and procedure of the court **1–407** (to be called "Court of Protection Rules") may be made in accordance with Part 1 of Schedule 1 to the Constitutional Reform Act 2003.]

(2) Court of Protection Rules may, in particular, make provision—

(a) as to the manner and form in which proceedings are to be commenced;
(b) as to the persons entitled to be notified of, and be made parties to, the proceedings;
(c) for the allocation, in such circumstances as may be specified, of any specified description of proceedings to a specified judge or to specified descriptions of judges;
(d) for the exercise of the jurisdiction of the court, in such circumstances as may be specified, by its officers or other staff;
(e) for enabling the court to appoint a suitable person (who may, with his consent, be the Official Solicitor) to act in the name of, or on behalf of, or to represent the person to whom the proceedings relate;
(f) for enabling an application to the court to be disposed of without a hearing;
(g) for enabling the court to proceed with, or with any part of, a hearing in the absence of the person to whom the proceedings relate;
(h) for enabling or requiring the proceedings or any part of them to be conducted in private and for enabling the court to determine who is to be admitted when the court sits in private and to exclude specified persons when it sits in public;
(i) as to what may be received as evidence (whether or not admissible apart from the rules) and the manner in which it is to be presented;
(j) for the enforcement of orders made and directions given in the proceedings.
(3) Court of Protection Rules may, instead of providing for any matter, refer to provision made or to be made about that matter by directions.
(4) Court of Protection Rules may make different provision for different areas.

AMENDMENT
1–408   Subs.(1) was substituted by SI 2006/1016, art.2, Sch.1, para.34.

DEFINITIONS
1–409   "the court": s.64(1)

GENERAL NOTE
1–410   The Court of Protection Rules 2007 (SI 2007/1744) have been made under this section. They are reproduced in Part 4 and are referred to throughout this work as "the CPR 2007".

[Practice directions

1–411   **52.**—(1) Directions as to the practice and procedure of the court may be given in accordance with Part 1 of Schedule 2 to the Constitutional Reform Act 2005.
(2) Practice directions given otherwise than under subsection (1) may not be given without the approval of—
(a) the Lord Chancellor, and
(b) the Lord Chief Justice.
(3) The Lord Chief Justice may nominate any of the following to exercise his functions under this section—
(a) the President of the Court of Protection;
(b) a judicial office holder (as defined in section 109(4) of the Constitutional Reform Act 2005).]

AMENDMENT
1–412   This section was substituted by SI 2006/1016, art.2, Sch.1, para.35.

DEFINITIONS
"the court": s.64(1)   **1–413**

GENERAL NOTE
This section provides for practice directions to be made regarding the court's practice **1–414**
and procedure. Section 51(3) enables the Court of Protection Rules, instead of providing
for any matter, to refer to provision made by a practice direction. The "intention is to
make rules accompanied by practice directions, on the model of the Civil Procedure
Rules 1998" (Explanatory Notes, para.138).

All of the practice directions that have been issued can be accessed in the forms and
booklets section of the website of the Office of the Public Guardian (see Annex A). The
numbering of the practice directions indicate the Part of the CPR 2007 that they
supplement.

Rights of appeal

53.—(1) Subject to the provisions of this section, an appeal lies to the Court of **1–415**
Appeal from any decision of the court.

(2) Court of Protection Rules may provide that where a decision of the court is
made by—

(a) a person exercising the jurisdiction of the court by virtue of rules made
    under section 51(2)(d),

(b) a district judge, or

(c) a circuit judge,

an appeal from that decision lies to a prescribed higher judge of the court and not
to the Court of Appeal.

(3) For the purposes of this section the higher judges of the court are—

(a) in relation to a person mentioned in subsection (2)(a), a circuit judge or a
    district judge;

(b) in relation to a person mentioned in subsection (2)(b), a circuit judge;

(c) in relation to any person mentioned in subsection (2), one of the judges
    nominated by virtue of section 46(2)(a) to (c).

(4) Court of Protection Rules may make provision—

(a) that, in such cases as may be specified, an appeal from a decision of the
    court may not be made without permission;

(b) as to the person or persons entitled to grant permission to appeal;

(c) as to any requirements to be satisfied before permission is granted;

(d) that where a higher judge of the court makes a decision on an appeal, no
    appeal may be made to the Court of Appeal from that decision unless the
    Court of Appeal considers that—

   (i) the appeal would raise an important point of principle or practice, or

   (ii) there is some other compelling reason for the Court of Appeal to hear it;

(e) as to any considerations to be taken into account in relation to granting or
    refusing permission to appeal.

DEFINITIONS
"the court": s.64(1)   **1–416**

GENERAL NOTE
This section, which is supplemented by Part 20 CPR 2007, is concerned with appeals **1–417**
from decisions of the Court of Protection. The appeal will either be to the Court of
Appeal or, if the decision was made by a judge at a lower level in the judicial hierarchy
of the court, to a higher judge within the court (subss.(1) and (2)).

Fees and costs

Fees

1–418 **54.**—(1) The Lord Chancellor may with the consent of the Treasury by order prescribe fees payable in respect of anything dealt with by the court.

(2) An order under this section may in particular contain provision as to—

(a) scales or rates of fees;

(b) exemptions from and reductions in fees;

(c) remission of fees in whole or in part.

(3) Before making an order under this section, the Lord Chancellor must consult—

(a) the President of the Court of Protection,

(b) the Vice-President of the Court of Protection, and

(c) the Senior Judge of the Court of Protection.

(4) The Lord Chancellor must take such steps as are reasonably practicable to bring information about fees to the attention of persons likely to have to pay them.

(5) Fees payable under this section are recoverable summarily as a civil debt.

DEFINITIONS

1–419 "the court": s.64(1)

GENERAL NOTE

1–420 The "Court of Protection and Office of the Public Guardian Fees", Department of Constitutional Affairs Consultation Paper CP 23/06 states at p.11:

> "In Her Majesty's Courts Service (HMCS), fees are set in line with the general principles of the Government's policy on charging fees for services. These are set out in the *Fee and Charges Guide* produced by HM Treasury. They require that fees should reflect a financial objective agreed by ministers, which should reflect (and not exceed) the cost to the organisation of providing the service. The new Court of Protection and Office of the Public Guardian will not be part of HMCS but will operate under the same principles. For the first year of their operation, the Court of Protection and the Office of Public Guardian's fees will be set at a level to recover approximately 80% of the costs of the two organisations, rather than pass on the full costs of operating the services to those applying to the new organisations. Fee exemptions and remissions will ensure that access to justice is protected for those who are unable to pay."

Subsection (1)

1–421 BY ORDER. See the Court of Protection Fees Order 2007 (SI 2007/1745) which is reproduced in Part 4.

Subsection (2)

1–422 The principle underpinning this provision was explained by the Parliamentary Under-Secretary of State: "[W]e believe that it is right that people should pay a fair price for the court's work on their behalf, but it is also right that fee reduction and remission arrangements exist so that no one is prevented from going to court if paying the fees would cause them financial hardship, or if there are other exceptional circumstances" (*Hansard*, HL Vol. 669, col.754).

Costs

1–423 **55.**—(1) Subject to Court of Protection Rules, the costs of and incidental to all proceedings in the court are in its discretion.

(2) The rules may in particular make provision for regulating matters relating to the costs of those proceedings, including prescribing scales of costs to be paid to legal or other representatives.

(3) The court has full power to determine by whom and to what extent the costs are to be paid.

(4) The court may, in any proceedings—

(a) disallow, or

(b) order the legal or other representatives concerned to meet,

the whole of any wasted costs or such part of them as may be determined in accordance with the rules.

(5) "Legal or other representative", in relation to a party to proceedings, means any person exercising a right of audience or right to conduct litigation on his behalf.

(6) "Wasted costs" means any costs incurred by a party—

(a) as a result of any improper, unreasonable or negligent act or omission on the part of any legal or other representative or any employee of such a representative, or

(b) which, in the light of any such act or omission occurring after they were incurred, the court considers it is unreasonable to expect that party to pay.

DEFINITIONS
"Court of Protection Rules": s.64(1)   1–424
"the court": s.64(1)

GENERAL NOTE
See Pt 19 of the CPR 2007.   1–425

Fees and costs: supplementary

56.—(1) Court of Protection Rules may make provision—   1–426

(a) as to the way in which, and funds from which, fees and costs are to be paid;

(b) for charging fees and costs upon the estate of the person to whom the proceedings relate;

(c) for the payment of fees and costs within a specified time of the death of the person to whom the proceedings relate or the conclusion of the proceedings.

(2) A charge on the estate of a person created by virtue of subsection (1)(b) does not cause any interest of the person in any property to fail or determine or to be prevented from recommencing.

DEFINITIONS
"Court of Protection Rules": s.64(1)   1–427

GENERAL NOTE
See Pt 19 of the CPR 2007.   1–428

The Public Guardian

The Public Guardian

57.—(1) For the purposes of this Act, there is to be an officer, to be known as the Public Guardian.   1–429

(2) The Public Guardian is to be appointed by the Lord Chancellor.

(3) There is to be paid to the Public Guardian out of money provided by Parliament such salary as the Lord Chancellor may determine.

(4) The Lord Chancellor may, after consulting the Public Guardian—

(a) provide him with such officers and staff, or

(b) enter into such contracts with other persons for the provision (by them or their sub-contractors) of officers, staff or services,

as the Lord Chancellor thinks necessary for the proper discharge of the Public Guardian's functions.

(5) Any functions of the Public Guardian may, to the extent authorised by him, be performed by any of his officers.

GENERAL NOTE

1–430   This section provides for a new public official, the Public Guardian, to be appointed by the Lord Chancellor, and for the Lord Chancellor either to provide the Public Guardian with officers and staff and/or to enter into contacts with other persons for the provision of officers, staff or services for the discharge of the Public Guardian's functions. The Public Guardian, who will be supported by the Office of the Public Guardian, an executive agency of the Ministry of Justice, has both administrative and supervisory functions. These are set out in s.58. The Public Guardian, who will be subject to the scrutiny of the Public Guardian Board (s.59), is required to produce annual reports (s.60).

The address of the Public Guardian is:

Archway Tower
Junction Road
London
N19 5SZ

tel: 0845 330 2900
fax: 0870 739 580

website: *www.publicguardian.gov.uk.*

Functions of the Public Guardian

1–431   **58.**—(1) The Public Guardian has the following functions—

(a) establishing and maintaining a register of lasting powers of attorney,

(b) establishing and maintaining a register of orders appointing deputies,

(c) supervising deputies appointed by the court,

(d) directing a Court of Protection Visitor to visit—

(i) a donee of a lasting power of attorney,

(ii) a deputy appointed by the court, or

(iii) the person granting the power of attorney or for whom the deputy is appointed (P),

and to make a report to the Public Guardian on such matters as he may direct,

(e) receiving security which the court requires a person to give for the discharge of his functions,

(f) receiving reports from donees of lasting powers of attorney and deputies appointed by the court,

(g) reporting to the court on such matters relating to proceedings under this Act as the court requires,

(h) dealing with representations (including complaints) about the way in which a donee of a lasting power of attorney or a deputy appointed by the court is exercising his powers,

(i) publishing, in any manner the Public Guardian thinks appropriate, any information he thinks appropriate about the discharge of his functions.

(2) The functions conferred by subsection (1)(c) and (h) may be discharged in co-operation with any other person who has functions in relation to the care or treatment of P.

(3) The Lord Chancellor may by regulations make provision—

(a) conferring on the Public Guardian other functions in connection with this Act;

(b) in connection with the discharge by the Public Guardian of his functions.

(4) Regulations made under subsection (3)(b) may in particular make provision as to—

(a) the giving of security by deputies appointed by the court and the enforcement and discharge of security so given;

(b) the fees which may be charged by the Public Guardian;

(c) the way in which, and funds from which, such fees are to be paid;

(d) exemptions from and reductions in such fees;

(e) remission of such fees in whole or in part;

(f) the making of reports to the Public Guardian by deputies appointed by the court and others who are directed by the court to carry out any transaction for a person who lacks capacity.

(5) For the purpose of enabling him to carry out his functions, the Public Guardian may, at all reasonable times, examine and take copies of—

(a) any health record,

(b) any record of, or held by, a local authority and compiled in connection with a social services function, and

(c) any record held by a person registered under Part 2 of the Care Standards Act 2000 (c.14),

so far as the record relates to P.

(6) The Public Guardian may also for that purpose interview P in private.

DEFINITIONS

"lasting power of attorney": s.64(1)   **1–432**

"deputy": s.64(1)

"the court": s.64(1)

"Court of ProtectionVisitor": s.64(1)

"health record": s.64(1)

"local authority": s.64(1)

"social services function": s.64(1)

GENERAL NOTE

The functions of the Public Guardian listed in subs.(1) are supplemented by regss.30 to **1–433** 48 of the Lasting Powers of Attorney, Enduring Powers of Attorney and Public Guardian Regulations 2007 (SI 2007/1253). Regulation 43 enables the Public Guardian to make applications to the Court of Protection. His functions include establishing and maintaining registers of LPAs and orders appointing deputies, supervising deputies to ensure that they exercise their responsibilities in line with the authority given to them, dealing with representations about the way both donees of LPAs and deputies are exercising their powers, and making enquiries or referring matters to the court where there are concerns that donees or deputies are not acting appropriately. The Public Guardian is given power to examine and take copies of relevant health or social services records, and also interview P in private (subss.(5) and (6)). Similar rights are provided for when the Public Guardian is reporting to the Court of Protection (s.49(7)–(8)).

The Public Guardian has no power of enforcement or sanction. An application to the court would have to be made if such power needs to be exercised.

The Public Guardian (Fees, etc) Regulations 2007 (SI 2007/2051), which are reproduced in Part 3, provide for fees to be charged in connection with the functions carried out by the Public Guardian. No fee is payable by the relevant person if that person is in receipt of income support, working tax credit, income-based job-seekers allowance, guarantee credit, council tax benefit or housing benefit. This exemption does not apply if the person has been awarded damages in excess of £16,000 which has been disregarded for the purposes of determining eligibility for any of these benefits (reg.8). Under reg.10, the Public Guardian has power to reduce or remit any fee if, "owing to the exceptional circumstances of the particular case", payment of the fee would "involve undue hardship".

Subsections (1)(a), (1)(b)

1–434   For the role of the Public Guardian in relation to the registers, see regs 20 to 32 of SI 2007/1253, above.

Subsection (1)(c)

1–435   After the appointment of the deputy, the Public Guardian must determine the level of supervision required. There are three levels of supervision: type I (highest), type II (lower) and type III (minimal); see SI 2007/2051, above, reg.8(3), the notes on s.16(2)(b) and the General Note to s.19.

For the power of the Public Guardian to require information from deputies, see reg.41 of SI 2007/1253, above. A deputy can require a review of decisions made by the Public Guardian, see reg.42.

Subsection (1)(d)

1–436   For visits by the Public Guardian or by Court of Protection Visitors at his direction, see reg.44 of SI 2007/1253, above. The Public Guardian can direct a Visitor to visit the donor or attorney of an EPA under reg.48.

Subsection (1)(f)

1–437   For reports from deputies, see regs 38 to 40 of SI 2007/1253, above. The Public Guardian can require the deputy to provide him with information (reg.41), and the deputy can require the Public Guardian to reconsider any decision that he has made in respect of him (reg.42).

Subsection (1)(h)

1–438   The Public Guardian might wish to refer a complaint concerning the personal welfare of P to the relevant health or social care agency. If the complaint suggests that a criminal offence has been committed, this will be referred to the police.

In the performance of his functions under this provision, the Public Guardian has the power to require information from a donee or deputy under regs 46 and 47 of SI 2007/1253, above.

Subsection (2)

1–439   It "is intended that the Public Guardian will work closely with organisations such as local authorities and NHS bodies" (Explanatory Notes, para.146). Although the Public Guardian's supervisory function will be mainly focused on financial affairs, he "would have a role in identifying and tackling possible abuse with other agencies by providing a focus for concerns and fielding them to the appropriate agency" (Department of Constitutional Affairs, Oral and written evidence, Ev 265).

Subsections (3), (4)

1–440   REGULATIONS. See SI 2007/1253, noted above.

Public Guardian Board

59.—(1) There is to be a body, to be known as the Public Guardian Board.   **1–441**

(2) The Board's duty is to scrutinise and review the way in which the Public Guardian discharges his functions and to make such recommendations to the Lord Chancellor about that matter as it thinks appropriate.

(3) The Lord Chancellor must, in discharging his functions under sections 57 and 58, give due consideration to recommendations made by the Board.

(4) [*Repealed by SI 2006/1016, art.2, Sch.1, para.36.*]

(5) The Board must have—

(a) at least one member who is a judge of the court, and

(b) at least four members who are persons appearing to the Lord Chancellor to have appropriate knowledge or experience of the work of the Public Guardian.

[(5A) Where a person to be appointed as a member of the Board is a judge of the court, the appointment is to be made by the Lord Chief Justice after consulting the Lord Chancellor.

(5B) In any other case, the appointment of a person as a member of the Board is to be made by the Lord Chancellor.]

(6) The Lord Chancellor may by regulations make provision as to—

(a) the appointment of members of the Board (and, in particular, the procedures to be followed in connection with appointments);

(b) the selection of one of the members to be the chairman;

(c) the term of office of the chairman and members;

(d) their resignation, suspension or removal;

(e) the procedure of the Board (including quorum);

(f) the validation of proceedings in the event of a vacancy among the members or a defect in the appointment of a member.

(7) Subject to any provision made in reliance on subsection (6)(c) or (d), a person is to hold and vacate office as a member of the Board in accordance with the terms of the instrument appointing him.

(8) The Lord Chancellor may make such payments to or in respect of members of the Board by way of reimbursement of expenses, allowances and remuneration as he may determine.

(9) The Board must make an annual report to the Lord Chancellor about the discharge of its functions.

[(10) The Lord Chief Justice may nominate any of the following to exercise his functions under this section—

(a) the President of the Court of Protection;

(b) a judicial office holder (as defined in section 109(4) of the Constitutional Reform Act 2005).]

AMENDMENTS

The amendments to this section were made by SI 2006/1016, art.2, Sch.1.   **1–442**

GENERAL NOTE

This section provides for the establishment of the Public Guardian Board which is **1–443** charged with the duty of scrutinising and reviewing the manner in which the Public Guardian discharges his or her functions. The Board may make recommendations to the Lord Chancellor who must, in discharging his or her functions under ss.57 and 58, give them due consideration.

Subsection (6)
1–444 The Public Guardian Board Regulations 2007 (SI 2007/1770) make provision in relation to the tenure of the office of members and as to the procedure of the Board. Regulation 9 provides that the Board must hold at least one meeting each year that is open to members of the public to attend.

Annual report
1–445 **60.**—(1) The Public Guardian must make an annual report to the Lord Chancellor about the discharge of his functions.

(2) The Lord Chancellor must, within one month of receiving the report, lay a copy of it before Parliament.

DEFINITIONS
1–446 "Public Guardian": s.64(1)

Court of Protection Visitors
1–447 **61.**—(1) A Court of Protection Visitor is a person who is appointed by the Lord Chancellor to—
  (a) a panel of Special Visitors, or
  (b) a panel of General Visitors.
(2) A person is not qualified to be a Special Visitor unless he—
  (a) is a registered medical practitioner or appears to the Lord Chancellor to have other suitable qualifications or training, and
  (b) appears to the Lord Chancellor to have special knowledge of and experience in cases of impairment of or disturbance in the functioning of the mind or brain.
(3) A General Visitor need not have a medical qualification.
(4) A Court of Protection Visitor—
  (a) may be appointed for such term and subject to such conditions, and
  (b) may be paid such remuneration and allowances,
as the Lord Chancellor may determine.

(5) For the purpose of carrying out his functions under this Act in relation to a person who lacks capacity (P), a Court of Protection Visitor may, at all reasonable times, examine and take copies of—
  (a) any health record,
  (b) any record of, or held by, a local authority and compiled in connection with a social services function, and
  (c) any record held by a person registered under Part 2 of the Care Standards Act 2000 (c.14),
so far as the record relates to P.

(6) A Court of Protection Visitor may also for that purpose interview P in private.

DEFINITIONS
1–448 "health record": s.64(1)
"local authority": s.64(1)
"social services function": s.64(1)

GENERAL NOTE
1–449 This section provides for the Lord Chancellor to appoint Special Visitors, who will be medical practitioners, and General Visitors. Their role is to carry out visits and produce

independent reports on matters relating to the exercise of powers under this Act as directed by the Court of Protection (s.49(2)) or the Public Guardian (s.58(1)(d)). The Visitors have the power to examine and take copies of relevant records, and to interview P in private.

PART 3

MISCELLANEOUS AND GENERAL

Declaratory provision

Scope of the Act

1–450   **62.**—For the avoidance of doubt, it is hereby declared that nothing in this Act is to be taken to affect the law relating to murder or manslaughter or the operation of section 2 of the Suicide Act 1961 (c. 60) (assisting suicide).

GENERAL NOTE

1–451   This section, which was inserted following representations from the Catholic Bishops' Conference of England and Wales, seeks to address the concerns that were expressed to the Joint Committee that this legislation might pave the way for "euthanasia by the back-door" (see para.196). Euthanasia, which is "a deliberate intervention with the express aim of ending life", is illegal (*Who Decides: Making Decisions on Behalf of Mentally Incapacitated Adults*, Cm.3803, para.1.8). Notwithstanding the declaration made in this section, it is the case that both a valid and applicable written advance decision to refuse life-sustaining treatment (see ss.24–26) and a refusal of such treatment by a donee under a lasting power of attorney, if such power is granted to the donee (see s.11(8)), are lawful and must be obeyed by healthcare professionals. A mentally capable patient can therefore use either of these mechanisms to bring about his or her death during a subsequent mental incapacity by refusing either the provision of nutrition and hydration by artificial means or other potentially life saving medical interventions in specified circumstances. In such an eventuality there can be no question of the person having committed suicide, nor therefore of the doctor having aided and abetted him or her in doing so (*Airedale NHS Trust v Bland* [1993] 1 All E.R. 821, HL, *per* Lord Goff at 866). However, if a donee "wanted to refuse consent to treatment and the doctors thought that this was with the intention of murder or manslaughter then the doctor could continue to treat", *per* the Parliamentary Under-Secretary of State in correspondence quoted at *Hansard*, HL Vol.688, col.1150.

Whether a decision to discontinue treatment that would inevitably lead to the patient's death constitutes euthanasia was considered by Lord Goff in *Bland* at 867:

"[T]he law draws a crucial distinction between cases in which a doctor decides not to provide, or continue to provide, for his patient treatment or care which could or might prolong his life and those in which he decides, for example by administering a lethal drug, actively to bring his patient's life to an end. As I have already indicated, the former may be lawful, either because the doctor is giving effect to his patient's wishes by with-holding the treatment or care, even in certain circumstances in which the patient is incapacitated from stating whether or not he gives his consent. But it is not lawful for a doctor to administer a drug to his patient to bring about his death, even though that course is prompted by a humanitarian desire to end his suffering, however great that suffering may be: see *R v Cox* (September 18,1992, unreported) *per* Ognall J in the Crown Court at Winchester. So to act is to cross the Rubicon which runs between on the one hand the care of the living patient and on the other hand euthanasia—actively causing his death to avoid or to end his suffering. Euthanasia is not lawful at common law. It is, of course well known that there are many responsible members of our society who believe that euthanasia should be made lawful; but that result could I believe, only be achieved by legislation which expresses the democratic will that so fundamental a change should be made in our law, and can, if enacted, ensure that such legalised killing can only be carried out subject to appropriate supervision and control. It is true that the drawing of this distinction may lead to a charge of hypocrisy, because it can be asked why, if the doctor, by discontinuing treatment, is entitled in consequence to let his patient die, it should not be lawful to put him out of his misery straight away, in a more humane manner, by a lethal injection, rather than to let him linger on in pain until he dies. But the law does not feel able to authorise euthanasia, even in circumstances such as these, for, once euthanasia is recognised as lawful in these circumstances, it is difficult to see any logical basis for excluding it in others."

In *Bland* the House of Lords held that treatment, including the provision of nutrition and hydration to the patient by artificial means, could be withheld from a mentally incapacitated patient who had no hope of recovery when it was known that the patient would shortly thereafter die, provided that responsible and competent medical opinion was of the view that it would be in the patient's best interests not to prolong his life by continuing the treatment because such treatment would be futile and would not confer any benefit on him.

Private international law

International protection of adults
    63.—Schedule 3—   **1–452**
    (a) gives effect in England and Wales to the Convention on the International Protection of Adults signed at the Hague on 13th January 2000 (Cm. 5881) (in so far as this Act does not otherwise do so), and
    (b) makes related provision as to the private international law of England and Wales.

GENERAL NOTE
    Schedule 3 makes provision as to the private international law of England and Wales in **1–453** relation to persons who cannot protect their interests. In particular, it gives effect in England and Wales to the Convention on the International Protection of Adults (Cm.5881) which was signed at the Hague on January 13, 2000. For the purposes of the Convention, England and Wales, Scotland and Northern Ireland are treated separately because they constitute separate jurisdictions. The provisions of Sch.3 are intended to be compatible with the provisions of Sch.3 to the Adults with Incapacity (Scotland) Act 2000 (asp 4) which provides for the private international law of Scotland in this field, and implemented the Convention in Scotland. The Explanatory Memorandum states at para.170:

"Scotland is as yet, the only country to have ratified the Convention, which will enter into force only once it has been ratified by three states. However, Sch.3 provides private international law rules to govern jurisdictional issues between Scotland and England/Wales, irrespective of whether the Convention is in force."

The aims of the Convention are set out in Art.1. They are to:

- provide for the protection in international situations of adults who, by reason of impairment or insufficiency in their personal faculties, are not in a position to defend their interests
- establish rules on jurisdiction, applicable law, international recognition and enforcement of protective measures which are to be respected by all Contracting States, and co-operation between Contracting States.

Interpretation

1–454　　**64.**—(1) In this Act—

"the 1985 Act" means the Enduring Powers of Attorney Act 1985 (c. 29),

"advance decision" has the meaning given in section 24(1),

["authorisation under Schedule A1" means either—

　(a) a standard authorisation under that Schedule, or

　(b) an urgent authorisation under that Schedule.]

"the court" means the Court of Protection established by section 45, "Court of Protection Rules" has the meaning given in section 51(1), "Court of Protection Visitor" has the meaning given in section 61, "deputy" has the meaning given in section 16(2)(b),

"enactment" includes a provision of subordinate legislation (within the meaning of the Interpretation Act 1978 (c. 30)),

"health record" has the meaning given in section 68 of the Data Protection Act 1998 (c. 29) (as read with section 69 of that Act),

"the Human Rights Convention" has the same meaning as "the Convention" in the Human Rights Act 1998 (c. 42),

"independent mental capacity advocate" has the meaning given in section 35(1),

"lasting power of attorney" has the meaning given in section 9,

"life-sustaining treatment" has the meaning given in section 4(10),

"local authority" [, except in Schedule A1,] means—

　(a) the council of a county in England in which there are no district councils,

　(b) the council of a district in England,

　(c) the council of a county or county borough in Wales,

　(d) the council of a London borough,

　(e) the Common Council of the City of London, or

　(f) the Council of the Isles of Scilly,

"Mental Health Act" means the Mental Health Act 1983 (c. 20),

"prescribed", in relation to regulations made under this Act, means prescribed by those regulations,

"property" includes any thing in action and any interest in real or personal property,

"public authority" has the same meaning as in the Human Rights Act 1998, "Public Guardian" has the meaning given in section 57,

"purchaser" and "purchase" have the meaning given in section 205(1) of the Law of Property Act 1925 (c. 20),

"social services function" has the meaning given in section 1A of the Local Authority Social Services Act 1970 (c. 42),

"treatment" includes a diagnostic or other procedure,

"trust corporation" has the meaning given in section 68(1) of the Trustee Act 1925 (c.19), and

"will" includes codicil.

(2) In this Act, references to making decisions, in relation to a donee of a lasting power of attorney or a deputy appointed by the court, include, where appropriate, acting on decisions made.

(3) In this Act, references to the bankruptcy of an individual include a case where a bankruptcy restrictions order under the Insolvency Act 1986 (c. 45) has effect in respect of him.

(4) "Bankruptcy restrictions order" includes an interim bankruptcy restrictions order.

[(5) In this Act, references to deprivation of a person's liberty have the same meaning as in Article 5(1) of the Human Rights Convention.

(6) For the purposes of such references, it does not matter whether a person is deprived of his liberty by a public authority or not.]

AMENDMENTS

The amendments to this section were made by the Mental Capacity Act 2007, s.50(7), **1–455** Sch.9, Pt.1, para.10.

GENERAL NOTE

Subsection (1)

TREATMENT. The provision of nutrition and hydration to a patient which involves the **1–456** application of a medical technique is "medical treatment" (*Airedale NHS Trust v Bland* [1993] 1 All E.R. 821, HL).

Rules, regulations and orders

65.—(1) Any power to make rules, regulations or orders under this Act [, other **1–457** than the powers in section 21]—

  (a) is exercisable by statutory instrument;
  (b) includes power to make supplementary, incidental, consequential, transitional or saving provision;
  (c) includes power to make different provision for different cases.

(2) Any statutory instrument containing rules, regulations or orders made by the Lord Chancellor or the Secretary of State under this Act, other than—

  (a) regulations under section 34 (loss of capacity during research project),
  (b) regulations under section 41 (adjusting role of independent mental capacity advocacy service),
  (c) regulations under paragraph 32(1)(b) of Schedule 3 (private international law relating to the protection of adults),
  (d) an order of the kind mentioned in section 67(6) (consequential amendments of primary legislation), or
  (e) an order under section 68 (commencement),

is subject to annulment in pursuance of a resolution of either House of Parliament.

(3) A statutory instrument containing an Order in Council under paragraph 31 of Schedule 3 (provision to give further effect to Hague Convention) is subject to annulment in pursuance of a resolution of either House of Parliament.

(4) A statutory instrument containing regulations made by the Secretary of State under section 34 or 41 or by the Lord Chancellor under paragraph 32(1)(b) of Schedule 3 may not be made unless a draft has been laid before and approved by resolution of each House of Parliament.

[(4A) Subsection (2) does not apply to a statutory instrument containing regulations made by the Secretary of State under Schedule A1.

(4B) If such a statutory instrument contains regulations under paragraph 42(2)(b), 129, 162 or 164 of Schedule A1 (whether or not it also contains other regulations), the instrument may not be made unless a draft has been laid before and approved by resolution of each House of Parliament.

(4C) Subject to that, such a statutory instrument is subject to annulment in pursuance of a resolution of either House of Parliament.]

[(5) An order under section 21—

(a) may include supplementary, incidental, consequential, transitional or saving provision;

(b) may make different provision for different cases;

(c) is to be made in the form of a statutory instrument to which the Statutory Instruments Act 1946 applies as if the order were made by a Minister of the Crown; and

(d) is subject to annulment in pursuance of a resolution of either House of Parliament.]

AMENDMENTS

1–458   The amendments to this section were made by SI 2006/1016, art.2, Sch.1 and the Mental Capacity Act 2005, s.50(7), Sch.9, Pt.1, para.11.

Existing receivers and enduring powers of attorney etc

1–459   **66.**—(1) The following provisions cease to have effect—

(a) Part 7 of the Mental Health Act,

(b) the Enduring Powers of AttorneyAct 1985 (c. 29).

(2) No enduring power of attorney within the meaning of the 1985 Act is to be created after the commencement of subsection (1)(b).

(3) Schedule 4 has effect in place of the 1985 Act in relation to any enduring power of attorney created before the commencement of subsection (1)(b).

(4) Schedule 5 contains transitional provisions and savings in relation to Part 7 of the Mental Health Act and the 1985 Act.

GENERAL NOTE

1–460   This section repeals Pt VII of the Mental Health Act 1983 and the whole of the Enduring Powers of Attorney Act 1985, but provides through transitional provisions contained in Schs 4 and 5 that those with valid powers as attorneys under the 1985 Act or receivers appointed under the 1983 Act do not lose their powers on the implementation of the repeals. It will no longer be possible to create an enduring power of attorney once the repeal of the 1985 Act has taken effect.

Subsection (3)

1–461   Schedule 4 has effect in relation to enduring powers of attorney created before the implementation of this Act. It ensures that such instruments will continue to have the same legal effect as they had at the time they were made. They will also continue to be governed by the same legal rules and procedures which were in place at the time they were made. The Schedule therefore reproduces, with amendments, the relevant provisions of the 1985 Act and provides that the principles set out in s.1 shall not retrospectively apply to EPAs. The amendments are directed to the way in which tasks performed by the replaced Court of Protection will, on implementation of this Act, be divided between the Court of Protection and the Office of Public Guardian.

Subsection (4)

1–462   Schedule 5 contains transitional provisions that apply to circumstances where a receiver was appointed under the Mental Health Act 1983 before October 1, 2007. From that date, existing receivers became deputies with the functions that they had as receivers (Sch.5, para.1(2)). Where a former receiver wishes to make a decision for P, but may not be reason of s.20(1), because P retains the capacity to make the decision in question, the former receiver must make an application to the Court of Protection for directions (Sch.5, para.1(4)).

Minor and consequential amendments and repeals

67.—(1) Schedule 6 contains minor and consequential amendments.   **1–463**

(2) Schedule 7 contains repeals.

(3) The Lord Chancellor may by order make supplementary, incidental, consequential, transitional or saving provision for the purposes of, in consequence of, or for giving full effect to a provision of this Act.

(4) An order under subsection (3) may, in particular—

(a) provide for a provision of this Act which comes into force before another provision of this Act has come into force to have effect, until the other provision has come into force, with specified modifications;

(b) amend, repeal or revoke an enactment, other than one contained in an Act or Measure passed in a Session after the one in which this Act is passed.

(5) The amendments that may be made under subsection (4)(b) are in addition to those made by or under any other provision of this Act.

(6) An order under subsection (3) which amends or repeals a provision of an Act or Measure may not be made unless a draft has been laid before and approved by resolution of each House of Parliament.

Commencement and extent

68.—(1) This Act, other than sections 30 to 41, comes into force in accordance **1–464** with provision made by order by the Lord Chancellor.

(2) Sections 30 to 41 come into force in accordance with provision made by order by—

(a) the Secretary of State, in relation to England, and

(b) the National Assembly for Wales, in relation to Wales.

(3) An order under this section may appoint different days for different provisions and different purposes.

(4) Subject to subsections (5) and (6), this Act extends to England and Wales only.

(5) The following provisions extend to the United Kingdom—

(a) paragraph 16(1) of Schedule 1(evidence of instruments and of registration of lasting powers of attorney),

(b) paragraph 15(3) of Schedule 4(evidence of instruments and of registration of enduring powers of attorney).

(6) Subject to any provision made in Schedule 6, the amendments and repeals made by Schedules 6 and 7 have the same extent as the enactments to which they relate.

GENERAL NOTE

The following commencement orders has been made under this section: the Mental **1–465** Capacity Act 2005 (Commencement No.1) Order 2006 (SI 2006/2814) (as amended by SI 2006/3473), the Mental Capacity Act 2005 (Commencement No.1) (England and Wales) Order 2007 (SI 2007/563), the Mental Capacity Act (Commencement) (Wales) Order 2007 (SI 2007/856) (W.79) and the Mental Capacity (Commencement No.2) Order 2007 (SI 2007/1897).

Subsection (2)(b)
1–466   The functions of the National Assembly for Wales are performed by the Welsh Ministers (Government of Wales Act 2006, s.162, Sch.11, para.30).

Short title

1–467   **69**. This Act may be cited as the Mental Capacity Act 2005.

SCHEDULES

[SCHEDULE A1

HOSPITAL AND CARE HOME RESIDENTS: DEPRIVATION OF LIBERTY

PART 1

AUTHORISATION TO DEPRIVE RESIDENTS OF LIBERTY ETC

Application of Part

1–468   **1.**—(1) This Part applies if the following conditions are met.

(2) The first condition is that a person ("P") is detained in a hospital or care home—for the purpose of being given care or treatment—

in circumstances which amount to deprivation of the person's liberty.

(3) The second condition is that a standard or urgent authorisation is in force.

(4) The third condition is that the standard or urgent authorisation relates—

(a) to P, and

(b) to the hospital or care home in which P is detained.

Authorisation to deprive P of liberty

1–469   **2.** The managing authority of the hospital or care home may deprive P of his liberty by detaining him as mentioned in paragraph 1(2).

No liability for acts done for purpose of depriving P of liberty

1–470   **3.**—(1) This paragraph applies to any act which a person ("D") does for the purpose of detaining P as mentioned in paragraph 1(2).

(2) D does not incur any liability in relation to the act that he would not have incurred if P—

(a) had had capacity to consent in relation to D's doing the act,

and

(b) had consented to D's doing the act.

No protection for negligent acts etc

1–471   **4.**—(1) Paragraphs 2 and 3 do not exclude a person's civil liability for loss or damage, or his criminal liability, resulting from his negligence in doing any thing.

(2) Paragraphs 2 and 3 do not authorise a person to do anything otherwise than for the purpose of the standard or urgent authorisation that is in force.

(3) In a case where a standard authorisation is in force, paragraphs 2 and 3 do not authorise a person to do anything which does not comply with the conditions (if any) included in the authorisation.

PART 2

INTERPRETATION: MAIN TERMS

Introduction

1–472   **5.**—This Part applies for the purposes of this Schedule.

Detained resident

    6. "Detained resident" means a person detained in a hospital or care home—for the purpose of being given care or treatment—in circumstances which amount to deprivation of the person's liberty.   **1–473**

Relevant person etc

    7. In relation to a person who is, or is to be, a detained resident—   **1–474**

    "relevant person" means the person in question;

    "relevant hospital or care home" means the hospital or care home in question;

    "relevant care or treatment" means the care or treatment in question.

Authorisations

    8. "Standard authorisation" means an authorisation given under Part 4.   **1–475**

    9. "Urgent authorisation" means an authorisation given under Part 5.   **1–476**

    10. "Authorisation under this Schedule" means either of the following—   **1–477**

    (a) a standard authorisation;

    (b) an urgent authorisation.

    11.—(1) The purpose of a standard authorisation is the purpose which is stated in the authorisation in accordance with paragraph 55(1)(d).   **1–478**

    (2) The purpose of an urgent authorisation is the purpose which is stated in the authorisation in accordance with paragraph 80(d).

PART 3

THE QUALIFYING REQUIREMENTS

The qualifying requirements

    12.—(1) These are the qualifying requirements referred to in this Schedule—   **1–479**

    (a) the age requirement;

    (b) the mental health requirement;

    (c) the mental capacity requirement;

    (d) the best interests requirement;

    (e) the eligibility requirement;

    (f) the no refusals requirement.

    (2) Any question of whether a person who is, or is to be, a detained resident meets the qualifying requirements is to be determined in accordance with this Part.

    (3) In a case where—

    (a) the question of whether a person meets a particular qualifying requirement arises in relation to the giving of a standard authorisation, and

    (b) any circumstances relevant to determining that question are expected to change between the time when the determination is made and the time when the authorisation is expected to come into force,

those circumstances are to be taken into account as they are expected to be at the later time.

The age requirement

    13. The relevant person meets the age requirement if he has reached 18.   **1–480**

The mental health requirement

    14.—(1) The relevant person meets the mental health requirement if he is suffering from mental disorder (within the meaning of the Mental Health Act, but disregarding any exclusion for persons with learning disability).   **1–481**

    (2) An exclusion for persons with learning disability is any provision of the Mental Health Act which provides for a person with learning disability not to be regarded as suffering from mental disorder for one or more purposes of that Act.

The mental capacity requirement

    15. The relevant person meets the mental capacity requirement if he lacks capacity in relation to the question whether or not he should be accommodated in the relevant hospital or care home for the purpose of being given the relevant care or treatment.   **1–482**

The best interests requirement

1–483 **16.**—(1) The relevant person meets the best interests requirement if all of the following conditions are met.

(2) The first condition is that the relevant person is, or is to be, a detained resident.

(3) The second condition is that it is in the best interests of the relevant person for him to be a detained resident.

(4) The third condition is that, in order to prevent harm to the relevant person, it is necessary for him to be a detained resident.

(5) The fourth condition is that it is a proportionate response to—

(a) the likelihood of the relevant person suffering harm, and

(b) the seriousness of that harm,

for him to be a detained resident.

The eligibility requirement

1–484 **17.**—(1) The relevant person meets the eligibility requirement unless he is ineligible to be deprived of liberty by this Act.

(2) Schedule 1A applies for the purpose of determining whether or not P is ineligible to be deprived of liberty by this Act.

The no refusals requirement

1–485 **18.** The relevant person meets the no refusals requirement unless there is a refusal within the meaning of paragraph 19 or 20.

1–486 **19.**—(1) There is a refusal if these conditions are met—

(a) the relevant person has made an advance decision;

(b) the advance decision is valid;

(c) the advance decision is applicable to some or all of the relevant treatment.

(2) Expressions used in this paragraph and any of sections 24, 25 or 26 have the same meaning in this paragraph as in that section.

1–487 **20.**—(1) There is a refusal if it would be in conflict with a valid decision of a donee or deputy for the relevant person to be accommodated in the relevant hospital or care home for the purpose of receiving some or all of the relevant care or treatment—

(a) in circumstances which amount to deprivation of the

person's liberty, or

(b) at all.

(2) A donee is a donee of a lasting power of attorney granted by the relevant person.

(3) A decision of a donee or deputy is valid if it is made—

(a) within the scope of his authority as donee or deputy, and

(b) in accordance with Part 1 of this Act.

PART 4

STANDARD AUTHORISATIONS

Supervisory body to give authorisation

1–488 **21.** Only the supervisory body may give a standard authorisation.

1–489 **22.** The supervisory body may not give a standard authorisation unless—

(a) the managing authority of the relevant hospital or care home have requested it, or

(b) paragraph 71 applies (right of third party to require consideration of whether authorisation needed).

1–490 **23.** The managing authority may not make a request for a standard authorisation unless—

(a) they are required to do so by paragraph 24 (as read with paragraphs 27 to 29),

(b) they are required to do so by paragraph 25 (as read with paragraph 28), or

(c) they are permitted to do so by paragraph 30.

Duty to request authorisation: basic cases

1–491 **24.**—(1) The managing authority must request a standard authorisation in any of the following cases.

(2) The first case is where it appears to the managing authority that the relevant person—

(a) is not yet accommodated in the relevant hospital or care home,

(b) is likely—at some time within the next 28 days—to be a detained resident in the relevant hospital or care home, and

(c) is likely—

(i) at that time, or

(ii) at some later time within the next 28 days,

to meet all of the qualifying requirements.

(3) The second case is where it appears to the managing authority that the relevant person—

(a) is already accommodated in the relevant hospital or care home,

(b) is likely—at some time within the next 28 days—to be a detained resident in the relevant hospital or care home,

and

(c) is likely—

(i) at that time, or

(ii) at some later time within the next 28 days,

to meet all of the qualifying requirements.

(4) The third case is where it appears to the managing authority that the relevant person—

(a) is a detained resident in the relevant hospital or care home, and

(b) meets all of the qualifying requirements, or is likely to do so at some time within the next 28 days.

(5) This paragraph is subject to paragraphs 27 to 29.

Duty to request authorisation: change in place of detention

25.—(1) The relevant managing authority must request a standard authorisation if it appears to them **1–492** that these conditions are met.

(2) The first condition is that a standard authorisation—

(a) has been given, and

(b) has not ceased to be in force.

(3) The second condition is that there is, or is to be, a change in the place of detention.

(4) This paragraph is subject to paragraph 28.

26.—(1) This paragraph applies for the purposes of paragraph 25. **1–493**

(2) There is a change in the place of detention if the relevant person—

(a) ceases to be a detained resident in the stated hospital or care home, and

(b) becomes a detained resident in a different hospital or care home ("the new hospital or care home").

(3) The stated hospital or care home is the hospital or care home to which the standard authorisation relates.

(4) The relevant managing authority are the managing authority of the new hospital or care home.

Other authority for detention: request for authorisation

27.—(1) This paragraph applies if, by virtue of section 4A(3), a decision of the court authorises the **1–494** relevant person to be a detained resident.

(2) Paragraph 24 does not require a request for a standard authorisation to be made in relation to that detention unless these conditions are met.

(3) The first condition is that the standard authorisation would be in force at a time immediately after the expiry of the other authority.

(4) The second condition is that the standard authorisation would not be in force at any time on or before the expiry of the other authority.

(5) The third condition is that it would, in the managing authority's view, be unreasonable to delay making the request until a time nearer the expiry of the other authority.

(6) In this paragraph—

(a) the other authority is—

(i) the decision mentioned in sub-paragraph (1), or

(ii) any further decision of the court which, by virtue of section 4A(3), authorises, or is expected to authorise, the relevant person to be a detained resident;

(b) the expiry of the other authority is the time when the other authority is expected to cease to authorise the relevant person to be a detained resident.

Request refused: no further request unless change of circumstances

28.—(1) This paragraph applies if— **1–495**

(a) a managing authority request a standard authorisation under paragraph 24 or 25, and

(b) the supervisory body are prohibited by paragraph 50(2) from giving the authorisation.

(2) Paragraph 24 or 25 does not require that managing authority to make a new request for a standard authorisation unless it appears to the managing authority that—

(a) there has been a change in the relevant person's case, and

(b) because of that change, the supervisory body are likely to give a standard authorisation if requested.

Authorisation given: request for further authorisation

1–496 **29.**—(1) This paragraph applies if a standard authorisation—

(a) has been given in relation to the detention of the relevant person, and

(b) that authorisation ("the existing authorisation") has not ceased to be in force.

(2) Paragraph 24 does not require a new request for a standard authorisation ("the new authorisation") to be made unless these conditions are met.

(3) The first condition is that the new authorisation would be in force at a time immediately after the expiry of the existing authorisation.

(4) The second condition is that the new authorisation would not be in force at any time on or before the expiry of the existing authorisation.

(5) The third condition is that it would, in the managing authority's view, be unreasonable to delay making the request until a time nearer the expiry of the existing authorisation.

(6) The expiry of the existing authorisation is the time when it is expected to cease to be in force.

Power to request authorisation

1–497 **30.**—(1) This paragraph applies if—

(a) a standard authorisation has been given in relation to the detention of the relevant person,

(b) that authorisation ("the existing authorisation") has not ceased to be in force,

(c) the requirement under paragraph 24 to make a request for a new standard authorisation does not apply, because of paragraph 29, and

(d) a review of the existing authorisation has been requested, or is being carried out, in accordance with Part 8.

(2) The managing authority may request a new standard authorisation which would be in force on or before the expiry of the existing authorisation; but only if it would also be in force immediately after that expiry.

(3) The expiry of the existing authorisation is the time when it is expected to cease to be in force.

(4) Further provision relating to cases where a request is made under this paragraph can be found in—

(a) paragraph 62 (effect of decision about request), and

(b) paragraph 124 (effect of request on Part 8 review).

Information included in request

1–498 **31.** A request for a standard authorisation must include the information (if any) required by regulations.

Records of requests

1–499 **32.**—(1) The managing authority of a hospital or care home must keep a written record of—

(a) each request that they make for a standard authorisation, and

(b) the reasons for making each request.

(2) A supervisory body must keep a written record of each request for a standard authorisation that is made to them.

Relevant person must be assessed

1–500 **33.**—(1) This paragraph applies if the supervisory body are requested to give a standard authorisation.

(2) The supervisory body must secure that all of these assessments are carried out in relation to the relevant person—

(a) an age assessment;

(b) a mental health assessment;

(c) a mental capacity assessment;

    (d) a best interests assessment;

    (e) an eligibility assessment;

    (f) a no refusals assessment.

    (3) The person who carries out any such assessment is referred to as the assessor.

    (4) Regulations may be made about the period (or periods) within which assessors must carry out assessments.

    (5) This paragraph is subject to paragraphs 49 and 133.

Age assessment

    34. An age assessment is an assessment of whether the relevant person meets the age requirement. **1–501**

Mental health assessment

    35. A mental health assessment is an assessment of whether the relevant person meets the mental **1–502** health requirement.

    36. When carrying out a mental health assessment, the assessor must also— **1–503**

    (a) consider how (if at all) the relevant person's mental health is likely to be affected by his being a detained resident, and

    (b) notify the best interests assessor of his conclusions.

Mental capacity assessment

    37. A mental capacity assessment is an assessment of whether the relevant person meets the mental **1–504** capacity requirement.

Best interests assessment

    38. A best interests assessment is an assessment of whether the relevant person meets the best inter- **1–505** ests requirement.

    39.—(1) In carrying out a best interests assessment, the assessor must comply with the duties in sub- **1–506** paragraphs (2) and (3).

    (2) The assessor must consult the managing authority of the relevant hospital or care home.

    (3) The assessor must have regard to all of the following—

    (a) the conclusions which the mental health assessor has notified to the best interests assessor in accordance with paragraph 36(b);

    (b) any relevant needs assessment;

    (c) any relevant care plan.

    (4) A relevant needs assessment is an assessment of the relevant person's needs which—

    (a) was carried out in connection with the relevant person being accommodated in the relevant hospital or care home, and

    (b) was carried out by or on behalf of—

       (i) the managing authority of the relevant hospital or care home, or

       (ii) the supervisory body.

    (5) A relevant care plan is a care plan which—

    (a) sets out how the relevant person's needs are to be met whilst he is accommodated in the relevant hospital or care home, and

    (b) was drawn up by or on behalf of—

       (i) the managing authority of the relevant hospital or care home, or

       (ii) the supervisory body.

    (6) The managing authority must give the assessor a copy of—

    (a) any relevant needs assessment carried out by them or on their behalf, or

    (b) any relevant care plan drawn up by them or on their behalf.

    (7) The supervisory body must give the assessor a copy of—

    (a) any relevant needs assessment carried out by them or on their behalf, or

    (b) any relevant care plan drawn up by them or on their behalf.

    (8) The duties in sub-paragraphs (2) and (3) do not affect any other duty to consult or to take the views of others into account.

    40.—(1) This paragraph applies whatever conclusion the best interests assessment comes to. **1–507**

    (2) The assessor must state in the best interests assessment the name and address of every interested person whom he has consulted in carrying out the assessment.

    41. Paragraphs 42 and 43 apply if the best interests assessment comes to the conclusion that the rel- **1–508** evant person meets the best interests requirement.

1–509   **42.**—(1) The assessor must state in the assessment the maximum authorisation period.

(2) The maximum authorisation period is the shorter of these periods—

    (a) the period which, in the assessor's opinion, would be the appropriate maximum period for the relevant person to be a detained resident under the standard authorisation that has been requested;

    (b) 1 year, or such shorter period as may be prescribed in regulations.

(3) Regulations under sub-paragraph (2)(b)—

    (a) need not provide for a shorter period to apply in relation to all standard authorisations;

    (b) may provide for different periods to apply in relation to different kinds of standard authorisations.

(4) Before making regulations under sub-paragraph (2)(b) the Secretary of State must consult all of the following—

    (a) each body required by regulations under paragraph 162 to monitor and report on the operation of this Schedule in relation to England;

    (b) such other persons as the Secretary of State considers it appropriate to consult.

(5) Before making regulations under sub-paragraph (2)(b) the National Assembly for Wales must consult all of the following—

    (a) each person or body directed under paragraph 163(2) to carry out any function of the Assembly of monitoring and reporting on the operation of this Schedule in relation to Wales;

    (b) such other persons as the Assembly considers it appropriate to consult.

1–510   **43.** The assessor may include in the assessment recommendations about conditions to which the standard authorisation is, or is not, to be subject in accordance with paragraph 53.

1–511   **44.**—(1) This paragraph applies if the best interests assessment comes to the conclusion that the relevant person does not meet the best interests requirement.

(2) If, on the basis of the information taken into account in carrying out the assessment, it appears to the assessor that there is an unauthorised deprivation of liberty, he must include a statement to that effect in the assessment.

(3) There is an unauthorised deprivation of liberty if the managing authority of the relevant hospital or care home are already depriving the relevant person of his liberty without authority of the kind mentioned in section 4A.

1–512   **45.** The duties with which the best interests assessor must comply are subject to the provision included in appointment regulations under Part 10 (in particular, provision made under paragraph 146).

Eligibility assessment

1–513   **46.** An eligibility assessment is an assessment of whether the relevant person meets the eligibility requirement.

1–514   **47.**—(1) Regulations may—

    (a) require an eligibility assessor to request a best interests assessor to provide relevant eligibility information, and

    (b) require the best interests assessor, if such a request is made, to provide such relevant eligibility information as he may have.

(2) In this paragraph—

"best interests assessor" means any person who is carrying out, or has carried out, a best interests assessment in relation to the relevant person;

"eligibility assessor" means a person carrying out an eligibility assessment in relation to the relevant person;

"relevant eligibility information" is information relevant to assessing whether or not the relevant person is ineligible by virtue of paragraph 5 of Schedule 1A.

No refusals assessment

1–515   **48.** A no refusals assessment is an assessment of whether the relevant person meets the no refusals requirement.

Equivalent assessment already carried out

1–516   **49.**—(1) The supervisory body are not required by paragraph 33 to secure that a particular kind of assessment ("the required assessment") is carried out in relation to the relevant person if the following conditions are met.

(2) The first condition is that the supervisory body have a written copy of an assessment of the relevant person ("the existing assessment") that has already been carried out.

(3) The second condition is that the existing assessment complies with all requirements under this Schedule with which the required assessment would have to comply (if it were carried out).

(4) The third condition is that the existing assessment was carried out within the previous 12 months; but this condition need not be met if the required assessment is an age assessment.

(5) The fourth condition is that the supervisory body are satisfied that there is no reason why the existing assessment may no longer be accurate.

(6) If the required assessment is a best interests assessment, in satisfying themselves as mentioned in sub-paragraph (5), the supervisory body must take into account any information given, or submissions made, by—

(a) the relevant person's representative,

(b) any section 39C IMCA, or

(c) any section 39D IMCA.

(7) It does not matter whether the existing assessment was carried out in connection with a request for a standard authorisation or for some other purpose.

(8) If, because of this paragraph, the supervisory body are not required by paragraph 33 to secure that the required assessment is carried out, the existing assessment is to be treated for the purposes of this Schedule—

(a) as an assessment of the same kind as the required assessment, and

(b) as having been carried out under paragraph 33 in connection with the request for the standard authorisation.

Duty to give authorisation

50.—(1) The supervisory body must give a standard authorisation if—   **1–517**

(a) all assessments are positive, and

(b) the supervisory body have written copies of all those assessments.

(2) The supervisory body must not give a standard authorisation except in accordance with sub-paragraph (1).

(3) All assessments are positive if each assessment carried out under paragraph 33 has come to the conclusion that the relevant person meets the qualifying requirement to which the assessment relates.

Terms of authorisation

51.—(1) If the supervisory body are required to give a standard authorisation, they must decide the   **1–518** period during which the authorisation is to be in force.

(2) That period must not exceed the maximum authorisation period stated in the best interests assessment.

52. A standard authorisation may provide for the authorisation to come into force at a time after it is   **1–519** given.

53.—(1) A standard authorisation may be given subject to conditions.   **1–520**

(2) Before deciding whether to give the authorisation subject to conditions, the supervisory body must have regard to any recommendations in the best interests assessment about such conditions.

(3) The managing authority of the relevant hospital or care home must ensure that any conditions are complied with.

Form of authorisation

54. A standard authorisation must be in writing.   **1–521**

55.—(1) A standard authorisation must state the following things—   **1–522**

(a) the name of the relevant person;

(b) the name of the relevant hospital or care home;

(c) the period during which the authorisation is to be in force;

(d) the purpose for which the authorisation is given;

(e) any conditions subject to which the authorisation is given;

(f) the reason why each qualifying requirement is met.

(2) The statement of the reason why the eligibility requirement is met must be framed by reference to the cases in the table in paragraph 2 of Schedule 1A.

56.—(1) If the name of the relevant hospital or care home changes, the standard authorisation is to be   **1–523** read as if it stated the current name of the hospital or care home.

(2) But sub-paragraph (1) is subject to any provision relating to the change of name which is made in any enactment or in any instrument made under an enactment.

Duty to give information about decision

1–524   **57.**—(1) This paragraph applies if—

(a) a request is made for a standard authorisation, and

(b) the supervisory body are required by paragraph 50(1) to give the standard authorisation.

(2) The supervisory body must give a copy of the authorisation to each of the following—

(a) the relevant person's representative;

(b) the managing authority of the relevant hospital or care home;

(c) the relevant person;

(d) any section 39A IMCA;

(e) every interested person consulted by the best interests assessor.

(3) The supervisory body must comply with this paragraph as soon as practicable after they give the standard authorisation.

1–525   **58.**—(1) This paragraph applies if—

(a) a request is made for a standard authorisation, and

(b) the supervisory body are prohibited by paragraph 50(2) from giving the standard authorisation.

(2) The supervisory body must give notice, stating that they are prohibited from giving the authorisation, to each of the following—

(a) the managing authority of the relevant hospital or care home;

(b) the relevant person;

(c) any section 39A IMCA;

(d) every interested person consulted by the best interests assessor.

(3) The supervisory body must comply with this paragraph as soon as practicable after it becomes apparent to them that they are prohibited from giving the authorisation.

Duty to give information about effect of authorisation

1–526   **59.**—(1) This paragraph applies if a standard authorisation is given.

(2) The managing authority of the relevant hospital or care home must take such steps as are practicable to ensure that the relevant person understands all of the following—

(a) the effect of the authorisation;

(b) the right to make an application to the court to exercise its jurisdiction under section 21A;

(c) the right under Part 8 to request a review;

(d) the right to have a section 39D IMCA appointed;

(e) how to have a section 39D IMCA appointed.

(3) Those steps must be taken as soon as is practicable after the authorisation is given.

(4) Those steps must include the giving of appropriate information both orally and in writing.

(5) Any written information given to the relevant person must also be given by the managing authority to the relevant person's representative.

(6) They must give the information to the representative as soon as is practicable after it is given to the relevant person.

(7) Sub-paragraph (8) applies if the managing authority is notified that a section 39D IMCA has been appointed.

(8) As soon as is practicable after being notified, the managing authority must give the section 39D IMCA a copy of the written information given in accordance with sub-paragraph (4).

Records of authorisations

1–527   **60.** A supervisory body must keep a written record of all of the following information—

(a) the standard authorisations that they have given;

(b) the requests for standard authorisations in response to which they have not given an authorisation;

(c) in relation to each standard authorisation given: the matters stated in the authorisation in accordance with paragraph 55.

Variation of an authorisation

1–528   **61.**—(1) A standard authorisation may not be varied except in accordance with Part 7 or 8.

(2) This paragraph does not affect the powers of the Court of Protection or of any other court.

Effect of decision about request made under paragraph 25 or 30

1–529   **62.**—(1) This paragraph applies where the managing authority request a new standard authorisation under either of the following—

(a) paragraph 25 (change in place of detention);

(b) paragraph 30 (existing authorisation subject to review).

(2) If the supervisory body are required by paragraph 50(1) to give the new authorisation, the existing authorisation terminates at the time when the new authorisation comes into force.

(3) If the supervisory body are prohibited by paragraph 50(2) from giving the new authorisation, there is no effect on the existing authorisation's continuation in force.

When an authorisation is in force

63.—(1) A standard authorisation comes into force when it is given.   **1–530**

(2) But if the authorisation provides for it to come into force at a later time, it comes into force at that
. time.

64.—(1) A standard authorisation ceases to be in force at the end of the period stated in the author- **1–531**
isation in accordance with paragraph 55(1)(c).

(2) But if the authorisation terminates before then in accordance with paragraph 62(2) or any other provision of this Schedule, it ceases to be in force when the termination takes effect.

(3) This paragraph does not affect the powers of the Court of Protection or of any other court.

65.—(1) This paragraph applies if a standard authorisation ceases to be in force.   **1–532**

(2) The supervisory body must give notice that the authorisation has ceased to be in force.

(3) The supervisory body must give that notice to all of the following—

(a) the managing authority of the relevant hospital or care home;

(b) the relevant person;

(c) the relevant person's representative;

(d) every interested person consulted by the best interests assessor.

(4) The supervisory body must give that notice as soon as practicable after the authorisation ceases to
be in force.

When a request for a standard authorisation is "disposed of"

66.—A request for a standard authorisation is to be regarded for the purposes of this Schedule as **1–533**
disposed of if the supervisory body have given—

(a) a copy of the authorisation in accordance with paragraph 57, or

(b) notice in accordance with paragraph 58.

Right of third party to require consideration of whether authorisation needed

67. For the purposes of paragraphs 68 to 73 there is an unauthorised deprivation of liberty if—   **1–534**

(a) a person is already a detained resident in a hospital or care home, and

(b) the detention of the person is not authorised as mentioned in section 4A.

68.—(1) If the following conditions are met, an eligible person may request the supervisory body to **1–535**
decide whether or not there is an unauthorised deprivation of liberty.

(2) The first condition is that the eligible person has notified the managing authority of the relevant hospital or care home that it appears to the eligible person that there is an unauthorised deprivation of liberty.

(3) The second condition is that the eligible person has asked the managing authority to request a standard authorisation in relation to the detention of the relevant person.

(4) The third condition is that the managing authority has not requested a standard authorisation within a reasonable period after the eligible person asks it to do so.

(5) In this paragraph "eligible person" means any person other than the managing authority of the relevant hospital or care home.

69.—(1) This paragraph applies if an eligible person requests the supervisory body to decide **1–536**
whether or not there is an unauthorised deprivation of liberty.

(2) The supervisory body must select and appoint a person to carry out an assessment of whether or not the relevant person is a detained resident.

(3) But the supervisory body need not select and appoint a person to carry out such an assessment in either of these cases.

(4) The first case is where it appears to the supervisory body that the request by the eligible person is frivolous or vexatious.

(5) The second case is where it appears to the supervisory body that—

(a) the question of whether or not there is an unauthorised deprivation of liberty has already been
decided, and

(b) since that decision, there has been no change of circumstances which would merit the question being decided again.

(6) The supervisory body must not select and appoint a person to carry out an assessment under this paragraph unless it appears to the supervisory body that the person would be—

(a) suitable to carry out a best interests assessment (if one were obtained in connection with a request for a standard authorisation relating to the relevant person), and

(b) eligible to carry out such a best interests assessment.

(7) The supervisory body must notify the persons specified in subparagraph (8)—

(a) that the supervisory body have been requested to decide whether or not there is an unauthorised deprivation of liberty;

(b) of their decision whether or not to select and appoint a person to carry out an assessment under this paragraph;

(c) if their decision is to select and appoint a person, of the person appointed.

(8) The persons referred to in sub-paragraph (7) are—

(a) the eligible person who made the request under paragraph 68;

(b) the person to whom the request relates;

(c) the managing authority of the relevant hospital or care home;

(d) any section 39A IMCA.

1–537   **70.**—(1) Regulations may be made about the period within which an assessment under paragraph 69 must be carried out.

(2) Regulations made under paragraph 129(3) apply in relation to the selection and appointment of a person under paragraph 69 as they apply to the selection of a person under paragraph 129 to carry out a best interests assessment.

(3) The following provisions apply to an assessment under paragraph 69 as they apply to an assessment carried out in connection with a request for a standard authorisation—

(a) paragraph 131 (examination and copying of records);

(b) paragraph 132 (representations);

(c) paragraphs 134 and 135(1) and (2) (duty to keep records and give copies).

(4) The copies of the assessment which the supervisory body are required to give under paragraph 135(2) must be given as soon as practicable after the supervisory body are themselves given a copy of the assessment.

1–538   **71.**—(1) This paragraph applies if—

(a) the supervisory body obtain an assessment under paragraph 69,

(b) the assessment comes to the conclusion that the relevant person is a detained resident, and

(c) it appears to the supervisory body that the detention of the person is not authorised as mentioned in section 4A.

(2) This Schedule (including Part 5) applies as if the managing authority of the relevant hospital or care home had, in accordance with Part 4, requested the supervisory body to give a standard authorisation in relation to the relevant person.

(3) The managing authority of the relevant hospital or care home must supply the supervisory body with the information (if any) which the managing authority would, by virtue of paragraph 31, have had to include in a request for a standard authorisation.

(4) The supervisory body must notify the persons specified in paragraph 69(8)—

(a) of the outcome of the assessment obtained under paragraph 69, and

(b) that this Schedule applies as mentioned in sub-paragraph (2).

1–539   **72.**—(1) This paragraph applies if—

(a) the supervisory body obtain an assessment under paragraph 69, and

(b) the assessment comes to the conclusion that the relevant person is not a detained resident.

(2) The supervisory body must notify the persons specified in paragraph 69(8) of the outcome of the assessment.

1–540   **73.**—(1) This paragraph applies if—

(a) the supervisory body obtain an assessment under paragraph 69,

(b) the assessment comes to the conclusion that the relevant person is a detained resident, and

(c) it appears to the supervisory body that the detention of the person is authorised as mentioned in section 4A.

(2) The supervisory body must notify the persons specified in paragraph 69(8)—

(a) of the outcome of the assessment, and

(b) that it appears to the supervisory body that the detention is authorised.

PART 5

Managing authority to give authorisation

74. Only the managing authority of the relevant hospital or care home may give an urgent **1–541** authorisation.

75. The managing authority may give an urgent authorisation only if they are required to do so by **1–542** paragraph 76 (as read with paragraph 77).

Duty to give authorisation

76.—(1) The managing authority must give an urgent authorisation in either of the following cases. **1–543**

(2) The first case is where—

(a) the managing authority are required to make a request under paragraph 24 or 25 for a standard authorisation, and

(b) they believe that the need for the relevant person to be a detained resident is so urgent that it is appropriate for the detention to begin before they make the request.

(3) The second case is where—

(a) the managing authority have made a request under paragraph 24 or 25 for a standard authorisation, and

(b) they believe that the need for the relevant person to be a detained resident is so urgent that it is appropriate for the detention to begin before the request is disposed of.

(4) References in this paragraph to the detention of the relevant person are references to the detention to which paragraph 24 or 25 relates.

(5) This paragraph is subject to paragraph 77.

77.—(1) This paragraph applies where the managing authority have given an urgent authorisation **1–544** ("the original authorisation") in connection with a case where a person is, or is to be, a detained resident ("the existing detention").

(2) No new urgent authorisation is to be given under paragraph 76 in connection with the existing detention.

(3) But the managing authority may request the supervisory body to extend the duration of the original authorisation.

(4) Only one request under sub-paragraph (3) may be made in relation to the original authorisation.

(5) Paragraphs 84 to 86 apply to any request made under subparagraph (3).

Terms of authorisation

78.—(1) If the managing authority decide to give an urgent authorisation, they must decide the **1–545** period during which the authorisation is to be in force.

(2) That period must not exceed 7 days.

Form of authorisation

79. An urgent authorisation must be in writing. **1–546**

80. An urgent authorisation must state the following things— **1–547**

(a) the name of the relevant person;

(b) the name of the relevant hospital or care home;

(c) the period during which the authorisation is to be in force;

(d) the purpose for which the authorisation is given.

81.—(1) If the name of the relevant hospital or care home changes, the urgent authorisation is to be **1–548** read as if it stated the current name of the hospital or care home.

(2) But sub-paragraph (1) is subject to any provision relating to the change of name which is made in any enactment or in any instrument made under an enactment.

Duty to keep records and give copies

82.—(1) This paragraph applies if an urgent authorisation is given. **1–549**

(2) The managing authority must keep a written record of why they have given the urgent authorisation.

(3) As soon as practicable after giving the authorisation, the managing authority must give a copy of the authorisation to all of the following—

(a) the relevant person;

(b) any section 39A IMCA.

Duty to give information about authorisation

1–550   **83.**—(1) This paragraph applies if an urgent authorisation is given.

(2) The managing authority of the relevant hospital or care home must take such steps as are practicable to ensure that the relevant person understands all of the following—
  (a) the effect of the authorisation;
  (b) the right to make an application to the court to exercise its jurisdiction under section 21A.

(3) Those steps must be taken as soon as is practicable after the authorisation is given.

(4) Those steps must include the giving of appropriate information both orally and in writing.

Request for extension of duration

1–551   **84.**—(1) This paragraph applies if the managing authority make a request under paragraph 77 for the supervisory body to extend the duration of the original authorisation.

(2) The managing authority must keep a written record of why they have made the request.

(3) The managing authority must give the relevant person notice that they have made the request.

(4) The supervisory body may extend the duration of the original authorisation if it appears to them that—
  (a) the managing authority have made the required request for a standard authorisation,
  (b) there are exceptional reasons why it has not yet been possible for that request to be disposed of, and
  (c) it is essential for the existing detention to continue until the request is disposed of.

(5) The supervisory body must keep a written record that the request has been made to them.

(6) In this paragraph and paragraphs 85 and 86—
  (a) "original authorisation" and "existing detention" have the same meaning as in paragraph 77;
  (b) the required request for a standard authorisation is the request that is referred to in paragraph 76(2) or (3).

1–552   **85.**—(1) This paragraph applies if, under paragraph 84, the supervisory body decide to extend the duration of the original authorisation.

(2) The supervisory body must decide the period of the extension.

(3) That period must not exceed 7 days.

(4) The supervisory body must give the managing authority notice stating the period of the extension.

(5) The managing authority must then vary the original authorisation so that it states the extended duration.

(6) Paragraphs 82(3) and 83 apply (with the necessary modifications) to the variation of the original authorisation as they apply to the giving of an urgent authorisation.

(7) The supervisory body must keep a written record of—
  (a) the outcome of the request, and
  (b) the period of the extension.

1–553   **86.**—(1) This paragraph applies if, under paragraph 84, the supervisory body decide not to extend the duration of the original authorisation.

(2) The supervisory body must give the managing authority notice stating—
  (a) the decision, and
  (b) their reasons for making it.

(3) The managing authority must give a copy of that notice to all of the following—
  (a) the relevant person;
  (b) any section 39A IMCA.

(4) The supervisory body must keep a written record of the outcome of the request.

No variation

1–554   **87.**—(1) An urgent authorisation may not be varied except in accordance with paragraph 85.

(2) This paragraph does not affect the powers of the Court of Protection or of any other court.

When an authorisation is in force

1–555   **88.** An urgent authorisation comes into force when it is given.

1–556   **89.**—(1) An urgent authorisation ceases to be in force at the end of the period stated in the authorisation in accordance with paragraph 80(c) (subject to any variation in accordance with paragraph 85).

(2) But if the required request is disposed of before the end of that period, the urgent authorisation ceases to be in force as follows.

(3) If the supervisory body are required by paragraph 50(1) to give the requested authorisation, the urgent authorisation ceases to be in force when the requested authorisation comes into force.

(4) If the supervisory body are prohibited by paragraph 50(2) from giving the requested authorisation, the urgent authorisation ceases to be in force when the managing authority receive notice under paragraph 58.

(5) In this paragraph—

"required request" means the request referred to in paragraph 76(2) or (3);

"requested authorisation" means the standard authorisation to which the required request relates.

(6) This paragraph does not affect the powers of the Court of Protection or of any other court.

90.—(1) This paragraph applies if an urgent authorisation ceases to be in force.   **1–557**

(2) The supervisory body must give notice that the authorisation has ceased to be in force.

(3) The supervisory body must give that notice to all of the following—

(a) the relevant person;

(b) any section 39A IMCA.

(4) The supervisory body must give that notice as soon as practicable after the authorisation ceases to be in force.

PART 6

ELIGIBILITY REQUIREMENT NOT MET: SUSPENSION OF STANDARD AUTHORISATION

91.—(1) This Part applies if the following conditions are met.   **1–558**

(2) The first condition is that a standard authorisation—

(a) has been given, and

(b) has not ceased to be in force.

(3) The second condition is that the managing authority of the relevant hospital or care home are satisfied that the relevant person has ceased to meet the eligibility requirement.

(4) But this Part does not apply if the relevant person is ineligible by virtue of paragraph 5 of Schedule 1A (in which case see Part 8).

92. The managing authority of the relevant hospital or care home must give the supervisory body **1–559** notice that the relevant person has ceased to meet the eligibility requirement.

93.—(1) This paragraph applies if the managing authority give the supervisory body notice under **1–560** paragraph 92.

(2) The standard authorisation is suspended from the time when the notice is given.

(3) The supervisory body must give notice that the standard authorisation has been suspended to the following persons—

(a) the relevant person;

(b) the relevant person's representative;

(c) the managing authority of the relevant hospital or care home.

94.—(1) This paragraph applies if, whilst the standard authorisation is suspended, the managing **1–561** authority are satisfied that the relevant person meets the eligibility requirement again.

(2) The managing authority must give the supervisory body notice that the relevant person meets the eligibility requirement again.

95.—(1) This paragraph applies if the managing authority give the supervisory body notice under **1–562** paragraph 94.

(2) The standard authorisation ceases to be suspended from the time when the notice is given.

(3) The supervisory body must give notice that the standard authorisation has ceased to be suspended to the following persons—

(a) the relevant person;

(b) the relevant person's representative;

(c) any section 39D IMCA;

(d) the managing authority of the relevant hospital or care home.

(4) The supervisory body must give notice under this paragraph as soon as practicable after they are given notice under paragraph 94.

96.—(1) This paragraph applies if no notice is given under paragraph 94 before the end of the rel- **1–563** evant 28 day period.

(2) The standard authorisation ceases to have effect at the end of the relevant 28 day period.

(3) The relevant 28 day period is the period of 28 days beginning with the day on which the standard authorisation is suspended under paragraph 93.

1–564   97. The effect of suspending the standard authorisation is that Part 1 ceases to apply for as long as the authorisation is suspended.

PART 7

STANDARD AUTHORISATIONS: CHANGE IN SUPERVISORY RESPONSIBILITY

Application of this Part

1–565   98.—(1) This Part applies if these conditions are met.

(2) The first condition is that a standard authorisation—

(a) has been given, and

(b) has not ceased to be in force.

(3) The second condition is that there is a change in supervisory responsibility.

(4) The third condition is that there is not a change in the place of detention (within the meaning of paragraph 25).

1–566   99. For the purposes of this Part there is a change in supervisory responsibility if—

(a) one body ("the old supervisory body") have ceased to be supervisory body in relation to the standard authorisation, and

(b) a different body ("the new supervisory body") have become supervisory body in relation to the standard authorisation.

Effect of change in supervisory responsibility

1–567   100.—(1) The new supervisory body becomes the supervisory body in relation to the authorisation.

(2) Anything done by or in relation to the old supervisory body in connection with the authorisation has effect, so far as is necessary for continuing its effect after the change, as if done by or in relation to the new supervisory body.

(3) Anything which relates to the authorisation and which is in the process of being done by or in relation to the old supervisory body at the time of the change may be continued by or in relation to the new supervisory body.

(4) But—

(a) the old supervisory body do not, by virtue of this paragraph, cease to be liable for anything done by them in connection with the authorisation before the change; and

(b) the new supervisory body do not, by virtue of this paragraph, become liable for any such thing.

PART 8

STANDARD AUTHORISATIONS: REVIEW

Application of this Part

1–568   101.—(1) This Part applies if a standard authorisation—

(a) has been given, and

(b) has not ceased to be in force.

(2) Paragraphs 102 to 122 are subject to paragraphs 123 to 125.

Review by supervisory body

1–569   102.—(1) The supervisory body may at any time carry out a review of the standard authorisation in accordance with this Part.

(2) The supervisory body must carry out such a review if they are requested to do so by an eligible person.

(3) Each of the following is an eligible person—

(a) the relevant person;

(b) the relevant person's representative;

(c) the managing authority of the relevant hospital or care home.

Request for review

1–570   103.—(1) An eligible person may, at any time, request the supervisory body to carry out a review of the standard authorisation in accordance with this Part.

(2) The managing authority of the relevant hospital or care home must make such a request if one or more of the qualifying requirements appear to them to be reviewable.

Grounds for review

104.—(1) Paragraphs 105 to 107 set out the grounds on which the qualifying requirements are **1–571** reviewable.

(2) A qualifying requirement is not reviewable on any other ground.

Non-qualification ground

105.—(1) Any of the following qualifying requirements is reviewable on the ground that the relevant **1–572** person does not meet the requirement—

   (a) the age requirement;
   (b) the mental health requirement;
   (c) the mental capacity requirement;
   (d) the best interests requirement;
   (e) the no refusals requirement.

(2) The eligibility requirement is reviewable on the ground that the relevant person is ineligible by virtue of paragraph 5 of Schedule 1A.

(3) The ground in sub-paragraph (1) and the ground in subparagraph (2) are referred to as the non-qualification ground.

Change of reason ground

106.—(1) Any of the following qualifying requirements is reviewable on the ground set out in sub- **1–573** paragraph (2)—

   (a) the mental health requirement;
   (b) the mental capacity requirement;
   (c) the best interests requirement;
   (d) the eligibility requirement;
   (e) the no refusals requirement.

(2) The ground is that the reason why the relevant person meets the requirement is not the reason stated in the standard authorisation.

(3) This ground is referred to as the change of reason ground.

Variation of conditions ground

107.—(1) The best interests requirement is reviewable on the ground that—   **1–574**

   (a) there has been a change in the relevant person's case, and
   (b) because of that change, it would be appropriate to vary the conditions to which the standard authorisation is subject.

(2) This ground is referred to as the variation of conditions ground.

(3) A reference to varying the conditions to which the standard authorisation is subject is a reference to—

   (a) amendment of an existing condition,
   (b) omission of an existing condition, or
   (c) inclusion of a new condition (whether or not there are already any existing conditions).

Notice that review to be carried out

108.—(1) If the supervisory body are to carry out a review of the standard authorisation, they must **1–575** give notice of the review to the following persons—

   (a) the relevant person;
   (b) the relevant person's representative;
   (c) the managing authority of the relevant hospital or care home.

(2) The supervisory body must give the notice—

   (a) before they begin the review, or
   (b) if that is not practicable, as soon as practicable after they have begun it.

(3) This paragraph does not require the supervisory body to give notice to any person who has requested the review.

Starting a review

109.—To start a review of the standard authorisation, the supervisory body must decide which, if **1–576** any, of the qualifying requirements appear to be reviewable.

No reviewable qualifying requirements

1–577 **110.**—(1) This paragraph applies if no qualifying requirements appear to be reviewable.

(2) This Part does not require the supervisory body to take any action in respect of the standard authorisation.

One or more reviewable qualifying requirements

1–578 **111.**—(1) This paragraph applies if one or more qualifying requirements appear to be reviewable.

(2) The supervisory body must secure that a separate review assessment is carried out in relation to each qualifying requirement which appears to be reviewable.

(3) But sub-paragraph (2) does not require the supervisory body to secure that a best interests review assessment is carried out in a case where the best interests requirement appears to the supervisory body to be non-assessable.

(4) The best interests requirement is non-assessable if—

(a) the requirement is reviewable only on the variation of conditions ground, and

(b) the change in the relevant person's case is not significant.

(5) In making any decision whether the change in the relevant person's case is significant, regard must be had to—

(a) the nature of the change, and

(b) the period that the change is likely to last for.

Review assessments

1–579 **112.**—(1) A review assessment is an assessment of whether the relevant person meets a qualifying requirement.

(2) In relation to a review assessment—

(a) a negative conclusion is a conclusion that the relevant person does not meet the qualifying requirement to which the assessment relates;

(b) a positive conclusion is a conclusion that the relevant person meets the qualifying requirement to which the assessment relates.

(3) An age review assessment is a review assessment carried out in relation to the age requirement.

(4) A mental health review assessment is a review assessment carried out in relation to the mental health requirement.

(5) A mental capacity review assessment is a review assessment carried out in relation to the mental capacity requirement.

(6) A best interests review assessment is a review assessment carried out in relation to the best interests requirement.

(7) An eligibility review assessment is a review assessment carried out in relation to the eligibility requirement.

(8) A no refusals review assessment is a review assessment carried out in relation to the no refusals requirement.

1–580 **113.**—(1) In carrying out a review assessment, the assessor must comply with any duties which would be imposed upon him under Part 4 if the assessment were being carried out in connection with a request for a standard authorisation.

(2) But in the case of a best interests review assessment, paragraphs 43 and 44 do not apply.

(3) Instead of what is required by paragraph 43, the best interests review assessment must include recommendations about whether — and, if so, how — it would be appropriate to vary the conditions to which the standard authorisation is subject.

Best interests requirement reviewable but non-assessable

1–581 **114.**—(1) This paragraph applies in a case where—

(a) the best interests requirement appears to be reviewable, but

(b) in accordance with paragraph 111(3), the supervisory body are not required to secure that a best interests review assessment is carried out.

(2) The supervisory body may vary the conditions to which the standard authorisation is subject in such ways (if any) as the supervisory body think are appropriate in the circumstances.

Best interests review assessment positive

1–582 **115.**—(1) This paragraph applies in a case where—

(a) a best interests review assessment is carried out, and

(b) the assessment comes to a positive conclusion.

(2) The supervisory body must decide the following questions—

(a) whether or not the best interests requirement is reviewable on the change of reason ground;

(b) whether or not the best interests requirement is reviewable on the variation of conditions ground;

(c) if so, whether or not the change in the person's case is significant.

(3) If the supervisory body decide that the best interests requirement is reviewable on the change of reason ground, they must vary the standard authorisation so that it states the reason why the relevant person now meets that requirement.

(4) If the supervisory body decide that—

(a) the best interests requirement is reviewable on the variation of conditions ground, and

(b) the change in the relevant person's case is not significant,

they may vary the conditions to which the standard authorisation is subject in such ways (if any) as they think are appropriate in the circumstances.

(5) If the supervisory body decide that—

(a) the best interests requirement is reviewable on the variation of conditions ground, and

(b) the change in the relevant person's case is significant,

they must vary the conditions to which the standard authorisation is subject in such ways as they think are appropriate in the circumstances.

(6) If the supervisory body decide that the best interests requirement is not reviewable on—

(a) the change of reason ground, or

(b) the variation of conditions ground,

this Part does not require the supervisory body to take any action in respect of the standard authorisation so far as the best interests requirement relates to it.

Mental health, mental capacity, eligibility or no refusals review assessment positive
116.—(1) This paragraph applies if the following conditions are met.   **1–583**

(2) The first condition is that one or more of the following are carried out—

(a) a mental health review assessment;

(b) a mental capacity review assessment;

(c) an eligibility review assessment;

(d) a no refusals review assessment.

(3) The second condition is that each assessment carried out comes to a positive conclusion.

(4) The supervisory body must decide whether or not each of the assessed qualifying requirements is reviewable on the change of reason ground.

(5) If the supervisory body decide that any of the assessed qualifying requirements is reviewable on the change of reason ground, they must vary the standard authorisation so that it states the reason why the relevant person now meets the requirement or requirements in question.

(6) If the supervisory body decide that none of the assessed qualifying requirements are reviewable on the change of reason ground, this Part does not require the supervisory body to take any action in respect of the standard authorisation so far as those requirements relate to it.

(7) An assessed qualifying requirement is a qualifying requirement in relation to which a review assessment is carried out.

One or more review assessments negative
117.—(1) This paragraph applies if one or more of the review assessments carried out comes to a   **1–584**
negative conclusion.

(2) The supervisory body must terminate the standard authorisation with immediate effect.

Completion of a review
118.—(1) The review of the standard authorisation is complete in any of the following cases.   **1–585**

(2) The first case is where paragraph 110 applies.

(3) The second case is where—

(a) paragraph 111 applies, and

(b) paragraph 117 requires the supervisory body to terminate the standard authorisation.

(4) In such a case, the supervisory body need not comply with any of the other provisions of paragraphs 114 to 116 which would be applicable to the review (were it not for this sub-paragraph).

(5) The third case is where—

(a) paragraph 111 applies,

(b) paragraph 117 does not require the supervisory body to terminate the standard authorisation, and

(c) the supervisory body comply with all of the provisions of paragraphs 114 to 116 (so far as they are applicable to the review).

Variations under this Part

1–586   **119.** Any variation of the standard authorisation made under this Part must be in writing.

Notice of outcome of review

1–587   **120.**—(1) When the review of the standard authorisation is complete, the supervisory body must give notice to all of the following—

(a) the managing authority of the relevant hospital or care home;

(b) the relevant person;

(c) the relevant person's representative;

(d) any section 39D IMCA.

(2) That notice must state—

(a) the outcome of the review, and

(b) what variation (if any) has been made to the authorisation under this Part.

Records

1–588   **121.** A supervisory body must keep a written record of the following information—

(a) each request for a review that is made to them;

(b) the outcome of each request;

(c) each review which they carry out;

(d) the outcome of each review which they carry out;

(e) any variation of an authorisation made in consequence of a review.

Relationship between review and suspension under Part 6

1–589   **122.**—(1) This paragraph applies if a standard authorisation is suspended in accordance with Part 6.

(2) No review may be requested under this Part whilst the standard authorisation is suspended.

(3) If a review has already been requested, or is being carried out, when the standard authorisation is suspended, no steps are to be taken in connection with that review whilst the authorisation is suspended.

Relationship between review and request for new authorisation

1–590   **123.**—(1) This paragraph applies if, in accordance with paragraph 24 (as read with paragraph 29), the managing authority of the relevant hospital or care home make a request for a new standard authorisation which would be in force after the expiry of the existing authorisation.

(2) No review may be requested under this Part until the request for the new standard authorisation has been disposed of.

(3) If a review has already been requested, or is being carried out, when the new standard authorisation is requested, no steps are to be taken in connection with that review until the request for the new standard authorisation has been disposed of.

1–591   **124.**—(1) This paragraph applies if—

(a) a review under this Part has been requested, or is being carried out, and

(b) the managing authority of the relevant hospital or care home make a request under paragraph 30 for a new standard authorisation which would be in force on or before, and after, the expiry of the existing authorisation.

(2) No steps are to be taken in connection with the review under this Part until the request for the new standard authorisation has been disposed of.

1–592   **125.** In paragraphs 123 and 124—

(a) the existing authorisation is the authorisation referred to in paragraph 101;

(b) the expiry of the existing authorisation is the time when it is expected to cease to be in force.

PART 9

ASSESSMENTS UNDER THIS SCHEDULE

Introduction

126. This Part contains provision about assessments under this Schedule.   **1–593**

127. An assessment under this Schedule is either of the following—

(a) an assessment carried out in connection with a request for a standard authorisation under Part 4;

(b) a review assessment carried out in connection with a review of a standard authorisation under Part 8.

128. In this Part, in relation to an assessment under this Schedule—   **1–594**

"assessor" means the person carrying out the assessment;

"relevant procedure" means—

(a) the request for the standard authorisation, or

(b) the review of the standard authorisation;

"supervisory body" means the supervisory body responsible for securing that the assessment is carried out.

Supervisory body to select assessor

129.—(1) It is for the supervisory body to select a person to carry out an assessment under this   **1–595**
Schedule.

(2) The supervisory body must not select a person to carry out an assessment unless the person—

(a) appears to the supervisory body to be suitable to carry out the assessment (having regard, in particular, to the type of assessment and the person to be assessed), and

(b) is eligible to carry out the assessment.

(3) Regulations may make provision about the selection, and eligibility, of persons to carry out assessments under this Schedule.

(4) Sub-paragraphs (5) and (6) apply if two or more assessments are to be obtained for the purposes of the relevant procedure.

(5) In a case where the assessments to be obtained include a mental health assessment and a best interests assessment, the supervisory body must not select the same person to carry out both assessments.

(6) Except as prohibited by sub-paragraph (5), the supervisory body may select the same person to carry out any number of the assessments which the person appears to be suitable, and is eligible, to carry out.

130.—(1) This paragraph applies to regulations under paragraph 129(3).   **1–596**

(2) The regulations may make provision relating to a person's—

(a) qualifications,

(b) skills,

(c) training,

(d) experience,

(e) relationship to, or connection with, the relevant person or any other person,

(f) involvement in the care or treatment of the relevant person,

(g) connection with the supervisory body, or

(h) connection with the relevant hospital or care home, or with any other establishment or undertaking.

(3) The provision that the regulations may make in relation to a person's training may provide for particular training to be specified by the appropriate authority otherwise than in the regulations.

(4) In sub-paragraph (3) the "appropriate authority" means—

(a) in relation to England: the Secretary of State;

(b) in relation to Wales: the National Assembly for Wales.

(5) The regulations may make provision requiring a person to be insured in respect of liabilities that may arise in connection with the carrying out of an assessment.

(6) In relation to cases where two or more assessments are to be obtained for the purposes of the relevant procedure, the regulations may limit the number, kind or combination of assessments which a particular person is eligible to carry out.

(7) Sub-paragraphs (2) to (6) do not limit the generality of the provision that may be made in the regulations.

Examination and copying of records

1–597   **131.** An assessor may, at all reasonable times, examine and take copies of—

(a) any health record,

(b) any record of, or held by, a local authority and compiled in accordance with a social services function, and

(c) any record held by a person registered under Part 2 of the Care Standards Act 2000,

which the assessor considers may be relevant to the assessment which is being carried out.

Representations

1–598   **132.** In carrying out an assessment under this Schedule, the assessor must take into account any information given, or submissions made, by any of the following—

(a) the relevant person's representative;

(b) any section 39A IMCA;

(c) any section 39C IMCA;

(d) any section 39D IMCA.

Assessments to stop if any comes to negative conclusion

1–599   **133.**—(1) This paragraph applies if an assessment under this Schedule comes to the conclusion that the relevant person does not meet one of the qualifying requirements.

(2) This Schedule does not require the supervisory body to secure that any other assessments under this Schedule are carried out in relation to the relevant procedure.

(3) The supervisory body must give notice to any assessor who is carrying out another assessment in connection with the relevant procedure that they are to cease carrying out that assessment.

(4) If an assessor receives such notice, this Schedule does not require the assessor to continue carrying out that assessment.

Duty to keep records and give copies

1–600   **134.**—(1) This paragraph applies if an assessor has carried out an assessment under this Schedule (whatever conclusions the assessment has come to).

(2) The assessor must keep a written record of the assessment.

(3) As soon as practicable after carrying out the assessment, the assessor must give copies of the assessment to the supervisory body.

1–601   **135.**—(1) This paragraph applies to the supervisory body if they are given a copy of an assessment under this Schedule.

(2) The supervisory body must give copies of the assessment to all of the following—

(a) the managing authority of the relevant hospital or care home;

(b) the relevant person;

(c) any section 39A IMCA;

(d) the relevant person's representative.

(3) If—

(a) the assessment is obtained in relation to a request for a standard authorisation, and

(b) the supervisory body are required by paragraph 50(1) to give the standard authorisation,

the supervisory body must give the copies of the assessment when they give copies of the authorisation in accordance with paragraph 57.

(4) If—

(a) the assessment is obtained in relation to a request for a standard authorisation, and

(b) the supervisory body are prohibited by paragraph 50(2) from giving the standard authorisation,

the supervisory body must give the copies of the assessment when they give notice in accordance with paragraph 58.

(5) If the assessment is obtained in connection with the review of a standard authorisation, the supervisory body must give the copies of the assessment when they give notice in accordance with paragraph 120.

1–602   **136.**—(1) This paragraph applies to the supervisory body if—

(a) they are given a copy of a best interests assessment, and

(b) the assessment includes, in accordance with paragraph 44(2), a statement that it appears to the assessor that there is an unauthorised deprivation of liberty.

(2) The supervisory body must notify all of the persons listed in subparagraph (3) that the assessment includes such a statement.

(3) Those persons are—

(a) the managing authority of the relevant hospital or care home;

(b) the relevant person;

(c) any section 39A IMCA;

(d) any interested person consulted by the best interests assessor.

(4) The supervisory body must comply with this paragraph when (or at some time before) they comply with paragraph 135.

PART 10

RELEVANT PERSON'S REPRESENTATIVE

The representative

137. In this Schedule the relevant person's representative is the person appointed as such in accord- **1–603** ance with this Part.

138.—(1) Regulations may make provision about the selection and appointment of representatives. **1–604**

(2) In this Part such regulations are referred to as "appointment regulations".

Supervisory body to appoint representative

139.—(1) The supervisory body must appoint a person to be the relevant person's representative as **1–605** soon as practicable after a standard authorisation is given.

(2) The supervisory body must appoint a person to be the relevant person's representative if a vacancy arises whilst a standard authorisation is in force.

(3) Where a vacancy arises, the appointment under sub-paragraph (2) is to be made as soon as practicable after the supervisory body becomes aware of the vacancy.

140.—(1) The selection of a person for appointment under paragraph 139 must not be made unless it **1–606** appears to the person making the selection that the prospective representative would, if appointed—

(a) maintain contact with the relevant person,

(b) represent the relevant person in matters relating to or connected with this Schedule, and

(c) support the relevant person in matters relating to or connected with this Schedule.

141.—(1) Any appointment of a representative for a relevant person is in addition to, and does not **1–607** affect, any appointment of a donee or deputy.

(2) The functions of any representative are in addition to, and do not affect—

(a) the authority of any donee,

(b) the powers of any deputy, or

(c) any powers of the court.

Appointment regulations

142. Appointment regulations may provide that the procedure for appointing a representative may **1–608** begin at any time after a request for a standard authorisation is made (including a time before the request has been disposed of).

143.—(1) Appointment regulations may make provision about who is to select a person for appoint- **1–609** ment as a representative.

(2) But regulations under this paragraph may only provide for the following to make a selection—

(a) the relevant person, if he has capacity in relation to the question of which person should be his representative;

(b) a donee of a lasting power of attorney granted by the relevant person, if it is within the scope of his authority to select a person;

(c) a deputy, if it is within the scope of his authority to select a person;

(d) a best interests assessor;

(e) the supervisory body.

(3) Regulations under this paragraph may provide that a selection by the relevant person, a donee or a deputy is subject to approval by a best interests assessor or the supervisory body.

(4) Regulations under this paragraph may provide that, if more than one selection is necessary in connection with the appointment of a particular representative—

(a) the same person may make more than one selection;

(b) different persons may make different selections.

187

(5) For the purposes of this paragraph a best interests assessor is a person carrying out a best interests assessment in connection with the standard authorisation in question (including the giving of that authorisation).

1–610   **144.**—(1) Appointment regulations may make provision about who may, or may not, be—

(a) selected for appointment as a representative, or

(b) appointed as a representative.

(2) Regulations under this paragraph may relate to any of the following matters—

(a) a person's age;

(b) a person's suitability;

(c) a person's independence;

(d) a person's willingness;

(e) a person's qualifications.

1–611   **145.** Appointment regulations may make provision about the formalities of appointing a person as a representative.

146. In a case where a best interests assessor is to select a person to be appointed as a representative, appointment regulations may provide for the variation of the assessor's duties in relation to the assessment which he is carrying out.

Monitoring of representatives

1–612   **147.** Regulations may make provision requiring the managing authority of the relevant hospital or care home to—

(a) monitor, and

(b) report to the supervisory body on,

the extent to which a representative is maintaining contact with the relevant person.

Termination

1–613   **148.** Regulations may make provision about the circumstances in which the appointment of a person as the relevant person's representative ends or may be ended.

149. Regulations may make provision about the formalities of ending the appointment of a person as a representative.

Suspension of representative's functions

1–614   **150.**—(1) Regulations may make provision about the circumstances in which functions exercisable by, or in relation to, the relevant person's representative (whether under this Schedule or not) may be—

(a) suspended, and

(b) if suspended, revived.

(2) The regulations may make provision about the formalities for giving effect to the suspension or revival of a function.

(3) The regulations may make provision about the effect of the suspension or revival of a function.

Payment of representative

1–615   **151.** Regulations may make provision for payments to be made to, or in relation to, persons exercising functions as the relevant person's representative.

Regulations under this Part

1–616   **152.** The provisions of this Part which specify provision that may be made in regulations under this Part do not affect the generality of the power to make such regulations.

Effect of appointment of section 39C IMCA

1–617   **153.** Paragraphs 159 and 160 make provision about the exercise of functions by, or towards, the relevant person's representative during periods when—

(a) no person is appointed as the relevant person's representative, but

(b) a person is appointed as a section 39C IMCA.

PART 11

IMCAS

Application of Part

154. This Part applies for the purposes of this Schedule.   **1–618**

The IMCAs

155. A section 39A IMCA is an independent mental capacity advocate appointed under section 39A. **1–619**
156. A section 39C IMCA is an independent mental capacity advocate appointed under section 39C. **1–620**
157. A section 39D IMCA is an independent mental capacity advocate appointed under section 39D. **1–621**
158. An IMCA is a section 39A IMCA or a section 39C IMCA or a section 39D IMCA.   **1–622**

Section 39C IMCA: functions

159.—(1) This paragraph applies if, and for as long as, there is a section 39C IMCA.   **1–623**

(2) In the application of the relevant provisions, references to the relevant person's representative are to be read as references to the section 39C IMCA.

(3) But sub-paragraph (2) does not apply to any function under the relevant provisions for as long as the function is suspended in accordance with provision made under Part 10.

(4) In this paragraph and paragraph 160 the relevant provisions are—

(a) paragraph 102(3)(b) (request for review under Part 8);

(b) paragraph 108(1)(b) (notice of review under Part 8);

(c) paragraph 120(1)(c) (notice of outcome of review under Part 8).

160.—(1) This paragraph applies if—   **1–624**

(a) a person is appointed as the relevant person's representative, and

(b) a person accordingly ceases to hold an appointment as a section 39C IMCA.

(2) Where a function under a relevant provision has been exercised by, or towards, the section 39C IMCA, there is no requirement for that function to be exercised again by, or towards, the relevant person's representative.

Section 39A IMCA: restriction of functions

161.—(1) This paragraph applies if—   **1–625**

(a) there is a section 39A IMCA, and

(b) a person is appointed under Part 10 to be the relevant person's representative (whether or not that person, or any person subsequently appointed, is currently the relevant person's representative).

(2) The duties imposed on, and the powers exercisable by, the section 39A IMCA do not apply.

(3) The duties imposed on, and the powers exercisable by, any other person do not apply, so far as they fall to be performed or exercised towards the section 39A IMCA.

(4) But sub-paragraph (2) does not apply to any power of challenge exercisable by the section 39A IMCA.

(5) And sub-paragraph (3) does not apply to any duty or power of any other person so far as it relates to any power of challenge exercisable by the section 39A IMCA.

(6) Before exercising any power of challenge, the section 39A IMCA must take the views of the relevant person's representative into account.

(7) A power of challenge is a power to make an application to the court to exercise its jurisdiction under section 21A in connection with the giving of the standard authorisation.

PART 12

MISCELLANEOUS

Monitoring of operation of Schedule

162.—(1) Regulations may make provision for, and in connection with, requiring one or more pre- **1–626**
scribed bodies to monitor, and report on, the operation of this Schedule in relation to England.

(2) The regulations may, in particular, give a prescribed body authority to do one or more of the following things—

(a) to visit hospitals and care homes;

(b) to visit and interview persons accommodated in hospitals and care homes;

(c) to require the production of, and to inspect, records relating to the care or treatment of persons.

(3) "Prescribed" means prescribed in regulations under this paragraph.

1–627   **163.**—(1) Regulations may make provision for, and in connection with, enabling the National Assembly for Wales to monitor, and report on, the operation of this Schedule in relation to Wales.

(2) The National Assembly may direct one or more persons or bodies to carry out the Assembly's functions under regulations under this paragraph.

Disclosure of information

1–628   **164.**—(1) Regulations may require either or both of the following to disclose prescribed information to prescribed bodies—

(a) supervisory bodies;

(b) managing authorities of hospitals or care homes.

(2) "Prescribed" means prescribed in regulations under this paragraph.

(3) Regulations under this paragraph may only prescribe information relating to matters with which this Schedule is concerned.

Directions by National Assembly in relation to supervisory functions

1–629   **165.**—(1) The National Assembly for Wales may direct a Local Health Board to exercise in relation to its area any supervisory functions which are specified in the direction.

(2) Directions under this paragraph must not preclude the National Assembly from exercising the functions specified in the directions.

(3) In this paragraph "supervisory functions" means functions which the National Assembly have as supervisory body, so far as they are exercisable in relation to hospitals (whether NHS or independent hospitals, and whether in Wales or England).

1–630   **166.**—(1) This paragraph applies where, under paragraph 165, a Local Health Board ("the specified LHB") is directed to exercise supervisory functions ("delegated functions").

(2) The National Assembly for Wales may give directions to the specified LHB about the Board's exercise of delegated functions.

(3) The National Assembly may give directions for any delegated functions to be exercised, on behalf of the specified LHB, by a committee, sub-committee or officer of that Board.

(4) The National Assembly may give directions providing for any delegated functions to be exercised by the specified LHB jointly with one or more other Local Health Boards.

(5) Where, under sub-paragraph (4), delegated functions are exercisable jointly, the National Assembly may give directions providing for the functions to be exercised, on behalf of the Local Health Boards in question, by a joint committee or joint subcommittee.

1–631   **167.**—(1) Directions under paragraph 165 must be given in regulations.

(2) Directions under paragraph 166 may be given—

(a) in regulations, or

(b) by instrument in writing.

1–632   **168.** The power under paragraph 165 or paragraph 166 to give directions includes power to vary or revoke directions given under that paragraph.

Notices

1–633   **169.** Any notice under this Schedule must be in writing.

Regulations

1–634   **170.**—(1) This paragraph applies to all regulations under this Schedule, except regulations under paragraph 162, 163, 167 or 183.

(2) It is for the Secretary of State to make such regulations in relation to authorisations under this Schedule which relate to hospitals and care homes situated in England.

(3) It is for the National Assembly for Wales to make such regulations in relation to authorisations under this Schedule which relate to hospitals and care homes situated in Wales.

1–635   **171.** It is for the Secretary of State to make regulations under paragraph 162.

1–636   **172.** It is for the National Assembly for Wales to make regulations under paragraph 163 or 167.

1–637   **173.**—(1) This paragraph applies to regulations under paragraph 183.

(2) It is for the Secretary of State to make such regulations in relation to cases where a question as to the ordinary residence of a person is to be determined by the Secretary of State.

(3) It is for the National Assembly for Wales to make such regulations in relation to cases where a question as to the ordinary residence of a person is to be determined by the National Assembly.

PART 13

INTERPRETATION

Introduction
174. This Part applies for the purposes of this Schedule.   **1–638**

Hospitals and their managing authorities
175.—(1) "Hospital" means—   **1–639**
(a) an NHS hospital, or
(b) an independent hospital.
(2) "NHS hospital" means—
(a) a health service hospital as defined by section 275 of the National Health Service Act 2006 or section 206 of the National Health Service (Wales) Act 2006, or
(b) a hospital as defined by section 206 of the National Health Service (Wales) Act 2006 vested in a Local Health Board.
(3) "Independent hospital" means a hospital as defined by section 2 of the Care Standards Act 2000 which is not an NHS hospital.
176.—(1) "Managing authority", in relation to an NHS hospital, means—   **1–640**
(a) if the hospital—
    (i) is vested in the appropriate national authority for the purposes of its functions under the National Health Service Act 2006 or of the National Health Service (Wales) Act 2006, or
    (ii) consists of any accommodation provided by a local authority and used as a hospital by or on behalf of the appropriate national authority under either of those Acts,
the Primary Care Trust, Strategic Health Authority, Local Health Board or Special Health Authority responsible for the administration of the hospital;
(b) if the hospital is vested in a Primary Care Trust, National Health Service trust or NHS foundation trust, that trust;
(c) if the hospital is vested in a Local Health Board, that Board.
(2) For this purpose the appropriate national authority is—
(a) in relation to England: the Secretary of State;
(b) in relation to Wales: the National Assembly for Wales;
(c) in relation to England and Wales: the Secretary of State and the National Assembly acting jointly.
177. "Managing authority", in relation to an independent hospital, means the person registered, or **1–641**
required to be registered, under Part 2 of the Care Standards Act 2000 in respect of the hospital.

Care homes and their managing authorities
178. "Care home" has the meaning given by section 3 of the Care Standards Act 2000.   **1–642**
179. "Managing authority", in relation to a care home, means the person registered, or required to be **1–643**
registered, under Part 2 of the Care Standards Act 2000 in respect of the care home.

Supervisory bodies: hospitals
180.—(1) The identity of the supervisory body is determined under this paragraph in cases where the **1–644**
relevant hospital is situated in England.
(2) If a Primary Care Trust commissions the relevant care or treatment, that Trust is the supervisory body.
(3) If the National Assembly for Wales or a Local Health Board commission the relevant care or treatment, the National Assembly are the supervisory body.
(4) In any other case, the supervisory body are the Primary Care Trust for the area in which the relevant hospital is situated.
(5) If a hospital is situated in the areas of two (or more) Primary Care Trusts, it is to be regarded for the purposes of sub-paragraph (4) as situated in whichever of the areas the greater (or greatest) part of the hospital is situated.
181.—(1) The identity of the supervisory body is determined under this paragraph in cases where the **1–645**
relevant hospital is situated in Wales.
(2) The National Assembly for Wales are the supervisory body.
(3) But if a Primary Care Trust commissions the relevant care or treatment, that Trust is the supervisory body.

Supervisory bodies: care homes

1–646   **182.**—(1) The identity of the supervisory body is determined under this paragraph in cases where the relevant care home is situated in England or in Wales.

(2) The supervisory body are the local authority for the area in which the relevant person is ordinarily resident.

(3) But if the relevant person is not ordinarily resident in the area of a local authority, the supervisory body are the local authority for the area in which the care home is situated.

(4) In relation to England "local authority" means—

(a) the council of a county;

(b) the council of a district for which there is no county council;

(c) the council of a London borough;

(d) the Common Council of the City of London;

(e) the Council of the Isles of Scilly.

(5) In relation to Wales "local authority" means the council of a county or county borough.

(6) If a care home is situated in the areas of two (or more) local authorities, it is to be regarded for the purposes of sub-paragraph (3) as situated in whichever of the areas the greater (or greatest) part of the care home is situated.

1–647   **183.**—(1) Subsections (5) and (6) of section 24 of the National Assistance Act 1948 (deemed place of ordinary residence) apply to any determination of where a person is ordinarily resident for the purposes of paragraph 182 as those subsections apply to such a determination for the purposes specified in those subsections.

(2) In the application of section 24(6) of the 1948 Act by virtue of subparagraph (1), section 24(6) is to be read as if it referred to a hospital vested in a Local Health Board as well as to hospitals vested in the Secretary of State and the other bodies mentioned in section 24(6).

(3) Any question arising as to the ordinary residence of a person is to be determined by the Secretary of State or by the National Assembly for Wales.

(4) The Secretary of State and the National Assembly must make and publish arrangements for determining which cases are to be dealt with by the Secretary of State and which are to be dealt with by the National Assembly.

(5) Those arrangements may include provision for the Secretary of State and the National Assembly to agree, in relation to any question that has arisen, which of them is to deal with the case.

(6) Regulations may make provision about arrangements that are to have effect before, upon, or after the determination of any question as to the ordinary residence of a person.

(7) The regulations may, in particular, authorise or require a local authority to do any or all of the following things—

(a) to act as supervisory body even though it may wish to dispute that it is the supervisory body;

(b) to become the supervisory body in place of another local authority;

(c) to recover from another local authority expenditure incurred in exercising functions as the supervisory body.

Same body managing authority and supervisory body

1–648   **184.**—(1) This paragraph applies if, in connection with a particular person's detention as a resident in a hospital or care home, the same body are both—

(a) the managing authority of the relevant hospital or care home, and

(b) the supervisory body.

(2) The fact that a single body are acting in both capacities does not prevent the body from carrying out functions under this Schedule in each capacity.

(3) But, in such a case, this Schedule has effect subject to any modifications contained in regulations that may be made for this purpose.

Interested persons

1–649   **185.** Each of the following is an interested person—

(a) the relevant person's spouse or civil partner;

(b) where the relevant person and another person of the opposite sex are not married to each other but are living together as husband and wife: the other person;

(c) where the relevant person and another person of the same sex are not civil partners of each other but are living together as if they were civil partners: the other person;

(d) the relevant person's children and step-children;

(e) the relevant person's parents and step-parents;

(f) the relevant person's brothers and sisters, half-brothers and half-sisters, and stepbrothers and stepsisters;

(g) the relevant person's grandparents;

(h) a deputy appointed for the relevant person by the court;

(i) a donee of a lasting power of attorney granted by the relevant person.

186.—(1) An interested person consulted by the best interests assessor is any person whose name is stated in the relevant best interests assessment in accordance with paragraph 40 (interested persons whom the assessor consulted in carrying out the assessment). **1–650**

(2) The relevant best interests assessment is the most recent best interests assessment carried out in connection with the standard authorisation in question (whether the assessment was carried out under Part 4 or Part 8).

187. Where this Schedule imposes on a person a duty towards an interested person, the duty does not apply if the person on whom the duty is imposed— **1–651**

(a) is not aware of the interested person's identity or of a way of contacting him, and

(b) cannot reasonably ascertain it.

188. The following table contains an index of provisions defining or otherwise explaining expressions used in this Schedule— **1–652**

age assessment	paragraph 34
age requirement	paragraph 13
age review assessment	paragraph 112(3)
appointment regulations	paragraph 138
assessment under this Schedule	paragraph 127
assessor (except in Part 9)	paragraph 33
assessor (in Part 9)	paragraphs 33 and 128
authorisation under this Schedule	paragraph 10
best interests (determination of)	section 4
best interests assessment	paragraph 38
best interests requirement	paragraph 16
best interests review assessment	paragraph 112(6)
care home	paragraph 178
change of reason ground	paragraph 106
complete (in relation to a review of a standard authorisation)	paragraph 118
deprivation of a person's liberty	section 64(5) and (6)
Deputy	section 16(2)(b)
detained resident	paragraph 6
disposed of (in relation to a request for a standard authorisation)	paragraph 66
eligibility assessment	paragraph 46
eligibility requirement	paragraph 17
eligibility review assessment	paragraph 112(7)
eligible person (in relation to paragraphs 68 to 73)	paragraph 68
eligible person (in relation to Part 8)	paragraph 102(3)
expiry (in relation to an existing authorisation)	paragraph 125(b)
existing authorisation (in Part 8)	paragraph 125(a)

Hospital	paragraph 175
IMCA	paragraph 158
in force (in relation to a standard authorisation)	paragraphs 63 and 64
in force (in relation to an urgent authorisation)	paragraphs 88 and 89
ineligible (in relation to the eligibility requirement)	Schedule 1A
interested person	paragraph 185
interested person consulted by the best interests assessor	paragraph 186
lack of capacity	section 2
lasting power of attorney	section 9
managing authority (in relation to a care home)	paragraph 179
managing authority (in relation to a hospital)	paragraph 176 or 177
maximum authorisation period	paragraph 42
mental capacity assessment	paragraph 37
mental capacity requirement	paragraph 15
mental capacity review assessment	paragraph 112(5)
mental health assessment	paragraph 35
mental health requirement	paragraph 14
mental health review assessment	paragraph 112(4)
negative conclusion	paragraph 112(2)(a)
new supervisory body	paragraph 99(b)
no refusals assessment	paragraph 48
no refusals requirement	paragraph 18
no refusals review assessment	paragraph 112(8)
non-qualification ground	paragraph 105
old supervisory body	paragraph 99(a)
positive conclusion	paragraph 112(2)(b)
purpose of a standard authorisation	paragraph 11(1)
purpose of an urgent authorisation	paragraph 11(2)
qualifying requirements	paragraph 12
refusal (for the purposes of the no refusals requirement)	paragraphs 19 and 20
relevant care or treatment	paragraph 7
relevant hospital or care home	paragraph 7
relevant managing authority	paragraph 26(4)
relevant person	paragraph 7
relevant person's representative	paragraph 137
relevant procedure	paragraph 128
review assessment	paragraph 112(1)
reviewable	paragraph 104

section 39A IMCA	paragraph 155
section 39C IMCA	paragraph 156
section 39D IMCA	paragraph 157
standard authorisation	paragraph 8
supervisory body (except in Part 9)	paragraph 180, 181 or 182
supervisory body (in Part 9)	paragraph 128 and paragraph 180, 181 or 182
unauthorised deprivation of liberty (in relation to paragraphs 68 to 73)	paragraph 67
urgent authorisation	paragraph 9
variation of conditions ground	paragraph 107]

AMENDMENT

This Schedule was inserted by the Mental Health Act 2007, s.50(5), Sch.7.   **1–653**

GENERAL NOTE

This Schedule is considered in Part 2.   **1–654**

SCHEDULE 1   **Section 9**

LASTING POWERS OF ATTORNEY: FORMALITIES

PART 1

MAKING INSTRUMENTS

General requirements as to making instruments

1.—(1) An instrument is not made in accordance with this Schedule unless—   **1–655**
   (a) it is in the prescribed form,
   (b) it complies with paragraph 2, and
   (c) any prescribed requirements in connection with its execution are satisfied.
  (2) Regulations may make different provision according to whether—
   (a) the instrument relates to personal welfare or to property and affairs (or to both);
   (b) only one or more than one donee is to be appointed (and if more than one, whether jointly or jointly and severally).
  (3) In this Schedule—
   (a) "prescribed" means prescribed by regulations, and
   (b) "regulations" means regulations made for the purposes of this Schedule by the Lord Chancellor.

Requirements as to content of instruments

2.—(1) The instrument must include—   **1–656**
   (a) the prescribed information about the purpose of the instrument and the effect of a lasting power of attorney,
   (b) a statement by the donor to the effect that he—
     (i) has read the prescribed information or a prescribed part of it (or has had it read to him), and
     (ii) intends the authority conferred under the instrument to include authority to make decisions on his behalf in circumstances where he no longer has capacity,
   (c) a statement by the donor—
     (i) naming a person or persons whom the donor wishes to be notified of any application for the registration of the instrument, or
     (ii) stating that there are no persons whom he wishes to be notified of any such application,

195

(d) a statement by the donee (or, if more than one, each of them) to the effect that he—
  (i) has read the prescribed information or a prescribed part of it (or has had it read to him), and
  (ii) understands the duties imposed on a donee of a lasting power of attorney under sections 1(the principles) and 4 (best interests), and
(e) a certificate by a person of a prescribed description that, in his opinion, at the time when the donor executes the instrument—
  (i) the donor understands the purpose of the instrument and the scope of the authority conferred under it,
  (ii) no fraud or undue pressure is being used to induce the donor to create a lasting power of attorney, and
  (iii) there is nothing else which would prevent a lasting power of attorney from being created by the instrument.
(2) Regulations may—
  (a) prescribe a maximum number of named persons;
  (b) provide that, where the instrument includes a statement under sub-paragraph (1)(c)(ii), two persons of a prescribed description must each give a certificate under sub-paragraph (1)(e).
(3) The persons who may be named persons do not include a person who is appointed as donee under the instrument.
(4) In this Schedule, "named person" means a person named under sub-paragraph (1)(c).
(5) A certificate under sub-paragraph (1)(e)—
(a) must be made in the prescribed form, and
(b) must include any prescribed information.
(6) The certificate may not be given by a person appointed as donee under the instrument.

Failure to comply with prescribed form

1–657 3.—(1) If an instrument differs in an immaterial respect in form or mode of expression from the prescribed form, it is to be treated by the Public Guardian as sufficient in point of form and expression.
(2) The court may declare that an instrument which is not in the prescribed form is to be treated as if it were, if it is satisfied that the persons executing the instrument intended it to create a lasting power of attorney.

PART 2

REGISTRATION

1–658 4.—(1) An application to the Public Guardian for the registration of an instrument intended to create a lasting power of attorney—
(a) must be made in the prescribed form, and
(b) must include any prescribed information.
(2) The application may be made—
(a) by the donor,
(b) by the donee or donees, or
(c) if the instrument appoints two or more donees to act jointly and severally in respect of any matter, by any of the donees.
(3) The application must be accompanied by—
(a) the instrument, and
(b) any fee provided for under section 58(4)(b).
(4) A person who, in an application for registration, makes a statement which he knows to be false in a material particular is guilty of an offence and is liable—
(a) on summary conviction, to imprisonment for a term not exceeding 12 months or a fine not exceeding the statutory maximum or both;
(b) on conviction on indictment, to imprisonment for a term not exceeding 2 years or a fine or both.

1–659 5. Subject to paragraphs 11 to 14, the Public Guardian must register the instrument as a lasting power of attorney at the end of the prescribed period.

1–660 6.—(1) A donor about to make an application under paragraph 4(2)(a) must notify any named persons that he is about to do so.
(2) The donee (or donees) about to make an application under paragraph 4(2)(b) or (c) must notify any named persons that he is (or they are) about to do so.

1–661 7. As soon as is practicable after receiving an application by the donor under paragraph 4(2)(a), the Public Guardian must notify the donee (or donees) that the application has been received.

8.—(1) As soon as is practicable after receiving an application by a donee (or donees) under para- **1–662** graph 4(2)(b), the Public Guardian must notify the donor that the application has been received.

(2) As soon as is practicable after receiving an application by a donee under paragraph 4(2)(c), the Public Guardian must notify—

(a) the donor, and

(b) the donee or donees who did not join in making the application,

that the application has been received.

9.—(1) A notice under paragraph 6 must be made in the prescribed form. **1–663**

(2) A notice under paragraph 6, 7 or 8 must include such information, if any, as may be prescribed.

10. The court may— **1–664**

(a) on the application of the donor, dispense with the requirement to notify under paragraph 6(1), or

(b) on the application of the donee or donees concerned, dispense with the requirement to notify under paragraph 6(2),

if satisfied that no useful purpose would be served by giving the notice.

11.—(1) If it appears to the Public Guardian that an instrument accompanying an application under **1–665** paragraph 4 is not made in accordance with this Schedule, he must not register the instrument unless the court directs him to do so.

(2) Sub-paragraph (3) applies if it appears to the Public Guardian that the instrument contains a provision which—

(a) would be ineffective as part of a lasting power of attorney, or

(b) would prevent the instrument from operating as a valid lasting power of attorney.

(3) The Public Guardian—

(a) must apply to the court for it to determine the matter under section 23(1), and

(b) pending the determination by the court, must not register the instrument.

(4) Sub-paragraph (5) applies if the court determines under section 23(1) (whether or not on an application by the Public Guardian) that the instrument contains a provision which—

(a) would be ineffective as part of a lasting power of attorney, or

(b) would prevent the instrument from operating as a valid lasting power of attorney.

(5) The court must—

(a) notify the Public Guardian that it has severed the provision, or

(b) direct him not to register the instrument.

(6) Where the court notifies the Public Guardian that it has severed a provision, he must register the instrument with a note to that effect attached to it.

12.—(1) Sub-paragraph (2) applies if it appears to the Public Guardian that— **1–666**

(a) there is a deputy appointed by the court for the donor, and

(b) the powers conferred on the deputy would, if the instrument were registered, to any extent conflict with the powers conferred on the attorney.

(2) The Public Guardian must not register the instrument unless the court directs him to do so.

13.—(1) Sub-paragraph (2) applies if a donee or a named person— **1–667**

(a) receives a notice under paragraph 6, 7 or 8 of an application for the registration of an instrument, and

(b) before the end of the prescribed period, gives notice to the Public Guardian of an objection to the registration on the ground that an event mentioned in section 13(3) or (6)(a) to (d) has occurred which has revoked the instrument.

(2) If the Public Guardian is satisfied that the ground for making the objection is established, he must not register the instrument unless the court, on the application of the person applying for the registration—

(a) is satisfied that the ground is not established, and

(b) directs the Public Guardian to register the instrument.

(3) Sub-paragraph (4) applies if a donee or a named person—

(a) receives a notice under paragraph 6, 7 or 8 of an application for the registration of an instrument, and

(b) before the end of the prescribed period—

(i) makes an application to the court objecting to the registration on a prescribed ground, and

(ii) notifies the Public Guardian of the application.

(4) The Public Guardian must not register the instrument unless the court directs him to do so.

14.—(1) This paragraph applies if the donor— **1–668**

(a) receives a notice under paragraph 8 of an application for the registration of an instrument, and

(b) before the end of the prescribed period, gives notice to the Public Guardian of an objection to the registration.

(2) The Public Guardian must not register the instrument unless the court, on the application of the donee or, if more than one, any of them—

(a) is satisfied that the donor lacks capacity to object to the registration, and

(b) directs the Public Guardian to register the instrument.

1–669 **15.** Where an instrument is registered under this Schedule, the Public Guardian must give notice of the fact in the prescribed form to—

(a) the donor, and

(b) the donee or, if more than one, each of them.

1–670 **16.**—(1) A document purporting to be an office copy of an instrument registered under this Schedule is, in any part of the United Kingdom, evidence of—

(a) the contents of the instrument, and

(b) the fact that it has been registered.

(2) Sub-paragraph (1) is without prejudice to—

(a) section 3 of the Powers of Attorney Act 1971 (c. 27) (proof by certified copy), and

(b) any other method of proof authorised by law.

1–671 **17.**—(1) The Public Guardian must cancel the registration of an instrument as a lasting power of attorney on being satisfied that the power has been revoked—

(a) as a result of the donor's bankruptcy, or

(b) on the occurrence of an event mentioned in section 13(6)(a) to (d).

(2) If the Public Guardian cancels the registration of an instrument he must notify—

(a) the donor, and

(b) the donee or, if more than one, each of them.

1–672 **18.** The court must direct the Public Guardian to cancel the registration of an instrument as a lasting power of attorney if it—

(a) determines under section 22(2)(a) that a requirement for creating the power was not met,

(b) determines under section 22(2)(b) that the power has been revoked or has otherwise come to an end, or

(c) revokes the power under section 22(4)(b) (fraud etc.).

1–673 **19.**—(1) Sub-paragraph (2) applies if the court determines under section 23(1) that a lasting power of attorney contains a provision which—

(a) is ineffective as part of a lasting power of attorney, or

(b) prevents the instrument from operating as a valid lasting power of attorney.

(2) The court must—

(a) notify the Public Guardian that it has severed the provision, or

(b) direct him to cancel the registration of the instrument as a lasting power of attorney.

1–674 **20.** On the cancellation of the registration of an instrument, the instrument and any office copies of it must be delivered up to the Public Guardian to be cancelled.

Partial revocation or suspension of power as a result of bankruptcy

1–675 **21.** If in the case of a registered instrument it appears to the Public Guardian that under section 13 a lasting power of attorney is revoked, or suspended, in relation to the donor's property and affairs (but not in relation to other matters), the Public Guardian must attach to the instrument a note to that effect.

Termination of appointment of donee which does not revoke power

1–676 **22.** If in the case of a registered instrument it appears to the Public Guardian that an event has occurred—

(a) which has terminated the appointment of the donee, but

(b) which has not revoked the instrument,

the Public Guardian must attach to the instrument a note to that effect.

Replacement of donee
   23. If in the case of a registered instrument it appears to the Public Guardian that the donee has been **1–677** replaced under the terms of the instrument the Public Guardian must attach to the instrument a note to that effect.

Severance of ineffective provisions
   24. If in the case of a registered instrument the court notifies the Public Guardian under paragraph **1–678** 19(2)(a) that it has severed a provision of the instrument, the Public Guardian must attach to it a note to that effect.

Notification of alterations
   25. If the Public Guardian attaches a note to an instrument under paragraph 21, 22, 23 or 24 he must **1–679** give notice of the note to the donee or donees of the power (or, as the case may be, to the other donee or donees of the power).

DEFINITIONS
   "lasting power of attorney": s.64(1)   **1–680**
   "Public Guardian": s.64(1)
   "the court": s.64(1)
   "deputy": s.64(1)
   "bankruptcy": s.64(3)

GENERAL NOTE
   This Schedule sets out the requirements with regard to the formalities of a LPA. A LPA is not created **1–681** unless it is made and registered in accordance with the provisions s.9(2).
   In summary, the requirements are:

Making instruments
- The LPA must be in the prescribed form.   **1–682**
- The form must contain statements by both the donor and donee to the effect that they have read (or in the case of the donor, had read to them) prescribed information.
- The LPA must include the names of any persons (a "named person"), not being a donee, whom the donor wishes to be notified of any application to register the LPA or a statement that there are no such persons.
- The form must include a certificate by a person of a prescribed description that, in his or her opinion, at the time when the donor executes the instrument the donor understands the purpose of the instrument and the scope of the authority conferred, that no fraud or undue pressure is being used to induce the donor to create a LPA, and that there is nothing else that would prevent a LPA being created.
- The Public Guardian may treat a LPA differing in an immaterial respect from the prescribed form as sufficient to create a LPA.
- The Court of Protection has the power to declare that an instrument not in the prescribed form is to be treated as if it were.

Registration
- The powers given in a LPA to the donee cannot be exercised until the document has been regis- **1–683** tered with the Public Guardian.
- The application, which must be in the prescribed form, can be made by the donor or donee.
- The named person must be notified of the pending registration by the donor or donee.
- The Public Guardian must notify the applicant that the application has been received unless the court has dispensed with this requirement.
- The donee or the named person may object to the LPA within a prescribed period.
- The objection is made to the either the Public Guardianor the court, depending upon the nature of the objection.
- If the LPA is registered, the Public Guardian must notify the donor and donee.

Cancellation of registration

1–684
- The Public Guardian will cancel the LPA if satisfied that the power has been revoked on the basis of the donor's bankruptcy, the donee disclaiming the appointment, the death or bankruptcy of the donee, the dissolution or annulment of a marriage or civil partnership between the donor and donee, and the lack of capacity of the donee.
- The court must direct the Public Guardian to cancel the registration of a LPA if the court decides that a requirement for creating the LPA was not met, decides that the LPA has been revoked or otherwise come to an end, or it revokes the power on fraud or undue pressure grounds.
- On cancellation the Public Guardian will notify both the donor and donee.

Records of alterations in registered powers

1–685
- The Public Guardian must attach a note to the LPA in the circumstances set out in paras 21–24.
- The Public Guardian must give the donor and donee notice of any notes attached.

Prescribed Forms

1–686 The prescribed forms for the making and registration of LPAs are set out in the Schs.1 to 5 to the Lasting Powers of Attorney, Enduring Powers of Attorney and Public Guardian Regulations 2007 (SI 2007/1253). For the loss or destruction of forms, see reg.19.

Paragraph 1(1)(c)

1–687 PRESCRIBED REQUIREMENTS IN CONNECTION WITH ITS EXECUTION. See SI 2007/1253, reg.9.

Paragraph 2(1)(c)

1–688 See SI 2007/1253, regs 6 and 7.

Paragraph 2(1)(e)

1–689 "The relevant person would interview the donor without the presence of the proposed [donee] and immediately before the signing of the LPA", *per* the Parliamentary Under-Secretary of State, St.Comm.A, para.142.

PERSON OF A PRESCRIBED DESCRIPTION. See SI 2007/1253, reg.8.

Paragraph 2(2)(a)

1–690 MAXIMUM NUMBER OF NAMED PERSONS. Is 5 (SI 2007/1253, reg.6).

Paragraph 2(2)(b)

1–691 See SI 2007/1253, reg.7.

Paragraph 5

1–692 PRESCRIBED PERIOD. See reg.12 of SI 2007/1253.

Paragraphs 6, 7 and 8

1–693 If a notified person wishes to make an objection to the registration to the Public Guardian, see regs.14 and 15 of SI 2007/1253.

Paragraph 13

1–694 OBJECTION. See SI 2007/1253, regs.14, 14A and 15.

Paragraph 15

1–695 REGISTERED. See SI 2007/1253, reg.17.

Paragraphs 21 to 24

1–696 NOTE TO THAT EFFECT. See SI 2007/1253, reg.18.

[SCHEDULE 1A

PERSONS INELIGIBLE TO BE DEPRIVED OF LIBERTY BY THIS ACT

PART 1

INELIGIBLE PERSONS

Application
   1. This Schedule applies for the purposes of—   **1–697**
   (a) section 16A, and
   (b) paragraph 17 of Schedule A1.

Determining ineligibility
   2. A person ("P") is ineligible to be deprived of liberty by this Act ("ineligible") if—   **1–698**
   (a) P falls within one of the cases set out in the second column of the following table, and
   (b) the corresponding entry in the third column of the table — or the provision, or one of the provisions, referred to in that entry — provides that he is ineligible.

	Status of P	*Determination of ineligibility*
Case A	P is— (a) subject to the hospital treatment regime, and (b) detained in a hospital under that regime.	P is ineligible.
Case B	P is— (a) subject to the hospital treatment regime, but (b) not detained in a hospital under that regime.	See paragraphs 3 and 4.
Case C	P is subject to the community treatment regime.	See paragraphs 3 and 4.
Case D	P is subject to the guardianship regime.	See paragraphs 3 and 5.
Case E	P is— (a) within the scope of the Mental Health Act, but (b) not subject to any of the mental health regimes.	See paragraph 5.

Authorised course of action not in accordance with regime
   3.—(1) This paragraph applies in cases B, C and D in the table in paragraph 2.   **1–699**
   (2) P is ineligible if the authorised course of action is not in accordance with a requirement which the relevant regime imposes.
   (3) That includes any requirement as to where P is, or is not, to reside.
   (4) The relevant regime is the mental health regime to which P is subject.

Treatment for mental disorder in a hospital
   4.—(1) This paragraph applies in cases B and C in the table in paragraph 2.   **1–700**
   (2) P is ineligible if the relevant care or treatment consists in whole or in part of medical treatment for mental disorder in a hospital.

P objects to being a mental health patient etc
   5.—(1) This paragraph applies in cases D and E in the table in paragraph 2.   **1–701**
   (2) P is ineligible if the following conditions are met.
   (3) The first condition is that the relevant instrument authorises P to be a mental health patient.
   (4) The second condition is that P objects—
   (a) to being a mental health patient, or
   (b) to being given some or all of the mental health treatment.
   (5) The third condition is that a donee or deputy has not made a valid decision to consent to each matter to which P objects.

(6) In determining whether or not P objects to something, regard must be had to all the circumstances (so far as they are reasonably ascertainable), including the following—

(a) P's behaviour;

(b) P's wishes and feelings;

(c) P's views, beliefs and values.

(7) But regard is to be had to circumstances from the past only so far as it is still appropriate to have regard to them.

PART 2

INTERPRETATION

Application

1–702   **6.** This Part applies for the purposes of this Schedule.

Mental health regimes

1–703   **7.** The mental health regimes are—

(a) the hospital treatment regime,

(b) the community treatment regime, and

(c) the guardianship regime.

Hospital treatment regime

1–704   **8.**—(1) P is subject to the hospital treatment regime if he is subject to—

(a) a hospital treatment obligation under the relevant enactment, or

(b) an obligation under another England and Wales enactment which has the same effect as a hospital treatment obligation.

(2) But where P is subject to any such obligation, he is to be regarded as not subject to the hospital treatment regime during any period when he is subject to the community treatment regime.

(3) A hospital treatment obligation is an application, order or direction of a kind listed in the first column of the following table.

(4) In relation to a hospital treatment obligation, the relevant enactment is the enactment in the Mental Health Act which is referred to in the corresponding entry in the second column of the following table.

Hospital treatment obligation	Relevant enactment
Application for admission for assessment	Section 2
Application for admission for assessment	Section 4
Application for admission for treatment	Section 3
Order for remand to hospital	Section 35
Order for remand to hospital	Section 36
Hospital order	Section 37
Interim hospital order	Section 38
Order for detention in hospital	Section 44
Hospital direction	Section 45A
Transfer direction	Section 47
Transfer direction	Section 48
Hospital order	Section 51

Community treatment regime

1–705   **9.** P is subject to the community treatment regime if he is subject to—

(a) a community treatment order under section 17A of the Mental Health Act, or

(b) an obligation under another England and Wales enactment which has the same effect as a community treatment order.

Guardianship regime

1–706   **10.** P is subject to the guardianship regime if he is subject to—

(a) a guardianship application under section 7 of the Mental Health Act,

(b) a guardianship order under section 37 of the Mental Health Act, or

(c) an obligation under another England and Wales enactment which has the same effect as a guardianship application or guardianship order.

England and Wales enactments

11.—(1) An England and Wales enactment is an enactment which extends to England and Wales **1–707** (whether or not it also extends elsewhere).

(2) It does not matter if the enactment is in the Mental Health Act or not.

P within scope of Mental Health Act

12.—(1) P is within the scope of the Mental Health Act if— **1–708**

(a) an application in respect of P could be made under section 2 or 3 of the Mental Health Act, and

(b) P could be detained in a hospital in pursuance of such an application, were one made.

(2) The following provisions of this paragraph apply when determining whether an application in respect of P could be made under section 2 or 3 of the Mental Health Act.

(3) If the grounds in section 2(2) of the Mental Health Act are met in P's case, it is to be assumed that the recommendations referred to in section 2(3) of that Act have been given.

(4) If the grounds in section 3(2) of the Mental Health Act are met in P's case, it is to be assumed that the recommendations referred to in section 3(3) of that Act have been given.

(5) In determining whether the ground in section 3(2)(c) of the Mental Health Act is met in P's case, it is to be assumed that the treatment referred to in section 3(2)(c) cannot be provided under this Act.

Authorised course of action, relevant care or treatment & relevant instrument

13. In a case where this Schedule applies for the purposes of section 16A— **1–709**

"authorised course of action" means any course of action amounting to deprivation of liberty which the order under section 16(2)(a) authorises;

"relevant care or treatment" means any care or treatment which—

(a) comprises, or forms part of, the authorised course of action, or

(b) is to be given in connection with the authorised course of action;

"relevant instrument" means the order under section 16(2)(a).

14. In a case where this Schedule applies for the purposes of paragraph 17 of Schedule A1— **1–710**

"authorised course of action" means the accommodation of the relevant person in the relevant hospital or care home for the purpose of being given the relevant care or treatment;

"relevant care or treatment" has the same meaning as in Schedule A1;

"relevant instrument" means the standard authorisation under Schedule A1.

15.—(1) This paragraph applies where the question whether a person is ineligible to be deprived of **1–711** liberty by this Act is relevant to either of these decisions—

(a) whether or not to include particular provision ("the proposed provision") in an order under section 16(2)(a);

(b) whether or not to give a standard authorisation under Schedule A1.

(2) A reference in this Schedule to the authorised course of action or the relevant care or treatment is to be read as a reference to that thing as it would be if—

(a) the proposed provision were included in the order, or

(b) the standard authorisation were given.

(3) A reference in this Schedule to the relevant instrument is to be read as follows—

(a) where the relevant instrument is an order under section 16(2)(a): as a reference to the order as it would be if the proposed provision were included in it;

(b) where the relevant instrument is a standard authorisation: as a reference to the standard authorisation as it would be if it were given.

Expressions used in paragraph 5

16.—(1) These expressions have the meanings given— **1–712**

"donee" means a donee of a lasting power of attorney granted by P;

"mental health patient" means a person accommodated in a hospital for the purpose of being given medical treatment for mental disorder;

"mental health treatment" means the medical treatment for mental disorder referred to in the definition of "mental health patient".

(2) A decision of a donee or deputy is valid if it is made—

(a) within the scope of his authority as donee or deputy, and

(b) in accordance with Part 1 of this Act.

Expressions with same meaning as in Mental Health Act

1–713 17.—(1) "Hospital" has the same meaning as in Part 2 of the Mental Health Act.

(2) "Medical treatment" has the same meaning as in the Mental Health Act.

(3) "Mental disorder" has the same meaning as in Schedule A1 (see paragraph 14).]

AMENDMENT

1–714 This Schedule was inserted by the Mental Health Act 2007, s.50(6), Sch.8.

GENERAL NOTE

1–715 This Schedule is considered in Part 2.

SCHEDULE 2   **Section 18(4)**

PROPERTY AND AFFAIRS: SUPPLEMENTARY PROVISIONS

1–716 1. Paragraphs 2 to 4 apply in relation to the execution of a will, by virtue of section 18, on behalf of P.

1–717 2. The will may make any provision (whether by disposing of property or exercising a power or otherwise) which could be made by a will executed by P if he had capacity to make it.

1–718 3.—(1) Sub-paragraph (2) applies if under section 16 the court makes an order or gives directions requiring or authorising a person (the authorised person) to execute a will on behalf of P.

(2) Any will executed in pursuance of the order or direction—

(a) must state that it is signed by P acting by the authorised person,

(b) must be signed by the authorised person with the name of P and his own name, in the presence of two or more witnesses present at the same time,

(c) must be attested and subscribed by those witnesses in the presence of the authorised person, and

(d) must be sealed with the official seal of the court.

1–719 4.—(1) This paragraph applies where a will is executed in accordance with paragraph 3.

(2) The Wills Act 1837 (c. 26) has effect in relation to the will as if it were signed by P by his own hand, except that—

(a) section 9 of the 1837 Act (requirements as to signing and attestation) does not apply, and

(b) in the subsequent provisions of the 1837 Act any reference to execution in the manner required by the previous provisions is to be read as a reference to execution in accordance with paragraph 3.

(3) The will has the same effect for all purposes as if—

(a) P had had the capacity to make a valid will, and

(b) the will had been executed by him in the manner required by the 1837 Act.

(4) But sub-paragraph (3) does not have effect in relation to the will—

(a) in so far as it disposes of immovable property outside England and Wales, or

(b) in so far as it relates to any other property or matter if, when the will is executed—

(i) P is domiciled outside England and Wales, and

(ii) the condition in sub-paragraph (5) is met.

(5) The condition is that, under the law of P's domicile, any question of his testamentary capacity would fall to be determined in accordance with the law of a place outside England and Wales.

1–720 5.—(1) If provision is made by virtue of section 18 for—

(a) the settlement of any property of P, or

(b) the exercise of a power vested in him of appointing trustees or retiring from a trust,

the court may also make as respects the property settled or the trust property such consequential vesting or other orders as the case may require.

(2) The power under sub-paragraph (1) includes, in the case of the exercise of such a power, any order which could have been made in such a case under Part 4 of theTrustee Act 1925 (c.19).

1–721 6.—(1) If a settlement has been made by virtue of section 18, the court may by order vary or revoke the settlement if—

(a) the settlement makes provision for its variation or revocation,

(b) the court is satisfied that a material fact was not disclosed when the settlement was made, or

(c) the court is satisfied that there has been a substantial change of circumstances.

(2) Any such order may give such consequential directions as the court thinks fit.

1–722 7.—(1) Sub-paragraph (2) applies if the court is satisfied—

(a) that under the law prevailing in a place outside England and Wales a person (M) has been appointed to exercise powers in respect of the property or affairs of P on the ground (however formulated) that P lacks capacity to make decisions with respect to the management and administration of his property and affairs, and

(b) that, having regard to the nature of the appointment and to the circumstances of the case, it is expedient that the court should exercise its powers under this paragraph.

(2) The court may direct—

(a) any stocks standing in the name of P, or

(b) the right to receive dividends from the stocks,

to be transferred into M's name or otherwise dealt with as required by M, and may give such directions as the court thinks fit for dealing with accrued dividends from the stocks.

(3) "Stocks" includes—

(a) shares, and

(b) any funds, annuity or security transferable in the books kept by any body corporate or unincorporated company or society or by an instrument of transfer either alone or accompanied by other formalities,

and "dividends" is to be construed accordingly.

8.—(1) Sub-paragraphs (2) and (3) apply if—   **1–723**

(a) P's property has been disposed of by virtue of section 18,

(b) under P's will or intestacy, or by a gift perfected or nomination taking effect on his death, any other person would have taken an interest in the property but for the disposal, and

(c) on P's death, any property belonging to P's estate represents the property disposed of.

(2) The person takes the same interest, if and so far as circumstances allow, in the property representing the property disposed of.

(3) If the property disposed of was real property, any property representing it is to be treated, so long as it remains part of P's estate, as if it were real property.

(4) The court may direct that, on a disposal of P's property—

(a) which is made by virtue of section 18, and

(b) which would apart from this paragraph result in the conversion of personal property into real property,

property representing the property disposed of is to be treated, so long as it remains P's property or forms part of P's estate, as if it were personal property.

(5) References in sub-paragraphs (1) to (4) to the disposal of property are to—

(a) the sale, exchange, charging of or other dealing (otherwise than by will) with property other than money;

(b) the removal of property from one place to another;

(c) the application of money in acquiring property;

(d) the transfer of money from one account to another;

and references to property representing property disposed of are to be construed accordingly and as including the result of successive disposals.

(6) The court may give such directions as appear to it necessary or expedient for the purpose of facilitating the operation of sub-paragraphs (1) to (3), including the carrying of money to a separate account and the transfer of property other than money.

9.—(1) Sub-paragraph (2) applies if the court has ordered or directed the expenditure of money—   **1–724**

(a) for carrying out permanent improvements on any of P's property, or

(b) otherwise for the permanent benefit of any of P's property.

(2) The court may order that—

(a) the whole of the money expended or to be expended, or

(b) any part of it,

is to be a charge on the property either without interest or with interest at a specified rate.

(3) An order under sub-paragraph (2) may provide for excluding or restricting the operation of paragraph 8(1) to (3).

(4) A charge under sub-paragraph (2) may be made in favour of such person as may be just and, in particular, where the money charged is paid out of P's general estate, may be made in favour of a person as trustee for P.

(5) No charge under sub-paragraph (2) may confer any right of sale or foreclosure during P's lifetime.

10.—(1) Any functions which P has as patron of a benefice may be discharged only by a person (R)   **1–725**
appointed by the court.

(2) R must be an individual capable of appointment under section 8(1)(b) of the 1986 Measure (which provides for an individual able to make a declaration of communicant status, a clerk in Holy Orders, etc. to be appointed to discharge a registered patron's functions).

(3) The 1986 Measure applies to R as it applies to an individual appointed by the registered patron of the benefice under section 8(1)(b) or (3) of that Measure to discharge his functions as patron.

(4) "The 1986 Measure" means the Patronage (Benefices) Measure 1986 (No.3).

DEFINITIONS

1–726   "will": s.64(1)
"property": s.64(1)
"the court": s.64(1)

GENERAL NOTE

1–727   This Schedule contains detailed provisions relating to the court's powers in relation to property and affairs, in particular the making of wills and settlements.

Paragraph 3(2)(b)

1–728   As the authorised person is not a witness, he or she would not be precluded from benefiting under s.15 of the Wills Act 1837 (c.26).

Paragraph 3(2)(d)

1–729   "The benefit of a court seal is that it provides authentication as to the originality of a document. It helps prevent fraud, and it reassures the financial institutions that they are dealing with the right person", *per* the Parliamentary Under-Secretary of State, St.Comm.A, para.188.

Paragraph 4(3)

1–730   A statutory will has the same effect as a will made by a competent testator.

Paragraph 7

1–731   The purpose of this provision is to enable the court to recognise judicially the operation of foreign law, whereby some form of curatorship has been constituted for a patient, without itself having to go into questions of mental status and capacity.

Paragraph 8

1–732   This ensures that those who have an interest in property that has been disposed of by virtue this Act should preserve that interest.

Paragraph 10

1–733   A "benefice" is a freehold office of the Church of England, such as the vicar of a parish. The patron of a benefice has the right to appoint a cleric to that office. The representative of P "will have to be an individual who is a communicant of the Church of England or a church in communion with it or a clerk in holy orders. The representative will fulfil the patron's role not only in presenting a priest to a vacant benefice under the Patronage Benefices Measure 1986 (m.3) but also in performing the other functions of a patron such as acting as a consultee when there is a proposal to suspend presentation under s.67 of the Pastoral Measure 1983 (m.1). In discharging his or her functions the representative will be subject to the provisions of the 1986 Measure in the same way that a registered patron would be", *per* the Under-Secretary of State (*Hansard*, HL Vol.670, col.1496).

SCHEDULE 3   **Section 63**

INTERNATIONAL PROTECTION OF ADULTS

PART 1

PRELIMINARY

Introduction

1–734   **1.** This Part applies for the purposes of this Schedule.

The Convention

2.—(1) "Convention" means the Convention referred to in section 63. **1–735**

(2) "Convention country" means a country in which the Convention is in force.

(3) A reference to an Article or Chapter is to an Article or Chapter of the Convention.

(4) An expression which appears in this Schedule and in the Convention is to be construed in accordance with the Convention.

Countries, territories and nationals

3.—(1) "Country" includes a territory which has its own system of law. **1–736**

(2) Where a country has more than one territory with its own system of law, a reference to the country, in relation to one of its nationals, is to the territory with which the national has the closer, or the closest, connection.

Adults with incapacity

4. "Adult" means a person who— **1–737**

(a) as a result of an impairment or insufficiency of his personal faculties, cannot protect his interests, and

(b) has reached 16.

Protective measures

5.—(1) "Protective measure" means a measure directed to the protection of the person or property **1–738** of an adult; and it may deal in particular with any of the following—

(a) the determination of incapacity and the institution of a protective regime,

(b) placing the adult under the protection of an appropriate authority,

(c) guardianship, curatorship or any corresponding system,

(d) the designation and functions of a person having charge of the adult's person or property, or representing or otherwise helping him,

(e) placing the adult in a place where protection can be provided,

(f) administering, conserving or disposing of the adult's property,

(g) authorising a specific intervention for the protection of the person or property of the adult.

(2) Where a measure of like effect to a protective measure has been taken in relation to a person before he reaches 16, this Schedule applies to the measure in so far as it has effect in relation to him once he has reached 16.

Central Authority

6.—(1) Any function under the Convention of a Central Authority is exercisable in England and **1–739** Wales by the Lord Chancellor.

(2) A communication may be sent to the Central Authority in relation to England and Wales by sending it to the Lord Chancellor.

PART 2

JURISDICTION OF COMPETENT AUTHORITY

7.—(1) The court may exercise its functions under this Act (in so far as it cannot otherwise do so) in **1–740** relation to—

(a) an adult habitually resident in England and Wales,

(b) an adult's property in England and Wales,

(c) an adult present in England and Wales or who has property there, if the matter is urgent, or

(d) an adult present in England and Wales, if a protective measure which is temporary and limited in its effect to England and Wales is proposed in relation to him.

(2) An adult present in England and Wales is to be treated for the purposes of this paragraph as habitually resident there if—

(a) his habitual residence cannot be ascertained,

(b) he is a refugee, or

(c) he has been displaced as a result of disturbance in the country of his habitual residence.

8.—(1) The court may also exercise its functions under this Act (in so far as it cannot otherwise do **1–741** so) in relation to an adult if sub-paragraph (2) or (3) applies in relation to him.

(2) This sub-paragraph applies in relation to an adult if—

(a) he is a British citizen,

(b) he has a closer connection with England and Wales than with Scotland or Northern Ireland, and

(c) Article 7 has, in relation to the matter concerned, been complied with.

(3) This sub-paragraph applies in relation to an adult if the Lord Chancellor, having consulted such persons as he considers appropriate, agrees to a request under Article 8 in relation to the adult.

1–742 **9.**—(1) This paragraph applies where jurisdiction is exercisable under this Schedule in connection with a matter which involves a Convention country other than England and Wales.

(2) Any Article on which the jurisdiction is based applies in relation to the matter in so far as it involves the other country (and the court must, accordingly, comply with any duty conferred on it as a result).

(3) Article 12 also applies, so far as its provisions allow, in relation to the matter in so far as it involves the other country.

1–743 **10.** A reference in this Schedule to the exercise of jurisdiction under this Schedule is to the exercise of functions under this Act as a result of this Part of this Schedule.

PART 3

APPLICABLE LAW

1–744 **11.** In exercising jurisdiction under this Schedule, the court may, if it thinks that the matter has a substantial connection with a country other than England and Wales, apply the law of that other country.

1–745 **12.** Where a protective measure is taken in one country but implemented in another, the conditions of implementation are governed by the law of the other country.

1–746 **13.**—(1) If the donor of a lasting power is habitually resident in England and Wales at the time of granting the power, the law applicable to the existence, extent, modification or extinction of the power is—

(a) the law of England and Wales, or

(b) if he specifies in writing the law of a connected country for the purpose, that law.

(2) If he is habitually resident in another country at that time, but England and Wales is a connected country, the law applicable in that respect is—

(a) the law of the other country, or

(b) if he specifies in writing the law of England and Wales for the purpose, that law.

(3) A country is connected, in relation to the donor, if it is a country—

(a) of which he is a national,

(b) in which he was habitually resident, or

(c) in which he has property.

(4) Where this paragraph applies as a result of sub-paragraph (3)(c), it applies only in relation to the property which the donor has in the connected country.

(5) The law applicable to the manner of the exercise of a lasting power is the law of the country where it is exercised.

(6) In this Part of this Schedule, "lasting power" means—

(a) a lasting power of attorney (see section 9),

(b) an enduring power of attorney within the meaning of Schedule 4, or

(c) any other power of like effect.

1–747 **14.**—(1) Where a lasting power is not exercised in a manner sufficient to guarantee the protection of the person or property of the donor, the court, in exercising jurisdiction under this Schedule, may disapply or modify the power.

(2) Where, in accordance with this Part of this Schedule, the law applicable to the power is, in one or more respects, that of a country other than England and Wales, the court must, so far as possible, have regard to the law of the other country in that respect (or those respects).

1–748 **15.** Regulations may provide for Schedule 1(lasting powers of attorney: formalities) to apply with modifications in relation to a lasting power which comes within paragraph 13(6)(c) above.

1–749 **16.**—(1) This paragraph applies where a person (a representative) in purported exercise of an authority to act on behalf of an adult enters into a transaction with a third party.

(2) The validity of the transaction may not be questioned in proceedings, nor may the third party be held liable, merely because—

(a) where the representative and third party are in England and Wales when entering into the transaction, sub-paragraph (3) applies;

(b) where they are in another country at that time, sub-paragraph (4) applies.

(3) This sub-paragraph applies if—

(a) the law applicable to the authority in one or more respects is, as a result of this Schedule, the law of a country other than England and Wales, and

(b) the representative is not entitled to exercise the authority in that respect (or those respects) under the law of that other country.

(4) This sub-paragraph applies if—

(a) the law applicable to the authority in one or more respects is, as a result of this Part of this Schedule, the law of England and Wales, and

(b) the representative is not entitled to exercise the authority in that respect (or those respects) under that law.

(5) This paragraph does not apply if the third party knew or ought to have known that the applicable law was—

(a) in a case within sub-paragraph (3), the law of the other country;

(b) in a case within sub-paragraph (4), the law of England and Wales.

17. Where the court is entitled to exercise jurisdiction under this Schedule, the mandatory pro- **1–750** visions of the law of England and Wales apply, regardless of any system of law which would otherwise apply in relation to the matter.

18. Nothing in this Part of this Schedule requires or enables the application in England and Wales of **1–751** a provision of the law of another country if its application would be manifestly contrary to public policy.

PART 4

RECOGNITION AND ENFORCEMENT

19.—(1) A protective measure taken in relation to an adult under the law of a country other than **1–752** England and Wales is to be recognised in England and Wales if it was taken on the ground that the adult is habitually resident in the other country.

(2) A protective measure taken in relation to an adult under the law of a Convention country other than England and Wales is to be recognised in England and Wales if it was taken on a ground mentioned in Chapter 2 (jurisdiction).

(3) But the court may disapply this paragraph in relation to a measure if it thinks that—

(a) the case in which the measure was taken was not urgent,

(b) the adult was not given an opportunity to be heard, and

(c) that omission amounted to a breach of natural justice.

(4) It may also disapply this paragraph in relation to a measure if it thinks that—

(a) recognition of the measure would be manifestly contrary to public policy,

(b) the measure would be inconsistent with a mandatory provision of the law of England and Wales, or

(c) the measure is inconsistent with one subsequently taken, or recognised, in England and Wales in relation to the adult.

(5) And the court may disapply this paragraph in relation to a measure taken under the law of a Convention country in a matter to which Article 33 applies, if the court thinks that that Article has not been complied with in connection with that matter.

20.—(1) An interested person may apply to the court for a declaration as to whether a protective **1–753** measure taken under the law of a country other than England and Wales is to be recognised in England and Wales.

(2) No permission is required for an application to the court under this paragraph.

21. For the purposes of paragraphs 19 and 20, any finding of fact relied on when the measure was **1–754** taken is conclusive.

22.—(1) An interested person may apply to the court for a declaration as to whether a protective **1–755** measure taken under the law of, and enforceable in, a country other than England and Wales is enforceable, or to be registered, in England and Wales in accordance with Court of Protection Rules.

(2) The court must make the declaration if—

(a) the measure comes within sub-paragraph (1) or (2) of paragraph 19, and

(b) the paragraph is not disapplied in relation to it as a result of sub-paragraph (3), (4) or (5).

(3) A measure to which a declaration under this paragraph relates is enforceable in England and Wales as if it were a measure of like effect taken by the court.

23.—(1) This paragraph applies where— **1–756**

(a) provision giving effect to, or otherwise deriving from, the Convention in a country other than England and Wales applies in relation to a person who has not reached 16, and

(b) a measure is taken in relation to that person in reliance on that provision.

(2) This Part of this Schedule applies in relation to that measure as it applies in relation to a protective measure taken in relation to an adult under the law of a Convention country other than England and Wales.

1–757   **24.** The court may not review the merits of a measure taken outside England and Wales except to establish whether the measure complies with this Schedule in so far as it is, as a result of this Schedule, required to do so.

1–758   **25.** Court of Protection Rules may make provision about an application under paragraph 20 or 22.

PART 5

CO-OPERATION

1–759   **26.**—(1) This paragraph applies where a public authority proposes to place an adult in an establishment in a Convention country other than England and Wales.

(2) The public authority must consult an appropriate authority in that other country about the proposed placement and, for that purpose, must send it—

(a) a report on the adult, and

(b) a statement of its reasons for the proposed placement.

(3) If the appropriate authority in the other country opposes the proposed placement within a reasonable time, the public authority may not proceed with it.

1–760   **27.** A proposal received by a public authority under Article 33 in relation to an adult is to proceed unless the authority opposes it within a reasonable time.

1–761   **28.**—(1) This paragraph applies if a public authority is told that an adult—

(a) who is in serious danger, and

(b) in relation to whom the public authority has taken, or is considering taking, protective measures,

is, or has become resident, in a Convention country other than England and Wales.

(2) The public authority must tell an appropriate authority in that other country about—

(a) the danger, and

(b) the measures taken or under consideration.

1–762   **29.** A public authority may not request from, or send to, an appropriate authority in a Convention country information in accordance with Chapter 5(co-operation) in relation to an adult if it thinks that doing so—

(a) would be likely to endanger the adult or his property, or

(b) would amount to a serious threat to the liberty or life of a member of the adult's family.

PART 6

GENERAL

1–763   **30.** A certificate given under Article 38 by an authority in a Convention country other than England and Wales is, unless the contrary is shown, proof of the matters contained in it.

1–764   **31.** Her Majesty may by Order in Council confer on the Lord Chancellor, the court or another public authority functions for enabling the Convention to be given effect in England and Wales.

1–765   **32.**—(1) Regulations may make provision—

(a) giving further effect to the Convention, or

(b) otherwise about the private international law of England and Wales in relation to the protection of adults.

(2) The regulations may—

(a) confer functions on the court or another public authority;

(b) amend this Schedule;

(c) provide for this Schedule to apply with specified modifications;

(d) make provision about countries other than Convention countries.

1–766   **33.** Nothing in this Schedule applies, and no provision made under paragraph 32 is to apply, to any matter to which the Convention, as a result of Article 4, does not apply.

1–767   **34.** A reference in this Schedule to regulations or an order (other than an Order in Council) is to regulations or an order made for the purposes of this Schedule by the Lord Chancellor.

1–768   **35.** The following provisions of this Schedule have effect only if the Convention is in force in accordance with Article 57—

(a) paragraph 8,

(b) paragraph 9,

    (c) paragraph 19(2) and (5),
    (d) Part 5,
    (e) paragraph 30.

DEFINITIONS
   "property": s.64(1)
   "the court": s.64(1)
   "Court of Protection Rules": s.64(1)

1–769

GENERAL NOTE
   See the notes to s.63. This Schedule is divided into six parts. Part 1 contains definitions and intro- **1–770** ductory provisions. Part 2 provides the grounds, based on Arts 5-11 of the Hague Convention on the International Protection of Adults, on which the Court of Protection will exercise its jurisdiction under this Act when dealing with cases with an international element. Part 3 makes provision as to the law of which country is to apply in various situations. It also provides protection for a third party who enters into a transaction with a representative on behalf of a person, where that representative was actually not entitled so to act under the law of a country other than England and Wales applicable by virtue of Pt 3. Part 4 provides for the recognition and enforcement of protective measures taken in other countries. Part 5 provides for co-operation between authorities in England and Wales and authorities in other Convention countries. Part 6 includes powers to make further provision as to private international by Order in Council and regulations and provisions on commencement.

SCHEDULE 4   Section 66(3)

PROVISIONS APPLYING TO EXISTING ENDURING POWERS OF ATTORNEY

PART 1

ENDURING POWERS OF ATTORNEY

Enduring power of attorney to survive mental incapacity of donor
   1.—(1) Where an individual has created a power of attorney which is an enduring power within the **1–771** meaning of this Schedule—
    (a) the power is not revoked by any subsequent mental incapacity of his,
    (b) upon such incapacity supervening, the donee of the power may not do anything under the authority of the power except as provided by sub-paragraph (2) unless or until the instrument creating the power is registered under paragraph 13, and
    (c) if and so long as paragraph (b) operates to suspend the donee's authority to act under the power, section 5 of the Powers of Attorney Act 1971 (c. 27) (protection of donee and third persons), so far as applicable, applies as if the power had been revoked by the donor's mental incapacity,
and, accordingly, section 1 of this Act does not apply.
   (2) Despite sub-paragraph (1)(b), where the attorney has made an application for registration of the instrument then, until it is registered, the attorney may take action under the power—
    (a) to maintain the donor or prevent loss to his estate, or
    (b) to maintain himselfor other persons in so far as paragraph 3(2) permits him to do so.
   (3) Where the attorney purports to act as provided by sub-paragraph (2) then, in favour of a person who deals with him without knowledge that the attorney is acting otherwise than in accordance with sub-paragraph (2)(a) or (b), the transaction between them is as valid as if the attorney were acting in accordance with sub-paragraph (2)(a) or (b).

Characteristics of an enduring power of attorney
   2.—(1) Subject to sub-paragraphs (5) and (6) and paragraph 20, a power of attorney is an enduring **1–772** power within the meaning of this Schedule if the instrument which creates the power—
    (a) is in the prescribed form,
    (b) was executed in the prescribed manner by the donor and the attorney, and
    (c) incorporated at the time of execution by the donor the prescribed explanatory information.
   (2) In this paragraph, "prescribed" means prescribed by such of the following regulations as applied when the instrument was executed—
    (a) the Enduring Powers of Attorney (Prescribed Form) Regulations 1986 (S.I.1986/ 126),

211

(b) the Enduring Powers of Attorney (Prescribed Form) Regulations 1987 (S.I.1987/ 1612),

(c) the Enduring Powers of Attorney (Prescribed Form) Regulations 1990 (S.I.1990/ 1376),

(d) the Enduring Powers of Attorney (Welsh Language Prescribed Form) Regulations 2000 (S.I. 2000/289).

(3) An instrument in the prescribed form purporting to have been executed in the prescribed manner is to be taken, in the absence of evidence to the contrary, to be a document which incorporated at the time of execution by the donor the prescribed explanatory information.

(4) If an instrument differs in an immaterial respect in form or mode of expression from the pre-scribed form it is to be treated as sufficient in point of form and expression.

(5) A power of attorney cannot be an enduring power unless, when he executes the instrument creat-ing it, the attorney is—

(a) an individual who has reached 18 and is not bankrupt, or

(b) a trust corporation.

(6) A power of attorney which gives the attorney a right to appoint a substitute or successor cannot be an enduring power.

(7) An enduring power is revoked by the bankruptcy of the donor or attorney.

(8) But where the donor or attorney is bankrupt merely because an interim bankruptcy restrictions order has effect in respect of him, the power is suspended for so long as the order has effect.

(9) An enduring power is revoked if the court—

(a) exercises a power under sections 16 to 20 in relation to the donor, and

(b) directs that the enduring power is to be revoked.

(10) No disclaimer of an enduring power, whether by deed or otherwise, is valid unless and until the attorney gives notice of it to the donor or, where paragraph 4(6) or 15(1) applies, to the Public Guardian.

Scope of authority etc. of attorney under enduring power

1–773 **3.**—(1) If the instrument which creates an enduring power of attorney is expressed to confer general authority on the attorney,the instrument operates to confer, subject to—

(a) the restriction imposed by sub-paragraph (3), and

(b) any conditions or restrictions contained in the instrument,

authority to do on behalf of the donor anything which the donor could lawfully do by an attorney at the time when the donor executed the instrument.

(2) Subject to any conditions or restrictions contained in the instrument, an attorney under an endur-ing power, whether general or limited, may (without obtaining any consent) act under the power so as to benefit himself or other persons than the donor to the following extent but no further—

(a) he may so act in relation to himself or in relation to any other person if the donor might be expected to provide for his or that person's needs respectively, and

(b) he may do whatever the donor might be expected to do to meet those needs.

(3) Without prejudice to sub-paragraph (2) but subject to any conditions or restrictions contained in the instrument, an attorney under an enduring power, whether general or limited, may (without obtain-ing any consent) dispose of the property of the donor by way of gift to the following extent but no further—

(a) he may make gifts of a seasonal nature or at a time, or on an anniversary, of a birth, a marriage or the formation of a civil partnership, to persons (including himself) who are related to or con-nected withthe donor, and

(b) he may make gifts to any charity to whom the donor made or might be expected to make gifts, provided that the value of each such gift is not unreasonable having regard to all the circumstances and in particular the size of the donor's estate.

PART 2

ACTION ON ACTUAL OR IMPENDING INCAPACITY OF DONOR

Duties of attorney in event of actual or impending incapacity of donor

1–774 **4.**—(1) Sub-paragraphs (2) to (6) apply if the attorney under an enduring power has reason to believe that the donor is or is becoming mentally incapable.

(2) The attorney must, as soon as practicable, make an application to the Public Guardian for the registration of the instrument creating the power.

(3) Before making an application for registration the attorney must comply with the provisions as to notice set out in Part 3 of this Schedule.

(4) An application for registration—

(a) must be made in the prescribed form, and

(b) must contain such statements as may be prescribed.

(5) The attorney—

(a) may, before making an application for the registration of the instrument, refer to the court for its determination any question as to the validity of the power, and

(b) must comply with any direction given to him by the court on that determination.

(6) No disclaimer of the power is valid unless and until the attorney gives notice of it to the Public Guardian; and the Public Guardian must notify the donor if he receives a notice under this subparagraph.

(7) A person who, in an application for registration, makes a statement which he knows to be false in a material particular is guilty of an offence and is liable—

(a) on summary conviction, to imprisonment for a term not exceeding 12 months or a fine not exceeding the statutory maximum or both;

(b) on conviction on indictment, to imprisonment for a term not exceeding 2 years or a fine or both.

(8) In this paragraph, "prescribed" means prescribed by regulations made for the purposes of this Schedule by the Lord Chancellor.

PART 3

NOTIFICATION PRIOR TO REGISTRATION

5. Subject to paragraph 7, before making an application for registration the attorney must give **1–775** notice of his intention to do so to all those persons (if any) who are entitled to receive notice by virtue of paragraph 6.

6.—(1) Subject to sub-paragraphs (2) to (4), persons of the following classes (relatives) are entitled **1–776** to receive notice under paragraph 5—

(a) the donor's spouse or civil partner,

(b) the donor's children,

(c) the donor's parents,

(d) the donor's brothers and sisters, whether of the whole or half blood,

(e) the widow, widower or surviving civil partner of a child of the donor,

(f) the donor's grandchildren,

(g) the children of the donor's brothers and sisters of the whole blood,

(h) the children of the donor's brothers and sisters of the half blood,

(i) the donor's uncles and aunts of the whole blood,

(j) the children of the donor's uncles and aunts of the whole blood.

(2) A person is not entitled to receive notice under paragraph 5 if—

(a) his name or address is not known to the attorney and cannot be reasonably ascertained by him, or

(b) the attorney has reason to believe that he has not reached 18 or is mentally incapable.

(3) Except where sub-paragraph (4) applies—

(a) no more than 3 persons are entitled to receive notice under paragraph 5, and

(b) in determining the persons who are so entitled, persons falling within the class in subparagraph (1)(a) are to be preferred to persons falling within the class in sub-paragraph (1)(b), those falling within the class in sub-paragraph (1)(b) are to be preferred to those falling within the class in sub-paragraph (1)(c), and so on.

(4) Despite the limit of 3 specified in sub-paragraph (3), where—

(a) there is more than one person falling within any of classes (a) to (j) of sub-paragraph (1), and

(b) at least one of those persons would be entitled to receive notice under paragraph 5, then, subject to sub-paragraph (2), all the persons falling within that class are entitled to receive notice under paragraph 5.

7.—(1) An attorney is not required to give notice under paragraph 5— **1–777**

(a) to himself, or

(b) to any other attorney under the power who is joining in making the application, even though he or, as the case may be, the other attorney is entitled to receive notice by virtue of paragraph 6.

(2) In the case of any person who is entitled to receive notice by virtue of paragraph 6, the attorney, before applying for registration, may make an application to the court to be dispensed from the requirement to give him notice; and the court must grant the application if it is satisfied—

(a) that it would be undesirable or impracticable for the attorney to give him notice, or

(b) that no useful purpose is likely to be served by giving him notice.

1–778   **8.**—(1) Subject to sub-paragraph (2), before making an application for registration the attorney must give notice of his intention to do so to the donor.

(2) Paragraph 7(2) applies in relation to the donor as it applies in relation to a person who is entitled to receive notice under paragraph 5.

1–779   **9.** A notice to relatives under this Part of this Schedule must—

(a) be in the prescribed form,

(b) state that the attorney proposes to make an application to the Public Guardian for the registration of the instrument creating the enduring power in question,

(c) inform the person to whom it is given of his right to object to the registration under paragraph 13(4), and

(d) specify, as the grounds on which an objection to registration may be made, the grounds set out in paragraph 13(9).

1–780   **10.** A notice to the donor under this Part of this Schedule—

(a) must be in the prescribed form,

(b) must contain the statement mentioned in paragraph 9(b), and

(c) must inform the donor that, while the instrument remains registered, any revocation of the power by him will be ineffective unless and until the revocation is confirmed by the court.

1–781   **11.**—(1) Subject to sub-paragraph (2), before making an application for registration an attorney under a joint and several power must give notice of his intention to do so to any other attorney under the power who is not joining in making the application; and paragraphs 7(2) and 9 apply in relation to attorneys entitled to receive notice by virtue of this paragraph as they apply in relation to persons entitled to receive notice by virtue of paragraph 6.

(2) An attorney is not entitled to receive notice by virtue of this paragraph if—

(a) his address is not known to the applying attorney and cannot reasonably be ascertained by him, or

(b) the applying attorney has reason to believe that he has not reached 18 or is mentally incapable.

1–782   **12.** Despite section 7 of the Interpretation Act 1978 (c. 30) (construction of references to service by post), for the purposes of this Part of this Schedule a notice given by post is to be regarded as given on the date on which it was posted.

PART 4

REGISTRATION

Registration of instrument creating power

1–783   **13.**—(1) If an application is made in accordance with paragraph 4(3) and (4) the Public Guardian must, subject to the provisions of this paragraph, register the instrument to which the application relates.

(2) If it appears to the Public Guardian that—

(a) there is a deputy appointed for the donor of the power created by the instrument, and

(b) the powers conferred on the deputy would, if the instrument were registered, to any extent conflict with the powers conferred on the attorney,

the Public Guardian must not register the instrument except in accordance with the court's directions.

(3) The court may, on the application of the attorney, direct the Public Guardian to register an instrument even though notice has not been given as required by paragraph 4(3) and Part 3 of this Schedule to a person entitled to receive it, if the court is satisfied—

(a) that it was undesirable or impracticable for the attorney to give notice to that person, or

(b) that no useful purpose is likely to be served by giving him notice.

(4) Sub-paragraph (5) applies if, before the end of the period of 5 weeks beginning with the date (or the latest date) on which the attorney gave notice under paragraph 5 of an application for registration, the Public Guardian receives a valid notice of objection to the registration from a person entitled to notice of the application.

(5) The Public Guardian must not register the instrument except in accordance with the court's directions.

(6) Sub-paragraph (7) applies if, in the case of an application for registration—

(a) it appears from the application that there is no one to whom notice has been given under paragraph 5, or

(b) the Public Guardian has reason to believe that appropriate inquiries might bring to light evidence on which he could be satisfied that one of the grounds of objection set out in subparagraph (9) was established.

(7) The Public Guardian—

(a) must not register the instrument, and

(b) must undertake such inquiries as he thinks appropriate in all the circumstances.

(8) If, having complied with sub-paragraph (7)(b), the Public Guardian is satisfied that one of the grounds of objection set out in sub-paragraph (9) is established—

(a) the attorney may apply to the court for directions, and

(b) the Public Guardian must not register the instrument except in accordance with the court's directions.

(9) A notice of objection under this paragraph is valid if made on one or more of the following grounds—

(a) that the power purported to have been created by the instrument was not valid as an enduring power of attorney,

(b) that the power created by the instrument no longer subsists,

(c) that the application is premature because the donor is not yet becoming mentally incapable,

(d) that fraud or undue pressure was used to induce the donor to create the power,

(e) that, having regard to all the circumstances and in particular the attorney's relationship to or connection with the donor, the attorney is unsuitable to be the donor's attorney.

(10) If any of those grounds is established to the satisfaction of the court it must direct the Public Guardian not to register the instrument, but if not so satisfied it must direct its registration.

(11) If the court directs the Public Guardian not to register an instrument because it is satisfied that the ground in sub-paragraph (9)(d) or (e) is established, it must by order revoke the power created by the instrument.

(12) If the court directs the Public Guardian not to register an instrument because it is satisfied that any ground in sub-paragraph (9) except that in paragraph (c) is established, the instrument must be delivered up to be cancelled unless the court otherwise directs.

Register of enduring powers

14. The Public Guardian has the function of establishing and maintaining a register of enduring **1–784** powers for the purposes of this Schedule.

PART 5

LEGAL POSITION AFTER REGISTRATION

Effect and proof of registration

15.—(1) The effect of the registration of an instrument under paragraph 13 is that— **1–785**

(a) no revocation of the power by the donor is valid unless and until the court confirms the revocation under paragraph 16(3);

(b) no disclaimer of the power is valid unless and until the attorney gives notice of it to the Public Guardian;

(c) the donor may not extend or restrict the scope of the authority conferred by the instrument and no instruction or consent given by him after registration, in the case of a consent, confers any right and, in the case of an instruction, imposes or confers any obligation or right on or creates any liability of the attorney or other persons having notice of the instruction or consent.

(2) Sub-paragraph (1) applies for so long as the instrument is registered under paragraph 13 whether or not the donor is for the time being mentally incapable.

(3) A document purporting to be an office copy of an instrument registered under this Schedule is, in any part of the United Kingdom, evidence of—

(a) the contents of the instrument, and

(b) the fact that it has been so registered.

(4) Sub-paragraph (3) is without prejudice to section 3 of the Powers of Attorney Act 1971 (c. 27) (proof by certified copies) and to any other method of proof authorised by law.

Functions of court with regard to registered power

16.—(1) Where an instrument has been registered under paragraph 13, the court has the following **1–786** functions with respect to the power and the donor of and the attorney appointed to act under the power.

(2) The court may—

(a) determine any question as to the meaning or effect of the instrument;

(b) give directions with respect to—

     (i) the management or disposal by the attorney of the property and affairs of the donor;

    (ii) the rendering of accounts by the attorney and the production of the records kept by him for the purpose;

  (iii) the remuneration or expenses of the attorney whether or not in default of or in accordance with any provision made by the instrument, including directions for the repayment of excessive or the payment of additional remuneration;

(c) require the attorney to supply information or produce documents or things in his possession as attorney;

(d) give any consent or authorisation to act which the attorney would have to obtain from a mentally capable donor;

(e) authorise the attorney to act so as to benefit himself or other persons than the donor otherwise than in accordance with paragraph 3(2) and (3) (but subject to any conditions or restrictions contained in the instrument);

(f) relieve the attorney wholly or partly from any liability which he has or may have incurred on account of a breach of his duties as attorney.

(3) On application made for the purpose by or on behalf of the donor, the court must confirm the revocation of the power if satisfied that the donor—

(a) has done whatever is necessary in law to effect an express revocation of the power, and

(b) was mentally capable of revoking a power of attorney when he did so (whether or not he is so when the court considers the application).

(4) The court must direct the Public Guardian to cancel the registration of an instrument registered under paragraph 13 in any of the following circumstances—

(a) on confirming the revocation of the power under sub-paragraph (3),

(b) on directing under paragraph 2(9)(b) that the power is to be revoked,

(c) on being satisfied that the donor is and is likely to remain mentally capable,

(d) on being satisfied that the power has expired or has been revoked by the mental incapacity of the attorney,

(e) on being satisfied that the power was not a valid and subsisting enduring power when registration was effected,

(f) on being satisfied that fraud or undue pressure was used to induce the donor to create the power,

(g) on being satisfied that, having regard to all the circumstances and in particular the attorney's relationship to or connection with the donor, the attorney is unsuitable to be the donor's attorney.

(5) If the court directs the Public Guardian to cancel the registration of an instrument on being satisfied of the matters specified in sub-paragraph (4)(f) or (g) it must by order revoke the power created by the instrument.

(6) If the court directs the cancellation of the registration of an instrument under sub-paragraph (4) except paragraph (c) the instrument must be delivered up to the Public Guardian to be cancelled, unless the court otherwise directs.

Cancellation of registration by Public Guardian

1–787   **17.** The Public Guardian must cancel the registration of an instrument creating an enduring power of attorney—

(a) on receipt of a disclaimer signed by the attorney;

(b) if satisfied that the power has been revoked by the death or bankruptcy of the donor or attorney or, if the attorney is a body corporate, by its winding up or dissolution;

(c) on receipt of notification from the court that the court has revoked the power;

(d) on confirmation from the court that the donor has revoked the power.

PART 6

PROTECTION OF ATTORNEY AND THIRD PARTIES

Protection of attorney and third persons where power is invalid or revoked

1–788   **18.**—(1) Sub-paragraphs (2) and (3) apply where an instrument which did not create a valid power of attorney has been registered under paragraph 13 (whether or not the registration has been cancelled at the time of the act or transaction in question).

(2) An attorney who acts in pursuance of the power does not incur any liability (either to the donor or to any other person) because of the non-existence of the power unless at the time of acting he knows—

(a) that the instrument did not create a valid enduring power,

(b) that an event has occurred which, if the instrument had created a valid enduring power, would have had the effect of revoking the power, or

(c) that, if the instrument had created a valid enduring power, the power would have expired before that time.

(3) Any transaction between the attorney and another person is, in favour of that person, as valid as if the power had then been in existence, unless at the time of the transaction that person has knowledge of any of the matters mentioned in sub-paragraph (2).

(4) If the interest of a purchaser depends on whether a transaction between the attorney and another person was valid by virtue of sub-paragraph (3), it is conclusively presumed in favour of the purchaser that the transaction was valid if—

(a) the transaction between that person and the attorney was completed within 12 months of the date on which the instrument was registered, or

(b) that person makes a statutory declaration, before or within 3 months after the completion of the purchase, that he had no reason at the time of the transaction to doubt that the attorney had authority to dispose of the property which was the subject of the transaction.

(5) For the purposes of section 5 of the Powers of Attorney Act 1971 (c. 27) (protection where power is revoked) in its application to an enduring power the revocation of which by the donor is by virtue of paragraph 15 invalid unless and until confirmed by the court under paragraph 16—

(a) knowledge of the confirmation of the revocation is knowledge of the revocation of the power, but

(b) knowledge of the unconfirmed revocation is not.

Further protection of attorney and third persons

19. (1) If—   **1–789**

(a) an instrument framed in a form prescribed as mentioned in paragraph 2(2) creates a power which is not a valid enduring power, and

(b) the power is revoked by the mental incapacity of the donor,

sub-paragraphs (2) and (3) apply, whether or not the instrument has been registered.

(2) An attorney who acts in pursuance of the power does not, by reason of the revocation, incur any liability (either to the donor or to any other person) unless at the time of acting he knows—

(a) that the instrument did not create a valid enduring power, and

(b) that the donor has become mentally incapable.

(3) Any transaction between the attorney and another person is, in favour of that person, as valid as if the power had then been in existence, unless at the time of the transaction that person knows—

(a) that the instrument did not create a valid enduring power, and

(b) that the donor has become mentally incapable.

(4) Paragraph 18(4) applies for the purpose of determining whether a transaction was valid by virtue of sub-paragraph (3) as it applies for the purpose or determining whether a transaction was valid by virtue of paragraph 18(3).

PART 7

JOINT AND JOINT AND SEVERAL ATTORNEYS

Application to joint and joint and several attorneys

20.—(1) An instrument which appoints more than one person to be an attorney cannot create an **1–790** enduring power unless the attorneys are appointed to act—

(a) jointly, or

(b) jointly and severally.

(2) This Schedule, in its application to joint attorneys, applies to them collectively as it applies to a single attorney but subject to the modifications specified in paragraph 21.

(3) This Schedule, in its application to joint and several attorneys, applies with the modifications specified in sub-paragraphs (4) to (7) and in paragraph 22.

(4) A failure, as respects any one attorney, to comply with the requirements for the creation of enduring powers—

(a) prevents the instrument from creating such a power in his case, but

(b) does not affect its efficacy for that purpose as respects the other or others or its efficacy in his case for the purpose of creating a power of attorney which is not an enduring power.

(5) If one or more but not both or all the attorneys makes or joins in making an application for registration of the instrument—

(a) an attorney who is not an applicant as well as one who is may act pending the registration of the instrument as provided in paragraph 1(2),

(b) notice of the application must also be given under Part 3 of this Schedule to the other attorney or attorneys, and

(c) objection may validly be taken to the registration on a ground relating to an attorney or to the power of an attorney who is not an applicant as well as to one or the power of one who is an applicant.

(6) The Public Guardian is not precluded by paragraph 13(5) or (8) from registering an instrument and the court must not direct him not to do so under paragraph 13(10) if an enduring power subsists as respects some attorney who is not affected by the ground or grounds of the objection in question; and where the Public Guardian registers an instrument in that case, he must make against the registration an entry in the prescribed form.

(7) Sub-paragraph (6) does not preclude the court from revoking a power in so far as it confers a power on any other attorney in respect of whom the ground in paragraph 13(9)(d) or (e) is established; and where any ground in paragraph 13(9) affecting any other attorney is established the court must direct the Public Guardian to make against the registration an entry in the prescribed form.

(8) In sub-paragraph (4), "the requirements for the creation of enduring powers" means the provisions of—

(a) paragraph 2 other than sub-paragraphs (8) and (9), and

(b) the regulations mentioned in paragraph 2.

Joint attorneys

1–791 **21.**—(1) In paragraph 2(5), the reference to the time when the attorney executes the instrument is to be read as a reference to the time when the second or last attorney executes the instrument.

(2) In paragraph 2(6) to (8), the reference to the attorney is to be read as a reference to any attorney under the power.

(3) Paragraph 13 has effect as if the ground of objection to the registration of the instrument specified in sub-paragraph (9)(e) applied to any attorney under the power.

(4) In paragraph 16(2), references to the attorney are to be read as including references to any attorney under the power.

(5) In paragraph 16(4), references to the attorney are to be read as including references to any attorney under the power.

(6) In paragraph 17, references to the attorney are to be read as including references to any attorney under the power.

Joint and several attorneys

1–792 **22.**—(1) In paragraph 2(7), the reference to the bankruptcy of the attorney is to be read as a reference to the bankruptcy of the last remaining attorney under the power; and the bankruptcy of any other attorney under the power causes that person to cease to be an attorney under the power.

(2) In paragraph 2(8), the reference to the suspension of the power is to be read as a reference to its suspension in so far as it relates to the attorney in respect of whom the interim bankruptcy restrictions order has effect.

(3) The restriction upon disclaimer imposed by paragraph 4(6) applies only to those attorneys who have reason to believe that the donor is or is becoming mentally incapable.

PART 8

INTERPRETATION

1–793 **23.**—(1) In this Schedule—

"enduring power" is to be construed in accordance with paragraph 2,

"mentally incapable" or "mental incapacity", except where it refers to revocation at common law, means in relation to any person, that he is incapable by reason of mental disorder [. . .] of managing and administering his property and affairs and "mentally capable"and "mental capacity"are to be construed accordingly,

"notice" means notice in writing, and

"prescribed", except for the purposes of paragraph 2, means prescribed by regulations made for the purposes of this Schedule by the Lord Chancellor.

[(1A) In sub-paragraph (1), "mental disorder" has the same meaning as in the Mental Health Act but disregarding the amendments made to that Act by the Mental Health Act 2007.]

(2) Any question arising under or for the purposes of this Schedule as to what the donor of the power might at any time be expected to do is to be determined by assuming that he had full mental capacity at the time but otherwise by reference to the circumstances existing at that time.

DEFINITIONS
"bankrupt": s.64(3)   **1–794**
"trust corporation": s.64(1)
"Public Guardian": s.64(1)
"the court": s.64(1)
"deputy": s.64(1)
"property": s.64(1)
"purchaser": s.64(1)
"Mental Health Act": s.64(1)

AMENDMENTS
The amendments to para.23 were made by the Mental Health Act 2007, s1(4), Sch.2, Pt.2, para.23.

GENERAL NOTE
The prescribed forms for the making and registration of LPAs are set out in the Schs 7 and 8 to the **1–795**
Lasting Powers of Attorney, Enduring Powers of Attorney and Public Guardian Regulations 2007 (SI
2007/1253). For the loss or destruction of forms, see reg.29. The purpose of this Schedule is explained
in the notes to s.66(3).

Paragraph 13(1)
REGISTER THE INSTRUMENT. See regs.23 to 27 of SI 2007/1253, above.   **1–796**

Paragraphs 13(2), 13(5), 13(7), and 24(2)
See reg.26 of SI 2007/1253.   **1–797**

Paragraph 13(4)
See reg.25 of SI 2007/1253.   **1–798**

PARAGRAPH 20(6),(7)
See reg.28 of SI 2007/1253.   **1–799**

SCHEDULE 5   **Section 66(4)**

TRANSITIONAL PROVISIONS AND SAVINGS

PART 1

REPEAL OF PART 7 OF THE MENTAL HEALTH ACT 1983

Existing receivers
1.—(1) This paragraph applies where, immediately before the commencement day, there is a **1–800**
receiver (R) for a person (P) appointed under section 99 of the Mental Health Act.

(2) On and after that day—
(a) this Act applies as if R were a deputy appointed for P by the court, but with the functions that R
had as receiver immediately before that day, and
(b) a reference in any other enactment to a deputy appointed by the court includes a person
appointed as a deputy as a result of paragraph (a).

(3) On any application to it by R, the court may end R's appointment as P's deputy.

(4) Where, as a result of section 20(1), R may not make a decision on behalf of P in relation to a
relevant matter, R must apply to the court.

(5) If, on the application, the court is satisfied that P is capable of managing his property and affairs
in relation to the relevant matter—
(a) it must make an order ending R's appointment as P's deputy in relation to that matter, but

(b) it may, in relation to any other matter, exercise in relation to P any of the powers which it has under sections 15 to 19.

(6) If it is not satisfied, the court may exercise in relation to P any of the powers which it has under sections 15 to 19.

(7) R's appointment as P's deputy ceases to have effect if P dies.

(8) "Relevant matter" means a matter in relation to which, immediately before the commencement day, R was authorised to act as P's receiver.

(9) In sub-paragraph (1), the reference to a receiver appointed under section 99 of the Mental Health Act includes a reference to a person who by virtue of Schedule 5 to that Act was deemed to be a receiver appointed under that section.

Orders, appointments etc

1–801 **2.**—(1) Any order or appointment made, direction or authority given or other thing done which has, or by virtue of Schedule 5 to the Mental Health Act was deemed to have, effect under Part 7 of the Act immediately before the commencement day is to continue to have effect despite the repeal of Part 7.

(2) In so far as any such order, appointment, direction, authority or thing could have been made, given or done under sections 15 to 20 if those sections had then been in force—

(a) it is to be treated as made, given or done under those sections, and

(b) the powers of variation and discharge conferred by section 16(7) apply accordingly.

(3) Sub-paragraph (1)—

(a) does not apply to nominations under section 93(1) or (4) of the Mental Health Act, and

(b) as respects receivers, has effect subject to paragraph 1.

(4) This Act does not affect the operation of section 109 of the Mental Health Act (effect and proof of orders etc.) in relation to orders made and directions given under Part 7 of that Act.

(5) This paragraph is without prejudice to section 16 of the Interpretation Act 1978 (c. 30) (general savings on repeal).

Pending proceedings

1–802 **3.**—(1) Any application for the exercise of a power under Part 7 of the Mental Health Act which is pending immediately before the commencement day is to be treated, in so far as a corresponding power is exercisable under sections 16 to 20, as an application for the exercise of that power.

(2) For the purposes of sub-paragraph (1) an application for the appointment of a receiver is to be treated as an application for the appointment of a deputy.

Appeals

1–803 **4.**—(1) Part 7 of the Mental Health Act and the rules made under it are to continue to apply to any appeal brought by virtue of section 105 of that Act which has not been determined before the commencement day.

(2) If in the case of an appeal brought by virtue of section 105(1) (appeal to nominated judge) the judge nominated under section 93 of the Mental Health Act has begun to hear the appeal, he is to continue to do so but otherwise it is to be heard by a puisne judge of the High Court nominated under section 46.

Fees

1–804 **5.** All fees and other payments which, having become due, have not been paid to the former Court of Protection before the commencement day, are to be paid to the new Court of Protection.

Court records

1–805 **6.**—(1) The records of the former Court of Protection are to be treated, on and after the commencement day, as records of the new Court of Protection and are to be dealt with accordingly under the Public Records Act 1958 (c. 51).

(2) On and after the commencement day, the Public Guardian is, for the purpose of exercising any of his functions, to be given such access as he may require to such of the records mentioned in sub-paragraph (1) as relate to the appointment of receivers under section 99 of the Mental Health Act.

Existing charges

1–806 **7.** This Act does not affect the operation in relation to a charge created before the commencement day of—

(a) so much of section 101(6) of the Mental Health Act as precludes a charge created under section 101(5) from conferring a right of sale or foreclosure during the lifetime of the patient, or

(b) section 106(6) of the Mental Health Act (charge created by virtue of section 106(5) not to cause interest to fail etc.).

Preservation of interests on disposal of property

8. Paragraph 8(1) of Schedule 2 applies in relation to any disposal of property (within the meaning **1–807** of that provision) by a person living on 1 st November 1960, being a disposal effected under the Lunacy Act 1890 (c.5) as it applies in relation to the disposal of property effected under sections 16 to 20.

Accounts

9. Court of Protection Rules may provide that, in a case where paragraph 1 applies, R is to have a **1–808** duty to render accounts—

(a) while he is receiver;

(b) after he is discharged.

Interpretation

10. In this Part of this Schedule— **1–809**

(a) "the commencement day" means the day on which section 66(1)(a) (repeal of Part 7 of the Mental Health Act) comes into force,

(b) "the former Court of Protection" means the office abolished by section 45, and

(c) "the new Court of Protection" means the court established by that section.

PART 2

REPEAL OF THE ENDURING POWERS OF ATTORNEY ACT 1985

Orders, determinations, etc

11.—(1) Any order or determination made, or other thing done, under the 1985 Act which has effect **1–810** immediately before the commencement day continues to have effect despite the repeal of that Act.

(2) In so far as any such order, determination or thing could have been made or done under Schedule 4 if it had then been in force—

(a) it is to be treated as made or done under that Schedule, and

(b) the powers of variation and discharge exercisable by the court apply accordingly.

(3) Any instrument registered under the 1985 Act is to be treated as having been registered by the Public Guardian under Schedule 4.

(4) This paragraph is without prejudice to section 16 of the Interpretation Act 1978 (c. 30) (general savings on repeal).

Pending proceedings

12.—(1) An application for the exercise of a power under the 1985 Act which is pending immedi- **1–811** ately before the commencement day is to be treated, in so far as a corresponding power is exercisable under Schedule 4, as an application for the exercise of that power.

(2) For the purposes of sub-paragraph (1)—

(a) a pending application under section 4(2) of the 1985 Act for the registration of an instrument is to be treated as an application to the Public Guardian under paragraph 4 of Schedule 4 and any notice given in connection with that application under Schedule 1 to the 1985 Act is to be treated as given under Part 3 of Schedule 4,

(b) a notice of objection to the registration of an instrument is to be treated as a notice of objection under paragraph 13 of Schedule 4, and

(c) pending proceedings under section 5 of the 1985 Act are to be treated as proceedings on an application for the exercise by the court of a power which would become exercisable in relation to an instrument under paragraph 16(2) of Schedule 4 on its registration.

Appeals

13.—(1) The 1985 Act and, so far as relevant, the provisions of Part 7 of the Mental Health Act and **1–812** the rules made under it as applied by section 10 of the 1985 Act are to continue to have effect in relation to any appeal brought by virtue of section 10(1)(c) of the 1985 Act which has not been determined before the commencement day.

(2) If, in the case of an appeal brought by virtue of section 105(1) of the Mental Health Act as applied by section 10(1)(c) of the 1985 Act (appeal to nominated judge), the judge nominated under section 93 of the Mental Health Act has begun to hear the appeal, he is to continue to do so but otherwise the appeal is to be heard by a puisne judge of the High Court nominated under section 46.

Exercise of powers of donor as trustee

1–813   **14.**—(1) Section 2(8) of the 1985 Act (which prevents a power of attorney under section 25 of the Trustee Act 1925 (c.19) as enacted from being an enduring power) is to continue to apply to any enduring power—

(a) created before 1 st March 2000, and

(b) having effect immediately before the commencement day.

(2) Section 3(3) of the 1985 Act (which entitles the donee of an enduring power to exercise the donor's powers as trustee) is to continue to apply to any enduring power to which, as a result of the provision mentioned in sub-paragraph (3), it applies immediately before the commencement day.

(3) The provision is section 4(3)(a) of the Trustee Delegation Act 1999 (c. 15) (which provides for section 3(3) of the 1985 Act to cease to apply to an enduring power when its registration is cancelled, if it was registered in response to an application made before 1 st March 2001).

(4) Even though section 4 of the 1999 Act is repealed by this Act, that section is to continue to apply in relation to an enduring power—

(a) to which section 3(3) of the 1985 Act applies as a result of sub-paragraph (2), or

(b) to which, immediately before the repeal of section 4 of the 1999 Act, section 1 of that Act applies as a result of section 4 of it.

(5) The reference in section 1(9) of the 1999 Act to section 4(6) of that Act is to be read with sub-paragraphs (2) to (4).

Interpretation

1–814   **15.** In this Part of this Schedule, "the commencement day" means the day on which section 66(1)(b) (repeal of the 1985 Act) comes into force.

DEFINITIONS

1–815   "Mental Health Act": s.64(1)
"deputy": s.64(1)
"the court": s.64(1)
"enactment": s.64(1)
"property": s.64(1)
"Public Guardian": s.64(1)
"Court of Protection Rules": s.64(1)
"the 1985 Act": s.64(1)

GENERAL NOTE

1–816   See the notes to s.66(4).

Paragraph 1(2)(a)

1–817   Where an existing receiver is treated as if he or she were a deputy appointed by the court under this provision, the fee prescribed in the Schedule to the Public Guardian (Fees, etc) Regulations 2007 (SI 2007/2051) shall be payable by P within 30 days of the date of the invoice for the fee (SI 2007/2051, regs.3,7). After the appointment, the Public Guardian must determine the level of supervision required by s.58(1)(c) and the level of fee as set out in the Schedule is payable accordingly. The three levels of supervision are type I (highest), type II (lower) and type III (minimal) (SI 2007/2051, reg.8; see further the General Note to s.19).

SCHEDULE 6 Section 67(1)

MINOR AND CONSEQUENTIAL AMENDMENTS

1–818   [*Not reproduced*]

SCHEDULE 7   **Section 67(2)**

REPEALS

[*Not reproduced*]   **1–819**

PART 2

THE DEPRIVATION OF LIBERTY SAFEGUARDS

Section 4A prohibits the deprivation of the liberty of a person under this Act **2–001** other than where the court has made an order under s.16(2)(a); where it is authorised for life-sustaining or other emergency treatment (s.4B); and where the deprivation is authorised under the deprivation of liberty safeguards set out in Sch.1A. This Part explains the background to the deprivation of liberty safeguards, describes how they are intended to operate, and considers their interface with the Mental Health Act 1983 (the 1983 Act).

HL v United Kingdom (the "Bournewood case")

In *HL v United Kingdom* (2004) 40 E.H.R.R. 761, Mr L, a mentally incapaci- **2–002** tated patient, alleged that he had been detained at the Bournewood Hospital as an informal patient in violation of Art.5(1) of the European Convention on Human Rights (ECHR) which is designed to ensure that no one should be arbitrarily deprived of his liberty. He also claimed that the procedures available to him for a review of the legality of his detention did not satisfy the requirements of Art.5(4) which provides a person who has been deprived of his or her liberty with a right to a speedy independent legal review of the detention. The facts of the case are remarkable. From the age of 13, for a period of over 30 years, Mr L, who had a profound intellectual disability, was autistic and lacked the capacity to consent or dissent from being in hospital, was a resident at the Bournewood Hospital. He was eventually discharged into the community to live with carers, Mr and Mrs E. Under their care Mr L flourished for three years until an incident occurred that led to his readmission to hospital. While attending a day centre one day, Mr L became particularly agitated and he could not be calmed. Mr and Mrs E, who were able to successfully deal with such incidents, could not be contacted. A doctor attended and administered a sedative to Mr L. On the advice of Mr L's social worker, he was taken to the Bournewood Hospital by which time the effect of the sedative was beginning to wear off and he was becoming increasingly agitated. He was assessed as requiring inpatient treatment. Mr L's psychiatrist considered whether it was necessary to detain him under the provisions of the 1983 Act but decided that this was not necessary because he appeared fully compliant and did not resist admission to hospital. He was therefore admitted informally. Mr and Mrs E made it plain that they wanted to take Mr L back into their care. The hospital were not prepared to countenance this and he remained in the hospital. Proceedings were commenced in the name of Mr L against the Bournewood NHS Trust for judicial review of the trust's decision to detain him and for a writ of habeas corpus to release him from detention. It was claimed that Mr L's detention was unlawful on the ground that the 1983 Act, which had not been invoked, was the only basis for the hospital's right to detain him. The hospital claimed Mr L was not being detained, but if he was, the detention was authorised under the common law doctrine of necessity.

Subsequent to the decision of the House of Lords ([1998] 3 All E.R. 289) to dismiss Mr L's claim, an application was made to European Court of Human Rights (ECtHR).

The decision of the ECtHR focussed on the findings of the House of Lords that the detention of a compliant mentally incapacitated patient could be justified under the common law doctrine of necessity, and that Mr L had not been detained while he was a patient at the Bournewood Hospital. The ECtHR held that:

1. In order to determine whether a person has been deprived of his or her liberty for the purposes of Art.5(1), the starting point must be the specific situation of the individual concerned and account must be taken of a whole range of factors arising in a particular case such as the type, duration, effects and manner of implementation of the measure in question. The distinction between a deprivation of, and a restriction upon, liberty is merely one of degree or intensity and not one of nature or substance (para.89).

2. The correspondence between HL's carers and his psychiatrist reflected both the carers' wish to have HL immediately released to their care and, equally, the clear intention of the health care professionals to exercise strict control over his assessment, treatment, contacts and, notably, movement and residence: HL would only be released from the hospital to the care of his carers as and when the professionals considered it appropriate. It followed that HL was being deprived of his liberty because he "was under continuous supervision and control and was not free to leave"(para.91). The fact that HL might have been on a ward which was not "locked" or "lockable" was not determinative (para.92). With regard to HL's compliance to his admission, the Court observed that "the right to liberty is too important in a democratic society for a person to lose the benefit of Convention protection for the single reason that he may have given himself up to be taken into detention, especially when it is not disputed that that person is legally incapable of consenting to, or disagreeing with, the proposed action" (para.90).

3. The Court found "striking the lack of any fixed procedural rules by which the admission and detention of compliant incapacitated patients is conducted" when contrasted with "the extensive network of safeguards applicable to psychiatric committals covered by the 1983 Act" (para.120). This absence of procedural safeguards in the doctrine of necessity failed to protect HL against arbitrary deprivations of his liberty. His detention therefore violated Art.5(1).

4. There had also been a violation of Art.5(4) of the Convention as HL did not have the opportunity to have the lawfulness of his detention reviewed by a court as neither judicial review nor other judicial remedies cited by the Government satisfied the requirements of Art.5(4) (para.141).

What constitutes a "deprivation of liberty"?

2–003   Section 64(5) of this Act states that "references to deprivations of a person's liberty have the same meaning as in Article 5(1) of the Human Rights Convention". It will therefore be necessary to examine the case law of both the ECtHR and domestic courts on the interpretation of the phrase "deprived of his liberty" in Art.5(1).

HL v United Kingdom was applied in *JE and DE v Surrey County Council* [2006] EWHC 3459 (Fam); [2007] M.H.L.R. 39, where Munby J. held, at para.77, that the following elements are relevant to the question of whether in the case of an adult there has been a deprivation of liberty engaging the State's obligations under Art.5(1):

1. An objective element of a person's confinement in a particular restricted space for a not negligible length of time. This involves assessing the facts of the case by applying the criteria identified in *HL*. The key factor in a case where a relative wishes to take over the care of the person is whether the person is, or is not free to leave the place where he or she is being cared for. This may be tested by determining whether those treating and managing the person exercise complete and effective control over the person's care and movement (*HL v United Kingdom*, para.91). A similar approach should be adopted if a main carer wished to take over the care of the person.

2. A subjective element, namely that the person has not validly consented to the confinement in question. Where a person lacks the capacity to give a valid consent to their confinement, consent cannot be inferred from the fact that the person does not object (*HL v United Kingdom*, para.90).

3. The deprivation of liberty must be imputable to the State, i.e. the State was responsible for the deprivation (*Storck v Germany* (2006) 43 E.H.R.R. 6, para.89).

Where a relative wished take over the care of a resident and the resident was indicating a willingness to be discharged to such care, his Lordship said, at para.115, that the crucial question is not so much whether (and, if so, to what extent) the person's freedom or liberty was or is curtailed within the institutional setting. The fundamental issue is whether the person is deprived of his liberty to leave the home where he was placed not in the sense of leaving for the purpose of some approved trip or outing, but rather "leaving in the sense of removing himself permanently in order to live where and with whom he chooses." If the person is not free to leave to live elsewhere, he is being deprived of his liberty. It follows from this that being "free to leave" in this context does not mean free to leave in the abstract because no mentally incapacitated person would be allowed just to wander out of a hospital or care home in a situation where there was nowhere for them to go. Rather, it means that the person is not free to leave to go to live in a specific alternative placement.

In *Guzzardi v Italy* (1980) 3 E.H.R.R. 33, para.93, the Court observed:

"The difference between deprivation of and restriction upon liberty is . . . merely one of degree or intensity, and not one of nature or substance. Although the process of classification into one or other of these categories sometimes proves to be no easy task in that in some borderline cases are a matter of pure opinion, the Court cannot avoid making the selection upon which the applicability of Art.5 depends."

This passage was cited by Collins J. in *R (on the application of G) v Mental* **2–004** *Health Review Tribunal* [2004] EWHC 2193 (Admin), para.20, as authority for the proposition "that there will be borderline cases when a decision either way cannot be said to be wrong in law. The court must be careful not to interfere unless persuaded that the decision is wrong in law". His Lordship said that it is important to bear in mind that the purpose of any measure of restriction, while a relevant consideration, must not be given too much weight. This consideration was identified by Keene L.J in *Secretary of State for the Home Department v Mental Health Review Tribunal and PH* [2002] EWCA Civ 1868; [2003] M.H.L.R. 2002, where his lordship identified the following principles which are applicable to the interpretation of Art.5(1):

1. A basic distinction is to be drawn between mere restrictions on liberty of movement and the deprivation of liberty.

2. The distinction is one merely of degree or intensity of restrictions, not of nature and substance.

3. The court must start with the concrete or actual situation of the individual concerned and take account of a range of criteria, such as type, duration, effects and manner of implementation of the measure in question.

4. Account must be taken of the cumulative effect of the various restrictions.

5. The purpose of any measures of restriction is a relevant consideration.

6. If the measures are taken principally in the interests of the individual who is being restricted, they may well be regarded as not amounting to a deprivation of liberty.

The sixth principle is taken from *HM v Switzerland* [2002] M.H.L.R. 209, where the ECtHR held that that an elderly mentally disordered patient who was required by a government order to reside in a "foster home" which allowed freedom of movement and encouraged contact with the outside world was not being deprived of her liberty. The court concluded that:

> "in the circumstances of the present case the applicant's placement in the foster home did not amount to a deprivation of liberty . . . but was a responsible measure taken by the competent authorities in the applicant's interests" (para.48).

2–005   In *Austin v Metropolitan Police Commissioner* [2007] EWCA Civ 989; [2008] 1 All E.R. 564, para.98, the court noted "in passing that, although the decision in *HM v Switzerland* was distinguished in *HL v United Kingdom*, the ECtHR did not disagree with the principle". Munby J., having reviewed recent Strasbourg case law in *JE and DE v Surrey County Council*, above, at para.70, said that the proposition must be approached with an "appropriate degree of caution" because it receives "absolutely no support" from the subsequent decisions of the Court in *HL v United Kingdom* and *Storck v Germany*.

Guzzardi was also cited in *Secretary of State for the Home Department v JJ and others* [2007] UKHL 45; [2008] 1 All E.R. 613, where it was common ground between the parties that the concept of "deprivation of liberty" has an autonomous meaning: "that is, it has a Council of Europe-wide meaning for the purposes of the Convention, whatever it might or might not be thought to mean in any member state" (per Lord Bingham at para.13). In *R. (on the application of Gillan) v Metropolitan Police Commissioner* [2006] UKHL 12; [2006] 4 All E.R. 1041, para.23, Lord Bingham said that the Strasbourg jurisprudence on what constitutes a deprivation of liberty "is closely focused on the facts of particular cases, and this makes it perilous to transpose the outcome of one case to another where the facts are different". In *Gillan*, it was held that a person who was detained for a short period by the police pursuant to a "stop and search" power was not deprived of his liberty for the purposes of Art.5.

Notwithstanding the decision in *HL*, the deprivation of a patient's liberty for a short period in order to respond to an emergency does not constitute a violation of Art.5(1) (*X v United Kingdom* (1982) 4 E.H.R.R. 188, para.41). In order to comply with Art.5(1), the authorisation of the deprivation in the absence of an emergency must be obtained before someone is detained (*City of Sunderland v PS and CA* [2007] EWHC 623 (Fam); [2007] M.H.L.R. 196, para.23). A subsequent review of detention under Art.5(4) cannot retrospectively authorise an unlawful detention (*HL v United Kingdom*).

Bearing in mind that there is no definitive legal test for what will amount to a **2–006** deprivation of liberty, relevant European and domestic case law suggests that it is unlikely that a court would find that a mentally incapacitated patient who has been taken to hospital or a care home has been being deprived of his or her liberty for the purposes of Art.5(1) in the absence of one or more of the following factors:

1. Force, threats or sedation being used to ensure that a resisting patient is taken to the hospital or care home.

2. Subterfuge being used to ensure the patient's co-operation in being taken to the hospital or care home, e.g. the patient being misled into believing that he will return home the next day.

3. The journey to the hospital or care home being either exceptionally long or otherwise being very onerous for the patient.

4. The decision to admit the patient to the hospital or care home being opposed by relatives or carers who live with the patient.

5. Force or threats being used to prevent the patient from leaving the hospital or care home in a situation where the patient is making a persistent and/or purposeful attempt to leave.

6. Sedation being used to prevent the patient from making an attempt to leave the hospital or care home.

7. Force being used in a non-emergency situation to ensure that a resisting patient receives necessary medical treatment.

8. The hospital or care home denying a request by relatives or carers for the patient to be discharged to their care. Given the judgment in *JE and DE v Surrey County Council,* above, the presence of this factor alone would suggest that the person is being deprived of his or her liberty. This would be the case even if the authorities had concerns about the quality of care that the patient would receive on being discharged. In *LLBC v TG, JG and HR* [2007] EWHC 2640 (Fam); [2007] M.H.L.R. 203, a case where members of the patient's family claimed that he was being unlawfully detained in a care home, McFarlane J. accepted a submission of the Official Solicitor that the fact that some family members opposed the placement was not sufficient to change the character of circumstances which would not otherwise amount to a deprivation of liberty.

9. A decision by the hospital or care home to deny or severely restrict access to the patient by relatives or carers.

10. The patient being denied freedom of association within the hospital or care home, or otherwise being subject to a care regime which severely restricts his autonomy.

11. The patient's access to the community being denied or severely restricted primarily due to concerns about public safety.

It is suggested that the following circumstances would not, by themselves, constitute a deprivation of liberty:

1. Benign force (i.e. force that is not being used to overcome resistance) being used to take a confused patient to the hospital or care home.

2. The patient being treated or cared for in a locked environment.

3. The design of door handles or the use of key pads making it difficult for a confused patient to leave the hospital or care home.

4. Staff bringing the patient who has wandered back to the hospital or care home.

5. The use of benign force to feed, dress or provide medical treatment for the patient.

6. The use of restraint, medication or seclusion in an emergency situation in order to respond to the patient's disturbed, threatening or self-harming behaviour.

7. Dissuading a confused patient from attempting to leave the hospital or care home, using benign force if necessary. This would be the case even if the confused patient had attempted to leave the premises on more than one occasion.

8. Placing reasonable limitations on the visiting of the patient by relatives or carers.

9. A temporary refusal to let the patient leave the hospital or care home in the absence of an escort whose role would be to support the patient rather than to protect the public.

The *Code of Practice* states at para.6.52:

"It is difficult to define the difference between actions that amount to a restriction of someone's liberty and those that result in a deprivation of liberty. In recent legal cases, the European Court of Human Rights said that the difference was 'one of degree or intensity, not one of nature or substance'. There must therefore be particular factors in the specific situation of the person concerned which provide the 'degree' or 'intensity' to result in a deprivation of liberty. In practice, this can relate to:

- the type of care being provided
- how long the situation lasts
- its effects, or

- the way in which a particular situation came about.

The European Court of Human Rights has identified the following as factors contributing to deprivation of liberty in its judgments on cases to date:

- restraint was used, including sedation, to admit a person who is resisting
- professionals exercised complete and effective control over care and movement for a significant period
- professionals exercised control over assessments, treatment, contacts and residence
- the person would be prevented from leaving if they made a meaningful attempt to do so
- a request by carers for the person to be discharged to their care was refused
- the person was unable to maintain social contacts because of restrictions placed on access to other people
- the person lost autonomy because they were under continuous supervision and control."

This guidance is expanded upon in Ch.2 of the supplement to the Code which is reproduced in Pt.5.

Phil Fennell argues that "if the person lacks capacity and the decision-maker is assuming complete control over treatment to the extent that they are making decisions about the administration of strong psychotropic medication or even ECT to a patient, then that is assuming complete control over treatment and would be a factor tipping the balance firmly towards there being a deprivation of liberty requiring the use of the Mental Health Act 1983 or at the very least use of the protective care provisions such as those proposed to fill the Bournewood Gap" ("The Mental Capacity Act 2005, the Mental Health Act, and the Common Law" (Nov 2005) Journal of Mental Health Law 167). As the provision of any medical treatment to an incapacitated patient involves a clinician assuming complete control over that patient's treatment, it is submitted that the provision of the treatments mentioned by Fennell in the absence of other factors confirming that "professionals treating and managing [the patient] exercised complete and effective control over his movements" (*HL v United Kingdom,* para.91) would not lead to a finding that there has been a deprivation of liberty. The case law of the ECtHR does not support the contention that a finding of a deprivation of liberty can be made solely on the basis that a particular treatment is being proposed for the patient: a "whole range of factors arising in a particular case" must be taken into account (*HL v United Kingdom,* para.89). In Peter Bartlett's opinion, "it would appear that electro-convulsive therapy can be given to an informal patient lacking capacity in his or her best interests, provided that the procedures in the [Mental Capacity Act 2005] are followed" (Blackstone's Guide to the Mental Capacity Act 2005 (Oxford University Press, 2005) para.3.43). The Mental Health Act Commission doubts "that there is anything inherent in the in the procedure for ECT treatment that amounts to a deprivation of liberty" (MHAC, *Twelfth Biennial Report* 2005–2007, para.6.86).

The response of the Government to the judgment in HL v United Kingdom

2–007   In order to remedy the breaches of Art.5 identified by the ECtHR in *HL v United Kingdom*, the Government undertook to provide additional procedural safeguards for incapacitated people who where not subject to the 1983 Act, but whose care and treatment involved a deprivation of liberty. Accordingly, in March 2005, a consultative document (*"Bournewood" Consultation: The approach to be taken in response to the judgment of the European Court of Human Rights in the "Bournewood" case*) was issued by the Government. The following options were identified:

1. A new form of "protective care" which would a basis for new procedures to govern admission and detention and therefore the circumstances in which a person might be lawfully deprived of liberty.

2. Extending the use of detention under the 1983 Act to the Bournewood group of patients.

3. Using existing arrangements for guardianship under the 1983 Act (modified as necessary).

A report of the outcome of the consultation was published in June 2006. At the same time, the Government announced its decision to proceed with the protective care option which had been favoured by the majority of respondents to the consultation, with a view to new deprivation of liberty safeguards being introduced into the Mental Capacity Act 2005. The Mental Health Bill (now the Mental Health Act 2007) was identified as a suitable vehicle through which to amend the 2005 Act for this purpose. The new safeguards are located in Schs A1 and 1A. They are extremely complex, and caused the Joint Committee on Human Rights to "question whether they will be readily understood by proprietors of residential care homes, even with the benefit of professional advice" (*Legislative Scrutiny: Mental Health Bill*, HL Paper 40; HC 288, para.90).

Schedule A1 – the deprivation of a person's liberty in a hospital or care home

2–008   Although Sch.A1 refers to the person who either is lacking capacity, or is thought to lack capacity as "the relevant person", to be consistent with the rest of the Act this person will be referred to as P.
A Code of Practice on the deprivation of liberty safeguards has been issued as a supplement to the main Code of Practice. This supplement is reproduced in Pt.5.

The requirements and procedure for requesting and granting a standard authorisation (Pts 3 and 4 of Sch.A1 – paras.12–73).

2–009   Part 2 of Sch.A1 sets out the "qualifying requirements" that must be met before a standard authorisation can be given to provide legal authority to detain a person in a hospital or care home. They are:

(a) *the age requirement* – the person must be aged 18 or over (para.13). For the eligibility of a person to carry out an age assessment, see reg.8 of SI 2008/1858.

(b) *the mental health requirement* – the person must be suffering from a mental disorder within the meaning of the 1983 Act (i.e. "any disorder or disability of mind") but disregarding any exclusion for persons with learning disability (para.14). This means that a person with a learning disability comes within the scope of Sch.A1 whether or not the disability is associated with abnormally aggressive or seriously irresponsible conduct. Dependence on alcohol or drugs is not considered to be a mental disorder for the purposes of the 1983 Act (see s.1(3) of that Act), although an alcoholic or a drug addict who suffers from an associated mental disorder would qualify.

This requirement is needed to satisfy the finding of the ECtHR in *Winterwerp v Netherlands* (1979–80) 2 E.H.R.R. that in order for a detention on the ground of unsoundness of mind to be lawful there must be medical evidence of mental disorder. When carrying out a mental health assessment, the assessor must consider how (if at all) the person's mental health is likely to be affected by his being a detained resident, and notify the best interests assessor of his conclusions (para.36). For the eligibility of a person to carry out a mental health assessment, see reg.4 of SI 2008/1858.

(c) *the mental capacity requirement* – the person must lack the capacity to decide whether or not he should be accommodated in the hospital or care home for the purpose of being given the relevant care or treatment (para.15). The assessment should be undertaken in accordance with ss.2 and 3, and the assessor must apply the principles set out in s.1. For the eligibility of a person to carry out a mental capacity assessment, see reg.6 of SI 2008/1858.

(d) *the best interests requirement* – the assessor must determine whether a deprivation of liberty is occurring, or is likely to occur. If this is the case, an assessment must be made as to whether the deprivation is in the best interests of the person, is necessary to prevent harm to him, and is a proportionate response to the likelihood and seriousness of that harm (para.16). Note that in relation to the prevention of harm the requirement is one of necessity, not desirability. The best interests assessor must consult with the managing authority of the hospital or care home, and that authority and the supervisory body must provide the assessor with any needs assessment or care plan that has been made by them, or on their behalf (para.39). The assessor must have regard to such documents, and of the opinion of the mental health assessor on the impact of the proposed course of action on the person's mental health. The assessor must state the maximum authorisation period (para.42), and the supervisory body may not grant an authorisation for longer than this period (para.51). The assessor may make recommendations about conditions relating to the deprivation to be attached to the authorisation (para.43). The supervisory body must "have regard" to such recommendations and, if the supervisory body accepts them, the managing authority must ensure they are complied with (para.53). When undertaking the assessment, the assessor will be bound by the general duty regarding the determination of a person's best interests which is set out in s.4. The assessor is subject to the principles set out in s.1 and should, in particular, consider whether "it is necessary for [P] to be a detained resident" (para.16(4)) or whether P's care could be provided in a less restrictive manner (s.1(6)). For the eligibility of a person to carry out a best interests assessment, see reg.5 of SI 2008/1858.

(e) *the eligibility requirement* – the person is ineligible to be deprived of his liberty under this Act if he is, or might be, subject to the 1983 Act in one of the circumstances set out in Sch.1A (para.17). Schedule 1A is considered below. For the eligibility of a person to carry out an eligibility assessment, see reg.7 of SI 2008/1858. Where the eligibility assessor and the best interests assessor are not the same person, reg.15 applies.

(f) *the no refusals requirement* – the purpose of this requirement is to establish whether an authorisation would conflict with an existing decision relating to the person. There are refusals if: (i) the authorisation is sought for the purpose of treatment for either a mental or physical disorder which is covered, either wholly or partially, by a valid and applicable advance decision made by the person, or (ii) to place the person in a hospital or care home would conflict with a valid decision of a donee of a lasting power of attorney or a deputy appointed by the Court of Protection (paras.18–20). The donee and the deputy would be governed by s.4 when reaching their decision. For the eligibility of a person to carry out a no refusals assessment, see reg.9 of SI 2008/1858.

Requests for a standard authorisation

2–010   The "managing authority" of a NHS hospital is the NHS body responsible for running the relevant hospital, and the managing authority of a private hospital or care home is the person registered under the Care Standards Act 2000 in respect of that hospital or home (paras.176–179). The managing authority must request authorisation from the relevant "supervisory body" if a person who meets or is likely to meet all of the qualifying requirements is, or is likely to be during the next 28 days, accommodated in their hospital or care home in circumstances that amount to a deprivation of liberty (para.24). In the meantime, an urgent authorisation may be issued by the managing authority if certain criteria are satisfied (see below). The information to be provided in a request for a standard authorisation is set out in SI 2008/1858, reg.16. If the person who is the subject of a standard authorisation becomes a detained resident in a different hospital or care home, the managing authority of that hospital or care home must request a new standard authorisation (paras.25–26). Managing authorities must keep written records of requests for authorisation and the reasons for them (para.32), and they should have systems in place to identify when a deprivation of liberty of a mentally incapacitated person may be taking place.

The supervisory body will be the relevant commissioning body for hospitals, and the relevant local authority for care homes, which will usually be the local authority for the area where the person is ordinarily resident (paras.180–183). Where a person is admitted to a care home or to an NHS hospital he continues to be ordinarily resident in the area in which he was ordinarily resident immediately before his admission (para.183). If there is a dispute about the person's place of ordinary residence, this is to be resolved by either the Secretary of State or the National Assembly for Wales (para.183(3)) If a local authority wishes to dispute whether it is the supervisory body, the provisions of SI 2008/1858 regs 17–19 apply. The managing authority and the supervisory body can be the same body (para.184). Schedule AI, Pt.7 (paras.98–100) applies if there is a change of supervisory body but the person does not move, for example because of changes in a local authority boundary.

With one exception, on a request for a standard authorisation being made to it the supervisory body must arrange for the person to be assessed within 21 days to determine whether each of the qualifying requirements are satisfied (para.33). The exception is that a particular assessment need not be undertaken if the supervisory body has in its possession an equivalent assessment that has been carried out within the previous year (apart from the age assessment (para.49(4)) and which meets the all of the requirements of the particular assessment, and it has no reason to believe that the assessment may no longer be accurate (paras.33(5) and 49). For example, a recent assessment for detention under the 1983 Act could be considered as being the equivalent of the mental health assessment. If the previous assessment is a best interests assessment, the supervisory body must take into account any information given, or submissions made by P's representative and any s.39C or s.39D IMCA (para.49(6)).

A standard authorisation request must be made if an order of the Court of Protection authorising a person's deprivation of liberty is about to expire and the person will continue to be deprived of his or her liberty (para.27). Provision is also made for a request to be made where there has been a previous refusal of a request for a standard authorisation but the managing authority considers that a fresh application would succeed (para.28).

Right of third party to require consideration of whether authorisation needed (paras 67–73)

A third party, such as a member of the person's family or a person inspecting the **2–011** hospital or care home, can trigger the assessment process by:

(a) informing the managing authority that it appears to him that the person is being deprived of his liberty without authorisation; and

(b) asking the managing authority to request a standard authorisation.

If the managing authority does not request the authorisation, the third party can request the supervisory body to decide whether there is an unauthorised deprivation of liberty (para.68). The supervisory body must then appoint a suitable qualified person to carry out an assessment of whether or not a deprivation of liberty exists, but need not do so if either:

(a) the request appears to be either frivolous or vexatious, or

(b) the question of whether the deprivation of liberty exists has already been determined and there is no change in circumstances that would merit the question being reconsidered (para.69(3) to (5)).

Subject to para.69(3) to (5), the assessment must be completed within 7 days of the request by the supervisory body (SI 2008/1858, reg.14). The supervisory body's response to the request must be notified to the person who made it, the person to whom the request relates, the managing authority and any s.39A IMCA (para.69(7),(8)). The same notifications need to be undertaken if the assessor concludes that there has been no deprivation of liberty (para.72). If the assessor concludes that the person is being deprived of his liberty, the full assessment process is triggered (para.71(2)), and the same people must be notified of that fact (para.71(4)). The same people must also be notified if a conclusion is reached that the detention is already authorised under s.4A (para.73).

The procedure for an urgent authorisation (Sch.AI, Pt.5 – paras.74–90)

2–012   Wherever possible, a request for a standard authorisation should be made before the deprivation of liberty commences. However, where the deprivation of liberty starts before the authorisation can be obtained, an urgent authorisation can be given which makes the deprivation lawful for a short period of time. The Government expects that an urgent authorisation "will be issued only in rare circumstances" (Hansard, HL Vol.703, col.390, per Baroness Thornton). An urgent authorisation is, in effect, a self authorisation. The managing authority of a care home or hospital can give itself an urgent authorisation to deprive a person of their liberty in cases of urgency for a maximum period of 7 days if the qualifying requirement are, or shortly will be, met (para.78). In exceptional circumstances, this period can be extended to 14 days by the supervisory body (paras.84, 85). The Explanatory Notes to the 2007 Act state, at para.231, that an extension "might occur for example if the best interests assessor has not been able to contact someone they are required to consult and considers that they cannot reach a judgment without doing so." If the supervisory body refuse the request for an extension they must notify the managing authority and give reasons for their decision. This notice must be copied to P and any s.39A IMCA (para.86). The supervisory body must complete the eligibility assessments within the period of the urgent authorisation.

Under para.76 a managing body must give an urgent authorisation where they:

(a) believe that the need for the person to be detained is so urgent that it is appropriate for the detention to begin before the request for a standard authorisation is made, or

(b) have made a request for a standard authorisation but believe that the need for the person to be detained is so urgent that it is appropriate for the detention to begin before the request is disposed of.

This means that an urgent authorisation must either follow a request for a standard authorisation or must immediately be followed by such a request. An urgent authorisation must be in writing (para.79) and must state the name of P, the name of the relevant hospital or care home, the period during which the authorisation is to be in force, and the purpose for which the authorisation is given (para.80). A copy of the authorisation must be sent to P and any s.39A IMCA (para.82(3)). The managing authority must keep a written record of their reasons for giving the authorisation (para.82(2)) and must take steps to ensure that P understands the effect of the authorisation and the right under s.21A to make an application to the Court of Protection (para.83).

An urgent authorisation ceases to be in force at the end of the specified period or earlier if a decision is reached on the application for a standard authorisation (para.89). If a request for a standard authorisation is refused, the urgent authorisation ceases to be in force when the managing authority receives notice of that fact under para.58 (para.89(4)). Notice that the authorisation has ended must be sent to P and any s.39A IMCA (para.90).

The assessors

2–013   Although the person assessing the mental health requirement cannot also be the best interests assessor (para.129(5)), the supervisory body can appoint the same assessor for other assessments.

Assessors may, at all reasonable times, examine and take copies of relevant records (para.131) and must take into account any information given, or submissions made, by a representative or any s.39A, 39C or 39D IMCA (para.132). The general eligibility requirements of assessors are set out in SI 2008/1858 , reg.3. Requirements relating to the selection of assessors are set out in regs10–12.

Generally speaking, the assessments must be completed within 21 calendar days of the request by the managing authority. However, where the managing authority has given an urgent authorisation, the assessments must be completed before the authorisation expires (SI 2008/1858, reg.13).

Appointment of an IMCA

Under s.39A, if the managing authority is satisfied that a person will become **2–014** subject to Sch.A1 and that person has no-one other than a paid or professional carer to be consulted with during the best interests assessment, the managing authority must notify the supervisory body which must instruct an Independent Mental Capacity Advocate (IMCA) to represent the person. A person becomes subject to Sch.A1 in the circumstances set out in s.39B.

An IMCA will also be appointed if P has an unpaid representative (s.39D), and if the appointment of P's representative ends and there is no other appropriate person to consult in determining P's best interests (s.39C). The appointment of a representative for P is considered below.

Refusal of standard authorisation

If any of the assessments concludes that a qualifying requirement is not met, no **2–015** further assessments should be undertaken (para.133) and the authorisation cannot be given (para.50(2)). The supervisory body is then required to notify P, the relevant managing authority, any IMCA instructed under s.39A, and any interested person consulted in the assessment process (para.58). If the best interests assessor concludes that the relevant person does not meet the best interests requirement but becomes aware that that person is being subjected to an unauthorised deprivation of liberty, he must include a statement to that effect in the assessment (para.44). A refusal could lead to P's detention under the 1983 Act or to an adjustment to P's care plan to avoid a deprivation of liberty.

The supervisory body is required to keep a written record of any requests that have not lead to authorisation being granted (para.60). A decision not to grant a request for a standard authorisation has no effect on the validity of an existing authorisation under Schedule A1 (para.62(3)).

The authorisation

An authorisation must be given if the assessments that have been commissioned **2–016** by the supervisory body conclude that all of the qualifying requirements have been satisfied (para.50). The effect of the authorisation is to provide legal authority for P's detention; it does not give authority to provide medical treatment to P, or to do anything else that would normally require P's consent.

The supervisory body must state in the authorisation the period during which the authorisation is in force. This may not be longer than the maximum period identified in the best interests assessment (para.51), and may start after the authorisation is given (para.52). The maximum authorisation period that the assessor can identify is a year, or such shorter period as may be prescribed by regulations (para.42(2)). The authorisation must also state the purpose for which authorisation is given, any conditions subject to which authorisation is given, and the reason why each qualifying requirement is met (para.55). The supervisory body must give copies of the authorisation to the relevant managing authority, P, any s.39A IMCA, and every interested person consulted by the best interests assessor (para.58(2)). It is for the managing authority to ensure that the conditions are complied with (para.53), to give relevant information to P and his representative (para.59), and to keep P's case under consideration and request a review if necessary (para.102). The information to P must be given both orally and in writing (para.59(4)).

If an authorisation is obtained, those who are carrying out the detention are protected against liability in battery or for wrongful imprisonment but not against liability in negligence, or for acting beyond the scope of the authorisation (paras 3, 4).

Conveyance to the hospital or care home

2–017   An authorisation does not provide authority for depriving people of their liberty when they are being conveyed from their home, or another location, to the hospital or care home. This point was taken up by the Joint Committee which, at para.99, recommended that a "take and convey" power be added to an authorisation. The Government responded as follows:

"We will reflect in the Code of Practice the importance of considering the impact of any transportation as part of assessing best interests. In practice, many people who will become subject to the proposed Mental Capacity Act deprivation of liberty safeguards will already be accommodated in hospitals or care homes at the time that a change in their care regime brings them within the scope of the safeguards, so the conveying issue will not arise.

We do accept, however, that, in a very few cases, there may be exceptional circumstances, for example where it is necessary to do more than persuade or restrain the person for the purpose of the conveyance, or perhaps if the journey was exceptionally long, where transportation may amount to a deprivation of liberty and it may be necessary to seek an order of the Court of Protection where additional consideration of the particular circumstances of the case would be an extra protection for the individual (or consider use of the 1983 Act). We do not therefore consider that it is desirable to extend authorisations to cover these rare cases, because we do not think it would strengthen the protections for the person concerned" (The Government's response to the report of the Joint Committee on Human Rights, Department of Health, April 13, 2007, paras.80,81).

The Joint Committee were not convinced by this response and remained of the view that in order to be compatible with Art.5 of the ECHR it was necessary for the legislation "to provide a procedure which precedes detention in all cases" (*Legislative Scrutiny: Seventh Progress Report*, HL Paper 112; HC 555, para.1.29). The issue here is not solely one of strengthening the "protections of the persons concerned"; those involved in transporting the person to the hospital or care home require legal justification for their action. If the act of transporting the person merely involves restricting a person's liberty, the authorisation for the restriction is to be found in ss.5 and 6. If, however, a person is being deprived of his liberty during the transportation, either the 1983 Act will need to be invoked or an application for an order authorising the deprivation should be made to the Court of Protection. If the person concerned is being transported to a care home, guardianship could provide the necessary authorisation as s.18(7) of the

1983 Act provides the applicant with a power to take and convey the person to a specified place of residence.

It is suggested that a deprivation of liberty occurs during transportation if:

(1) either force, medication, or threats have to be used to overcome the person's resistance to being transported;

(2) subterfuge has to be resorted to, e.g. the person is falsely informed that he will be returning to his home in the near future; or

(3) the circumstances of the transportation are very onerous for the person.

In *Sunderland City Council v PS and CA* [2007], above, para.23, Munby J. said that, in order to comply with Art.5 of the ECHR, the detention must be authorised before the detention commences. However, Art.5 is not violated if a person is subjected to a deprivation of liberty for a short period in order to respond to an emergency (*X v United Kingdom* (1982) 4 E.H.R.R. 188, para.41).

This issue is considered in the supplement to the *Code of Practice* at paras.2.14 and 2.15.

The appointment of representatives (Sch.A1, Pt.10 – paras.137–153)

As soon as practicable after a standard authorisation is given, the supervisory **2–018** body must appoint a person to be P's representative (para.139). The role of the representative is to maintain contact with P and to support and represent him in matters relating to the authorisation, including requesting a review, using the organisations complaint's procedure or applying to the Court of Protection on his behalf (para.140). Decisions by the representative are governed by the best interests principle set out in s.1(5). To enable the representative to perform this role, the representative will receive a copy of the authorisation (para.57(2)), and must be informed by the managing authority of its effect (para.59(5)). The functions of a representative are in addition to, and do not affect the authority of a donee of a lasting power of attorney or the powers of a court appointed deputy (para.141).

The Mental Capacity (Deprivation of Liberty: Appointment of Relevant Person's Representative) Regulations 2008 (SI 2008/1315), which are reproduced in Pt.3, provide details in relation to the selection, appointment and termination of the appointment of a representative. In most cases, the representative will be a friend, relative or informal carer of P but a paid appointment can be made where the person has no one else to fulfil the role. The supplement to the *Code of Practice* suggests, at para.4.76, that, where possible, the best interests assessor should recommend someone to be appointed as P's representative.

If the representative is unpaid, an IMCA must be appointed in the circumstances identified in s.39D to provide support to P and/or his representative. For the circumstances where an IMCA will be appointed when the appointment of the representative ends, see s.39C.

Renewal of standard authorisation

2–019   The managing authority must apply for a further authorisation to begin if the existing authorisation is about to expire (para.29). Such a request will result in the full assessment process being repeated. The existing authorisation terminates at the time when the new authorisation comes into force (para.62(2)). If no request for a further authorisation is made, the authorisation will come to an end at the expiration of the authorised period.

Suspension of authorisation (Sch.AI, Pt.6 – paras.91–97)

2–020   A standard authorisation may be suspended for up to 28 days if P has ceased to meet the eligibility requirement set out in Sch.1A for reasons other than his objection to becoming a mental health patient, in which case the authorisation will be reviewed (para.91(4)) The authorisation will end if P continues to be ineligible at the end of the 28 days (para.96(2)). Notice of the suspension must be sent to P, his representative and the managing authority (para.93(3)), who, along with any s.39D IMCA, must also be informed when the suspension has come to an end (para.95(3)). The suspension will come to an end if during the 28 day period the managing authority are satisfied that P meets the eligibility requirement again (para.94). The purpose of a suspension is to allow for a short period of treatment under the 1983 Act.

Review by supervisory body (Sch.AI, Pt.8 – paras.101–125)

2–021   The supervisory body may review a standard authorisation at any time and must do so if requested to do by P, his representative, an IMCA or the managing authority of the hospital or care home (para.102). The managing authority, which is required to keep the person's case under review, must request a review if one or more of the qualifying requirements appear to them to be reviewable (para.103). The qualifying requirements are reviewable if:

(a) P no longer meets the age, mental health, mental capacity, best interests or no refusals requirements, or

(b) P no longer meets the eligibility requirement because he now objects to receiving treatment for his mental health in hospital and he meets the criteria for detention under s.2 or 3 of the 1983 Act, or

(c) the reason why P meets a qualifying requirement is not the reason stated in the authorisation, or

(d) there has been a change in P's case and, because of that change, it would be appropriate to vary the conditions of the authorisation (this ground only applies to the best interests requirement) (paras.104–107).

The supervisory body, which must give notice of the review to P, his representative and to the managing authority (para.108), is not automatically obliged to re-assess all of the qualifying requirements when it receives a request for a review. Rather, it must determine which, if any, "appear to be reviewable" (para.109), and appoint assessors to review those requirements (para.111). There is no requirement to carry out a review of the best interests requirement if that requirement is only reviewable on the "variation of conditions" ground (see (d), above) and the change in P's case is not significant (para.111). If none of the requirements appear to be reviewable, no further action is required (para.110) and the review ends (para.118(2)).

The assessment process on a review is the same as applies when an application for an authorisation is made, with the exception that the best interests assessor is not obliged to include a statement that there is an unauthorised deprivation of liberty under para.44, and rather than make recommendations about what conditions should apply under para.33, the assessor must include recommendations about whether it would be appropriate to vary the conditions (para.113).

If the assessments are positive, the supervisory body must consider whether the authorisation needs to be varied on the change of reason ground or, for the best interests review only, the variation of conditions ground (paras.115–116). If one or more of the review assessments comes to a negative conclusion, the authorisation must be terminated with immediate effect (para.117).

When the review is complete, the supervisory body must give notice to the managing authority, P, his or her representative and any s.39D IMCA. The notice must state the outcome of the review and what variation (if any) has been made to the authorisation (para.120).

As an alternative to requesting a review, the managing authority could make a request for a fresh standard authorisation. Such a request would have to be made if the authorisation is about to expire (para.29). A request for a fresh authorisation may be made even if a review has already been requested or is being carried out (para.30), in which case the request for the fresh authorisation takes precedence (para.124).

Review by the Court of Protection

Neither the standard nor urgent authorisation procedure requires the approval **2–022** of the Court of Protection.

Article 5(4) of the ECHR requires that everyone "who is deprived of his liberty . . . shall be entitled to take proceedings by which the lawfulness of his detention shall be decided speedily by a court and his release ordered if the detention is not lawful". Section 21A gives the Court of Protection jurisdiction for this purpose.

Monitoring (paras.162,163)

Regulations may be made to enable Sch.A1 to be monitored by one or more **2–023** prescribed bodies. A prescribed body will have the power to:

(a) monitor, and report on, the operation of the new procedures;

(b) visit hospitals and care homes;

(c) visit and interview persons accommodated in hospitals and care homes; and

(d) require the production of, and to inspect, records relating to the care and treatment of patients.

Regulations will be made to require supervisory bodies and managing authorities to disclose information to the monitoring body (or bodies).

Schedule 1A – persons ineligible to be deprived of liberty by the Mental Capacity Act

This Act cannot be used to deprive P of his liberty if P is "ineligible": see s.16A **2–024** for the Court of Protection and Sch.A1, paras.12(e) and 17 for the authorisation procedure. P is ineligible if he falls within Cases A to E of Sch.1A. These Cases identify when the Mental Health Act 1983 takes precedence over this Act.

Case A (Patients detained under the Mental Health Act 1983)

2–025   P is ineligible if he is subject to the "hospital treatment regime" and is detained under that regime in either an independent or NHS hospital. P is subject to the "hospital treatment regime" if he is subject to a "hospital treatment obligation" i.e. he is detained under ss.2, 4, 3, 35, 36, 37, 38, 44, 45A, 47, 48 or 51 of the 1983 Act or under "another England and Wales enactment which has the same effect as a hospital treatment obligation" (paras.2,8). The consequence of this is that if P is detained under the 1983 Act he is ineligible for detention under this Act even if he requires treatment for a physical disorder. In this situation, P will be detained and treated for his mental disorder under the 1983 Act and treated for any physical disorder under Part 1 of this Act.

Case B (Patients on Leave of Absence or Conditional Discharge)

2–026   This Case applies if P is subject to the "hospital treatment regime" (i.e. he is subject to a "hospital treatment obligation") but is not detained in hospital under that regime. This covers patients who have been granted leave of absence under s.17 of the 1983 Act or who have been granted a conditional discharge under either s.42 or 73 of that Act. P will be ineligible if:

(a)   the proposed course of action under this Act is "not in accordance with a requirement" which the 1983 Act imposes, such as a requirement as to where P is, or is not, to reside (para.3). This means that P would be ineligible if, for example, there is a conflict between where P is required to reside under the conditions of a conditional discharge and where he would be required to reside under a standard authorisation; or

(b)   the proposed care and treatment to be administered under this Act "consists in whole or in part of medical treatment for mental disorder in a hospital" (para.4). This means that an authorisation cannot be used as an alternative to the procedures for a patient's recall to hospital under the 1983 Act. However, the patient would be eligible if he required treatment in hospital for a physical disorder.

Case C (Patients on a Community Treatment Order)

2–027   P is ineligible if:

(a)   he is subject to a "community treatment regime", i.e. a community treatment order under s.17A of the 1983 Act or its equivalent (para.9); and

(b)   either of the situations set out in paras.(a) or (b) of Case B, above, apply.

Case D (Patients subject to Guardianship)

2–028   If P is subject to a guardianship application under s.7 of the 1983 Act, a guardianship order under s.37 of that Act, or an obligation under another England and Wales enactment which has similar effect (para.10), he will be ineligible if :

(a)   the proposed course of action under this Act is not in accordance with a requirement imposed by the guardianship, including any requirement where P is to reside (para.3). This means that P would be ineligible if, for example, there is a conflict between where P is required to reside under the terms of the guardianship and where he would be required to reside under a standard authorisation; or

(b) the standard authorisation would authorise P to be a mental health patient (i.e. a person accommodated in a hospital for the purpose of being given medical treatment for mental disorder (para.16)), P objects (or would be likely to object if he was in a position to do so) to being a mental patient or to being given some or all of the mental health treatment, and no valid consent has been given by a donee of a lasting power of attorney or a court deputy to each matter to which P objects. The donee and the deputy will be governed by s.4 when making their decision. In determining whether P would be likely to object, regard must be had to all the circumstances, including P's behaviour, his wishes and feelings and his views values and beliefs, although circumstances from the past only need to be considered in so far as it is appropriate to consider them (para.5).

Case E (Patients who are "within the scope" of the 1983 Act but are not subject to it)

P is "within the scope" of the 1983 Act if an application under s.2 or 3 of that **2–029** Act could be made in respect of him if practitioners were minded to do so, and P could be detained in a hospital in pursuance of such an application, were one made (para.12(1)). In making this assessment it is to be assumed that the necessary medical recommendations are in place (para.12(3),(4)) and that the treatment referred to in s.3(2)(c) of the 1983 Act, which is treatment that "is necessary for the health or safety of the patient or for the protection of other persons", cannot be provided under this Act (para.12(5)). Such a person would be ineligible if the situation set out in para.(b) of Case D, above, applies, i.e. he objects to being admitted to hospital or to being treated for his mental disorder there and no valid consent has been given by a donee or a deputy. Determining whether P objects "will inevitably call for a judgment on the part of the relevant decision-maker. The fact that a person cannot (or does not) express a view (or otherwise communicate an objection) does not of itself mean that the person should not be taken to object" (Explanatory Notes to the Mental Health Act 2007, para.203).

The "purpose of this provision is to treat people in this situation as if they had capacity to consent but are refusing to be admitted (or stay in) hospital or are not consenting to the treatment for mental disorder they are to be given there. In such cases, they would either have to be detained under the 1983 Act, or another way of giving treatment would have to be found. A person's objections will not make them ineligible if a donee of a lasting power of attorney . . . or a deputy appointed by the Court of Protection (or the Court of Protection itself) has made a valid decision to consent to the hospitalisation and treatment on their behalf" (*ibid.*, paras.204,205).

It is not the role of the assessor to consider whether any objection made by P is reasonable, or whether it would be appropriate to make an application in respect of him under the 1983 Act.

Deprivations of liberty – the Mental Capacity Act 2005 or the Mental Health Act 1983?

Deprivations of liberty in hospitals

2–030   Schedule 1A sets out the circumstances that prevent a person who is being deprived of his liberty from being the subject of a standard authorisation. If Sch. 1A applies, the 1983 Act must be used. However, there is nothing in either Act that prevents the 1983 Act from being used to authorise a deprivation of liberty in a situation where Sch. 1A does not apply. In this situation, either this Act or the 1983 Act can be invoked if the patient satisfies the relevant statutory criteria. In other words, in most circumstances the decision as to which Act to use will be a matter of professional discretion. The following factors provide cogent reasons for exercising choice in favour of using the powers of detention in the 1983 Act:

- Parts IV and IVA of the 1983 Act provide patients with significant protections relating to the provision of treatment for the patient's mental disorder. The provision of such treatment to patients detained under this Act is not subject to any external regulation.

- The 1983 Act provides a patient's nearest relative with significant protective powers relating to the patient's detention, including the power to discharge the patient from detention. The nearest relative has no role to play under this Act.

- A patient detained under the 1983 Act has a right to make an application to a Mental Health Review Tribunal, which has the power to discharge the patient from detention, and his case will be referred to the tribunal if this right is not exercised. This Act provides for no automatic judicial oversight of the patient's detention.

- A patient who is detained under the 1983 Act can apply for a hearing before the hospital managers who have the power to order the patient's discharge from detention. There is no similar power under this Act.

- The 1983 Act, in s.6(1), contains explicit authority for the applicant for the patient's detention to "take and convey" the patient to the hospital named in the application and, in s.18(1), for the hospital authority to return the patient to the hospital in the event of the patient absconding. This Act contains no equivalent powers.

- Patients detained under the 1983 Act and who are subject to s.117 of that Act receive after-care services provided under that section free of charge. Patients who are detained under this Act and who are discharged from hospital will be subject to a mandatory charging regime if they are placed in a care home (National Assistance Act 1948, s.22) and a discretionary charging regime if they receive domiciliary care services (Health and Social Services and Social Security Adjudications Act 1983, s.17).

Section 3(2)(c) of the 1983 Act states that an application under that section may be made on the ground that "it is necessary for the health or safety of the patient or for the protection of other persons that he should receive [medical treatment in a hospital] and it *cannot be provided unless he is detained under this section*" (emphasis added). It has been said that if mental health professionals are satisfied that a patient can safely and effectively be assessed or treated by relying on the Mental Capacity Act, "it is likely to be difficult to demonstrate that the criteria for detaining them under s.3(2)(c) are met" (Phil Fennell, *Mental Health: the new law* (2007), para.6.18). Although this is undoubtedly correct in relation to patients who are not already detained under the 1983 Act, most patients who are being assessed for detention under s.3 will already be detained under s.2 of the that Act. Such patients cannot be made subject to the authorisation procedure because they will be ineligible by virtue of Sch.1A, Case A.

The 1983 Act provides detained patients with a far greater degree of protection, both in relation to treatment and detention, than that provided for under this Act. If the approach outlined above is adopted, the deprivation of liberty provisions of this Act need only be invoked for the small number of patients who are either being deprived of their liberty while being treated in hospital for a physical disorder or who require hospital treatment for a mental disorder but fail to satisfy the criteria for detention under the 1983 Act, for example, a learning disabled patient who requires detention under s.3 of that Act but whose disability is not "associated with abnormally aggressive or seriously irresponsible conduct" (see s.1(2A),(2B),(4) of the 1983 Act).

Deprivations of liberty in care homes

In its response to the Bournewood consultation exercise, the Government rejec- **2–031** ted the option of using the guardianship provisions of the 1983 Act as a vehicle that could be used to authorise detention. This decision is reinforced by para.13.16 of the *Code of Practice* which states that guardianship cannot be used to deprive a person of their liberty. This is a commonly held opinion, but is it correct? The 1983 Act provides the guardian of a mentally incapacitated person with the following powers:

- a power to take the person to where he does not want to go, using force if necessary (ss.18(7) and 137).

- a power to insist that the person remains at that place (s.8(1)(a)).

- a power to return the person to that place if he leaves without authority, using force if necessary (ss.18(4), 137).

- a power to take the person to a place where he will receive medical treatment under the authority of this Act (s.8(1)(b)).

Put bluntly, a person under guardianship, who must be over the age of 16, can be forced to leave his home to go to a place where he does not want to go to, can be required to stay at that place and can be returned to that place if he leaves without being given permission to do so. Given the interpretation that the ECtHR and the High Court have given to the meaning of a deprivation of liberty (see above), how can it possibly be argued that a person who is subject to the operation of such powers is not being deprived of his liberty? Such a person is clearly subject to the continuous control of the guardian and is not free to leave the specified place of residence (*HL v United Kingdom*, above, para.91). The Joint Committee on Human Rights said that it "is possible to envisage circumstances where a guardianship patient might be subject to a degree of control of the requisite degree and intensity to amount to a deprivation of liberty" (*Legislative Scrutiny: Seventh Progress Report*, HL Paper 112; HC 555, para.1.30). The fact that the 1983 Act does not specifically state that guardianship can be used to authorise the deprivation of a patient's liberty is not legally relevant to the question of whether it can have that effect.

2–032   In *JE and DE v Surrey County Council*, above, Munby J. held that the crucial issue in determining whether a mentally incapacitated person who is being cared for in a care home is being deprived of his liberty is not so much whether the person's freedom within the home is curtailed but rather whether or not the person is free to leave. His Lordship said, at para.117, that the person concerned, who had not been received into the guardianship of the local authority, was not free to leave and "was and is, in that sense, completely under the control of the [local authority]", because it is the local authority who decides the essential matters of where he should live, whether he can leave and whether he can be with his wife. Guardianship would have provided the authority with the power to make such decisions. It follows from *DE* that if guardianship is being used to ensure that a person does not leave the place where he is required by the guardian to reside in order to take up residence in an alternative placement, it is being used to deprive that person of his liberty.

Does guardianship comply with the requirements of Art.5 of the ECHR? Guardianship is clearly a "procedure prescribed by law" for the purposes of Art.5(1), and the House of Lords has heldin *R. (on the application of MH) v Secretary of State for Health* [2005] UKHL 60; [2005] 4 All E.R. 1311 that Art.5(4), which provides that a person who has been deprived of his liberty must be entitled to take proceedings to challenge the lawfulness of the detention, is not breached by virtue of the fact that the person concerned lacks the mental capacity to institute such proceedings. It is also the case that the procedure for making a guardianship application under s.7 of the 1983 Act meets the substantive and procedural requirements for the lawful detention of persons of unsound mind which were established by the ECtHR in *Winterwerp v Netherlands* (1979–80) 2 E.H.R.R. 387.

The Government could be faced with a compatibility issue under the Convention if a person who is has been deprived of his liberty by virtue of the operation of the guardianship provisions makes an application to a MHRT. Subsequent to the decision of the Court of Appeal in *R. (on the application of H) v Mental Health Review Tribunal, North and East London* Region [2001] EWCA Civ 415, which declared that ss.72(1) and 73(1) of the 1983 Act were incompatible with Arts.5(1) and 5(4) because they placed the burden upon the patient to prove that the criteria justifying detention no longer exist, Parliament passed the Mental Health Act 1983 (Remedial) Order 2001 (SI 2001/3712) which placed the burden of proof on the detaining authority. As this Order did not reverse the burden of proof in s.72(4), which deals with applications made by guardianship patients, the Government might have to make a further remedial order to ensure compatibility with Art.5.

If a guardianship application, together with a requirement that the person reside at a particular place, can have the effect of depriving that person of his liberty, is it necessary for the deprivation to be authorised by the procedure set out in Sch.A1? The Government's view is that both Acts would have to be used because the scheme of the 1983 Act, together with the lack of an explicit power to detain a patient under guardianship, mean that guardianship cannot be used to authorise the deprivation of a person's liberty; also see the *Code of Practice* on the 1983 Act at para.26.30. Counter arguments are:

1. As Phil Fennell has said, there "is nothing in the MHA 1983 to say that guardianship cannot authorise deprivation of liberty" (*Mental Health: the new law* (2007), para.6.104).

2. If the legitimate use of the guardianship provisions can have the effect of depriving a person of his liberty, it would be surprising if the Act did not authorise what it allows for.

From a practical perspective, it is surely a bureaucratic nonsense to require two **2–033** sets of professionals to undertake two sets of procedures under separate Acts in order to provide the necessary authority to deprive a guardianship patient of his liberty. The nonsense is compounded by the fact that the authorisation procedure provides the patient with a weaker set of safeguards than those provided for under guardianship.

Paragraph 13.20 of the *Code of Practice* states that decision-makers "must never consider guardianship as a way to avoid applying the MCA". This is a strange statement as this Act will always be applicable to a mentally incapacitated person irrespective of whether a guardianship application has been made in respect of that person. Compared with guardianship the authorisation procedure is Byzantine in its complexity, but this factor alone would not provide a "cogent reason" for departing from the guidance in the Code (*R. (on the application of Munjaz v Mersey Care National Health Service Trust* [2005] UKHL 58; [2006] 4 All E.R. 736). The following factors provide such reasons:

- There is an argument in favour of the contention that the statement in the Code at para.13.16 that guardianship cannot be used to deprive a person of his or her liberty does not represent the true legal position.

- Guardianship provides a greater degree of protection than that provided for under the authorisation procedure to both professional and lay carers and to P in that:

  (i) unlike the authorisation procedure, guardianship provides explicit legal authority to deprive a person of his or her liberty during conveyance from that person's home to the specified place of residence (s.18(7) of the 1983 Act). To ensure compliance with Art.5, the procedure authorising a deprivation of liberty must be initiated before the deprivation takes place (*Sunderland City Council v PS and CA*, above);

  (ii) unlike the authorisation procedure, guardianship provides explicit authority for the person to be returned to the specified place of residence in the event of the person leaving that place without authority (s.18(3) of the 1983 Act);

  (iii) the responsible local social services authority must arrange for a person under guardianship to be visited at intervals of not more than 3 months, and at least one such visit in any year shall be by an approved clinician or a "section 12 doctor": see reg.23 of the Mental Health (Hospital, Guardianship and Treatment) Regulations 2008 (SI 2008/ 1184). No similar obligation is to be found in the authorisation procedure; and

  (iv) the 1983 Act provides a patient's nearest relative with significant powers with respect to guardianship that are intended to protect the interests of the patient, including the power to discharge the patient from guardianship. The nearest relative has no role to play under the authorisation procedure.

Although the issue might eventually have to be determined by the courts, there is an argument in favour of the contention that guardianship with a condition of residence can be used as the sole authority for authorising the deprivation of a patient's liberty in the designated care home. As Fennell points out, the main limitations on using guardianship as an alternative to the authorisation procedure "are the exclusion in relation to learning disability without abnormally aggressive or seriously irresponsible conduct, and the right of the nearest relative to block a guardianship application" (see above, para.6.106).

PART 3

DELEGATED LEGISLATION

THE MENTAL CAPACITY ACT 2005 (INDEPENDENT MENTAL CAPACITY ADVOCATES) (GENERAL) REGULATIONS 2006

(SI 2006/1832)

Dated July 7, 2006 and made by the Secretary of State for Health under the Mental Capacity Act 2005 (c.9), ss.35(2), (3), 36, 37(6), (7), 38(8), 64(1) and 65(1).

GENERAL NOTE

These Regulations define "NHS body" and "serious medical treatment" for the pur- **3–001** poses of certain provisions the Mental Capacity Act 2005 which deal with independent mental capacity advocates ("IMCAs"). The Regulations also contain provision as to who can be appointed to act as an IMCA and as to an IMCA's functions when he has been instructed to represent a person in a particular case. The provisions about the IMCA's appointment and functions apply where the IMCA is instructed under ss.37 to 39 of the Act or under regulations made by virtue of s.41 of the Act (see reg.2(2)).

Regulation 3 defines "NHS body". This term is used in ss.37 and 38 of the Act. Those sections impose an obligation on NHS bodies to instruct an IMCA in certain circumstances involving acts or decisions relating to serious medical treatment or to accommodation.

Regulation 4 defines "serious medical treatment". Under s.37 of the Act, an NHS body must instruct an IMCA where it is proposing to provide, or secure the provision of, such treatment.

Regulation 5 provides that a person can only act as an IMCA if he has been approved by a local authority or is a member of a class which has been so approved. For an IMCA to be appointed, he must satisfy certain requirements as to experience, training, good character and independence.

Regulation 6 sets out the steps an IMCA must take once he has been instructed to act in a particular case. He must obtain and evaluate information about the person he has been instructed to represent ("P") and about P's wishes, feelings, beliefs or values. He must then report to the person who instructed him.

Under *regulation 7,* an IMCA who is instructed to represent P in relation to any matter may challenge a decision made in that matter in relation to P, including any decision as to whether P is a person who lacks capacity. For the purpose of making a challenge, the IMCA is treated in the same way as any other person caring for P or interested in his welfare.

The equivalent to regs 3 to 7 with respect to Wales are regs 3 to 7 of the Mental Capacity Act 2005 (Independent Mental Capacity Advocates) (Wales) Regulations 2007 (SI 2007/852 (W.77)).

Citation, commencement and extent

1.—(1) These Regulations may be cited as the Mental Capacity Act 2005 **3–002** (Independent Mental Capacity Advocates) (General) Regulations 2006.

(2) These Regulations shall come into force—

    (a) for the purpose of enabling the Secretary of State to make arrangements under section 35 of the Act, and for the purpose of enabling local authorities to approve IMCAs, on 1st November 2006, and

    (b) for all other purposes, on 1st April 2007.

    (3) These Regulations apply in relation to England only.

Interpretation

3–003   **2.**—(1) In these Regulations—

"the Act" means the Mental Capacity Act 2005; and

"IMCA" means an independent mental capacity advocate.

    (2) In these Regulations, references to instructions given to a person to act as an IMCA are to instructions given under sections 37 to 39 of the Act or under regulations made by virtue of section 41 of the Act.

Meaning of NHS Body

3–004   **3.**—(1) For the purposes of sections 37 and 38 of the Act, "NHS body" means a body in England which is—

    (a) a Strategic Health Authority;

    (b) an NHS foundation trust;

    (c) a Primary Care Trust;

    (d) an NHS Trust; or

    (e) a Care Trust.

    (2) In this regulation—

"Care Trust" means a body designated as a Care Trust under section 45 of the Health and Social Care Act 2001;

"NHS foundation trust" has the meaning given in section 1 of the Health and Social Care (Community Health and Standards) Act 2003;

"NHS trust" means a body established under section 5 of the National Health Service and Community Care Act 1990;

"Primary Care Trust" means a body established under section 16A of the National Health Service Act 1977; and

"Strategic Health Authority" means a Strategic Health Authority established under section 8 of the National Health Service Act 1977.

Meaning of serious medical treatment

3–005   **4.**—(1) This regulation defines serious medical treatment for the purposes of section 37 of the Act.

    (2) Serious medical treatment is treatment which involves providing, withdrawing or withholding treatment in circumstances where—

    (a) in a case where a single treatment is being proposed, there is a fine balance between its benefits to the patient and the burdens and risks it is likely to entail for him,

    (b) in a case where there is a choice of treatments, a decision as to which one to use is finely balanced, or

    (c) what is proposed would be likely to involve serious consequences for the patient.

Appointment of independent mental capacity advocates

5.—(1) No person may be appointed to act as an IMCA for the purposes of sec- **3–006** tions 37 to 39 of the Act, or regulations made by virtue of section 41 of the Act, unless—

(a) he is for the time being approved by a local authority on the grounds that he satisfies the appointment requirements, or

(b) he belongs to a class of persons which is for the time being approved by a local authority on the grounds that all persons in that class satisfy the appointment requirements.

(2) The appointment requirements, in relation to a person appointed to act as an IMCA, are that—

(a) he has appropriate experience or training or an appropriate combination of experience and training;

(b) he is a person of integrity and good character; and

(c) he is able to act independently of any person who instructs him.

(3) Before a determination is made in relation to any person for the purposes of paragraph (2)(b), there must be obtained in respect of that person—

(a) an enhanced criminal record certificate issued pursuant to section 113B of the Police Act 1997; or

(b) if the purpose for which the certificate is required is not one prescribed under subsection (2) of that section, a criminal record certificate issued pursuant to section 113A of that Act.

Functions of an independent mental capacity advocate

6.—(1) This regulation applies where an IMCA has been instructed by an auth- **3–007** orised person to represent a person ("P").

(2) "Authorised person" means a person who is required or enabled to instruct an IMCA under sections 37 to 39 of the Act or under regulations made by virtue of section 41of the Act.

(3) The IMCA must determine in all the circumstances how best to represent and support P.

(4) In particular, the IMCA must—

(a) verify that the instructions were issued by an authorised person;

(b) to the extent that it is practicable and appropriate to do so—

  (i) interview P, and

  (ii) examine the records relevant to P to which the IMCA has access under section 35(6) of the Act;

(c) to the extent that it is practicable and appropriate to do so, consult—

  (i) persons engaged in providing care or treatment for P in a professional capacity or for remuneration, and

  (ii) other persons who may be in a position to comment on P's wishes, feelings, beliefs or values; and

(d) take all practicable steps to obtain such other information about P, or the act or decision that is proposed in relation to P, as the IMCA considers necessary.

(5) The IMCA must evaluate all the information he has obtained for the purpose of—

(a) ascertaining the extent of the support provided to P to enable him to participate in making any decision about the matter in relation to which the IMCA has been instructed;

    (b) ascertaining what P's wishes and feelings would be likely to be, and the beliefs and values that would be likely to influence P, if he had capacity in relation to the proposed act or decision;

    (c) ascertaining what alternative courses of action are available in relation to P;

    (d) where medical treatment is proposed for P, ascertaining whether he would be likely to benefit from a further medical opinion.

(6) The IMCA must prepare a report for the authorised person who instructed him.

(7) The IMCA may include in the report such submissions as he considers appropriate in relation to P and the act or decision which is proposed in relation to him.

Challenges to decisions affecting persons who lack capacity

3–008   **7.**—(1) This regulation applies where—

    (a) an IMCA has been instructed to represent a person ("P") in relation to any matter, and

    (b) a decision affecting P (including a decision as to his capacity) is made in that matter.

(2) The IMCA has the same rights to challenge the decision as he would have if he were a person (other than an IMCA) engaged in caring for P or interested in his welfare.

THE MENTAL CAPACITY ACT 2005 (INDEPENDENT MENTAL CAPACITY ADVOCATES) (EXPANSION OF ROLE) REGULATIONS 2006

(SI 2006/2883)

Dated October 30, 2006 and made by the Secretary of State for Health under the Mental Capacity Act 2005 (c.9), ss.41(1), (2), 64(1) and 65(1).

GENERAL NOTE

These Regulations adjust the obligation to make arrangements as to the availability of **3–009** independent mental capacity advocates ("IMCAs") which is imposed by s.35 of the Mental Capacity Act 2005. Under the Regulations, the Secretary of State may also make arrangements to enable IMCAs to be available to represent a person ("P") who lacks capacity to agree to the outcome of an accommodation review or to protective measures taken in adult protection cases.

Regulation 2 provides that arrangements under s.35 of the Act may extend to cover IMCAs who are instructed in the circumstances specified in reg.3 or 4.

Regulation 3 specifies circumstances where an NHS body has made, or a local authority have made, arrangements as to P's accommodation and it is then proposed to review those arrangements. In addition, P must not have capacity to participate in the review and there must be no one else who can be consulted as to matters affecting his best interests.

Regulation 4 specifies circumstances where it is alleged that P is or has been abused or neglected by another person or that he is abusing or has abused another person. In addition, protective measures affecting P must have been taken, or be proposed, by an NHS body or local authority in accordance with any adult protection procedures which have been set up pursuant to certain statutory guidance. The guidance current when these Regulations were made is entitled "No secrets: guidance on developing and implementing multi-agency policies and procedures to protect vulnerable adults from abuse".

Regulation 5 provides that an NHS body or local authority may instruct an IMCA to represent P if the NHS body considers, or the local authority consider, that that would be of particular benefit to P. The NHS body or local authority must take account of information provided by the IMCA and of any submissions made by him.

Paragraph 10.61 of the *Code of Practice* states:

"Responsible bodies are expected to take a strategic approach in deciding whether they will use IMCAs in [the situations set out in regs 3 and 4]. They should establish a policy locally for determining these decisions, setting out the criteria for appointing an IMCA including the issues to be taken into account when deciding if an IMCA will be of particular benefit to the person concerned. However, decision-makers will need to consider each case separately to see if the criteria are met. Local authorities or NHS bodies may wish to publish their approach for ease of access, setting out the ways they intend to use these additional powers and review it periodically."

The equivalent to regs 3 and 4 with respect to Wales are regs 8 and 9 of the Mental Capacity Act 2005 (Independent Mental Capacity Advocates) (Wales) Regulations 2007 (SI 2007/852 (W.77)).

Citation, commencement, extent and interpretation

1.—(1) These Regulations may be cited as the Mental Capacity Act 2005 **3–010** (Independent Mental Capacity Advocates) (Expansion of Role) Regulations 2006.

(2) These Regulations shall come into force—

(a) for the purpose of enabling the Secretary of State to make arrangements by virtue of regulation 2, on 1st November 2006, and

(b) for all other purposes, on 1st April 2007.

(3) These Regulations apply in relation to England only.

(4) In these Regulations—

"the Act" means the Mental Capacity Act 2005;

"IMCA" means an independent mental capacity advocate; and

"NHS body" means a body in England which is—

(a) a Strategic Health Authority;

(b) an NHS foundation trust;

(c) a Primary Care Trust;

(d) an NHS Trust; or

(e) a Care Trust.

(5) In the definition of "NHS body" in paragraph (4)—

"Care Trust" means a body designated as a Care Trust under section 45 of the Health and Social Care Act 2001;

"NHS foundation trust" has the meaning given in section 1 of the Health and Social Care (Community Health and Standards) Act 2003;

"NHS trust" means a body established under section 5 of the National Health Service and Community Care Act 1990;

"Primary Care Trust" means a body established under section 16A of the National Health Service Act 1977; and

"Strategic Health Authority" means a Strategic Health Authority established under section 8 of the National Health Service Act 1977.

Adjustment of the obligation to make arrangements imposed by section 35 of the Act

3–011   **2.** Arrangements made by the Secretary of State under section 35 of the Act may include such provision as she considers reasonable for the purpose of enabling IMCAs to be available to represent and support persons in the circumstances specified in regulation 3 or 4.

Review of arrangements as to accommodation

3–012   **3.**—(1) The circumstances specified in this regulation are where—

(a) qualifying arrangements have been made by an NHS body or local authority as to the accommodation of a person ("P") who lacks capacity to agree to the arrangements;

(b) a review of the arrangements is proposed or in progress (whether under a care plan or otherwise);

(c) the NHS body is satisfied, or the local authority are satisfied, that there is no person, other than a person engaged in providing care or treatment for P in a professional capacity or for remuneration, whom it would be appropriate to consult in determining what would be in P's best interests;

(d) none of the following exist—

(i) a person nominated by P (in whatever manner) as a person to be consulted in matters affecting his interests,

   (ii) a donee of a lasting power of attorney created by P,

   (iii) a deputy appointed by the Court of Protection for P, or

   (iv) a donee of an enduring power of attorney (within the meaning of Schedule 4 to the Act) created by P; and

   (e) sections 37, 38 and 39 of the Act do not apply.

(2) In this regulation—

"accommodation" means—

(a) accommodation in a care home or hospital, or

(b) residential accommodation provided in accordance with—

   (i) section 21 or 29 of the National Assistance Act 1948, or

   (ii) section 117 of the Mental Health Act 1983,

as the result of a decision taken by a local authority under section 47 of the National Health Service and Community Care Act 1990;

"care home" and "hospital" have the same meaning as in section 38 of the Act; and

"qualifying arrangements" means arrangements—

(a) under which accommodation has been provided for P for a continuous period of 12 weeks or more, and

(b) which are not made as a result of an obligation imposed on P under the Mental Health Act 1983.

Adult protection cases

4.—(1) The circumstances specified in this regulation are where—   **3–013**

(a) an NHS body proposes to take or has taken, or a local authority propose to take or have taken, protective measures in relation to a person ("P") who lacks capacity to agree to one or more of the measures;

(b) the proposal is made or the measures have been taken—

   (i) following the receipt of an allegation or evidence that P is being, or has been, abused or neglected by another person or that P is abusing, or has abused, another person, and

   (ii) in accordance with arrangements relating to the protection of vulnerable adults from abuse which are made pursuant to guidance issued under section 7 of the Local Authority Social Services Act 1970; and

(c) none of the following provisions apply—

   (i) section 37, 38 or 39 of the Act, or

   (ii) regulation 3 of these Regulations.

(2) The reference to protective measures in relation to P includes measures to minimise the risk that any abuse or neglect of P, or abuse by P, will continue.

GENERAL NOTE

Under this Regulation, an IMCA may be appointed even where P has family or friends **3–014**
whom it might be appropriate to consult.

Instructing an IMCA

5.—(1) In the circumstances specified in regulation 3 or 4, an NHS body or **3–015**
local authority may instruct an IMCA to represent P if the NHS body is satisfied,

or the local authority are satisfied, that it would be of particular benefit to P to be so represented.

(2) An NHS body which instructs, or a local authority which instruct, an IMCA under paragraph (1) must—

(a) in making any decision resulting from a review of arrangements as to P's accommodation, or

(b) in making any decision, or further decision, about protective measures in relation to P,

take into account any information given, or submissions made, by the IMCA.

THE MENTAL CAPACITY ACT 2005 (LOSS OF CAPACITY DURING RESEARCH PROJECT) (ENGLAND) REGULATIONS 2007

(SI 2007/679)

Dated March 3, 2007 and made by the Secretary of State for Health under the Mental Capacity Act 2005 (c.9), ss.30(6)(a), 34(1), (2) and (3)(b), 64(1) and 65(1)(c).

GENERAL NOTE

These Regulations are made under s.34 of the Mental Capacity Act 2005. They provide **3–016** for certain research, relating to people without capacity to consent to it, to be carried out lawfully where otherwise the requirements of s.30 of the Act would have to be complied with.

Regulation 1 provides for the Regulations to come into force on 1 July 2007 for the purpose of enabling applications for approval of research protocols under the Regulations to be made and determined and on 1 October 2007 for all other purposes.

Regulation 2 provides that the Regulations apply where a research project began before 1 October 2007 and a person ("P") consented, prior to 31 March 2008, to take part in the project but has subsequently lost capacity to continue to consent.

Regulation 3 provides that research under such a project may be carried out using information or material collected prior to P's loss of capacity. The information or material must be either data within the meaning of the Data Protection Act 1998 (c. 29) or material which consists of or includes human cells or DNA. In addition the requirements of Schedules 1 and 2 must be complied with.

Schedule 1 provides that an appropriate body must have approved a protocol for the project which provides for research to be carried out in relation to a person who has consented to take part and then lost capacity. The appropriate body must also be satisfied that there are reasonable arrangements for ensuring that Schedule 2 will be complied with.

Schedule 2, which repeats the relevant safeguards from s.32 and 33 of the Act, sets out requirements as to consultation about P's involvement in the project, as to respecting his wishes and objections and as to assuming that his interests outweigh those of science and society.

Provision for Wales, which in all material respects replicates these regulations, is contained in the Mental Capacity Act 2005 (Loss of Capacity during Research Project) (Wales) Regulations 2007 (SI 2007/837 (W.72)).

Citation, commencement, territorial application and interpretation

1.—(1) These Regulations may be cited as the Mental Capacity Act 2005 (Loss **3–017** of Capacity during Research Project) (England) Regulations 2007 and shall come into force on—

(a) 1 July 2007 for the purpose of enabling applications for approval for the purposes of Schedule 1 to be made to, and determined by, an appropriate body,

(b) 1 October 2007 for all other purposes.

(2) These Regulations apply in relation to the carrying out of research in England.

(3) In these Regulations—

"the Act" means the Mental Capacity Act 2005;

"appropriate body" has the meaning given by section 30(4) of the Act and the Mental Capacity Act 2005 (Appropriate Body) (England) Regulations 2006.

Application

3–018   **2.** These Regulations apply where—

(a) a person ("P")—

    (i) has consented before 31 March 2008 to take part in a research project ("the project") begun before 1st October 2007, but

    (ii) before the conclusion of the project, loses capacity to consent to continue to take part in it, and

    (iii) research for the purposes of the project in relation to P would, apart from these Regulations, be unlawful by virtue of section 30 of the Act.

Research which may be carried out despite a participant's loss of capacity

3–019   **3.** Despite P's loss of capacity, research for the purposes of the project may be carried out using information or material relating to him if—

(a) that information or material was obtained before P's loss of capacity,

(b) that information or material is either—

    (i) data within the meaning given in section 1(1) of the Data Protection Act 1998, or

    (ii) material which consists of or includes human cells or human DNA,

(c) the project satisfies the requirements set out in Schedule 1, and

(d) the person conducting the project ("R") takes in relation to P such steps as are set out in Schedule 2.

SCHEDULE 1   **Regulation 3(c)**

REQUIREMENTS WHICH THE PROJECT MUST SATISFY

3–020   **1.** A protocol approved by an appropriate body and having effect in relation to the project makes provision for research to be carried out in relation to a person who has consented to take part in the project but loses capacity to consent to continue to take part in it.

3–021   **2.** The appropriate body is satisfied that there are reasonable arrangements in place for ensuring that the requirements of Schedule 2 will be met.

SCHEDULE 2   **Regulation 3(d)**

STEPS WHICH THE PERSON CONDUCTING THE PROJECT MUST TAKE

3–022   **1.** R must take reasonable steps to identify a person who—

(a) otherwise than in a professional capacity or for remuneration, is engaged in caring for P or is interested in P's welfare, and

(b) is prepared to be consulted by R under this Schedule.

3–023   **2.** If R is unable to identify such a person he must, in accordance with guidance issued by the Secretary of State, nominate a person who—

(a) is prepared to be consulted by R under this Schedule, but

(b) has no connection with the project.

3–024   **3.** R must provide the person identified under paragraph 1, or nominated under paragraph 2, with information about the project and ask him—

(a) for advice as to whether research of the kind proposed should be carried out in relation to P, and

(b) what, in his opinion, P's wishes and feelings about such research being carried out would be likely to be if P had capacity in relation to the matter.

3–025   **4.** If, at any time, the person consulted advises R that in his opinion P's wishes and feelings would be likely to lead him to wish to withdraw from the project if he had capacity in relation to the matter, R must ensure that P is withdrawn from it.

3–026   **5.** The fact that a person is the donee of a lasting power of attorney given by P, or is P's deputy, does not prevent him from being the person consulted under paragraphs 1 to 4.

3–027   **6.** R must ensure that nothing is done in relation to P in the course of the research which would be contrary to—

(a) an advance decision of his which has effect, or

(b) any other form of statement made by him and not subsequently withdrawn,

of which R is aware.

7. The interests of P must be assumed to outweigh those of science and society.   **3–028**

8. If P indicates (in any way) that he wishes the research in relation to him to be discontinued, it must **3–029** be discontinued without delay.

9. The research in relation to P must be discontinued without delay if at any time R has reasonable **3–030** grounds for believing that the requirement set out in paragraph 1 of Schedule 1 is no longer met or that there are no longer reasonable arrangements in place for ensuring that the requirements of this Schedule are met in relation to P.

10. R must conduct the research in accordance with the provision made in the protocol referred to in **3–031** paragraph 1 of Schedule 1 for research to be carried out in relation to a person who has consented to take part in the project but loses capacity to consent to continue to take part in it.

THE LASTING POWERS OF ATTORNEY, ENDURING POWERS OF ATTORNEY AND PUBLIC GUARDIAN REGULATIONS 2007

(SI 2007/1253)

Dated April 16, 2007 and made by the Lord Chancellor under the Mental Capacity Act 2005 (c.9), sections 13(6)(a), 58(3) and 64(1), Schedules 1 and 4.

GENERAL NOTE

These Regulations supplement the requirements set out in Schedule 1 to the Mental **3–032** Capacity Act 2005 which apply to the making and registration of lasting powers of attorney and the requirements set out in Schedule 4 to the Act which apply to the registration of enduring powers or attorney. The Regulations also confer functions on the Public Guardian and make other provision in connection with functions conferred on him by the Act or by these Regulations.

Part 1 of the Regulations is general and contains a number of definitions and interpretative provisions.

Part 2 of, and Schedules 1 to 6 to, the Regulations deal with lasting powers of attorney. Under section 9(2)(b) of the Act, a lasting power of attorney is not created unless it has (amongst other things) been made and registered in accordance with Schedule 1 to the Act. Regulation 5 (and Schedule 1) set out the forms of instruments to be used to make a lasting power of attorney. A different form must be used according to whether the instrument is intended to confer authority to make decisions about the donor's personal welfare, or about his property and affairs. Regulations 6 to 8 make detailed provision about the content of the instrument. Regulation 9 specifies the steps that must be taken to execute the instrument and the sequence in which those steps must be taken. Regulations 10 to 17 make provision about the procedure for registering an instrument as a lasting power of attorney, and Schedules 2 to 5 set out the application form and the form of notices to be used at different stages of the process. There are also certain other requirements specified which relate to the registration process.

Regulations 18 to 22 contain a number of miscellaneous provisions that apply to instruments which have been registered as lasting powers of attorney. These provisions specify steps to be taken if an instrument is changed, revoked, lost or destroyed. Regulation 20 (and Schedule 6) set out the form to be used by the donee of a lasting power when he wishes to disclaim his appointment.

Part 3 of, and Schedules 7 and 8 to, the Regulations deal with enduring powers of attorney. No new enduring power of attorney may be created after the commencement of section 66(1)(b) of the Act, but Schedules 4 and 5 to the Act apply to any power that was created before then. Regulation 23 (and Schedule 7) set out the form of notice to be given to the donor, and to his relatives, when an attorney under an enduring power intends to apply for registration. Regulation 23 also requires that the notice be given to the donor personally, together with an explanation of its effect. Regulations 24 to 28 (and Schedule 8) specify certain other requirements applying to the registration process and regulation 29 specifies steps to be taken if an instrument creating an enduring power of attorney is lost or destroyed after it has been registered.

Part 4 of the Regulations confers a number of specific functions on the Public Guardian. It also makes provision in connection with functions conferred on him by the Act or by these Regulations.

Additional functions are conferred by regulations 43, 45 and 48. Regulation 43 deals with the making of applications to the Court of Protection, regulation 45 sets out functions in relation to persons who are authorised to carry out a particular transaction and regulation 48 sets out functions in relation to enduring powers of attorney.

There are also provisions relating to the registers which the Public Guardian is required to maintain under the Act (regulations 30 to 32); relating to the giving of any security and the replacement, maintenance, enforcement or discharge of a security which has been endorsed (regulations 33 to 37); relating to the information that a deputy appointed by the Court of Protection must give to the Public Guardian (regulations 38 to 41); and relating to the review of a decision made by the Public Guardian in relation to a deputy (regulation 42). Regulations 44, 46 and 47 make provision in connection with a number of other areas where the Public Guardian has functions, including the requirements to be met when visits on any person are carried out by, or at the direction of, the Public Guardian (regulation 48).

CONTENTS

PART 1

Preliminary

PART 2

LASTING POWERS OF ATTORNEY

Instruments intended to create a lasting power of attorney

Registering the instrument

Post-registration

PART 1

PRELIMINARY

Citation and commencement

3–033   **1.**—(1) These Regulations may be cited as the Lasting Powers of Attorney, Enduring Powers of Attorney and Public Guardian Regulations 2007.

(2) These Regulations shall come into force on 1 October 2007.

Interpretation

3–034   **2.**—(1) In these Regulations—

"the Act" means the Mental Capacity Act 2005;

"court" means the Court of Protection;

"LPA certificate", in relation to an instrument made with a view to creating a lasting power of attorney, means the certificate which is required to be included in the instrument by virtue of paragraph 2(1)(e) of Schedule 1 to the Act;

"named person", in relation to an instrument made with a view to creating a lasting power of attorney, means a person who is named in the instrument as being a person to be notified of any application for the registration of the instrument;

"prescribed information", in relation to any instrument intended to create a lasting power of attorney, means the information contained in the form used for the instrument which appears under the heading "prescribed information".

Minimal differences from forms prescribed in these Regulations

3–035   **3.**—(1) In these Regulations, any reference to a form—

    (a) in the case of a form set out in Schedules 1 to 7 to these Regulations, is to be regarded as including a Welsh version of that form; and

(b) in the case of a form set out in Schedules 2 to 7 to these Regulations, is to be regarded as also including—
  (i) a form to the same effect but which differs in an immaterial respect in form or mode of expression;
  (ii) a form to the same effect but with such variations as the circumstances may require or the court or the Public Guardian may approve; or
  (iii) a Welsh version of a form within (i) or (ii).

Computation of time

4.—(1) This regulation shows how to calculate any period of time which is **3–036** specified in these Regulations.

(2) A period of time expressed as a number of days must be computed as clear days.

(3) Where the specified period is 7 days or less, and would include a day which is not a business day, that day does not count.

(4) When the specified period for doing any act at the office of the Public Guardian ends on a day on which the office is closed, that act will be done in time if done on the next day on which the office is open.

(5) In this regulation—

"business day" means a day other than—
(a) a Saturday, Sunday, Christmas Day or Good Friday; or
(b) a bank holiday under the Banking and Financial Dealings Act 1971, in England and Wales; and

"clear days" means that in computing the number of days—
(a) the day on which the period begins, and
(b) if the end of the period is defined by reference to an event, the day on which that event occurs,

are not included.

PART 2

LASTING POWERS OF ATTORNEY

Instruments intended to create a lasting power of attorney

Forms for lasting powers of attorney

5.—(1) The forms set out in Parts 1 and 2 of Schedule 1 to these Regulations **3–037** are the forms which, in the circumstances to which they apply, are to be used for instruments intended to create a lasting power of attorney.

Maximum number of named persons

6.— The maximum number of named persons that the donor of a lasting power **3–038** of attorney may specify in the instrument intended to create the power is 5.

Requirement for two LPA certificates where instrument has no named persons

3–039 **7.** Where an instrument intended to create a lasting power of attorney includes a statement by the donor that there are no persons whom he wishes to be notified of any application for the registration of the instrument—

(a) the instrument must include two LPA certificates; and

(b) each certificate must be completed and signed by a different person.

Persons who may provide an LPA certificate

3–040 **8.**—(1) Subject to paragraph (3), the following persons may give an LPA certificate—

(a) a person chosen by the donor as being someone who has known him personally for the period of at least two years which ends immediately before the date on which that person signs the LPA certificate;

(b) a person chosen by the donor who, on account of his professional skills and expertise, reasonably considers that he is competent to make the judgments necessary to certify the matters set out in paragraph (2)(1)(e) of Schedule 1 to the Act.

(2) The following are examples of persons within paragraph (1)(b)—

(a) a registered health care professional;

(b) a barrister, solicitor or advocate called or admitted in any part of the United Kingdom;

(c) a registered social worker; or

(d) an independent mental capacity advocate.

(3) A person is disqualified from giving an LPA certificate in respect of any instrument intended to create a lasting power of attorney if that person is—

(a) a family member of the donor;

(b) a donee of that power;

(c) a donee of—

(i) any other lasting power of attorney, or

(ii) an enduring power of attorney,

which has been executed by the donor (whether or not it has been revoked);

(d) a family member of a donee within sub-paragraph (b);

(e) a director or employee of a trust corporation acting as a donee within sub-paragraph (b);

(f) a business partner or employee of—

(i) the donor, or

(ii) a donee within sub-paragraph (b);

(g) an owner, director, manager or employee of any care home in which the donor is living when the instrument is executed; or

(h) a family member of a person within sub-paragraph (g).

(4) In this regulation—

"care home" has the meaning given in section 3 of the Care Standards Act 2000;

"registered health care professional" means a person who is a member of a profession regulated by a body mentioned in section 25(3) of the National Health Service Reform and Health Care Professions Act 2002; and

"registered social worker" means a person registered as a social worker in a register maintained by—

(a) the General Social Care Council;

(b) the Care Council for Wales;

(c) the Scottish Social Services Council; or

(d) the Northern Ireland Social Care Council.

Execution of instrument

9.—(1) An instrument intended to create a lasting power of attorney must be **3–041** executed in accordance with this regulation.

(2) The donor must read (or have read to him) all the prescribed information.

(a) 2000 c.14.

(b) 2002 c.17.

(3) As soon as reasonably practicable after the steps required by paragraph (2) have been taken, the donor must—

(a) complete the provisions of Part A of the instrument that apply to him (or direct another person to do so); and

(b) subject to paragraph (7), sign Part A of the instrument in the presence of a witness.

(4) As soon as reasonably practicable after the steps required by paragraph (3) have been taken—

(a) the person giving an LPA certificate, or

(b) if regulation 7 applies (two LPA certificates required), each of the persons giving a certificate,

must complete the LPA certificate at Part B of the instrument and sign it.

(5) As soon as reasonably practicable after the steps required by paragraph (4) have been taken—

(a) the donee, or

(b) if more than one, each of the donees,

must read (or have read to him) all the prescribed information.

(6) As soon as reasonably practicable after the steps required by paragraph (5) have been taken, the donee or, if more than one, each of them—

(a) must complete the provisions of Part C of the instrument that apply to him (or direct another person to do so); and

(b) subject to paragraph (7), must sign Part C of the instrument in the presence of a witness.

(7) If the instrument is to be signed by any person at the direction of the donor, or at the direction of any donee, the signature must be done in the presence of two witnesses.

(8)For the purposes of this regulation—

(a) the donor may not witness any signature required for the power;

(b) a donee may not witness any signature required for the power apart from that of another donee.

(9) A person witnessing a signature must—

(a) sign the instrument; and

(b) give his full name and address.

(10) Any reference in this regulation to a person signing an instrument (however expressed) includes his signing it by means of a mark made on the instrument at the appropriate place.

Notice to be given by a person about to apply for registration of lasting power of attorney

3–042   **10.** Schedule 2 to these Regulations sets out the form of notice ("LPA 001") which must be given by a donor or donee who is about to make an application for the registration of an instrument intended to create a lasting power of attorney.

Application for registration

3–043   **11.**—(1) Schedule 3 to these Regulations sets out the form ("LPA 002") which must be used for making an application to the Public Guardian for the registration of an instrument intended to create a lasting power of attorney.

(2) Where the instrument to be registered which is sent with the application is neither—

(a) the original instrument intended to create the power, nor

(b) a certified copy of it,

the Public Guardian must not register the instrument unless the court directs him to do so.

(3) In paragraph (2) "a certified copy" means a photographic or other facsimile copy which is certified as an accurate copy by—

(a) the donor; or

(b) a solicitor or notary.

GENERAL NOTE

The fee prescribed in the Schedule to the Public Guardian (Fees, etc) Regulations 2007 (SI 2007/2051) shall be payable upon the application to register (SI 2007/2051, regs 3, 5).

Period to elapse before registration in cases not involving objection or defect

3–044   **12.** The period at the end of which the Public Guardian must register an instrument in accordance with paragraph 5 of Schedule 1 to the Act is the period of 6 weeks beginning with—

(a) the date on which the Public Guardian gave the notice or notices under paragraph 7 or 8 of Schedule 1 to the Act of receipt of an application for registration; or

(b) if notices were given on more than one date, the latest of those dates.

Notice of receipt of application for registration

3–045   **13.**—(1) Part 1 of Schedule 4 to these Regulations sets out the form of notice ("LPA 003A") which the Public Guardian must give to the donee (or donees) when the Public Guardian receives an application for the registration of a lasting power of attorney.

(2) Part 2 of Schedule 4 sets out the form of notice ("LPA 003B") which the Public Guardian must give to the donor when the Public Guardian receives such an application.

(3) Where it appears to the Public Guardian that there is good reason to do so, the Public Guardian must also provide (or arrange for the provision of) an explanation to the donor of—

(a) the notice referred to in paragraph (2) and what the effect of it is; and

(b) why it is being brought to his attention.

(4) Any information provided under paragraph (3) must be provided—

(a) to the donor personally; and

(b) in a way that is appropriate to the donor's circumstances (for example using simple language, visual aids or other appropriate means).

Objection to registration: notice to Public Guardian [to be given by the donee of the power or a named person]

14.—(1) This regulation deals with any objection to the registration of an **3–046** instrument as a lasting power of attorney which is to be made to the Public Guardian [to be given by the donee of the power or a named person].

(2) Where [the donee of the power or a named person]

(a) is entitled to receive notice under paragraph 6, 7 or 8 of Schedule 1 to the Act of an application for the registration of the instrument, and

(b) wishes to object to registration on a ground set out in paragraph 13(1) of Schedule 1 to the Act,

he must do so before the end of the period of 5 weeks beginning with the date on which the notice is given.

(3) A notice of objection must be given in writing, setting out—

(a) the name and address of the objector;

(b) [. . .] the name and address of the donor of the power;

(c) if known, the name and address of the donee (or donees); and

(d) the ground for making the objection.

(4) The Public Guardian must notify the objector as to whether he is satisfied that the ground of the objection is established.

(5) At any time after receiving the notice of objection and before giving the notice required by paragraph (4), the Public Guardian may require the objector to provide such further information,
or produce such documents, as the Public Guardian reasonably considers necessary to enable him to determine whether the ground for making the objection is established.

(6) Where—

(a) the Public Guardian is satisfied that the ground of the objection is established, but

(b) by virtue of section 13(7) of the Act, the instrument is not revoked,

the notice under paragraph (4) must contain a statement to that effect.

(7) Nothing in this regulation prevents an objector from making a further objection under paragraph 13 of Schedule 1 to the Act where—

(a) the notice under paragraph (4) indicates that the Public Guardian is not satisfied that the particular ground of objection to which that notice relates is established; and

(b) the period specified in paragraph (2) has not expired.

AMENDMENTS
The amendments to this regulation were made by SI 2007/2161, reg.3. **3–047**

[Objection to registration: notice to Public Guardian to be given by the donor

14A.—(1) This regulation deals with any objection to the registration of an instrument as a lasting power of attorney which is to be made to the Public Guardian by the donor of the power.

(2) Where the donor of the power—

(a) is entitled to receive notice under paragraph 8 of Schedule 1 to the Act of an application for the registration of the instrument, and

(b) wishes to object to the registration, he must do so before the end of the period of 5 weeks beginning with the date on which the notice is given.

(3) The donor of the power must give notice of his objection in writing to the Public Guardian, setting out—

(a) the name and address of the donor of the power;

(b) if known, the name and address of the donee (or donees); and

(c) the ground for making the objection.]

AMENDMENT

This regulation was inserted by SI 2007/2161, reg.4.

Objection to registration: application to the court

3–048   **15.**—(1) This regulation deals with any objection to the registration of an instrument as a lasting power of attorney which is to be made to the court.

(2) The grounds for making an application to the court are—

(a) that one or more of the requirements for the creation of a lasting power of attorney have not been met;

(b) that the power has been revoked, or has otherwise come to an end, on a ground other than the grounds set out in paragraph 13(1) of Schedule 1 to the Act;

(c) any of the grounds set out in paragraph (a) or (b) of section 22(3) of the Act.

(3) Where any person—

(a) is entitled to receive notice under paragraph 6, 7 or 8 of Schedule 1 to the Act of an application for the registration of the instrument, and

(b) wishes to object to registration on one or more of the grounds set out in paragraph (2),

he must make an application to the court before the end of the period of 5 weeks beginning with the date on which the notice is given.

(4) The notice of an application to the court, which a person making an objection to the court is required to give to the Public Guardian under paragraph 13(3)(b)(ii) of Schedule 1 to the Act, must be in writing.

Notifying applicants of non-registration of lasting power of attorney

3–049   **16.** Where the Public Guardian is prevented from registering an instrument as a lasting power of attorney by virtue of—

(a) paragraph 11(1) of Schedule 1 to the Act (instrument not made in accordance with Schedule),

(b) paragraph 12(2) of that Schedule (deputy already appointed),

(c) paragraph 13(2) of that Schedule (objection by donee or named person on grounds of bankruptcy, disclaimer, death etc),

(d) paragraph 14(2) of that Schedule (objection by donor), or

(a) regulation 11(2) of these Regulations (application for registration not accompanied by original instrument or certified copy),

he must notify the person (or persons) who applied for registration of that fact.

Notice to be given on registration of lasting power of attorney

3–050   **17.**—(1) Where the Public Guardian registers an instrument as a lasting power of attorney, he must—

(a) retain a copy of the instrument; and

(b) return to the person (or persons) who applied for registration the original instrument, or the certified copy of it, which accompanied the application for registration.

(2) Schedule 5 to these Regulations sets out the form of notice ("LPA 004") which the Public Guardian must give to the donor and donee (or donees) when the Public Guardian registers an instrument.

(3) Where it appears to the Public Guardian that there is good reason to do so, the Public Guardian must also provide (or arrange for the provision of) an explanation to the donor of—

(a) the notice referred to in paragraph (2) and what the effect of it is; and

(b) why it is being brought to his attention.

(4) Any information provided under paragraph (3) must be provided—

(a) to the donor personally; and

(b) in a way that is appropriate to the donor's circumstances (for example using simple language, visual aids or other appropriate means).

(5) "Certified copy" is to be construed in accordance with regulation 11(3).

Post-registration

Changes to instrument registered as lasting power of attorney

18.—(1) This regulation applies in any case where any of paragraphs 21 to 24 of   **3–051** Schedule 1 to the Act requires the Public Guardian to attach a note to an instrument registered as a lasting power of attorney.

(2) The Public Guardian must give a notice to the donor and the donee (or, if more than one, each of them) requiring him to deliver to the Public Guardian—

(a) the original of instrument which was sent to the Public Guardian for registration;

(b) any office copy of that registered instrument; and

(c) any certified copy of that registered instrument.

(3) On receipt of the document, the Public Guardian must—

(a) attach the required note; and

(b) return the document to the person from whom it was obtained.

Loss or destruction of instrument registered as lasting power of attorney

19.—(1) This regulation applies where—   **3–052**

(a) a person is required by or under the Act to deliver up to the Public Guardian any of the following documents—

  (i) an instrument registered as a lasting power of attorney;

  (ii) an office copy of that registered instrument;

  (iii) a certified copy of that registered instrument; and

(b) the document has been lost or destroyed.

(2) The person required to deliver up the document must provide to the Public Guardian in writing—

(a) if known, the date of the loss or destruction and the circumstances in which it occurred;

(b) otherwise, a statement of when he last had the document in his possession.

Disclaimer of appointment by a donee of lasting power of attorney

3–053   **20.**—(1) Schedule 6 to these Regulations sets out the form ("LPA 005") which a donee of an instrument registered as a lasting power of attorney must use to disclaim his appointment as donee.

(2) The donee must send—

(a) the completed form to the donor; and

(b) a copy of it to—

    (i) the Public Guardian; and

    (ii) any other donee who, for the time being, is appointed under the power.

Revocation by donor of lasting power of attorney

3–054   **21.**—(1)A donor who revokes a lasting power to attorney must—

(a) notify the Public Guardian that he has done so; and

(b) notify the donee (or, if more than one, each of them) of the revocation.

(2) Where the Public Guardian receives a notice under paragraph (1)(a), he must cancel the registration of the instrument creating the power if he is satisfied that the donor has taken such steps as are necessary in law to revoke it.

(3) The Public Guardian may require the donor to provide such further information, or produce such documents, as the Public Guardian reasonably considers necessary to enable him to determine whether the steps necessary for revocation have been taken.

(4) Where the Public Guardian cancels the registration of the instrument he must notify—

(a) the donor; and

(b) the donee or, if more than one, each of them.

Revocation of a lasting power of attorney on death of donor

3–055   **22.**—(1) The Public Guardian must cancel the registration of an instrument as a lasting power of attorney if he is satisfied that the power has been revoked as a result of the donor's death.

(2) Where the Public Guardian cancels the registration of an instrument he must notify the donee or, if more than one, each of them.

PART 3

ENDURING POWERS OF ATTORNEY

Notice of intention to apply for registration of enduring power of attorney

3–056   **23.**—(1) Schedule 7 to these Regulations sets out the form of notice ("EP1PG") which an attorney (or attorneys) under an enduring power of attorney must give of his intention to make an application for the registration of the instrument creating the power.

(2) In the case of the notice to be given to the donor, the attorney must also provide (or arrange for the provision of) an explanation to the donor of—

(a) the notice and what the effect of it is; and

(b) why it is being brought to his attention.

(3) The information provided under paragraph (2) must be provided—

(a) to the donor personally; and

(b) in a way that is appropriate to the donor's circumstances (for example using simple language, visual aids or other appropriate means).

Application for registration
24.—(1) Schedule 8 to these Regulations sets out the form ("EP2PG") which **3–057**
must be used for making an application to the Public Guardian for the registration
of an instrument creating an enduring power of attorney.
(2) Where the instrument to be registered which is sent with the application is
neither—
(a) the original instrument creating the power, nor
(b) a certified copy of it,
the Public Guardian must not register the instrument unless the court directs
him to do so.
(3) "Certified copy", in relation to an enduring power of attorney, means a
copy certified in accordance with section 3 of the Powers of Attorney Act 1971.

GENERAL NOTE
The fee prescribed in the Schedule to the Public Guardian (Fees, etc) Regulations 2007
(SI 2007/2051) shall be payable upon the application to register (2007/2051, regs 3, 4).

Notice of objection to registration
25.—(1) This regulation deals with any objection to the registration of an **3–058**
instrument creating an enduring power of attorney which is to be made to the
Public Guardian under paragraph 13(4) of Schedule 4 to the Act.
(2) A notice of objection must be given in writing, setting out—
(a) the name and address of the objector;
(b) if different, the name and address of the donor of the power;
(c) if known, the name and address of the attorney (or attorneys); and
(d) the ground for making the objection.

Notifying applicants of non-registration of enduring power of attorney
26. Where the Public Guardian is prevented from registering an instrument **3–059**
creating an enduring power of attorney by virtue of—
(a) paragraph 13(2) of Schedule 4 to the Act (deputy already appointed),
(b) paragraph 13(5) of that Schedule (receipt by Public Guardian of valid notice
of objection from person entitled to notice of application to register),
(c) paragraph 13(7) of that Schedule (Public Guardian required to undertake
appropriate enquiries in certain circumstances), or
(d) regulation 24(2) of these Regulations (application for registration not
accompanied by original instrument or certified copy),
he must notify the person (or persons) who applied for registration of that fact.

Registration of instrument creating an enduring power of attorney
27.—(1) Where the Public Guardian registers an instrument creating an endur- **3–060**
ing power of attorney, he must—
(a) retain a copy of the instrument; and
(b) return to the person (or persons) who applied for registration the original
instrument, or the certified copy of it, which accompanied the application.
(2) "Certified copy" has the same meaning as in regulation 24(3).

Objection or revocation not applying to all joint and several attorneys
28. In a case within paragraph 20(6) or (7) of Schedule 4 to the Act, the form of **3–061**
the entry to be made in the register in respect of an instrument creating the

enduring power of attorney is a stamp bearing the following words (inserting the information indicated, as appropriate)—

"THE REGISTRATION OF THIS ENDURING POWER OF ATTORNEY IS QUALIFIED AND EXTENDS TO THE APPOINTMENT OF . . . . (insert name of attorney(s) not affected by ground(s) of objection or revocation) ONLY AS THE ATTORNEY(S) OF . . . . (insert name of donor)".

Loss or destruction of instrument registered as enduring power of attorney
3–062   **29.**—(1)This regulation applies where—
  (a) a person is required by or under the Act to deliver up to the Public Guardian any of the following documents—
      (i) an instrument registered as an enduring power of attorney;
      (ii) an office copy of that registered instrument; or
      (iii) a certified copy of that registered instrument; and
  (b) the document has been lost or destroyed.
  (2) The person who is required to deliver up the document must provide to the Public Guardian in writing—
  (a) if known, the date of the loss or destruction and the circumstances in which it occurred;
  (b) otherwise, a statement of when he last had the document in his possession.

PART 4

FUNCTIONS OF THE PUBLIC GUARDIAN

The registers

Establishing and maintaining the registers
3–063   **30.**—(1) In this Part "the registers" means—
  (a)   the register of lasting powers of attorney,
  (b)   the register of enduring powers of attorney, and (c) the register of court orders appointing deputies,
which the Public Guardian must establish and maintain.
  (2) On each register the Public Guardian may include—
  (a)   such descriptions of information about a registered instrument or a registered order as the
  Public Guardian considers appropriate; and
  (b)   entries which relate to an instrument or order for which registration has been cancelled.

Disclosure of information on a register: search by the Public Guardian
3–064   **31.**—(1)Any person may, by an application made under paragraph (2), request the Public Guardian to carry out a search of one or more of the registers. (2) An application must—
  (a) state—
      (i) the register or registers to be searched;
      (ii) the name of the person to whom the application relates; and
      (iii)   such other details about that person as the Public Guardian may require for the purpose of carrying out the search; and

(b) be accompanied by any fee provided for under section 58(4)(b) of the Act.

(3) The Public Guardian may require the applicant to provide such further information, or produce such documents, as the Public Guardian reasonably considers necessary to enable him to carry out the search.

(4) As soon as reasonably practicable after receiving the application—

(a) the Public Guardian must notify the applicant of the result of the search; and

(b) in the event that it reveals one or more entries on the register, the Public Guardian must disclose to the applicant all the information appearing on the register in respect of each entry.

GENERAL NOTE

With the exception of applications made by a registered health care professional or a representative of a health authority, the fee prescribed in the Schedule to the Public Guardian (Fees, etc) Regulations 2007 (SI 2007/2051) shall be payable upon the application to search the registers (SI 2007/2051, regs 3, 6).

Disclosure of additional information held by the Public Guardian

32.—(1) This regulation applies in any case where, as a result of a search made **3–065** under regulation 31, a person has obtained information relating to a registered instrument or a registered order which confers authority to make decisions about matters concerning a person ("P").

(2) On receipt of an application made in accordance with paragraph (4), the Public Guardian may, if he considers that there is good reason to do so, disclose to the applicant such additional information as he considers appropriate.

(3) "Additional information" means any information relating to P—

(a) which the Public Guardian has obtained in exercising the functions conferred on him under the Act; but

(b) which does not appear on the register.

(4) An application must state—

(a) the name of P;

(b) the reasons for making the application; and

(c) what steps, if any, the applicant has taken to obtain the information from P.

(5) The Public Guardian may require the applicant to provide such further information, or produce such documents, as the Public Guardian reasonably considers necessary to enable him to determine the application.

(6) In determining whether to disclose any additional information to P, the Public Guardian must, in particular, have regard to—

(a) the connection between P and the applicant;

(b) the reasons for requesting the information (in particular, why the information cannot or should not be obtained directly from P);

(c) the benefit to P, or any detriment he may suffer, if a disclosure is made; and

(d) any detriment that another person may suffer if a disclosure is made.

Security for discharge of functions

Persons required to give security for the discharge of their functions

33.—(1) This regulation applies in any case where the court orders a person **3–066** ("S") to give to the Public Guardian security for the discharge of his functions.

(2) The security must be given by S—

(a) by means of a bond which is entered into in accordance with regulation 34; or

(b) in such other manner as the court may direct.

(3) For the purposes of paragraph (2)(a), S complies with the requirement to give the security only if—

(a) the endorsement required by regulation 34(2) has been provided; and

(b) the person who provided it has notified the Public Guardian of that fact.

(4) For the purposes of paragraph (2)(b), S complies with the requirement to give the security—

(a) in any case where the court directs that any other endorsement must be provided, only if—

(i) that endorsement has been provided; and

(ii) the person who provided it has notified the Public Guardian of that fact;

(b) in any case where the court directs that any other requirements must be met in relation to the giving of the security, only if the Public Guardian is satisfied that those other requirements have been met.

Security given under regulation 33(2)(a): requirement for endorsement

3–067   **34.**—(1) This regulation has effect for the purposes of regulation 33(2)(a).

(2) A bond is entered into in accordance with this regulation only if it is endorsed by—

(a) an authorised insurance company; or

(b) an authorised deposit-taker.

(3) A person may enter into the bond under—

(a) arrangements made by the Public Guardian; or

(b) other arrangements which are made by the person entering into the bond or on his behalf.

(4) The Public Guardian may make arrangements with any person specified in paragraph (2) with a view to facilitating the provision by them of bonds which persons required to give security to the Public Guardian may enter into.

(5) In this regulation—

"authorised insurance company" means—

(a) a person who has permission under Part 4 of the Financial Services and Markets Act 2000 to effect or carry out contracts of insurance;

(b) an EEA firm of the kind mentioned in paragraph 5(d) of Schedule 3 to that Act, which has permission under paragraph 15 of that Schedule to effect or carry out contracts of insurance;

(c) a person who carries on insurance market activity (within the meaning given in section 3 16(3) of that Act); and

"authorised deposit-taker" means—

(a) a person who has permission under Part 4 of the Financial Services and Markets Act 2000 to accept deposits;

(b) an EEA firm of the kind mentioned in paragraph 5(d) of Schedule 3 to that Act, which has permission under paragraph 15 of that Schedule to accept deposits.

(6) The definitions of "authorised insurance company" and "authorised deposit-taker" must be read with—

(a) section 22 of the Financial Services and Markets Act 2000;

(b) any relevant order under that section; and

(c) Schedule 2 to that Act.

Security given under regulation 33(2)(a): maintenance or replacement

35.—(1) This regulation applies to any security given under regulation 3–068
33(2)(a).

(2) At such times or at such intervals as the Public Guardian may direct by
notice in writing, any person ("S") who has given the security must satisfy the
Public Guardian that any premiums payable in respect of it have been paid.

(3) Where S proposes to replace a security already given by him, the new security is not to be regarded as having been given until the Public Guardian is satisfied
that—
  (a) the requirements set out in sub-paragraphs (a) and (b) of regulation 3 3(3)
      have been met in relation to it; and
  (b) no payment is due from S in connection with the discharge of his functions.

Enforcement following court order of any endorsed security

36.—(1) This regulation applies to any security given to the Public Guardian in 3–069
respect of which an endorsement has been provided.

(2) Where the court orders the enforcement of the security, the Public Guardian
must—
  (a) notify any person who endorsed the security of the contents of the order; and
  (b) notify the court when payment has been made of the amount secured.

Discharge of any endorsed security

37.—(1) This regulation applies to any security given by a person ("S") to the 3–070
Public Guardian in respect of which an endorsement has been provided.

(2) The security may be discharged if the court makes an order discharging it.

(3) In any other case, the security may not be discharged until the end of the
period of 7 years commencing with whichever of the following dates first
occurs—
  (a) if the person on whose behalf S was appointed to act dies, the date of his
      death;
  (b) if S dies, the date of his death;
  (c) if the court makes an order which discharges S but which does not also dis-
      charge the security under paragraph (2), the date of the order;
  (d) the date when S otherwise ceases to be under a duty to discharge the func-
      tions in respect of which he was ordered to give security.

(4) For the purposes of paragraph (3), if a person takes any step with a view to
discharging the security before the end of the period specified in that paragraph,
the security is to be treated for all purposes as if it were still in place.

Deputies

Application for additional time to submit a report

38.—(1) This regulation applies where the court requires a deputy to submit a 3–071
report to the Public Guardian and specifies a time or interval for it to be submitted.

(2) A deputy may apply to the Public Guardian requesting more time for sub-
mitting a particular report.

(3) An application must—
  (a) state the reason for requesting more time; and

(b) contain or be accompanied by such information as the Public Guardian may reasonably require to determine the application.

(4) In response to an application, the Public Guardian may, if he considers it appropriate to do so, undertake that he will not take steps to secure performance of the deputy's duty to submit the report at the relevant time on the condition that the report is submitted on or before such later date as he may specify.

Content of reports

3–072   **39.**—(1) Any report which the court requires a deputy to submit to the Public Guardian must include such material as the court may direct.

(2) The report must also contain or be accompanied by—

(a) specified information or information of a specified description; or

(b) specified documents or documents of a specified description.

(3) But paragraph (2)—

(a) extends only to information or documents which are reasonably required in connection with the exercise by the Public Guardian of functions conferred on him under the Act; and

(b) is subject to paragraph (1) and to any other directions given by the court.

(4) Where powers as respects a person's property and affairs are conferred on a deputy under section 16 of the Act, the information specified by the Public Guardian under paragraph (2) may include accounts which—

(a) deal with specified matters; and

(b) are provided in a specified form.

(5) The Public Guardian may require—

(a) any information provided to be verified in such manner, or

(b) any document produced to be authenticated in such manner, as he may reasonably require.

(6) "Specified" means specified in a notice in writing given to the deputy by the Public Guardian.

Power to require final report on termination of appointment

3–073   **40.**—(1) This regulation applies where—

(a) the person on whose behalf a deputy was appointed to act has died;

(b) the deputy has died;

(c) the court has made an order discharging the deputy; or

(d) the deputy otherwise ceases to be under a duty to discharge the functions to which his appointment relates.

(2) The Public Guardian may require the deputy (or, in the case of the deputy's death, his personal representatives) to submit a final report on the discharge of his functions.

(3) A final report must be submitted—

(a) before the end of such reasonable period as may be specified; and

(b) at such place as may be specified.

(4) The Public Guardian must consider the final report, together with any other information that he may have relating to the discharge by the deputy of his functions.

(5) Where the Public Guardian is dissatisfied with any aspect of the final report he may apply to the court for an appropriate remedy (including enforcement of security given by the deputy).

(6) "Specified" means specified in a notice in writing given to the deputy or his personal representatives by the Public Guardian.

Power to require information from deputies

41.—(1) This regulation applies in any case where—   **3–074**
(a) the Public Guardian has received representations (including complaints) about—
    (i) the way in which a deputy is exercising his powers; or
    (ii) any failure to exercise them; or
(b) it appears to the Public Guardian that there are other circumstances which—
    (i) give rise to concerns about, or dissatisfaction with, the conduct of the deputy (including any failure to act); or
    (ii) otherwise constitute good reason to seek information about the deputy's discharge of his functions.

(2) The Public Guardian may require the deputy—
(a) to provide specified information or information of a specified description; or
(b) to produce specified documents or documents of a specified description.
(3) The information or documents must be provided or produced—
(a) before the end of such reasonable period as may be specified; and
(b) at such place as may be specified.
(4) The Public Guardian may require—
(a) any information provided to be verified in such manner, or
(b) any document produced to be authenticated in such manner,
as he may reasonably require.
(5) "Specified" means specified in a notice in writing given to the deputy by the Public Guardian.

Right of deputy to require review of decisions made by the Public Guardian

42.—(1) A deputy may require the Public Guardian to reconsider any decision **3–075**
he has made in relation to the deputy.
(2) The right under paragraph (1) is exercisable by giving notice of exercise of the right to the Public Guardian before the end of the period of 14 days beginning with the date on which notice of the decision is given to the deputy.
(3) The notice of exercise of the right must—
(a) state the grounds on which reconsideration is required; and
(b) contain or be accompanied by any relevant information or documents.
(4) At any time after receiving the notice and before reconsidering the decision to which it relates, the Public Guardian may require the deputy to provide him with such further information, or to produce such documents, as he reasonably considers necessary to enable him to reconsider the matter.
(5) The Public Guardian must give to the deputy—
(a) written notice of his decision on reconsideration, and
(b) if he upholds the previous decision, a statement of his reasons.

Miscellaneous functions

Applications to the Court of Protection

3–076   **43.** The Public Guardian has the function of making applications to the court in connection with his functions under the Act in such circumstances as he considers it necessary or appropriate to do so.

Visits by the Public Guardian or by Court of Protection Visitors at his direction

3–077   **44.**—(1) This regulation applies where the Public Guardian visits, or directs a Court of Protection Visitor to visit, any person under any provision of the Act or these Regulations.

(2) The Public Guardian must notify (or make arrangements to notify) the person to be visited of—

  (a) the date or dates on which it is proposed that the visit will take place;
  (b) to the extent that it is practicable to do so, any specific matters likely to be covered in the course of the visit; and
  (c) any proposal to inform any other person that the visit is to take place.

(3) Where the visit is to be carried out by a Court of Protection Visitor—

  (a) the Public Guardian may—
    (i) give such directions to the Visitor, and
    (ii) provide him with such information concerning the person to be visited, as the Public Guardian considers necessary for the purposes of enabling the visit to take place and the Visitor to prepare any report the Public Guardian may require; and
  (b) the Visitor must seek to carry out the visit and take all reasonable steps to obtain such other information as he considers necessary for the purpose of preparing a report.

(4) A Court of Protection Visitor must submit any report requested by the Public Guardian in accordance with any timetable specified by the Public Guardian.

(5) If he considers it appropriate to do so, the Public Guardian may, in relation to any person interviewed in the course of preparing a report—

  (a) disclose the report to him; and
  (b) invite him to comment on it.

Functions in relation to persons carrying out specific transactions

3–078   **45.**—(1) This regulation applies where, in accordance with an order made under section 16(2)(a) of the Act, a person ("T") has been authorised to carry out any transaction for a person who lacks capacity.

(2) The Public Guardian has the functions of—

  (a) receiving any reports from T which the court may require;
  (b) dealing with representations (including complaints) about—
    (i) the way in which the transaction has been or is being carried out; or
    (ii) any failure to carry it out.

(3) Regulations 38 to 41 have effect in relation to T as they have effect in relation a deputy.

Power to require information from donees of lasting power of attorney

46.—(1) This regulation applies where it appears to the Public Guardian that **3–079** there are circumstances suggesting that the donee of a lasting power of attorney may—

(a) have behaved, or may be behaving, in a way that contravenes his authority or is not in the best interests of the donor of the power,

(b) be proposing to behave in a way that would contravene that authority or would not be in the donor's best interests, or

(c) have failed to comply with the requirements of an order made, or directions given, by the court.

(2) The Public Guardian may require the donee—

(a) to provide specified information or information of a specified description; or

(b) to produce specified documents or documents of a specified description.

(3) The information or documents must be provided or produced—

(a) before the end of such reasonable period as may be specified; and

(b) at such place as may be specified.

(4) The Public Guardian may require—

(a) any information provided to be verified in such manner, or

(b) any document produced to be authenticated in such manner,

as he may reasonably require.

(5) "Specified" means specified in a notice in writing given to the donee by the Public Guardian.

Power to require information from attorneys under enduring power of attorney

47.—(1) This regulation applies where it appears to the Public Guardian that **3–080** there are circumstances suggesting that, having regard to all the circumstances (and in particular the attorney's relationship to or connection with the donor) the attorney under a registered enduring power of attorney may be unsuitable to be the donor's attorney.

(2) The Public Guardian may require the attorney—

(a) to provide specified information or information of a specified description; or

(b) to produce specified documents or documents of a specified description.

(3) The information or documents must be provided or produced—

(a) before the end of such reasonable period as may be specified; and

(b) at such place as may be specified.

(4) The Public Guardian may require—

(a) any information provided to be verified in such manner, or

(b) any document produced to be authenticated in such manner,

as he may reasonably require.

(5) "Specified" means specified in a notice in writing given to the attorney by the Public Guardian.

Other functions in relation to enduring powers of attorney

48. The Public Guardian has the following functions— **3–081**

(a) directing a Court of Protection Visitor—

(i) to visit an attorney under a registered enduring power of attorney, or

(ii) to visit the donor of a registered enduring power of attorney, and to make a report to the Public Guardian on such matters as he may direct;

(b) dealing with representations (including complaints) about the way in which an attorney under a registered enduring power of attorney is exercising his powers.

SCHEDULES 1 TO 8

[Not reproduced]

THE MENTAL CAPACITY ACT 2005 (TRANSFER OF PROCEEDINGS) ORDER 2007

(SI 2007/1899)

Dated June 25, 2007 and made by the President of the Family Division of the High Court with the agreement of the Lord Chancellor under the Mental Capacity Act 2005 (c.9), ss.21 and 65(5).

GENERAL NOTE

This Order provides for transfers of proceedings between the Court of Protection and a **3–082** court having jurisdiction under the Children Act 1989 (c. 41) ("the Children Act").

Article 2 specifies the circumstances in which proceedings in the Court of Protection may be transferred to a court having jurisdiction under the Children Act and sets out how proceedings are to be dealt with when a transfer is made.

Article 3 specifies the circumstances in which proceedings in a court having jurisdiction under the Children Act may be transferred to the Court of Protection and sets out how proceedings are to be dealt with when a transfer is made.

Article 4 makes provision for treating any fee paid to start the proceedings which are transferred as if it had been the fee payable to start proceedings in the court to which the transfer is made.

Citation and commencement

1.—(1) This Order may be cited as the Mental Capacity Act 2005 (Transfer of **3–083** Proceedings) Order 2007.

(2) This Order shall come into force on 1st October 2007.

(3) In this Order "the Children Act" means the Children Act 1989.

Transfers from the Court of Protection to a court having jurisdiction under the Children Act

2.—(1) This article applies to any proceedings in the Court of Protection which **3–084** relate to a person under 18.

(2) The Court of Protection may direct the transfer of the whole or part of the proceedings to a court having jurisdiction under the Children Act where it considers that in all the circumstances, it is just and convenient to transfer the proceedings.

(3) In making a determination, the Court of Protection must have regard to—

(a) whether the proceedings should be heard together with other proceedings that are pending in a court having jurisdiction under the Children Act;

(b) whether any order that may be made by a court having jurisdiction under that Act is likely to be a more appropriate way of dealing with the proceedings;

(c) the need to meet any requirements that would apply if the proceedings had been started in a court having jurisdiction under the Children Act; and

(d) any other matter that the court considers relevant.

(4) The Court of Protection—

(a) may exercise the power to make an order under paragraph (2) on an application or on its own initiative; and

(b) where it orders a transfer, must give reasons for its decision.

(5) Any proceedings transferred under this article—

(a) are to be treated for all purposes as if they were proceedings under the Children Act which had been started in a court having jurisdiction under that Act; and

(b) are to be dealt with after the transfer in accordance with directions given by a court having jurisdiction under that Act.

Transfers from a court having jurisdiction under the Children Act to the Court of Protection

3–085   **3.**—(1) This article applies to any proceedings in a court having jurisdiction under the Children Act which relate to a person under 18.

(2) A court having jurisdiction under the Children Act may direct the transfer of the whole or part of the proceedings to the Court of Protection where it considers that in all circumstances, it is just and convenient to transfer the proceedings.

(3) In making a determination, the court having jurisdiction under the Children Act must have regard to—

(a) whether the proceedings should be heard together with other proceedings that are pending in the Court of Protection;

(b) whether any order that may be made by the Court of Protection is likely to be a more appropriate way of dealing with the proceedings;

(c) the extent to which any order made as respects a person who lacks capacity is likely to continue to have effect when that person reaches 18; and

(d) any other matter that the court considers relevant.

(4) A court having jurisdiction under the Children Act—

(a) may exercise the power to make an order under paragraph (2) on an application or on its own initiative; and

(b) where it orders a transfer, must give reasons for its decision.

(5) Any proceedings transferred under this article—

(a) are to be treated for all purposes as if they were proceedings under the Mental Capacity Act 2005 which had been started in the Court of Protection; and

(b) are to be dealt with after the transfer in accordance with directions given by the Court of Protection.

Avoidance of double liability for fees

3–086   **4.** Any fee paid for the purpose of starting any proceedings that are transferred under article 2 or 3 is to be treated as if it were the fee that would have been payable if the proceedings had started in the court to which the transfer is made.

THE PUBLIC GUARDIAN (FEES, ETC) REGULATIONS 2007

(SI 2007/2051)

Dated June 26, 2007 and made by the Lord Chancellor under the Mental Capacity Act 2005 (c.9), sections 58(3), (4) and 65(1)(b).

Citation and commencement

1. These Regulations may be cited as the Public Guardian (Fees, etc) **3–087** Regulations 2007 and shall come into force on 1 October 2007.

Interpretation

2. In these Regulations— **3–088**

"the Act" means the Mental Capacity Act 2005; "court" means the Court of Protection;

"P" means the person in respect of whom a deputy has been appointed under section 16 of the Act; and

"Public Guardian" means the officer appointed in accordance with section 57 of the Act;

"the registers" means—
(a) the register of lasting powers of attorney,
(b) the register of enduring powers of attorney, and (c) the register of court orders appointing deputies,
established and maintained by the Public Guardian under section 58(1)(a) and (b) of and paragraph 14 of Schedule 4 to the Act.

Schedule of fees

3. The fees set out in the Schedule to these Regulations shall apply in accord- **3–089** ance with the following provisions of these Regulations.

Enduring power of attorney registration fee

4.—(1) A fee for the registration of an enduring power of attorney shall be pay- **3–090** able by the person seeking to register the enduring power of attorney under regulation 24 of the Lasting Powers of Attorney, Enduring Powers of Attorney and Public Guardian Regulations 2007 (application for registration).

(2) The fee prescribed by paragraph (1) shall be payable upon the application to register the enduring power of attorney.

Lasting power of attorney registration fee

5.—(1) A fee for the registration of a lasting power of attorney shall be payable **3–091** by the person seeking to register the lasting power of attorney under regulation 11 of the Lasting Powers of Attorney, Enduring Powers of Attorney and Public Guardian Regulations 2007 (application for registration).

(2) The fee prescribed by paragraph (1) shall be payable upon the application to register the lasting power of attorney.

Application to search the registers fee

3–092   **6.**—(1) A fee for an application to search the registers made under regulation 31 of the Lasting Powers of Attorney, Enduring Powers of Attorney and Public Guardian Regulations 2007 (disclosure of information on a register: search by the Public Guardian) shall be payable by the person making the application.

(2) The fee prescribed by paragraph (1) shall be payable upon the application to search the registers.

(3) The fee prescribed by paragraph (1) shall not be payable where the person making the application is a:

(a) registered health care professional; or

(b) a representative of a public authority.

(4) In paragraph (3) "registered health care professional" means a person who is a member of a profession regulated by a body mentioned in section 25(3) of the National Health Service Reform and Health Care Professions Act 2002.

Appointment of deputy fee

3–093   **7.**—(1) This regulation applies where—

(a) the court has appointed a deputy under section 16 of the Act (powers to make decisions and appoint deputies: general); or

(b) an existing receiver is treated as if he were a deputy appointed by the court under paragraph 1(2)(a) of Schedule 5 to the Act.

(2) Where paragraph (1) applies a fee shall be payable by P.

(3) The fee prescribed by paragraph (2) shall be payable by P within 30 days of the date of the invoice for the fee.

Appointment of deputy: supervision fees

3–094   **8.**—(1) This regulation applies where—

(a) the court has appointed a deputy under section 16 of the Act (powers to make decisions and appoint deputies: general); or

(b) an existing receiver is treated as if he were a deputy appointed by the court under paragraph 1(2)(a) of Schedule 5 to the Act.

(2) Where paragraph (1) applies the Public Guardian shall determine the level of supervision required under section 58(1)(c) of the Act.

(3) The levels of supervision are—

(a) type I (highest);

(b) type II (lower); and

(c) type III (minimal).

(4) Where the level of supervision determined by the Public Guardian in accordance with paragraph (2) is type I (highest) or type II (lower) an annual supervision fee shall be payable by P until the appointment of the deputy is terminated.

(5) Subject to paragraphs (6) and (7), the appropriate supervision fee prescribed by paragraph (2) shall be due on 31 March each year and shall be payable by P within 30 days of the date of the invoice for the fee.

(6) Where the period for which the fee prescribed by paragraph (4) is payable is less than one year, the amount of the fee payable shall be such proportion of the full fee as that period bears to one year.

(7) Where the deputy's appointment terminates, the appropriate fee prescribed by paragraph (4) shall be due on the date of termination and shall be payable within 30 days of the date of the invoice for the fee.

(8) In the event of termination of the appointment due to P's death, the appropriate fee prescribed by paragraph (2) shall be payable by P's estate.

Exemptions

9.—(1) Subject to paragraph (2) no fee shall be payable under these regulations **3–095** when, at the time when the fee would otherwise become payable, the relevant person is in receipt of any qualifying benefit.

(2) Paragraph (1) does not apply to a person who has an award of damages in excess of £16,000 which has been disregarded for the purposes of determining eligibility for that benefit.

(3) For the purposes of regulation 4 the relevant person is the donor of the enduring power of attorney.

(4) For the purposes of regulation 5 the relevant person is the donor of the lasting power of attorney.

(5) For the purposes of regulation 6 the relevant person is the person making the application.

(6) For the purposes of regulations 7 and 8 the relevant person is P.

(7) The following are qualifying benefits for the purposes of paragraph (1)—

(a) income support under the Social Security Contributions and Benefits Act 1992

(b) working tax credit, provided that—

   (i) child tax credit is being paid to the relevant person, or to a couple (as defined in section 3(5)(A) of the Tax Credits Act 2002 which includes the relevant person; or

   (ii) there is a disability element or severe disability element (or both) to the [. . .] tax credit received by the relevant person;

(c) income-based job-seeker's allowance under the Jobseekers Act 1995;

(d) guarantee credit under the State Pensions Credit Act 2002;

(e) council tax benefit under the Social Security Contributions and Benefits Act 1992; and

(f) housing benefit under the Social Security Contributions and Benefits Act 1992.

AMENDMENT
The word omitted in para. (b)(ii) was revoked by SI 2007/2616, reg.2.

Reductions and remissions in exceptional circumstances

10. Where it appears to the Public Guardian that the payment of any fee pre- **3–096** scribed by these Regulations would, owing to the exceptional circumstances of the particular case, involve undue hardship, he may reduce or remit the fee in that case.

Transitional provision

11.—(1) In respect of the administration fee that would have been payable **3–097** under rule 78 of the Court of Protection Rules 2001 on 31 March 2008, the appropriate proportion of that fee shall be due on 30 September 2007 and shall be payable within 30 days of the date of the invoice for the fee.

(2) Where the period for which the fee prescribed by paragraph (1) is payable is less than six months, the amount of the fee payable shall be such proportion of that fee as that period bears to six months.

Amendment to Schedule 7 of the Lasting Powers of Attorney, Enduring Powers of Attorney and Public Guardian Regulations 2007

12. [Not reproduced]

SCHEDULE   **Regulation 3**

FEES TO BE TAKEN

3–098

Column 1	Column 2
Enduring power of attorney registration (regulation 4)	£120.00
Lasting power of attorney registration (regulation 5)	£150.00
Application to search the registers (regulation 6)	£25.00
Appointment of deputy (regulation 7)	£125.00
Type I (highest) supervision (regulation 8)	£800.00 per annum
Type II (lower) supervision (regulation 8)	£175.00 per annum
Type III (minimal) supervision (regulation 8)	No fee

THE MENTAL CAPACITY (DEPRIVATION OF LIBERTY: APPOINTMENT OF REVELANT PERSON'S REPRESENTATIVE) REGULATIONS 2008

(SI 2008/1315)

Dated May 14, 2008, and made by the Secretary of State for Health under the Mental Capacity Act 2005 (c.9), section 65(1) and Schedule A1, paras.138 (1), 142 to 145, 148, 149 and 151.

GENERAL NOTE

Where the deprivation of the liberty of a mentally incapacitated has been authorised **3–099** under s.4A and Schedule AI to the Mental Capacity Act 2005, paragraph 139 of Schedule A1 requires that the supervisory body appoint a representative to a person in respect of whom a standard authorisation has been issued. Supervisory bodies are only able to appoint representatives who have been selected for that purpose. The role of the representative is to maintain contact with the person and to support and represent them in matters relating to their deprivation of liberty.

These Regulations provide for the selection and appointment of representatives and the circumstances in which they may be paid, by—

(a) detailing the eligibility requirements for appointment as a representative (reg.3);

(b) enabling the best interests assessor to determine whether the person deprived, or potentially deprived of, liberty ("the relevant person") has capacity to select a person to be their representative (reg. 4);

(c) enabling the relevant person to select a family member, friend or carer to be their representative, where they have capacity to make that decision (reg.5);

(d) enabling a donee or deputy of a relevant person who lacks capacity to select a representative, to select a family member, friend, carer or him or herself to be the representative, where their scope of authority permits that (reg.6);

(e) requiring that the best interests assessor confirms the eligibility for appointment of any selection made by a relevant person, donee or deputy. Where confirmation is given, the best interests assessor must recommend the selected person for appointment. Where confirmation cannot be given, the selector must be advised why that is the case and invited to make another selection (reg.7);

(f) enabling the best interests assessor to select a relevant person's family member, friend or carer as the representative when one is not, or cannot, be selected by the relevant person, a donee or a deputy (reg.8);

(g) enabling the supervisory body to select a person in a professional capacity to be a representative where one cannot be selected from the relevant person's family, friends or carers (reg.9);

(h) requiring that the procedure for appointing a representative begin as soon as a best interests assessor is selected in relation to a request for a standard authorisation or as soon as an existing representative's appointment terminates or is about to terminate (reg.10);

(i) requiring that the supervisory body only appoints a person approved by the best interests assessor, unless such approval cannot be given (reg.11);

(j) detailing the formalities of appointment and termination of appointment (regs 12 to 14); and

(k) enabling the supervisory body to pay a person who has been selected to be a representative in a professional capacity (reg.15)

Citation, commencement and application

3–100   **1.**—(1) These Regulations may be cited as the Mental Capacity (Deprivation of Liberty: Appointment of Relevant Person's Representative) Regulations 2008 and shall come into force on 3rd November 2008.

(2) These Regulations apply in relation to England only.

Interpretation

3–101   **2.** In these Regulations—

"best interests assessor" means a person selected to carry out a best interests assessment under paragraph 38 of Schedule A1 to the Act;

"donee" is a person who has a lasting power of attorney conferred on them by the relevant person, giving that donee the authority to make decisions about the relevant person's personal welfare;

"the Act" means the Mental Capacity Act 2005; and

"the relevant person's managing authority" means the managing authority that has made the application for a standard authorisation in respect of the relevant person.

PART 1

SELECTION OF REPRESENTATIVES

Selection of a person to be a representative—general

3–102   **3.**—(1) In addition to any requirements in regulations 6 to 9 and 11, a person can only be selected to be a representative if they are—

(a) 18 years of age or over;

(b) able to keep in contact with the relevant person;

(c) willing to be the relevant person's representative;

(d) not financially interested in the relevant person's managing authority;

(e) not a relative of a person who is financially interested in the managing authority;

(f) not employed by, or providing services to, the relevant person's managing authority, where the relevant person's managing authority is a care home);

(g) not employed to work in the relevant person's managing authority in a role that is, or could be, related to the relevant person's case, where the relevant person's managing authority is a hospital; and

(h) not employed to work in the supervisory body that is appointing the representative in a role that is, or could be, related to the relevant person's case.

(2) For the purposes of this regulation a "relative" means—

(a) a spouse, ex-spouse, civil partner or ex-civil partner;

(b) a person living with the relevant person as if they were a spouse or a civil partner;

(c) a parent or child;

(d) a brother or sister;

(e) a child of a person falling within sub-paragraphs (a), (b) or (d);

(f) a grandparent or grandchild;

(g) a grandparent-in-law or grandchild-in-law;

(h) an uncle or aunt;

(i) a brother-in-law or sister-in-law;
(j) a son-in-law or daughter-in-law;
(k) a first cousin; or
(l) a half-brother or half-sister.
(3) For the purposes of this regulation—
(a) the relationships in paragraph (2)(c) to (k) include step relationships;
(b) references to step relationships and in-laws in paragraph (2) are to be read in
     accordance with section 246 of the Civil Partnership Act 2004;
(c) a person has a financial interest in a managing authority where—
     (i) that person is a partner, director, other office-holder or major share-
          holder of the managing authority that has made the application for a
          standard authorisation, and
     (ii) the managing authority is a care home or independent hospital; and
(d) a major shareholder means—
     (i) any person holding one tenth or more of the issued shares in the manag-
          ing authority, where the managing authority is a company limited by
          shares, and
     (ii) in all other cases, any of the owners of the managing authority.

AMENDMENT
    Para.1(f) was substituted by SI 2008/2368, reg.2.

Determination of capacity
    4. The best interests assessor must determine whether the relevant person has **3–103**
capacity to select a representative.

Selection by the relevant person
    5.—(1) Where the best interests assessor determines that the relevant person **3–104**
has capacity, the relevant person may select a family member, friend or carer.
    (2) Where the relevant person does not wish to make a selection under para-
graph (1), regulation 8 applies.

Selection by a donee or deputy
    6.—(1) Where—   **3–105**
(a) the best interests assessor determines that the relevant person lacks capacity
     to select a representative; and
(b) the relevant person has a donee or deputy and the donee's or deputy's scope
     of authority permits the selection of a family member, friend or carer of the
     relevant person,
the donee or deputy may select such a person.
    (2) A donee or deputy may select himself or herself to be the relevant person's
representative.
    (3) Where a donee or deputy does not wish to make a selection under paragraph
(1) or (2), regulation 8 applies.

Confirmation of eligibility of family member, friend or carer and recommendation to the supervisory body
    7.—(1)The best interests assessor must confirm that a person selected under **3–106**
regulation 5(1) or 6(1) or (2) is eligible to be a representative.

(2) Where the best interests assessor confirms the selected person's eligibility under paragraph (1), the assessor must recommend the appointment of that person as a representative to the supervisory body.

(3) Where the best interests assessor is unable to confirm the selected person's eligibility under paragraph (1), the assessor must—

(a) advise the person who made the selection of that decision and give the reasons for it; and

(b) invite them to make a further selection.

Selection by the best interests assessor

3–107   **8.**—(1)The best interests assessor may select a family member, friend or carer as a representative where paragraph (2) applies.

(2) The best interests assessor may make a selection where—

(a) the relevant person has the capacity to make a selection under regulation 5(1) but does not wish to do so;

(b) the relevant person's donee or deputy does not wish to make a selection under regulation 6(1) or (2); or

(c) the relevant person lacks the capacity to make a selection and—

(i) does not have a donee or deputy, or

(ii) has a donee or deputy but the donee's or deputy's scope of authority does not permit the selection of a representative.

(3) Where the best interests assessor selects a person in accordance with paragraph (2), the assessor must recommend that person for appointment as a representative to the supervisory body.

(4) But the best interests assessor must not select a person under paragraph (2) where the relevant person, donee or deputy objects to that selection.

(5) The best interests assessor must notify the supervisory body if they do not select a person who is eligible to be a representative.

Selection by the supervisory body

3–108   **9.**—(1)Where a supervisory body is given notice under regulation 8(5), it may select a person to be the representative, who—

(a) would be performing the role in a professional capacity;

(b) has satisfactory skills and experience to perform the role;

(c) is not a family member, friend or carer of the relevant person;

(d) is not employed by, or providing services to, the relevant person's managing authority, where the relevant person's managing authority is a care home;

(e) is not employed to work in the relevant person's managing authority in a role that is, or could be, related to the relevant person's case, where the relevant person's managing authority is a hospital; and

(f) [is not employed by the supervisory body].

(2) The supervisory body must be satisfied that there is in respect of the person—

(a) an enhanced criminal record certificate issued pursuant to section 113B of the Police Act 1997 (enhanced criminal record certificates);or

(b) if the purpose for which the certificate is required is not one prescribed under subsection (2) of that section, a criminal record certificate issued pursuant to section 113A of that Act (criminal record certificates).

PART 2

APPOINTMENT OF REPRESENTATIVES

Commencement of appointment procedure

10. The procedure for appointing a representative must begin as soon as— **3–109**
(a) a best interests assessor is selected by the supervisory body for the purposes of a request for a standard authorisation; or
(b) a relevant person's representative's appointment terminates, or is to be terminated, under regulation 14 and the relevant person remains subject to a standard authorisation.

Appointment of representative

11. Except where regulation 9 applies, a supervisory body may not appoint a **3–110** representative unless the person is recommended to it under regulations 7 or 8.

Formalities of appointing a representative

12.—(1) The offer of an appointment to a representative must be made in writ- **3–111** ing and state—
(a) the duties of a representative to—
   (i) maintain contact with the relevant person,
   (ii) represent the relevant person in matters relating to, or connected with, the deprivation of liberty, and
   (iii) support the relevant person in matters relating to, or connected with, the deprivation of liberty; and
(b) the length of the period of the appointment.
(2) The representative must inform the supervisory body in writing that they are willing to accept the appointment and that they have understood the duties set out in sub-paragraph (1)(a).
(3) The appointment must be made for the period of the standard authorisation.
(4) The supervisory body must send copies of the written appointment to—
(a) the appointed person;
(b) the relevant person;
(c) the relevant person's managing authority;
(d) any donee or deputy of the relevant person;
(e) any independent mental capacity advocate appointed in accordance with sections 37 to 39D of the Act), involved in the relevant person's case; and
(f) every interested person named by the best interests assessor in their report as somebody the assessor has consulted in carrying out the assessment.

Termination of representative's appointment

13. A person ceases to be a representative if— **3–112**
(a) the person dies;
(b) the person informs the supervisory body that they are no longer willing to continue as representative;
(c) the period of the appointment ends;
(d) a relevant person who has selected a family member, friend or carer under regulation 5(1) who has been appointed as their representative informs the supervisory body that they object to the person continuing to be a representative;

(e) a donee or deputy who has selected a family member, friend or carer of the relevant person under regulation 6(1) who has been appointed as a representative informs the supervisory body that they object to the person continuing to be a representative;

(f) the supervisory body terminates the appointment because it is satisfied that the representative is not maintaining sufficient contact with the relevant person in order to support and represent them;

(g) the supervisory body terminates the appointment because it is satisfied that the representative is not acting in the best interests of the relevant person; or

(h) the supervisory body terminates the appointment because it is satisfied that the person is no longer eligible or was not eligible at the time of appointment, to be a representative.

Formalities of termination of representative's appointment

3–113　　**14.**—(1) Where a representative's appointment is to be terminated for a reason specified in paragraphs (c) to (h) of regulation 13, the supervisory body must inform the representative of—

(a) the pending termination of the appointment;

(b) the reasons for the termination of the appointment; and

(c) the date on which the appointment terminates.

(2) The supervisory body must send copies of the termination of the appointment to—

(a) the relevant person;

(b) the relevant person's managing authority;

(c) any donee or deputy of the relevant person;

(d) any independent mental capacity advocate appointed in accordance with sections 37 to 39D of the Act, involved in the relevant person's case; and

(e) every interested person named by the best interests assessor in their report as somebody the assessor has consulted in carrying out the assessment.

Payment to a representative

3–114　　**15.** A supervisory body may make payments to a representative appointed following a selection under regulation 9.

THE MENTAL CAPACITY (DEPRIVATION OF LIBERTY: STANDARD AUTHORISATIONS, ASSESSMENTS AND ORDINARY RESIDENCE) REGULATIONS 2008

(SI 2008/1858)

Dated July 9, 2008, and made by the Secretary of State for Health under s.65(1) of, and paras.31, 33(4), 47, 70, 129(3), 130 and 183(6) and (7) of Sch. A1 to, the Mental Capacity Act 2005(c.9).

GENERAL NOTE

The Mental Capacity Act 2005 provides for the deprivation of liberty of people lacking **3–115** capacity to consent to the arrangements made for their care or treatment where authorisation under section 4A of and Schedule A1 to the Act exists. Under Schedule A1, where it appears that a person who lacks capacity is detained, or is likely to be detained, in a care home or hospital, the managing authority of the care home or hospital must request an authorisation from the supervisory body. On receiving such a request the supervisory body must ensure that various assessments are carried out in relation to the individual concerned in order to determine whether it is appropriate to grant the authorisation. The supervisory body must select people to carry out those assessments in accordance with paragraph 129 of Schedule A1 and may only select people who are eligible in accordance with these Regulations which require that—

(a) all assessors are adequately insured and that the supervisory body is satisfied that they have suitable skills and have undergone a Criminal Record Bureau check (reg.3);

(b) mental health assessments can only be carried out by medical practitioners who have been approved under section 12 of the Mental Health Act 1983 or registered medical practitioners who have similar mental health experience to practitioners approved under section 12 of the Mental Health Act and the supervisory body is satisfied that the person has the required training (reg.4);

(c) best interests assessments can only be carried out by mental health practitioners who have been approved under section 114(1) of the Mental Health Act, certain health professionals or social workers, with specialised and relevant skills and with at least two years post registration experience. The supervisory body must be satisfied that the person has the required training (reg.5);

(d) mental capacity assessments can only be carried out by people who are eligible to carry out a mental health assessment or a best interests assessment (reg.6);

(e) eligibility assessments can only be carried out by medical practitioners who have been approved under section 12 of the Mental Health Act or an approved mental health professional and the supervisory body is satisfied that the person has the required training (reg.7);

(f) age assessments and no refusals assessments can only be carried out by people who are

(g) eligible to carry out a best interests assessment (regs 8 and 9).

These Regulations provide some limitations on the ability of a supervisory body to select people to carry out assessments, even if the person meets the eligibility requirements. They do so by preventing the selection of—

(a) people who have, or are related to a person who has, a personal financial interest in the care of the individual in need of assessment or are a relative of the individual (regs 10 and 11); and

(b) a best interests assessor who is involved in the care of the individual in need of assessment, or is employed by the supervisory body where the managing authority and the supervisory body are the same (reg.12).

These Regulations contain provisions relating to the assessments required in response to a request for—

(a) a standard authorisation by requiring that all of the required assessments be completed within 21 days from the date on which the supervisory body receives the request, except where an urgent authorisation is in force, in which case assessments must be completed during the period of the urgent authorisation (reg.13); and

(b) a decision as to whether or not there is an unauthorised deprivation of liberty by requiring that the assessment be completed within 7 days from the date the supervisory body receives the request (reg.14).

Regulation 15 enables the person carrying out the eligibility assessment to require the person conducting the best interests assessment to provide them with information relevant to their assessment.

Regulation 16 specifies the information that must be included in a request for a standard authorisation and information that must be included if it is available or could reasonably be obtained by the managing authority.

Paragraph 182 of Sch.A1 makes provision for identifying the supervisory body where the managing authority is a care home. In the case of a care home the supervisory body will be the local authority in which the person is ordinarily resident. Part 6 of these Regulations applies in specified circumstances where a local authority wishes to dispute that it is the supervisory body (reg.17).

Regulation 18 sets out who is to act as supervisory body until the question of ordinary residence is determined. Regulation 19 provides for the effect of a change in supervisory body following the determination of a question as to the ordinary residence of a relevant person.

PART 1

PRELIMINARY

Citation, commencement and application

3–116 **1.**—(1) These Regulations may be cited as the Mental Capacity (Deprivation of Liberty: Standard Authorisations, Assessments and Ordinary Residence) Regulations 2008 and shall come into force on 3rd November 2008.

(2) These Regulations apply in relation to England only.

Interpretation

3–117 **2.** In these Regulations—

"approved mental health professional" means a person approved under section 114(1) of the Mental Health Act 1983 to act as an approved mental health professional for the purposes of that Act;

"best interests assessor" means a person selected to carry out a best interests assessment under paragraph 38 of Schedule A1 to the Act;

"General Social Care Council" has the meaning given by section 54(1) of the Care Standards Act 2000; and

"the Act" means the Mental Capacity Act 2005.

PART 2

ELIGIBILITY TO CARRY OUT ASSESSMENTS

Eligibility—general

3.—(1) In addition to any requirement in regulations 4 to 9, a person is eligible **3–118**
to carry out an assessment where paragraphs (2) to (4) are met.

(2) The person must—
(a) be insured in respect of any liabilities that might arise in connection with
    carrying out the assessment; and
(b) satisfy the supervisory body that he or she has such insurance.

(3) The supervisory body must be satisfied that the person has the skills and
experience appropriate to the assessment to be carried out which must include,
but are not limited to, the following—
(a) an applied knowledge of the Mental Capacity Act 2005 and related Code of
    Practice; and
(b) the ability to keep appropriate records and to provide clear and reasoned
    reports in accordance with legal requirements and good practice.

(4) The supervisory body must be satisfied that there is in respect of the
person—

(a) an enhanced criminal record certificate issued under section 113B of the
    Police Act 1997 (enhanced criminal record certificates); or
(b) if the purpose for which the certificate is required is not one prescribed
    under subsection (2) of that section, a criminal record certificate issued pur-
    suant to section 113A of that Act (criminal record certificates).

Eligibility to carry out a mental health assessment

4.—(1) A person is eligible to carry out a mental health assessment if para- **3–119**
graphs (2) and (3) are met.

(2) The person must be—
(a) approved under section 12 of the Mental Health Act 1983; or
(b) a registered medical practitioner who the supervisory body is satisfied has at
    least three years post registration experience in the diagnosis or treatment of
    mental disorder.

(3) The supervisory body must be satisfied that the person has successfully
completed the Deprivation of Liberty Safeguards Mental Health Assessors training programme made available by the Royal College of Psychiatrists

(4) Except in the 12 month period beginning with the date the person has successfully completed the programme referred to in paragraph (3), the supervisory
body must be satisfied that the person has, in the 12 months prior to selection,
completed further training relevant to their role as a mental health assessor.

Eligibility to carry out a best interests assessment

5.—(1) A person is eligible to carry out a best interests assessment if paragraphs **3–120**
(2) and (3) are met.

(2) The person must be one of the following—
(a) an approved mental health professional;
(b) a social worker registered with the General Social Care Council;

(c) a first level nurse, registered in Sub-Part 1 of the Nurses Part of the Register maintained under article 5 of the Nursing and Midwifery Order 2001;

(d) an occupational therapist registered in Part 6 of the register maintained under article 5 of the Health Professions Order 2001; or

(e) a chartered psychologist who is listed in the British Psychological Society's Register of Chartered Psychologists and who holds a relevant practising certificate issued by that Society.

(3) The supervisory body must be satisfied that the person—

(a) is not suspended from the register or list relevant to the person's profession mentioned in paragraph (2);

(b) has at least two years post registration experience in one of the professions mentioned in paragraph (2);

(c) has successfully completed training that has been approved by the Secretary of State to be a best interests assessor;

(d) except in the 12 month period beginning with the date the person has successfully completed the training referred to in sub-paragraph (c), the supervisory body must be satisfied that the person has, in the 12 months prior to selection, completed further training relevant to their role as a best interests assessor; and

(e) has the skills necessary to obtain, evaluate and analyse complex evidence and differing views and to weigh them appropriately in decision making.

Eligibility to carry out a mental capacity assessment

3–121   **6.** A person is eligible to carry out a mental capacity assessment if that person is eligible to carry out—

(a) a mental health assessment; or

(b) a best interests assessment.

Eligibility to carry out an eligibility assessment

3–122   **7.** A person is eligible to carry out an eligibility assessment if that person is—

(a) approved under section 12 of the Mental Health Act 1983 and is eligible to carry out a mental health assessment; or

(b) an approved mental health professional and is eligible to carry out a best interests assessment.

Eligibility to carry out an age assessment

3–123   **8.** A person is eligible to carry out an age assessment if that person is eligible to carry out a best interests assessment.

Eligibility to carry out a no refusals assessment

3–124   **9.** A person is eligible to carry out a no refusals assessment if that person is eligible to carry out a best interests assessment.

PART 3

SELECTION OF ASSESSORS

Selection of assessors–relatives

3–125   **10.**—(1) A supervisory body must not select a person to carry out an assessment if the person is—

(a) a relative of the relevant person; or

(b) a relative of a person who is financially interested in the care of the relevant person.

(2) For the purposes of this regulation a "relative" means—

(a) a spouse, ex-spouse, civil partner or ex-civil partner;

(b) a person living with the relevant person as if they were a spouse or a civil partner;

(c) a parent or child;

(d) a brother or sister;

(e) a child of a person falling within sub-paragraphs (a), (b) or (d);

(f) a grandparent or grandchild;

(g) a grandparent-in-law or grandchild-in-law;

(h) an uncle or aunt;

(i) a brother-in-law or sister-in-law;

(j) a son-in-law or daughter-in-law;

(k) a first cousin; or

(l) a half-brother or half-sister.

(3) For the purposes of this regulation—

(a) the relationships in paragraph (2)(c) to (k) include step relationships;

(b) references to step relationships and in-laws in paragraph (2) are to be read in accordance with section 246 of the Civil Partnership Act 2004; and

(c) financial interest has the meaning given in regulation 11.

Selection of assessors—financial interest

11.—(1)A supervisory body must not select a person to carry out an assessment **3–126** where the person has a financial interest in the case.

(2) A person has a financial interest in a case where—

(a) that person is a partner, director, other office-holder or major shareholder of the managing authority that has made the application for a standard authorisation; and

(b) the managing authority is a care home or independent hospital.

(3) A major shareholder means—

(a) any person holding one tenth or more of the issued shares in the managing authority, where the managing authority is a company limited by shares; and

(b) in all other cases, any of the owners of the managing authority.

Selection of best interests assessors

12.—(1) A supervisory body must not select a person to carry out a best inter- **3–127** ests assessment if that person is involved in the care, or making decisions about the care, of the relevant person.

(2) Where the managing authority and supervisory body are both the same body, the supervisory body must not select a person to carry out a best interests assessment who is employed by it or who is providing services to it.

PART 4

ASSESSMENTS

Time frame for assessments

3–128   **13.**—(1)Except as provided in paragraph (2), all assessments required for a standard authorisation must be completed within the period of 21 days beginning with the date that the supervisory body receives a request for such an authorisation.

(2) Where a supervisory body receives a request for a standard authorisation and the managing authority has given an urgent authorisation under paragraph 76 of Schedule A1 to the Act, the assessments required for that standard authorisation must be completed within the period during which the urgent authorisation is in force.

Time limit for carrying out an assessment to decide whether or not there is an unauthorised deprivation of liberty

3–129   **14.** Subject to paragraph 69(3) to (5) of Schedule A1 to the Act, an assessment required under that paragraph must be completed within the period of 7 days beginning with the date that the supervisory body receives the request from an eligible person.

Relevant eligibility information

3–130   **15.**—(1) This regulation applies where an individual is being assessed and the eligibility assessor and the best interests assessor are not the same person.

(2) The eligibility assessor must request that the best interests assessor provides any relevant eligibility information that the best interests assessor may have.

(3) The best interests assessor must comply with any request made under this regulation.

(4) In this regulation "eligibility assessor" means a person selected to carry out the eligibility assessment under paragraph 46 of Schedule A1 to the Act.

PART 5

REQUESTS FOR A STANDARD AUTHORISATION

Information to be provided in a request for a standard authorisation

3–131   **16.**—(1) A request for a standard authorisation must include the following information—

(a) the name and gender of the relevant person;

(b) the age of the relevant person or, where this is not known, whether the managing authority believes that the relevant person is aged 18 years or older;

(c) the address and telephone number where the relevant person is currently located;

(d) the name, address and telephone number of the managing authority and the name of the person within the managing authority who is dealing with the request;

(e) the purpose for which the authorisation is requested;

(f) the date from which the standard authorisation is sought; and

(g) whether the managing authority has given an urgent authorisation under paragraph 76 of Schedule A1 to the Act and, if so, the date on which it expires.

(2) Except as provided for in paragraph (3), a request for a standard authorisation must include the following information if it is available or could reasonably be obtained by the managing authority—

(a) any medical information relating to the relevant person's health that the managing authority considers to be relevant to the proposed restrictions to the relevant person's liberty;

(b) the diagnosis of the mental disorder (within the meaning of the Mental Health Act 1983 but disregarding any exclusion for persons with learning disability) that the relevant person is suffering from;

(c) any relevant care plans and relevant needs assessments;

(d) the racial, ethnic or national origins of the relevant person;

(e) whether the relevant person has any special communication needs;

(f) details of the proposed restrictions on the relevant person's liberty;

(g) whether section 39A of the Act (person becomes subject to Schedule A1) applies;

(h) where the purpose of the proposed restrictions to the relevant person's liberty is to give treatment, whether the relevant person has made an advance decision that may be valid and applicable to some or all of that treatment;

(i) whether the relevant person is subject to—
   (i) the hospital treatment regime,
   (ii) the community treatment regime, or
   (iii) the guardianship regime;

(j) the name, address and telephone number of—
   (i) anyone named by the relevant person as someone to be consulted about his welfare,
   (ii) anyone engaged in caring for the person or interested in his welfare,
   (iii) any donee of a lasting power of attorney granted by the person,
   (iv) any deputy appointed for the person by the court, and
   (v) any independent mental capacity advocate appointed in accordance with sections 37 to 39D of the Act; and

(k) whether there is an existing authorisation in relation to the detention of the relevant person and, if so, the date of the expiry of that authorisation.

(3) Where—

(a) there is an existing authorisation in force in relation to the detention of the relevant person; and

(b) the managing authority makes a request in accordance with paragraph 30 of Schedule A1 to the Act for a further standard authorisation in relation to the same relevant person,

the request need not include any of the information mentioned in paragraph (2)(a) to (j) if that information remains the same as that supplied in relation to the request for the existing authorisation.

(4) In this regulation "existing authorisation" has the same meaning as in paragraph 29 of Schedule A1 to the Act.

PART 6

SUPERVISORY BODIES: CARE HOMES

Disputes about the Place of Ordinary Residence

Application and Interpretation of Part 6

3–132   **17.**—(1) This Part applies where—
  (a) a local authority ("local authority A") receives a request from—
    (i) a care home for a standard authorisation under paragraph 24, 25 or 30 of Schedule A1 to the Act, or
    (ii) an eligible person to decide whether or not there is an unauthorised deprivation of liberty in a care home under paragraph 68 of Schedule A1 to the Act;
  (b) local authority A wishes to dispute that it is the supervisory body; and
  (c) a question as to the ordinary residence of the relevant person is to be determined by the Secretary of State under paragraph 183 of Schedule A1 to the Act.
  (2) In this Part—
  (a) "local authority A" has the meaning given in paragraph (1); and
  (b) "local authority C" has the meaning given in regulation 18(2).

Arrangements where there is a question as to the ordinary residence

3–133   **18.**—(1) Local authority A must act as supervisory body in relation to a request mentioned in regulation 17(1)(a) until the determination of the question as to the ordinary residence of the relevant person.
  (2) But where another local authority ("local authority C") agrees to act as the supervisory body in place of local authority A, that local authority shall become the supervisory body until the determination of the question as to the ordinary residence of the relevant person.
  (3) When the question about the ordinary residence of the relevant person has been determined, the local authority which has been identified as the supervisory body shall become the supervisory body.

Effect of change in supervisory body following determination of any question about ordinary residence

3–134   **19.**—(1) Where the question of ordinary residence of the relevant person is determined in accordance with paragraph 183(3) of Schedule A1 to the Act, and another local authority ("local authority B") becomes the supervisory body in place of local authority A or local authority C, as the case may be, paragraphs (3) to (6) shall apply.
  (2) Where the question of ordinary residence of the relevant person is determined in accordance with paragraph 183(3) of Schedule A1 to the Act and local authority C remains the supervisory body, paragraphs (7) to (9) shall apply.
  (3) Local authority B shall be treated as the supervisory body that received the request mentioned in regulation 17(1)(a) and must comply with the time limits specified in—
  (a) regulation 13 for carrying out the assessments required for a standard authorisation; or

(b) regulation 14 for carrying out an assessment required under paragraph 69 of Schedule A1 to the Act,

as the case may be, where the assessments have still to be completed.

(4) Anything done by or in relation to local authority A or local authority C in connection with the authorisation or request, as the case may be, has effect, so far as is necessary for continuing its effect after the change, as if done by or in relation to local authority B.

(5) Anything which relates to the authorisation or request and which is in the process of being done by or in relation to local authority A or local authority C at the time of the change may be continued by or in relation to local authority B.

(6) But—

(a) local authority A or local authority C does not, by virtue of this regulation, cease to be liable for anything done by it in connection with the authorisation or request before the change; and

(b) local authority B does not, by virtue of this regulation, become liable for any such thing.

(7) Local authority C shall be treated as the supervisory body that received the request mentioned in regulation 17(1)(a) and must comply with the time limits specified in—

(a) regulation 13 for carrying out the assessments required for a standard authorisation; or

(b) regulation 14 for carrying out an assessment required under paragraph 69 of Schedule A1 to the Act,

as the case may be, where the assessments have still to be completed.

(8) Anything done by or in relation to local authority A in connection with the authorisation or request, as the case may be, has effect, so far as is necessary for continuing its effect after the change, as if done by or in relation to local authority C.

(9) Anything which relates to the authorisation or request and which is in the process of being done by or in relation to local authority A at the time of the change may be continued by or in relation to local authority C.

(10) But—

(a) local authority A does not, by virtue of this regulation, cease to be liable for anything done by it in connection with the authorisation or request before the change; and

(b) local authority C does not, by virtue of this regulation, become liable for any such thing.

PART 4

PRACTICE AND PROCEDURE

THE COURT OF PROTECTION RULES 2007

(SI 2007/1744)

Dated June 25, 2007 and made by the President of the Family Division of the High Court with the agreement of the Lord Chancellor under the Mental Capacity Act 2005 (c.9) ss.49(5), 50(2), 51, 53(2) and (4), 55, 56 and 65(1), and in accordance with the Constitutional Reform Act 2005 (c.4), Sch.1, Pt.1.

GENERAL NOTE

These Rules set out the practice and procedure to be followed in the new Court of **4–001** Protection. Section 45 of the Mental Capacity Act 2005 establishes a new, superior court of record called the Court of Protection which replaces the office of the Supreme Court known as the Court of Protection. These Rules revoke the rules governing procedure in the former Court of Protection (the Court of Protection Rules 2001 (SI 2001/824)) and the Court of Protection (Enduring Power of Attorney Rules) 2001 (SI 2001/825).

Part 2 of the Rules sets out the overriding objective that is to be applied whenever the court exercises its powers under the Rules, or interprets any rule or practice direction. Part 3 contains provisions for interpreting the Rules and for the Civil Procedure Rules 1998 to be applied insofar as may be necessary to further the overriding objective. Part 4 makes provision as to court documents, including the requirement for certain documents to be verified by a statement of truth. Part 5 sets out the court's general case management powers, and includes the power to dispense with the requirement of any rule. The Rules provide procedures for serving documents (Part 6), notifying the person who lacks capacity and who is the subject matter of the application of certain documents and events (Part 7), seeking permission to start proceedings (Part 8), starting proceedings (Part 9), making interim applications and applications within proceedings (Part 10), as to how applications will be dealt with (Part 12) and as to hearings (Part 13), including provisions as to publication of information and as to privacy and publicity of proceedings.

The Rules set out procedures to be followed in relation to evidence (Parts 14 and 15), disclosure (Part 16), appointment of litigation friends (Part 17), change of solicitor (Part 18), costs (Part 19), appeals (Part 20), the enforcement of orders (Part 21) and transitory and transitional matters (Part 22). The detail of the transitional and transitory procedures is provided in the practice directions. The fees to be charged in connection with the Court are set out in the Court of Protection Fees Order 2007 (SI 2007/1745).

Practice Directions

The practice directions that have been issued to supplement these Rules are noted in the General Note to the relevant Part. All of the practice directions that have been issued can be accessed in the forms and booklets section of the website of the Office of the Public Guardian (see Annex A).

Forms

The following forms have been prescribed for use in the Court of Protection. They can be downloaded from the website of the Office of the Public Guardian.

COP1	Application Form
COP1A	Annex A: Supporting information for property and affairs applications
COP1B	Annex B: Supporting information for health and welfare applications
COP2	Permission form
COP3	Assessment of capacity
COP4	Deputy's declaration
COP5	Acknowledgement of service / notification
COP7	Application to object to the registration of a Lasting Power of Attorney (LPA)
COP8	Application relating to the registration of an enduring power of attorney (EPA)
COP9	Application notice for applications within proceedings
COP10	Application notice for applications to be joined as a party
COP12	Special undertaking by trustees
COP14	Proceedings about you in the Court of Protection
COP14A	Guidance notes on completing form COP14
COP15	Notice that an application form has been issued
COP15A	Guidance notes for completing form COP15
COP17	Request for directions relating to an objection to the registration of an Enduring Power of Attorney
COP20	Certificate of service/non-service. Certificate of notification/ non-notification
COP22	Certificate of suitability of litigation friend
COP23	Certificate of failure or refusal of witness to attend before an examiner
COP24	Witness statement
COP25	Affidavit
COP29	Notice of hearing for committal order
COP30	Notice of change of solicitor
COP31	Notice of intention to file evidence by deposition
COP28	Notice of hearing
COP35	Appellants notice
COP36	Respondents notice
COP37	Skeleton Argument

SI 2007/1744

CONTENTS

PART 9

HOW TO START PROCEEDINGS

Initial steps

Steps following issue of application form

Responding to an application

The parties to the proceedings

PART 10

APPLICATIONS WITHIN PROCEEDINGS

Interim Remedies

PART 11

HUMAN RIGHTS

PART 12

DEALING WITH APPLICATIONS

Allocation of proceedings

Disputing the jurisdiction of the court

Participation in hearings

Reconsideration of court orders

PART 13

HEARINGS

Private hearings

Power to order a public hearing

Supplementary

PART 14

ADMISSIONS, EVIDENCE AND DEPOSITIONS

Admissions

PART 16

DISCLOSURE

PART 17

LITIGATION FRIEND

PART 18

CHANGE OF SOLICITOR

PART 19

COSTS

PART 23

MISCELLANEOUS

PART 1

PRELIMINARY

Title and commencement
1. These Rules may be cited as the Court of Protection Rules 2007 and come **4–002**
into force on 1 October 2007.

Revocations
2. The following rules are revoked— **4–003**
(a) the Court of Protection Rules 2001; and
(b) the Court of Protection (Enduring Powers of Attorney) Rules 2001.

PART 2

THE OVERRIDING OBJECTIVE

The overriding objective
3.—(1) These Rules have the overriding objective of enabling the court to deal **4–004**
with a case justly, having regard to the principles contained in the Act.
(2) The court will seek to give effect to the overriding objective when it—
(a) exercises any power under these Rules; or
(b) interprets any rule or practice direction.
(3) Dealing with a case justly includes, so far as is practicable—
(a) ensuring that it is dealt with expeditiously and fairly;
(b) ensuring that P's interests and position are properly considered;
(c) dealing with the case in ways which are proportionate to the nature, importance and complexity of the issues;
(d) ensuring that the parties are on an equal footing;
(e) saving expense; and
(f) allotting to it an appropriate share of the court's resources, while taking
account of the need to allot resources to other cases.

The duty of the parties
4. The parties are required to help the court to further the overriding objective. **4–005**

Court's duty to manage cases
5.—(1) The court will further the overriding objective by actively managing **4–006**
cases.
(2) Active case management includes—
(a) encouraging the parties to co-operate with each other in the conduct of the
proceedings;
(b) identifying at an early stage—
(i) the issues; and
(ii) who should be a party to the proceedings;
(c) deciding promptly—
(i) which issues need a full investigation and hearing and which do not; and
(ii) the procedure to be followed in the case;
(d) deciding the order in which issues are to be resolved;

   (e) encouraging the parties to use an alternative dispute resolution procedure if the court considers that appropriate;

   (f) fixing timetables or otherwise controlling the progress of the case;

   (g) considering whether the likely benefits of taking a particular step justify the cost of taking it;

   (h) dealing with as many aspects of the case as the court can on the same occasion;

   (i) dealing with the case without the parties needing to attend at court;

   (j) making use of technology; and

   (k) giving directions to ensure that the case proceeds quickly and efficiently.

PART 3

INTERPRETATION AND GENERAL PROVISIONS

Interpretation

4–007   **6.** In these Rules—

"the Act" means the Mental Capacity Act 2005;

"applicant" means a person who makes, or who seeks permission to make, an application to the court;

"application form" means the document that is to be used to begin proceedings in accordance with Part 9 of these Rules or any other provision of these Rules or the practice directions which requires the use of an application form;

"application notice" means the document that is to be used to make an application in accordance with Part 10 of these Rules or any other provision of these Rules or the practice directions which requires the use of an application notice;

"attorney" means the person appointed as such by an enduring power of attorney created, or purporting to have been created, in accordance with the regulations mentioned in paragraph 2 of Schedule 4 to the Act;

"business day" means a day other than—

   (a) a Saturday, Sunday, Christmas Day or Good Friday; or

   (b) a bank holiday in England and Wales, under the Banking and Financial Dealings Act 1971;

"child" means a person under 18;

"court" means the Court of Protection;

"deputy" means a deputy appointed under the Act; "donee" means the donee of a lasting power of attorney;

"donor" means the donor of a lasting power of attorney, except where this expression is used in rule 68 or 201(5) (where it means the donor of an enduring power of attorney);

"enduring power of attorney" means an instrument created in accordance with such of the regulations mentioned in paragraph 2 of Schedule 4 to the Act as applied when it was executed;

"filing" in relation to a document means delivering it, by post or otherwise, to the court office; "judge" means a judge nominated to be a judge of the court under the Act;

"lasting power of attorney" has the meaning given in section 9 of the Act;

"legal representative" means a barrister or a solicitor, solicitor's employee or other authorised litigator (as defined in the Courts and Legal Services Act 1990 who has been instructed to act for a party in relation to any application;

"LSC funded client" means an individual who receives services funded by the Legal Services Commission as part of the Community Legal Service within the meaning of Part I of the Access to Justice Act 1999);

"order" includes a declaration made by the court;

"P" means any person (other than a protected party) who lacks or, so far as consistent with the context, is alleged to lack capacity to make a decision or decisions in relation to any matter that is the subject of an application to the court and references to a person who lacks capacity are to be construed in accordance with the Act;

"party" is to be construed in accordance with rule 73;

"permission form" means the form that is to be used to make an application for permission to begin proceedings in accordance with Part 8 of these Rules;

"personal welfare" is to be construed in accordance with section 17 of the Act;

"President" and "Vice-President" refer to those judges appointed as such under section 46(3)(a) and (b) of the Act;

"property and affairs" is to be construed in accordance with section 18 of the Act;

"protected party" means a party or an intended party (other than P or a child) who lacks capacity to conduct the proceedings;

"respondent" means a person who is named as a respondent in the application form or notice, as the case may be;

"Senior Judge" means the judge who has been nominated to be Senior Judge under section 46(4) of the Act, and references in these Rules to a circuit judge include the Senior Judge;

"Visitor" means a person appointed as such by the Lord Chancellor under section 61 of the Act.

Court officers

7.—(1) Where these Rules permit or require the court to perform an act of a **4–008** purely formal or administrative character, that act may be performed by a court officer.

(2) A requirement that a court officer carry out any act at the request of any person is subject to the payment of any fee required by a fees order for the carrying out of that act.

Computation of time

4–009   **8.** This rule shows how to calculate any period of time which is specified—

(a) by these Rules;

(b) by a practice direction; or

(c) in an order or direction of the court.

(2) A period of time expressed as a number of days must be computed as clear days.

(3) In this rule "clear days" means that in computing the number of days—

(a) the day on which the period begins; and

(b) if the end of the period is defined by reference to an event, the day on which that event occurs,

are not included.

(4) Where the specified period is 7 days or less, and would include a day which is not a business day, that day does not count.

(5) When the specified period for doing any act at the court office ends on a day on which the office is closed, that act will be done in time if done on the next day on which the court office is open.

Application of the Civil Procedure Rules

4–010   **9.** In any case not expressly provided for by these Rules or the practice directions made under them, the Civil Procedure Rules 1998 (including any practice directions made under them) may be applied with any necessary modifications, insofar as is necessary to further the overriding objective.

PART 4

Practice Directions

4A Court Documents

4B Statements of Truth

COURT DOCUMENTS

Documents used in court proceedings

4–011   **10.**—(1) The court will seal or otherwise authenticate with the stamp of the court the following documents on issue—

(a) a permission form;

(b) an application form;

(c) an application notice;

(d) an order; and

(e) any other document which a rule or practice direction requires to be sealed or stamped.

(2) Where these Rules or any practice direction require a document to be signed, that requirement is satisfied if the signature is printed by computer or other mechanical means.

(3) A practice direction may make provision for documents to be filed or sent to the court by—

(a) facsimile; or

(b) other means.

Documents required to be verified by a statement of truth

11.—(1) The following documents must be verified by a statement of truth— **4–012**
(a) a permission form, an application form or an application notice, where the applicant seeks to rely upon matters set out in the document as evidence;
(b) a witness statement;
(c) a certificate of—
    (i) service or non-service; or
    (ii) notification or non-notification;
(d) a deputy's declaration; and
(e) any other document required by a rule or practice direction to be so verified.
(2) Subject to paragraph (3), a statement of truth is a statement that—
(a) the party putting forward the document;
(b) in the case of a witness statement, the maker of the witness statement; or
(c) in the case of a certificate referred to in paragraph (1)(c), the person who signs the certificate,
believes that the facts stated in the document being verified are true.
(3) If a party is conducting proceedings with a litigation friend, the statement of truth in—
(a) a permission form;
(b) an application form; or
(c) an application notice,
is a statement that the litigation friend believes the facts stated in the document being verified are true.
(4) The statement of truth must be signed—
(a) in the case of a permission form, an application form or an application notice—
    (i) by the party or litigation friend; or
    (ii) by the legal representative on behalf of the party or litigation friend; and
(b) in the case of a witness statement, by the maker of the statement.
(5) A statement of truth which is not contained in the document which it verifies must clearly identify that document.
(6) A statement of truth in a permission form, an application form or an application notice may be made by—
(a) a person who is not a party; or
(b) two or more parties jointly,
where this is permitted by a relevant practice direction.

Failure to verify a document

12. If a permission form, application form or application notice is not verified **4–013** by a statement of truth, the applicant may not rely upon the document as evidence of any of the matters set out in it unless the court permits.

Failure to verify a witness statement

13. If a witness statement is not verified by a statement of truth, it shall not be **4–014** admissible in evidence unless the court permits.

False statements

14.—(1) Proceedings for contempt of court may be brought against a person if **4–015** he makes, or causes to be made, a false statement in a document verified by a statement of truth without an honest belief in its truth.

(2) Proceedings under this rule may be brought only—

(a) by the Attorney General; or

(b) with the permission of the court.

Personal details

4–016 **15.**—(1) Where a party does not wish to reveal—

(a) his home address or telephone number;

(b) P's home address or telephone number;

(c) the name of the person with whom P is living (if that person is not the applicant); or

(d) the address or telephone number of his place of business, or the place of business of any of the persons mentioned in sub-paragraphs (b) or (c),

he must provide those particulars to the court.

(2) Where paragraph (1) applies, the particulars given will not be revealed to any person unless the court so directs.

(3) Where a party changes his home address during the course of the proceedings, he must give notice of the change to the court.

(4) Where a party does not reveal his home address, he must nonetheless provide an address for service which must be within the jurisdiction of the court.

Supply of documents to a party from court records

4–017 **16.** Unless the court orders otherwise, a party to proceedings may inspect or obtain from the records of the court a copy of—

(a) any document filed by a party to the proceedings; or

(b) any communication in the proceedings between the court and—

(i) a party to the proceedings; or

(ii) another person.

Supply of documents to a non-party from court records

4–018 **17.**—(1) Subject to rules 20 and 92(2), a person who is not a party to proceedings may inspect or obtain from the court records a copy of any judgment or order given or made in public.

(2) The court may, on an application made to it, authorise a person who is not a party to proceedings to—

(a) inspect any other documents in the court records; or

(b) obtain a copy of any such documents, or extracts from such documents.

(3) A person making an application for an authorisation under paragraph (2) must do so in accordance with Part 10.

(4) Before giving an authorisation under paragraph (2), the court will consider whether any document is to be provided on an edited basis.

Subsequent use of court documents

4–019 **18.**—(1) Where a document has been filed or disclosed, a party to whom it was provided may use the document only for the purpose of the proceedings in which it was filed or disclosed, except where—

(a) the document has been read to or by the court or referred to at a public hearing; or

(b) the court otherwise permits.

(2) Paragraph (1)(a) is subject to any order of the court made under rule 92(2).

Editing information in court documents

19.—(1) A party may apply to the court for an order that a specified part of a **4–020** document is to be edited prior to the document's service or disclosure.

(2) An order under paragraph (1) may be made at any time.

(3) Where the court makes an order under this rule any subsequent use of that document in the proceedings shall be of the document as edited, unless the court directs otherwise.

(4) An application under this rule must be made in accordance with Part 10.

Public Guardian to be supplied with court documents relevant to supervision of deputies

20.—(1) This rule applies in any case where the court makes an order— **4–021**

(a) appointing a person to act as a deputy; or

(b) varying an order under which a deputy has been appointed.

(2) Subject to paragraphs (3) and (6), the Public Guardian is entitled to be supplied with a copy of qualifying documents if he reasonably considers that it is necessary for him to have regard to them in connection with the discharge of his functions under section 58 of the Act in relation to the supervision of deputies.

(3) The court may direct that the right to be supplied with documents under paragraph (2) does not apply in relation to such one or more documents, or descriptions of documents, as the court may specify.

(4) A direction under paragraph (3) or (6) may be given—

(a) either on the court's own initiative or on an application made to it; and

(b) either—

    (i) at the same time as the court makes the order which appoints the deputy, or which varies it; or

    (ii) subsequently.

(5) "Qualifying documents" means documents which—

(a) are filed in court in connection with the proceedings in which the court makes the order referred to in paragraph (1); and

(b) are relevant to—

    (i) the decision to appoint the deputy;

    (ii) any powers conferred on him;

    (iii) any duties imposed on him; or

    (iv) any other terms applying to those powers and duties which are contained in the order.

(6) The court may direct that any document is to be provided to the Public Guardian on an edited basis.

Provision of court order to Public Guardian

21. Any order of the court requiring the Public Guardian to do something, or **4–022** not to do something, will be served by the court on the Public Guardian as soon as practicable and in any event not later than 7 days after the order was made.

Amendment of application

22.—(1) The court may allow or direct an applicant, at any stage of the pro- **4–023** ceedings, to amend his application form or notice.

(2) The amendment may be effected by making in writing the necessary alterations to the application form or notice, but if the amendments are so numerous or of such a nature or length that written alteration would make it difficult or inconvenient to read, a fresh document amended as allowed or directed may be issued.

Clerical mistakes or slips

4–024   **23.** The court may at any time correct any clerical mistakes in an order or direction or any error arising in an order or direction from any accidental slip or omission.

Endorsement of amendment

4–025   **24.** Where an application form or notice, order or direction has been amended under this Part, a note shall be placed on it showing the date on which it was amended and the alteration shall be sealed.

PART 5

GENERAL CASE MANAGEMENT POWERS

The court's general powers of case management

4–026   **25.**—(1) The list of powers in this rule is in addition to any powers given to the court by any other rule or practice direction or by any other enactment or any powers it may otherwise have.

(2) The court may—

(a) extend or shorten the time for compliance with any rule, practice direction, or court order or direction (even if an application for extension is made after the time for compliance has expired);

(b) adjourn or bring forward a hearing;

(c) require P, a party, a party's legal representative or litigation friend, to attend court;

(d) hold a hearing and receive evidence by telephone or any other method of direct oral communication;

(e) stay the whole or part of any proceedings or judgment either generally or until a specified date or event;

(f) consolidate proceedings;

(g) hear two or more applications on the same occasion;

(h) direct a separate hearing of any issue;

(i) decide the order in which issues are to be heard;

(j) exclude an issue from consideration;

(k) dismiss or give judgment on an application after a decision is made on a preliminary basis;

(l) direct any party to file and serve an estimate of costs; and

(m) take any step or give any direction for the purpose of managing the case and furthering the overriding objective.

(3) A judge to whom a matter is allocated may, if he considers that the matter is one which ought properly to be dealt with by another judge, transfer the matter to such a judge.

(4) Where the court gives directions it may take into account whether or not a party has complied with any rule or practice direction.

(5) The court may make any order it considers appropriate even if a party has not sought that order.

(6) A power of the court under these Rules to make an order includes a power to vary or revoke the order;

(7) Rules 25.12 to 25.15 of the Civil Procedure Rules 1998 (which make provision about security for costs) apply in proceedings to which these Rules apply as if the references in those Rules to "defendant" and "claimant" were to "respondent" and "applicant" respectively.

Court's power to dispense with requirement of any rule

26. In addition to its general powers and the powers listed in rule 25, the court **4–027** may dispense with the requirement of any rule.

Exercise of powers on the court's own initiative

27.—(1) Except where these Rules or some other enactment make different **4–028** provision, the court may exercise its powers on its own initiative.

(2) The court may make an order on its own initiative without hearing the parties or giving them the opportunity to make representations.

(3) Where the court proposes to make an order on its own initiative it may give the parties and any person it thinks fit an opportunity to make representations and, where it does so, it will specify the time by which, and the manner in which, the representations must be made.

(4) Where the court proposes—

 (a) to make an order on its own initiative; and

 (b) to hold a hearing to decide whether to make the order,

it will give the parties and may give any other person it thinks likely to be affected by the order at least 3 days' notice of the hearing.

General power of the court to rectify matters where there has been an error of procedure

28. Where there has been an error of procedure, such as a failure to comply **4–029** with a rule or practice direction—

 (a) the error does not invalidate any step taken in the proceedings unless the court so orders; and

 (b) the court may waive the error or require it to be remedied or may make such other order as appears to the court to be just.

PART 6

Practice Direction
 6A Service

SERVICE OF DOCUMENTS

Service generally

Scope

29.—(1) Subject to paragraph (2), the rules in this Part apply to— **4–030**

 (a) the service of documents; and

(b) to the requirement under rule 70 for a person to be notified of the issue of an application form,

and references to 'serve', 'service', 'notice' and 'notify', and kindred expressions shall be construed accordingly.

(2) The rules in this Part do not apply where—

(a) any other enactment, a rule in another Part or a practice direction makes different provision; or

(b) the court directs otherwise.

Who is to serve

4–031   **30.**—(1) The general rule is that the following documents will be served by the court—

(a) an order or judgment of the court;

(b) an acknowledgment of service or notification; and

(c) except where the application is for an order for committal, a notice of hearing.

(2) Any other document is to be served by the party seeking to rely upon it, except where—

(a) a rule or practice direction provides otherwise; or

(b) the court directs otherwise.

(3) Where the court is to serve a document—

(a) it is for the court to decide which of the methods of service specified in rule 31 is to be used; and

(b) if the document is being served on behalf of a party, that party must provide sufficient copies.

Methods of service

4–032   **31.**—(1) A document may be served by any of the methods specified in this rule.

(2) Where it is not known whether a solicitor is acting on behalf of a person, the document may be served by—

(a) delivering it to the person personally;

(b) delivering it at his home address or last known home address; or

(c) sending it to that address, or last known address, by first class post (or by an alternative method of service which provides for delivery on the next working day).

(3) Where a solicitor—

(a) is authorised to accept service on behalf of a person; and

(b) has informed the person serving the document in writing that he is so authorised,

the document must be served on the solicitor, unless personal service is required by an enactment, rule, practice direction or court order.

(4) Where it appears to the court that there is a good reason to authorise service by a method other than those specified in paragraphs (2) or (3), the court may direct that service is effected by that method.

(5) A direction that service is effected by an alternative method must specify—

(a) the method of service; and

(b) the date when the document will be deemed to be served.

(6) A practice direction may set out how documents are to be served by document exchange, electronic communication or other means.

Service of documents on children and protected parties

32.—(1) The following table shows the person on whom a document must be **4–033** served if it is a document which would otherwise be served on—

(a) a child; or

(b) a protected party.

Type of document	Nature of party	Person to be served
Application form	Child	—A person who has parental responsibility for the child within the meaning of the Children Act 1989; or —if there is no such person, a person with whom the child resides or in whose care the child is.
Application form	Protected party	—The person who is authorised to conduct the proceedings in the protected party's name or on his behalf; or —a person who is a duly appointed attorney, donee or deputy of the protected party; or —if there is no such person, a person with whom the protected party lives or in whose care the latter is.
Application for an order appointing a litigation friend, where a child or protected party has no litigation friend	Child or protected party	—See rule 145 (appointment of litigation friend by court order—supplementary).
Any other document	Child or protected party	—The litigation friend or other duly authorised person who is conducting the proceedings on behalf of the child or protected party.

(2) The court may make an order for service on a child or a protected party by permitting the document to be served on some person other than the person specified in the table set out in paragraph (1) above (which may include service on the child or the protected party).

(3) An application for an order under paragraph (2) may be made without notice.

(4) The court may order that, although a document has been served on someone other than the person specified in the table, the document is to be treated as if it had been properly served.

(5) This rule does not apply in relation to the service of documents upon a child in any case where the court has made an order under rule 141(4) permitting the child to conduct proceedings without a litigation friend.

Service of documents on P if he becomes a party

33.—(1) If P becomes a party to the proceedings, all documents to be served on **4–034** him must be served on his litigation friend or other person duly authorised to conduct proceedings on P's behalf.

(2) The court may make an order for service on P by permitting the document to be served on some person other than the person specified in paragraph (1) above (which may include service on P).

(3) An application for an order under paragraph (2) may be made without notice.

(4) The court may order that, although a document has been served on someone other than a person specified in paragraph (1), the document is to be treated as if it had been properly served.

(5) This rule does not apply in relation to the service of documents upon P in any case where the court has made an order under rule 147(2) (procedure where appointment of a litigation friend comes to an end—for P).

Substituted service

4–035   **34.** Where it appears to the court that it is impracticable for any reason to serve a document in accordance with any of the methods provided under rule 31, the court may make an order for substituted service of the document by taking such steps as the court may direct to bring it to the notice of the person to be served.

Deemed service

4–036   **35.**—(1) A document which is served in accordance with these Rules or any relevant practice direction shall be deemed to be served on the day shown in the following table—

Method of service	Deemed day of service
First class post (or other service for next-day delivery)	The second day after it was posted.
Document exchange	The second day after it was left at the document exchange.
Delivering the document to a permitted address	The day after it was delivered to that address.
Fax	If it is transmitted on a business day before 4p.m., on that day; or in any other case, on the business day after the day on which it is transmitted.
Other electronic means	The second day after the day on which it is transmitted.

(2) If a document is served personally—
(a) after 5 p.m., on a business day; or
(b) at any time on a Saturday, Sunday or a Bank Holiday,
it will be treated as being served on the next business day.

Certificate of service

4–037   **36.**—(1) Where a rule, practice direction or court order requires a certificate of service for the document, the certificate must state the details set out in the following table—

Method of service	Details to be certified
First class post (or any other service for next-day delivery)	Date of posting.
Personal service	Date of personal service
Document exchange	Date when the document was left at the document exchange.

Method of service	Details to be certified
Delivery of document to permitted address	Date when the document was delivered to that address.
Fax	Date of transmission.
Other electronic means	Date of transmission and the means used.
Alternative method permitted by the court	As required by the court.

(2) The certificate must be filed within 7 days after service of the document to which it relates.

Certificate of non-service

37.—(1) Where an applicant or other person is unable to serve any document under these Rules or as directed by the court, he must file a certificate of non-service stating the reasons why service has not been effected. **4–038**

(2) The certificate of non-service must be filed within 7 days of the latest date on which service should have been effected.

Power of court to dispense with service

38.—(1) The court may dispense with any requirement to serve a document. **4–039**

(2) An application for an order to dispense with service may be made without notice.

Service out of the jurisdiction

Application of Family Procedure (Adoption) Rules 2005

39.—(1) The rules in Section 2 of Part 6 of the Family Procedure (Adoption) Rules 2005 ('the 2005 Rules') apply, with the modifications set out in this rule, to the service of documents out of the jurisdiction. **4–040**

(2) References in the 2005 Rules to the Hague Convention shall be read in these Rules as references to the Convention on the International Protection of Adults signed at the Hague on 13th January 2000 (Cm. 5881).

(3) References in the 2005 Rules to the Senior Master of the Queen's Bench Division shall be read in these Rules as references to the Senior Judge.

PART 7

Practice Direction
7A Notifying P

NOTIFYING P

General requirement to notify P

General

40.—(1) Subject to paragraphs (2) and (3), the rules in this Part apply where P is to be given notice of any matter or document, or is to be provided with any document, either under the Rules or in accordance with an order or direction of the court. **4–041**

(2) If P becomes a party, the rules in this Part do not apply and service is to be effected in accordance with Part 6 or as directed by the court.

(3) In any case the court may, either on its own initiative or on application, direct that P must not be notified of any matter or document, or provided with any document, whether in accordance with this Part or at all.

Who is to notify P

4–042   **41.**—(1) Where P is to be notified under this Part, notification must be effected by—

(a) the applicant;

(b) the appellant (where the matter relates to an appeal);

(c) an agent duly appointed by the applicant or the appellant; or

(d) such other person as the court may direct.

(2) The person within paragraph (1) is referred to in this Part as "the person effecting notification".

Circumstances in which P must be notified

Application forms

4–043   **42.**—(1) P must be notified—

(a) that an application form has been issued by the court;

(b) that an application form has been withdrawn; and

(c) of the date on which a hearing is to be held in relation to the matter, where that hearing is for disposing of the application.

(2) Where P is to be notified that an application form has been issued, the person effecting notification must explain to P—

(a) who the applicant is;

(b) that the application raises the question of whether P lacks capacity in relation to a matter or matters, and what that means;

(c) what will happen if the court makes the order or direction that has been applied for; and

(d) where the application contains a proposal for the appointment of a person to make decisions on P's behalf in relation to the matter to which the application relates, details of who that person is.

(3) Where P is to be notified that an application form has been withdrawn, the person effecting notification must explain to P—

(a) that the application form has been withdrawn; and

(b) the consequences of that withdrawal.

(4) The person effecting notification must also inform P that he may seek advice and assistance in relation to any matter of which he is notified.

Appeals

4–044   **43.**—(1) P must be notified—

(a) that an appellant's notice has been issued by the court;

(b) that an appellant's notice has been withdrawn; and

(c) of the date on which a hearing is to be held in relation to the matter, where that hearing is for disposing of the appellant's notice.

(2) Where P is to be notified that an appellant's notice has been issued, the person effecting notification must explain to P—

(a) who the appellant is;

(b) the issues raised by the appeal; and

(c) what will happen if the court makes the order or direction that has been applied for.

(3) Where P is to be notified that an appellant's notice has been withdrawn, the person effecting notification must explain to P—

(a) that the appellant's notice has been withdrawn; and

(b) the consequences of that withdrawal.

(4) The person effecting notification must also inform P that he may seek advice and assistance in relation to any matter of which he is notified.

Final orders

44.—(1) P must be notified of a final order of the court.   **4–045**

(2) Where P is notified in accordance with this rule, the person effecting notification must explain to P the effect of the order.

(3) The person effecting notification must also inform P that he may seek advice and assistance in relation to any matter of which he is notified.

Other matters

45.—(1) This rule applies where the court directs that P is to be notified of any **4–046** other matter.

(2) The person effecting notification must explain to P such matters as may be directed by the court.

(3) The person effecting notification must also inform P that he may seek advice and assistance in relation to any matter of which he is notified.

Manner of notification, and accompanying documents

Manner of notification

46.—(1) Where P is to be notified under this Part, the person effecting notifi- **4–047** cation must provide P with the information specified in rules 42 to 45 in a way that is appropriate to P's circumstances (for example, using simple language, visual aids or any other appropriate means).

(2) The information referred to in paragraph (1) must be provided to P personally.

(3) P must be provided with the information mentioned in paragraph (1) as soon as practicable and in any event within 21 days of the date on which—

(a) the application form or appellant's notice was issued or withdrawn;

(b) the order was made; or

(c) the person effecting notification received the notice of hearing from the court and in any event no later than 14 days before the date specified in the notice of the hearing,

as the case may be.

Acknowledgment of notification

47. When P is notified that an application form or an appellant's notice has **4–048** been issued, he must also be provided with a form for acknowledging notification.

Certificate of notification

4–049   **48.** The person effecting notification must, within 7 days beginning with the date on which notification in accordance with this Part was given, file a certificate of notification which certifies—

(a) the date on which P was notified; and

(b) that he was notified in accordance with this Part.

Dispensing with requirement to notify, etc

4–050   **49.**—(1) The applicant, the appellant or other person directed by the court to effect notification may apply to the court seeking an order—

(a) dispensing with the requirement to comply with the provisions in this Part; or

(b) requiring some other person to comply with the provisions in this Part.

(2) An application under this rule must be made in accordance with Part 10.

PART 8

Practice Direction
8A Permission

PERMISSION

General

4–051   **50.** Subject to these Rules and to section 50(1) of, and paragraph 20 of Schedule 3 to, the Act, the applicant must apply for permission to start proceedings under the Act.

(Section 50(1) of the Act specifies persons who do not need to apply for permission. Paragraph 20 of Schedule 3 to the Act specifies an application for which permission is not needed.)

Where the court's permission is not required

4–052   **51.** The permission of the court is not required—

(1) where an application is made by—

(a) the Official Solicitor; or

(b) the Public Guardian;

(2) where the application concerns—

(a) P's property and affairs, unless the application is of a kind specified in rule 52;

(b) a lasting power of attorney which is, or purports to be, created under the Act; or (c) an instrument which is, or purports to be, an enduring power of attorney;

(3) where an application is made in accordance with Part 10; or

(4) where a person files an acknowledgment of service or notification in accordance with this Part or Part 9, for any order proposed that is different from that sought by the applicant.

Exceptions to rule 51(2)(a)

4–053   **52.**—(1) For the purposes of rule 5 1(2)(a), the permission of the court is required to make any of the applications specified in this rule.

(2) An application for the exercise of the jurisdiction of the court under section 54(2) of the Trustee Act 1925, where the application is made by a person other than—

(a) a person who has made an application for the appointment of a deputy;

(b) a continuing trustee; or

(c) any other person who, according to the practice of the Chancery Division, would have been entitled to make the application if it had been made in the High Court.

(3) An application under section 36(9) of the Trustee Act 1925 for leave to appoint a new trustee in place of P, where the application is made by a person other than—

(a) a co-trustee; or

(b) another person with the power to appoint a new trustee.

(4) An application seeking the exercise of the court's jurisdiction under section 18(1)(b) (where the application relates to making a gift of P's property), (h) or (i) of the Act, where the application is made by a person other than—

(a) a person who has made an application for the appointment of a deputy;

(b) a person who, under any known will of P or under his intestacy, may become entitled to any property of P or any interest in it;

(c) a person who is an attorney appointed under an enduring power of attorney which has been registered in accordance with the Act or the regulations referred to in Schedule 4 to the Act;

(d) a person who is a donee of a lasting power of attorney which has been registered in accordance with the Act; or

(e) a person for whom P might be expected to provide if he had capacity to do so.

(5) An application under section 20 of the Trusts of Land and Appointment of Trustees Act 1996, where the application is made by a person other than a beneficiary under the trust or, if there is more than one, by both or all of them.

Permission—supplementary

53.—(1) The provisions of rule 52(2) apply with such modifications as may be **4–054** necessary to an application under section 18(1)(j) of the Act for an order for the exercise of any power vested in P of appointing trustees or retiring from a trust.

(2) Where part of the application concerns a matter which requires permission, and part of it does not, permission need only be sought for that part of it which requires permission.

Application for permission

54. The applicant must apply for permission by filing a permission form and **4–055** must file with it—

(a) any information or documents specified in the relevant practice direction;

(b) a draft of the application form which he seeks permission to have issued; and

(c) an assessment of capacity form, where this is required by the relevant practice direction.

What the court will do when an application for permission to start proceedings is filed

4–056   **55.** Within 14 days of a permission form being filed, the court will issue it and—

(a) grant the application in whole or in part, or subject to conditions, without a hearing and may give directions in connection with the issue of the application form;

(b) refuse the application without a hearing; or

(c) fix a date for the hearing of the application.

Persons to be notified of the hearing of an application for permission

4–057   **56.**—(1) Where the court fixes a date for a hearing under rule 55(c), it will notify the applicant and such other persons as it thinks fit, and provide them with—

(a) subject to paragraph (2), the documents mentioned in rule 54; and

(b) a form for acknowledging notification.

(2) The court may direct that any document is to be provided on an edited basis.

Acknowledgment of notification of permission application

4–058   **57.**—(1) Any person who is notified of an application for permission and who wishes to take part in the permission hearing must file an acknowledgment of notification in accordance with the following provisions of this rule.

(2) The acknowledgment of notification must be filed not more than 21 days after notice of the application was given.

(3) The court will serve the acknowledgment of notification on the applicant and on any other person who has filed such an acknowledgment.

(4) The acknowledgment of notification must—

(a) state whether the person acknowledging notification consents to the application for permission;

(b) state whether he opposes the application for permission, and if so, set out the grounds for doing so;

(c) state whether he proposes that permission should be granted to make an application for a different order, and if so, set out what that order is;

(d) provide an address for service, which must be within the jurisdiction of the court; and (e) be signed by him or his legal representative.

(5) The acknowledgment of notification may include or be accompanied by an application for directions.

(6) Subject to rules 120 and 123 (restrictions on filing an expert's report and court's power to restrict expert evidence), where a person opposes the application for permission or proposes that permission is granted for a different order, the acknowledgment of notification must be accompanied by a witness statement containing any evidence upon which that person intends to rely.

Failure to file acknowledgment of notification

4–059   **58.** Where a person notified of the application for permission has not filed an acknowledgment of notification in accordance with rule 57, he may not take part in a hearing to decide whether permission should be given unless the court permits him to do so.

Service of an order giving or refusing permission

59. The court will serve— **4–060**

(a) the order granting or refusing permission;

(b) if refusing permission without a hearing, the reasons for its decision in summary form; and

(c) any directions,

on the applicant and on any other person notified of the application who filed an acknowledgment of notification.

Appeal against a permission decision following a hearing

60. Where the court grants or refuses permission following a hearing, any **4–061** appeal against the permission decision shall be dealt with in accordance with Part 20 (appeals).

PART 9

Practice Directions

9A The application form

9B Notification of other persons that an application has been issued

9C Responding to an application

9D Application by currently appointed Deputies, Attorneys and Donees in relation to P's property and affairs

9E Application relating to serious medical treatment

9F Applications relating to statutory wills, codicils, settlements and other dealings with P's property

9G Applications to appoint or discharge a trustee

9H Application relating to the registration of Enduring Powers of Attorney

HOW TO START PROCEEDINGS

Initial steps

General

61.—(1) Applications to the court to start proceedings shall be made in accord- **4–062** ance with this Part and, as applicable, Part 8 and the relevant practice directions.

(2) The appropriate forms must be used in the cases to which they apply, with such variations as the case requires, but not so as to omit any information or guidance which any form gives to the intended recipient.

(3) If permission to make an application is required, the court shall not issue the application form until permission is granted.

When proceedings are started

62.—(1) The general rule is that proceedings are started when the court issues **4–063** an application form at the request of the applicant.

(2) An application form is issued on the date entered on the application form by the court.

Contents of the application form

63. The application form must— **4–064**

(a) state the matter which the applicant wants the court to decide;

(b) state the order which the applicant is seeking;

(c) name—

(i) the applicant;

(ii) P;

(iii) as a respondent, any person (other than P) whom the applicant reasonably believes to have an interest which means that he ought to be heard in relation to the application (as opposed to being notified of it in accordance with rule 70); and

(iv) any person whom the applicant intends to notify in accordance with rule 70; and

(d) if the applicant is applying in a representative capacity, state what that capacity is.

Documents to be filed with the application form

4–065   **64.** When an applicant files his application form with the court, he must also file—

(a) in accordance with the relevant practice direction, any evidence upon which he intends to rely;

(b) if permission was required to make the application, a copy of the court's order granting permission;

(c) an assessment of capacity form, where this is required by the relevant practice direction;

(d) any other documents referred to in the application form; and

(e) such other information and material as may be set out in a practice direction.

What the court will do when an application form is filed

4–066   **65.** As soon as practicable after an application form is filed the court will issue the application form in any case where permission—

(a) is not required; or

(b) has been granted by the court; and

do anything else that may be set out in a practice direction.

Steps following issue of application form

Applicant to serve the application form on named respondents

4–067   **66.**—(1) As soon as practicable and in any event within 21 days of the date on which the application form was issued, the applicant must serve a copy of the application form on any person who is named as a respondent in the application form, together with copies of any documents filed in accordance with rule 64 and a form for acknowledging service.

(2) The applicant must file a certificate of service within 7 days beginning with the date on which the documents were served.

Applications relating to lasting powers of attorney

4–068   **67.**—(1) Where the application concerns the powers of the court under section 22 or 23 of the Act (powers of the court in relation to the validity and operation of lasting powers of attorney) the applicant must serve a copy of the application form, together with copies of any documents filed in accordance with rule 64 and a form for acknowledging service—

(a) unless the applicant is the donor or donee of the lasting power of attorney ("the power"), on the donor and every donee of the power;

(b) if he is the donor, on every donee of the power; and

(c) if he is a donee, on the donor and any other donee of the power,

but only if the above-mentioned persons have not been served or notified under any other rule.

(2) Where the application is solely in respect of an objection to the registration of a power, the requirements of rules 66 and 70 do not apply to an application made under this rule by—

(a) a donee of the power; or

(b) a person named in a statement made by the donor of the power in accordance with paragraph 2(1)(c)(i) of Schedule 1 to the Act.

(3) The applicant must comply with paragraph (1) as soon as practicable and in any event within 21 days of date on which the application form was issued.

(4) The applicant must file a certificate of service within 7 days beginning with the date on which the documents were served.

(5) Where the applicant knows or has reasonable grounds to believe that the donor of the power lacks capacity to make a decision in relation to any matter that is the subject of the application, he must notify the donor in accordance with Part 7.

Applications relating to enduring powers of attorney

68.—(1) Where the application concerns the powers of the court under paragraphs 2(9), 4(5)(a) and (b), 7(2), 10(c), 13, or 16(2), (3), (4) and (6) of Schedule 4 to the Act, the applicant must serve a copy of the application form, together with copies of any documents filed in accordance with rule 64 and a form for acknowledging service— **4–069**

(a) unless the applicant is the donor or attorney under the enduring power of attorney ("the power"), on the donor and every attorney of the power;

(b) if he is the donor, on every attorney under the power; or

(c) if he is an attorney, on the donor and any other attorney under the power,

but only if the above-mentioned persons have not been served or notified under any other rule.

(2) Where the application is solely in respect of an objection to the registration of a power, the requirements of rules 66 and 70 do not apply to an application made under this rule by—

(a) an attorney under the power; or

(b) a person listed in paragraph 6(1) of Schedule 4 to the Act.

(3) The applicant must comply with paragraph (1) as soon as practicable and in any event within 21 days of the date on which the application form was issued.

(4) The applicant must file a certificate of service within 7 days beginning with the date on which the documents were served.

(5) Where the applicant knows or has reasonable grounds to believe that the donor of the power lacks capacity to make a decision in relation to any matter that is the subject of the application, he must notify the donor in accordance with Part 7.

Applicant to notify P of an application

4–070   **69.** P must be notified in accordance with Part 7 that an application form has been issued, unless the requirement to do so has been dispensed with under rule 49.

Applicant to notify other persons of an application

4–071   **70.**—(1) As soon as practicable and in any event within 21 days of the date on which the application form was issued, the applicant must notify the persons specified in the relevant practice direction—

(a) that an application form has been issued;

(b) whether it relates to the exercise of the court's jurisdiction in relation to P's property and affairs, or his personal welfare, or to both; and

(c) of the order or orders sought.

(2) Notification of the issue of the application form must be accompanied by a form for acknowledging notification.

(3) The applicant must file a certificate of notification within 7 days beginning with the date on which notification was given.

Requirements for certain applications

4–072   **71.** A practice direction may make additional or different provision in relation to specified applications.

Responding to an application

Responding to an application

4–073   **72.**—(1) A person who is served with or notified of an application form and who wishes to take part in proceedings must file an acknowledgment of service or notification in accordance with this rule.

(2) The acknowledgment of service or notification must be filed not more than 21 days after the application form was served or notification of the application was given.

(3) The court will serve the acknowledgment of service or notification on the applicant and on any other person who has filed such an acknowledgment.

(4) The acknowledgment of service or notification must—

(a) state whether the person acknowledging service or notification consents to the application;

(b) state whether he opposes the application and, if so, set out the grounds for doing so;

(c) state whether he seeks a different order from that set out in the application form and, if so, set out what that order is;

(d) provide an address for service, which must be within the jurisdiction of the court; and (e) be signed by him or his legal representative.

(5) Subject to rules 120 and 123 (restriction on filing an expert's report and court's power to restrict expert evidence), where a person who has been served in accordance with rule 66, 67 or 68 opposes the application or seeks a different order, the acknowledgment of service must be accompanied by a witness statement containing any evidence upon which that person intends to rely.

(6) In addition to complying with the other requirements of this rule, an acknowledgment of notification filed by a person notified of the application in accordance with rule 67(5), 68(5), 69 or 70 must—

(a) indicate whether the person wishes to be joined as a party to the proceedings; and

(b) state the person's interest in the proceedings.

(7) Subject to rules 120 and 123 (restriction on filing an expert's report and court's power to restrict expert evidence), where a person has been notified in accordance with rule 67(5), 68(5), 69, 70, the acknowledgment of notification must be accompanied by a witness statement containing any evidence of his interest in the proceedings and, if he opposes the application or seeks a different order, any evidence upon which he intends to rely.

(8) The court will consider whether to join a person mentioned in paragraph (6) as a party to the proceedings and, if it decides to do so, will make an order to that effect.

(9) Where a person who is notified in accordance with rule 67(5), 68(5), 69 or 70 complies with the requirements of this rule, he need not comply with the requirements of rule 75 (application to be joined as a party).

(10) Where a person has filed an acknowledgment of notification in accordance with rule 57 (acknowledgment of notification of permission application) he must still acknowledge service or notification of an issued application form in accordance with this rule.

(11) A practice direction may make provision about responding to applications.

The parties to the proceedings

Parties to the proceedings

73.—(1) Unless the court otherwise directs, the parties to any proceedings **4–074** are—

(a) the applicant; and

(b) any person who is named as a respondent in the application form and who files an acknowledgment of service in respect of the application form.

(2) The court may order a person to be joined as a party if it considers that it is desirable to do so for the purpose of dealing with the application.

(3) The court may at any time direct that any person who is a party to the proceedings is to be removed as a party.

(4) Unless the court orders otherwise, P shall not be named as a respondent to any proceedings.

(5) A party to the proceedings is bound by any order or direction of the court made in the course of those proceedings.

Persons to be bound as if parties

74.—(1) The persons mentioned in paragraph (2) shall be bound by any order **4–075** made or directions given by the court in the same way that a party to the proceedings is so bound.

(2) The persons referred to in paragraph (1) are—

(a) P; and

(b) any person who has been served with or notified of an application form in accordance with these Rules.

Application to be joined as a party

75.—(1) Any person with sufficient interest may apply to the court to be joined **4–076** as a party to the proceedings.

(2) An application to be joined as a party must be made by filing an application notice in accordance with Part 10 which must—

(a) state the full name and address of the person seeking to be joined as a party to the proceedings;

(b) state his interest in the proceedings;

(c) state whether he consents to the application;

(d) state whether he opposes the application and, if so, set out the grounds for doing so;

(e) state whether he proposes that an order different from that set out in the application form should be made and, if so, set out what that order is;

(f) provide an address for service, which must be within the jurisdiction of the court; and (g) be signed by him or his legal representative.

(3) Subject to rules 120 and 123 (restriction on filing an expert's report and court's power to restrict expert evidence), an application to be joined must be accompanied by—

(a) a witness statement containing evidence of his interest in the proceedings and, if he proposes that an order different from that set out in the application form should be made, the evidence on which he intends to rely; and

(b) a sufficient number of copies of the application notice to enable service of the application on every other party to the proceedings.

(4) The court will serve the application notice and any accompanying documents on all parties to the proceedings.

(5) The court will consider whether to join a person applying under this rule as a party to the proceedings and, if it decides to do so, will make an order to that effect.

Applications for removal as a party to proceedings
4-077   **76.** A person who wishes to be removed as a party to the proceedings must apply to the court for an order to that effect in accordance with Part 10.

PART 10

Practice Directions
10A Applications within proceedings
10B Urgent and interim applications

APPLICATIONS WITHIN PROCEEDINGS

Types of applications for which the Part 10 procedure may be used
4-078   **77.**—(1) The Part 10 procedure is the procedure set out in this Part.

(2) The Part 10 procedure may be used if the application is made by any person—

(a) in the course of existing proceedings; or

(b) as provided for in a rule or practice direction.

(3) The court may grant an interim remedy before an application form has been issued only if—

(a) the matter is urgent; or

(b) it is otherwise necessary to do so in the interests of justice.

(4) An application made during the course of existing proceedings includes an application made during appeal proceedings.

Application notice to be filed

78.—(1) Subject to paragraph (5), the applicant must file an application notice **4–079** to make an application under this Part.

(2) The applicant must, when he files the application notice, file the evidence upon which he relies (unless such evidence has already been filed).

(3) The court will issue the application notice and, if there is to be a hearing, give notice of the date on which the matter is to be heard by the court.

(4) Notice under paragraph (3) must be given to—

(a) the applicant;

(b) anyone who is named as a respondent in the application notice (if not otherwise a party to the proceedings);

(c) every party to the proceedings; and

(d) any other person, as the court may direct.

(5) An applicant may make an application under this Part without filing an application notice if—

(a) this is permitted by any rule or practice direction; or

(b) the court dispenses with the requirement for an application notice.

(6) If the applicant makes an application without giving notice, the evidence in support of the application must state why notice has not been given.

What an application notice must include

79. An application notice must state—   **4–080**

(a) what order or direction the applicant is seeking;

(b) briefly, the grounds on which the applicant is seeking the order or direction; and (c) such other information as may be required by any rule or a practice direction.

Service of an application notice

80.—(1) Subject to paragraphs (4) and (5), the applicant must serve a copy of **4–081** the application notice on—

(a) anyone who is named as a respondent in the application notice (if not otherwise a party to the proceedings);

(b) every party to the proceedings; and

(c) any other person, as the court may direct,

as soon as practicable and in any event within 21 days of the date on which it was issued.

(2) The application notice must be accompanied by a copy of the evidence filed in support.

(3) The applicant must file a certificate of service within 7 days beginning with the date on which the documents were served.

(4) This rule does not require a copy of evidence to be served on a person upon whom it has already been served, but the applicant must in such a case give to that person notice of the evidence upon which he intends to rely.

(5) An application may be made without serving a copy of the application notice if this is permitted by—

(a) a rule;

(b) a practice direction; or (c) the court.

Applications without notice

4–082 **81.**—(1) This rule applies where the court has dealt with an application which was made without notice having been given to any person.

(2) Where the court makes an order, whether granting or dismissing the application, the applicant must, as soon as practicable or within such period as the court may direct, serve the documents mentioned in paragraph (3) on—

(a) anyone named as a respondent in the application notice (if not otherwise a party to the proceedings);

(b) every party to the proceedings; and

(c) any other person, as the court may direct.

(3) The documents referred to in paragraph (2) are—

(a) a copy of the application notice;

(b) the court's order; and

(c) any evidence filed in support of the application.

(Rule 89 provides for reconsideration of orders made without a hearing or without notice to a person.)

Interim Remedies

Orders for interim remedies

4–083 **82.**—(1) The court may grant the following interim remedies—

(a) an interim injunction;

(b) an interim declaration; or

(c) any other interim order it considers appropriate.

(2) Unless the court orders otherwise, a person on whom an application form is served under Part 9, or who is given notice of such an application, may not apply for an interim remedy before he has filed an acknowledgment of service or notification in accordance with Part 9.

(3) This rule does not limit any other power of the court to grant interim relief.

PART 11

Practice Direction
11A Human Rights Act 1998

HUMAN RIGHTS

General

4–084 **83.**—(1) A party who seeks to rely upon any provision of or right arising under the Human Rights Act 1998 ("the 1998 Act") or who seeks a remedy available under that Act must inform the court in the manner set out in the relevant practice direction specifying—

(a) the Convention right (within the meaning of the 1998 Act) which it is alleged has been infringed and details of the alleged infringement; and

(b) the remedy sought and whether this includes a declaration of incompatibility under section 4 of the 1998 Act.

(2) The court may not make a declaration of incompatibility unless 21 days notice, or such other period of notice as the court directs, has been given to the Crown.

(3) Where notice has been given to the Crown, a Minister or other person permitted by the 1998 Act will be joined as a party on filing an application in accordance with rule 75 (application to be joined as a party).

PART 12

DEALING WITH APPLICATIONS

Dealing with the application

84.—(1) As soon as practicable after any application has been issued the court **4–085** shall consider how to deal with it.

(2) The court may deal with an application or any part of an application at a hearing or without a hearing.

(3) In considering whether it is necessary to hold a hearing, the court shall, as appropriate, have regard to—

(a) the nature of the proceedings and the orders sought;

(b) whether the application is opposed by a person who appears to the court to have an interest in matters relating to P's best interests;

(c) whether the application involves a substantial dispute of fact;

(d) the complexity of the facts and the law;

(e) any wider public interest in the proceedings;

(f) the circumstances of P and of any party, in particular as to whether their rights would be adequately protected if a hearing were not held;

(g) whether the parties agree that the court should dispose of the application without a hearing; and

(h) any other matter specified in the relevant practice direction.

(4) Where the court considers that a hearing is necessary, it will—

(a) give notice of the hearing date to the parties and to any other person it directs; and

(b) state whether the hearing is for disposing of the matter or for directions.

(5) Where the court decides that it can deal with the matter without a hearing it will do so and serve a copy of its order on the parties and on any other person it directs.

Directions

85.—(1) The court may—   **4–086**

(a) give directions in writing; or

(b) set a date for a directions hearing; and

(c) do anything else that may be set out in a practice direction.

(2) When giving directions, the court may do any of the following—

(a) require a report under section 49 of the Act and give directions as to any such report;

(b) give directions as to any requirements contained in these Rules or a practice direction for the giving of notification to any person or for that person to do anything in response to a notification;

(c) if the court considers that P should be a party to the proceedings, give directions joining him as a party;

(d) if P is joined as a party to proceedings, give directions as to the appointment of a litigation friend;

(e) if the court considers that any other person or persons should be a party to the proceedings, give directions joining them as a party;

(f) if the court considers that any party to the proceedings should not be a party, give directions for that person's removal as a party;

(g) give directions for the management of the case and set a timetable for the steps to be taken between the giving of directions and the hearing;

(h) subject to rule 86, give directions as to the type of judge who is to hear the case;

(i) give directions as to whether the proceedings or any part of them are to be heard in public, or as to whether any particular person should be permitted to attend the hearing, or as to whether any publication of the proceedings is to be permitted;

(j) give directions as to the disclosure of documents, service of witness statements and any expert evidence;

(k) give directions as to the attendance of witnesses and as to whether, and the extent to which, cross-examination will be permitted at any hearing; and

(l) give such other directions as the court thinks fit.

(3) The court may give directions at any time—

(a) on its own initiative; or

(b) on the application of a party.

(4) Subject to paragraphs (5) and (6) and unless these Rules or a practice direction provide otherwise or the court directs otherwise, the time specified by a rule or by the court for a person to do any act may be varied by the written agreement of the parties.

(5) A party must apply to the court if he wishes to vary –

(a) the date the court has fixed for the final hearing; or

(a) the period within which the final hearing is to take place.

(6) The time specified by a rule or practice direction or by the court may not be varied by the parties if the variation would make it necessary to vary the date the court has fixed for any hearing or the period within which the final hearing is to take place.

Allocation of proceedings

Court's jurisdiction in certain kinds of case to be exercised by certain judges

4–087   **86.**—(1) The court will consider whether the application is of a type specified in the relevant practice direction as being one which must be dealt with by—

(a) the President;

(b) the Vice-President; or

(c) one of the other judges nominated by virtue of section 46(2)(a) to (c) of the Act.

(2) The practice direction made under this rule shall specify the categories of case which must be dealt with by a judge mentioned in paragraph (1).

(3) Applications in any matter other than those specified in the relevant practice direction may be dealt with by any judge.

Disputing the jurisdiction of the court

Procedure for disputing the court's jurisdiction
   87.—(1) A person who wishes to—   **4–088**
  (a) dispute the court's jurisdiction to hear an application; or
  (b) argue that the court should not exercise its jurisdiction,
   may apply to the court at any time for an order declaring that it has no such jurisdiction or should not exercise any jurisdiction that it may have.
   (2) An application under this rule must be—
  (a) made by using the form specified in the relevant practice direction; and
  (b) supported by evidence.
   (3) An order containing a declaration that the court has no jurisdiction or will not exercise its jurisdiction may also make further provision, including—
  (a) setting aside the application;
  (b) discharging any order made; and
  (c) staying the proceedings.

Participation in hearings

Participation in hearings
   88.—(1) The court may hear P on the question of whether or not an order **4–089**
should be made, whether or not he is a party to the proceedings.
   (2) The court may proceed with a hearing in the absence of P if it considers that it would be appropriate to do so.
   (3) A person other than P who is served with or notified of the application may only take part in a hearing if—
  (a) he files an acknowledgment in accordance with the Rules and is made a party to the proceedings; or
  (b) the court permits.

Reconsideration of court orders

Orders made without a hearing or without notice to any person
   89.—(1) This rule applies where the court makes an order—   **4–090**
  (a) without a hearing; or
  (b) without notice to any person who is affected by it.
   (2) Where this rule applies—
  (a) P;
  (b) any party to the proceedings; or
  (c) any other person affected by the order,
   may apply to the court for reconsideration of the order made.
   (3) An application under paragraph (2) must be made—
  (a) within 21 days of the order being served or such other period as the court may direct; and
  (b) in accordance with Part 10.
   (4) The court will—
  (a) reconsider the order without directing a hearing; or
  (b) fix a date for the matter to be heard, and notify all parties to the proceedings and such other persons as the court may direct, of that date.

(5) Where an application is made in accordance with this rule, the court may affirm, set aside or vary any order made.

(6) Reconsideration may be by any judge of the court—

(a) including the judge who made the decision in respect of which the reconsideration is sought; but

(b) may not be by a judge who is not a prescribed higher judge within the meaning of section 53(3) of the Act in relation to the first-mentioned judge.

(7) No application may be made seeking a reconsideration of a decision that has been made under paragraph (5).

(8) An appeal against a decision made under paragraph (5) may be made in accordance with Part 20 (appeals).

(9) Any order made without a hearing or without notice to any person, other than one made under paragraph (5), must contain a statement of the right to apply for a reconsideration of the decision in accordance with this rule.

(10) An application made under this rule may include a request that the court reconsider the matter at a hearing.

PART 13

Practice Direction
13A Hearings (including reporting restrictions)

HEARINGS

Private hearings

General rule—hearing to be in private

4–091   **90.**—(1) The general rule is that a hearing is to be held in private.

(2) A private hearing is a hearing which only the following persons are entitled to attend—

(a) the parties;

(b) P (whether or not a party);

(c) any person acting in the proceedings as a litigation friend;

(d) any legal representative of a person specified in any of sub-paragraphs (a) to (c); and (e) any court officer.

(3) In relation to a private hearing, the court may make an order—

(a) authorising any person, or class of persons, to attend the hearing or a part of it; or

(b) excluding any person, or class of persons, from attending the hearing or a part of it.

Court's general power to authorise publication of information about proceedings

4–092   **91.**—(1) For the purposes of the law relating to contempt of court, information relating to proceedings held in private may be published where the court makes an order under paragraph (2).

(2) The court may make an order authorising—

(a) the publication of such information relating to the proceedings as it may specify; or

(b) the publication of the text or a summary of the whole or part of a judgment or order made by the court.

(3) Where the court makes an order under paragraph (2) it may do so on such terms as it thinks fit, and in particular may—

(a) impose restrictions on the publication of the identity of—
   (i) any party;
   (ii) P (whether or not a party);
   (iii) any witness; or
   (iv) any other person;
(b) prohibit the publication of any information that may lead to any such person being identified;
(c) prohibit the further publication of any information relating to the proceedings from such date as the court may specify; or
(d) impose such other restrictions on the publication of information relating to the proceedings as the court may specify.

Power to order a public hearing

Court's power to order that a hearing be held in public

92.—(1) The court may make an order—   **4–093**

(a) for a hearing to be held in public;
(b) for a part of a hearing to be held in public; or
(c) excluding any person, or class of persons, from attending a public hearing or a part of it.

(2) Where the court makes an order under paragraph (1), it may in the same order or by a subsequent order—

(a) impose restrictions on the publication of the identity of—
   (i) any party;
   (ii) P (whether or not a party);
   (iii) any witness; or
   (iv) any other person;
(b) prohibit the publication of any information that may lead to any such person being identified;
(c) prohibit the further publication of any information relating to the proceedings from such date as the court may specify; or
(d) impose such other restrictions on the publication of information relating to the proceedings as the court may specify.

Supplementary

Supplementary provisions relating to public or private hearings

93.—(1) An order under rule 90, 91 or 92 may be made—   **4–094**

(a) only where it appears to the court that there is good reason for making the order;
(b) at any time; and
(c) either on the court's own initiative or on an application made by any person in accordance with Part 10.

(2) A practice direction may make further provision in connection with—

(a) private hearings;
(b) public hearings; or

(c) the publication of information about any proceedings.

PART 14

ADMISSIONS, EVIDENCE AND DEPOSITIONS

Admissions

Making an admission

4–095   **94.**—(1) Without prejudice to the ability to make an admission in any other way, a party may
admit the truth of the whole or part of another party's case by giving notice in writing. (2) The court may allow a party to amend or withdraw an admission.

Evidence

Power of court to control evidence

4–096   **95.**—(1) The court may—
  (a) control the evidence by giving directions as to—
    (i) the issues on which it requires evidence;
    (ii) the nature of the evidence which it requires to decide those issues; and
    (iii) the way in which the evidence is to be placed before the court;
  (b) use its power under this rule to exclude evidence that would otherwise be admissible;
  (c) allow or limit cross-examination; and
  (d) admit such evidence, whether written or oral, as it thinks fit.

Evidence of witnesses—general rule

4–097   **96.**—(1) The general rule is that any fact which needs to be proved by evidence of a witness is to be proved—
  (a) where there is a final hearing, by their oral evidence; or
  (b) at any other hearing, or if there is no hearing, by their evidence in writing.
    (2) Where a witness is called to give oral evidence under paragraph (1)(a), his witness statement shall stand as his evidence in chief unless the court directs otherwise.
    (3) A witness giving oral evidence at the final hearing may, if the court permits—
  (a) amplify his witness statement; and
  (b) give evidence in relation to new matters which have arisen since the witness statement was made.
    (4) The court may so permit only if it considers that there is good reason not to confine the evidence of the witness to the contents of his witness statement.

(5) This rule is subject to—

(a) any provision to the contrary in these Rules or elsewhere; or

(b) any order or direction of the court.

Written evidence—general rule

97. A party may not rely upon written evidence unless—   **4–098**

(a) it has been filed in accordance with these Rules or a practice direction;

(b) it is expressly permitted by these Rules or a practice direction; or

(c) the court gives permission.

Evidence by video link or other means

98. The court may allow a witness to give evidence through a video link or by **4–099** other communication technology.

Service of witness statements for use at final hearing

99.—(1) A witness statement is a written statement which contains the evi- **4–100** dence which that person would be allowed to give orally.

(2) The court will give directions about the service of any witness statement that a party intends to rely upon at the final hearing.

(3) The court may give directions as to the order in which witness statements are to be served. (Rules 11 and 100 require witness statements to be verified by a statement of truth.)

Form of witness statement

100. A witness statement must contain a statement of truth and comply with the **4–101** requirements set out in the relevant practice direction.

Witness summaries

101.—(1) A party who wishes to file a witness statement for use at final hear- **4–102** ing, but is unable to do so, may apply, without notice, to be permitted to file a witness summary instead.

(2) A witness summary is a summary of—

(a) the evidence, if known, which would otherwise be included in a witness statement; or

(b) if the evidence is not known, the matters about which the party filing the witness summary proposes to question the witness.

(3) Unless the court directs otherwise, a witness summary must include the name and address of the intended witness.

(4) Unless the court directs otherwise, a witness summary must be filed within the period in which a witness statement would have had to be filed.

(5) Where a party files a witness summary, so far as practicable, rules 96(3)(a) (amplifying witness statements) and 99 (service of witness statements for use at a final hearing) shall apply to the summary.

Affidavit evidence

102. Evidence must be given by affidavit instead of or in addition to a witness **4–103** statement if this is required by the court, a provision contained in any rule, a practice direction or any other enactment.

Form of affidavit

4–104   **103.** An affidavit must comply with the requirements set out in the relevant practice direction.

Affidavit made outside the jurisdiction

4–105   **104.** A person may make an affidavit outside the jurisdiction in accordance with—

(a) this Part; or

(b) the law of the place where he makes the affidavit.

Notarial acts and instruments

4–106   **105.** A notarial act or instrument may, without further proof, be received in evidence as duly authenticated in accordance with the requirements of law unless the contrary is proved.

Summoning of witnesses

4–107   **106.**—(1) The court may allow or direct any party to issue a witness summons requiring the person named in it to attend before the court and give oral evidence or produce any document to the court.

(2) An application by a party for the issue of a witness summons may be made by filing an application notice which includes—

(a) the name and address of the applicant and of his solicitor, if any;

(b) the name, address and occupation of the proposed witness;

(c) particulars of any document which the proposed witness is to be required to produce; and

(d) the grounds on which the application is made.

(3) The general rule is that a witness summons is binding if it is served at least 7 days before the date on which the witness is required to attend before the court, and the requirements of paragraph (6) have been complied with.

(4) The court may direct that a witness summons shall be binding although it will be served less than 7 days before the date on which the witness is required to attend before the court.

(5) Unless the court directs otherwise, a witness summons is to be served by the person making the application.

(6) At the time of service the witness must be offered or paid—

(a) a sum reasonably sufficient to cover his expenses in travelling to and from the court; and

(b) such sum by way of compensation for loss of time as may be specified in the relevant practice direction.

(7) The court may order that the witness is to be paid such general costs as it considers appropriate.

Power of court to direct a party to provide information

4–108   **107.**—(1) Where a party has access to information which is not reasonably available to the other party, the court may direct that party to prepare and file a document recording the information.

(2) The court will give directions about serving a copy of that document on the other parties.

Depositions

Evidence by deposition

108.—(1) A party may apply for an order for a person to be examined before **4–109** the hearing takes place.

(2) A person from whom evidence is to be obtained following an order under this rule is referred to as a 'deponent' and the evidence is referred to as a 'deposition'.

(3) An order under this rule shall be for a deponent to be examined on oath before—

  (a) a circuit judge or a district judge, whether or not nominated as a judge of the court;

  (b) an examiner of the court; or

  (c) such other person as the court appoints.

(4) The order may require the production of any document which the court considers is necessary for the purposes of the examination.

(5) The order will state the date, time and place of the examination.

(6) At the time of service of the order, the deponent must be offered or paid—

  (a) a sum reasonably sufficient to cover his expenses in travelling to and from the place of examination; and

  (b) such sum by way of compensation for loss of time as may be specified in the relevant practice direction.

(7) Where the court makes an order for a deposition to be taken, it may also order the party who obtained the order to file a witness statement or witness summary in relation to the evidence to be given by the person to be examined.

Conduct of examination

109.—(1) Subject to any directions contained in the order for examination, the **4–110** examination must be conducted in the same way as if the witness were giving evidence at a final hearing.

(2) If all the parties are present, the examiner may conduct the examination of a person not named in the order for examination if all the parties and the person to be examined consent.

(3) The examiner must ensure that the evidence given by the witness is recorded in full.

(4) The examiner must send a copy of the deposition—

  (a) to the person who obtained the order for the examination of the witness; and

  (b) to the court.

(5) The court will give directions as to the service of a copy of the deposition on the other parties.

Fees and expenses of examiners of the court

110.—(1) An examiner of the court may charge a fee for the examination and **4–111** he need not send the deposition to the court until the fee is paid, unless the court directs otherwise.

(2) The examiner's fees and expenses must be paid by the party who obtained the order for examination.

(3) If the fees and expenses due to an examiner are not paid within a reasonable time, he may report that fact to the court.

(4) The court may order the party who obtained the order for examination to deposit in the court office a specified sum in respect of the examiner's fees and, where it does so, the examiner will not be asked to act until the sum has been deposited.

(5) An order under this rule does not affect any decision as to the person who is ultimately to bear the costs of the examination.

Examiners of the court

4–112   **111.**—(1) The Lord Chancellor shall appoint persons to be examiners of the court.

(2) The persons appointed shall be barristers or solicitor-advocates who have been practising for a period of not less than 3 years.

(3) The Lord Chancellor may revoke an appointment at any time.

(4) In addition to appointing persons in accordance with this rule, examiners appointed under rule 34.15 of the Civil Procedure Rules 1998 may act as examiners in the court.

Enforcing attendance of a witness

4–113   **112.**—(1) If a person served with an order to attend before an examiner—

(a) fails to attend; or

(b) refuses to be sworn for the purpose of the examination or to answer any lawful question or produce any document at the examination,

a certificate of his failure or refusal, signed by the examiner, must be filed by the party requiring the deposition.

(2) On the certificate being filed, the party requiring the deposition may apply to the court for an order requiring that person to attend or to be sworn or to answer any question or produce any document, as the case may be.

(3) An application for an order under this rule may be made without notice.

(4) The court may order the person against whom an order is sought or made under this rule to pay any costs resulting from his failure or refusal.

Use of deposition at a hearing

4–114   **113.**—(1) A deposition ordered under rule 108, 115 or 116 may be put in evidence at a hearing unless the court orders otherwise.

(2) A party intending to put a deposition in evidence at a hearing must file notice of his intention to do so on the court and serve the notice on every other party.

(3) Unless the court directs otherwise, he must file the notice at least 14 days before the day fixed for the hearing.

(4) The court may require a deponent to attend the hearing and give evidence orally.

Taking evidence outside the jurisdiction

Interpretation

4–115   **114.** In this Section—

(a) "Regulation State" has the same meaning as "Member State" in the Taking of Evidence Regulation, that is all Member States except Denmark; and

(b) "the Taking of Evidence Regulation" means Council Regulation (EC) No. 1206/200 1 of 28 May 2001 on co-operation between the courts of Member States in the taking of evidence in civil and commercial matters.

Where a person to be examined is in another Regulation State

115.—(1) This rule applies where a party wishes to take a deposition from a **4–116** person who is—

(a) outside the jurisdiction; and

(a) in a Regulation State.

(2) The court may order the issue of the request to a designated court ("the requested court") in the Regulation State in which the proposed deponent is.

(3) If the court makes an order for the issue of a request, the party who sought the order must file—

(a) a draft Form A as set out in the annex to the Taking of Evidence Regulation (request for the taking of evidence);

(b) except where paragraph (4) applies, a translation of the form;

(c) an undertaking to be responsible for the costs sought by the requested court in relation to—

(i) fees paid to experts and interpreters; and

(ii) where requested by that party, the use of special procedure or communications technology; and

(d) an undertaking to be responsible for the court's expenses.

(4) There is no need to file a translation if—

(a) English is one of the official languages of the Regulation State where the examination is to take place; or

(b) the Regulation State has indicated, in accordance with the Taking of Evidence Regulation, that English is a language which it will accept.

(5) Where article 17 of the Taking of Evidence Regulation (direct taking of evidence by the requested court) allows evidence to be taken directly in another Regulation State, the court may make an order for the submission of a request in accordance with that article.

(6) If the court makes an order for the submission of a request under paragraph (5), the party who sought the order must file—

(a) draft Form I as set out in the annex to the Taking of Evidence Regulation (request for direct taking of evidence);

(b) except where paragraph (4) applies, a translation of the form; and

(c) an undertaking to be responsible for the requested court's expenses.

Where a person to be examined is out of the jurisdiction—letter of request

116.—(1) This rule applies where a party wishes to take a deposition from a **4–117** person who is—

(a) out of the jurisdiction; and

(b) not in a Regulation State within the meaning of rule 114.

(2) The court may order the issue of a letter of request to the judicial authorities of the country in which the proposed deponent is.

(3) A letter of request is a request to a judicial authority to take the evidence of that person, or arrange for it to be taken.

(4) If the government of a country permits a person appointed by the court to examine a person in that country, the court may make an order appointing a special examiner for that purpose.

(5) A person may be examined under this rule on oath or affirmation in accordance with any procedure permitted in the country in which the examination is to take place.

(6) If the court makes an order for the issue of a letter of request, the party who sought the order must file—

(a) the following documents and, except where paragraph (7) applies, a translation of them—

    (i) a draft letter of request;

    (ii) a statement of the issues relevant to the proceedings; and

    (iii) a list of questions or the subject matter of questions to be put to the person to be examined; and

(b) an undertaking to be responsible for the Secretary of State's expenses.

(7) There is no need to file a translation if—

(a) English is one of the official languages of the country where the examination is to take place; or

(b) a practice direction has specified that country is a country where no translation is necessary.

Section 49 reports

Reports under section 49 of the Act

4–118   **117.**—(1) This rule applies where the court requires a report to be made to it under section 49 of the Act.

(2) It is the duty of the person who is required to make the report to help the court on the matters within his expertise.

(3) Unless the court directs otherwise, the person making the report must—

(a) contact or seek to interview such persons as he thinks appropriate or as the court directs;

(b) to the extent that it is practicable and appropriate to do so, ascertain what P's wishes and feelings are, and the beliefs and values that would be likely to influence P if he had the capacity to make a decision in relation to the matter to which the application relates;

(c) describe P's circumstances; and

(d) address such other matters as are required in a practice direction or as the court may direct.

(4) The court will send a copy of the report to the parties and to such persons as the court may direct.

(5) Subject to paragraphs (6) and (7), the person who is required to make the report may examine and take copies of any document in the court records.

(6) The court may direct that the right to inspect documents under this rule does not apply in relation to such documents, or descriptions of documents, as the court may specify.

(7) The court may direct that any information is to be provided to the maker of the report on an edited basis.

Written questions to person making a report under section 49

4–119   **118.**—(1) Where a report is made under section 49 the court may, on the application of any party, permit written questions relevant to the issues before the court to be put to the person by whom the report was made.

(2) The questions sought to be put to the maker of the report shall be submitted to the court, and the court may put them to the maker of the report with such amendments (if any) as it thinks fit and the maker of the report shall give his replies in writing to the questions so put.

(3) The court will send a copy of the replies given by the maker of the report under this rule to the parties and to such other persons as the court may direct.

PART 15

Practice Direction
 15A Expert evidence

EXPERTS

References to expert
  119. A reference to an expert in this Part—   **4–120**
  (a) is to an expert who has been instructed to give or prepare evidence for the purpose of court proceedings; but
  (b) does not include any person instructed to make a report under section 49 of the Act.

Restriction on filing an expert's report
  120.—(1) No person may file expert evidence unless the court or a practice **4–121** direction permits, or if it is filed with the permission form or application form and is evidence—
  (a) that P is a person who lacks capacity to make a decision or decisions in relation to the matter or matters to which the application relates;
  (b) as to P's best interests; or
  (c) that is required by any rule or practice direction to be filed with the permission form or application form.

  (2) An applicant may only rely upon any expert evidence so filed in support of the permission form or application form to the extent and for the purposes that the court allows.

  (Rule 64(a) requires the applicant to file any evidence upon which he wishes to rely with the application form and rule 54 requires certain documents to be filed with the application for permission form.)

Duty to restrict expert evidence
  121. Expert evidence shall be restricted to that which is reasonably required to **4–122** resolve the proceedings.

Experts—overriding duty to the court
  122. It is the duty of the expert to help the court on the matters within his **4–123** expertise.

Court's power to restrict expert evidence
  123.—(1) Subject to rule 120, no party may file or adduce expert evidence **4–124** unless the court or a practice direction permits.
  (2) When a party applies for a direction under this rule he must—

(a) identify the field in respect of which he wishes to rely upon expert evidence;
(b) where practicable, identify the expert in that field upon whose evidence he wishes to rely;
(c) provide any other material information about the expert; and
(d) provide a draft letter of instruction to the expert.

(3) Where a direction is given under this rule, the court shall specify the field or fields in respect of which the expert evidence is to be provided.

(4) The court may specify the person who is to provide the evidence referred to in paragraph (3).

(5) Where a direction is given under this rule for a party to call an expert or put in evidence an expert's report, the court shall give directions for the service of the report on the parties and on such other persons as the court may direct.

(6) The court may limit the amount of the expert's fees and expenses that the party who wishes to rely upon the expert may recover from any other party.

General requirement for expert evidence to be given in a written report

4–125   **124.** Expert evidence is to be given in a written report unless the court directs otherwise.

Written questions to experts

4–126   **125.**—(1) A party may put written questions to—
(a) an expert instructed by another party; or
(b) a single joint expert appointed under rule 130,
about a report prepared by such person.

(2) Written questions under paragraph (1)—
(a) may be put once only;
(b) must be put within 28 days beginning with the date on which the expert's report was served; and
(c) must be for the purpose only of clarification of the report.

(3) Paragraph (2) does not apply in any case where—
(a) the court permits it to be done on a further occasion;
(b) the other party or parties agree; or
(c) any practice direction provides otherwise.

(4) An expert's answers to questions put in accordance with paragraph (1) shall be treated as part of the expert's report.

(5) Paragraph (6) applies where—
(a) a party has put a written question to an expert instructed by another party in accordance with this rule; and
(b) the expert does not answer that question.

(6) The court may make one or both of the following orders in relation to the party who instructed the expert—
(a) that the party may not rely upon the evidence of that expert; or
(b) that the party may not recover the fees and expenses of that expert, or part of them, from any other party.

(7) Unless the court otherwise directs, and subject to any final costs order that may be made, the instructing party is responsible for the payment of the expert's fees and expenses, including the expert's costs of answering questions put by any other party.

Contents of expert's report

126.—(1) The court may give directions as to the matters to be covered in an **4–127** expert's report.

(2) An expert's report must comply with the requirements set out in the relevant practice direction.

(3) At the end of an expert's report there must be a statement that—

(a) the expert understands his duty to the court; and

(b) he has complied with that duty.

(4) The expert's report must state the substance of all material instructions, whether written or oral, on the basis of which the report was written.

(5) The instructions to the expert shall not be privileged against disclosure.

Use by one party of expert's report disclosed by another

127. Where a party has disclosed an expert's report, any party may use that **4–128** expert's report as evidence at any hearing in the proceedings.

Discussions between experts

128.—(1) The court may, at any stage, direct a discussion between experts for **4–129** the purpose of requiring the experts to—

(a) identify and discuss the expert issues in the proceedings; and

(b) where possible, reach an agreed opinion on those issues.

(2) The court may specify the issues which the experts must discuss.

(3) The court may direct that following a discussion between the experts they must prepare a statement for the court showing—

(a) those issues on which they agree; and

(b) those issues on which they disagree and a summary of their reasons for disagreeing.

(4) Unless the court otherwise directs, the content of the discussions between experts may be referred to at any hearing or at any stage in the proceedings.

Expert's right to ask court for directions

129.—(1) An expert may file a written request for directions to assist him in **4–130** carrying out his function as an expert.

(2) An expert must, unless the court directs otherwise, provide a copy of any proposed request for directions under paragraph (1)—

(a) to the party instructing him, at least 7 days before he files the request; and

(b) to all other parties, at least 4 days before he files it.

(3) The court, when it gives directions, may also direct that a party be served with a copy of the directions.

Court's power to direct that evidence is to be given by a single joint expert

130.—(1) Where two or more parties wish to submit expert evidence on a par- **4–131** ticular issue, the court may direct that the evidence on that issue is to be given by one expert only.

(2) The parties wishing to submit the expert evidence are called 'the instructing parties'.

(3) Where the instructing parties cannot agree who should be the expert, the court may—

(a) select the expert from a list prepared or identified by the instructing parties; or

(b) direct the manner by which the expert is to be selected.

Instructions to a single joint expert

4–132   **131.**—(1) Where the court gives a direction under rule 130 for a single joint expert to be used, each party may give instructions to the expert.

(2) Unless the court otherwise directs, when an instructing party gives instructions to the expert he must, at the same time, send a copy of the instructions to the other instructing parties.

(3) The court may give directions about—

(a) the payment of the expert's fees and expenses; and

(b) any inspection, examination or experiments which the expert wishes to carry out.

(4) The court may, before an expert is instructed, limit the amount that can be paid by way of fees and expenses to the expert.

(5) Unless the court otherwise directs, and subject to any final costs order that may be made, the instructing parties are jointly and severally liable for the payment of the expert's fees and expenses.

PART 16

DISCLOSURE

Meaning of disclosure

4–133   **132.** A party discloses a document by stating that the document exists or has existed.

General or specific disclosure

4–134   **133.**—(1) The court may either on its own initiative or on the application of a party make an order to give general or specific disclosure.

(2) General disclosure requires a party to disclose—

(a) the documents on which he relies; and

(b) the documents which—

   (i) adversely affect his own case;

   (ii) adversely affect another party's case; or

   (iii) support another party's case.

(3) An order for specific disclosure is an order that a party must do one or more of the following things—

(a) disclose documents or classes of documents specified in the order;

(b) carry out a search to the extent stated in the order; or

(c) disclose any document located as a result of that search.

(4) A party's duty to disclose documents is limited to documents which are or have been in his control.

(5) For the purpose of paragraph (4) a party has or has had a document in his control if—

(a) it is or was in his physical possession;

(b) he has or has had possession of it; or

(c) he has or has had a right to inspect or take copies of it.

Procedure for general or specific disclosure

134.—(1) This rule applies where the court makes an order under rule 133 to **4–135** give general or specific disclosure.

(2) Each party must make, and serve on every other party, a list of documents to be disclosed.

(3) A copy of each list must be filed within 7 days of the date on which it is served.

(4) The list must identify the documents in a convenient order and manner and as concisely as possible.

(5) The list must indicate—

(a) the documents in respect of which the party claims a right or duty to withhold inspection (see rule 138); and

(b) the documents that are no longer in his control, stating what has happened to them.

Ongoing duty of disclosure

135.—(1) Where the court makes an order to give general or specific disclos- **4–136** ure under rule 133, any party to whom the order applies is under a continuing duty to provide such disclosure as is required by the order until the proceedings are concluded.

(2) If a document to which the duty of disclosure imposed by paragraph (1) extends comes to a party's notice at any time during the proceedings, he must immediately notify every other party.

Right to inspect documents

136.—(1) A party to whom a document has been disclosed has a right to **4–137** inspect any document disclosed to him except where—

(a) the document is no longer in the control of the party who disclosed it; or

(b) the party disclosing the document has a right or duty to withhold inspection of it.

(2) The right to inspect disclosed documents extends to any document mentioned in—

(a) a document filed or served in the course of the proceedings by any other party; or

(b) correspondence sent by any other party.

Inspection and copying of documents

137.—(1) Where a party has a right to inspect a document, he— **4–138**

(a) must give the party who disclosed the document written notice of his wish to inspect it; and

(b) may request a copy of the document.

(2) Not more than 14 days after the date on which the party who disclosed the document received the notice under paragraph (1)(a), he must permit inspection of the document at a convenient place and time.

(3) Where a party has requested a copy of the document, the party who disclosed the document must supply him with a copy not more than 14 days after the date on which he received the request.

(4) For the purposes of paragraph (2), the party who disclosed the document must give reasonable notice of the time and place for inspection.

(5) For the purposes of paragraph (3), the party requesting a copy of the document is responsible for the payment of reasonable copying costs, subject to any final costs order that may be made.

Claim to withhold inspection or disclosure of document

4–139   **138.**—(1) A party who wishes to claim that he has a right or duty to withhold inspection of a document, or part of a document, must state in writing—

(a) that he has such a right or duty; and

(b) the grounds on which he claims that right or duty.

(2) The statement must be made in the list in which the document is disclosed (see rule 134(2)).

(3) A party may, by filing an application notice in accordance with Part 10, apply to the court to decide whether the claim made under paragraph (1) should be upheld.

Consequence of failure to disclose documents or permit inspection

4–140   **139.** A party may not rely upon any document which he fails to disclose or in respect of which he fails to permit inspection unless the court permits.

PART 17

Practice Direction
17A Litigation friend

LITIGATION FRIEND

Who may act as a litigation friend

4–141   **140.**—(1) A person may act as a litigation friend on behalf of a person mentioned in paragraph (2) if he—

(a) can fairly and competently conduct proceedings on behalf of that person; and

(b) has no interests adverse to those of that person.

(2) The persons for whom a litigation friend may act are—

(a) P;

(b) a child; or

(c) a protected party.

Requirement for a litigation friend

4–142   **141.**—(1) Subject to rule 147, P (if a party to proceedings) must have a litigation friend.

(2) A protected party (if a party to the proceedings) must have a litigation friend.

(3) A child (if a party to proceedings) must have a litigation friend to conduct those proceedings on his behalf unless the court makes an order under paragraph (4).

(4) The court may make an order permitting the child to conduct proceedings without a litigation friend.

(5) An application for an order under paragraph (4)—

(a) may be made by the child;

(b) if the child already has a litigation friend, must be made on notice to the litigation friend; and

(c) if the child has no litigation friend, may be made without notice.

(6) Where—

(a) the court has made an order under paragraph (4); and

(b) it subsequently appears to the court that it is desirable for a litigation friend to conduct the proceedings on behalf of the child,

the court may appoint a person to be the child's litigation friend.

Litigation friend without a court order

142.—(1) This rule does not apply—   **4–143**

(a) in relation to P;

(b) where the court has appointed a person under rule 143 or 144; or (c) where the Official Solicitor is to act as litigation friend.

(2) A deputy with the power to conduct legal proceedings in the name of the protected party or on the protected party's behalf is entitled to be a litigation friend of the protected party in any proceedings to which his power relates.

(3) If no one has been appointed by the court, or in the case of a protected party, there is no deputy with the power to conduct proceedings, a person who wishes to act as a litigation friend must—

(a) file a certificate of suitability stating that he satisfies the conditions specified in rule 140(1); and

(b) serve the certificate of suitability on—

(i) the person on whom an application form is to be served in accordance with rule 32 (service on children and protected parties); and

(ii) every other person who is a party to the proceedings.

(4) If the person referred to in paragraph (2) wishes to act as a litigation friend for the protected party, he must file and serve a copy of the court order which appointed him on those persons mentioned in paragraph (3)(b).

Litigation friend by court order

143.—(1) The court may make an order appointing—   **4–144**

(a) the Official Solicitor; or

(b) some other person,

to act as a litigation friend.

(2) The court may act under paragraph (1)—

(a) either on its own initiative or on the application of any person; but

(b) only with the consent of the person to be appointed.

(3) An application for an order under paragraph (1) must be supported by evidence.

(4) The court may not appoint a litigation friend under this rule unless it is satisfied that the person to be appointed satisfies the conditions specified in rule 140(1).

(5) The court may at any stage of the proceedings give directions as to the appointment of a litigation friend.

Court's power to prevent a person from acting as litigation friend or to order change

4–145   **144.**—(1) The court may either on its own initiative or on the application of any person—

(a) direct that a person may not act as a litigation friend;

(b) terminate a litigation friend's appointment; or

(c) appoint a new litigation friend in place of an existing one.

(2) An application for an order under paragraph (1) must be supported by evidence.

(3) The court may not appoint a litigation friend under this rule unless it is satisfied that the person to be appointed satisfies the conditions specified in rule 140(1).

Appointment of litigation friend by court order—supplementary

4–146   **145.** The applicant must serve a copy of an application for an order under rule 143 or 144 on—

(a) the person on whom an application form is to be served in accordance with rule 32 (service on children and protected parties);

(b) every other person who is a party to the proceedings;

(c) any person who is the litigation friend, or who is purporting to act as the litigation friend, when the application is made; and

(d) unless he is the applicant, the person who it is proposed should be the litigation friend, as soon as practicable and in any event within 21 days of the date on which it was issued.

Procedure where appointment of litigation friend comes to an end—for a child or protected party

4–147   **146.**—(1) This rule applies—

(a) when a child reaches 18, provided he is neither—

(i) P; nor

(ii) a protected party; and

(b) where a protected party ceases to be a person who lacks capacity to conduct the proceedings himself.

(2) Where paragraph (1)(a) applies, the litigation friend's appointment ends.

(3) Where paragraph (1)(b) applies, the litigation friend's appointment continues until it is brought to an end by a court order

(4) An application for an order under paragraph (3) may be made by—

(a) the former protected party;

(b) his litigation friend; or

(c) any other person who is a party to the proceedings.

(5) The applicant must serve a copy of the application notice seeking an order under this rule on all parties to the proceedings as soon as practicable and in any event within 21 days of the date on which it was issued.

(6) Where paragraph (2) applies the child must serve notice on every other party—

(a) stating that he has reached full age;

(b) stating that the appointment of the litigation friend has ended; and (c) providing his address for service.

(7) Where paragraph (3) applies, the former protected party must provide his address for service to all other parties to the proceedings.

Procedure where appointment of litigation friend comes to an end—for P

147.—(1) This rule applies where P ceases to be a person who lacks capacity to conduct the proceedings himself but continues to lack capacity in relation to the matter or matters to which the application relates. **4–148**

(2) The litigation friend's appointment continues until it is brought to an end by a court order.

(3) An application for an order under paragraph (2) may be made by—

(a) P;

(b) his litigation friend; or

(c) any other person who is a party to the proceedings.

(4) The applicant must serve a copy of the application notice seeking an order under this rule on all other parties to the proceedings as soon as practicable and in any event within 21 days of the date on which it was issued.

(5) Where the court makes an order under this rule, P must provide his address for service to all other parties to the proceedings.

Procedure where P ceases to lack capacity

148.—(1) This rule applies where P ceases to lack capacity both to conduct the proceedings himself and in relation to the matter or matters to which the application relates. **4–149**

(2) The litigation friend's appointment continues until it is brought to an end by a court order.

(3) An application may be made by—

(a) P;

(b) his litigation friend; or

(c) any other person who is a party to the proceedings,

for the proceedings to come to an end.

(4) The applicant must serve a copy of the application notice seeking an order under this rule on all parties to the proceedings as soon as practicable and in any event within 21 days of the date on which it was issued.

Practice direction in relation to litigation friends

149.—(1) A practice direction may make additional or different provision in relation to litigation friends. **4–150**

PART 18

Practice Direction
18A Change of solicitor

CHANGE OF SOLICITOR

Change of solicitor

150.—(1) This rule applies where a party to proceedings— **4–151**

(a) for whom a solicitor is acting wants to change his solicitor or act in person; or

(b) after having conducted the proceedings in person, appoints a solicitor to act on his behalf (except where the solicitor is appointed only to act as an advocate for a hearing).

(2) The party proposing the change must—

(a) file a notice of the change with the court; and

(b) serve the notice of the change on every other party to the proceedings and, if there is one, on the solicitor who will cease to act.

(3) The notice must state the party's address for service.

(4) The notice filed at court must state that it has been served as required by paragraph (2)(b).

(5) Where there is a solicitor who will cease to act, he will continue to be considered the party's solicitor unless and until—

(a) the notice is filed and served in accordance with paragraphs (2), (3) and (4); or

(b) the court makes an order under rule 152 and the order is served in accordance with that rule.

LSC funded clients

4–152   **151.**—(1) Where the certificate of any person ("A") who is an LSC funded client is revoked or discharged—

(a) the solicitor who acted for A will cease to be the solicitor acting in the case as soon as his retainer is determined under regulation 4 of the Community Legal Services (Costs) Regulations 2000; and

(b) if A wishes to continue and appoints a solicitor to act on his behalf, rule 150(2), (3) and (4) will apply as if A had previously conducted the application in person.

(2) In this rule, "certificate" means a certificate issued under the Funding Code (approved under section 9 of the Access to Justice Act 1999.

Order that a solicitor has ceased to act

4–153   **152.**—(1) A solicitor may apply for an order declaring that he has ceased to be the solicitor acting for a party.

(2) Where an application is made under this rule—

(a) the solicitor must serve the application notice on the party for whom the solicitor is acting, unless the court directs otherwise; and

(b) the application must be supported by evidence.

(3) Where the court makes an order that a solicitor has ceased to act, the solicitor must—

(a) serve a copy of the order on every other party to the proceedings; and

(b) file a certificate of service.

Removal of solicitor who has ceased to act on application of another party

4–154   **153.**—(1) Where—

(a) a solicitor who has acted for a party—

(i) has died;

(ii) has become bankrupt;

(iii) has ceased to practice; or

(iv) cannot be found; and

(b) the party has not served a notice of a change of solicitor or notice of intention to act in person as required by rule 150,

any other party may apply for an order declaring that the solicitor has ceased to be the solicitor acting for the other party in the case.

(2) Where an application is made under this rule, the applicant must serve the application on the party to whose solicitor the application relates, unless the court directs otherwise.

(3) Where the court makes an order under this rule—

(a) the court will give directions about serving a copy of the order on every other party to the proceedings; and

(b) where the order is served by a party, that party must file a certificate of service.

Practice direction relating to change of solicitor

154. A practice direction may make additional or different provision in relation to change of solicitor. **4–155**

PART 19

Practice Directions
19A Costs in the Court of Protection
19B Fixed costs in the Court of Protection

COSTS

Interpretation

155.—(1) In this Part— **4–156**

(a) 'additional liability' means the percentage increase, the insurance premium, or the additional amount in respect of provision made by a membership organisation, as the case may be;

(b) 'authorised court officer' means any officer of the Supreme Court Costs Office, whom the Lord Chancellor has authorised to assess costs;

(c) 'costs' include fees, charges, disbursements, expenses, reimbursement permitted to a litigant in person, any additional liability incurred under a funding arrangement and any fee or reward charged by a lay representative for acting on behalf of a party in proceedings;

(d) 'costs judge' means a taxing Master of the Supreme Court;

(e) 'costs officer' means a costs judge or an authorised court officer;

(f) 'detailed assessment' means the procedure by which the amount of costs or remuneration is decided by a costs officer in accordance with Part 47 of the Civil Procedure Rules 1998 (which are applied to proceedings under these Rules, with modifications, by rule 160);

(g) 'fixed costs' are to be construed in accordance with the relevant practice direction;

(h) 'fund' includes any estate or property held for the benefit of any person or class of persons and any fund to which a trustee or personal representative is entitled in his capacity as such;

(i) 'funding arrangement' means an arrangement where a person has–

(i) entered into a conditional fee agreement or a collective conditional fee agreement which provides for a success fee within the meaning of section 5 8(2) of the Courts and Legal Services Act 1990;

(ii) taken out an insurance policy to which section 29 of the Access to Justice Act 1999 (recovery of insurance premiums by way of costs) applies; or

(iii) made an agreement with a membership organisation to meet his legal costs;

(j) 'insurance premium' means a sum of money paid or payable for insurance against the risk of incurring a costs liability in the proceedings, taken out after the event that is the subject matter of the claim;

(k) 'membership organisation' means a body prescribed for the purposes of section 30 of the Access to Justice Act 1999 (recovery where body undertakes to meet costs liabilities);

(l) 'paying party' means a party liable to pay costs;

(m) 'percentage increase' means the percentage by which the amount of a legal representative's fee can be increased in accordance with a conditional fee agreement which provides for a success fee;

(n) 'receiving party' means a party entitled to be paid costs;

(o) 'summary assessment' means the procedure by which the court, when making an order about costs, orders payment of a sum of money instead of fixed costs or 'detailed assessment'.

(2) The costs to which the rules in this Part apply include—

(a) where the costs may be assessed by the court, costs payable by a client to his solicitor; and

(b) costs which are payable by one party to another party under the terms of a contract, where the court makes an order for an assessment of those costs.

(3) Where advocacy or litigation services are provided to a client under a conditional fee agreement, costs are recoverable under this Part notwithstanding that the client is liable to pay his legal representative's fees and expenses only to the extent that sums are recovered in respect of the proceedings, whether by way of costs or otherwise.

(4) In paragraph (3), the reference to a conditional fee agreement is to an agreement which satisfies all the conditions applicable to it by virtue of section 58 of the Courts and Legal Services Act 1990.

Property and affairs—the general rule

4–157 **156.** Where the proceedings concern P's property and affairs the general rule is that the costs of the proceedings or of that part of the proceedings that concerns P's property and affairs, shall be paid by P or charged to his estate.

Personal welfare—the general rule

4–158 **157.** Where the proceedings concern P's personal welfare the general rule is that there will be no order as to the costs of the proceedings or of that part of the proceedings that concerns P's personal welfare.

Apportioning costs—the general rule

4–159 **158.** Where the proceedings concern both property and affairs and personal welfare the court, insofar as practicable, will apportion the costs as between the respective issues.

Departing from the general rule

159.—(1) The court may depart from rules 156 to 158 if the circumstances so **4–160** justify, and in deciding whether departure is justified the court will have regard to all the circumstances, including—

(a) the conduct of the parties;

(b) whether a party has succeeded on part of his case, even if he has not been wholly successful; and

(c) the role of any public body involved in the proceedings.

(2) The conduct of the parties includes—

(a) conduct before, as well as during, the proceedings;

(b) whether it was reasonable for a party to raise, pursue or contest a particular issue;

(c) the manner in which a party has made or responded to an application or a particular issue; and

(d) whether a party who has succeeded in his application or response to an application, in whole or in part, exaggerated any matter contained in his application or response.

(3) Without prejudice to rules 156 to 158 and the foregoing provisions of this rule, the court may permit a party to recover their fixed costs in accordance with the relevant practice direction.

Rules about costs in the Civil Procedure Rules to apply

160.—(1) Subject to the provisions of these Rules, Parts 44, 47 and 48 of the **4–161** Civil Procedure Rules 1998 ("the 1998 Rules") shall apply with the modifications in this rule and such other modifications as may be appropriate, to costs incurred in relation to proceedings under these Rules as they apply to costs incurred in relation to proceedings in the High Court.

(2) The provisions of Part 47 of the 1998 Rules shall apply with the modifications in this rule and such other modifications as may be appropriate, to a detailed assessment of the remuneration of a deputy under these Rules as they apply to a detailed assessment of costs in proceedings to which the 1998 Rules apply.

(3) Where the definitions in Part 43 (referred to in Parts 44, 47 and 48) of the 1998 Rules are different from the definitions in rule 155 of these Rules, the latter shall prevail.

(4) Rules 44.1, 44.3(1) to (5), 44.6, 44.7, 44.9, 44.10, 44.11. 44.12 and 44.12A of the 1998 Rules do not apply.

(5) In rule 44.17 of the 1998 Rules, the references to Parts 45 and 46 do not apply.

(6) In rule 47.3(1)(c) of the 1998 Rules, the words "unless the costs are being assessed under rule 48.5 (costs where money is payable to a child or a patient)" are removed.

(7) In rule 47.3(2) of the 1998 Rules, the words "or a district judge" are removed.

(8) Rule 47.4(3) and (4) of the 1998 Rules do not apply.

(9) Rules 47.9(4), 47.10 and 47.11 of the 1998 Rules do not apply where the costs are to be paid by P or charged to his estate.

(10) Rules 48.2, 48.3, 48.6A, and 48.10 of the 1998 Rules do not apply.

(11) Rule 48.1(1) of the 1998 Rules is removed and is replaced by the following: "This paragraph applies where a person applies for an order for specific disclosure before the commencement of proceedings".

Detailed assessment of costs
4–162 **161.**—(1) Where the court orders costs to be assessed by way of detailed assessment, the detailed assessment proceedings shall take place in the High Court.

(2) A fee is payable in respect of the detailed assessment of costs and on an appeal against a decision made in a detailed assessment of costs.

(3) Where a detailed assessment of costs has taken place, the amount payable by P is the amount which the court certifies as payable.

Employment of a solicitor by two or more persons
4–163 **162.** Where two or more persons having the same interest in relation to a matter act in relation to the proceedings by separate legal representatives, they shall not be permitted more than one set of costs of the representation unless and to the extent that the court certifies that the circumstances justify separate representation.

Costs of the Official Solicitor
4–164 **163.** Any costs incurred by the Official Solicitor in relation to proceedings under these Rules or in carrying out any directions given by the court and not provided for by remuneration under rule 167 shall be paid by such persons or out of such funds as the court may direct.

Procedure for assessing costs
4–165 **164.** Where the court orders a party, or P, to pay costs to another party it may either—
(a) make a summary assessment of the costs; or
(b) order a detailed assessment of the costs by a costs officer,
unless any rule, practice direction or other enactment provides otherwise.

Costs following P's death
4–166 **165.** An order or direction that costs incurred during P's lifetime be paid out of or charged on his estate may be made within 6 years after P's death.

Costs orders in favour of or against non-parties
4–167 **166.**—(1) Where the court is considering whether to make a costs order in favour of or against a person who is not a party to proceedings—
(a) that person must be added as a party to the proceedings for the purposes of costs only; and
(b) he must be given a reasonable opportunity to attend a hearing at which the court will consider the matter further.

(2) This rule does not apply where the court is considering whether to make an order against the Legal Services Commission.

Remuneration of a deputy, donee or attorney
4–168 **167.**—(1) Where the court orders that a deputy, donee or attorney is entitled to remuneration out of P's estate for discharging his functions as such, the court may make such order as it thinks fit, including an order that—

(a) he be paid a fixed amount;

(b) he be paid at a specified rate; or

(c) the amount of the remuneration shall be determined in accordance with the schedule of fees set out in the relevant practice direction.

(2) Any amount permitted by the court under paragraph (1) shall constitute a debt due from P's estate.

(3) The court may order a detailed assessment of the remuneration by a costs officer, in accordance with rule 164(b).

Practice direction as to costs

168. A practice direction may make further provision in respect of costs in **4–169** proceedings.

PART 20

Practice Direction
20A Appeals

APPEALS

Scope of this Part

169. This Part applies to an appeal against any decision of the court except **4–170** where, in relation to those cases that are to be dealt with in accordance with Part 22 (transitory and transitional provisions), Part 22 makes different provision.

Interpretation

170.—(1) In the following provisions of this Part—   **4–171**

(a) "appeal judge" means a judge of the court to whom an appeal is made;

(b) "first instance judge" means the judge of the court from whose decision an appeal is brought;

(c) "appellant" means the person who brings or seeks to bring an appeal;

(d) "respondent" means—

  (i) a person other than the appellant who was a party to the proceedings before the first instance judge and who is affected by the appeal; or

  (ii) a person who is permitted or directed by the first instance judge or the appeal judge to be a party to the appeal.

(2) In this Part, where the expression "permission" is used it means "permission to appeal" unless otherwise stated.

Dealing with appeals

171.—(1) The court may deal with an appeal or any part of an appeal at a hear- **4–172** ing or without a hearing.

(2) In considering whether it is necessary to hold a hearing, the court shall have regard to the matters set out in rule 84(3).

(Rule 89 provides for reconsideration of orders made without a hearing or without notice to a person.)

Permission to appeal

4–173   **172.**—(1) Subject to paragraph (8), an appeal against a decision of the court may not be made without permission.

(2) Any person bound by an order of the court by virtue of rule 74 (persons to be bound as if parties) may seek permission to appeal under this Part.

(3) Permission is to be granted or refused in accordance with this Part.

(4) An application for permission to appeal may be made to the first instance judge or the appeal judge.

(5) Where an application for permission is refused by the first instance judge, a further application for permission may be made in accordance with paragraphs (6) and (7).

(6) Where the decision sought to be appealed is a decision of a district judge, permission may be granted or refused by—

(a) the President;

(b) the Vice-President;

(c) one of the other judges nominated by virtue of section 46(2)(a) to (c) of the Act; or

(d) a circuit judge.

(7) Where the decision sought to be appealed is a decision of a circuit judge, permission may only be granted or refused by one of the judges mentioned in paragraph (6)(a) to (c).

(8) Permission is not required to appeal against an order for committal to prison.

Matters to be taken into account when considering an application for permission

4–174   **173.**—(1) Permission to appeal shall be granted only where—

(a) the court considers that the appeal would have a real prospect of success; or

(b) there is some other compelling reason why the appeal should be heard.

(2) An order giving permission may—

(a) limit the issues to be heard; and

(b) be made subject to conditions.

Parties to comply with the practice direction

4–175   **174.** All parties to an appeal must comply with any relevant practice direction.

Appellant's notice

4–176   **175.**—(1) Where the appellant seeks permission from the appeal judge, it must be requested in the appellant's notice.

(2) The appellant must file an appellant's notice at the court within—

(a) such period as may be directed or specified in the order of the first instance judge; or

(b) where that judge makes no such direction or order, 21 days after the date of the decision being appealed.

(3) The court will issue the appellant's notice and unless it orders otherwise, the appellant must serve the appellant's notice on each respondent and on such other persons as the court may direct, as soon as practicable and in any event within 21 days of the date on which it was issued.

(4) The appellant must file a certificate of service within 7 days beginning with the date on which he served the appellant's notice.

Respondent's notice

176.—(1) A respondent who— 4–177

(a) is seeking permission from the appeal judge to appeal; or

(b) wishes to ask the appeal judge to uphold the order of the first instance judge for reasons different from or additional to those given by the first instance judge,

must file a respondent's notice.

(2) Where the respondent seeks permission from the appeal judge, permission must be requested in the respondent's notice.

(3) A respondent's notice must be filed within—

(a) such period as may be directed by the first instance judge; or

(b) where the first instance judge makes no such direction, 21 days beginning with the date referred to in paragraph (4).

(4) The date is the soonest of—

(a) the date on which the respondent is served with the appellant's notice where—

(i) permission to appeal was given by the first instance judge; or

(ii) permission to appeal is not required;

(b) the date on which the respondent is served with notification that the appeal judge has given the appellant permission to appeal; or

(c) the date on which the respondent is served with the notification that the application for permission to appeal and the appeal itself are to be heard together.

(5) The court will issue a respondent's notice and, unless it orders otherwise, the respondent must serve the respondent's notice on the appellant, any other respondent and on such other parties as the court may direct, as soon as practicable and in any event within 21 days of the date on which it was issued.

(6) The respondent must file a certificate of service within 7 days beginning with the date on which the copy of the respondent's notice was served.

Variation of time

177.—(1) An application to vary the time limit for filing an appellant's or 4–178 respondent's notice must be made to the appeal judge.

(2) The parties may not agree to extend any date or time limit for or in respect of an appeal set by—

(a) these Rules;

(b) the relevant practice direction; or

(c) an order of the appeal judge or the first instance judge.

Power of appeal judge on appeal

178.—(1) In relation to an appeal, an appeal judge has all the powers of the first 4–179 instance judge whose decision is being appealed.

(2) In particular, the appeal judge has the power to—

(a) affirm, set aside or vary any order made by the first instance judge;

(b) refer any claim or issue to that judge for determination;

(c) order a new hearing;

(d) make a costs order.

(3) The appeal judge may exercise his powers in relation to the whole or part of an order made by the first instance judge.

Determination of appeals

4–180   **179.**—(1) An appeal will be limited to a review of the decision of the first instance judge unless—

(a) a practice direction makes different provision for a particular category of appeal; or

(b) the appeal judge considers that in the circumstances of the appeal it would be in the interests of justice to hold a re-hearing.

(2) Unless he orders otherwise, the appeal judge will not receive—

(a) oral evidence; or

(b) evidence that was not before the first instance judge.

(3) The appeal judge will allow an appeal where the decision of the first instance judge was—

(a) wrong; or

(b) unjust, because of a serious procedural or other irregularity in the proceedings before the first instance judge.

(4) The appeal judge may draw any inference of fact that he considers justified on the evidence.

(5) At the hearing of the appeal a party may not rely upon a matter not contained in his appellant's or respondent's notice unless the appeal judge gives permission.

Allocation

4–181   **180.** Except in accordance with the relevant practice direction—

(a) an appeal from a first instance decision of a circuit judge shall be heard by a judge of the court nominated by virtue of section 46(2)(a) to (c) of the Act; and

(b) an appeal from a decision of a district judge shall be heard by a circuit judge.

Appeals to the Court of Appeal

Appeals against decision of a puisne judge of the High Court, etc

4–182   **181.**—(1) Where the decision sought to be appealed is a decision of a judge nominated by virtue of section 46(2)(a) to (c) of the Act, an appeal will lie only to the Court of Appeal.

(2) The judge nominated by virtue of section 46(2)(a) to (c) of the Act may grant permission to appeal to the Court of Appeal in accordance with this Part, where the decision sought to be appealed was a decision made by a judge so nominated as a first instance judge.

Second appeals

4–183   **182.**—(1) A decision of a judge of the court which was itself made on appeal from a judge of the court may only be appealed further to the Court of Appeal.

(2) Permission is required from the Court of Appeal for such an appeal.

(3) The Court of Appeal will not give permission unless it considers that—

(a) the appeal would raise an important point of principle or practice; or

(b) there is some other compelling reason for the Court of Appeal to hear it.

(4) Nothing in this rule or in rule 181 applies to a second appeal from a decision of a nominated officer.

PART 21

Practice Direction
21A Enforcement

ENFORCEMENT

Enforcement methods—general

183.—(1) The rules in this Part make provision for the enforcement of judg- **4–184** ments and orders.

(2) The relevant practice direction may set out methods of enforcing judgments or orders.

(3) An application for an order for enforcement may be made on application by any person in accordance with Part 10.

Application of the Civil Procedure Rules 1998 and RSC Orders

184.—(1)The following provisions apply, as far as they are relevant and with **4–185** such modifications as may be necessary, to the enforcement of orders made in proceedings under these Rules—

(a) Parts 70 (General Rules about Enforcement of Judgments and Orders), 71 (Orders to Obtain Information from Judgment Debtors), 72 (Third Party Debt Orders) and 73 (Charging Orders, Stop Orders and Stop Notices) of the Civil Procedure Rules 1998; and

(b) Orders 45 (Enforcement of Judgments and Orders: General), 46 (Writs of Execution: General) and 47 (Writs of Fieri Facias) of the Rules of the Supreme Court.

Orders for committal

Contempt of court—generally

185. An application relating to the committal of a person for contempt of court **4–186** shall be made to a judge and the power to punish for contempt may be exercised by an order of committal.

Application for order of committal

186.—(1) An application for an order of committal must be made by filing an **4–187** application notice, stating the grounds of the application, and must be supported by an affidavit made in accordance with the relevant practice direction.

(2) Subject to paragraph (3), the application notice, a copy of the affidavit in support thereof and notice of the date of the hearing of the application must be served personally on the person sought to be committed.

(3) Without prejudice to its powers under Part 6, the court may dispense with service under this rule if it thinks it just to do so.

Oral evidence

187.—(1) If on the hearing of the application the person sought to be commit- **4–188** ted expresses a wish to give oral evidence on his own behalf, he shall be entitled to do so.

Hearing for committal order

4–189   **188.**—(1) Except where the court permits, no grounds shall be relied upon at the hearing except the grounds set out in the application notice.

(2) Notwithstanding rule 90(1) (general rule—hearing to be in private), when determining an application for committal the court will hold the hearing in public unless it directs otherwise.

(3) If the court hearing an application in private decides that a person has committed a contempt of court, it shall state publicly—

(a) the name of that person;

(b) in general terms the nature of the contempt in respect of which the order of committal is being made; and

(c) any punishment imposed.

(4) If the person sought to be committed does not attend the hearing, the court may fix a date and time for the person to be brought before the court.

Power to suspend execution of committal order

4–190   **189.**—(1) A judge who has made an order of committal may direct that the execution of the order of committal shall be suspended for such period or on such terms and conditions as may be specified.

(2) Where an order is suspended under paragraph (1), the applicant for the order of committal must, unless the court otherwise directs, serve on the person against whom it was made a notice informing him of the making and terms of the direction under that paragraph.

Warrant for arrest

4–191   **190.**—(1)A warrant for the arrest of a person against whom an order of committal has been made shall not, without further order of the court, be enforced more than 2 years after the date on which the warrant is issued.

Discharge of person committed

4–192   **191.**—(1)The court may, on the application of any person committed to prison for contempt of court, discharge him.

(2) Where a person has been committed for failing to comply with a judgment or order requiring him to deliver any thing to some other person or to deposit it in court or elsewhere, and a writ of sequestration has also been issued to enforce that judgment or order, then, if the thing is in the custody or power of the person committed, the commissioners appointed by the writ of sequestration may take possession of it as if it were the property of that person and, without prejudice to the generality of paragraph (1), the court may discharge the person committed and may give such directions for dealing with the thing taken by the commissioners as it thinks fit.

Penal notices

4–193   **192.**—(1) The court may direct that a penal notice is to be attached to any order warning the person on whom the copy of the order is served that disobeying the order would be a contempt of court punishable by imprisonment or a fine.

(2) Unless the court gives a direction under paragraph (1), a penal notice may not be attached to any order.

(3) A penal notice is to be in the following terms: "You must obey this order. If you do not, you may be sent to prison for contempt of court.".

Saving for other powers

193. The rules in this Part do not limit the power of the court to make an order **4–194** requiring a person guilty of contempt to pay a fine or give security for his good behaviour and those rules, so far as applicable, shall apply in relation to an application for such an order as they apply in relation to an application for an order of committal.

Power of court to commit on its own initiative

194. The preceding provisions of these Rules shall not be taken as affecting **4–195** the power of the court to make an order for committal on its own initiative against a person guilty of contempt of court.

PART 22

TRANSITORY AND TRANSITIONAL PROVISIONS

Transitory provision: applications by former receivers

195.—(1) This rule and rule 196—   **4–196**
  (a) apply in any case where a person becomes a deputy by virtue of paragraph 1(2) of Schedule 5 to the Act; but
  (b) shall cease to have effect at the end of the period specified in the relevant practice direction.
  (2) The deputy may make an application to the court in connection with—
  (a) any decision in connection with the day-to-day management of P's property and affairs; or
  (b) any supplementary decision which is necessary to give full effect to any order made, or directions given, before 1st October 2007 under Part 7 of the Mental Health Act 1983.
  (3) Decisions within paragraph (2) include those that may be specified in the relevant practice direction.
  (4) An application—
  (a) may relate only to a particular decision or decisions to be made on P's behalf;
  (b) must specify details of the decision or decisions to be made; and
  (c) must be made using the application form set out in the relevant practice direction.

Transitory provision: dealing with applications under rule 195

196.—(1) The court may, in determining an application under rule 195, treat the **4–197** application as if it were an application to vary the functions of the deputy which is made in accordance with the relevant practice direction made under rule 71, and dispose of it accordingly.

(2) In any other case, an application under rule 195 may be determined by an order made or directions given by—

(a) the court; or

(b) a person nominated under paragraph (3).

(3) The Senior Judge or the President may nominate an officer or officers of the court for the purpose of determining applications under rule 195.

(4) Where an officer has been nominated under paragraph (3) to determine an application, he may refer to a judge any proceedings or any question arising in any proceedings which ought, in the officer's opinion, to be considered by a judge.

Appeal against a decision of a nominated officer

4–198   **197.**—(1) This rule applies in relation to decisions made under rules 195 and 196 by a nominated officer.

(2) An appeal from a decision to which this rule applies lies to a judge of the court nominated by virtue of section 46(2)(e) of the Act.

(3) No permission is required for an appeal under paragraph (2).

(4) A judge determining an appeal under paragraph (2) has all the powers that an appeal judge on appeal has by virtue of rule 178.

(5) An appeal from a decision made under paragraph (2) ("a second appeal") lies to a judge of the court nominated by virtue of section 46(2)(d) of the Act.

(6) A second appeal may be made from a decision of a nominated officer, and a judge to whom such an appeal is made may, if he considers the matter is one which ought to be heard by a judge of the court nominated by virtue of section 46(2)(a) to (c), transfer the matter to such a judge.

(7) An appeal from a decision made on a second appeal lies to the Court of Appeal.

Application of Rules to proceedings within paragraphs 3 and 12 of Schedule 5 to the Act

4–199   **198.**—(1) In this rule, "pending proceedings" means proceedings on an application within paragraph 3 or 12 of Schedule 5 to the Act.

(2) A practice direction shall make provision for the extent to which these Rules shall apply to pending proceedings.

Practice direction

4–200   **199.**A practice direction may make additional or different provision in relation to transitory and transitional matters.

PART 23

Practice Directions

23A Request for directions where notice of objection prevents Public Guardian from registering Enduring Power of Attorney

23B Where P ceases to lack capacity or dies

MISCELLANEOUS

Order or directions requiring a person to give security for discharge of functions

200.—(1) This rule applies where the court makes an order or gives a direction—

4–201

(a) conferring functions on any person (whether as deputy or otherwise); and

(b) requiring him to give security for the discharge of those functions.

(2) The person on whom functions are conferred must give the security before he undertakes to discharge his functions, unless the court permits it to be given subsequently.

(3) Paragraphs (4) to (6) apply where the security is required to be given before any action can be taken.

(4) Subject to paragraph (5), the security must be given in accordance with the requirements of regulation 33(2)(a) of the Public Guardian Regulations (which makes provision about the giving of security by means of a bond that is endorsed by an authorised insurance company or deposit-taker).

(5) The court may impose such other requirements in relation to the giving of the security as it considers appropriate (whether in addition to, or instead of, those specified in paragraph (4)).

(6) In specifying the date from which the order or directions referred to in paragraph (1) are to take effect, the court will have regard to the need to postpone that date for such reasonable period as would enable the Public Guardian to be satisfied that—

(a) if paragraph (4) applies, the requirements of regulation 34 of the Public Guardian Regulations have been met in relation to the security; and

(b) any other requirements imposed by the court under paragraph (5) have been met.

(7) "The Public Guardian Regulations" means the Lasting Powers of Attorney, Enduring Powers of Attorney and Public Guardian Regulations 2007.

Objections to registration of an enduring power of attorney: request for directions

201.—(1) This rule applies in any case where—

4–202

(a) the Public Guardian (having received a notice of objection to the registration of an instrument creating an enduring power of attorney) is prevented by paragraph 13(5) of Schedule 4 to the Act from registering the instrument except in accordance with the court's directions; and

(b) on or before the relevant day, no application for the court to give such directions has been made under Part 9 (how to start proceedings).

(2) In paragraph (1)(b) the relevant day is the later of—

(a) the final day of the period specified in paragraph 13(4) of Schedule 4 to the Act; or

(b) the final day of the period of 14 days beginning with the date on which the Public Guardian receives the notice of objection.

(3) The Public Guardian may seek the court's directions about registering the instrument by filing a request in accordance with the relevant practice direction.

(4) As soon as practicable and in any event within 21 days of the date on which the request was made, the court will notify—

(a) the person (or persons) who gave the notice of objection; and

(b) the attorney or, if more than one, each of them.

(5) As soon as practicable and in any event within 21 days of the date on which the request is filed, the Public Guardian must notify the donor of the power that the request has been so filed.

(6) The notice under paragraph (4) must—

(a) state that the Public Guardian has requested the court's directions about registration;

(b) state that the court will give directions in response to the request unless an application under Part 9 is made to it before the end of the period of 21 days commencing with the date on which the notice is issued; and

(c) set out the steps required to make such an application.

(7) "Notice of objection" means a notice of objection which is made in accordance with paragraph 13(4) of Schedule 4 to the Act.

Disposal of property where P ceases to lack capacity

4–203   **202.**—(1) This rule applies where P ceases to lack capacity.

(2) In this rule, "relevant property" means any property belonging to P and forming part of his estate, and which—

(a) remains under the control of anyone appointed by order of the court; or

(b) is held under the direction of the court.

(3) The court may at any time make an order for any relevant property to be transferred to P, or at P's direction, provided that it is satisfied that P has the capacity to make decisions in relation to that property.

(4) An application for an order under this rule is to be made in accordance with Part 10.

THE COURT OF PROTECTION FEES ORDER 2007

(SI 2007/1745)

Dated July 26, 2007 and made by the Lord Chancellor under the Mental Capacity Act 2005 (c.9), ss.54(1) and (2), 65(1), with the consent of the Treasury and after consulting in accordance with s.54(3) of that Act.

GENERAL NOTE

This Order provides for fees to be charged in connection with the Court of Protection. Article 10 provides that where a hearing that takes place on or after 1 October 2007 was listed by the former Court of Protection (which ceases to exist under section 45(6) of the Act), no hearing fee is payable.

Citation and commencement

1. This Order may be cited as the Court of Protection Fees Order 2007 and **4–204** comes into force on 1 October 2007.

Interpretation

2. In this Order— **4–205**

"the Act" means the Mental Capacity Act 2005;

"appellant" means the person who brings or seeks to bring an appeal; "court" means the Court of Protection;

"P" means any person (other than a protected party) who lacks or, so far as consistent with the context, is alleged to lack capacity to make a decision or decisions in relation to any matter that is the subject of an application to the court and references to a person who lacks capacity are to be construed in accordance with the Act;

"protected party" means a party or an intended party (other than P or a child) who lacks capacity to conduct the proceedings;

"the Regulations" means the Lasting Powers of Attorney, Enduring Powers of Attorney and Public Guardian Regulations 2007; and

"the Rules" means the Court of Protection Rules 2007.

Schedule of fees

3. The fees set out in the Schedule to this Order shall apply in accordance with the following provisions of this Order.

Application fee

4.—(1) An application fee shall be payable by the applicant on making an **4–206** application under Part 9 of the Rules (how to start proceedings) in accordance with the following provisions of this article.

(2) Where permission to start proceedings is required under Part 8 of the Rules (permission), the fee prescribed by paragraph (1) shall be payable on making an application for permission.

(3) The fee prescribed by paragraph (1) shall not be payable where the application is made under—

   (a) rule 67 of the Rules (applications relating to lasting powers of attorney)
     by—
      (i) the donee of a lasting power of attorney, or
     (ii) a person named in a statement made by the donor of a lasting power of
        attorney in accordance with paragraph 2(1)(c)(i) of Part 1 of Schedule 1
        to the Act,

and is solely in respect of an objection to the registration of a lasting power of
attorney; or
    (b) rule 68 of the Rules (applications relating to enduring powers of attorney)
      by—
      (i) a donor of an enduring power of attorney,
     (ii) an attorney under an enduring power of attorney, or
    (iii) a person listed in paragraph 6(1) of Part 3 of Schedule 4 to the Act,

and is solely in respect of an objection to the registration of an enduring power of
attorney.

(4) The fee prescribed by paragraph (1) shall not be payable where the application is made by the Public Guardian.

(5) Where a fee has been paid under paragraph (1) it shall be refunded where P dies within five days of the application being filed.

Appeal fee

4–207   **5.**—(1) An appeal fee shall be payable by the appellant on the filing of an appellant's notice under Part 20 of the Rules (appeals) in accordance with the following provisions of this article.

(2) The fee prescribed by paragraph (1) shall not be payable where the appeal is—
    (a) brought by the Public Guardian; or
    (b) an appeal against a decision of a nominated officer made under rule 197 of
      the Rules (appeal against a decision of a nominated officer).

(3) The fee prescribed by paragraph (1) shall be refunded where P dies within five days of the appellant's notice being filed.

Hearing fees

4—208   **6.**—(1) A hearing fee shall be payable by the applicant where the court has—
    (a) held a hearing in order to determine the case; and
    (b) made a final order, declaration or decision.

(2) A hearing fee shall be payable by the appellant in relation to an appeal where the court has—
    (a) held a hearing in order to determine the appeal; and
    (b) made a final order, declaration or decision in relation to the appeal.

(3) The fees prescribed by paragraphs (1) and (2) shall not be payable where the hearing is in respect of an application or appeal brought by the Public Guardian.

(4) The fee prescribed by paragraph (2) shall not be payable where the hearing is in respect of an appeal against a decision of a nominated officer made under rule 197 of the Rules (appeal against a decision of a nominated officer).

(5) The fee prescribed by paragraph (1) shall not be payable where the applicant was not required to pay an application fee under Article 4(1) by virtue of Article 4(3).

(6) The fees prescribed by paragraphs (1) and (2) shall be payable by the applicant or appellant as the case may be within 30 days of the date of the invoice for the fee.

Fee for request for copy of court document
7.—(1) A fee for a copy of a court document shall be payable by the person **4–209** requesting the copy of the document.

(2) A fee for a certified copy of a court document shall be payable by the person requesting the certified copy of the document.

(3) The fees prescribed by paragraphs (1) and (2) shall be payable at the time the request for the copy is made to the court.

Exemptions
8.—(1) Subject to paragraph (2) no fee shall be payable under this Order by a **4–210** person who, at the time when a fee would otherwise become payable, is in receipt of any qualifying benefit.

(2) Paragraph (1) does not apply to a person who has an award of damages in excess of £16,000 which has been disregarded for the purposes of determining eligibility for that benefit.

(3) The following are qualifying benefits for the purposes of paragraph 1 above—
- (a) income support under the Social Security Contributions and Benefits Act 1992;
- (b) working tax credit, provided that—
  - (i) child tax credit is being paid to the person, or to a couple (as defined in section 3(5)(A) of the Tax Credits Act 2002) which includes the person; or
  - (ii) there is a disability element or severe disability element (or both) to the tax credit received by the person;
- (c) income-based jobseeker's allowance under the Jobseekers Act 1995;
- (d) guarantee credit under the State Pensions Credit Act 2002;
- (e) council tax benefit under the Social Security Contributions and Benefits Act 1992; and
- (f) housing benefit under the Social Security Contributions and Benefits Act 1992.

Reductions and remissions in exceptional circumstances
9. Where it appears to the Lord Chancellor that the payment of any fee pre- **4–211** scribed by this Order would, owing to the exceptional circumstances of the particular case, involve undue hardship, he may reduce or remit the fee in that case.

Transitional provision
10.—(1) In this article "Court of Protection" means the office of the Supreme **4–212** Court called the Court of Protection which ceases to exist under section 45(6) of the Act.

(2) Where a hearing that takes place on or after 1 October 2007 was listed by the Court of Protection before 1 October 2007, no hearing fee shall be payable under Article 6.

SCHEDULE **Article 3**

FEES TO BE TAKEN

4–213

Column 1	Column 2
Application fee (Article 4)	£400.00
Appeal fee (Article 5)	£400.00
Hearing fees (Article 6)	£500.00
Copy of a document fee (Article 7(1))	£5.00
Certified copy of a document fee (Article 7(2))	£25.00

PART 5

DEPRIVATION OF LIBERTY SAFEGUARDS

CODE OF PRACTICE TO SUPPLEMENT THE MAIN MENTAL CAPACITY
ACT 2005 CODE OF PRACTICE

LAID BEFORE PARLIAMENT IN DRAFT JUNE 2008, PURSUANT TO
SECTIONS 42 AND 43 OF THE ACT

This Code of Practice has been prepared and laid before Parliament by the Lord Chancellor in accordance with sections 42 and 43 of the Mental Capacity Act 2005, after having consulted Welsh Ministers and such other persons as he considered appropriate.

The Code of Practice remains in draft form until it has been laid before both Houses of Parliament for a 40-day period during which neither House has resolved not to approve it. Once the 40-day period has expired the Code of Practice will be formally issued and published in such a way as the Lord Chancellor considers appropriate for bringing it to the attention of persons likely to be concerned with its provisions.

London: TSO

FOREWORD BY IVAN LEWIS AND EDWINA HART MBE

The Mental Capacity Act 2005 ('the Act') provides a statutory framework for **5–001** acting and making decisions on behalf of individuals who lack the mental capacity to do so for themselves. It introduced a number of laws to protect these individuals and ensure that they are given every chance to make decisions for themselves. The Act came into force in October 2007.

The Government has added new provisions to the Act: the deprivation of liberty safeguards. The safeguards focus on some of the most vulnerable people in our society: those who for their own safety and in their own best interests need to be accommodated under care and treatment regimes that may have the effect of depriving them of their liberty, but who lack the capacity to consent.

The deprivation of a person's liberty is a very serious matter and should not happen unless it is absolutely necessary, and in the best interests of the person concerned. That is why the safeguards have been created: to ensure that any decision to deprive someone of their liberty is made following defined processes and in consultation with specific authorities.

The new provisions in the Act set out the legal framework of the deprivation of liberty safeguards. This Code of Practice is formally issued by the Lord Chancellor as a Code of Practice under the Mental Capacity Act 2005. It provides guidance and information for those implementing the deprivation of liberty safeguards legislation on a daily basis. In some cases, this will be paid staff, in others those who have been appointed in law to represent individuals who lack capacity to make decisions for themselves (such as deputies or donees of a Lasting Power of Attorney).

Because of this broad audience, the Code of Practice has been written so as to make it as user-friendly as possible—like the main Mental Capacity Act 2005 Code of Practice, issued in April 2007. We are grateful to all those who commented on earlier drafts of the Code to help it achieve that goal.

Ivan Lewis   Edwina Hart

INTRODUCTION

The Mental Capacity Act 2005 ('the Act'), covering England and Wales, pro- **5–002** vides a statutory framework for acting and making decisions on behalf of people who lack the capacity to make those decisions for themselves. These can be small decisions—such as what clothes to wear—or major decisions, such as where to live.

In some cases, people lack the capacity to consent to particular treatment or care that is recognised by others as being in their best interests, or which will protect them from harm. Where this care might involve depriving vulnerable people of their liberty in either a hospital or a care home, extra safeguards have been introduced, in law, to protect their rights and ensure that the care or treatment they receive is in their best interests.

This Code of Practice helps explain how to identify when a person is, or is at risk of, being deprived of their liberty and how deprivation of liberty may be avoided. It also explains the safeguards that have been put in place to ensure that deprivation of liberty, where it does need to occur, has a lawful basis. In addition, it provides guidance on what someone should do if they suspect that a person who lacks capacity is being deprived of their liberty unlawfully.

These safeguards are an important way of protecting the rights of many vulnerable people and should not be viewed negatively. Depriving someone of their liberty can be a necessary requirement in order to provide effective care or treatment. By following the criteria set out in the safeguards, and explained in this Code of Practice, the decision to deprive someone of their liberty can be made lawfully and properly.

HOW DOES THIS CODE OF PRACTICE RELATE TO THE MAIN MENTAL CAPACITY ACT 2005 CODE OF PRACTICE?

This document adds to the guidance in the main Mental Capacity Act 2005 **5–003** Code of Practice ('the main Code'), which was issued in April 2007, and should be used in conjunction with the main Code. It focuses specifically on the deprivation of liberty safeguards added to the Act. These can be found in sections 4A and 4B of, and Schedules A1 and 1A to, the Act.

Though these safeguards were mentioned in the main Code (particularly in chapters 6 and 13), they were not covered in any detail. That was because, at the time the main Code was published, the deprivation of liberty safeguards were still going through the Parliamentary process as part of the Mental Health Bill.[1]

Although the main Code does not cover the deprivation of liberty safeguards, the principles of that Code, and much of its content, are directly relevant to the deprivation of liberty safeguards. It is important that both the Act and the main Code are adhered to whenever capacity and best interests issues, and the deprivation of liberty safeguards, are being considered. The deprivation of liberty safeguards are in addition to, and do not replace, other safeguards in the Act.

---

[1] The Mental Health Bill was used as a vehicle to amend the Mental Capacity Act 2005 in order to introduce the deprivation of liberty safeguards. The Bill became the Mental Health Act 2007 following completion of its Parliamentary passage.

HOW SHOULD THIS CODE OF PRACTICE BE USED?

5–004   This Code of Practice provides guidance to anyone working with and/or caring for adults who lack capacity, but it particularly focuses on those who have a 'duty of care' to a person who lacks the capacity to consent to the care or treatment that is being provided, where that care or treatment may include the need to deprive the person of their liberty. This Code of Practice is also intended to provide information for people who are, or could become, subject to the deprivation of liberty safeguards, and for their families, friends and carers, as well as for anyone who believes that someone is being deprived of their liberty unlawfully.

In this Code of Practice, as throughout the main Code, references to 'lack of capacity' refer to the capacity to make a particular decision at the time it needs to be made. In the context of the deprivation of liberty safeguards, the capacity is specifically the capacity to decide whether or not to consent to care or treatment which involves being kept in a hospital or care home in circumstances that amount to a deprivation of liberty, at the time that decision needs to be made.

WHAT IS THE LEGAL STATUS OF THIS CODE OF PRACTICE?

5–005   As with the main Code, this Code of Practice is published by the Lord Chancellor, under sections 42 and 43 of the Mental Capacity Act 2005. The purpose of the main Code is to provide guidance and information about how the Act works in practice.

Both this Code and the main Code have statutory force, which means that certain people are under a legal duty to have regard to them. More details can be found in the Introduction to the main Code, which explains the legal status of the Code and who should have regard to it.

In addition to those for whom the main Code is intended, this Code of Practice specifically focuses on providing guidance for:

- people exercising functions relating to the deprivation of liberty safeguards, and

- people acting as a relevant person's representative[1] under the deprivation of liberty safeguards (see chapter 7).

SCENARIOS USED IN THIS CODE OF PRACTICE

5–006   This Code of Practice includes boxes within the main text containing scenarios, using imaginary characters and situations. These are intended to help illustrate what is meant in the main text. They should not in any way be taken as templates for decisions that need to be made in similar situations. Decisions must always be made on the facts of each individual case.

ALTERNATIVE FORMATS AND FURTHER INFORMATION

5–007   This Code of Practice is also available in Welsh and can be made available in other formats on request.

---

[1] A 'relevant person' is a person who is, or may become, deprived of their liberty in accordance with the deprivation of liberty safeguards.

CONTENTS

What are the responsibilities of the managing authority and the commissioners of care if a request for an authorisation is turned down?

6.   When can urgent authorisations of deprivation of liberty be given? (5–191)

When can an urgent authorisation be given?
What records should be kept about urgent authorisations?
Who should be consulted before giving an urgent authorisation?
Can a person be moved into care under an urgent authorisation?
What happens at the end of an urgent authorisation period?
How and when can an urgent authorisation be extended?

7.   What is the role of the relevant person's representative? (5–222)

What is the role of the relevant person's representative?
How should managing authorities work with the relevant person's representative?
Who can be the relevant person's representative?
When should the relevant person's representative be identified?
How should the relevant person's representative be selected?
How should the relevant person's representative be appointed?
How should the work of the relevant person's representative be supported and monitored?
When can the appointment of the relevant person's representative be terminated?
What happens when there is no relevant person's representative available?
When should an IMCA be instructed?

8.   When should an authorisation be reviewed and what happens when it ends? (5–264)

When should a standard authorisation be reviewed?
What happens when a review is going to take place?
How should standard authorisations be reviewed?
What happens if any of the requirements are not met?
Is a review necessary when the relevant person's capacity fluctuates?
What happens when an authorisation ends?

9.   What happens if someone thinks a person is being deprived of their liberty without authorisation? (5–295)

What action should someone take if they think a person is being deprived of their liberty without authorisation?
What happens if somebody informs the supervisory body directly that they think a person is being deprived of their liberty without authorisation?
How will the assessment of unlawful deprivation of liberty be conducted?
What happens once the assessment has been conducted?

10.   What is the Court of Protection and when can people apply to it? (5–310)

When can people apply to the Court of Protection about the deprivation of liberty safeguards and who can apply?
How should people apply to the Court of Protection?
What orders can the Court of Protection make?
What is the role of the Court of Protection in respect of people lacking

capacity who are deprived of their liberty in settings other than hospitals or care homes?

Is legal aid available to support applications to the Court of Protection in deprivation of liberty safeguards cases?

11.   How will the safeguards be monitored? (5–324)
Who will monitor the safeguards?
What will the inspection bodies do and what powers will they have?

Checklists (5–333)

Key points for care homes and hospitals (managing authorities)

Key points for local authorities and NHS bodies (supervisory bodies)

Key points for managing authorities and supervisory bodies

Annexes (5–336)

Annex 1—Overview of the deprivation of liberty safeguards process

Annex 2—What should a managing authority consider before applying for authorisation of deprivation of liberty?

Annex 3—Supervisory body action on receipt of a request for a standard deprivation of liberty authorisation or to determine whether there is an unauthorised deprivation of liberty

Annex 4—Standard authorisation review process

Key words and phrases used in the Code of Practice

1.   WHAT ARE THE DEPRIVATION OF LIBERTY SAFEGUARDS AND WHY WERE THEY INTRODUCED?

The deprivation of liberty safeguards were introduced to provide a legal frame- **5–008** work around the deprivation of liberty. Specifically, they were introduced to prevent breaches of the European Convention on Human Rights (ECHR) such as the one identified by the judgment of the European Court of Human Rights (ECtHR) in the case of *HL v the United Kingdom*[1] (commonly referred to as the 'Bournewood' judgment). The case concerned an autistic man (HL) with a learning disability, who lacked the capacity to decide whether he should be admitted to hospital for specific treatment. He was admitted on an informal basis under common law in his best interests, but this decision was challenged by HL's carers. In its judgment, the ECtHR held that this admission constituted a deprivation of HL's liberty and, further, that:

- the deprivation of liberty had not been in accordance with 'a procedure prescribed by law' and was, therefore, in breach of Article 5(1) of the ECHR, and

- there had been a contravention of Article 5(4) of the ECHR because HL had no means of applying quickly to a court to see if the deprivation of liberty was lawful.

---

[1] (2004) Application No: 00045508/99.

To prevent further similar breaches of the ECHR, the Mental Capacity Act 2005 has been amended to provide safeguards for people who lack capacity specifically to consent to treatment or care in either a hospital or a care home[1] that, in their own best interests, can only be provided in circumstances that amount to a deprivation of liberty, and where detention under the Mental Health Act 1983 is not appropriate for the person at that time. These safeguards are referred to in this Code of Practice as 'deprivation of liberty safeguards'.

What are the deprivation of liberty safeguards?

5–009   1.1   The deprivation of liberty safeguards provide legal protection for those vulnerable people who are, or may become, deprived of their liberty within the meaning of Article 5 of the ECHR in a hospital or care home, whether placed under public or private arrangements. They do not apply to people detained under the Mental Health Act 1983. The safeguards exist to provide a proper legal process and suitable protection in those circumstances where deprivation of liberty appears to be unavoidable, in a person's own best interests.

5–010   1.2   Every effort should be made, in both commissioning and providing care or treatment, to prevent deprivation of liberty. If deprivation of liberty cannot be avoided, it should be for no longer than is necessary.

5–011   1.3   The safeguards provide for deprivation of liberty to be made lawful through 'standard' or 'urgent' authorisation processes. These processes are designed to prevent arbitrary decisions to deprive a person of liberty and give a right to challenge deprivation of liberty authorisations.

5–012   1.4   The deprivation of liberty safeguards mean that a 'managing authority' (i.e. the relevant hospital or care home—see paragraph 3.1) must seek authorisation from a 'supervisory body' in order to be able lawfully to deprive someone of their liberty. Before giving such an authorisation, the supervisory body must be satisfied that the person has a mental disorder[2] and lacks capacity to decide about their residence or treatment. The supervisory body could be a primary care trust, a local authority, Welsh Ministers or a local health board (LHB) (see paragraph 3.3).

5–013   1.5   A decision as to whether or not deprivation of liberty arises will depend on all the circumstances of the case (as explained more fully in chapter 2). It is neither necessary nor appropriate to apply for a deprivation of liberty authorisation for everyone who is in hospital or a care home simply because the person concerned lacks capacity to decide whether or not they should be there. In deciding whether or not an application is necessary, a managing authority should carefully consider whether any restrictions that are, or will be, needed to provide ongoing care or treatment amount to a deprivation of liberty when looked at together.

5–014   1.6   The deprivation of liberty safeguards cover:
- how an application for authorisation should be applied for

---

[1] Throughout this document, the term 'care home' means a care home registered under the Care Standards Act 2000.

[2] As defined in section 1 of the Mental Health Act 1983, a mental disorder is any disorder or disability of the mind, apart from dependence on alcohol and drugs. This includes all learning disabilities. The distinction in the Mental Health Act 1983 between learning disabilities depending on whether or not they are associated with abnormally aggressive or seriously irresponsible behaviour is not relevant.

- how an application for authorisation should be assessed
- the requirements that must be fulfilled for an authorisation to be given
- how an authorisation should be reviewed
- what support and representation must be provided for people who are subject to an authorisation, and
- how people can challenge authorisations.

Who is covered by these safeguards?

1.7 The safeguards apply to people in England and Wales who have a mental **5–015** disorder and lack capacity to consent to the arrangements made for their care or treatment, but for whom receiving care or treatment in circumstances that amount to a deprivation of liberty may be necessary to protect them from harm and appears to be in their best interests. A large number of these people will be those with significant learning disabilities, or older people who have dementia or some similar disability, but they can also include those who have certain other neurological conditions (for example as a result of a brain injury).

1.8 In order to come within the scope of a deprivation of liberty authorisation, **5–016** a person must be detained in a hospital or care home, for the purpose of being given care or treatment in circumstances that amount to a deprivation of liberty. The authorisation must relate to the individual concerned and to the hospital or care home in which they are detained.

1.9 For the purposes of Article 5 of the ECHR, there is no distinction in prin- **5–017** ciple between depriving a person who lacks capacity of their liberty for the purpose of treating them for a physical condition, and depriving them of their liberty for treatment of a mental disorder. There will therefore be occasions when people who lack capacity to consent to admission are taken to hospital for treatment of physical illnesses or injuries, and then need to be cared for in circumstances that amount to a deprivation of liberty. In these circumstances, a deprivation of liberty authorisation must be applied for. Consequently, this Code of Practice must be followed and applied in acute hospital settings as well as care homes and mental health units.

1.10 It is important to bear in mind that, while the deprivation of liberty might **5–018** be for the purpose of giving a person treatment, a deprivation of liberty authorisation does not itself authorise treatment. Treatment that is proposed following authorisation of deprivation of liberty may only be given with the person's consent (if they have capacity to make the decision) or in accordance with the wider provisions of the Mental Capacity Act 2005. More details of this are contained in paragraphs 5.10 to 5.13 of this Code.

1.11 The safeguards cannot apply to people while they are detained in hospital **5–019** under the Mental Health Act 1983. The safeguards can, however, apply to a person who has previously been detained in hospital under the Mental Health Act 1983. There are other cases in which people who are—or could be—subject to the Mental Health Act 1983 will not meet the eligibility requirement for the safeguards. Chapter 13 of the main Code contains guidance on the relationship between the Mental Capacity Act 2005 and the Mental Health Act 1983 generally, as does the Code of

Practice to the Mental Health Act 1983 itself. Paragraphs 4.40 to 4.57 of the present Code explain the relationship of the deprivation of liberty safeguards to the Mental Health Act 1983, and in particular how to assess if a person is eligible to be deprived of their liberty under the safeguards.

5–020 1.12 The safeguards relate only to people aged 18 and over. If the issue of depriving a person under the age of 18 of their liberty arises, other safeguards must be considered—such as the existing powers of the court, particularly those under section 25 of the Children Act 1989, or use of the Mental Health Act 1983.

When can someone be deprived of their liberty?

5–021 1.13 Depriving someone who lacks the capacity to consent to the arrangements made for their care or treatment of their liberty is a serious matter, and the decision to do so should not be taken lightly. The deprivation of liberty safeguards make it clear that a person may only be deprived of their liberty:

- in their own best interests to protect them from harm
- if it is a proportionate response to the likelihood and seriousness of the harm, and
- if there is no less restrictive alternative.

5–022 1.14 Under no circumstances must deprivation of liberty be used as a form of punishment, or for the convenience of professionals, carers or anyone else. Deprivation of liberty should not be extended due to delays in moving people between care or treatment settings, for example when somebody awaits discharge after completing a period of hospital treatment.

Are there any cultural considerations in implementing the safeguards?

5–023 1.15 The deprivation of liberty safeguards should not impact in any different way on different racial or ethnic groups, and care should be taken to ensure that the provisions are not operated in a manner that discriminates against particular racial or ethnic groups. It is up to managing authorities and supervisory bodies to ensure that their staff are aware of their responsibilities in this regard and of the need to ensure that the safeguards are operated fairly and equitably.

5–024 1.16 Assessors who carry out deprivation of liberty assessments to help decide whether a person should be deprived of their liberty (see chapter 4) should have the necessary skills and experience to take account of people's diverse backgrounds. Accordingly, they will need to have an understanding of, and respect for, the background of the relevant person. Supervisory bodies must take these factors into account when appointing assessors and must seek to appoint the most suitable available person for each case.

5–025 1.17 Interpreters should be available, where necessary, to help assessors to communicate not only with the relevant person but also with people with an interest in their care and treatment. An interpreter should be suitably qualified and experienced to enable them to provide effective language and communication support in the particular case concerned, and to offer appropriate assistance to the assessors involved. Information should be made available in other languages where relevant.

1.18 Any decision about the instruction of Independent Mental Capacity **5–026** Advocates (see paragraphs 3.22 to 3.28) or relevant person's representatives (see chapter 7) should take account of the cultural, national, racial or ethnic background of the relevant person.

Where do the safeguards apply?

1.19 Although the Bournewood judgment was specifically about a patient who **5–027** lacked capacity to consent to admission to hospital for mental health treatment, the judgment has wider implications that extend to people who lack capacity and who might be deprived of their liberty either in a hospital or in a care home.

1.20 It will only be lawful to deprive somebody of their liberty elsewhere (for **5–027** example, in their own home, in supported living arrangements other than in a care home, or in a day centre) when following an order of the Court of Protection on a personal welfare matter. In such a case, the Court of Protection order itself provides a legal basis for the deprivation of liberty. This means that a separate deprivation of liberty authorisation under the processes set out in this Code of Practice is not required. More information about applying to the Court of Protection regarding personal welfare matters is given in chapter 10.

How do the safeguards apply to privately arranged care or treatment?

1.21 Under the Human Rights Act 1998, the duty to act in accordance with the **5–029** ECHR applies only to public authorities. However, all states that have signed up to the ECHR are obliged to make sure that the rights set out in the ECHR apply to all of their citizens. The Mental Capacity Act 2005 therefore makes it clear that the deprivation of liberty safeguards apply to both publicly and privately arranged care or treatment.

How do the safeguards relate to the rest of the Mental Capacity Act 2005?

1.22 The deprivation of liberty safeguards are in addition to, and do not **5–030** replace, other safeguards in the Mental Capacity Act 2005. This means that decisions made, and actions taken, for a person who is subject to a deprivation of liberty authorisation must fulfil the requirements of the Act in the same way as for any other person. In particular, any action taken under the deprivation of liberty safeguards must be in line with the principles of the Act:

- A person must be assumed to have capacity to make a decision unless it is established that they lack the capacity to make that decision.
- A person is not to be treated as unable to make a decision unless all practicable steps to help them to do so have been taken without success.
- A person is not to be treated as unable to make a decision merely because they make an unwise decision.
- An act done, or decision made, under the Act for or on behalf of a person who lacks capacity must be done, or made, in their best interests.

- Before the act is done, or the decision is made, regard must be had to whether the purpose for which it is needed can be as effectively achieved in a way that is less restrictive of the person's rights and freedom of action.

These principles are set out in chapter 2 of the main Code and explained in more detail in chapters 3 to 6 of the same document. Paragraph 5.13 of the main Code contains a checklist of factors that need to be taken into account in determining a person's best interests.

2. WHAT IS DEPRIVATION OF LIBERTY?

5–031   There is no simple definition of deprivation of liberty. The question of whether the steps taken by staff or institutions in relation to a person amount to a deprivation of that person's liberty is ultimately a legal question, and only the courts can determine the law. This guidance seeks to assist staff and institutions in considering whether or not the steps they are taking, or proposing to take, amount to a deprivation of a person's liberty. The deprivation of liberty safeguards give best interests assessors the authority to make recommendations about proposed deprivations of liberty, and supervisory bodies the power to give authorisations that deprive people of their liberty.

This chapter provides guidance for staff and institutions on how to assess whether particular steps they are taking, or proposing to take, might amount to a deprivation of liberty, based on existing case law. It also considers what other factors may be taken into account when considering the issue of deprivation of liberty, including, importantly, what is permissible under the Mental Capacity Act 2005 in relation to restraint or restriction. Finally, it provides a summary of some of the most important cases to date.

Further legal developments may occur after this guidance has been issued, and healthcare and social care staff need to keep themselves informed of legal developments that may have a bearing on their practice.

What does case law say to date?

5–032   2.1   The European Court of Human Rights (ECtHR) has drawn a distinction between the deprivation of liberty of an individual (which is unlawful, unless authorised) and restrictions on the liberty of movement of an individual.

5–033   2.2   The ECtHR made it clear that the question of whether someone has been deprived of liberty depends on the particular circumstances of the case. Specifically, the ECtHR said in its October 2004 judgment in *HL v the United Kingdom:*

> "to determine whether there has been a deprivation of liberty, the starting-point must be the specific situation of the individual concerned and account must be taken of a whole range of factors arising in a particular case such as the type, duration, effects and manner of implementation of the measure in question. The distinction between a deprivation of, and restriction upon, liberty is merely one of degree or intensity and not one of nature or substance."

2.3 The difference between deprivation of liberty and restriction upon liberty **5–034** is one of degree or intensity. It may therefore be helpful to envisage a scale, which moves from 'restraint' or 'restriction' to 'deprivation of liberty'. Where an individual is on the scale will depend on the concrete circumstances of the individual and may change over time. For more information on how the Act defines restraint, see paragraphs 2.8–2.12.

2.4 Although the guidance in this chapter includes descriptions of past **5–035** decisions of the courts, which should be used to help evaluate whether deprivation of liberty may be occurring, each individual case must be assessed on its own circumstances. No two cases are likely to be identical, so it is important to be aware of previous court judgments and the factors that the courts have identified as important.

2.5 The ECtHR and UK courts have determined a number of cases about **5–036** deprivation of liberty. Their judgments indicate that the following factors can be relevant to identifying whether steps taken involve more than restraint and amount to a deprivation of liberty. It is important to remember that this list is not exclusive; other factors may arise in future in particular cases.
- Restraint is used, including sedation, to admit a person to an institution where that person is resisting admission.
- Staff exercise complete and effective control over the care and movement of a person for a significant period.
- Staff exercise control over assessments, treatment, contacts and residence.
- A decision has been taken by the institution that the person will not be released into the care of others, or permitted to live elsewhere, unless the staff in the institution consider it appropriate.
- A request by carers for a person to be discharged to their care is refused.
- The person is unable to maintain social contacts because of restrictions placed on their access to other people.
- The person loses autonomy because they are under continuous supervision and control.

There is more information on some relevant cases at the end of this chapter (paragraphs 2.17–2.23).

How can deprivation of liberty be identified?

2.6 In determining whether deprivation of liberty has occurred, or is likely to **5–037** occur, decision-makers need to consider all the facts in a particular case. There is unlikely to be any simple definition that can be applied in every case, and it is probable that no single factor will, in itself, determine whether the overall set of steps being taken in relation to the relevant person amount to a deprivation of liberty. In general, the decision-maker should always consider the following:
- All the circumstances of each and every case
- What measures are being taken in relation to the individual? When are they required? For what period do they endure? What are the effects of any restraints or restrictions on the individual? Why are they necessary? What aim do they seek to meet?

- What are the views of the relevant person, their family or carers? Do any of them object to the measures?
- How are any restraints or restrictions implemented? Do any of the constraints on the individual's personal freedom go beyond 'restraint' or 'restriction' to the extent that they constitute a deprivation of liberty?
- Are there any less restrictive options for delivering care or treatment that avoid deprivation of liberty altogether?
- Does the cumulative effect of all the restrictions imposed on the person amount to a deprivation of liberty, even if individually they would not?

What practical steps can be taken to reduce the risk of deprivation of liberty occurring?

5–038   2.7   There are many ways in which providers and commissioners of care can reduce the risk of taking steps that amount to a deprivation of liberty, by minimising the restrictions imposed and ensuring that decisions are taken with the involvement of the relevant person and their family, friends and carers. The processes for staff to follow are:
- Make sure that all decisions are taken (and reviewed) in a structured way, and reasons for decisions recorded.
- Follow established good practice for care planning.
- Make a proper assessment of whether the person lacks capacity to decide whether or not to accept the care or treatment proposed, in line with the principles of the Act (see chapter 3 of the main Code for further guidance).
- Before admitting a person to hospital or residential care in circumstances that may amount to a deprivation of liberty, consider whether the person's needs could be met in a less restrictive way. Any restrictions placed on the person while in hospital or in a care home must be kept to the minimum necessary, and should be in place for the shortest possible period.
- Take proper steps to help the relevant person retain contact with family, friends and carers. Where local advocacy services are available, their involvement should be encouraged to support the person and their family, friends and carers.
- Review the care plan on an ongoing basis. It may well be helpful to include an independent element, possibly via an advocacy service, in the review.

What does the Act mean by 'restraint'?

5–039   2.8   Section 6(4) of the Act states that someone is using restraint if they:
- use force—or threaten to use force—to make someone do something that they are resisting, or
- restrict a person's freedom of movement, whether they are resisting or not.

5–040   2.9   Paragraphs 6.40 to 6.48 of the main Code contain guidance about the appropriate use of restraint. Restraint is appropriate when it is used to prevent harm to the person who lacks capacity and it is a proportionate response to the likelihood and seriousness of harm. Appropriate use of restraint falls short of deprivation of liberty.

2.10 Preventing a person from leaving a care home or hospital unaccompanied **5–041** because there is a risk that they would try to cross a road in a dangerous way, for example, is likely to be seen as a proportionate restriction or restraint to prevent the person from coming to harm. That would be unlikely, in itself, to constitute a deprivation of liberty. Similarly, locking a door to guard against immediate harm is unlikely, in itself, to amount to a deprivation of liberty.

2.11 The ECtHR has also indicated that the duration of any restrictions is a rel- **5–042** evant factor when considering whether or not a person is deprived of their liberty. This suggests that actions that are immediately necessary to prevent harm may not, in themselves, constitute a deprivation of liberty.

2.12 However, where the restriction or restraint is frequent, cumulative and **5–043** ongoing, or if there are other factors present, then care providers should consider whether this has gone beyond permissible restraint, as defined in the Act. If so, then they must either apply for authorisation under the deprivation of liberty safeguards (as explained in chapter 3) or change their care provision to reduce the level of restraint.

How does the use of restraint apply within a hospital or when taking someone to a hospital or a care home?

Within a hospital

2.13 If a person in hospital for mental health treatment, or being considered for **5–044** admission to a hospital for mental health treatment, needs to be restrained, this is likely to indicate that they are objecting to treatment or to being in hospital. The care providers should consider whether the need for restraint means the person is objecting (see paragraph 4.46 of this Code for guidance on how to decide whether a person is objecting for this purpose). A person who objects to mental health treatment, and who meets the criteria for detention under the Mental Health Act 1983, is normally ineligible for an authorisation under the deprivation of liberty safeguards. If the care providers believe it is necessary to detain the person, they may wish to consider use of the Mental Health Act 1983.

Taking someone to a hospital or a care home

2.14 Transporting a person who lacks capacity from their home, or another **5–045** location, to a hospital or care home will not usually amount to a deprivation of liberty (for example, to take them to hospital by ambulance in an emergency.) Even where there is an expectation that the person will be deprived of liberty within the care home or hospital, it is unlikely that the journey itself will constitute a deprivation of liberty so that an authorisation is needed before the journey commences. In almost all cases, it is likely that a person can be lawfully taken to a hospital or a care home under the wider provisions of the Act, as long as it is considered that being in the hospital or care home will be in their best interests.

5–046   2.15   In a very few cases, there may be exceptional circumstances where taking a person to a hospital or a care home amounts to a deprivation of liberty, for example where it is necessary to do more than persuade or restrain the person for the purpose of transportation, or where the journey is exceptionally long. In such cases, it may be necessary to seek an order from the Court of Protection to ensure that the journey is taken on a lawful basis.

How should managing authorities avoid unnecessary applications for standard authorisations?

5–047   2.16   While it is unlawful to deprive a person of their liberty without authorisation, managing authorities should take into consideration that unnecessary applications for standard authorisations in cases that do not in fact involve depriving a person of liberty may place undue stress upon the person being assessed and on their families or carers. Moreover, consideration must always be given to the possibility of less restrictive options for delivering care or treatment that avoid deprivation of liberty altogether.

Examples of case law

5–048   2.17   To provide further guidance, the following paragraphs contain short descriptions of what appear to be the significant features of recent or important cases in England and Wales and the ECtHR dealing with deprivation of liberty. Remember that:

- these descriptions are for guidance only
- only the courts can authoritatively determine the law; and
- the courts are likely to give judgments in cases after this guidance is issued. Staff will need to keep up to date and take account of further relevant legal developments.

Cases where the courts found that the steps taken did not involve a deprivation of liberty

5–049   2.18   *LLBC v TG* (judgment of High Court of 14 November 2007)

TG was a 78-year-old man with dementia and cognitive impairment. TG was resident in a care home, but was admitted to hospital with pneumonia and septicaemia. While he was in hospital, there was a dispute between the local authority and TG's daughter and granddaughter about TG's future. The daughter and granddaughter wanted TG to live with them, but the local authority believed that TG needed 24-hour care in a residential care home.

The council obtained an order from the court, directing that TG be delivered to the care home identified as appropriate by the council. Neither the daughter nor granddaughter was informed that a court hearing was taking place. That order was subsequently changed and TG was able to live with his daughter and granddaughter.

TG's daughter and granddaughter claimed that the period of time he had spent at the care home amounted to a deprivation of his liberty.

The judge considered that there was no deprivation of liberty, but the case was borderline. The key factors in his decision included:

- The care home was an ordinary care home where only ordinary restrictions of liberty applied.
- The family were able to visit TG on a largely unrestricted basis and were entitled to take him out from the home for outings.
- TG was personally compliant and expressed himself as happy in the care home. He had lived in a local authority care home for over three years and was objectively content with his situation there.
- There was no occasion where TG was objectively deprived of his liberty.

The judge said:

"Whilst I agree that the circumstances of the present case may be near the borderline between mere restrictions of liberty and Article 5 detention, I have come to the conclusion that, looked at as a whole and having regard to all the relevant circumstances, the placement of TG in Towerbridge falls short of engaging Article 5."

2.19 *Nielsen v Denmark (ECtHR; (1988) 11 EHRR 175)*   **5–050**

The mother of a 12-year-old boy arranged for his admission to the state hospital's psychiatric ward. The boy had a nervous disorder and required treatment in the form of regular talks and environmental therapy. The treatment given, and the conditions under which it was administered, was appropriate. The duration of treatment was 51/2 months. The boy, however, applied to the ECtHR, feeling that he had been deprived of his liberty.

The restrictions placed on the applicant's freedom of movement and contacts with the outside world were not much different from restrictions that might be imposed on a child in an ordinary hospital. The door of the ward was locked to prevent children exposing themselves to danger or running around disturbing other patients. The applicant was free to leave the ward with permission and to go out if accompanied by a member of staff. He was able to visit his family and friends, and towards the end of his stay to go to school.

The Court held:

"The restrictions imposed on the applicant were not of a nature or degree similar to the cases of deprivation of liberty specified in paragraph (1) of Article 5. In particular, he was not detained as a person of unsound mind. .... Indeed, the restrictions to which the applicant was subject were no more than the normal requirements for the care of a child of 12 years of age receiving treatment in hospital. The conditions in which the applicant stayed thus did not, in principle, differ from those obtaining in many hospital wards where children with physical disorders are treated."

It concluded:

"the hospitalisation of the applicant did not amount to a deprivation of liberty within the meaning of Article 5, but was a responsible exercise by his mother of her custodial rights in the interests of the child."

5–051   2.20   *HM v Switzerland (ECtHR; (2002) 38 EHRR 314)*

An 84-year-old woman was placed indefinitely in a nursing home by state authorities. She had had the possibility of staying at home and being cared for there, but she and her son had refused to co-operate with the relevant care association, and her living conditions had subsequently deteriorated. The state authorities placed her in the home in order to provide her with necessary medical care and satisfactory living conditions and hygiene.

The woman was not placed in the secure ward of the home but was free to move within the home and to have social contacts with the outside world. She was initially undecided as to what solution she preferred and, after moving into the home, the applicant had agreed to stay there. However, she subsequently applied to the courts saying that she had been deprived of her liberty.

The Court held that she had not been deprived of her liberty:

"Bearing these elements in mind, in particular the fact that [the authorities] had ordered the applicant's placement in the nursing home in her own interests in order to provide her with the necessary medical care and satisfactory living conditions and standards of hygiene, and also taking into consideration the comparable circumstances of *Nielsen v Denmark* [see case summary above], the Court concludes that in the circumstances of the present case the applicant's placement in the nursing home did not amount to a deprivation of liberty within the meaning of Article 5(1), but was a responsible measure taken by the competent authorities in the applicant's best interests."

Cases where the courts have found that the steps taken involve a deprivation of liberty

5–052   2.21   *DE and JE v Surrey County Council (SCC)* (High Court judgment of 29 December 2006)

DE was a 76-year-old man who, following a major stroke, had become blind and had significant short-term memory impairment. He also had dementia and lacked capacity to decide where he should live, but was still often able to express his wishes with some clarity and force.

DE was married to JE. In August 2003, DE was living at home with JE. There was an occasion when JE felt that she could not care for DE, and placed him on a chair on the pavement in front of the house and called the police. The local authority then placed him in two care homes, referred to in the judgment of the court as the X home and the Y home.

Within the care homes, DE had a very substantial degree of freedom and lots of contact with the outside world. He was never subject to physical or chemical restraint.

DE repeatedly expressed the wish to live with JE, and JE also wanted DE to live with her. SCC would not agree to DE returning to live with, or visit, JE and made it clear that if JE were to persist in an attempt to remove

DE, SCC would contact the police. DE and JE applied to the courts that this was a deprivation of his liberty.

In his judgment, Justice Munby said:

"The fundamental issue in this case ... is whether DE has been and is deprived of his liberty to leave the X home and whether DE has been and is deprived of his liberty to leave the Y home. And when I refer to leaving the X home and the Y home, I do not mean leaving for the purpose of some trip or outing approved by SCC or by those managing the institution; I mean leaving in the sense of removing himself permanently in order to live where and with whom he chooses, specifically removing himself to live at home with JE."

He then said:

"DE was not and is not "free to leave", and was and is, in that sense, completely under the control of [the local authority], because, as [counsel for DE] put it, it was and is [the local authority] who decides the essential matters of where DE can live, whether he can leave and whether he can be with JE."

He concluded:

"The simple reality is that DE will be permitted to leave the institution in which [the local authority] has placed him and be released to the care of JE only as and when,—if ever; probably never,—[the local authority] considers it appropriate. [The local authority's] motives may be the purest, but in my judgment, [it] has been and is continuing to deprive DE of his liberty."

2.22 *HL v United Kingdom (ECtHR; (2004) 40 EHRR 761)* **5–053**

A 48-year-old man who had had autism since birth was unable to speak and his level of understanding was limited. He was frequently agitated and had a history of self-harming behaviour. He lacked the capacity to consent to treatment.

For over 30 years, he was cared for in Bournewood Hospital. In 1994, he was entrusted to carers and for three years he lived successfully with his carers. Following an incident of self-harm at a day centre on 22 July 1997, the applicant was taken to Bournewood Hospital where he was re-admitted informally (not under the Mental Health Act 1983).

The carers wished to have the applicant released to their care, which the hospital refused. The carers were unable to visit him.

In its judgment in *HL v the United Kingdom,* the ECtHR said that:

"the key factor in the present case [is] that the health care professionals treating and managing the applicant exercised complete and effective control over his care and movements from the moment he presented acute behavioural problems on July 22, 1997 to the date when he was compulsorily detained on October 29, 1997."

"His responsible medical officer (Dr M) was clear that, had the applicant resisted admission or tried to leave thereafter, she would have prevented him from doing so and would have considered his involuntary committal under s. 3 of the 1983 Act; indeed, as soon as the Court of Appeal indicated that his appeal would be allowed, he was compulsorily detained under the 1983 Act. The correspondence between the applicant's carers and Dr M reflects both the carer's wish to have the applicant immediately released to their care and, equally, the clear intention of Dr M and the other relevant health care professionals to exercise strict control over his assessment, treatment, contacts and, notably, movement and residence; the applicant would only be released from hospital to the care of Mr and Mrs E as and when those professionals considered it appropriate. ... it was clear from the above noted correspondence that the applicant's contact with his carers was directed and controlled by the hospital, his carers visiting him for the first time after his admission on 2 November 1997."

"Accordingly, the concrete situation was that the applicant was under continuous supervision and control and was not free to leave."

5–054   2.23   *Storck v Germany (ECtHR; (2005) 43 EHRR 96)*

A young woman was placed by her father in a psychiatric institution on occasions in 1974 and 1975. In July 1977, at the age of 18, she was placed again in a psychiatric institution. She was kept in a locked ward and was under the continuous supervision and control of the clinic personnel and was not free to leave the clinic during her entire stay of 20 months. When she attempted to flee, she was shackled. When she succeeded one time, she was brought back by the police. She was unable to maintain regular contact with the outside world.

She applied to the courts on the basis that she had been deprived of her liberty. There was a dispute about whether she consented to her confinement.

The Court noted:

"the applicant, on several occasions, had tried to flee from the clinic. She had to be shackled in order to prevent her from absconding and had to be brought back to the clinic by the police when she managed to escape on one occasion. Under these circumstances, the Court is unable to discern any factual basis for the assumption that the applicant—presuming that she had the capacity to consent—agreed to her continued stay in the clinic. In the alternative, assuming that the applicant was no longer capable of consenting following her treatment with strong medication, she cannot, in any event, be considered to have validly agreed to her stay in the clinic."

5–055   2.24   These cases reinforce the need to carefully consider all the specific circumstances of the relevant individual before deciding whether or not a person is being deprived of their liberty. They also underline the vital importance of involving family, friends and carers in this decision-making process: a significant feature of a number of the cases that have come before the courts is a difference of opinion or communication issue between the commissioners or providers of care and family members and carers.

3. HOW AND WHEN CAN DEPRIVATION OF LIBERTY BE APPLIED FOR AND AUTHORISED?

There are some circumstances in which depriving a person, who lacks capacity **5–056** to consent to the arrangements made for their care or treatment, of their liberty is necessary to protect them from harm, and is in their best interests.

Deprivation of liberty can be authorised by supervisory bodies (primary care trusts (PCTs), local authorities, Welsh Ministers or local health boards (LHBs). To obtain authorisation to deprive someone of their liberty, managing authorities have to apply for an authorisation following the processes set out in this chapter.[1] Once an application has been received, the supervisory body must then follow the assessment processes set out in chapter 4 before it can authorise deprivation of liberty. It should be borne in mind that a deprivation of liberty authorisation does not, in itself, give authority to treat someone. This issue is covered in paragraphs 5.10 to 5.13.

In the vast majority of cases, it should be possible to plan in advance so that a standard authorisation can be obtained before the deprivation of liberty begins. There may, however, be some exceptional cases where the need for the deprivation of liberty is so urgent that it is in the best interests of the person for it to begin while the application is being considered. In that case, the care home or hospital may give an urgent authorisation for up to seven days (see chapter 6).

How, in summary, can deprivation of liberty be authorised?

3.1 A **managing authority** has responsibility for applying for authorisation **5–057** of deprivation of liberty for any person who may come within the scope of the deprivation of liberty safeguards:
   - In the case of an NHS hospital, the managing authority is the NHS body responsible for the running of the hospital in which the relevant person is, or is to be, a resident.
   - In the case of a care home or a private hospital, the managing authority will be the person registered, or required to be registered, under part 2 of the Care Standards Act 2000 in respect of the hospital or care home.

3.2 If a healthcare or social care professional thinks that an authorisation is **5–058** needed, they should inform the managing authority. This might be as a result of a care review or needs assessment but could happen at any other time too. (See chapter 9 for guidance on action to take if there is a concern that a person is already being deprived of their liberty, without authorisation.)

3.3 A **supervisory body** is responsible for considering requests for authorisa- **5–059** tions, commissioning the required assessments (see chapter 4) and, where all the assessments agree, authorising the deprivation of liberty:
   - Where the deprivation of liberty safeguards are applied to a person in a hospital situated in England, the supervisory body will be:

---

[1] If a person is lawfully deprived of liberty in a care home or hospital as **a consequence of an order of the Court of Protection,** there is no need to apply for an authorisation. However, once the order of the Court of Protection has expired, for lawful deprivation of liberty to continue authorisation must be obtained by following the processes set out in this chapter.

—if a PCT commissions[1] the relevant care or treatment (or it is commissioned on the PCT's behalf), that PCT

—if the Welsh Ministers or an LHB commissions the relevant care and treatment in England, the Welsh Ministers, or

—in any other case, the PCT for the area in which the hospital is situated.

- Where the deprivation of liberty safeguards are applied to a person in a hospital situated in Wales, the supervisory body will be the Welsh Ministers or an LHB **unless** a PCT commissions the relevant care and treatment in Wales, in which case the PCT will be the supervisory body.

- Where the deprivation of liberty safeguards are applied to a person in a care home, whether situated in England or Wales, the supervisory body will be the local authority for the area in which the person is ordinarily resident. However, if the person is not ordinarily resident in the area of any local authority (for example a person of no fixed abode), the supervisory body will be the local authority for the area in which the care home is situated.[2]

5–060 3.4 There are two types of authorisation: standard and urgent. A managing authority must request a standard authorisation when it appears likely that, at some time during the next 28 days, someone will be accommodated in its hospital or care home in circumstances that amount to a deprivation of liberty within the meaning of Article 5 of the European Convention on Human Rights. The request must be made to the supervisory body. Whenever possible, authorisation should be obtained in advance. Where this is not possible, and the managing authority believes it is necessary to deprive someone of their liberty in their best interests **before** the standard authorisation process can be completed, the managing authority must itself give an urgent authorisation and then obtain standard authorisation within seven calendar days (see chapter 6).

5–061 3.5 The flowchart at Annex 1 gives an overview of how the deprivation of liberty safeguards process should operate.

---

[1] Guidance on establishing the responsible commissioner can be found at http://www.dh.gov.uk/en/ Publicationsandstatistics/Publications/ PublicationsPolicyAndGuidance/DH_078466

[2] To work out the place of ordinary residence, the usual mechanisms under the National Assistance Act 1948 apply (see http://www.dh.gov.uk/en/SocialCare/Deliveringadultsocialcare/ Ordinaryresidence/ DH_079346). Any unresolved questions about the ordinary residence of a person will be handled by the Secretary of State or by the Welsh Ministers. Until a decision is made, the local authority that received the application must act as the supervisory body. After the decision is made, the local authority of ordinary residence must become the supervisory body. Regulations 17 to 19 of the Mental Capacity (Deprivation of Liberty: Standard Authorisations, Assessments and Ordinary Residence) Regulations 2008 set out, for England, arrangements that are to have effect while any question as to the ordinary residence of a person is determined in a case in which a local authority has received a request for a standard authorisation or a request to decide whether there is an unauthorised deprivation of liberty.

How should managing authorities decide whether to apply for an authorisation?

3.6 Managing authorities should have a procedure in place that identifies: **5–062**
- whether deprivation of liberty is or may be necessary in a particular case
- what steps they should take to assess whether to seek authorisation
- whether they have taken all practical and reasonable steps to avoid a deprivation of liberty
- what action they should take if they do need to request an authorisation
- how they should review cases where authorisation is or may be necessary, and
- who should take the necessary action.

A flowchart that can be used to help develop such a procedure is at Annex 2.

What is the application process?

3.7 A managing authority must apply for a standard authorisation. The application should be made in writing to the supervisory body. A standard form is available for this purpose.   **5–063**

3.8 In England, the request from a managing authority for a standard authorisation must include: **5–064**
- the name and gender of the relevant person
- the age of the relevant person or, where this is not known, whether the managing authority reasonably believes that the relevant person is aged 18 years or older
- the address at which the relevant person is currently located, and the telephone number at the address
- the name, address and telephone number of the managing authority and the name of the person within the managing authority who is dealing with the request
- the purpose for which the authorisation is requested
- the date from which the authorisation is sought, and
- whether the managing authority has given an urgent authorisation and, if so, the date on which it expires.

3.9 A request for a standard authorisation must also include, if it is available or could reasonably be obtained by the managing authority: **5–065**
- any medical information relating to the relevant person's health that the managing authority reasonably considers to be relevant to the proposed restrictions to their liberty
- the diagnosis of the mental disorder (within the meaning of the Mental Health Act 1983 but disregarding any exclusion for persons with learning disability) from which the relevant person is suffering
- any relevant care plans and needs assessments
- the racial, ethnic or national origins of the relevant person
- whether the relevant person has any special communication needs
- details of the proposed restrictions on the relevant person's liberty
- whether it is necessary for an Independent Mental Capacity Advocate (IMCA) to be instructed

- where the purpose of the proposed restrictions to the relevant person's liberty is to give treatment, whether the relevant person has made an advance decision that may be valid and applicable to some or all of that treatment
- whether there is an existing standard authorisation in relation to the detention of the relevant person and, if so, the date of the expiry of that authorisation
- whether the relevant person is subject to any requirements of the Mental Health Act 1983, and
- the name, address and telephone number of:
  —anyone named by the relevant person as someone to be consulted about their welfare
  —anyone engaged in caring for the person or interested in their welfare any donee of a Lasting Power of Attorney ('donee') granted by the person
  —any deputy appointed for the person by the court, and
  —any IMCA who has already been instructed.

  If there is an existing authorisation, information that has not changed does not have to be resupplied.

5–066 3.10 In Wales, the request from a managing authority for a standard authorisation must include:
- the name of the relevant person
- the name, address and telephone number of the managing authority
- the reasons why the managing authority considers that the relevant person is being or will be detained in circumstances which amount to a deprivation of liberty
- the reasons why the managing authority considers that the relevant person satisfies the qualifying requirements
- details of any urgent authorisation
- information or documents in support of why the relevant person satisfies the qualifying requirements
- the name, address and telephone number of any person who has an interest in the welfare of the relevant person, and
- details of any relevant valid and applicable advance decision.

Where should applications be sent?

5–067 3.11 If the application is being made by a care home, the application must be sent to the local authority for the area in which the relevant person is ordinarily resident. If the relevant person is not ordinarily resident in the area of any local authority (for example, is of no fixed abode), if the care home does not know where the person currently lives, or if the person does not live in England or Wales, the application should be sent to the local authority in whose area the care home is located.

5–068 3.12 When the application is being made by a hospital:
- if the care is commissioned by a PCT, the application should be sent to that PCT
- if the care is commissioned by the Welsh Ministers, the application should be sent to the LHB for the area in which the relevant person is ordinarily resident

- if the care is commissioned by an LHB, the application should be sent to that LHB, and
- in any other case (for example, care that is commissioned privately), the application should be sent to the PCT for the area in which the relevant hospital is situated.

3.13 An application sent to the wrong supervisory body can be passed on to the **5–069** correct supervisory body without the managing authority needing to reapply. But the managing authority should make every effort to establish which is the correct supervisory body to minimise delays in handling the application. (Footnote 8 explains how place of ordinary residence is determined and how disputes about the place of ordinary residence will be resolved.)

3.14 The managing authority must keep a written record of each request made **5–070** for a standard authorisation and the reasons for making the request.

Who should be informed that an application has been made?

3.15 The managing authority should tell the relevant person's family, friends **5–071** and carers, and any IMCA already involved in the relevant person's case, that it has applied for an authorisation of deprivation of liberty, unless it is impractical or impossible to do so, or undesirable in terms of the interests of the relevant person's health or safety. Anyone who is engaged in caring for the relevant person or interested in their welfare, or who has been named by them as a person to consult, must be given the opportunity to input their views on whether deprivation of liberty is in the best interests of the relevant person, as part of the best interests assessment (see paragraphs 4.58 to 4.76), as far as is practical and appropriate. The views of the relevant person about who to inform and consult should be taken into account.

3.16 The managing authority must notify the supervisory body if it is satisfied **5–072** that there is no one who should be consulted in determining the relevant person's best interests, except those providing care and treatment for the relevant person in a professional capacity or for remuneration. In such a case, the supervisory body must instruct an IMCA to represent and support the relevant person before any assessments take place (see paragraphs 3.22 to 3.27 regarding the rights and role of an IMCA instructed in these circumstances).

What action does the supervisory body need to take when it receives an application for authorisation?

3.17 When it receives an application for authorisation of deprivation of liberty, **5–073** the supervisory body must, as soon as is practical and possible:
- consider whether the request is appropriate and should be pursued, and
- seek any further information that it requires from the managing authority to help it with the decision.

If the supervisory body has any doubts about proceeding with the request, it should seek to resolve them with the managing authority.

3.18 Supervisory bodies should have a procedure in place that identifies the **5–074** action they should take, who should take it and within what timescale.

As far as practical and possible, they should communicate the procedure to managing authorities and give them the relevant contact details for making an application. The flowchart at Annex 3 summarises the process that a supervisory body should follow on receipt of a request from a managing authority for a standard deprivation of liberty authorisation.

Can an application for authorisation be made in advance?

5–075   3.19   A standard authorisation comes into force when it is given, or at any later time specified in the authorisation. Paragraph 3.4 refers to the timescales for initially applying for authorisations: 28 days are allowed so that authorisations can usually be sought as part of care planning (such as planning of discharge from hospital). There is no statutory limit on how far in advance of the expiry of one authorisation a fresh authorisation can be sought. Clearly, however, an authorisation should not be applied for too far in advance as this may prevent an assessor from making an accurate assessment of what the person's circumstances will be at the time the authorisation will come into force.

5–076   3.20   If a supervisory body considers that an application for an authorisation has been made too far in advance, it should raise the matter with the managing authority. The outcome may be an agreement with the managing authority that the application should be withdrawn, to be resubmitted at a more appropriate time.

What happens when the managing authority and the supervisory body are the same organisation?

5–077   3.21   In some cases, a single organisation will be both supervisory body and managing authority—for example, where a local authority itself provides a residential care home, rather than purchasing the service from another organisation. This does not prevent it from acting in both capacities. However, in England the regulations specify that in such a situation the best interests assessor cannot be an employee of the supervisory body/ managing authority, or providing services to it. For example, in a case involving a local authority care home, the best interests assessor could be an NHS employee or an independent practitioner. (See paragraphs 4.13 and 4.60 for full details of who can be a best interests assessor.) There are similar provisions for Wales.

When should an IMCA be instructed?

5–078   3.22   If there is nobody appropriate to consult, other than people engaged in providing care or treatment for the relevant person in a professional capacity[1] or for remuneration, the managing authority must notify the supervisory body when it submits the application for the deprivation of liberty authorisation. The supervisory body must then instruct an IMCA straight away to represent the person. It is particularly important that

---

[1] A friend or family member is **not** considered to be acting in a professional capacity simply because they have been appointed as the person's representative for a previous authorisation.

the IMCA is instructed quickly if an urgent authorisation has been given, so that they can make a meaningful input at a very early stage in the process. (See paragraph 3.28 for other stages in the deprivation of liberty safeguards process when an IMCA must or may be instructed.)

3.23 Chapter 10 of the main Code ('What is the new Independent Mental **5–079** Capacity Advocate service and how does it work?') describes the wider rights and role of an IMCA. Supervisory bodies should follow the guidance in that chapter in identifying an IMCA who is suitably qualified to represent the relevant person. However, it is also important to note that an IMCA instructed at this initial stage of the deprivation of liberty safeguards process has additional rights and responsibilities compared to an IMCA more generally instructed under the Mental Capacity Act 2005. IMCAs in this context have the right to:

- as they consider appropriate, give information or make submissions to assessors, which assessors must take into account in carrying out their assessments
- receive copies of any assessments from the supervisory body
- receive a copy of any standard authorisation given by the supervisory body
- be notified by the supervisory body if they are unable to give a standard authorisation because one or more of the deprivation of liberty assessments did not meet the qualifying requirements
- receive a copy of any urgent authorisation from the managing authority
- receive from the managing authority a copy of any notice declining to extend the duration of an urgent authorisation
- receive from the supervisory body a copy of any notice that an urgent authorisation has ceased to be in force, and
- apply to the Court of Protection for permission to take the relevant person's case to the Court in connection with a matter relating to the giving or refusal of a standard or urgent authorisation (in the same way as any other third party can).

The assessment and authorisation processes are described in chapters 4 and 5.

3.24 IMCAs will need to familiarise themselves with the relevant person's cir- **5–080** cumstances and to consider what they may need to tell any of the assessors during the course of the assessment process. They will also need to consider whether they have any concerns about the outcome of the assessment process.

3.25 Differences of opinion between an IMCA and an assessor should ideally **5–081** be resolved while the assessment is still in progress. Where there are significant disagreements between an IMCA and one or more of the assessors that cannot be resolved between them, the supervisory body should be informed before the assessment is finalised. The supervisory body should then consider what action might be appropriate, including perhaps convening a meeting to discuss the matter. Wherever possible, differences of opinion should be resolved informally in order to minimise the need for an IMCA to make an application to the Court of Protection. However, an IMCA should not be discouraged from making an application to the Court of Protection should they consider it necessary. (Chapter 15 of the main Code ('What are the best ways to settle disagreements and disputes about issues covered in the Act?') contains general guidance about the resolution of disputes arising under the Act.)

5–082 3.26 An IMCA will also need to consider whether they have any concerns about the giving of an urgent authorisation (see chapter 6), and whether it would be appropriate to challenge the giving of such an authorisation via the Court of Protection.

5–083 3.27 Once a relevant person's representative is appointed (see chapter 7), the duties imposed on the IMCA cease to apply. The IMCA may, however, still apply to the Court of Protection for permission to take the relevant person's case to the Court in connection with the giving of a standard authorisation; but, in doing so, the IMCA must take account of the views of the relevant person's representative.

Other circumstances in which an IMCA must or may be instructed

5–084 3.28 An IMCA must also be instructed during gaps in the appointment of a relevant person's representative (for instance, if a new representative is being sought—see paragraphs 7.34 to 7.36). In addition, an IMCA may be instructed at any time where:
- the relevant person does not have a paid 'professional' representative
- the relevant person or their representative requests that an IMCA is instructed to help them, or
- a supervisory body believes that instructing an IMCA will help to ensure that the person's rights are protected (see paragraphs 7.37 to 7.41).

4. WHAT IS THE ASSESSMENT PROCESS FOR A STANDARD AUTHORISATION OF DEPRIVATION OF LIBERTY?

5–085 When a supervisory body gives a standard authorisation of deprivation of liberty, the managing authority may lawfully deprive the relevant person of their liberty in the hospital or care home named in the authorisation.

This chapter describes the assessments that have to be undertaken in order for a standard authorisation to be given. It also sets out who is eligible to undertake the assessments.

What assessments are required before giving a standard authorisation?

5–086 4.1 As soon as the supervisory body has confirmed that the request for a standard authorisation should be pursued, it must obtain the relevant assessments to ascertain whether the qualifying requirements of the deprivation of liberty safeguards are met. The supervisory body has a legal responsibility to select assessors who are both suitable and eligible. Assessments must be completed within 21 days for a standard deprivation of liberty authorisation, or, where an urgent authorisation has been given, before the urgent authorisation expires.

5–087 4.2 The assessments (described in paragraphs 4.23 to 4.76) are:
- age assessment (paragraphs 4.23 and 4.24)
- no refusals assessment (paragraphs 4.25 to 4.28).
- mental capacity assessment (paragraphs 4.29 to 4.32)

- mental health assessment (paragraphs 4.33 to 4.39)
- eligibility assessment (paragraphs 4.40 to 4.57), and
- best interests assessment (paragraphs 4.58 to 4.76).

Standard forms are available for completion by each of the assessors.

4.3 If the person being assessed is not currently in the supervisory body's **5–088** area, the supervisory body should seek, as far as is practical and possible, to arrange to use assessors based near where the person currently is.

Using equivalent assessments

4.4 The Act states that where an 'equivalent assessment' to any of these **5–089** assessments has already been obtained, it may be relied upon instead of obtaining a fresh assessment.

4.5 An equivalent assessment is an assessment: **5–090**
- that has been carried out in the last 12 months, not necessarily for the purpose of a deprivation of liberty authorisation (where the required assessment is an age assessment, there is no time limit on the use of an equivalent assessment)
- that meets all the requirements of the deprivation of liberty assessment,
- of which the supervisory body is satisfied that there is no reason to believe that it is no longer accurate, and
- of which the supervisory body has a written copy.

An example would be a recent assessment carried out for the purposes of the Mental Health Act 1983, which could serve as an equivalent to a mental health assessment.

4.6 Great care should be taken in deciding to use an equivalent assessment **5–091** and this should not be done routinely. The older the assessment is, even if it took place within the last 12 months, the less likely it is to represent a valid equivalent assessment (unless it is an age assessment). For example, only a very recent mental capacity assessment would be appropriate where capacity is known to fluctuate, since one of the principles of the Act is that a person must be assumed to have capacity unless it is established that they lack capacity.

4.7 If an equivalent best interests assessment is used, the supervisory body **5–092** must also take into account any information given, or submissions made, by the relevant person's representative or an Independent Mental Capacity Advocate (IMCA) instructed under the deprivation of liberty safeguards.

4.8 Supervisory bodies should record the reasons why they have used any **5–093** equivalent assessment. A standard form is available for this purpose.

When must assessments take place?

4.9 The regulations for England[1] specify that all assessments required for a **5–094** standard authorisation must be completed within 21 calendar days from the date on which the supervisory body receives a request from a managing authority. The regulations for Wales specify that all assessments

---

[1] The Mental Capacity (Deprivation of Liberty: Standard Authorisations, Assessments and Ordinary Residence) Regulations 2008.

required for a standard authorisation must be completed within 21 days from the date the assessors were instructed by the supervisory body.

5–095　4.10　However, if an urgent authorisation is already in force, the assessments must be completed before the urgent authorisation expires. The regulations for Wales specify that, where the managing authority has given itself an urgent authorisation and applies for a standard authorisation, the assessors must complete the assessments within five days of the date of instruction.

5–096　4.11　Urgent authorisations may be given by managing authorities for an initial period not exceeding seven days. If there are exceptional reasons why it has not been possible to deal with the request for a standard authorisation within the period of the urgent authorisation, they may be extended **by the supervisory body** for up to a further seven days. It is for the supervisory body to decide what constitutes an 'exceptional reason', taking into account all the circumstances of an individual case.

5–097　4.12　Supervisory bodies must keep a record of all requests for standard authorisations that they receive and should acknowledge the receipt of requests from managing authorities for standard authorisations.

How should assessors be selected?

5–098　4.13　The six assessments do not have to be completed by different assessors. In fact, it is highly unlikely that there will be six separate assessors—not least because it is desirable to minimise the burden on the person being assessed. However, each assessor must make their own decisions, and to ensure that an appropriate degree of objectivity is brought to the assessment process:

- there **must** be a minimum of two assessors
- the mental health and best interests assessors **must** be different people
- the best interests assessor can be an employee of the supervisory body or managing authority, but **must not** be involved in the care or treatment of the person they are assessing nor in decisions about their care
- a potential best interests assessor should not be used if they are in a line management relationship with the professional proposing the deprivation of liberty or the mental health assessor
- none of the assessors may have a financial interest in the case of the person they are assessing (a person is considered to have a financial interest in a case where that person is a partner, director, other office-holder or major shareholder of the managing authority that has made the application for a standard authorisation)
- an assessor **must not** be a relative of the person being assessed, nor of a person with a financial interest in the person's care. For this purpose, a 'relative' is:
  - a. a spouse, ex-spouse, civil partner or ex-civil partner
  - b. a person living with the relevant person as if they were a spouse or a civil partner
  - c. a parent or child
  - d. a brother or sister
  - e. a child of a person falling within definitions a, b or d
  - f. a grandparent or grandchild

    g. a grandparent-in-law or grandchild-in-law

    h. an aunt or uncle

    i. a sister-in-law or brother-in-law

    j. a son-in-law or daughter-in-law

    k. a first cousin, or

    l. a half-brother or half-sister.

These relationships include step-relationships

- where the managing authority and supervisory body are both the same body (see paragraph 3.21), the supervisory body may not select to carry out a best interests assessment a person who is employed by the body, or providing services to it, and
- the supervisory body should seek to avoid appointing assessors in any other possible conflict of interests situations that might bring into question the objectivity of an assessment.

4.14 Other relevant factors for supervisory bodies to consider when appointing **5–099** assessors include:

- the reason for the proposed deprivation of liberty
- whether the potential assessor has experience of working with the service user group from which the person being assessed comes (for example, older people, people with learning disabilities, people with autism, or people with brain injury)
- whether the potential assessor has experience of working with people from the cultural background of the person being assessed, and
- any other specific needs of the person being assessed, for example communication needs.

4.15 Supervisory bodies should ensure that sufficient assessors are available to **5–100** meet their needs, and must be satisfied in each case that the assessors have the skills, experience, qualifications and training required by regulations to perform the function effectively. The regulations also require supervisory bodies to be satisfied that there is an appropriate criminal record certificate issued in respect of an assessor. It will be useful to keep a record of qualified assessors and their experience and availability. Supervisory bodies should consider making arrangements to ensure that assessors have the necessary opportunities to maintain their skills and knowledge (of legal developments, for example) and share, audit and review their practice.

4.16 Assessors act as individual professionals and are personally accountable **5–101** for their decisions. Managing authorities and supervisory bodies must not dictate or seek to influence their decisions.

4.17 There is no reason in principle why interviews, examinations and fact- **5–102** finding required as part of any deprivation of liberty safeguards assessment cannot serve more than one purpose, in order to avoid unnecessary burdens both on the person being assessed and on staff. However, if this does happen, all purposes of the interview or examination should be made clear to the relevant person, and to any family members, friends, carers or advocates supporting them.

Protection against liability

5–103   4.18   Nobody can or should carry out an assessment unless they are protected against any liabilities that might arise in connection with carrying out the assessment. Individual assessors will need to satisfy themselves, and any supervisory body that selects them as an assessor, that they are appropriately covered by either employers' or personal insurance.

What is the assessment process?

5–104   4.19   As indicated in paragraph 4.2, there are six assessments that must be conducted before a supervisory body can give an authorisation.

5–105   4.20   The assessments are set out in the order in which it will normally be most appropriate to complete them. In particular, it is recommended that the best interests assessment, which is likely to be the most time-consuming, is not started until there is a reasonable expectation that the other five qualifying requirements will be met.

5–106   4.21   But, ultimately, it is for the supervisory body to decide on the order in which the assessments should be undertaken and, in the light of the time available to complete the overall assessment process, the extent to which they should be undertaken to separate or simultaneous timescales. The supervisory body's decision about how many assessors will undertake the assessments (see paragraph 4.13) will also be a relevant factor.

5–107   4.22   The following paragraphs explain the assessment process.

Age assessment

5–108   4.23   The purpose of the age assessment is simply to confirm whether the relevant person is aged 18 or over. This is because, as paragraph 1.12 explains, the deprivation of liberty safeguards apply only to people aged 18 or over. For people under the age of 18, a different safeguards process applies. In most cases, this is likely to be a fairly straightforward assessment. If there is any doubt, age should be established by a birth certificate or other evidence that the assessor considers reliable. Where it is not possible to verify with any certainty whether a person is aged 18 or over, the assessor should base the assessment on the best of their knowledge and belief.

5–109   4.24   This assessment can be undertaken by anybody whom the supervisory body is satisfied is eligible to be a best interests assessor.

No refusals assessment

5–110   4.25   The purpose of the no refusals assessment is to establish whether an authorisation to deprive the relevant person of their liberty would conflict with other existing authority for decision-making for that person.

5–111   4.26   The following are instances of a conflict that would mean that a standard authorisation could not be given:
- If the relevant person has made **an advance decision to refuse treatment** that remains valid and is applicable to some or all of the treatment that is the purpose for which the authorisation is requested, then a

standard authorisation cannot be given. See sections 24 to 26 of the Mental Capacity Act 2005 and chapter 9 of the main Code ('What does the Act say about advance decisions to refuse treatment?') for more information about advance decisions and when they are valid and applicable. Remember too that the deprivation of liberty authorisation does not, in itself, provide authority to treat the person (see paragraphs 5.10 to 5.13 of this Code).

- If any part of the proposal to deprive the person of their liberty (including any element of the care plan) would be in conflict with a **valid decision of a donee or a deputy** made within the scope of their authority, then a standard authorisation cannot be given. For example, if a donee or deputy decides that it would not be in the best interests of the relevant person to be in a particular care home, and that decision is within the scope of their authority, then the care plan will need to be reviewed with the donee or deputy.

4.27   If there is any such conflict, the no refusals assessment qualifying require-   **5–112**
ment will not be met and a standard authorisation for deprivation of liberty cannot be given.

4.28   The no refusals assessment can be undertaken by anybody that the super-   **5–113**
visory body is satisfied is eligible to be a best interests assessor.

Mental capacity assessment

4.29   The purpose of the mental capacity assessment is to establish whether the   **5–114**
relevant person lacks capacity to decide whether or not they should be accommodated in the relevant hospital or care home to be given care or treatment. The assessment refers specifically to the relevant person's capacity to make this decision at the time it needs to be made. The starting assumption should always be that a person has the capacity to make the decision.

4.30   Sections 1 to 3 of the Act set out how a person's capacity to make   **5–115**
decisions should be determined. Chapter 4 of the main Code ('How does the Act define a person's capacity to make a decision and how should capacity be assessed?') gives further guidance on ways to assess capacity. When assessing the capacity of a person being considered for the deprivation of liberty safeguards, these guidelines should be followed.

4.31   The regulations for England specify that the mental capacity assessment   **5–116**
can be undertaken by anyone who is eligible to act as a mental health or best interests assessor. In deciding who to appoint for this assessment, the supervisory body should take account of the need for understanding and practical experience of the nature of the person's condition and its impact on decision-making.

4.32   Supervisory bodies may wish to consider using an eligible assessor who   **5–117**
already knows the relevant person to undertake this assessment, if they think it would be of benefit. This will primarily arise if somebody involved in the person's care is considered best placed to carry out a reliable assessment, using their knowledge of the person over a period of time. It may also help in reducing any distress that might be caused to the person if they were assessed by somebody they did not know.

Mental health assessment

5–118 4.33 The purpose of the mental health assessment is to establish whether the relevant person has a mental disorder within the meaning of the Mental Health Act 1983. That means any disorder or disability of mind, apart from dependence on alcohol or drugs. It includes all learning disabilities. This is not an assessment to determine whether the person requires mental health treatment.

5–119 4.34 A distinction can be drawn between the mental health assessment and the mental capacity assessment:
  • Although a person must have an impairment or disturbance of the functioning of the mind or brain in order to lack capacity, it does not follow that they automatically have a mental disorder within the meaning of the Mental Health Act 1983.
  • The objective of the mental health assessment is to ensure that the person is medically diagnosed as being of 'unsound mind' and so comes within the scope of Article 5 of the European Convention on Human Rights.

5–120 4.35 In both England and Wales, the regulations specify that:
  • the mental health assessment must be carried out by a doctor, and
  • the assessing doctor has to either be approved under section 12 of the Mental Health Act 1983, or be a registered medical practitioner with at least three years' post-registration experience in the diagnosis or treatment of mental disorder, such as a GP with a special interest. This includes doctors who are automatically treated as being section 12 approved because they are approved clinicians under the Mental Health Act 1983.

5–121 4.36 To be eligible to undertake assessments, in England a doctor will need to have completed the standard training for deprivation of liberty mental health assessors. Except in the 12 month period beginning with the date the doctor has successfully completed the standard training, the regulations for England also require the supervisory body to be satisfied that the doctor has, in the 12 months prior to selection, completed further training relevant to their role as a mental health assessor. In Wales, a doctor will need to have completed appropriate training and have appropriate skills and experience.

5–122 4.37 Supervisory bodies must consider the suitability of the assessor for the particular case (for example, whether they have experience relevant to the person's condition).

5–123 4.38 As with the mental capacity assessment, supervisory bodies may wish to consider using an eligible assessor who already knows the relevant person to undertake this assessment, if they think it would be of benefit.

5–124 4.39 The mental health assessor is required to consider how the mental health of the person being assessed is likely to be affected by being deprived of their liberty, and to report their conclusions to the best interests assessor. The mental health and best interests assessments cannot be carried out by the same person.

Eligibility assessment

4.40 This assessment relates specifically to the relevant person's status, or **5–125** potential status, under the Mental Health Act 1983.

4.41 A person is not eligible for a deprivation of liberty authorisation if: **5–126**
- they are detained as a hospital in-patient under the Mental Health Act 1983, or
- the authorisation, if given, would be inconsistent with an obligation placed on them under the Mental Health Act 1983, such as a requirement to live somewhere else. This will only affect people who are on leave of absence from detention under the Mental Health Act 1983 or who are subject to guardianship, supervised community treatment or conditional discharge.

4.42 Where the proposed authorisation relates to a care home, or to deprivation **5–127** of liberty in a hospital for non-mental health treatment, the eligibility assessment will simply be a matter of checking that authorisation would not be inconsistent with an obligation placed on the person under the Mental Health Act 1983.

4.43 When a person is subject to guardianship under the Mental Health Act **5–128** 1983, their guardian can decide where they are to live, but cannot authorise deprivation of liberty and cannot require them to live somewhere where they are deprived of liberty unless that deprivation of liberty is authorised.

4.44 Occasionally, a person who is subject to guardianship and who lacks **5–129** capacity to make the relevant decisions may need specific care or treatment in a care home or hospital that cannot be delivered without deprivation of liberty. This may be in a care home in which they are already living or in which the guardian thinks they ought to live, or it may be in a hospital where they need to be for physical health care. It may also apply if they need to be in hospital for mental health care. The process for obtaining a deprivation of liberty authorisation and the criteria to be applied are the same as for any other person.

4.45 If the proposed authorisation relates to deprivation of liberty in a hospital **5–130** **wholly or partly for the purpose of treatment of mental disorder,** then the relevant person will not be eligible if:
- they object to being admitted to hospital, or to some or all the treatment they will receive there for mental disorder, **and**
- they meet the criteria for an application for admission under section 2 or section 3 of the Mental Health Act 1983 (unless an attorney or deputy, acting within their powers, had consented to the things to which the person is objecting).

4.46 In many cases, the relevant person will be able to state an objection. **5–131** However, where the person is unable to communicate, or can only communicate to a limited extent, assessors will need to consider the person's behaviour, wishes, feelings, views, beliefs and values, both present and past, so far as they can be ascertained (see paragraphs 5.37 to 5.48 of the main Code for guidance on how to do this). If there is reason to think that a person would object if able to do so, then the person should be assumed to be objecting. Occasionally, it may be that the person's behaviour initially suggests an objection, but that this objection is in fact not directed at the treatment at all. In that case, the person should **not** be taken to be objecting.

5–132   4.47   Assessors should always bear in mind that their job is simply to establish whether the person objects to treatment or to being in hospital: whether that objection is reasonable or not is not the issue.

5–133   4.48   Even where a person does not object and a deprivation of liberty authorisation is possible, it should not be assumed that such an authorisation is invariably the correct course. There may be other factors that suggest that the Mental Health Act 1983 should be used (for example, where it is thought likely that the person will recover relevant capacity and will then refuse to consent to treatment, or where it is important for the hospital managers to have a formal power to retake a person who goes absent without leave). Further guidance on this is given in the Mental Health Act 1983 Code of Practice.

5–134   4.49   The eligibility assessor is not required to decide (or even consider) whether an application under the Mental Health Act 1983 would be in the person's best interests.

5–135   4.50   If the proposed authorisation relates to deprivation of liberty in a hospital **wholly or partly for the purpose of treatment of mental disorder,** then the person will also not be eligible if they are:
- currently on leave of absence from detention under the Mental Health Act 1983
- subject to supervised community treatment, or
- subject to conditional discharge,

in which case powers of recall under the Mental Health Act 1983 should be used.

5–136   4.51   People on leave of absence from detention under the Mental Health Act 1983 or subject to supervised community treatment or conditional discharge are, however, eligible for the deprivation of liberty safeguards if they require treatment in hospital for a physical disorder.

Who can conduct an eligibility assessment?

5–137   4.52   The regulations for England specify that the eligibility assessment must be completed by:
- a mental health assessor who is also a section 12 doctor, or
- a best interests assessor who is also an approved mental health professional (AMHP).

5–138   4.53   The assessment cannot be carried out by a non-section 12 doctor, even if they are qualified to be a mental health assessor, nor by a nonAMHP, even if they are qualified to be a best interests assessor. This will ensure that the eligibility assessor is sufficiently familiar with the Mental Health Act 1983, which will be particularly important in cases in which it appears that the powers available under the Mental Health Act 1983 may be more appropriate than the deprivation of liberty safeguards.

5–139   4.54   The eligibility assessment will often be carried out by the best interests assessor but, where this is not the case, the eligibility assessor must request the best interests assessor to provide any relevant eligibility information that the best interests assessor may have, and the best interests assessor must comply with this request.

What happens when people are assessed as ineligible?

4.55   If the eligibility assessor believes that the relevant person is not eligible, **5–140** but (on the basis of the report of the best interests assessor) that they should nevertheless be deprived of liberty in their best interests, the eligibility assessor should immediately inform the supervisory body.

4.56   In the case of someone already subject to the Mental Health Act 1983, the **5–141** eligibility assessor should inform the supervisory body with a view to contact being made with the relevant responsible clinician (i.e. the clinician in overall charge of the person's treatment) or, if the person is subject to guardianship, the relevant local social services authority. Otherwise, the assessor or supervisory body should take steps to arrange for the person to be assessed further with a view to an application being made for admission to hospital under the Mental Health Act 1983. Assessors will need to be familiar with local arrangements for doing this.

4.57   In some cases, even before the eligibility assessment is undertaken, it may **5–142** be known that there is a chance that the person will have to be assessed with a view to an application under the Mental Health Act 1983 because the eligibility assessment might conclude that they are ineligible for a deprivation of liberty authorisation. In such cases, steps should be taken, where practical and possible, to arrange assessments in a way that minimises the number of separate interviews or examinations the person has to undergo.

Best interests assessment

4.58   The purpose of the best interests assessment is to establish, firstly, **5–143** whether deprivation of liberty is occurring or is going to occur and, if so, whether:

- it is in the best interests of the relevant person to be deprived of liberty
- it is necessary for them to be deprived of liberty in order to prevent harm to themselves, and
- deprivation of liberty is a proportionate response to the likelihood of the relevant person suffering harm and the seriousness of that harm.

4.59   The best interests assessor is the person who is responsible for assessing **5–144** what is in the best interests of a relevant person.

4.60   In both England and Wales, the best interests assessment must be under- **5–145** taken by an AMHP, social worker, nurse, occupational therapist or chartered psychologist with the skills and experience specified in the regulations. In England, this includes at least two years' post-registration experience. In England, the supervisory body must also be satisfied that the assessor:

- is not suspended from the register or list relevant to the person's profession
- has successfully completed training that has been approved[1] by the Secretary of State to be a best interests assessor

---

[1] Approved courses can be found at: http://www.dh.gov.uk/en/SocialCare/Deliveringadultsocialcare/ MentalCapacity/ MentalCapacityActDeprivationofLibertySafeguards/index.htm

- except in the 12 month period beginning with the date the person has successfully completed the approved training, has, in the 12 months prior to selection, completed further training relevant to their role as a best interests assessor, and
- has the skills necessary to obtain, evaluate and analyse complex evidence and differing views and to weigh them appropriately in decision-making.

5–146   4.61   Section 4 of the Mental Capacity Act 2005 sets out the best interests principles that apply for the purpose of the Act. Chapter 5 of the main Code ('What does the Act mean when it talks about "best interests"?') explains this in more detail, and, in particular, paragraph 5.13 of the main Code includes a checklist of factors that need to be taken into account in working out what is in a person's best interests. These principles and guidance apply equally to working out a person's best interests for the purpose of the deprivation of liberty safeguards. However, when it comes to best interests around deprivation of liberty, additional factors apply, including:

- whether any harm to the person could arise if the deprivation of liberty does not take place
- what that harm would be
- how likely that harm is to arise (i.e. is the level of risk sufficient to justify a step as serious as depriving a person of liberty?)
- what other care options there are which could avoid deprivation of liberty, and
- if deprivation of liberty is currently unavoidable, what action could be taken to avoid it in future.

Establishing whether deprivation of liberty is occurring

5–147   4.62   The first task of a best interests assessor is to establish whether deprivation of liberty is occurring, or is likely to occur, since there is no point in the assessment process proceeding further if deprivation of liberty is not at issue. If the best interests assessor concludes that deprivation of liberty is **not** occurring and is not likely to occur, they should state in their assessment report to the supervisory body that deprivation of liberty is not in the person's best interests because there is obviously a less restrictive option available. The best interests requirement will therefore not be met in such a case.

5–148   4.63   To establish whether deprivation of liberty is occurring, or is likely to occur, the best interests assessor must consult the managing authority of the hospital or care home where the person is, or will be, accommodated and examine any relevant needs assessments and care plans prepared for the person. The best interests assessor must consider whether the care plan and the manner in which it is being, or will be, implemented constitutes a deprivation of liberty. If not, then no deprivation of liberty authorisation is required for that care plan.

5–149   4.64   The managing authority and supervisory body must provide the best interests assessor with any needs assessments or care plans that they have undertaken or which have been undertaken on their behalf.

The best interests assessment process

4.65 If the best interests assessor considers that deprivation of liberty is **5–150** occurring, or is likely to occur, they should start a full best interests assessment. In line with section 4(7) of the Act this involves seeking the views of a range of people connected to the relevant person to find out whether they believe that depriving the relevant person of their liberty is, or would be, in the person's best interests to protect them from harm or to enable them to follow the care plan proposed. The best interests assessor should, as far as is practical and possible, seek the views of:
- anyone the person has previously named as someone they want to be consulted
- anyone involved in caring for the person
- anyone interested in the person's welfare (for example, family carers, other close relatives, or an advocate already working with the person), and
- any donee or deputy who represents the person.

4.66 This may mean that the best interests assessor needs to explain key **5–151** aspects of the care plan and what it aims to do to the people being consulted. The best interests assessor should then take the views received into account as far as is practical and appropriate. It is essential that the best interests assessor provides an independent and objective view of whether or not there is a genuine justification for deprivation of liberty, taking account of all the relevant views and factors.

4.67 The best interests assessor must state in their assessment the name and **5–152** address of every interested person whom they have consulted in carrying out the assessment.

4.68 Family and friends may not be confident about expressing their views: it **5–153** is the responsibility of the best interests assessor to enable them to do so—using support to meet communication or language needs as necessary.

Scenario: Consulting around best interests   **5–154**

Mr Simpson is 60 and has dementia with particularly poor short-term memory, which clinicians agree is most likely to be related to chronic excessive alcohol intake. After initial treatment in hospital, he has been admitted to a care home—a decision which he consented to.

However, though he had the mental capacity to consent to hospital admission, he has no insight into his dementia. He is unable to understand the health and safety implications of continuing to drink, and will do so heavily whenever he has access to alcohol and the money to buy it.

Although Mr Simpson had no access to alcohol in hospital, there is a pub within walking distance of the care home, which he visits and drinks in. When he returns to the home intoxicated, his behaviour can be very distressing and potentially dangerous to other residents. The care home staff believe that if this continues, there may be no other option than to return him to hospital under the Mental Health Act 1983.

Scenario: Consulting around best interests *(continued)*

The care home staff have asked Mr Simpson to drink only in moderation, but this has not proved successful; and the landlord has been asked not to serve him more than one drink but has refused to do so. The manager of the home is now considering a care plan to prevent Mr Simpson from leaving the home without an escort, and to prevent visits from friends who bring alcohol. He believes this would be in Mr Simpson's best interests.

As the pub is open all day, if this new care plan was adopted, Mr Simpson would be stopped from going out at all without an escort, even though he often goes to the shops and the park as well as the pub. Staffing levels are such that an escort would only be available on some days and for limited periods.

Mr Simpson's daughter, his closest relative, is concerned that these restrictions are excessive and would amount to a deprivation of liberty. She believes that having a drink and socialising in the pub is her father's 'only remaining pleasure', and is sure that, if he still had capacity, he would choose to carry on drinking, regardless of the health risks.

She requests a best interests meeting to consider whether a less restrictive care plan could still meet his needs.

At this meeting, Mr Simpson's community mental health nurse confirms that Mr Simpson is likely to lack capacity in relation to this particular issue, and advises that if he continues to drink to excess his dementia is likely to advance rapidly and his life expectancy will be reduced. However, small amounts of alcohol will not be significantly harmful.

The consensus is that the proposed restrictions would severely limit Mr Simpson's ability to maintain social contact and to carry on the life he has been used to, and that this would amount to deprivation of liberty. Bearing in mind his daughter's view, it is felt that it would not be in Mr Simpson's best interests to prevent him from having any alcohol at all. However, in view of the health risks and the likelihood that he would otherwise have to be detained in hospital, it would be in Mr Simpson's best interests to ensure that he does not get intoxicated. (The possibility of limiting his access to his money would be unacceptable since he retains the capacity to decide how to spend it in other ways.)

Discussion then focuses on ways of minimising restrictions so that he is still able to visit the pub, but drinks in moderation. The care home key worker says that when she has gone to the pub with Mr Simpson he has been fully co-operative and has had just one drink before coming back with her. It is therefore agreed that the home will provide an escort for him to visit the pub at least three times a week, and the shops and the park at other times, and that his daughter will be able to take him out at any time.

It is agreed that care home staff (in consultation with his daughter) will review Mr Simpson's care plan in two months' time and, if it is felt that increased restrictions are required, consider whether it is then necessary to request an authorisation for deprivation of liberty.

4.69 The best interests assessor must involve the relevant person in the assess- **5–155** ment process as much as is possible and practical, and help them to participate in decision-making. The relevant person should be given the support needed to participate, using non-verbal means of communication where needed (see paragraphs 3.10 and 3.11 of the main Code) or the support of speech and language therapists. It may also help to involve others whom the relevant person already trusts and who are used to communicating with the relevant person.

4.70 The best interests assessor will need to consider the conclusions of the **5–156** mental health assessor about how the person being assessed is likely to be affected by being deprived of their liberty. If the proposed care would involve the person being moved, then the assessor should consider the impact of the upheaval and of the journey itself on the person.

4.71 If the best interests assessment supports deprivation of liberty in the care **5–157** home or hospital in question, the assessor must state what the maximum authorisation period should be in the case concerned. This must not exceed 12 months. The assessor should set out the reasons for selecting the period stated. This decision will be based on the information obtained during the consultation process—but should also reflect information from the person's care plan about how long any treatment or care will be required in circumstances that amount to a deprivation of liberty. It should also take into account any available indication of how likely it is that the relevant person's circumstances will change, including the expected progression of the illness or disability. The underlying principle is that deprivation of liberty should be for the minimum period necessary so, for the maximum 12-month period to apply, the assessor will need to be confident that there is unlikely to be a change in the person's circumstances that would affect the authorisation within that timescale.

The report of the best interests assessor

4.72 The best interests assessor must provide a report that explains their con- **5–158** clusion and their reasons for it. If they do not support deprivation of liberty, then their report should aim to be as useful as possible to the commissioners and providers of care in deciding on future action (for example, recommending an alternative approach to treatment or care in which deprivation of liberty could be avoided). It may be helpful for the best interests assessor to discuss the possibility of any such alternatives with the providers of care **during the assessment process**.

4.73 If the best interests assessor does not support deprivation of liberty, it **5–159** would be good practice for their report to be included in the relevant person's care plan or case notes, to ensure that any views about how deprivation of liberty can be avoided are made clear to the providers of care and all relevant staff on an ongoing basis.

4.74 The best interests assessor may recommend that conditions should be **5–160** attached to the authorisation. For example, they may make recommendations around contact issues, issues relevant to the person's culture or other major issues related to the deprivation of liberty, which—if not dealt with—would mean that the deprivation of liberty would cease to be in the person's best interests. The best interests assessor may also recommend conditions in order to work towards avoiding deprivation of liberty in future. But it is not the best interests assessor's role to specify conditions that do not directly relate to the issue of deprivation of liberty.

4.75 Conditions should not be a substitute for a properly constructed care plan (see paragraph 2.7 on good practice for care planning). In recommending conditions, best interests assessors should aim to impose the minimum necessary constraints, so that they do not unnecessarily prevent or inhibit the staff of the hospital or care home from responding appropriately to the person's needs, whether they remain the same or vary over time. It would be good practice for the best interests assessor to discuss any proposed conditions with the relevant personnel at the home or hospital before finalising the assessment, and to make clear in their report whether the rejection or variation of recommended conditions by the supervisory body would significantly affect the other conclusions they have reached.

4.76 Where possible, the best interests assessor should recommend someone to be appointed as the relevant person's representative (see chapter 7). The assessor should be well placed, as a result of the consultation process, to identify whether there is anybody suitable to take on this role. The appointment of the relevant person's representative cannot take place unless and until an authorisation is given. However, by identifying someone to take on this role at an early stage, the best interests assessor can help to ensure that a representative is appointed as soon as possible.

5–163

Scenario: Application for standard authorisation

Mrs Jackson is 87 years old and lives by herself in an isolated bungalow in a rural area. Over the past few years, staff at her local health centre have become increasingly concerned about her wellbeing and ability to look after herself. Her appearance has become unkempt, she does not appear to be eating properly and her house is dirty.

The community mental health team have attempted to gain her trust, but she is unwilling to engage with them. She has refused care workers entry to her home and declined their help with personal hygiene and household chores.

Because it is believed that she is a potential risk to herself, she is admitted to psychiatric hospital under section 2 of the Mental Health Act 1983 for assessment of her mental disorder.

Following the assessment, it is felt that Mrs Jackson requires further treatment for mental disorder. An application is made for her detention to be continued under section 3 of the Mental Health Act 1983. She is prescribed antipsychotic medication, but this seems to have little effect on her behaviour. She remains extremely suspicious of people to the point of being delusional. She is assessed as potentially having mild dementia, most probably of the Alzheimer type, but because there is no obvious benefit from anti-dementia medication, further treatment for mental disorder is felt unnecessary.

Mrs Jackson insists that she wishes to return to her own home, but given past failed attempts to gain her acceptance of support at home and her likely future mental deterioration, transfer to a care home is believed to be most appropriate.

Scenario: Application for standard authorisation *(continued)*

A best interests meeting is held by the mental health team to consider her future care and placement, and the team's approved social worker and the instructed IMCA are invited. The meeting concludes that Mrs Jackson does not have sufficient mental capacity to make an informed decision on her stated wish to return home. There is no advance decision in existence, no Lasting Power of Attorney or court deputy appointed and no practical way of contacting her immediate family.

An appropriate care home is identified. A care plan is developed to give Mrs Jackson as much choice and control over her daily living as possible. However, it is felt that the restrictions still necessary to ensure Mrs Jackson's wellbeing will be so intense and of such duration that a request for a standard deprivation of liberty authorisation should be made by the care home manager (the relevant managing authority).

The best interests assessor agrees that the proposed course of action is in Mrs Jackson's best interests and recommends a standard authorisation for six months in the first instance.

What guidelines are there relating to the work of assessors?

Access to records

4.77 All assessors may, at any reasonable time, examine and take copies of: **5–164**
- any health record
- any record of, or held by, a local authority that was compiled in accordance with a social services function, and
- any record held by a care home

which they consider may be relevant to their assessment. Assessors should list in their assessment report what records they examined.

Recording and reporting assessments

4.78 As soon as possible after carrying out their assessments, assessors must **5–165** keep a written record of the assessment and must give copies of their assessment report(s) to the supervisory body. The supervisory body must in turn give copies of the assessment report(s) to:
- the managing authority
- the relevant person and their representative, and
- any IMCA instructed

at the same time that it gives them copies of the deprivation of liberty authorisation or notification that an authorisation is not to be given (see paragraphs 5.7 and 5.18 respectively).

5. WHAT SHOULD HAPPEN ONCE THE ASSESSMENTS ARE COMPLETE?

5–166   If all the assessments in the standard authorisation assessment process indicate that the relevant person meets all the qualifying requirements, then the supervisory body will give a deprivation of liberty authorisation. If any of the qualifying requirements are not met, however, different actions will need to be taken, depending on the circumstances of the individual case.

This chapter identifies potential outcomes of the assessment process and offers guidance on what should happen next.

What action should the supervisory body take if the assessments conclude that the person meets the requirements for authorisation?

5–167   5.1   If all the assessments conclude that the relevant person meets the requirements for authorisation, and the supervisory body has written copies of all the assessments, it must give a standard authorisation. A standard form is available for this purpose.

5–168   5.2   The supervisory body cannot give a standard authorisation if any of the requirements are not fulfilled.

5–169   5.3   The supervisory body must set the period of the authorisation, which may not be longer than that recommended by the best interests assessor (see paragraph 4.71).

5–170   5.4   When the supervisory body gives a standard authorisation, it must do so in writing and must state the following:

- the name of the relevant person
- the name of the relevant hospital or care home
- the period during which the authorisation is to be in force (which may not exceed the period recommended by the best interests assessor)
- the purpose for which the authorisation is given (i.e. why the person needs to be deprived of their liberty)
- any conditions subject to which the authorisation is given (see paragraph 5.5), and
- the reason why each qualifying requirement is met.

5–171   5.5   The supervisory body may attach conditions to the authorisation. Before deciding whether to give the authorisation subject to conditions, the supervisory body must consider any recommendations made by the best interests assessor (see paragraph 4.74). Where the supervisory body does not attach conditions as recommended by the best interests assessor, it should discuss the matter with the best interests assessor in case the rejection or variation of the conditions would significantly affect the other conclusions the best interests assessor reached in their report.

5–172   5.6   It is the responsibility of the supervisory body to appoint a representative for the relevant person (see chapter 7).

5–173   5.7   As soon as possible after giving the authorisation, the supervisory body must give a copy of the authorisation to:

- the managing authority
- the relevant person
- the relevant person's representative
- any Independent Mental Capacity Advocate (IMCA) involved, and

- every interested person named by the best interests assessor in their report as somebody they have consulted in carrying out their assessment.

The supervisory body must also keep a written record of any standard authorisation that it gives and of the matters referred to in paragraph 5.4.

5.8 The managing authority must take all practical and possible steps to **5–174** ensure that the relevant person understands the effect of the authorisation and their rights around it. These include their right to challenge the authorisation via the Court of Protection, their right to request a review, and their right to have an IMCA instructed, along with the process for doing so (see paragraphs 7.37 to 7.41). Appropriate information must be given to the relevant person both orally and in writing. Any written information must also be given to the relevant person's representative. This must happen as soon as possible and practical after the authorisation is given.

How long can an authorisation last?

5.9 A deprivation of liberty should last for the shortest period possible. The **5–175** best interests assessor should only recommend authorisation for as long as the relevant person is likely to meet all the qualifying requirements. The authorisation may be for quite a short period. A short period may, for example, be appropriate if:

- the reason that the deprivation of liberty is in the person's best interests is because their usual care arrangements have temporarily broken down, or
- there are likely to be changes in the person's mental disorder in the relatively near future (for example, if the person is in rehabilitation following brain injury).

What restrictions exist on authorisations?

5.10 A deprivation of liberty authorisation—whether urgent or standard— **5–176** relates solely to the issue of deprivation of liberty. It does not give authority to treat people, nor to do anything else that would normally require their consent. The arrangements for providing care and treatment to people in respect of whom a deprivation of liberty authorisation is in force are subject to the wider provisions of the Mental Capacity Act 2005.

5.11 This means that any treatment can only be given to a person who has not **5–177** given their consent if:

- it is established that the person lacks capacity to make the decision concerned
- it is agreed that the treatment will be in their best interests, having taken account of the views of the person and of people close to them, and, where relevant in the case of serious medical treatment, of any IMCA involved
- the treatment does not conflict with a valid and applicable advance decision to refuse treatment, and

- the treatment does not conflict with a decision made by a donee of Lasting Power of Attorney or a deputy acting within the scope of their powers.

5–178   5.12   In deciding what is in a person's best interests, section 4 of the Act applies in the same way as it would if the person was not deprived of liberty. The guidance in chapter 5 of the main Code on assessing best interests is also relevant.

5–179   5.13   Life-sustaining treatment, or treatment to prevent a serious deterioration in the person's condition, may be provided while a decision in respect of any relevant issue is sought from the Court of Protection. The need to act in the best interests of the person concerned will continue to apply in the meantime.

Can a person be moved to a different location under a standard authorisation?

5–180   5.14   If a person who is subject to a standard authorisation moves to a different hospital or care home, the managing authority of the new hospital or care home must request a new standard authorisation. The application should be made **before** the move takes place.

5–181   5.15   If the move has to take place so urgently that this is impossible, the managing authority of the new hospital or care home will need to give an urgent authorisation (see chapter 6).

5–182   5.16   The only exception is if the care regime in the new facility will not involve deprivation of liberty.

5–183   5.17   These arrangements are not an alternative to applying the provisions of sections 38 and 39 of the Act regarding change of residence.

What happens if an assessment concludes that one of the requirements is not met?

5–184   5.18   If any of the assessments conclude that one of the requirements is not met, then the assessment process should stop immediately and authorisation may not be given. The supervisory body should:
- inform anyone still engaged in carrying out an assessment that they are not required to complete it
- notify the managing authority, the relevant person, any IMCA involved and every interested person consulted by the best interests assessor that authorisation has not been given (a standard form is available for this purpose), and
- provide the managing authority, the relevant person and any IMCA involved with copies of those assessments that have been carried out. This must be done as soon as possible, because in some cases different arrangements will need to be made for the person's care.

5–185   5.19   If the reason the standard authorisation cannot be given is because the eligibility requirement is not met, it may be necessary to consider making the person subject to the Mental Health Act 1983. If this is the case, it may be possible to use the same assessors to make that decision, thereby minimising the assessment processes.

What are the responsibilities of the managing authority and the commissioners of care if a request for an authorisation is turned down?

5.20 The managing authority is responsible for ensuring that it does not **5–186** deprive a person of their liberty without an authorisation. The managing authority must comply with the law in this respect: where a request for an authorisation is turned down, it will need to review the relevant person's actual or proposed care arrangements to ensure that a deprivation of liberty is not allowed to either continue or commence.

5.21 Supervisory bodies and other commissioners of care will need to purchase **5–187** care packages in a way that makes it possible for managing authorities to comply with the outcome of the deprivation of liberty safeguards assessment process when a request for a standard authorisation is turned down.

5.22 The actions that both managing authorities and commissioners of care **5–188** should consider if a request for an authorisation is turned down will depend on the reason why the authorisation has not been given:

- If the best interests assessor concluded that the relevant person was not in fact being, or likely to be, deprived of liberty, no action is likely to be necessary.
- If the best interests assessor concluded that the proposed or actual deprivation of liberty was not in the relevant person's best interests, the managing authority, in conjunction with the commissioner of the care, will need to consider how the care plan could be changed to avoid deprivation of liberty. (See, for example, the guidance on practical ways to reduce the risk of deprivation of liberty in paragraph 2.7.) They should examine carefully the reasons given in the best interests assessor's report, and may find it helpful to discuss the matter with the best interests assessor. Where appropriate, they should also discuss the matter with family and carers. If the person is not yet a resident in the care home or hospital, the revised care plan may not involve admission to that facility unless the conditions of care are adapted to be less restrictive and deprivation of liberty will not occur.
- If the mental capacity assessor concluded that the relevant person **has** capacity to make decisions about their care, the care home or hospital will need to consider, in conjunction with the commissioner of the care, how to support the person to make such decisions.
- If the relevant person was identified as not eligible to be subject to a deprivation of liberty authorisation, it may be appropriate to assess whether an application should be made to detain the person under the Mental Health Act 1983.
- If the relevant person does not have a mental disorder as defined in the Mental Health Act 1983, the care plan will need to be modified to avoid a deprivation of liberty, since there would be no lawful basis for depriving a person of liberty in those circumstances.
- Where there is a valid refusal by a donee or deputy, or an applicable and valid advance decision (see paragraphs 4.25 to 4.28), alternative care arrangements will need to be made. If there is a question about the refusal, a decision may be sought from the Court of Protection.

- If the person is under 18, use of the Children Act 1989 may be considered.

5–189 5.23 Working out what action should be taken where a request for a standard deprivation of liberty authorisation is turned down in respect of a 'self-funder' may present particular problems, because the managing authority may not be able to make alternative care arrangements without discussing them with those controlling the funding, whether relatives of the person concerned or others. The desired outcome should be the provision of a care regime that does not constitute deprivation of liberty.

5–190 5.24 Where the best interests assessor comes to the conclusion that the best interests requirement is not met, but it appears to the assessor that the person being assessed is already being deprived of their liberty, the assessor must inform the supervisory body and explain in their report why they have reached that conclusion. The supervisory body must then inform the managing authority to review the relevant person's care plan immediately so that unauthorised deprivation of liberty does not continue. Any necessary changes must be made urgently to stop what would be an unlawful deprivation of liberty. The steps taken to stop the deprivation of liberty should be recorded in the care plan. Where possible, family, friends and carers should be involved in deciding how to prevent the unauthorised deprivation of liberty from continuing. If the supervisory body has any doubts about whether the matter is being satisfactorily resolved within an appropriately urgent timescale, it should alert the inspection body (see chapter 11).

6. WHEN CAN URGENT AUTHORISATIONS OF DEPRIVATION OF LIBERTY BE GIVEN?

5–191 Wherever possible, applications for deprivation of liberty authorisations should be made before the deprivation of liberty commences. However, where deprivation of liberty unavoidably needs to commence before a standard authorisation can be obtained, an urgent authorisation can be given which will make the deprivation of liberty lawful for a short period of time.

This chapter contains guidance on the rules around urgent authorisations.

When can an urgent authorisation be given?

5–192 6.1 A managing authority can itself give an urgent authorisation for deprivation of liberty where:
- it is required to make a request to the supervisory body for a standard authorisation, but believes that the need for the person to be deprived of their liberty is so urgent that deprivation needs to begin before the request is made, or
- it has made a request for a standard authorisation, but believes that the need for a person to be deprived of liberty has now become so urgent that deprivation of liberty needs to begin before the request is dealt with by the supervisory body.

This means that an urgent authorisation can never be given without a request for a standard authorisation being made simultaneously. Therefore, before giving an urgent authorisation, a managing authority will need to have a reasonable expectation that the six qualifying requirements for a standard authorisation are likely to be met.

6.2 Urgent authorisations should normally only be used in response to sudden **5–193** unforeseen needs. However, they can also be used in care planning (for example, to avoid delays in transfer for rehabilitation, where delay would reduce the likely benefit of the rehabilitation).

6.3 However, an urgent authorisation should not be used where there is no **5–194** expectation that a standard deprivation of liberty authorisation will be needed. Where, for example:

- a person who lacks capacity to make decisions about their care and treatment has developed a mental disorder as a result of a physical illness, and
- the physical illness requires treatment in hospital in circumstances that amount to a deprivation of liberty, and
- the treatment of that physical illness is expected to lead to rapid resolution of the mental disorder such that a standard deprivation of liberty authorisation would not be required,

it would not be appropriate to give an urgent authorisation simply to legitimise the short-term deprivation of liberty.

6.4 Similarly, an urgent deprivation of liberty authorisation should not be **5–195** given when a person is, for example, in an accident and emergency unit or a care home, and it is anticipated that within a matter of a few hours or a few days the person will no longer be in that environment.

6.5 Any decision to give an urgent authorisation and take action that deprives **5–196** a person of liberty must be in the person's best interests, as set out in section 4 of the Mental Capacity Act 2005. Where restraint is involved, all actions must comply with the additional conditions in section 6 of the Act (see chapter 6 of the main Code).

6.6 The managing authority must decide the period for which the urgent auth- **5–197** orisation is given, but this must not exceed seven days (see paragraphs 6.20 to 6.28 regarding the possible extension of the seven-day period). The authorisation must be in writing and must state:

- the name of the relevant person
- the name of the relevant hospital or care home
- the period for which the authorisation is to be in force, and
- the purpose for which the authorisation is given.

A standard form is available for a managing authority to use to notify a supervisory body that it has given an urgent authorisation.

6.7 Supervisory bodies and managing authorities should have a procedure in **5–198** place that identifies:

- what actions should be taken when an urgent authorisation needs to be made
- who should take each action, and
- within what timescale.

What records should be kept about urgent authorisations?

5–199   6.8   The managing authority must keep a written record of any urgent authorisations given, including details of why it decided to give an urgent authorisation. They must give a copy of the authorisation to the relevant person and any IMCA instructed, and place a copy in the relevant person's records. The managing authority must also seek to ensure that, as far as possible, the relevant person understands the effect of the authorisation and the right to challenge the authorisation via the Court of Protection. Appropriate information must be given both orally and in writing.

5–200   6.9   The managing authority should, as far as possible and appropriate, notify the relevant person's family, friends and carers when an urgent authorisation is given in order to enable them to offer informed support to the person.

5–201   6.10   The processes surrounding the giving and receiving of urgent authorisations should be clearly recorded, and regularly monitored and audited, as part of a managing authority's or supervisory body's governance structure.

Who should be consulted before giving an urgent authorisation?

5–202   6.11   If the managing authority is considering depriving a person of liberty in an emergency and giving an urgent authorisation, they must, as far as is practical and possible, take account of the views of anyone engaged in caring for the relevant person or interested in their welfare. The aim should be to consult carers and family members at as early a stage as possible so that their views can be properly taken into account before a decision to give an urgent authorisation is taken.

5–203   6.12   The steps taken to involve family, friends or carers should be recorded in the relevant person's records, along with their views. The views of the carers will be important because their knowledge of the person will put them in a good position to gauge how the person will react to the deprivation of their liberty, and the effect it will have on their mental state. It may also be appropriate to consult any staff who may have some involvement in the person's case.

5–204   6.13   The ultimate decision, though, will need to be based on a judgement of what is in the relevant person's best interests. The decision-maker from the managing authority will need to be able to show that they have made a reasonable decision based on their professional judgement and taking account of all the relevant factors. This is an important decision, because it could mean the deprivation of a person's liberty without, at this stage, the full deprivation of liberty safeguards assessment process having taken place. The decision should therefore be taken at a senior level within the managing authority.

Scenario: Urgent authorisation followed by short-term standard authorisation 5–205

Mr Baker is 75, widowed and lives near his only family—his daughter. He is admitted to hospital having been found by his daughter on his kitchen floor. He is uncharacteristically confused and is not able to give a reliable history of what has happened. He has a routine physical examination, as well as blood and urine investigations, and is diagnosed as having a urinary tract infection. He is given antibiotics, but his nursing care is complicated by his fluctuating confusion. Once or twice he removes his clothes and walks through the ward naked, and at times he tries to leave the ward, unaware that he is in hospital, and believing that he is late for an important work meeting. During more lucid moments, however, he knows where he is and accepts the need for investigation and treatment in hospital.

The responsible consultant, in consultation with ward nursing staff and Mr Baker's daughter, feels that it would be in his best interests to place him in a side room to protect his dignity, and restrict his movements to ensure he remains on the ward.

However, after two days, his confusion appears to worsen: he starts having hallucinations and has to be restrained more often by staff to prevent him leaving the ward. After assessment by a doctor from the liaison psychiatry team, Mr Baker is prescribed antipsychotic medication for his own and other patients' safety. He does not resist taking this medication. The likely benefits and possible side effects are discussed with his daughter and, on balance, the medication is felt to be in his best interests in order to continue his medical investigations.

Staff become concerned about the level of restriction of liberty Mr Baker is now subject to. In particular, they are concerned about the duration of the restrictions; the fact that Mr Baker no longer has lucid intervals when he can give his consent to ongoing care and treatment in hospital; and the physical restraint that is still being required on occasion.

After discussion between the ward manager and Mr Baker's daughter, the managing authority gives an urgent authorisation and submits a request for a standard authorisation to the supervisory body (PCT). A best interests assessor is appointed, and the liaison psychiatrist provides the mental health and mental capacity assessments. In making all the deprivation of liberty safeguards assessments to see whether the qualifying requirements are met, it is considered that although restraint is being used, this does not mean he is objecting having regard to all the circumstances, so he is not ineligible and a standard authorisation is given.

Can a person be moved into care under an urgent authorisation?

6.14 There may be cases in which managing authorities are considering giving 5–206
an urgent authorisation to enable them to move the relevant person to a
new type of care. This may occur, for example, when considering whether
to admit a person living at home or with relatives into a hospital care
regime that would deprive them of their liberty, and when the need for

admission appears to be so urgent that there would not be enough time to follow the standard authorisation process.

5–207   6.15   For some people, such a change of location may have a detrimental effect on their mental health, which might significantly distort the way they come across during any assessment process. In such a case, managing authorities should consider whether giving the urgent authorisation and admitting the person to hospital would outweigh the benefits of leaving the person in their existing location, where any assessment of their needs might be more accurate. This will involve looking carefully at the existing care arrangements and consulting with any carers involved, to establish whether or not the person could safely and beneficially be cared for in their home environment while the assessment process takes place. Where the relevant person is already known to statutory care providers, for example the community mental health team or social services, it will be important to involve them in this decision-making process. The relevant person's GP may also be an important source of knowledge about the person's situation, and may be able to offer a valuable opinion when the appropriateness of moving the person into a different care setting is under consideration.

What happens at the end of an urgent authorisation period?

5–208   6.16   An urgent authorisation will terminate at the end of the period for which it is given. As noted above, this is normally a maximum of seven days, but in exceptional circumstances an urgent authorisation can be extended to a maximum of 14 days **by the supervisory body,** as explained in paragraphs 6.20 to 6.28.

5–209   6.17   An urgent authorisation will terminate before this time if the standard authorisation applied for is given.

5–210   6.18   An urgent authorisation will also terminate if a managing authority receives notice from the supervisory body that the standard authorisation will not be given. It will not then be lawful to continue to deprive the relevant person of their liberty.

5–211   6.19   The supervisory body must inform the relevant person and any IMCA instructed that the urgent authorisation has ended. This notification can be combined with the notification to them of the outcome of the application for standard authorisation.

5–212 | **Scenario: Considering an urgent authorisation**

Mr Watson is 35. He has autism and learning disabilities. He lives in the family home with his parents. Although he is well settled and generally calm at home, Mr Watson sometimes becomes disturbed when in an unfamiliar and crowded environment.

While his parents are away for a couple of days, and Mr Watson is in the care of a paid carer, he has an accident at home. His carer is concerned that he may have broken his arm and takes him to the A&E department at the local hospital, where it is decided that his arm needs to be X-rayed to check for a break. The outcome is that there is no break, just bad bruising, so there is no medical need to admit him.

Scenario: Considering an urgent authorisation *(continued)*

However, because of the pain he is in and the crowded environment,
Mr Watson has become very agitated to the extent that hospital security personnel feel a need to control him physically. The carer tries to restrain him and lead him outside where she says he is likely to be more settled and calm down.

Because restraint is being used, the A&E doctor wonders whether it his duty to use an urgent authorisation or other measure to detain Mr Watson in hospital if he believes it is in his best interests.

He consults a liaison psychiatry nurse, who reassures him that such restraint is permitted under the Mental Capacity Act 2005 where it is necessary to prevent harm to the person himself and so long as it is a proportionate response. The nurse assists the carer with gentle restraint to take Mr Watson to a quieter area. She suggests the doctor phone Mr Watson's parents for further information, and obtains painkillers for Mr Watson.

The doctor speaks to Mr Watson's parents, who believe that Mr Watson does not have the mental capacity to decide on his care and treatment in the current circumstances. They have experienced similar situations many times, and are confident that Mr Watson will calm down once he is back in his home environment. They state that if any more detailed assessment of his mental state is required it should take place there, in the company of the carer whom they know and trust. They reassure the doctor that Mr Watson is highly unlikely to present a danger to himself, his carer or the general public.

The doctor decides that it will be in Mr Watson's best interests to return home with his carer.

How and when can an urgent authorisation be extended?

6.20   If there are exceptional reasons why the request for a standard authoris- **5–213** ation cannot be dealt with within the period of the original urgent authorisation, the managing authority may ask the supervisory body to extend the duration of the urgent authorisation for a maximum of a further seven days. The managing authority must keep a written record of the reason for making the request and must notify the relevant person, in writing, that they have made the request. Standard forms are available for managing authorities to request the extension of an urgent authorisation from a supervisory body and for supervisory bodies to record their decision in response to such a request.

6.21   Unless the duration of the urgent authorisation is extended by the super- **5–214** visory body, or a standard authorisation is given before the urgent authorisation expires, the authority to deprive the person of liberty will cease once the urgent authorisation period has expired. It is therefore essential that any request for an extension of an urgent authorisation is made promptly. This will necessitate good communication between the managing authority and the supervisory body regarding the progress of the standard authorisation assessment process. Particular care may need to be taken where an urgent authorisation is due to expire over the weekend or on a bank holiday, when appropriate people at the managing authority and supervisory body may not be immediately available.

5–215 6.22 The supervisory body may only extend the duration of the urgent authorisation if:

- the managing authority has made a request for a standard authorisation
- there are exceptional reasons why it has not yet been possible to make a standard authorisation, and
- it is essential for the deprivation of liberty to continue while the supervisory body makes its decision.

5–216 6.23 Extensions can only be granted for exceptional reasons. An example of when an extension would be justified might be where:

- it was not possible to contact a person whom the best interests assessor needed to contact
- the assessment could not be relied upon without their input, and
- extension for the specified period would enable them to be contacted.

5–217 6.24 It is for the supervisory body to decide what constitutes an 'exceptional reason', but because of the seriousness of the issues involved, the supervisory body's decision must be soundly based and defensible. It would not, for example, be appropriate to use staffing shortages as a reason to extend an urgent authorisation.

5–218 6.25 An urgent authorisation can only be extended once.

5–219 6.26 The supervisory body must notify the managing authority of the length of any extension granted and must vary the original urgent authorisation so that it states the extended duration. The supervisory body must also keep a written record of the outcome of the request and the period of the extension.

5–220 6.27 The managing authority must give a copy of the varied urgent authorisation to the relevant person and any IMCA instructed, and must seek to ensure that, as far as possible, the relevant person understands the effect of the varied authorisation and the right to challenge the authorisation via the Court of Protection. The appropriate information must be given both orally and in writing.

5–221 6.28 If the supervisory body decides not to extend the urgent authorisation, it must inform the managing authority of its decision and the reasons for it. The managing authority must give a copy of the notice to the relevant person and any IMCA involved.

7. WHAT IS THE ROLE OF THE RELEVANT PERSON'S REPRESENTATIVE?

5–222 Once a standard deprivation of liberty authorisation has been given, supervisory bodies must appoint the relevant person's representative as soon as possible and practical to represent the person who has been deprived of their liberty.

This chapter explains the role of the relevant person's representative and gives guidance on their selection and appointment.

What is the role of the relevant person's representative?

5–223 7.1 The supervisory body must appoint a relevant person's representative for every person to whom they give a standard authorisation for deprivation of liberty. It is important that the representative is appointed at the time the authorisation is given or as soon as possible and practical thereafter.

7.2 The role of the relevant person's representative, once appointed, is: **5–224**
- to maintain contact with the relevant person, and
- to represent and support the relevant person in all matters relating to the deprivation of liberty safeguards, including, if appropriate, triggering a review, using an organisation's complaints procedure on the person's behalf or making an application to the Court of Protection.

This is a crucial role in the deprivation of liberty process, providing the relevant person with representation and support that is independent of the commissioners and providers of the services they are receiving.

7.3 The best interests principle of the Act applies to the relevant person's rep- **5–225** resentative in the same way that it applies to other people acting or making decisions for people who lack capacity.

How should managing authorities work with the relevant person's representative?

7.4 As soon as possible and practical after a standard deprivation of liberty **5–226** authorisation is given, the managing authority must seek to ensure that the relevant person and their representative understand:
- the effect of the authorisation
- their right to request a review (see chapter 8)
- the formal and informal complaints procedures that are available to them
- their right to make an application to the Court of Protection to seek variation or termination of the authorisation (see chapter 10), and
- their right, where the relevant person does not have a paid 'professional' representative, to request the support of an Independent Mental Capacity Advocate (IMCA) (see paragraphs 7.37 to 7.41).

7.5 When providing information to the person and their representative, the **5–227** managing authority should take account of the communication and language needs of both the person and their representative. Provision of information should be seen as an ongoing responsibility, rather than a one-off activity.

Who can be the relevant person's representative?[1]

7.6 To be eligible to be the relevant person's representative, a person must be: **5–228**
- 18 years of age or over
- able to keep in contact with the relevant person, and
- willing to be appointed.

The person must not be:

---

[1] Requirements relating to the eligibility, selection and appointment of relevant person's representatives are covered in regulations. The regulations for England are The Mental Capacity (Deprivation of Liberty: Appointment of Relevant Person's Representative) Regulations 2008. The regulations for Wales are The Mental Capacity (Deprivation of Liberty: Appointment of Relevant Person's Representative) (Wales) Regulations 2008.

- financially interested in the relevant person's managing authority (a person is considered to be financially interested where that person is a partner, director, other office-holder or major shareholder of the managing authority)
- a relative of a person who has a financial interest in the relevant person's managing authority (paragraph 4.13 explains what is meant by 'relative')
- employed by, or providing services to, the care home in which the person relevant person is residing
- employed by the hospital in a role that is, or could be, related to the treatment or care of the relevant person, or
- employed to work in the relevant person's supervisory body in a role that is, or could be, related to the relevant person's case.

5-229   7.7   The appointment of the relevant person's representative is in addition to, and does not affect, any appointment of a donee or deputy. Similarly, the functions of the representative are in addition to, and do not affect, the authority of any donee, the powers of any deputy or any powers of the court. A donee or deputy may themselves be appointed as the relevant person's representative if they meet the eligibility criteria set out in paragraph 7.6.

5-230   7.8   There is no presumption that the relevant person's representative should be the same as the person who is their nearest relative for the purposes of the Mental Health Act 1983, even where the relevant person is likely to be subject simultaneously to an authorisation under these safeguards and a provision of the Mental Health Act 1983. This is because the relevant person's representative is not selected in the same way as the nearest relative under the Mental Health Act 1983, nor do they perform the same role. However, there is nothing to stop the relevant person's representative being the same as their nearest relative under the Mental Health Act 1983.

When should the relevant person's representative be identified?

5-231   7.9   The process of identifying a representative must begin as soon as possible.

5-232   7.10   Normally, this should be when the best interests assessor is appointed— even if one or more of the other assessments has not yet been completed. This is because the best interests assessor must, as part of the assessment process, identify if there is anyone they would recommend to become the relevant person's representative. The best interests assessor should discuss the representative role with the people interviewed as part of the assessment.

5-233   7.11   This does leave a risk that the process to identify a representative might begin in cases where authorisation is not given. Nevertheless, it is important that the process begins, so that the representative can be appointed immediately the authorisation is given or as soon as possible and practical thereafter.

How should the relevant person's representative be selected?

5-234   7.12   The best interests assessor should first establish whether the relevant person has the capacity to select their own representative and, if so, invite them to do so. If the relevant person has capacity and selects an eligible person (according to the criteria set out in paragraph 7.6), the best interests assessor must recommend that person to the supervisory body for appointment.

7.13 Alternatively, if the relevant person lacks capacity and there is a donee or **5–235** deputy with the appropriate authority, the donee or deputy may select the person to be recommended as the relevant person's representative, again subject to the criteria set out in paragraph 7.6.

If a donee or deputy selects an eligible person, then the best interests assessor must recommend that person to the supervisory body for appointment.

7.14 It is up to the best interests assessor to confirm whether any representative **5–236** proposed by the relevant person, a donee or a deputy is eligible. If the best interests assessor decides that a proposed representative is not eligible, they must advise the person who made the selection and invite them to make a further selection.

7.15 If neither the relevant person, nor a donee or deputy, selects an eligible **5–237** person, then the best interests assessor must consider whether they are able to identify someone eligible who could act as the relevant person's representative.

7.16 In making a recommendation, the assessor should consider, and balance, **5–238** factors such as:

- Does the relevant person have a preference?
- If they do not have the capacity to express a preference now, is there any written statement made by the relevant person when they had capacity that indicates who they may now want to be their representative?
- Will the proposed representative be able to keep in contact with the relevant person?
- Does the relevant person appear to trust and feel comfortable with the proposed representative?
- Would the proposed representative be able to represent the relevant person effectively?
- Is the proposed representative likely to represent the relevant person's best interests?

In most cases, the best interests assessor will be able to check at the same time that the proposed representative is willing to take on the role.

7.17 It should not be assumed that the representative needs to be someone who **5–239** supports the deprivation of liberty.

7.18 The best interests assessor must not select a representative where the rel- **5–240** evant person, if they have the capacity to do so, or a donee or a deputy acting within the scope of their authority, states they are not content with that selection.

7.19 If the best interests assessor is unable to recommend anybody to be the **5–241** relevant person's representative, they must notify the supervisory body accordingly. The supervisory body must then itself identify an eligible person to be appointed as the representative. In doing so, the supervisory body may select a person who:

- would be performing the role in a professional capacity
- has satisfactory skills and experience to perform the role

- is not a family member, friend or carer of the relevant person
- is not employed by, or providing services to, the relevant person's managing authority, where the relevant person's managing authority is a care home
- is not employed to work in the relevant person's managing authority in a role that is, or could be, related to the relevant person's case, where the relevant person's managing authority is a hospital
- is not employed to work in the supervisory body that is appointing the representative in a role that is, or could be, related to the relevant person's case, and
- the supervisory body is satisfied that an appropriate criminal record certificate has been issued in respect of.

5–242 7.20 The supervisory body may pay a person they select to be the relevant person's representative in the circumstances set out in paragraph 7.19. This service could be commissioned, for example, through an advocacy services provider, ensuring that the service provides effective independent representation for the relevant person.

5–243 7.21 When selecting a suitable representative for the relevant person, the best interests assessor or supervisory body should pay particular attention to the communication and cultural needs of the relevant person.

How should the relevant person's representative be appointed?

5–244 7.22 The supervisory body must invite, in writing, the person recommended by the best interests assessor to become the relevant person's representative. If the best interests assessor does not recommend anyone, then the supervisory body should identify and appoint someone to undertake the role. If the person is willing to become the representative, the supervisory body must formally appoint them. If the person refuses, a further eligible person must be identified and invited to become the representative. This process must continue until an eligible person is appointed.

5–245 7.23 The appointment of the relevant person's representative by the supervisory body must be in writing and set out the role and responsibilities of the relevant person's representative. The letter of appointment should also state the name of the appointed person and the date of expiry of the appointment, which must be for the period of the standard authorisation that has been given. The supervisory body must send copies of the written appointment to:
- the appointed person
- the relevant person
- any donee or deputy of the relevant person
- any IMCA involved
- every interested person named by the best interests assessor in their report as somebody they have consulted in carrying out their assessment, and
- the managing authority of the relevant hospital or care home.

5–246 7.24 The relevant person's representative must confirm to the supervisory body in writing that they are willing to accept the appointment and have understood their roles and responsibilities in respect of the relevant person.

How should the work of the relevant person's representative be supported and monitored?

7.25 It is important that the representative has sufficient contact with the rel- **5–247** evant person to ensure that the relevant person's best interests are being safeguarded. In order to fulfil their role, therefore, the representative will need to be able to have face-to-face contact with the relevant person. That means that the care home or hospital should accommodate visits by the representative at reasonable times. The name of the person's representative should be recorded in the person's health and social care records.

7.26 Managing authorities and supervisory bodies should inform the relevant **5–248** person's representative about sources of support and information available to help them in the role, including how to access the support of an IMCA (see paragraphs 7.37 to 7.41).

7.27 If the representative has insufficient contact with the relevant person, for **5–249** whatever reason, the person may effectively be unable to access important review and appeal rights. For this reason, if the representative does not maintain an appropriate level of contact with the person, the managing authority will need to consider informing the supervisory body. When the managing authority is reviewing the person's care plan, it should consider whether the representative is in sufficient contact with the relevant person to offer effective support. Records kept by managing authorities about frequency of contact will support this consideration.

7.28 Because the appropriate levels and methods of contact between a relevant **5–250** person and their representative will vary from case to case, this is a matter about which the managing authority will need to exercise discretion. If the managing authority has any concerns, it may be best to raise the matter with the representative initially to see whether any perceived problems can be resolved informally. If after this the representative still does not maintain what the managing authority considers to be an appropriate level of contact with the relevant person, then the managing authority should notify the supervisory body.

When can the appointment of the relevant person's representative be terminated?

7.29 The appointment of the relevant person's representative will be termina- **5–251** ted in any of the following circumstances:
- The standard authorisation comes to an end and a new authorisation is not applied for or, if applied for, is not given.
- The relevant person, if they have capacity to do so, objects to the representative continuing in their role and a different person is selected to be their representative instead.
- A donee or deputy, if it is within their authority to do so and the relevant person lacks the capacity to decide, objects to the representative continuing in their role and a different person is selected to be the representative instead.
- The supervisory body becomes aware that the representative is no longer willing or eligible to continue in the role.

- The supervisory body becomes aware that the relevant person's representative is not keeping in touch with the person, is not representing and supporting them effectively or is not acting in the person's best interests.
- The relevant person's representative dies.

5–252 7.30 If the supervisory body becomes aware that the representative may not be keeping in touch with the person, is not acting in the relevant person's best interests, or is no longer eligible, it should contact the representative to clarify the position before deciding whether to terminate the appointment.

5–253 7.31 When the appointment of the relevant person's representative ends, the supervisory body must give notice to all those listed in paragraph 7.23. This notice should be given as soon as possible, stating when the appointment ended and the reason why.

5–254 7.32 When the appointment of a relevant person's representative ends but the lawful deprivation of liberty continues, the supervisory body must appoint a suitable replacement to be the relevant person's representative as soon as possible and practical after they become aware of the vacancy. As before, a person qualified to be a best interests assessor should make a recommendation to the supervisory body and the supervisory body should take account of any such recommendations.

5–255 7.33 If the reason for the termination of the former representative's appointment is that they are no longer eligible, the views of the former representative on who might replace them should be sought. The person identified as most suitable should then be invited to accept the appointment. This process should continue until an eligible person is willing to accept appointment.

What happens when there is no relevant person's representative available?

5–256 7.34 A person who is being deprived of their liberty will be in a particularly vulnerable position during any gaps in the appointment of the relevant person's representative, since there may be nobody to represent their interests or to apply for a review on their behalf. In these circumstances, if there is nobody who can support and represent the person (other than a person engaged in providing care and treatment for the relevant person in a professional capacity or for remuneration), the managing authority must notify the supervisory body, who must instruct an IMCA to represent the relevant person until a new representative is appointed.

5–257 7.35 The role of an IMCA instructed in these circumstances is essentially the same as that of the relevant person's representative. The role of the IMCA in this situation ends when the new relevant person's representative is appointed.

5–258 7.36 At any time when the relevant person does not have a representative, it will be particularly important for supervisory bodies to consider exercising their discretion to carry out a review if there is any significant change in the person's circumstances.

When should an IMCA be instructed?

7.37 Both the person who is deprived of liberty under a standard authorisation **5–259** and their representative have a statutory right of access to an IMCA. It is the responsibility of the supervisory body to instruct an IMCA if the relevant person or their representative requests one. The intention is to provide extra support to the relevant person or a family member or friend acting as their representative if they need it, and to help them make use of the review process or access the Court of Protection safeguards. Where the relevant person has a paid 'professional' representative (see paragraphs 7.19 and 7.20), the need for additional advocacy support should not arise and so there is no requirement for an IMCA to be provided in those circumstances.

7.38 The role of the IMCA is to help represent the relevant person and, in par- **5–260** ticular, to assist the relevant person and their representative to understand the effect of the authorisation, what it means, why it has been given, why the relevant person meets the criteria for authorisation, how long it will last, any conditions to which the authorisation is subject and how to trigger a review or challenge in the Court of Protection. The IMCA can also provide support with a review (see chapter 8) or with an application to the Court of Protection (see chapter 10), for example to help the person to communicate their views.

7.39 The IMCA will have the right to make submissions to the supervisory **5–261** body on the question of whether a qualifying requirement should be reviewed, or to give information, or make submissions, to any assessor carrying out a review assessment. Both the person and their representative must be told about the IMCA service and how to request an IMCA.

7.40 An IMCA must be instructed whenever requested by the relevant person **5–262** or their representative. A request may be made more than once during the period of the authorisation. For example, help may be sought at the start of the authorisation and then again later in order to request a review.

7.41 In addition, if the supervisory body has reason to believe that the review **5–263** and Court of Protection safeguards might not be used without the support of an IMCA, then they must instruct an IMCA. For example, if the supervisory body is aware that the person has selected a representative who needs support with communication, it should consider whether an IMCA is needed.

8. WHEN SHOULD AN AUTHORISATION BE REVIEWED AND WHAT HAPPENS WHEN IT ENDS?

When a person is deprived of their liberty, the managing authority has a **5–264** duty to monitor the case on an ongoing basis to see if the person's circumstances change—which may mean they no longer need to be deprived of their liberty.

The managing authority must set out in the care plan clear roles and responsibilities for monitoring and confirm under what circumstances a review is necessary. For example, if a person's condition is changing frequently, then their situation should be reviewed more frequently.

This chapter explains the duties of managing authorities and supervisory bodies in relation to reviewing cases, and what happens when an authorisation ends. The review process is set out in flowchart form at Annex 4.

When should a standard authorisation be reviewed?

5–265   8.1   A standard authorisation can be reviewed at any time. The review is carried out by the supervisory body.

8.2   There are certain statutory grounds for carrying out a review. If the statutory grounds for a review are met, the supervisory body must carry out a review. If a review is requested by the relevant person, their representative or the managing authority, the supervisory body must carry out a review. Standard letters are available for the relevant person or their representative to request a review. There is also a standard form available for the managing authority to request a review. A supervisory body can also decide to carry out a review at its own discretion.

5–266   8.3   The statutory grounds for a review are:
- The relevant person no longer meets the age, no refusals, mental capacity, mental health or best interests requirements.
- The relevant person no longer meets the eligibility requirement because they now object to receiving mental health treatment in hospital and they meet the criteria for an application for admission under section 2 or section 3 of the Mental Health Act 1983 (see paragraphs 4.45 to 4.48).
- There has been a change in the relevant person's situation and, because of the change, it would be appropriate to amend an existing condition to which the authorisation is subject, delete an existing condition or add a new condition.
- The reason(s) the person now meets the qualifying requirement(s) is(are) different from the reason(s) given at the time the standard authorisation was given.

5–267   8.4   Different arrangements apply if the person no longer meets the eligibility requirement because they have been detained under the Mental Health Act, or become subject to a requirement under that Act that conflicts with the authorisation. (See paragraphs 8.19 to 8.21 regarding the short-term suspension of a standard authorisation.)

5–268   8.5   A managing authority must request a review if it appears to it that one or more of the qualifying requirements is no longer met, or may no longer be met.

What happens when a review is going to take place?

5–269   8.6   The supervisory body must tell the relevant person, their representative and the managing authority if they are going to carry out a review. This must be done either before the review begins or as soon as possible and practical after it has begun. A standard form is available for this purpose.

5–270   8.7   The relevant person's records must include information about any formal reviews that have been requested, when they were considered, and the outcome. These records must be retained by the supervisory body.

8.8   Deprivation of liberty can be ended before a formal review. An authoris-   **5–271**
ation only **permits** deprivation of liberty: it does not mean that a person
must be deprived of liberty where circumstances no longer necessitate it.
If a care home or hospital decides that deprivation of liberty is no longer
necessary then they must end it immediately, by adjusting the care regime
or implementing whatever other change is appropriate. The managing
authority should then apply to the supervisory body to review and, if
appropriate, formally terminate the authorisation.

How should standard authorisations be reviewed?

8.9   When a supervisory body receives a request for a review, it must first   **5–272**
decide which, if any, of the qualifying requirements need to be reviewed.
A standard form is available for recording this decision.

8.10 If the supervisory body concludes that none of the qualifying require-   **5–273**
ments need to be reviewed, no further action is necessary. For example,
if there has been a very recent assessment or review and no new evidence
has been submitted to show that the relevant person does not meet the criteria, or that circumstances have changed, no review is required.

8.11 If it appears that one or more of the qualifying requirements should be   **5–274**
reviewed, the supervisory body must arrange for a separate review assessment to be carried out for each of these requirements.

8.12 The supervisory body must record when a review is requested, what it   **5–275**
decides to do (whether it decides to carry out a review or not) and the
reasons for its decision.

8.13 In general, review processes should follow the standard authorisation pro-   **5–276**
cesses—so supervisory bodies should conduct the assessments outlined in
chapter 4 of this Code of Practice for each of the qualifying requirements
that need to be reviewed.

8.14 Where the supervisory body decides that the best interests requirement   **5–277**
should be reviewed solely because details of the **conditions** attached to
the authorisation need to be changed, and the review request does not
include evidence that there is a significant change in the relevant person's
overall circumstances, there is no need for a full reassessment of best
interests. The supervisory body can simply vary the conditions attached
to the authorisation as appropriate. In deciding whether a full reassessment is necessary, the supervisory body should consider whether the
grounds for the authorisation, or the nature of the conditions, are being
contested by anyone as part of the review request.

8.15 If the review relates to any of the other requirements, or to a significant   **5–278**
change in the person's situation under the best interests requirement,
the supervisory body must obtain a new assessment.

8.16 If the assessment shows that the requirement is still met, the supervisory   **5–279**
body must check whether the reason that it is met has changed from the
reason originally stated on the authorisation. If it
has, the supervisory body should make any appropriate amendments to
the authorisation. In addition, if the review relates to the best interests
requirement, the supervisory body must consider whether any conditions
should be changed following the new assessment.

5–280

Scenario: The review process

Jo is 29 and sustained severe brain damage in a road traffic collision that killed her parents. She has great difficulty in verbal and written communication. Jo can get very frustrated and has been known to lash out at other people in the nursing care home where she now lives. At first, she regularly attempted to leave the home, but the view of the organisation providing Jo's care was that such a move would place her at serious risk, so she should be prevented from leaving.

Jo was assessed under the deprivation of liberty safeguards and an authorisation was made for six months. That authorisation is not due to end for another three months. However, Jo has made huge progress at the home and her representative is no longer sure that the restrictions are necessary. Care home staff, however, do not think that her improvement reduces the best interests requirement of the deprivation of liberty authorisation.

Jo is assisted by her representative to request a review, in the form of a letter with pictures. The pictures appear to describe Jo's frustration with the legal processes that she perceives are preventing her from moving into her own accommodation.

The supervisory body appoints a best interests assessor to coordinate the review. The best interests assessor considers which of the qualifying requirements needs to be reviewed and by whom. It appears that the best interests assessment, as well as possibly the mental health and mental capacity assessments, should be reviewed.

To assess Jo's mental capacity and her own wishes for the best interests assessment, the best interests assessor feels that specialist help would be beneficial. A speech and language therapist meets with Jo and uses a visual communication system with her. Using this system, the therapist is able to say that in her view Jo is unlikely to have capacity to make the decision to leave the care home. The mental health assessment also confirmed that Jo was still considered to have a mental disorder.

The best interests assessor was uncertain, however, whether it was still in Jo's best interests to remain under the deprivation of liberty authorisation. It was not possible to coordinate full updated assessments from the rehabilitation team, who knew her well, in the time limits required. So, because the care home believed that the standard authorisation was still required, and it was a complex case, the best interests assessor recommended to the supervisory body that two conditions should be applied to the standard authorisation:

- assessments must be carried out by rehabilitation specialists on Jo's clinical progress, and
- a full case review should be held within one month.

At this review meeting, to which Jo's representative and the best interests assessor were invited, it was agreed that Jo had made such good progress that deprivation of liberty was no longer necessary, because the risks of her having increased freedom had reduced. The standard authorisation was therefore terminated, and a new care plan was prepared which focused on working towards more independent living.

What happens if any of the requirements are not met?

8.17 If any of the requirements are not met, then the authorisation must be ter- **5–281**
      minated immediately.

8.18 The supervisory body must give written notice of the outcome of a review **5–282**
      and any changes that have been made to the deprivation of liberty auth-
      orisation to:
      • the managing authority and the care home or hospital itself
      • the relevant person
      • the relevant person's representative, and
      • any Independent Mental Capacity Advocate (IMCA) involved.

Short-term suspension of authorisation

8.19 There are separate review arrangements for cases in which the eligibility **5–283**
      requirement ceases to be met for a short period of time for reasons other
      than that the person is objecting to receiving mental health treatment in
      hospital. For example, if the relevant person is detained as a hospital
      in-patient under the Mental Health Act 1983, the managing authority
      must notify the supervisory body, who will suspend the authorisation.

8.20 If the relevant person then becomes eligible again within 28 days, the **5–284**
      managing authority must notify the supervisory body who will remove
      the suspension. If no such notice is given within 28 days, then the author-
      isation will be terminated. Standard forms are available for managing
      authorities to notify supervisory bodies about the need for suspension
      of an authorisation, or that a suspension should be lifted.

8.21 If the person ceases to meet the eligibility requirement because they begin **5–285**
      to object to receiving mental health treatment in hospital and they meet
      the criteria for an application for admission under section 2 or section 3
      of the Mental Health Act 1983, a review should be started immediately
      (see paragraph 8.3).

Is a review necessary when the relevant person's capacity fluctuates?

8.22 Guidance about people with fluctuating or temporary capacity is con- **5–286**
      tained in paragraphs 4.26 and 4.27 of the main Code. In the context of
      deprivation of liberty safeguards, where a relevant person's capacity to
      make decisions about the arrangements made for their care and treatment
      fluctuates on a short-term basis, a balance needs to be struck between:
      • the need to review and terminate an authorisation if a person regains
        capacity, and
      • spending time and resources constantly reviewing, terminating and
        then seeking fresh deprivation of liberty authorisations as the relevant
        person's capacity changes.

8.23 Each case must be treated on its merits. Managing authorities should keep **5–287**
      all cases under review: where a person subject to an authorisation is
      deemed to have regained the capacity to decide about the arrangements
      made for their care and treatment, the managing authority must assess
      whether there is consistent evidence of the regaining of capacity on a

longer-term basis. This is a clinical judgement that will need to be made by a suitably qualified person.

5–288   8.24   Where there is consistent evidence of regaining capacity on this longer-term basis, deprivation of liberty should be lifted immediately, and a formal review and termination of the authorisation sought. However, it should be borne in mind that a deprivation of liberty authorisation carries with it certain safeguards that the relevant person will lose if the authorisation is terminated. Where the regaining of capacity is likely to be temporary, and the authorisation will be required again within a short period of time, the authorisation should be left in place, but with the situation kept under ongoing review.

5–289 | **Scenario: Fluctuating capacity**

Walter, an older man with severe depression, is admitted to hospital from a care home. He seems confused and bewildered, but does not object. His family are unable to look after him at home, but they would prefer him to go into a different care home rather than stay in hospital. However, there is no alternative placement available, so when the assessment concludes that Walter lacks capacity to make decisions about his care and treatment, the only option seems to be that he should stay on the ward.

Because the care regime in the ward is extremely restrictive—Walter is not allowed to leave the hospital and his movement within the hospital is restricted for his own safety—ward staff think that they need to apply for a deprivation of liberty authorisation which is subsequently given.

However, over time Walter starts to experience lucid passages, during which he expresses relief at being on the ward rather than in the care home. A review meeting is convened and the participants agree that Walter now sometimes has capacity to make decisions about the arrangements made for his care and treatment. As this capacity fluctuates, it is decided, in consultation with his family, that the deprivation of liberty authorisation should remain in place for the time being.

Walter remains on the ward and his progress is such that his family feel they could look after him at home. Walter seems happy with this proposal and the consultant psychiatrist with responsibility for his care agrees to this. The deprivation of liberty authorisation is reviewed and terminated.

What happens when an authorisation ends?

5–290   8.25   When an authorisation ends, the managing authority cannot lawfully continue to deprive a person of their liberty.

5–291   8.26   If the managing authority considers that a person will still need to be deprived of liberty after the authorisation ends, they need to request a further standard authorisation to begin immediately after the expiry of the existing authorisation.

5–292   8.27   There is no statutory time limit on how far in advance of the expiry of one authorisation the managing authority can apply for a renewal authorisation. It will need to be far enough in advance for the renewal authorisation to be given before the existing authorisation ends (but see paragraphs 3.19 and 3.20 about not applying for authorisations too far in advance).

8.28 Once underway, the process for renewing a standard authorisation is the **5–293** same as that for obtaining an original authorisation, and the same assessment processes must take place. However, the need to instruct an IMCA will not usually arise because the relevant person should at this stage have a representative appointed.

8.29 When the standard authorisation ends, the supervisory body must inform **5–294** in writing:

- the relevant person
- the relevant person's representative
- the managing authority, and
- every interested person named by the best interests assessor in their report as somebody they have consulted in carrying out their assessment.

9. WHAT HAPPENS IF SOMEONE THINKS A PERSON IS BEING DEPRIVED OF THEIR LIBERTY WITHOUT AUTHORISATION?

It is a serious issue to deprive someone of their liberty without authorisation if **5–295** they lack the capacity to consent. If anyone believes that a person is being deprived of their liberty without authorisation, they should raise this with the relevant authorities.

If the conclusion is that the person is being deprived of their liberty unlawfully, this will normally result in a change in their care arrangements, or in an application for a deprivation of liberty authorisation being made.

This chapter explains the process for reporting concerns and for assessing whether unauthorised deprivation of liberty is occurring. The flowchart at Annex 3 summarises the process that a supervisory body should follow when it receives a request from somebody other than the managing authority to examine whether or not there is a current unauthorised deprivation of liberty.

What action should someone take if they think a person is being deprived of their liberty without authorisation?

9.1 If the relevant person themselves, any relative, friend or carer or any other **5–296** third party (such as a person carrying out an inspection visit or a member of an advocacy organisation) believes that a person is being deprived of liberty without the managing authority having applied for an authorisation, they should draw this to the attention of the managing authority. A standard letter is available for this purpose. In the first instance, they should ask the managing authority to apply for an authorisation if it wants to continue with the care regime, or to change the care regime immediately. Given the seriousness of deprivation of liberty, a managing authority must respond within a reasonable time to the request. This would normally mean within 24 hours.

9.2 It may be possible for the managing authority to resolve the matter infor- **5–297** mally with the concerned person. For example, the managing authority could discuss the case with the concerned person, and perhaps make some adjustment to the care arrangements so that concerns that a deprivation of liberty may be occurring are removed. However, if the managing authority is unable to resolve the issue with the concerned person quickly, they should submit a request for a standard authorisation to the supervisory body.

5–298   9.3   If the concerned person has raised the matter with the managing authority, and the managing authority does not apply for an authorisation within a reasonable period, the concerned person can ask the supervisory body to decide whether there is an unauthorised deprivation of liberty. They should:

- tell the supervisory body the name of the person they are concerned about and the name of the hospital or care home, and
- as far as they are able, explain why they think that the person is deprived of their liberty.

A standard letter is available for this purpose.

5–299   9.4   In such circumstances, the supervisory body must select and appoint a person who is suitable and eligible to carry out a best interests assessment to consider whether the person is deprived of liberty.

5–300   9.5   The supervisory body does not, however, need to arrange such an assessment where it appears to the supervisory body that:

- the request they have received is frivolous or vexatious (for example, where the person is very obviously not deprived of their liberty) or where a very recent assessment has been carried out and repeated requests are received, or
- the question of whether or not there is an unauthorised deprivation of liberty has already been decided, and since that decision, there has been no change of circumstances that would merit the question being considered again.

The supervisory body should record the reasons for their decisions. A standard form is available for this purpose.

5–301   9.6   The supervisory body must notify the person who raised the concern, the relevant person, the managing authority of the relevant hospital or care home and any IMCA involved:

- that it has been to asked to assess whether or not there is an unauthorised deprivation of liberty
- whether or not it has decided to commission an assessment, and
- where relevant, who has been appointed as assessor.

What happens if somebody informs the supervisory body directly that they think a person is being deprived of their liberty without authorisation?

5–302   9.7   If a person raises concerns about a potential unauthorised deprivation of liberty directly with the supervisory body, the supervisory body should immediately arrange a preliminary assessment to determine whether a deprivation of liberty is occurring. The supervisory body should then immediately notify the managing authority, rather than asking the concerned person to contact the managing authority themselves, to ask them to request a standard authorisation in respect of the person who is possibly deprived of liberty. The supervisory body should agree with the managing authority what is a reasonable period within which a standard authorisation should be requested (unless the managing authority is able to resolve the matter informally with the concerned person as described in paragraph 9.2). If the managing authority does not submit an application within the agreed period, and the matter has not been resolved informally, the supervisory body should follow the process set out in paragraphs 9.3 to 9.6 to assess whether unlawful deprivation of liberty is occurring. Even if the concerned person prefers to deal directly with the managing authority, the supervisory body should monitor what happens very closely to ensure that no unlawful deprivation of liberty may be occurring without proper action being taken.

How will the assessment of unlawful deprivation of liberty be conducted?

9.8 An assessment of whether an unlawful deprivation of liberty is occurring **5–303** must be carried out within seven calendar days. Although the assessment must be completed by somebody who is suitable and eligible to carry out a best interests assessment, it is not a best interests assessment as such. The purpose of the assessment is simply to establish whether unlawful deprivation of liberty is occurring.

9.9 The person nominated to undertake the assessment must consult the man- **5–304** aging authority of the relevant hospital or care home, and examine any relevant needs assessments and care plans to consider whether they constitute a deprivation of liberty. They should also speak to the person who raised the concern about why they believe that the relevant person is being deprived of their liberty and consult, as far as is possible, with the relevant person's family and friends. If there is nobody appropriate to consult among family and friends, they should inform the supervisory body who must arrange for an IMCA to be instructed to support and represent the person. A standard form is available for the assessor to record the outcome of their assessment.

What happens once the assessment has been conducted?

9.10 There are three possible outcomes of this assessment. The assessor may **5–305** conclude that:
- the person is not being deprived of their liberty
- the person is being lawfully deprived of their liberty because authorisation exists (this, though, is an unlikely outcome since the supervisory body should already be aware if any authorisation exists, thus rendering any assessment in response to a third party request unnecessary), or
- the person is being deprived of their liberty unlawfully.

9.11 The supervisory body must notify the following people of the outcome of **5–306** the assessment:
- the concerned third party who made the request
- the relevant person
- the managing authority of the relevant hospital or care home, and
- any IMCA involved. A standard form is available for this purpose.

9.12 If the outcome of the assessment is that there is an unauthorised depri- **5–307** vation of liberty, then the full assessment process should be completed as if a standard authorisation for deprivation of liberty had been applied for—unless the managing authority changes the care arrangements so that it is clear that there is no longer any deprivation of liberty.

5–308   9.13   If, having considered what could be done to avoid deprivation of liberty, the managing authority decides that the need to continue the deprivation of liberty is so urgent that the care regime should continue while the assessments are carried out, it must give an urgent authorisation and seek a standard authorisation within seven days. The managing authority must supply the supervisory body with the same information it would have had to include in a request for a standard authorisation.

5–309   9.14   If the concerned person does not accept the outcome of their request for assessment, they can apply to the Court of Protection to hear their case. See chapter 10 for more details of the role of the Court of Protection.

10.   WHAT IS THE COURT OF PROTECTION AND WHEN CAN PEOPLE APPLY TO IT?

5–310   To comply with Article 5(4) of the European Convention on Human Rights, anybody deprived of their liberty in accordance with the safeguards described in this Code of Practice is entitled to the right of speedy access to a court that can review the lawfulness of their deprivation of liberty. The Court of Protection, established by the Mental Capacity Act 2005, is the court for this purpose. Chapter 8 of the main Code provides more details on its role, powers and responsibilities.

When can people apply to the Court of Protection about the deprivation of liberty safeguards and who can apply? Applying before an authorisation is given

5–311   10.1   The relevant person, or someone acting on their behalf, may make an application to the Court of Protection **before** a decision has been reached on an application for authorisation to deprive a person of their liberty. This might be to ask the court to declare whether the relevant person has capacity, or whether an act done or proposed to be done in relation to that person is lawful (this may include whether or not the act is or would be in the best interests of the relevant person). It is up to the Court of Protection to decide whether or not to consider such an application in advance of the decision on authorisation.

Applying after an authorisation has been given

5–312   10.2   Once a standard authorisation has been given, the relevant person or their representative has the right to apply to the Court of Protection to determine any question relating to the following matters:
- whether the relevant person meets one or more of the qualifying requirements for deprivation of liberty
- the period for which the standard authorisation is to be in force
- the purpose for which the standard authorisation is given, or
- the conditions subject to which the standard authorisation is given.

5–313   10.3   Where an urgent authorisation has been given, the relevant person or certain persons acting on their behalf, such as a donee or deputy, has the right to apply to the Court of Protection to determine any question relating to the following matters:

- whether the urgent authorisation should have been given
- the period for which the urgent authorisation is to be in force, or
- the purpose for which the urgent authorisation has been given.

10.4 Where a standard or urgent authorisation has been given, any other person **5–314** may also apply to the Court of Protection for permission to take the relevant person's case to court to determine whether an authorisation should have been given. However, the Court of Protection has discretion to decide whether or not to consider an application from these people.

10.5 Wherever possible, concerns about the deprivation of liberty should be **5–315** resolved informally or through the relevant supervisory body's or managing authority's complaints procedure, rather than through the Court of Protection. Chapter 15 of the main Code ('What are the best ways to settle disagreements and disputes about issues covered in the Act?') contains general guidance on how to settle disputes about issues covered in the Mental Capacity Act 2005. The review processes covered in chapter 8 of this Code also provide a way of resolving disputes or concerns, as explained in that chapter.

10.6 The aim should be to limit applications to the Court of Protection to cases **5–316** that genuinely need to be referred to the court. However, with deprivation of liberty at stake, people should not be discouraged from making an application to the Court of Protection if it proves impossible to resolve concerns satisfactorily through other routes in a timely manner.

How should people apply to the Court of Protection?

10.7 Guidance on the court's procedures, including how to make an appli- **5–317** cation, is given in the Court of Protection Rules and Practice Directions issued by the court.[1]

10.8 The following people have an automatic right of access to the Court of **5–318** Protection and do not have to obtain permission from the court to make an application:

- a person who lacks, or is alleged to lack, capacity in relation to a specific decision or action
- the donor of a Lasting Power of Attorney to whom an application relates, or their donee
- a deputy who has been appointed by the court to act for the person concerned
- a person named in an existing court order[2] to which the application relates, and
- the person appointed by the supervisory body as the relevant person's representative.

---

[1] There will usually be a fee for applications to the court. Details of the fees charged by the court and the circumstances in which fees may be waived or remitted are available from the Office of the Public Guardian (http://www.publicguardian.gov.uk/)

[2] Examples of existing court orders include orders appointing a deputy or declarations made by the court in relation to treatment issues.

5–319 10.9 All other applicants must obtain the permission of the court before making an application. (See section 50 of the Mental Capacity Act 2005, as amended.) This can be done by completing the appropriate application form.

What orders can the Court of Protection make?

5–320 10.10 The court may make an order:
- varying or terminating a standard or urgent authorisation, or
- directing the supervisory body (in the case of a standard authorisation) or the managing authority (in the case of an urgent authorisation) to vary or terminate the authorisation.

What is the role of the Court of Protection in respect of people lacking capacity who are deprived of their liberty in settings other than hospitals or care homes?

5–321 10.11 The deprivation of liberty safeguards relate only to circumstances where a person is deprived of their liberty in a hospital or care home. Depriving a person who lacks capacity to consent to the arrangements made for their care or treatment of their liberty in other settings (for example in a person's own home, in supported living arrangements other than in care homes or in a day centre) will only be lawful following an order of the Court of Protection on a best interests personal welfare matter (see paragraph 6.51 of the main Code).

5–322 10.12 In such a case, application to the Court of Protection should be made before deprivation of liberty begins. A Court of Protection order will then itself provide a legal basis for the deprivation of liberty. A separate deprivation of liberty authorisation under the processes set out in this Code will not be required.

Is legal aid available to support applications to the Court of Protection in deprivation of liberty safeguards cases?

5–323 10.13 Legal aid will be available both for advice and representation before the Court of Protection.

11. HOW WILL THE SAFEGUARDS BE MONITORED?

5–324 The deprivation of a person's liberty is a significant issue. The deprivation of liberty safeguards are designed to ensure that a person who lacks capacity to consent to the arrangements made for their care or treatment is suitably protected against arbitrary detention. In order to provide reassurance that the safeguards processes are being correctly operated, it is important for there to be an effective mechanism for monitoring the implementation of the safeguards.

Who will monitor the safeguards?

5–325 11.1 Regulations[1] will confer the responsibility for the inspection process of the operation of the deprivation of liberty safeguards in England on a new regulator, the Care Quality Commission, bringing together functions from the existing Commission for Social Care Inspection, the Healthcare Commission and the Mental Health Act Commission. The new body will be established during 2008, subject to the passage of the relevant legislation through Parliament, and is expected to be fully operational by 2009/10 in line with the deprivation of liberty safeguards coming into force.

11.2   In Wales, the functions of monitoring the operation of the deprivation of **5–326** liberty safeguards will fall to Welsh Ministers. These functions will be performed on their behalf by Healthcare Inspectorate Wales and the Care and Social Services Inspectorate Wales.

What will the inspection bodies do and what powers will they have?

11.3   The inspection bodies for care homes and hospitals will be expected to: **5–327**
 • monitor the manner in which the deprivation of liberty safeguards are being operated by:
   —visiting hospitals and care homes in accordance with their existing visiting programme
   —interviewing people accommodated in hospitals and care homes to the extent that they consider it necessary to do so, and
   —requiring the production of, and inspecting, relevant records relating to the care or treatment of people accommodated in hospitals and care homes
 • report annually, summarising their activity and their findings about the operation of the deprivation of liberty safeguards. In England this report will be made to the Secretary of State for Health, and in Wales the report will be made to the Welsh Ministers. It will be for each monitoring body to decide whether there should be a deprivation of liberty safeguards specific report or whether the report should form part of a wider report on the monitoring body's activities.

11.4   The inspection bodies will have the power to require supervisory **5–328** bodies and managing authorities of hospitals or care homes to disclose information to them.

11.5   The inspection process will not cover the revisiting of individual assess- **5–329** ments (other than by way of a limited amount of sampling).

11.6   The inspection process will not constitute an alternative review or appeal **5–330** process. However, if the inspection body comes across a case where they believe deprivation of liberty may be occurring without an authorisation, they should inform the supervisory body in the same way as any other third party may do.

11.7   The inspection bodies will look at the deprivation of liberty protocols and **5–331** procedures in place within managing authorities and supervisory bodies. The aim is to use a small amount of sampling to evaluate the effect of these protocols and procedures on individual cases. Monitoring should take place at a time when the monitoring body is visiting the care home or in-patient setting as part of routine operations, not as an exception.

---

[1]   Draft regulations for England will be consulted upon later. Welsh Ministers are currently considering how they will use their regulation-making powers for Wales.

5-332   11.8 Supervisory bodies and managing authorities should keep their protocols and procedures under review and supervisory bodies should assess the nature of the authorisations they are giving in light of their local population. This information may be relevant to policy decisions about commissioning care and support services.

CHECKLISTS

Key points for care homes and hospitals (managing authorities)

5-333
- Managing authorities need to adapt their care planning processes to incorporate consideration of whether a person has capacity to consent to the services which are to be provided and whether their actions are likely to result in a deprivation of liberty.
- A managing authority must not, except in an urgent situation, deprive a person of liberty unless a standard authorisation has been given by the supervisory body for that specific situation, and remains in force.
- It is up to the managing authority to request such authorisation and implement the outcomes.
- Authorisation should be obtained from the supervisory body in advance of the deprivation of liberty, except in circumstances considered to be so urgent that the deprivation of liberty needs to begin immediately. In such cases, authorisation must be obtained within seven calendar days of the start of the deprivation of liberty.
- A managing authority must ensure that they comply with any conditions attached to the authorisation.
- A managing authority should monitor whether the relevant person's representative maintains regular contact with the person.
- Authorisation of deprivation of liberty should only be sought if it is genuinely necessary for a person to be deprived of liberty in their best interests in order to keep them safe. It is not necessary to apply for authorisations for all admissions to hospitals and care homes simply because the person concerned lacks capacity to decide whether to be admitted.

Key points for local authorities and NHS bodies (supervisory bodies)

5-334
- Supervisory bodies will receive applications from managing authorities for standard authorisations of deprivation of liberty. Deprivation of liberty cannot lawfully begin until the supervisory body has given authorisation, or the managing authority has itself given an urgent authorisation.
- Before an authorisation for deprivation of liberty may be given, the supervisory body must have obtained written assessments of the relevant person in order to ensure that they meet the qualifying requirements (including that the deprivation of liberty is necessary to protect them from harm and will be in their best interests).
- Supervisory bodies will need to ensure that sufficient assessors are available to meet the needs of their area and that these assessors have the skills, qualifications, experience and training to perform the function.
- Authorisation may not be given unless all the qualifying requirements are met.

- In giving authorisation, the supervisory body must specify its duration, which may not exceed 12 months and may not be for longer than recommended by the best interests assessor. Deprivation of liberty should not continue for longer than is necessary.
- The supervisory body may attach conditions to the authorisation if it considers it appropriate to do so.
- The supervisory body must give notice of its decision in writing to specified people, and notify others.
- The supervisory body must appoint a relevant person's representative to represent the interests of every person for whom they give a standard authorisation for deprivation of liberty.
- When an authorisation is in force, the relevant person, the relevant person's representative and any IMCA representing the individual have a right at any time to request that the supervisory body reviews the authorisation.

Key points for managing authorities and supervisory bodies

In addition to the above, both managing authorities and supervisory bodies **5–335** should be aware of the following key points:
- An authorisation may last for a maximum period of 12 months.
- Anyone engaged in caring for the person, anyone named by them as a person to consult, and anyone with an interest in the person's welfare must be consulted in decision-making.
- Before the current authorisation expires, the managing authority may seek a fresh authorisation for up to another 12 months, provided it is established, on the basis of further assessment, that the requirements continue to be met.
- The authorisation should be reviewed, and if appropriate revoked, before it expires if there has been a significant change in the person's circumstances. To this end, the managing authority will be required to ensure that the continued deprivation of liberty of a person remains necessary in the best interests of the person.
- A decision to deprive a person of liberty may be challenged by the relevant person, or by the relevant person's representative, by an application to the Court of Protection. However, managing authorities and supervisory bodies should always be prepared to try to resolve disputes locally and informally. No one should be forced to apply to the court because of failure or unwillingness on the part of a managing authority or supervisory body to engage in constructive discussion.
- If the court is asked to decide on a case where there is a question about whether deprivation of liberty is lawful or should continue to be authorised, the managing authority can continue with its current care regime where it is necessary:
  —for the purpose of giving the person life-sustaining treatment, or
  —to prevent a serious deterioration in their condition while the court makes its decision.
- The complete process of assessing and authorising deprivation of liberty should be clearly recorded, and regularly monitored and audited, as part of an organisation's governance structure.

- Management information should be recorded and retained, and used to measure the effectiveness of the deprivation of liberty processes. This information will also need to be shared with the inspection bodies.

Annex 1

Overview of the deprivation of liberty safeguards process

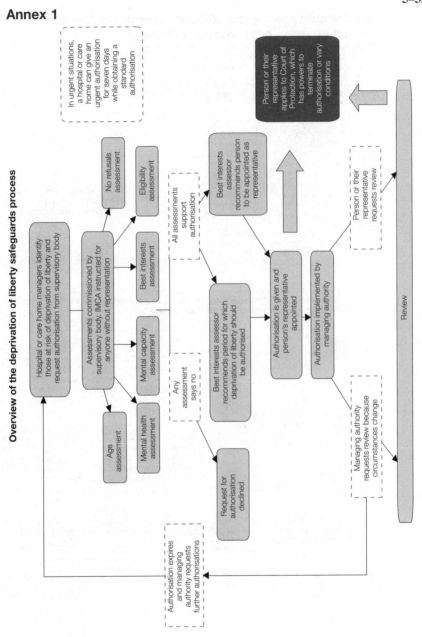

5–337

Annex 2

What should a managing authority consider before applying for authorisation of deprivation of liberty?

These questions are relevant **both** at admission **and** when reviewing the care of patients and residents. By considering the following questions in the following order, a managing authority will be helped to know whether an application for authorisation is required.

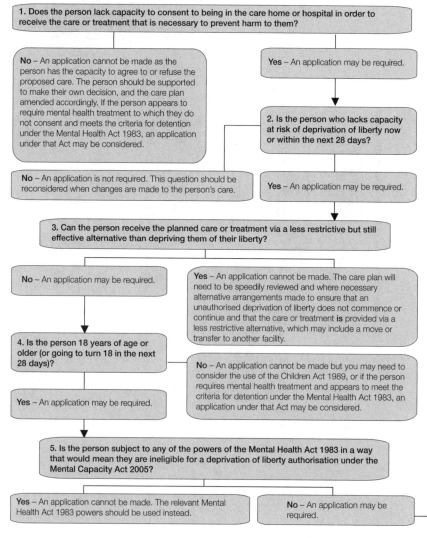

1. Does the person lack capacity to consent to being in the care home or hospital in order to receive the care or treatment that is necessary to prevent harm to them?

No – An application cannot be made as the person has the capacity to agree to or refuse the proposed care. The person should be supported to make their own decision, and the care plan amended accordingly. If the person appears to require mental health treatment to which they do not consent and meets the criteria for detention under the Mental Health Act 1983, an application under that Act may be considered.

Yes – An application may be required.

2. Is the person who lacks capacity at risk of deprivation of liberty now or within the next 28 days?

No – An application is not required. This question should be reconsidered when changes are made to the person's care.

Yes – An application may be required.

3. Can the person receive the planned care or treatment via a less restrictive but still effective alternative than depriving them of their liberty?

No – An application may be required.

Yes – An application cannot be made. The care plan will need to be speedily reviewed and where necessary alternative arrangements made to ensure that an unauthorised deprivation of liberty does not commence or continue and that the care or treatment **is** provided via a less restrictive alternative, which may include a move or transfer to another facility.

4. Is the person 18 years of age or older (or going to turn 18 in the next 28 days)?

No – An application cannot be made but you may need to consider the use of the Children Act 1989, or if the person requires mental health treatment and appears to meet the criteria for detention under the Mental Health Act 1983, an application under that Act may be considered.

Yes – An application may be required.

5. Is the person subject to any of the powers of the Mental Health Act 1983 in a way that would mean they are ineligible for a deprivation of liberty authorisation under the Mental Capacity Act 2005?

Yes – An application cannot be made. The relevant Mental Health Act 1983 powers should be used instead.

No – An application may be required.

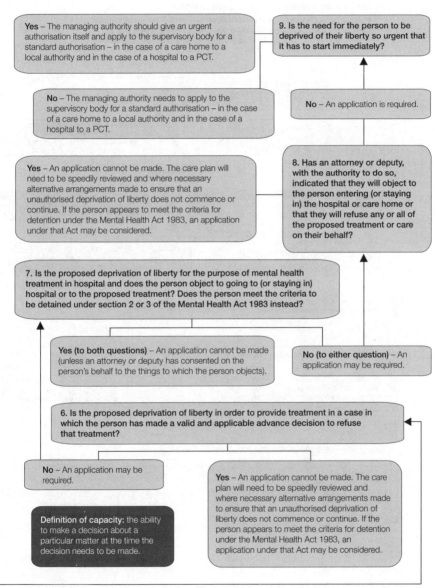

Yes – The managing authority should give an urgent authorisation itself and apply to the supervisory body for a standard authorisation – in the case of a care home to a local authority and in the case of a hospital to a PCT.

9. Is the need for the person to be deprived of their liberty so urgent that it has to start immediately?

No – The managing authority needs to apply to the supervisory body for a standard authorisation – in the case of a care home to a local authority and in the case of a hospital to a PCT.

No – An application is required.

Yes – An application cannot be made. The care plan will need to be speedily reviewed and where necessary alternative arrangements made to ensure that an unauthorised deprivation of liberty does not commence or continue. If the person appears to meet the criteria for detention under the Mental Health Act 1983, an application under that Act may be considered.

8. Has an attorney or deputy, with the authority to do so, indicated that they will object to the person entering (or staying in) the hospital or care home or that they will refuse any or all of the proposed treatment or care on their behalf?

7. Is the proposed deprivation of liberty for the purpose of mental health treatment in hospital and does the person object to going to (or staying in) hospital or to the proposed treatment? Does the person meet the criteria to be detained under section 2 or 3 of the Mental Health Act 1983 instead?

Yes (to both questions) – An application cannot be made (unless an attorney or deputy has consented on the person's behalf to the things to which the person objects).

No (to either question) – An application may be required.

6. Is the proposed deprivation of liberty in order to provide treatment in a case in which the person has made a valid and applicable advance decision to refuse that treatment?

No – An application may be required.

Yes – An application cannot be made. The care plan will need to be speedily reviewed and where necessary alternative arrangements made to ensure that an unauthorised deprivation of liberty does not commence or continue. If the person appears to meet the criteria for detention under the Mental Health Act 1983, an application under that Act may be considered.

Definition of capacity: the ability to make a decision about a particular matter at the time the decision needs to be made.

NB: An authorisation only relates to deprivation of liberty and does not give authority for any course of treatment.

5–338

Annex 3

Supervisory body action on receipt of a request from:

a) a managing authority for a standard deprivation of liberty authorisation
b) somebody other than a managing authority (an eligible person) to determine whether or not there is a current unauthorised deprivation of liberty

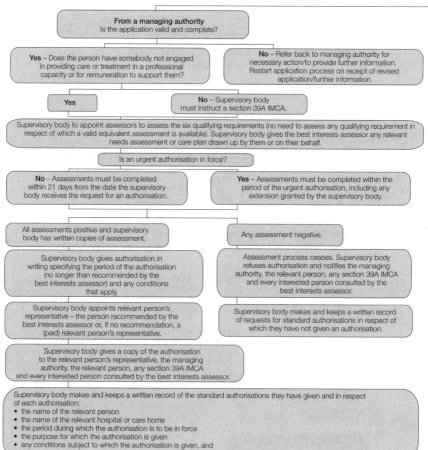

From a managing authority
Is the application valid and complete?

Yes – Does the person have somebody not engaged in providing care or treatment in a professional capacity or for remuneration to support them?

No – Refer back to managing authority for necessary action/to provide further information. Restart application process on receipt of revised application/further information.

Yes

No – Supervisory body must instruct a section 39A IMCA.

Supervisory body to appoint assessors to assess the six qualifying requirements (no need to assess any qualifying requirement in respect of which a valid equivalent assessment is available). Supervisory body gives the best interests assessor any relevant needs assessment or care plan drawn up by them or on their behalf.

Is an urgent authorisation in force?

No – Assessments must be completed within 21 days from the date the supervisory body receives the request for an authorisation.

Yes – Assessments must be completed within the period of the urgent authorisation, including any extension granted by the supervisory body.

All assessments positive and supervisory body has written copies of assessment.

Any assessment negative.

Supervisory body gives authorisation in writing specifying the period of the authorisation (no longer than recommended by the best interests assessor) and any conditions that apply.

Assessment process ceases. Supervisory body refuses authorisation and notifies the managing authority, the relevant person, any section 39A IMCA and every interested person consulted by the best interests assessor.

Supervisory body appoints relevant person's representative – the person recommended by the best interests assessor or, if no recommendation, a (paid) relevant person's representative.

Supervisory body makes and keeps a written record of requests for standard authorisations in respect of which they have not given an authorisation.

Supervisory body gives a copy of the authorisation to the relevant person's representative, the managing authority, the relevant person, any section 39A IMCA and every interested person consulted by the best interests assessor.

Supervisory body makes and keeps a written record of the standard authorisations they have given and in respect of each authorisation:
- the name of the relevant person
- the name of the relevant hospital or care home
- the period during which the authorisation is to be in force
- the purpose for which the authorisation is given
- any conditions subject to which the authorisation is given, and
- the reason why each qualifying requirement is met.

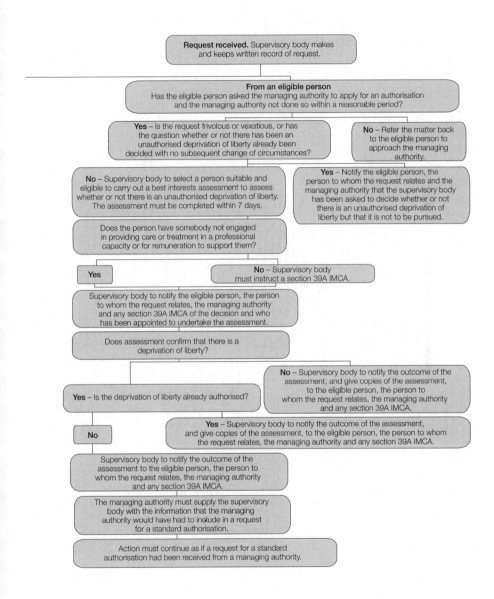

Request received. Supervisory body makes and keeps written record of request.

From an eligible person
Has the eligible person asked the managing authority to apply for an authorisation and the managing authority not done so within a reasonable period?

Yes – Is the request frivolous or vexatious, or has the question whether or not there has been an unauthorised deprivation of liberty already been decided with no subsequent change of circumstances?

No – Refer the matter back to the eligible person to approach the managing authority.

No – Supervisory body to select a person suitable and eligible to carry out a best interests assessment to assess whether or not there is an unauthorised deprivation of liberty. The assessment must be completed within 7 days.

Yes – Notify the eligible person, the person to whom the request relates and the managing authority that the supervisory body has been asked to decide whether or not there is an unauthorised deprivation of liberty but that it is not to be pursued.

Does the person have somebody not engaged in providing care or treatment in a professional capacity or for remuneration to support them?

Yes

No – Supervisory body must instruct a section 39A IMCA.

Supervisory body to notify the eligible person, the person to whom the request relates, the managing authority and any section 39A IMCA of the decision and who has been appointed to undertake the assessment.

Does assessment confirm that there is a deprivation of liberty?

No – Supervisory body to notify the outcome of the assessment, and give copies of the assessment, to the eligible person, the person to whom the request relates, the managing authority and any section 39A IMCA.

Yes – Is the deprivation of liberty already authorised?

Yes – Supervisory body to notify the outcome of the assessment, and give copies of the assessment, to the eligible person, the person to whom the request relates, the managing authority and any section 39A IMCA.

No

Supervisory body to notify the outcome of the assessment to the eligible person, the person to whom the request relates, the managing authority and any section 39A IMCA.

The managing authority must supply the supervisory body with the information that the managing authority would have had to include in a request for a standard authorisation.

Action must continue as if a request for a standard authorisation had been received from a managing authority.

461

5–339

Annex 4

Standard authorisation review process

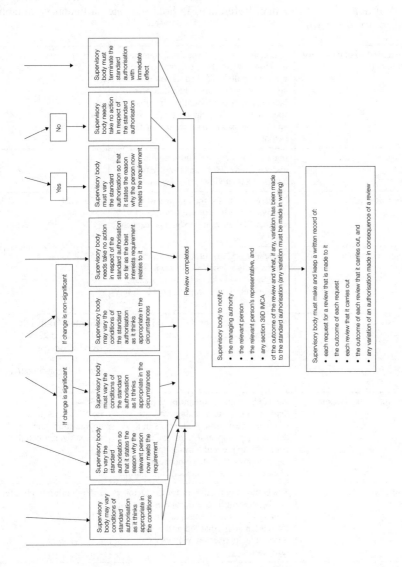

KEY WORDS AND PHRASES USED IN THE CODE OF PRACTICE

5–340   The table below is not a full index or glossary. Instead, it is a list of key terms used in this Code of Practice. References in bold indicate particularly valuable content for that term.

Advance decision to refuse treatment	A decision to refuse specified treatment made in advance by a person who has capacity to do so. This decision will then apply at a future time when that person lacks capacity to consent to, or refuse, the specified treatment. Specific rules apply to advance decisions to refuse life sustaining treatment.	4.26
Advocacy	Independent help and support with understanding issues and putting forward a person's own views, feelings and ideas.	2.7
Age assessment	An assessment, for the purpose of the deprivation of liberty safeguards, of whether the relevant person has reached age 18.	**4.23–4.24**
Approved mental health professional	A social worker or other professional approved by a local social services authority to act on behalf of a local social services authority in carrying out a variety of functions.	4.52, 4.53, 4.60
Assessor	A person who carries out a deprivation of liberty safeguards assessment	**Chapter 4 (all)** 1.16–1.17, 3.21, 5.22, 9.10 Best interests, and appointing a relevant person's representative: 7.10–7.23
Best interests assessment	An assessment, for the purpose of the deprivation of liberty safeguards, of whether deprivation of liberty is in a detained person's best interests, is necessary to prevent harm to the person and is a proportionate response to the likelihood and seriousness of that harm.	**4.58–4.76** Best interests, and appointing a relevant person's representative: 7.10–7.23
Bournewood judgment	The commonly used term for the October 2004 judgment by the European Court of Human Rights in the case of HL v the United Kingdom that led to the introduction of the deprivation of liberty safeguards.	**Introduction to chapter 1** 1.19, 2.2, 2.22
Capacity	Short for mental capacity. The ability to make a decision about a particular matter at the time the decision needs to be made. A legal definition is contained in section 2 of the Mental Capacity Act 2005.	Throughout
Care home	A care facility registered under the Care Standards Act 2000.	Throughout
Care Quality Commission	The new integrated regulator for health and adult social care that, subject to the	Chapter 11

	passage of legislation, will take over regulation of health and adult social care from 1 April 2009.	
Carer	Someone who provides unpaid care by looking after a friend or neighbour who needs support because of sickness, age or disability. In this document, the term carer does not mean a paid care worker.	Throughout
Children Act 1989	A law relating to children and those with parental responsibility for children.	1.12, 5.22
Conditions	Requirements that a supervisory body may impose when giving a standard deprivation of liberty authorisation, after taking account of any recommendations made by the best interests assessor.	**4.74–4.75** 5.5 Review of: 8.14, 8.16
Consent	Agreeing to a course of action—specifically in this document, to a care plan or treatment regime. For consent to be legally valid, the person giving it must have the capacity to take the decision, have been given sufficient information to make the decision, and not have been under any duress or inappropriate pressure.	Throughout
Court of Protection	The specialist court for all issues relating to people who lack capacity to make specific decisions.	**Chapter 10**
Deprivation of liberty	Deprivation of liberty is a term used in the European Convention on Human Rights about circumstances when a person's freedom is taken away. Its meaning in practice is being defined through case law.	**Chapter 2** Throughout
Deprivation of liberty safeguards	The framework of safeguards under the Mental Capacity Act 2005 for people who need to be deprived of their liberty in a hospital or care home in their best interests for care or treatment and who lack the capacity to consent to the arrangements made for their care or treatment.	Throughout
Deprivation of liberty safeguards assessment	Any one of the six assessments that need to be undertaken as part of the standard deprivation of liberty authorisation process.	**Chapter 4**
Deputy	Someone appointed by the Court of Protection with ongoing legal authority, as prescribed by the Court, to make decisions on behalf of a person who lacks capacity to make particular decisions.	4.26, 4.65, 5.11, 5.22, 7.7, 7.13–7.15, 7.18, 7.23, 7.29, 10.3, 10.8
Donee	Someone appointed under a Lasting Power of Attorney who has the legal right to make decisions within the scope of their authority on behalf of the person (the donor) who made the Lasting Power of Attorney.	3.9, 4.26, 4.65, 5.11, 5.22, 7.7, 7.13–7.15, 7.18, 7.23, 7.29, 10.3, 10.8

Eligibility assessment	An assessment, for the purpose of the deprivation of liberty safeguards, of whether or not a person is rendered ineligible for a standard deprivation of liberty authorisation because the authorisation would conflict with requirements that are, or could be, placed on the person under the Mental Health Act 1983.	**4.40–4.57**
European Convention on Human Rights	A convention drawn up within the Council of Europe setting out a number of civil and political rights and freedoms, and setting up a mechanism for the enforcement of the obligations entered into by contracting states.	Chapter 1, Chapter 2
European Court of Human Rights	The court to which any contracting state or individual can apply when they believe that there has been a violation of the European Convention on Human Rights.	Introduction to Chapter 1, 2.1–2.2
Guardianship under the Mental Health Act 1983	The appointment of a guardian to help and supervise patients in the community for their own welfare or to protect other people. The guardian may be either a local authority or a private individual approved by the local authority.	4.43, 4.44
Independent Mental Capacity Advocate (IMCA)	Someone who provides support and representation for a person who lacks capacity to make specific decisions, where the person has no-one else to support them. The IMCA service was established by the Mental Capacity Act 2005 and is not the same as an ordinary advocacy service.	**3.22–3.28, 7.34–7.41** 3.16, 4.7, 5.7–5.8, 5.18, 6.8, 6.19, 6.27–6.28, 7.4, 7.23, 7.26, 8.18, 8.28, 9.6, 9.9
Lasting Power of Attorney	A Power of Attorney created under the Mental Capacity Act 2005 appointing an attorney (donee), or attorneys, to make decisions about the donor's personal welfare, including health care, and/or deal with the donor's property and affairs.	10.8
Life-sustaining treatment	Treatment that, in the view of the person providing health care, is necessary to keep a person alive.	5.13
Local authority	In the deprivation of liberty safeguards context, the local council responsible for social services in any particular area of the country.	1.4, 2.18, 2.21, 3.3, 3.11, 3.21, 4.77
Local health board (LHB)	Local health boards cover the same geographic areas as local authorities in Wales. They work alongside their respective local authorities in planning long-term strategies for dealing with issues of health and wellbeing in their areas.	1 .4, 3.3
Main Code	The Code of Practice for the Mental Capacity Act 2005.	Throughout

Managing authority	The person or body with management responsibility for the hospital or care home in which a person is, or may become, deprived of their liberty.	**1.4–1.5, 3.1** Throughout
Maximum authorisation period	The maximum period for which a supervisory body may give a standard deprivation of liberty authorisation, which must not exceed the period recommended by the best interests assessor, and which cannot be for more than 12 months.	4.71
Mental Capacity Act 2005	Legislation that governs decision-making for people who lack capacity to make decisions for themselves or who have capacity and want to make preparations for a time when they may lack capacity in the future. It sets out who can take decisions, in which situations, and how they should go about this.	Throughout
Mental capacity assessment	An assessment, for the purpose of the deprivation of liberty safeguards, of whether a person lacks capacity in relation to the question of whether or not they should be accommodated in the relevant hospital or care home for the purpose of being given care or treatment.	4.29–4.32
Mental disorder	Any disorder or disability of the mind, apart from dependence on alcohol or drugs. This includes all learning disabilities.	1.4, 1.7, 1.9, 3.9, 4.33–4.35, 4.45, 4.50, 5.9, 5.22, 6.3
Mental Health Act 1983	Legislation mainly about the compulsory care and treatment of patients with mental health problems. It covers detention in hospital for mental health treatment, supervised community treatment and guardianship.	**4.33–4.57** 1.1, 1.11–1.12, 2.13, 4.5, 5.19, 5.22, 7.8, 8.3, 8.19–8.21
Mental health assessment	An assessment, for the purpose of the deprivation of liberty safeguards, of whether a person has a mental disorder.	**4.33–4.39**
No refusals assessment	An assessment, for the purpose of the deprivation of liberty safeguards, of whether there is any other existing authority for decision-making for the relevant person that would prevent the giving of a standard deprivation of liberty authorisation. This might include any valid advance decision, or valid decision by a deputy or donee appointed under a Lasting Power of Attorney.	**4.25–4.28**
Qualifying requirement	Any one of the six qualifying requirements (age, mental health, mental capacity, best interests, eligibility and no refusals) that need to be assessed and met in order for a standard deprivation of liberty authorisation to be given.	4.1

Relevant hospital or care home	The hospital or care home in which the person is, or may become, deprived of their liberty.	Throughout
Relevant person	A person who is, or may become, deprived of their liberty in a hospital or care home.	Throughout
Relevant person's representative	A person, independent of the relevant hospital or care home, appointed to maintain contact with the relevant person, and to represent and support the relevant person in all matters relating to the operation of the deprivation of liberty safeguards.	**Chapter 7**
Restraint	The use or threat of force to help carry out an act that the person resists. Restraint may only be used where it is necessary to protect the person from harm and is proportionate to the risk of harm.	2.8–2.15
Restriction of liberty	An act imposed on a person that is not of such a degree or intensity as to amount to a deprivation of liberty.	Chapter 2
Review	A formal, fresh look at a relevant person's situation when there has been, or may have been, a change of circumstances that may necessitate an amendment to, or termination of, a standard deprivation of liberty authorisation.	**Chapter 8**
Standard authorisation	An authorisation given by a supervisory body, after completion of the statutory assessment process, giving lawful authority to deprive a relevant person of their liberty in the relevant hospital or care home.	**Chapter 4** Throughout
Supervised community treatment	Arrangements under which people can be discharged from detention in hospital under the Mental Health Act 1983, but remain subject to the Act in the community rather than in hospital. Patients on supervised community treatment can be recalled to hospital if treatment in hospital is necessary again.	4.41, 4.50, 4.51
Supervisory body	A primary care trust, local authority, Welsh Ministers or a local health board that is responsible for considering a deprivation of liberty request received from a managing authority, commissioning the statutory assessments and, where all the assessments agree, authorising deprivation of liberty.	**1.4, 3.3** Throughout
Unauthorised deprivation of liberty	A situation in which a person is deprived of their liberty in a hospital or care home without the deprivation being authorised by either a standard or urgent deprivation of liberty authorisation.	Chapter 9

Urgent authorisation	An authorisation given by a managing authority for a maximum of seven days, which may subsequently be extended by a maximum of a further seven days by a supervisory body, that gives the managing authority lawful authority to deprive a person of their liberty in a hospital or care home while the standard deprivation of liberty authorisation process is undertaken.	**Chapter 6** Throughout

ANNEX A

CONTACT DETAILS

The following list provides contact details for relevant organisations.   **A–001**

Action on Elder Abuse

web: *www.elderabuse.org.uk*
telephone helpline: 0808 808 8141
switchboard: 020 8765 7000

Age Concern

web: *www.ace.org.uk*
telephone helpline: 0800 009966
switchboard: 020 8765 7200

Alzheimers Society

web: *www.alzheimers.org.uk*
telephone: 020 7306 0606

British Banking Association

web: *www.bba.org.uk*
telephone: 020 7216 8800

British Institute of Learning Disabilities

web: *www.bild.org.uk*
telephone: 01562 723025

British Psychological Society

web: *www.bps.org.uk*
telephone: 0116 254 9568

Care and Social Services Inspectorate Wales

web: *www.csiw.wales.gov.uk*
telephone: 01443 848450

Carers UK

web: *www.carersuk.org*
telephone carers line: 0808 808 7777
switchboard: 020 7490 8818

Commission for Social Care Inspection

web: *www.csci.org.uk*
telephone: 0845 015 0120 / 0191 233 3323
textphone: 0845 015 2255 / 0191 233 3588

Community Legal Services Direct

web: *www.clsdirect.org.uk*
telephone helpline: 0845 345 4345

Criminal Records Bureau

web: *www.crb.org.uk*
tel: 0870 909 0811

Department of Health

web: *www.dh.gov.uk*

Department for Work and Pensions

web: *www.dwp.gov.org*

Disability Rights Commission

web: *www.drc-gb.org*
telephone helpline: 08457 622 633
textphone: 08457 622 644

Down's Syndrome Association

web: *www.downs-syndrome.org.uk*
telephone helpline: 0845 230 0372
switchboard: 0845 230 0372

Foundation for People with Leaning Difficulties

web: *www.learningdisabilities.org.uk*
telephone: 020 7803 1100

Headway—the Brain Injury Association

web: *www.headway.org.uk*
telephone helpline: 0808 800 2244
switchboard: 0115 924 0800

Healthcare Commission

web: *www.healthcarecommission.org.uk*
telephone helpline: 0845 601 3012
switchboard: 020 7448 9200

Healthcare Inspectorate for Wales

web: *www.hiw.org.uk*
telephone: 029 2092 8850

Help the Aged

web: *www.helptheaged.org.uk*
telephone: 020 7278 1114

Information Commissioner's Office

web: *www.ico.gov.uk*
telephone helpline: 0845 630 6060
switchboard: 01625 545700

Local Government Ombudsman

web: *www.lgo.org.uk*
telephone advice line: 0845 602 1983

Mencap

web: *www.mencap.org.uk*
telephone: 020 7454 0454

Mental Health Act Commission

web: *www.mhac.org.uk*
telephone: 0115 943 7100

Mind

web: *www.mind.org.uk*
telephone infoline: 0845 766 0163
switchboard: 020 8519 2122

Ministry of Justice

telephone: 020 7210 8500

Morgan Cole Mental Capacity Act website

web: *www.mental-capacity.com*
switchboard: 02920 385385

National Autistic Society

web: *www.nas.org.uk*
telephone helpline: 0845 070 4004
switchboard: 020 7833 2299

Office of the Public Guardian

web: *www.publicguardian.gov.uk*
switchboard: 0845 330 2900

Official Solicitor

web: *www.officialsolicitor.gov.uk*
telephone: 020 7911 7127

Parliamentary and Health Service Ombudsman

web: *www.ombudsman.org.uk*
complaints helpline: 0845 015 4033

Public Service Ombudsman for Wales

web: *www.ombudsman-wales.org.uk*
telephone: 01656 641150

Rethink

web: *www.rethink.org*
telephone: 0845 456 0455

Royal College of Psychiatrists

web: *www.rcpsych.ac.uk*
telephone: 020 7235 2351

Solicitors for the Elderly

web: *www.solicitorsfortheelderly.com*
telephone: 01992 471568

Young Minds

web: *www.youngminds.org.uk*
telephone: 020 7336 8445

Index

LEGAL TAXONOMY
FROM SWEET & MAXWELL

This index has been prepared using Sweet and Maxwell's Legal Taxonomy. Main index entries conform to keywords provided by the Legal Taxonomy except where references to specific documents or non-standard terms (denoted by quotation marks) have been included. These keywords provide a means of identifying similar concepts in other Sweet & Maxwell publications and online services to which keywords from the Legal Taxonomy have been applied. Readers may find some minor differences between terms used in the text and those which appear in the index. Suggestions to *sweetandmaxwell.taxonomy@thomson.com*.

(All references are to paragraph number)

Accommodation
  see **Residential accommodation**
Adults with incapacity
  see **Persons lacking capacity**
Advance decisions
  advance directives, 1–211
  advance statements, 1–214
  applicability
    see validity
  approach to legislation, 1–210
  consideration of all relevant maters, 1–215
  contacting relatives, 1–213
  controversy, 1–213
  effect
    apparent advance decisions, 1–239
    definitions, 1–234
    general, 1–212, 1–235
    liability, 1–233
    meaning of "satisfied", 1–236
    patient's best interests, 1–238
    reasonable belief, 1–237
  form of advance decision, 1–212
  health professionals
    conscientious objection, 1–213
  lasting powers of attorney
    restrictions, 1–117
  liability for providing treatment, 1–220—
    1–232
  meaning of "advance decision", 1–208
  meaning of "treatment", 1–209
  Mental Health Act 1983
    overriding provisions, 1–212

  oral decisions, 1–212
  persons under 18, 1–215
  specified circumstances, 1–216
  specified treatment, 1–216
  treatment described in lay terms, 1–217
  validity
    advance directives made before October 1,
      2007, 1–232
    applicable circumstances, 1–229—1–230
    decisions made before October 1, 2007,
      1–223
    definitions, 1–221
    health professional aware of existence,
      1–224
    inconsistent behaviour, 1–227
    lasting powers of attorney, 1–226
    liability for providing treatment, 1–220—
      1–232
    oral advance decisions, 1–232
    oral withdrawal of written decision, 1–225
    refusal of life-sustaining treatment, 1–223
    suicide notes, 1–228
    treatment until issue determined, 1–231
    unborn children, 1–231
  withdrawal, 1–218—1–219
Age
  authorisations to detain persons
    assessments, 1–501, 3–123, 5–108—5–109
    qualifying requirements, 1–480
  lasting powers of attorney
    donees, 1–105

475